Animal behaviour in the laboratory

Animal behaviour in the laboratory

PAUL SILVERMAN

PICA PRESS
NEW YORK

TO RINA, DEBRA AND RUTH

Published in the United States of America in 1978 by
PICA PRESS
Distributed by Universe Books
381 Park Avenue South, New York, N.Y. 10016

© 1978 A. P. Silverman

All rights reserved. No part of this publication may be reproduced, stored in a retrieval system, or transmitted, in any form or by any means, electronic, mechanical, photocopying, recording, or otherwise, without the prior permission of the publishers.

Library of Congress Catalog Card Number: 77-088842
ISBN 0-87663-727-6

Printed in Great Britain

Contents

	Acknowledgements	*page* xi
1.	**Introduction**	1
	Is behaviour a science?	3
	Language	5
	Relationship of animal behaviour to human	6
2.	**Language, truth, and science**	8
	What you say influences what you see	10
	A question of numbers	13
	Conclusions	14
3.	**What to watch – the units of behaviour**	15
	Obtaining behaviour on demand	15
	The rat race	16
	Behaviour as a search for reflexes	18
	Drinking, a survey of a typical kind of behaviour	21
	Summary	24
4.	**Some questions of ethics and experimental design**	25
	The case against experimentation	25
	The case against the case against	26
	Pain and behaviour	28
	Caging, care, and choice	29
	Pharmacological models: drugs in animals and man	31
	Conclusions	33
5.	**A gallop through physiological psychology**	35
	Sleep	35
	Feeding	39
	Excretion	47
	Grooming or care of the body surface	49

Social behaviour *page* 53
Aggression 53
Sexual behaviour 53
Parental behaviour 56

6. Drug screening and brain pharmacology **58**
Some general screening batteries 59
Some specialised pharmacological tests 64
An excursion into brain pharmacology 71
Discussion 75

7. Motor activity **79**
Methods of measuring activity 80
Rhythms of activity 85
Experiments on activity 87
Summary and comment 91

8. Choice and self-administration **93**
Preference tests in temperature control 93
Strength of drive and companion preferences 93
Food preferences 95
Statistics of preference 96
Drug dosing by sugaring the pill 96
Hunting 97
Addiction to alcohol 99
Some comments on addiction 101
Self-administration of drugs 102
Self-stimulation 103
Summary 105

9. Interlude: conditioned and unconditioned **106**

10. Approach to a conditioned stimulus: mazes **110**
The first maze 110
Subways and superstructures 111
Procedure 112
Temporal mazes 115
Heredity, nutrition, and political relevance 116
Straightforward simplicity 118
Summary 119

Contents vii

11.	Conditioned reflexes	*page*	**120**
	Part 1: Pavlov and conditioned reflexes		120
	Comments		133
	Part 2: Motor–food conditioned reflexes		135
	Application of conditioned reflexes in toxicology		138
	Summary		139

12.	Operant conditioning	**141**
	Apparatus: the 'Skinner Box' and its control	141
	Continuous reinforcement (CRF)	147
	Extinction	149
	Fixed Ratio (FR)	149
	Fixed Interval (FI)	150
	Variable Ratio (VR)	151
	Variable Interval (VI)	151
	Differential reinforcement of low rates of response (DRL)	152
	Comparison of some simple schedules	154
	Combinations of schedules	160
	Summary	163

13.	Comments on operant and other behaviour	**164**

14.	Discrimination	**179**
	Discriminative abilities	179
	Tests for discrimination – conditioned reflexes	181
	Internal discrimination	185
	Discrimination without errors	186
	Operant thresholds	187
	Discrimination as an indicator of concepts	189
	Go/No Go discrimination	190
	Summary	191

15.	Behaviour after aversive stimuli: suppression, punishment, and withdrawal	**192**
	Definitions	192
	Stimuli which lead to withdrawal	194
	Direct responses to shock	197
	Conditioned emotional response	200
	Conditioned suppression	201
	Punishment	202
	Conflict	203

16.	**Conditioned avoidance of aversive stimuli** *page*	**204**
	Escape	204
	Pole-climbing avoidance	204
	Shuttle avoidance	206
	Instrumental avoidance	209
	Free-operant avoidance	211
	Passive or one-trial avoidance	215
	Unconditioned avoidance	218
	Summary of Chapters 15 and 16	219
17.	**Conditioned conflict with aversive stimuli**	**220**
	Approach–avoidance conflict	220
	Measurement of drives	222
	Operant conflict	223
	Conflict of response but not of stimulus	224
	Two-lever approach and avoidance. Experiments on the interpretation of drug effects	225
	Summary	229
18.	**Exploration**	**230**
	Match and mismatch. Some physiology of motor control	232
	The basis of practical tests	234
	The open field	235
	Measurement of exploration	236
	Why mazes?	238
	Exploration and unconditioned caution	240
	Activity and exploration	240
	Hole boards and tunnel boards	241
	Exploration as a search for novelty	244
	Exploration as behaviour with high priority	246
	Summary	252
19.	**Some aspects of learning**	**254**
	Some definitions	254
	State dependence	255
	Chemical transfer of learning	256
	Learning pills. Can a drug improve short-term learning?	258
	Getting over the shock	259
	Exploration and latent learning – Ye know not what ye seek	261
	Exploration as a one-trial learning	261
	Imprinting	263
	Habituation	266

Contents ix

Reversal learning – comparative 'intelligence'	page	266
Maze learning and cholinesterase		268
Discussion		269
Summary		270

20. Tests of behaviour in groups and of stimulated aggression — 271

Some differences between grouped and solitary rats and mice	272
Dominance by fighting	274
Rank-orders in rats and mice	275
Rank-order measured by feeding	278
The Frustration–Aggression hypothesis – is fighting frustrated feeding?	280
The aggressions induced by drugs: and some definitions	282
Defensive fighting induced by shock	284
Mouse-killing	285
Aggression induced by brain lesions	286
Electrical stimulation in the brain	288
Tests of territorial aggression in mice	289
Summary	292

21. Analysis of behaviour in a social situation. — 294

Checklist observation	294
Objective observation	295
Early studies of aggressive behaviour in laboratory rats	296
Rats' social encounters portrayed as drama	298
Behaviour in a social situation	299
A technical interlude: recording the data	300
Elements in the social behaviour of laboratory rats	301
A note on nomenclature and on what is being named	305
Sequences of elements	307
The organisation of social behaviour	310
Summary of the argument	314
Laboratories and species compared	314
Territory in the laboratory	316

22. Social behaviour as an experimental method — 319

Introduction of isolated male rats	320
Interpreting drug effects: chlorpromazine	322
Multi-variate analysis	326
Observation of selected elements	328

Repeated observations on rats – introducing isolates and parting pairs *page* 329
Separation and return: nicotine 330
Development of the social behaviour test 334
Cross-introductions of paired mice 335
Summary 336

23. Sociobiology: ecology and the function of social aggression 338

Population explosions 339
The population problem and social behaviour 339
The genetics of 'altruism' 342
Behaviour, nutrition, and ecology 344
Social behaviour disrupted 346

24. A comparison of laboratory and wild rodents 349

The rat-catchers' stories 349
Feeding patterns, neophobia, and the division of labour 351
The sociology and biology of the Norway rat 353
Burrows 356
The Black rat (*Rattus rattus*) 358
Confirmation of laboratory conclusions 359
The difference between laboratory and wild rats 359
Strain-specific behaviour in mice 363
Summary 365

25. Finale 366

An end and a beginning 367
Comparing animals and man 371
Trends in the study of behaviour, and the four questions of biology 372

References 376

General index 389

Chemicals index 397

Species index 400

Author index 402

Acknowledgements

Hannah Steinberg, Susan Iverson, David Humphries, Victor Laties, and David McFarland read earlier versions of this book, which has greatly benefited from their constructive criticism. David Buxton, Keith Extance, Ken Fletcher, David Greenwood, and Terry Weight have also made useful comments on parts of the manuscript. I am very grateful to all these for their help, and hope they will bear with me for everything that needs further improvement and for the places where I have chosen the advice I liked best. The book was written while I was at ICI's Central Toxicology Laboratory, and I would like to express my appreciation to Andrew Swan for my time there. Sheila Scarrot deserves special thanks for turning my handwriting into accurate typescript. Georgina Godley has added immeasurably to the book with her cartoons and some figures. I thank John Carpenter for Figs. 25.1 and 25.2, and *The New York Academy of Sciences, Prentice-Hall Inc., E. J. Brill NV* and *The British Pharmacological Society* for Figs. 12.2 and 12.5, 21.11 and 21.12, and 22.1 respectively. Sketches of rats were mostly traced from photographs by myself.

A.P.S.

ONE
Introduction

Animal behaviour makes a fascinating study both for its own sake and in a conscious search for models of human behaviour. Although we all have a lifetime's practical experience in the observation, analysis, and prediction of what other people do, we like to practise and to improve our understanding with simpler models. The study of animal behaviour is like story-telling and television soap opera in this respect, although it is rather harder work for the observer.

Animal behaviour is also used experimentally to observe the results of doing something else, and the principal aim of this book is to serve as a guide to behaviour as an applied science. Experimenters who may not be especially interested in behaviour for its own sake may nevertheless need to investigate, for example, a supposedly psychotropic drug. Similarly the functions of some part of the brain may be studied with surgical or chemical lesions or by mild electric stimulation in animals; since the animals cannot say what the treatment feels like, it is necessary to detect and measure any changes in what they do. Children who have suffered a period of starvation or of protein-deficiency diseases like kwashiorkor may appear – physically – to recover completely; yet they may still have problems, and it is said, sadly, that other children rarely choose them as friends. Obviously such children should have the best available treatment – and obtaining it for them or preventing the need for it are political problems more important than anything in this book. But to improve the treatment, indeed to understand the real nature of the damage, experiments are necessary which obviously cannot be done on human beings. What sort of behavioural changes should be looked for in animals and how can they be detected, measured, and interpreted?

There are many excellent books concerned with behaviour for its own sake. As an introduction that can be read for amusement in 2 or 3 hours, it would be hard to improve on Konrad Lorenz's *King Solomon's Ring* (1953). It conveys a greater understanding of how animals behave and of the fun of observing them than dozens of weighty tomes. For a more systematic approach, a good short introduction is probably still Niko Tinbergen's *The Study of Instinct* (1951), although it is badly out of date in detail. The general principles of how a zoologist observes gulls, wasps, and sticklebacks and wonders how their behaviour contributes to their survival, does not change; but the stimulus which this book gave to the subject was enormous, and I suspect that Tinbergen himself has changed his mind about nearly all the specific hypotheses he suggested then. For a detailed modern synthesis of ethology and psychology I know of no rival to Robert Hinde's *Animal Behaviour* (1970).

None of these books gives direct practical guidance to the applied scientist who innocently wishes to use behavioural methods for other purposes. For him, these books are like discussing nutrition and the importance of unsaturated fats and essential amino acids when he only wants a recipe for boiling an egg. Everyone needs to select the right materials for a balanced diet, but everyone could also get some help from a cookery book to convert the ingredients into appetising meals to satisfy the family.

Many pharmacology textbooks include a chapter or two on behavioural methods, but most are only adequate at the boiled-egg level. Specialised psychopharmacology texts are better, notably the *Handbook of Psychopharmacology* (Iverson, Iverson and Snyder, 1977). However, most psychopharmacology texts give what I believe to be a one-sided view of the subject. They are apt to concentrate heavily on conditioned behaviour, where all that the experimenter observes is what he has himself trained the animal to perform. Valuable as this approach is, as we shall see, the alternative approach of watching what animals do of their own accord needs to be explored.

There seems to be room for a book which will give practical guidance on methods of detecting changes in animal behaviour, describing each method in just enough detail to let the reader use it without constantly referring to the original publication. There is sufficient discussion of theory and of typical results to allow critical evaluation. It would be futile to try to list all possible variations of method but the selection is wide enough to let the reader place an unfamiliar technique into the general scheme and appreciate its likely pros and cons. I have described ethological methods in greater detail than others, since the literature on the application of this approach in the laboratory is sparse and it is the area where my own experience is greatest and most likely to be useful.

Similarly I have concentrated on rats and, to some extent, other laboratory rodents, partly because I know them best. The main reason lies in the very comprehensive information already available on the behaviour of these animals in the laboratory – from a variety of points of view – and in the wild, on their physiology and ecology. There are great advantages in comparing the results of a new experiment with all the old ones. I have seldom wanted to illustrate an argument without being able to find an example using rats.

Only by understanding how and why other animals are different from rats, however, can we understand rats properly. We may study rats as a model for man, but rats are not just a representative for all animals, and can only be appreciated in their own right if other species are appreciated too.

Introduction

The reader may find it sufficient to dip into most chapters, but the early ones present a simple theoretical introduction to the principles of persuading animals to perform for our convenient observation. What I have to say is fairly obvious, but I have not seen it written elsewhere and it seems a helpful way of expressing the practical issues; those who find all theories tedious will no doubt omit these chapters.

principles of persuading animals to perform

Methods using essentially 'simple observations' come first. Because this proved to have limitations, methods were developed for conditioning behaviour and these are described next. These too have limitations, and a return can be made with ethology to improved and objective observation. Finally behaviour in the laboratory is compared with that in the wild.

Even the best methods are of little value if they do not lead to useful results, just as results are only as valid as the methods used to obtain them. I have therefore discussed some of the more interesting topics, briefly within chapters or as background comment on more general principles, in order to encourage a deeper interest and, most important, an intelligently critical attitude to anything I or any expert may say.

Note that most such discussions are limited in depth. The reader will be able to appreciate the problem concerned, but the theory will not always be enough to satisfy the experts.

The book will certainly arm the reader with a comprehensive set of questions. Examples are quoted throughout the book of different methods applied to a few commonly-used drugs, and it is noticeable that the results of two methods may lead to apparently quite different conclusions about a drug's mode of action. While science advances through the resolution of such conflicts, it can only do so if we try to deepen our understanding of what it is that the experiments have really measured.

Is behaviour a science?

It is commonly stated, mostly by scientists in other disciplines, that behaviour is too variable, too flexible, too shapeless to be suitable for objective scientific study. This view would be disputed in practice by many non-scientists who are professionally concerned with animals. Farmers, shepherds, lion-tamers and other circus people, horsemen and jockeys, racegoers, and bookies have a pretty shrewd idea of just how predictable the behaviour of a species can be, and of the limitations on any individual animal's predictability in detail. Nearly all horses, suitably trained, will race; they may baulk occasionally but the main unpredictability is in the fine detail of how fast. A shepherd relies on the skill and the instinctive urges of his dog, and of the sheep, and can do so very successfully within certain limits. Unfortunately such people are generally rather inarticulate within the academic terminology that scientists require; their own language may be fluent but anthropomorphic.

Behaviour may be regarded as the relationship between the organism and its environment, and must adjust according to the requirements of either or both. Since many variables have an influence, some of them invisibly within the animal, it is not surprising that it takes long and patient observation before the regularities in spontaneous behaviour become obvious, though once recognised, they are never forgotten. However, it is not easy to give animals the scope to show the full range of their behaviour in a laboratory. They do not need to go hunting for their dinner; in steel or plastic cages they have no room to burrow; and single-sex groups prohibit normal reproductive behaviour. Only hints of their full behaviour appear without the appropriate stimuli and are too abbreviated to be easily visible or clearly understood in isolation.

Nevertheless, the spontaneous behaviour even of laboratory animals is remarkably well-organised, no doubt partly as a relic of the behaviour of the wild but also partly as a positive adaptation to a particular environment. But if the structure of 'natural' behaviour is, to first appearances, only hinted at, we might invent something new. Hence the popularity of conditioning in laboratory tests, where the animal is trained to make very reliably predictable responses to an environment tightly controlled in minute detail. In fact, so reliable as perhaps to lose sensitivity to mild experimental disturbances.

The organisation of behaviour is real but it is elaborate, because the

deep thought in a deep armchair

Introduction

animal has to earn its living in a complicated world. The requirements of the real world are too varied and complex for the organisation to be deduced merely by deep thought in a deep armchair, it has to be discovered by observation. While it is important that hypotheses to explain the observed behaviour should be tested and disproved experimentally, analysis of the observed facts is proportionately more important and experimentation less than in most sciences – other than the oldest-established of all, astronomy.

Language

Anthony Barnett (1963) in his excellent short book *The Rat, a Study of Behaviour* said he aimed always to be clear, even at the risk of sometimes being clearly wrong. He succeeded admirably in both aims and I only hope to do half as well.

Animal behaviour is a science which has suffered as well as gained from a surfeit of great men, or more accurately from multiple creation. Each creative observer has seen comparable phenomena from a different viewpoint and has described them in a newly-invented language. The new words represent new concepts and therefore new advances in our understanding, but are confusing unless it is possible to translate from one jargon to another. I have used something of all jargons where they seemed to express concepts simply and accurately, but I have tried my best to use plain English. For the simpler the language, the less the risk of confusing what is actually seen with its theoretical implications; it is because these are important that they must be clearly distinguished. For example there are subtle distinctions between the words 'instinct' (in one of its several meanings), 'drive', and 'tendency' when they are used to discuss reproductive or feeding behaviour. I have used the awkward phrase 'kind of behaviour' (more or less equivalent to 'tendency') in order to refer to the easily observable differences between behaviours of different form and with different functions, and to avoid (or postpone) any speculation about a physiological 'drive' behind what you can see. The words illustrate how jargon can increase precision of thought, just as it can be used to obscure the vagueness of waffle.

One reason for using a precise technical language is that it makes it easier to be objective, that is to say, to describe the behaviour in a way which will allow someone else to repeat the experiment and be sure he has seen the same thing. If to be scientific means to be falsifiable, an objective description is one which leads to a hypothesis which can be proved wrong. If it cannot in principle be proved wrong, it is too vague to be helpful. However, there is a problem of swings and roundabouts. The more objective the jargon, the harder it is for the inexperienced reader to visualise precisely what the procedure entails. He cannot understand the method and the results it obtains unless he appreciates it from the animal's point of view.

For this reason I have, with some hesitation, expressed many arguments anthropomorphically. I believe that, with care, introspection can be a valuable corrective to blind reliance on objective terminology, for only by a controlled exercise of the imagination can we appreciate the constraints facing the animal, and the full variety of the options open to it. An experimental situation can be visualised more clearly and expressed more vividly to the reader if he imagines how a human being might respond.

However, anthropomorphism is a good servant but a bad master. It can be a powerful tool to help us appreciate how we might feel and therefore how complex are the possible explanations of the animal's response. But a danger is that we might postulate that the animal has subjective feelings – we might then say that the animal is doing so-and-so 'because he is hungry', 'frightened', or whatever. Now animals may well have emotions more vivid than human beings, but they are not observable and cannot be used to 'explain' the behaviour without the argument becoming circular.

In short, because we can imagine one – or several – of the possible explanations it does not follow that we have found the correct one. Objective experimentation without imagination is premature, it will certainly answer the wrong question. But only objective analysis after observation and experiment will let us choose between the hypotheses we have invented and approach a little closer to the real truth. I have therefore used anthropomorphic descriptions purely as a means of expressing an argument vividly. Once the argument has been understood the description should be abandoned, and I have been as careful as I can to phrase the description in objective terms first, in my own mind, terms to which it can easily be translated back without ambiguity.

It might be worth adding that many people appear to think in subjective terms and translate into objective language when they write. Sometimes this is done consciously and is therefore acceptable, because the writer who is aware is in control. Some writers use the most rigidly objective phraseology, but in spoken discussions give the impression of thinking quite subjectively without being aware of it. The objective language is used as if to hide the anthropomorphism from the person himself, and can therefore be not only useless but misleading.

Relationship of animal behaviour to human

It is better to discuss this at the end of the book, except for some basic propositions. Man is descended from animals, and therefore human behaviour must have evolved from animal behaviour. This does not mean that man is merely an animal. For one thing, any two animal species may differ from each other at least as widely as either does from man. And after a lifetime's experience of human behaviour we can appreciate how much more complex it is than anything we know of animals.

But if we can discover the laws governing animal behaviour in general, and if we can understand the ecological constraints which explain how and why two closely-related species may differ in their behaviour, then we have a framework for understanding ourselves. We are subject to the same necessities as any animal, but we have far more complex and subtle ways of achieving comparable goals.

Tests of animal behaviour may be merely predictive or they may be explanatory. For example, clinically useful antidepressant drugs nearly all antagonise the effects of reserpine in animals, such as the fall in body temperature, so that reserpine provides a practical predictive screening test. Reserpine also has an effect on the stores of noradrenaline held by sympathetic nerve terminals, and some antidepressant drugs seem to act by preventing the loss of noradrenaline. A behavioural test which showed us more precisely how subjective mood is related to adrenergic function would have explanatory value.

The reader of this book will be somewhat better equipped to devise tests of animal behaviour which will not only reveal an effect sensitively but allow him or her to understand it. A full knowledge of the technology of testing implies an understanding of animal behaviour for its own sake as a pure science, no matter how indirectly it is obtained; but I believe the methods will only work if the experimenter likes animals.

TWO
Language, truth and science

It all depends what you mean by behaviour

Words are the scientist's most important tools, in obtaining new knowledge as much as in communicating it to others, and the use of words requires some attention.

Suppose you want to give some laboratory rats an experimental treatment, and to discover any behavioural effects. Whatever sort of treatment it is – feeding them on a low-protein diet, housing them 1, 2, 8, or 16 to a cage, injecting an antibiotic drug, ovariectomy, or bringing them up with toys to play with – the most obvious way of finding behavioural effects is simply to go and look. So off you go. You peer into the cage and the rats are sleeping. You tap on the sides of the cage with a pencil. The animals get up one by one, and stroll over to look for a moment, then curl up and go back to sleep. You tap louder and more vigorously. When one of the rats wearily gets up and comes to look at you again, you poke the pencil through the bars of the cage and the rat bites it. If it is one of the experimental rats, you note that the treatment tends to make some of the animals irritable and aggressive. If this rat is an untreated control, while the experimental rats merely raise an eyelid quizzically, or lick a paw and snooze off again, then you call them subdued.

What do you call behaviour?

Behavioural experiments are not really designed as crudely as this, but some are not so very much better. After writing this I looked through the current issues of some reputable journals for papers reporting behavioural effects. The authors of the two I found do not claim to be experts on behaviour of course, and will forgive me for using their examples for constructive criticism of a poor state of affairs.

In a study of the cardiovascular effects of 6-hydroxydopamine injected intraventricularly, Haeusler, Gerold, and Thoenen (1972) stated that 'compared with vehicle-injected controls, the phentolamine-treated rats showed an increased irritability and aggressiveness'. The words were left quite undefined.

In the narrow sense, 'irritability' could mean a lowered threshold of response to stimuli. If so, what stimuli, and what was the response? In the colloquial sense, irritability means nearly the same as aggressiveness, but the response requires a little provocation. If so, why use two words when one would do? And aggressive to whom or what? Did the animals actually attack and bite someone or something (a pencil stuck into the cage?) without provocation, or did they merely defend themselves against the experimenter? Was he just trying to pick them up? I have the impression that many older rats suffer from what you might call abdominal subcutaneous hyperalgesia: grasping what should be the loose skin of the back and flanks seems to be distinctly painful and an otherwise docile rat may struggle, squeal, and bite. The 'irritability and aggressiveness' referred to in this paper may not have been as trivial as this. But without some description of what the animals actually did, how can the reader know?

It is perhaps unfair to criticise a passing comment. There must be many statements in this book equally open to question. Nevertheless, if something is worth saying, it is worth at least trying to make it comprehensible.

The other example concerns the 'biological effects of prolonged exposure to deuterium oxide' (Peng, Ho, and Taylor, 1972). Rats were given drinking water for 7 months in which various proportions had been replaced by 'heavy water'. 'The behaviour, food, and water consumption, and body weights . . . were carefully observed and recorded daily', and there were 'no abnormal behavioural changes' in the animals drinking 2 or 5 per cent D_2O.

This description of their method sounds perfunctory to an earnest behavioural scientist. Nevertheless, it is clear that the observation really was very careful. One of eighteen rats drinking 10 per cent deuterium oxide and three on 20 per cent '. . . showed ataxia and a peculiar head movement somewhat similar to . . . chorea; . . . jerking circular movements of the head, as the rat sought his food. Later his head movements became more pronounced. Furthermore, the rat developed a tendency to fall to one side while moving. When the rat was suspended by the tail, the body of the rat would rotate continuously on its long axis.'

This is admirably clear. It reminds me of the symptoms of an infection of the semicircular canals of the middle ear, and I suspect that I would have jumped to the hasty conclusion that the rats were suffering from 'middle ear disease' and left it at that; which illustrates how often a convenient name can substitute for a proper description of the phenomenon. The main point is that the experimenters described exactly what they saw rather than what they thought it meant. This is surprisingly difficult and even if this has once been achieved, it is very easy to slip back into slipshod verbal shorthand.

Peng, Ho, and Taylor did this in describing the other apparent effect of deuterium oxide. In the highest concentration, 20 per cent, the behaviour effects were 'more striking; most of the rats became hyper-irritable and hyper-excitable 2 to 3 days after the commencement of deuterium oxide feeding. Some rats became more aggressive, wild, and very difficult to handle. However, no convulsions occurred . . .' After 3 to 5 months, 'the rats became more withdrawn and lethargic but less excitable'. Never use one word where three will do, especially if none of the three is defined well enough for the reader to know how to repeat the observation with any confidence. As in the previous example, we want to ask if hyper-excitable, hyper-irritable, aggressive, and wild all mean merely difficult to handle? If not, how could each symptom be recognised and differentiated from all the others?

What you say influences what you see

The problem of language is partly one of communication to others, and partly one of its role in our own acquisition of information. To oversimplify a complex phenomenon, our perception is not just a matter of gratefully accepting sense-data. We actively look more than we passively see, we listen rather than hear. This is not the place to recapitulate centuries of philosophical debate, nor is this a textbook of sensory neurophysiology. What I wish to suggest is that there is a parallel, reasonably enough, between the way we deal with trivial moment-to-moment sensory information and with, let us say, important behavioural experiments. At any rate the idea will help us make sense of some technical points in the design of experiments and perhaps of some differences between science and religion. As it is not capable of proof or disproof, the idea can be discarded at the end of the next chapter.

If something catches our attention – we hear a car passing, or see a blackbird hopping about the garden, or a girl – we have to classify the information. We listen and watch. What is it? Does it need action now or later this evening? When it is identified and its priority for action assigned, we can stop observing and return to what we were doing. And successful identification is accompanied by a momentary feeling of relief, a sense that we are in control. Of course, in trivial examples like these, the emotional sensation is too small to be noticeable. But the more difficult the task of identification, the greater the wave of emotional relief. In the ultimate case: Eureka!

Essentially the same thing happens, I suggest, when we observe the behaviour of experimental animals. We watch. We think we can identify – put a name to – what the animal is doing. And then we stop intensive observation. Although we may continue to watch, once we know what we are looking at, much of the carefulness has gone. I saw striking examples of this in Michael Chance's pharmacology demonstrations (Chance and Humphries, 1967).We would take four pairs of rats, inject one of each pair with saline and the other with one of four assorted drugs. Medical students had half an hour to observe the rats, decide which one of each pair had been dosed, and describe the effects of all four drugs. It was remarkable how accurate the descriptions were when the students could not identify the drugs. It was even more remarkable how sketchy, inaccurate, and even wrong, the descriptions were when a student guessed the identity of a drug (against advice), irrespective of whether he guessed right or wrong.

Language, truth and science

It is not only primitive tribesmen who think they have power over an object or a beastie in the bush, as soon as they have given it a name. We all do. But an internal, subjective sense of achievement is not sufficient in science, we also have to communicate it to others.

Normally when we impart information, for instance to a baby, we observe when his attention has been caught by something, and couple what we think he sees with the sound of the appropriate name: this is a nose, that is a red car, there is a man running. To a slightly older little child, we demonstrate a process: this is how you write a letter A, here are 1, 2, 3, 4, 5 sweets; give two to your little brother; how many have you got left? Yes, 1, 2, 3 . . . this is how you cut one of your sweets exactly in half. We assume that if we tell someone the name of an object or a process, the name will symbolise the same sense-data for him as for us.

In simple cases it usually does, although even simple language misunderstandings can be embarrassing, like to the honest British boxer whose manager went to the United States 'to fix a fight' for him. In more complicated cases, we can never be sure. Most of us can be painfully inarticulate when we try to describe something we know perfectly well in a non-spoken context, even when it is as concrete as the route a stranger should take to the railway station or how to make pastry for a pie. When it is as abstract as 'intelligence' we all know what we mean, though we cannot define it; and only when we get deep into an argument do we discover that the other fellow clearly has not the slightest idea of what the words mean.

It is for this reason that scientists emphasise the need for objectivity. Objectivity means, in effect, that when we try to describe a phenomenon, we try as carefully as possible to describe the actual sense-data we receive. An essential corollary is that we also describe the relevant characteristics of the methods we have used to obtain our sense-data.

Admittedly, our selection of what to observe is still biased by our preconceptions. It is also true that, since we can only communicate about factual matters through language, we are bound to use words which are misunderstood. Nevertheless, the nearer we can get to a physical description of what we see, the better will other people be able to distinguish between the facts we observe and the conclusions we draw from them. If they then arrive at a new sensation of understanding, it will be solidly based because they will have achieved it for themselves.

Both science and religion attempt to explain the universe and to evoke as much as possible of the emotion of understanding. Religion may be said to attempt to arouse it as directly as possible by Faith, and may be impatient of attempts to analyse the objectivity of the evidence. Evidence is largely irrelevant, it is the subjective feeling which matters, and the moral codes for human behaviour that follow. Science on the other hand concentrates on the analysis of the evidence and the logic of its interpretation; the emotion accompanying the acceptance of an explanation, if it is acknowledged at all, is considered irrelevant. But it is not evidence which finally determines whether a scientist continues to gather further information or whether he submits his paper for publication; it is the emotional satisfaction that terminates the study. Since emotions are notoriously liable to exaggeration or depreciation, disproportionately to what an onlooker might think justified, the scientific concern for objectivity represents the need to communicate the reasons for the emotion rather than the satisfaction itself.

Objectivity, on this view, need not mean avoiding a direct description of behaviour. There are some scientists who seem to believe that an observation is not objective unless it is weighed in milligrams. Certainly test-tube observations are easier to repeat, or retain for long periods for re-checking. But observation of colour change in a chemical titration is not in principle more reliable than colour change in a chameleon. The angle of the pointer needle of a meter is not in principle more reliable than the angles between the bill, neck, and body of a herring gull in a territorial dispute. If the behaviour is described accurately in a way that other people can recognise, which means in practice if it is described in physical terms, then it is just as objective as a physical object.

Science is prediction

All this implies that behaviour is predicted, that a piece of behaviour seen and described once can be seen again. Yet is not behaviour notoriously unpredictable? And if there are no predictable regularities, there is mumbo-jumbo but no science.

There is some excuse for this doubt. Certainly the factors which influence any observable behaviour are numerous, and can be enormously complex. True as this is in animals, behaviour is surely even more complex in human beings. We are aware of so many possible constraints on our behaviour – the need to earn a living, or to sleep, the expectations of our companions – that we hesitate to examine them closely. Even more, it is precisely when we are not aware of the constraints that we are reluctant to probe, for if our behaviour is determinate, where is the free will we feel we possess?

This sense of freedom should not inhibit us from looking for the considerable regularities in our behaviour. We risk our lives every day on the almost absolute predictability that hundreds of virtually unselected car drivers drive on the correct side of the road, though our behaviour may be less predictable where the Darwinian selection-pressure is not so obvious. Nevertheless, market researchers and the gentlemen at the sides of horse race-tracks have very profitable evidence of just how far human (and animal) behaviour is predictable – as well as of how far it is not.

Language, truth and science

A question of numbers

Science is supposed to be numerical knowledge, but the units you count must measure the same characteristics, relevant for a given purpose. If you are counting your money, a few foreign coins will not help to buy your beer in this country. However, a bank can transform them into more suitable units. You can then start measuring in your penny units, how many volumetric units you can buy; the volumetric units representing convenient divisions of a continuously variable liquid.

It is worth emphasising that units can come in all shapes and sizes, and that if you mix pennies with pints, you get some funny answers. Stevens (1951) classified the various grades of units, and Siegel (1956), in that most straightforward of introductory statistical textbooks *Non-Parametric Statistics*, added a commentary on the statistical methods valid at each grade.

Nominal units are the simplest possible, where numbers are used only as names, with no implications that they represent quantities – car registration numbers, for instance, or route numbers for the roads they drive on. The only measures that can be taken of them are of contingency or frequency, the number of cases in group 1 compared with the number in group 2, using binomial, chi-squared or similar tests to discover whether the distribution is non-random.

On an *ordinal* scale, units can be ranked one above another in some sense that is not measurable. Thus, an army sergeant ranks higher than a corporal who is in turn, by some military criterion, superior to a private soldier, but a sergeant with three stripes on his sleeve is not three times as good as a lance-corporal with one.

On an *interval* scale, successive units are not only ranked, but are of equal size; however the zero point is arbitrary and has no absolute meaning. For example on the Celsius or Fahrenheit scales, a rise in temperature of 1° always means the same absolute rise, but because 0° is set arbitrarily, 10 °C does not mean 10 times as hot as 1 °C. Where there is a true zero, there is a *ratio* scale. 400 °K is in a real sense twice as hot as 200 °K, since there can be nothing colder than absolute zero in the Kelvin scale. On interval and ratio scales, parametric tests are valid and a concept like standard deviation has a real meaning.

In behavioural studies the commonest units are nominal, and if there are many kinds, it may be necessary to group them. For statistical analysis, the fewer the variables the more reliable the results from a given number of animals; and of course the fewer the kinds of behaviour to explain, the easier it is to think of an explanation. In fact, if you reduce the variables to one, an effect can have many possible interpretations, all fitting the available data, but only one is likely to be correct. So you have to be careful to establish as reasonably valid a grouping of the units as can be judged, for an interesting pattern could otherwise be hidden in a mush of miscellaneous meanderings.

In some methods, only one type of unit is observed, but can be recorded in very large numbers. In some versions of operant conditioning, the animal may press a lever hundreds of times a session, and the patterning of the behaviour, in time or in relation to external stimuli, then becomes interesting.

The way in which units are grouped, so far as this is under the experimenter's control, is clearly as important as the original selection of units, but it will be easier to discuss these problems for each method in turn. There seems to be no general way of deciding whether a given grouping or patterning is 'natural' and corresponds to the real structure of the behaviour in the animal.

Conclusions

I have claimed that the reader considers a scientific proof truly proved, when the evidence releases a specific emotional satisfaction (though the evidence has to be good to achieve such success). This is in principle a scientific hypothesis about the working of the brain, but in practice it is not easy to test. Paradoxically, therefore, I have had to argue the case for the hypothesis, not in a scientific manner, but as if it were an 'arts' subject or even a quasi-religious one. That is, I have appealed to what should be common experience, hoping to release the 'Eureka' emotion, in which you find the answer and stop looking for more information. Since I cannot provide hard evidence, I can only suggest that whether or not the idea is true or original, you may find it a useful way of looking at things.

The other issues illustrate how often debates that are supposed to be about facts boil down to discussions on the meaning of words. The converse can occur, since the meaning of the word hyper-excitable could well be decided by observation, analysis and (in principle) experiment. But time and again, we are brought back to the central issue, that it is essential to define your words, in particular to define what you will treat as a unit.

THREE
What to watch – the units of behaviour

A keen young psychopharmacologist, you stride into the laboratory in the morning – and your animals are fast asleep. You have to decide what to observe and record and how to find it.

If you observe long enough, you will see everything the animals are capable of. At least, everything they can do in the restricted environment of a laboratory cage, and this can still be remarkably varied. A day in the life of albino rat might start when he wakes at twilight (or when the humans have just gone home) and explores the cage a little, just to make sure that everything is as it should be. He might wash his face and paws, have a short quarrel with a cage-mate to see how the dominance relationships are this evening, and then settle down to breakfast. Meals are customarily followed in due course by sleep. There are several such cycles of activity in 24 hours, and the relative durations of exploration, grooming, fighting, eating, and sleep vary considerably according to the time of day. Sexual and parental behaviour follow longer-term rhythms, while food-hoarding and burrow-digging vary, among other things, according to the facilities available.

The would-be experimenter has two basic problems: to select behavioural units which can be relied on to provide trustworthy evidence; and to persuade the animal to perform them at a time of the experimenter's choice.

To discover the place of a particular piece of behaviour on the animal's own order of priorities, you have to wait for the animal to perform it at a time of his own convenience. You can then discern some features of the situation which may govern its appearance. There will almost certainly be both internal factors (e.g. hormone levels or the time since the previous performance) and external stimuli involved. You can make a hypothesis about these and then devise experiments to test it. But if you want to use the behaviour to indicate the effect of some other treatment, then you have to persuade the animal to perform it when you are ready to observe it, with your paper and pencil or on-line computer at the ready.

Obtaining behaviour on demand

Most kinds of behaviour require specific stimuli, and those for exploration in rats and aggression in mice are easier to present than most others. There are two general ways of inducing behaviour on demand, not logically distinct from presenting specific stimuli, but convenient to describe separately as I will do in the rest of this book. You can deprive the animal of something you believe it needs, and then offer it. The something is usually food or water, but other things have been used – warmth, a social companion of the same or opposite sex, a lactating female's pups. Rats have even been deprived of air by releasing them into an underwater maze.

Deprivation of air or of a comfortable environmental temperature could be regarded not as the removal of a positive stimulus, but from the opposite point of view, as the presentation of a negative one. The animal would be expected to escape from somewhere much too hot or cold, or to avoid entering it in the first place. The usual negative stimulus is electric shock, because of its flexibility in use and the ease of its control, but puffs of air and bursts of loud noise have also been used satisfactorily.

Electric shock or deprivation of food, water, or air can be quite mild. They can be used very effectively to get useful results, but also to an extent which amounts to cruelty. Ethical questions deserve a chapter to themselves, but I hope this book will help to suggest techniques giving more information to man at lower cost to the animal.

The rat race

If you put a rat into a situation where the specific stimuli for a particular kind of behaviour are present, then that is what will be available for observation. Thus if you have deprived the animals of water and then offer them water, then it is quite possible to watch them drinking. But as I shall discuss in a moment, the most obvious behaviour to watch is not always interesting except for itself alone, and is not the most useful for more general purposes. So it is usual not to give water to a thirsty animal directly, but to give him the opportunity to do something to obtain it, something which becomes the subject-matter of all those routines that the word 'rat-race' was invented for. The animal has to run through a maze or jump through a hoop marked

teaching rats to jump through hoops

The units of behaviour

in vertical stripes. 'I've got my professor well trained,' says one white rat in the famous cartoon to the other. 'Every time I press this lever, he gives me a pellet of food.'

The advantage gained by this indirect approach is twofold. In the first place, not every drug (or other treatment) affects behaviour by altering motivation, though many do. The treatment might have altered the speed of motor responses, or the animal might have gone limp, for some drugs specifically relax muscle. It might have altered the animal's ability to discriminate between two sensory stimuli, or (probably very commonly) the attention that he pays to such stimuli as come his way. These are not closely related to what the animal wants to do, as it were, but they could severely affect his ability to achieve it. It is usually easier to test for and measure such effects on the behaviour an animal shows well before it attains its goal. When licking or chewing is all that needs doing, it is too late to interfere.

The first advantage of the indirect approach is that it covers an area much more sensitive to certain types of experimental intervention, some of them not easily accessible in any other way. The second advantage is that the units of some kinds of 'rat-race' routines are easier to record objectively and even automatically. The time taken to run a maze can be recorded on a stopwatch, or even by photocells and an electronic timer. Pressing a lever can switch an electric circuit and be counted, recorded, timed, and rewarded electrically without the intervention of human hand almost from start to finish.

When I outlined a day in the life of a laboratory rat, I was beginning to try to identify units in the animal's own behaviour. It was implied that a set of specific actions can be found in grooming, for example, which can be described in physical terms, without confusion with anything else. Thus, licking the forepaws and wiping the inner side of each forearm alternately along the sides of the face seem to form one grooming unit, and scratching the flank with the extended claws of a hindleg another. The fact that they occur in an essentially all-or-nothing form suggests that they are genuine units of behaviour under the control of a single on/off switch somewhere in the central nervous system.

Historically, units seen in the animal's own behaviour seemed subjective, before ethologists like Tinbergen showed how to define them adequately. In the first half of the twentieth century, the dominant concern of animal psychology was objectivity, but instead of making the observation of the animal's actions more objective, the tendency was to develop artificial units.

Pavlov avoided the problem of the subjectivity of 'natural' units of behaviour by not measuring behaviour at all. In the main, he measured a physiological correlate of behaviour instead, namely the volume of saliva secreted by a hungry dog allowed to smell meat. Pavlov then used, not the original unconditioned smell stimulus, but an artificial one, a light or sound that was at first quite meaningless to the dog. The new stimulus, after repeated association with the old, came to acquire the significance of the original smell of meat: it could evoke the flow of saliva.

Measuring the flow of saliva is technically feasible but a little awkward. Moreover, salivation is normally an automatic component of the process of eating, without any particular behavioural consequences apart from not getting a sore dry mouth (though the dogs no doubt expect to get the experimenter's approval too). In real life, so to speak, behaviour is a means to an end, to the finding of a mate, a nest, some food, and so on. Whatever the animal does has consequences which may be beneficial or otherwise, and the animal can modify his behaviour appropriately in future.

Conditioned stimuli therefore lead logically to a conditioned response. In the laboratory, this has to be somewhat artificial, a rat-race routine which the animal would be unlikely to perform quite spontaneously. There must, of course, be something for the experimenter to select, modify, and develop by suitable rewards, but he needs to be sure that it has occurred because of the experimental procedure and not in response to some unnoticed and accidental stimulus. An artificial unit can also be arranged to be easy to detect and record, but to be reliable it must produce beneficial consequences for the animal. Thus, until the rat has run through a maze to the goal box, he gets no food. If he does not climb a wooden pole within 5 seconds of the light coming on, he gets a strong electric shock. If he does not press a lever at the right time, he has a much longer wait for a lick of water.

Behaviour as a search for reflexes

These so-called 'natural' and 'artificial' units can best be compared in the framework of a simple example of the normal structure of behaviour. Wallace Craig (1918) is said (e.g. by Kennedy, 1954) to have first distinguished between 'appetitive' and 'consummatory' phases of instinctive behaviour. The consummatory phase, as you might expect, is the actual consumption of food, the consummation of sexual behaviour in copulation, the goals which give each kind of behaviour its name. These (chewing, swallowing, and so on) would be a fairly rigid series of reflex actions. Appetitive behaviour is much more complicated and variable, and consists of all those actions from the time of the first internal stimulus for feeding, i.e. when the animal first 'feels hungry', until it has worked its way into a situation where the consummatory reflexes can take over.

Consider breathing. Helen Spurway and J. B. S. Haldane (1953) pointed out how it is usually a reflex system quite simple to study physiologically. In man, in the absence of illness, breathing is a reflex cycle depending on the distension or relaxation of receptors in the lungs and ribcage. Low oxygen tension in the carotid sinus accelerates the cycle, lowered pH (due to extra dissolved carbon dioxide) makes breathing deeper. But if this reflex system is blocked, under water perhaps, there develops an increasingly strong drive

The units of behaviour 19

to exercise the breathing reflex. There is no mistaking how apt the strong word 'drive' is.

In newts, breathing can be clearly seen to be a miniature instinct. When partly or wholly out of water, *Triturus cristatus* breathes by reflex like man. In water, the newt is slightly buoyant, but can become denser than the water by 'guffing' out a bubble of air, by compressing the lungs in active diving, or by gradually absorbing the oxygen from the lungs. It can become less dense by ascending towards the surface (decompressing the lungs) or by breathing. The interval between ascents is shortened by reducing the oxygen concentration in the air, or by raising the temperature or pressure. The interval is lengthened, Spurway and Haldane found, by increasing the oxygen tension in air or water, since much of the gas exchange takes place through the skin. Carbon dioxide, for this reason, does not affect a newt's breathing. The newt's lungs act as buoyancy tanks at least as much as gas exchangers.

A newt may show signs that he is beginning to need to breathe before he actually does so. He may interrupt feeding or courtship under water with 'intention movements', lifting his head and maybe his chest briefly before resuming courtship. Eventually he breaks off for longer, and swims up slowly with his legs or quickly with the tail. He may rise to just below the surface, or climb out, breathe, and dive again, perhaps to find the female has lost patience and departed (cf. Halliday and Sweatman, 1976).

Spurway and Haldane point out how this behaviour bears most of the signs of a classical instinct. The final consummatory fixed-action pattern based on reflexes is relatively invariable. To bring the animal into a position to perform this, there is a relatively long period of appetitive behaviour, variable according to circumstances. It contains reflex or other innate components (chemical stimuli from oxygen tension in the blood, and from tension receptors in the chest) and movements of the head, legs, and tail. There are other components varying with the immediate external stimuli. (Is the pond bank closer than that flat underwater stone? If not, is the stone near enough to the surface to be worth standing on?) It includes competition from tendencies to do something else and, perhaps, influences from the individual's past experience (i.e. learning. Although lower vertebrates like newts have not been shown to learn an entirely new response, they may well modify what they have always been capable of in relation to a new stimulus). Except that learning is not so important in amphibia as in most mammals, breathing in newts is therefore a microcosm of the structure of many kinds of behaviour.

Suppose we were to use newts as the experimental animal and breathing as the variable to test. Breathing is easy to observe visually but difficult to record automatically (we could use photography or videotape, of course, but this would only postpone the problem to another occasion). The consummatory phase would have to be estimated as the number and duration of periods in air or as carbon dioxide output into the air and water of a closed aquarium. But detectable changes in these might be because a warmer environment had increased the newts' metabolic rate and therefore motor activity and respiration in general. It might be easier to measure motor activity directly.

The appetitive phase is necessarily more flexible and sensitive to changes either in the need to breathe or in any competing tendencies. The newt must respond, for instance, to any source of information about where to go. Intention movements are by definition likely to show where the tendency to breathe is just about in balance with whatever the newt submerged for in the first place.

Thus Halliday and Sweatman (1976) show how a male newt courting an unresponsive female may continue until courtship is inhibited by increasing competition from the need to breathe. These bouts are interrupted at variable points in the sequence, the interruptions being presumably by intention movements of ascent. If the female responds, particularly if she stimulates the male to deposit a spermatophore by touching his tail, breathing is delayed until the end of a stage in the courtship sequence; it is then disinhibited and the male ascends directly to the surface without the need for intention movements.

As a rough generalisation, and with all the caution this implies, tests of the consummatory phase are most suited to measure the 'strength' of the particular tendency involved. They might do so in absolute terms (e.g. how much oxygen is consumed?) or compared to other kinds of behaviour (e.g. when does breathing become more urgent than courtship?). Because they use relatively fixed sequences of actions, they are perhaps less sensitive than the corresponding tests of the appetitive phase but validate the results more reliably.

Tests of the appetitive phase might be classifiable as 'natural' or 'artificial'. Those using units recognised in unconditioned behaviour might be particularly suitable for assessing the balance between competing tendencies – courtship bouts are shorter in newts with low 'libido' after they have used up most of their spermatophores, and more easily interrupted by the need to breathe; conversely, sexual behaviour is a little faster if less oxygen is available (Halliday, 1977).

Artificial units conditioned by the experimenter may be better for discovering the animal's capabilities than its priorities. They can be tailored to test the particular skills needed for a task, the limits of what it can be trained to do or the stimuli it can distinguish. The degree to which the animal actually uses the skills is strongly affected by the conditioning process (this is discussed in Chapter 13) and may therefore be less sensitive.

I should emphasise, of course, that the words 'appetitive' and 'consummatory' are not to be rigidly separated. They are labels for the extremes of a continuous spectrum, used in order to make the arguments clear, not to

The units of behaviour 21

divide all behaviour into two distinct classes. 'Natural' and 'artificial' are, even more emphatically, words used to convey an argument, a convenient shorthand, and nothing more. Behaviour I have labelled artificial will certainly have been especially conditioned by the experimenter, but there must have been a pre-existing foundation to build on. Units I have called 'natural' have not been conditioned deliberately, but may well have been conditioned by the environment in which the individual was born and bought up, in the routine of the laboratory colony. Their development is a subject for research in its own right, but if the units exist they can be exploited.

Drinking, a survey of a typical kind of behaviour

Most of the rest of this book will describe actual tests of animal behaviour, but this chapter should have explained some of the underlying logic. A brief review of experiments on a single behaviour may help to relate different behavioural methods to each other and to physiology. A rat drinks by licking. The usual laboratory system allows a lick to remove a drop of water, held in by surface tension, from the bottom of the inverted water-bottle spout

Fig. 3.1.

(Fig. 3.1). Corbit and Luschei (1969) showed that rats lick at remarkably constant rates. Inter-lick intervals in their sample were 150 ± 15 milliseconds and rats obtained about 0.03 ml of water per second in six or seven licks. Drinking must be a simple on/off cycle, and the quantity of water drunk fairly simply related to the sheer length of time spent drinking. However, in my own observations the first and last few licks of a bout of drinking often have somewhat longer intervals than the rest. Also, if three or four rats are drinking simultaneously, each one must lick at slightly longer intervals (slightly out of phase with the others) so they can lick in turn.

The general uniformity of licking rates implies that if a treatment lengthens the time taken for 100 licks (e.g. Vogel, Hughes, and Carlton, 1967), then the animal probably breaks up the 100 licks into a greater number of bouts, or bouts further apart in time. The effective unit is the bout of licking, not the single lick itself.

In the short term, a rat stops drinking through stimuli in the mouth, especially cooling of the tongue (Kapatos and Gold, 1972), and swallowing. 'Air drinking', when the spout delivers a puff of air, can temporarily satisfy a rat (Oatley and Dickenson, 1970). Water passed directly into the stomach through a fistula does not act as a reward for the performance of a learned task: at least in Barbary doves, a thirsty bird only works if he can swallow (McFarland, 1969).

In the longer term it is possible to distinguish two causes of thirst (Campbell and Misanin, 1969), although they usually occur together. First, as water is lost from the blood through breathing, excretion, and so on, its volume must be replaced, and isotonic saline would be suitable. However, when water is lost in the exhaled breath or when blood sugar concentration rises after a meal, the osmotic pressure goes up. Osmotic thirst arises rapidly and is sensitive to a 1 per cent rise in solute concentration; it can of course only be relieved by water, not saline solution.

The rate of water loss, formerly thought to be proportional to body surface area, was shown by Siegel and Stuckey (1947) and Bolles (1961) to be more directly related to food consumption, though this is in turn related to heat loss and thence to surface area. Much of a laboratory rat's water is required to digest a dry laboratory diet, and a rat deprived of food need not be thirsty. A rat deprived of water, on the other hand, cannot eat and digest his food and is therefore both thirsty and hungry.

Experiments to elucidate physiological control mechanisms must be fascinating in their own right. David McFarland and his colleagues (1971) have concentrated on drinking as a problem in control engineering, and have used 'black box' mathematics to describe the drinking of doves quantitatively, down to surprisingly small details.

Many psychologists are not concerned with drinking in its own right, rather they have utilised it as an indicator of some other effect. Thirst provides the driving force for an elaborate learned appetitive behaviour, but a force that need be of no specific interest. According to one theory, such thirst could in principle be replaced by half a dozen other drives without the slightest apparent difference to the results.

Drinking can be altered by many different treatments and it is instructive to briefly review a few of them. Khavari and Russell (1969) found the anticholinergic drugs atropine and scopolamine to depress drinking. They probably did not act directly on the brain, as their methyl bromide derivatives (which do not cross the 'blood–brain barrier') had the same effect. But while these drugs reduced the number of licks and hence the intake of water, they did not alter the time taken by 100 licks, as a noise warning of electric shock did (Vogel et al., 1967) – not surprisingly, fear and

The units of behaviour

thirst are different phenomena with independent effects on the same dependent variable. Antihistamines also depress deprivation-induced drinking, which is restored if histamine itself is injected directly into the brain ventricles (Gerald and Maickel, 1972).

As we might expect, diuretic drugs deplete the body of water and stimulate drinking, but drinking specifically of water, of course, not of alcohol (Ericksson, 1967). So although treated rats drank the same absolute amount of alcohol their preference (alcohol as a percentage of total fluid) appeared to decline – note the danger of jumping to the conclusion that a diuretic might alleviate a drinking problem. Water consumption can also be raised surgically: ligature of the inferior vena cava restricts blood flow to the kidneys, mimicking a low blood volume and stimulating a hormone to induce drinking (Fitzsimons, 1966).

Barbiturates, especially after repeated dosing (Schmidt, Kleinman, and Douthitt, 1967), also increase drinking but by a quite different mechanism. It depends on 'sensitising the drinking response' in the brain, as shown by permuting training and testing with or without phenobarbitone and/or water deprivation. This idea matches a finding of Richard Tomkiewicz (1972). He deprived groups of four male rats of water for 21 hours a day, and gave them 3 minutes access to a water bottle that only one rat could drink from at a time. The rats formed hierarchies in terms of who got how much water in that 3 minutes. A small dose (7.5 mg/kg) of amylobarbitone daily for 2 weeks abolished the hierarchy, the subordinates achieved as much access as the dominants, yet the hierarchies appeared again 2 weeks later. However, the sensitisation of a response is probably not specific to drinking: Silverman (1966b) found barbiturates to disinhibit aggression and reduce submission or escape in rats and this phenomenon may have helped Tomkiewicz's subordinate rats too.

A more complex interaction is suggested by an experiment with dexamphetamine. This is a motor stimulant which also reduces eating and drinking, and in large doses can be generally disruptive. Glick and Jarvik (1969) trained monkeys on a delayed-matching task to obtain water. Dexamphetamine upset the monkeys' accuracy on this task even in the low doses of 0.1–0.4 mg/kg intramuscularly. At the same time 0.1 mg/kg increased their rate of working while 0.2–0.4 mg/kg depressed it. Longer deprivation of water, on the other hand, made the monkeys try harder: it increased both accuracy and response rate, so the larger doses of amphetamine acted as if to reduce 'thirst'.

The fact that the complex, learned task was appetitive to drinking was relevant: the monkeys could have been trained to give the same performance to avoid shock, but the same drug would probably have then had different effects. However Cathleen Morrison (1967) trained rats on four different lever-pressing schedules for water. Nicotine, usually found to be a stimulant in animal experiments, duly increased response rates on all the schedules (with transient reductions in some). Since the response rate did not greatly change how much water the rats obtained, and for other reasons, Morrison concluded that the drug had not altered the tendency to drink as such. The effects were more closely related to the task the animals were called on to perform, to the means rather than the end.

It follows that we have to study not only the units of behaviour, but also the way they are organised into a larger structure. The stimuli that can be responded to, and the responses that can be made, differ qualitatively and quantitatively between species. They probably also differ between different kinds of behaviour, between the appetitive and consummatory phases of each kind, and possibly within these too. It is therefore necessary to be as careful in interpreting results from one level or one 'kind' of behaviour as from one species to another. Yet there is, I believe, sufficient similarity in the organisation of behaviour between species to enable meaningful (if cautious) comparisons to be made. The complex organisation of behaviour means that any one treatment (e.g. a drug) may have superficially different effects in different tests. But that very complexity ought to lend confidence when various tests give the same result, and it should also help to formulate and test a unitary hypothesis when they differ.

Summary

Behaviour sequences end in a functional goal, either a state (e.g. having escaped from danger, a state where certain stimuli are absent) or in the opportunity to perform some fixed action pattern (e.g. chewing and swallowing, assuming certain stimuli are also present). The fixed action patterns are virtually reflexes, but are preceded by a long and variable appetitive sequence which can therefore include a mixture of elements. Some of these exist relatively uniformly in all members of a species, whether they are strictly innate or learned during the normal course of development, but the dependence of this appetitive behaviour on environmental stimuli means that we can condition a relatively artificial action to suit the experiment. Essentially 'natural' actions can be exploited experimentally mainly in relation to the specific kind of behaviour concerned and its place in the animal's behaviour as a whole. Artificial units reveal what the animal is able to do more than what it does spontaneously, its capabilities more than its motivation.

FOUR

Some questions of ethics and experimental design

I would not be writing this book and you would not continue to read it if we did not both believe that, in some circumstances, experiments on living animals are justified. Many people do not take this view. A few do not even consider the question: some experiments are interesting and some are essential, and if they cannot be done on man for any reason, then let us use animals without further ado. At the other extreme, many people say that any experiment on a defenceless animal, or even mere captivity, is inevitably cruel and therefore wrong. While I disagree, I believe that the issue is important. My conclusions are of course personal, but open discussion will help the reader to reach his own on rational grounds.

Briefly, the argument is that some experiments seem to cause unnecessary suffering. One or two examples are given in this book, though I am sure that the experimenters were not intentionally cruel and I may, after all, be misinterpreting the facts. But the case needs answering even if the examples are mistaken.

The intention of this book is therefore to encourage future experimenters in animal behaviour to consider carefully what they hope to find out. By displaying the methods available, it should help them obtain the most information at the lowest cost, both to the experimenter and to the animals.

The case against experimentation

The 'anti-vivisectionists' argue from a simple principle, sentimental but still disturbing, that it is wrong to deliberately inflict pain on other living creatures. It is equally wrong to deliberately do something without caring: pain caused by accident is just as painful. The wrong is even greater if that living creature is in your power, unable either to stop you or to escape. The problem does not only arise from science, of course, but also from battery chickens unable to stretch their wings, from *pâté de foie gras* prepared from forcibly fed geese, from lobsters boiled alive. The logical anti-vivisectionist will have none of this either. She will not use drugs developed by testing in animals, she is a vegetarian and will not eat meat or exploit animals in any way she knows how to avoid.

How can pain be recognised? The signs of pain that we take most notice of, are audible squeals or screams. These are usually alarm signals which seem to be shared by many mammals and birds. It may be that each species independently evolved a signal with similar characteristics (sounds of a pitch high but audible to man travel well but are hard to localise for physical reasons, so that the animal can warn its friends and relatives without attracting too close attention from a prowling cat); or because the more species respond to common alarm signals, the more potential sentries there are. So we too are likely to respond when an experimental animal screeches suddenly, and it is likely that the screech really is a response to pain – or to tissue damage that in man would probably be accompanied by pain – or to the anticipation of pain. At least the animal is responding as if it thinks there is something to be alarmed about.

It does not follow that there is no pain if there is no squeal, for not all pain requires a predator to be startled or a neighbour warned. Rats may squeal when picked up or injected, but not afterwards – even when an arched back and laterally compressed abdomen suggest a severe internal pain. Rats with tumours whose counterparts in man would be treated with large doses of pain-killing drugs may show little sign beyond an obvious handicap in walking round the cage. Conversely, the lowing of a cow that has lost her calf sounds subjectively mournful to us but may merely be a summoning call that the calf could detect and localise from a long way off. We simply cannot tell, in many cases, whether the animal is suffering or not; but if suffering is to be expected, can we take a chance?

Pain is not the only intolerable discomfort. In man, drugs like apomorphine cause vomiting. Rats cannot vomit, but after apomorphine they may lift their head repeatedly as if retching, so that head-lifting can be taken as a sign of nausea. What looks like a surprising degree of fear can come merely by leaving a rat alone and undisturbed in its cage for a week or two and then trying to pick it up. In other situations where you might plausibly suspect a rat to be terrified, a motionless, straight-backed crouch (alternating with very fast running only if it is disturbed) has been apparently mistaken in more than one pharmacological report for sedation.

At the same time, what we imagine to be unpleasant may not really be so. Something may be considered very disturbing for man, but may be trivial to an animal. Even if the triviality is given a nasty name, it may still be trivial.

The case against the case against

The first answer to the anti-vivisectionists is that pain or other cruelty is not necessarily involved at all, and perhaps the majority of experiments are trivial. In fact, even if a scientist wished to be cruel, it would not be in his interest, for excessive stress can make the response untypical and the experiment uninformative.

The second answer contradicts the first to some extent, but it could be claimed that we owe no duty to other species, only to our own. Some people arguing this way also suggest that animals may not feel pain as we do.

The third argument, given that there is a real risk of unavoidable cruelty, is that it can be necessary because in the long run it will be of benefit to man or indeed to other animals. It is possible to misuse this answer, for the equivalent is the classic excuse in a police state for the torture of suspected dissidents. Nevertheless, it is the answer I prefer because it implies a quantitative balance – how much benefit can be weighed against how much pain?

It may indeed be difficult to draw a line between human beings of your own family or nation and strangers, or between human beings and creatures so intelligent and so like us (apart from being so rare) as chimpanzees, or between them and monkeys, or dogs, cats, and horses .... There is admittedly no easy line to be drawn between any two groups or species, except of course for the sentimental distinction between pets and others. Nevertheless, it is absurd to refuse to make a distinction at all. Do you refuse to swat a fly or a mosquito? And if so, do you condemn them to lingering convulsions with anticholinesterase insecticides? Some people claim that even vegetables have feelings – when you bite a crisp stick of celery, is the crackle really a scream of pain? To avoid drawing a line as ridiculous as to draw it in any single place.

Moreover, we cannot avoid exploiting animals even if we avoid meat and drugs. Much as I dislike the use of rare primates by drug companies, I cannot deny that poliomyelitis became a rare disease after the 1960s largely through the large-scale use of a vaccine that could at first be grown only on monkey kidneys. If it comes to that, we cannot avoid exploiting other human beings, for we cannot opt out of society. Using animals is legitimate, I believe, so long as they are not wasted. The experiments had better be good.

Experiments should be planned so as to stand a good chance of yielding useful results in any case. To illustrate the present issue with the testing of potential pain-killing drugs, the risk of pain should be set against the analgesic effectiveness that can reasonably be expected. If the chemicals to be screened are quite new and untested, I suggest that the worst pain you should inflict on control animals (or on those given 'drugs' that turn out useless) is a pain mild enough for a weak analgesic like aspirin to deal with. If you hope to relieve such intense or long-term conditions as some terminal cancers or a phantom limb, then candidate drugs ought to have been already proved effective in milder screens; there should be prior evidence that the compounds stand a real chance of being found as effective as morphine. And there should be a rational means of selecting the candidate compounds in the first place from research into the neurology of pain or the pharmacology of 'enkephalin', rather than randomly testing everything in sight.

In short, there is a distinction between the probability of inflicting suffering and its likely severity. If the pain is likely to be severe, then not only should the potential benefit to man be correspondingly great, but only very few animals should be exposed to the risk; control animals should nearly all be given a standard drug known to be effective rather than a 'placebo' known to be useless. If a high proportion of the animals are at risk, then the pain must only be mild.

Routine testing in toxicology therefore makes me uneasy. The first time the safety of a new chemical is considered, the standard test is to estimate the LD_{50}, the dose lethal to 50 per cent of a (small) group of animals. Certainly it is important to discover the dose of a potential drug or pesticide that might kill human beings exposed to it, for if the dose is low, the compound is too dangerous for common use. But this is almost the last thing we need to know about a serious candidate compound, not the first. For a quick, crude measure of safety, I would like to consider replacing the LD_{50} with something we might call the UD_{50}, the lowest dose to produce an 'unacceptable' effect in 50 per cent of a group of animals. This would be any effect which would make the compound unacceptable for its proposed use in man; death would clearly be an especially unacceptable effect, but any lesser side-effect should be discovered and considered sooner rather than later.

In brief a cost–benefit analysis is necessary at the planning stage of an experiment. How great is the likely benefit to mankind at large? What is the private benefit to the experimenter, in terms of money, prestige, or a PhD? And what is the cost to the animal?

Pain and behaviour

Behavioural experiments do not usually cause pain, and when they do, it is sometimes because of the experimenter's carelessness or ignorance. Such experiments should not have been performed or published unless they give information which is both important and could not have been otherwise obtained. It is not always possible to make a fair judgement from the published description but an example is given (p. 197) which at face value seems unacceptable to me. Rats were subjected to electroshock strong enough to evoke 'the maximal overt response' at unpredictable intervals over periods of up to 7 hours. The sheer duration seems wrong for animals whose own periods of sustained activity last for perhaps half an hour. The objective was to find a model for the stress (as the hypothesis went at the time) that raises free fatty acid concentrations in blood plasma and so leads to coronary thrombosis in business executives, and to see if tranquillising drugs inhibit the rise. The expected effects were found, but to such a slight degree as to cast doubt (in my personal view, with hindsight) on the value of the experiment.

Similarly when investigating shock-induced aggression (see p. 284), was it necessary to give a pair of rats a shock every 1.5 seconds for 7.5 hours just to see them respond with a fighting gesture to 80 per cent of the shocks at

Some questions of ethics and experimental design

first but to less than 40 per cent after 6 hours? Or to expose them to physically damaging intensity (135 dB) of noise for over a minute at a time to show that noise is not an effective stimulus?

A further example (p. 161) does not involve pain but suggests an unacceptable degree of discomfort. If I understand the report correctly, monkeys were held in restraining chairs and given a repeated cycle of tests for 6 months continuously with no opportunity for more than a few minutes snatched sleep. This seems absurd and I should learn how to read; if it were true, it would be serious.

On the other hand there is a large class of behavioural experiments involving the risk of pain, but for which there is every justification in principle. These are studies of 'punishment' where a certain action by the animal is followed by a stimulus that the animal tends to escape from or avoid altogether in future. The argument is nicely expressed by Azrin and Holz (1966): every time you put your finger in the fire you get burned, every time you pluck a rose you risk the thorns. It is not a cruel human law but one of nature which punishes certain actions inevitably and immediately without implying immorality or disapproval. Since we are constructed to feel pain it must have survival value, and its most obvious function is to act as a graded but powerful 'negative reinforcer' to inhibit actions which could lead to physical damage.

Behaviour in relation to painful stimuli is therefore a phenomenon which requires study. In many respects the actual degree of apparent pain is surprisingly unimportant – especially, of course, when the animal successfully avoids the painful stimulus altogether. In most cases there is nothing to be gained by using an intense stimulus, whose effects may be due to actual tissue damage, where a mild one will do. In fact the electrical stimuli establishing and maintaining avoidance behaviour (see Chapters 15–17) can be remarkably slight. If you put your own hand on the grid floor, the stimulus can hardly be felt, your arm jumps off the grid by reflex before you are aware of the stimulus as a slight tingle or tickle. It would be quite tolerable if there was any advantage to be gained, and though rats may not feel as we do, they still accept shock in some circumstances.

So it is not the mere use of electroshock that makes a procedure cruel, nor does the use of the word 'pain' as a shorthand label for 'aversive reinforcement'. The critical questions are numerical, the intensity and duration of the shock. The risk is magnified because electroshock is given automatically by a suitable machine, usually without any need for the experimenter actually to observe what he has made happen.

Caging, care and choice

If wild rats travel a matter of kilometres every night and migrate to the country in summer (see Chapter 24), and laboratory rats run similar distances in activity wheels, is confinement to a cage itself a case of cruelty? But perhaps such long journeys are forced, in the one case by the unwilling search for food and in the other by some stimuli from the wheel. For other laboratory measures of activity do not confirm the distances run in wheels, and it may equally well be that rats are content to live a life of warmth and well-fed leisure in a confined space (like people?) if born and brought up in the same conditions. Kavanau showed (see p. 91) how the important question for deermice is not the distance or timing of their run, but how far they control it themselves.

Behaviour is after all the means by which animals adapt to their environment, and perhaps there is no absolutely 'correct' environment in which behaviour is 'natural' but only various conditions which are more or less sub-optimal or indeed super-optimal. Rats, in particular, are useful laboratory animals precisely because they are so adaptable in the wild, making the ideal both harder to discover and (up to a point) less important.

In the wild, rats normally live in groups (Chapter 24) and in the laboratory there are differences (Chapter 20) between rats caged singly and those in small groups, some of which suggest that the latter are usually better off. One kind of exception seems reasonable. In operant conditioning experiments (Chapter 12) rats are caged singly for months at a time and seem not to suffer. Perhaps it is crucial that the animals are handled daily and given some task to perform. Brain chemistry is different in rats given a variety of 'toys' and it may be that rats are intelligent enough to suffer from boredom, which social companionship or a variety of things to do can ameliorate.

Hamsters cause a problem because in the wild they seem to adopt individual but neighbouring territories. Living in groups in small laboratory

individual attention

cages, they can fight viciously since the victim cannot run away home and continues to present the stimuli provoking attack. Yet hamsters are surely equally liable to boredom.

Whatever 'intelligence' may be, dogs and cats surely have more of it than any rodent, and the higher monkeys and apes more still. In their different ways, all these are also group-living animals. Dogs can be kept very successfully in laboratories, as Pavlov showed (Chapter 11), but the individual attention they need is widely recognised. The questions of boredom and a suitable social structure matter so overwhelmingly for the higher primates that I doubt if the ordinary laboratory can legitimately keep true monkeys or apes in solitary confinement. A solitary monkey is fine if someone is willing to spend his working life attending to it as the nineteenth-century organ-grinders did; a single chimpanzee is fine if taken into a human family like Washoe, taught deaf-and-dumb language and patiently reintroduced to chimpanzees. Conversely, a caged group of monkeys and apes can do well in a laboratory if they have the facilities to occupy themselves busily. But even zoos with a good reputation for trying to get conditions right are apt to show their primates gloomy, apathetic, or pacing a stereotyped repetitive path. It is not surprising if a monkey left solitary and bored in a cramped cage should alternate between depression and sudden attacks on the rare person bold enough to try and handle it.

In my opinion, those who wish to use primates ought to demonstrate that they can do so without inadvertent cruelty. There is also a conservation problem in finding primates for experiment from habitats dwindling daily in the face of civilisation. While the best laboratories, especially those breeding their own animals, are clearly legitimate, the difficulties of reaching an adequate standard are far greater for primates than for rodents. It is correspondingly harder to give a valid reason for using primates to obtain information that rodents give more cheaply. For all laboratory animals, the right conditions are important, and the UFAW Handbook (1976) should be consulted.

Pharmacological models: drugs in animals and man

Human behaviour has evolved from that of animals, and the protean forms our behaviour takes are in principle merely ever more complicated and versatile ways of solving the same problems. When we come to the use of animals for pharmacological and other testing, however, the first question is not their validity as a model for man, but whether the treatment affects the animal, and if so, how. There may be differences between species, but at this stage the animal is considered as if it were a test-tube and taxonomic relationships are hardly relevant. A mouse may on occasion make a better model of man than a monkey, clearer like a cartoon sketch even if not truly closer. Experiments are easier in mice and certainly cheaper.

The dosage of drugs is usually calculated on the ratio between weight of drug and body-weight of animal, but this is an approximation that works better within species than between them. The notorious story is of an elephant given LSD in a microgram per kilogram dose which had had virtually no observable effect in mice; the elephant died. Weighing the drug in terms of the animal's surface area gives, for a given shape, a more constant concentration at the relevant target organ. But the brain, if this is the target, is not always the same relative size, and when the real target may be receptors on some specific type of neuron of unknown number and protected behind the blood–brain barrier, then the correct dosage is impossible to predict. For a first approximation, a weight for weight basis is probably right, remembering that some species – cats, horses, and presumably elephants – seem to be more sensitive than others.

Man is also usually said to be more sensitive than most animals, perhaps partly out of pride, mostly because doses effective in laboratory animal tests are indeed higher than those clinically effective in man. Barbiturates usually help people to sleep at less than 1 mg/kg but 10 mg/kg in animals usually leads to the paradoxical excitement of a small dose. LSD works in man at 1 or 2 μg/kg but the lowest dose proven effective in animals is 12·5 μg/kg and twice that is usual. But very often the discrepancy arises, I suspect, because of the contrast between a formal objective test in animals and the dose a physician finds effective in stopping his patients complaining, or coming back. Many clinically important effects of CNS-active drugs are subjective, none more so than pain, depressive mood, or anxiety, which the patient can usually talk about directly but the animal cannot. Further, it is common for people (and presumably animals) to know perfectly well that they have been 'doped' and to be very conscious of it while nothing is visible on the surface. The converse is of course equally common, as anyone knows who has been accused of being intoxicated by so-called friends and carried home to bed while stone-cold sober.

The dose–species–response relation depends on the drug too. Chlorpromazine seems effective in rats and men at doses over about 0·5 mg/kg, and doses of 10 mg/kg a day have been used clinically as well as in animals. The difference between this and other drugs may not be pharmacological so much as in the tests that can be applied to the relevant effect. Chlorpromazine's actions include a clear decrease in motor activity in all species whereas more subjective actions require subtle indirect tests to measure them. It may be the tests that are less sensitive to the drugs, not the animals. The best of the methods described in this book – operant conditioning, exploratory and social behaviour – can be sensitive for example to air-pollution from solvents in factories and dry-cleaners, and to nicotine in doses comparable to those a human obtains from a cigarette, when used appropriately. No doubt these could be special cases, but they disprove any universal lack of sensitivity in animals.

Some drugs do not act directly but are transformed in the body to active metabolites, and not every species modifies a particular foreign chemical along the same routes. So if man and mouse oxidise a given drug and it is the oxidation product that is pharmacologically active, while monkeys deaminate the drug, there is no point in studying it in the monkey, no matter how close a relative of ours it may be. And vice versa, no matter how convenient an experimental animal the mouse may be.

Metabolic pathways are not often predictable for a newly-invented chemical and are not relevant for purely behavioural or surgical treatments, but metabolism illustrates the general principle of matching the test to the problem. It is not worthwhile to test sedative drugs on the motor activity of a snail or to look for hunting behaviour in a sheep.

Behaviour is intricately adapted to the species' way of earning a living and can therefore illustrate clearly the problems for which a given system is a solution. But no one species is the only true model for man, because man is so versatile. I do not mean merely that human beings and human societies are far more complex than any animal model, for if model-making did not simplify it would not help. The point is that the search for an animal model clarifies the human behaviour that we wish to understand. We may never find the right model but the attempt makes us consider the issues as a whole.

Conclusions

It is necessary to ask of any proposed experiment, what is the benefit to mankind (if that is not too grandiose a phrase)? What is the benefit to the experimenter in money or prestige? And what are the consequences to the animal? What is painful or uncomfortable to man may not be so to an animal, but may be worse, and a procedure that is trivial in small 'doses' may amount to cruelty in large ones. It is necessary to attempt to balance benefits against costs and to obtain information that is useful.

The first question to ask of an experimental treatment is whether it has had an effect at all. If so, what is the relationship between 'dose' and duration of treatment and time of onset and degree of response? Tests to answer these questions require sensitivity but little else. Secondly one asks what kind of effect is it? Tests in this class must discriminate: they may be broad-spectrum and sensitive to many kinds of experimental interference, but if so they must distinguish between them. Note the distinction between explanations at different levels: a behavioural effect has to be explained behaviourally (e.g. the animal eats less because it is exploring the cage), and also physiologically (certain neurons in the midbrain are firing at a higher rate), pharmacologically (the metabolism of noradrenaline has been slowed down), biochemically (monoamine oxidase is inhibited) and so on; any of these explanations could be wrong without affecting the others.

Finally and crucially the effect has to be interpreted. Is it important in helping us to understand what is going on, or does it merely indicate that something is happening which needs to be explained? Or merely that an explanation previously thought to be explanatory is really no more than an indicator after all? In short, how does it alter what we do next?

FIVE
A gallop through physiological psychology

Sleep, scratching and sex

If you want to see the effect of a treatment on an animal's behaviour the simplest way is to go and look.

Sleep

What you may find is sleep, and since laboratory animals are not hidden down a burrow, sleep is easy to observe and recognise. But it does not make a very useful measure, it is not numerical and cannot be counted. Even timing its duration accurately is awkward, since the processes of going to sleep and waking up can be imperceptibly gradual.

In practice it can be measured indirectly, when some more mobile activity stops or begins again. Most work on sleep uses electrophysiological methods, principally electroencephalography (EEG), outside the scope of this book. The present short account will be just sufficient to illustrate that sleep is in many ways a kind of behaviour like any other. For that matter, the EEG has some of the same difficulties of objectivity as behaviour, except that a machine records signs of electrical activity on paper. Alpha-rhythm and K-complexes may be defined as subjectively as irritability but independent observers can identify them at leisure.

Deprivation of sleep causes an increasing tendency to sleep (subjectively an increasingly irresistible 'drive'), and there is a characteristic appetitive behaviour preceding it, the classic criterion for an 'instinct' in Tinbergen's sense (1951). Most animals and people have to go through a fairly stereotyped appetitive ritual before going to sleep. Dogs circle their bedding as though treading down grass, cats claw at it until the bedding is comfortably fluffed, apes weave a nest every night. Rodents often construct a nest of straw or paper (remarkably elaborate in some females with newborn litters), and even pile up sawdust with the back of their paws, closing up the draughty and conspicuous front door of the burrow.

Sleep ends, as well as begins, with a ritual. The animal yawns, stretches, explores, and washes its face before breakfast. We are reminded that behaviour is a continuous chain, each link interesting both for its own sake and for its place in the whole.

There are at least two subdivisions of sleep and there may be several functions. Most of the classical suggestions relate to deep sleep, when the

sleep ends as well as starts with a ritual

EEG shows slow waves and the body is generally motionless but not quite limp. Apparently the patterns of changes in cell division and in the blood concentration of sugars, protein, some hormones, lymphocytes, and so on are consistent with the suggestion that slow-wave sleep is the time for physical growth and structural repair, and is increased during recovery from illness.

Several times a night, slow-wave sleep is interrupted by a paradoxical phase of rapid eye movements, a desynchronised 'waking' EEG, secretion of some sex hormones, and the skeletal muscles become profoundly relaxed, especially in the neck. People awakened from paradoxical, rapid eye movement (REM) sleep commonly report that they had just been dreaming; from deep sleep, they recall only rare or fragmentary dreams. The functions of REM sleep must be related to dreaming. Christopher Evans made a fascinating computer analogy, to the 'housekeeping' periodically necessary for tidying the files, amending programs in the light of experience, cross-indexing data under all useful headings.

Sigmund Freud, to oversimplify his argument crudely, thought that dreams are attempts by the subconscious mind to relate the most significant events of the day to our private symbols for instinctive urges. We reorganise the symbolically important features of events until they fit our preconceptions. Tinbergen (1951) suggested that tendencies incompatible with sleep (sex, hunger, etc.) are periodically aroused spontaneously. They would interfere with the functions of deep sleep, whatever these are, and are therefore disconnected from the motor system, becoming neural events only. We eat at intervals during the day, and may also do so symbolically in dreams at night. The periodic rises in blood androgen concentration and the penile erections of males suggest that other kinds of behaviour operate similarly. These three suggestions seem to express much the same concept from different points of view.

Yet it is curious that these two kinds of sleep should coexist, competing for a share of one part of our time, and that the time spent in sleep should vary so widely both in individuals (from 4 to 12 hours a night is quite usual in adult humans) and between species. Ray Meddis (1975) suggested that all physiological and data-housekeeping functions are secondary, taking advantage of a time when it is convenient for them to occur. The primary function of sleep is the simplest and most blindingly obvious – sleeping animals are inactive.

A period of energy conservation is necessary, because food is not always equally available. If you need to see your food, you might consume more energy than you obtain by looking for it on a moonless night. Similarly, if you feed by hunting other animals which are only available in daylight because of their own needs. A grass eater sleeps little because it must chew large amounts of low-quality food. A predator like a lion sleeps a long time because a frequent big kill of high-quality protein is neither needed nor possible but it must still conserve energy. A system where a period of inactivity starts quite automatically would be too rigid: inactivity may be better when predators are a little too readily available, but a better system employs merely a progressively increasing tendency to become inactive. It can be geared to daylight (and to tides in seashore animals), but lets sleep be postponed in emergency. The need to allow growth and repair can take over the predominant role in case of illness or injury, but it is secondary. Even the sleep of babies and small children, Meddis suggests, is more for the benefit of the parents than for their own direct use.

If sleep is one of the basic kinds of behaviour, it should be possible to utilise it experimentally. Certainly the human use of hypnotic drugs is relevant ('I can't seem to get to sleep, doctor'), and it has been estimated that sedative tablets are used for one night's sleep in every ten for the whole population of Great Britain, man, woman, and child.

Many drugs interfere selectively with REM sleep. Ian Oswald (1968, 1973) stated that antidepressants like imipramine, hypnotics like phenobarbitone, or tranquillisers like nitrazepam, all reduced both frequency and duration of REM sleep while deep sleep was hardly affected. There is little tolerance to this effect, repeated doses continue to reduce REM sleep to brief, delayed bursts, but a 'rebound' of a few nights' enhanced REM sleep and vivid dreaming often follows withdrawal from the drugs.

A few drugs can 'dissociate' EEG patterns from behaviour. Thus, atropine can produce a slow-wave EEG while the animal appears highly

perchance to dream

excited, and physostigmine causes a waking pattern on the EEG while the animal sleeps (see the discussion in Bradley, 1964). Domino, Yamamoto, and Dren (1968) suggested that the dissociated EEG represents REM sleep, that physostigmine causes sleeping cats to dream, perchance of catching mice.

para Chlorophenylalanine (*p*COA) lowers the brain concentration of catecholamines and serotonin and, among others, Elizabeth Shillito (1969, 1970a) showed that it increased play-fighting and sexual behaviour in juvenile and young adult male rats. Mouret, Bobillier, and Jouvet (1968) found that the rather large dose of 500 mg/kg of *p*CPA also caused insomnia, decreasing both REM and deep sleep, without rebound when the effect eventually wore off. *p*CPA seems to be a general activity-intensifier, since it also increased eating, drinking, and biting the experimenters.

The paradox of the barbiturates

Phenobarbitone does more than help an animal to get to sleep. If you inject a dose above about 30 mg/kg, it is in a state of surgical anaesthesia for a short time. Obviously 30 mg/kg is too high a dose, but if you give a smaller dose, you do not induce normal sleep, on the contrary the animal becomes highly excited, just as it does before and after anaesthesia. Between about 5 and 20 mg/kg animals will be ataxic (limp, floppy), though dose-for-dose, amylobarbitone causes much less ataxia than phenobarbitone. Despite the limpness, the animal rushes round faster than usual. This is not like the stereotyped running due to amphetamine, since other kinds of behaviour are enhanced – eating, drinking, even fighting. Curiously enough, it is said that the only way to cage two adult buck rabbits together (who are liable to fight to the death if confined so that they cannot run away) is to let them wake up together from anaesthesia.

The smallest effective doses of barbiturates in animals seem to be about 5 to 10 mg/kg and are almost always excitatory. Why then should these drugs, given by the less efficient oral route, be quite powerful 'sleeping pills' in man at about 1 to 2 mg/kg?

Man is usually said to be more sensitive to drugs than animals, but the effect of other psychotropic drugs is seldom actually reversed. The paradox depends partly on the context, including the person's or the animal's expectations. A person taking a sleeping tablet expects it to help her to get to sleep (the well-known placebo effect). She will be in a familiar, dark, quiet environment, or at least will pay as little attention to the surroundings as possible. Tests on animals, on the other hand, stimulate them. A rat may have been picked up to its surprise, injected, and put into an unfamiliar maze requiring exploration or work for food or water. What is common to all these situations may be an exaggeration of what would occur in any case.

There is, unfortunately, little solid evidence for the suggestion. In a Y-maze, amylobarbitone at 15 mg/kg usually causes a marked increase in activity (Kumar, 1971). Steinberg, Rushton, and Tinson (1961) found only a slight stimulation on the first trial, but other rats were first given the drug on their thirty-second trial in the maze and it reduced their activity by half. Peter Dews (1955) found a small dose of pentobarbitone (1 mg per pigeon) to increase the rate of pecking for a grain of corn when the task induced high rates of pecking anyway; but when the birds had to wait a quarter of an hour before a peck would produce any corn, the same dose reduced the rate even further and must have put the pigeon virtually to sleep. Even so, on both tasks, an even smaller dose of 0·5 mg/bird had a stimulant action.

These experiments are rather weak evidence for a sedative effect of barbiturates in animals at something near sedative doses for man, but they seem to be the best available.

Indirect measures of sleep
A simple direct test of sleep is impracticable, either because sleep and waking grade into each other too imperceptibly, or because the very process of trying to demonstrate sedation tends to antagonise it. It is worth trying an indirect measure, not of sleep, but the motor activity that represents its converse.

Methods of monitoring motor activity are discussed in Chapter 7, but it is best to follow the animals for several days at a time. The first few hours in a new apparatus will detect mostly exploration and the sleep pattern will be abnormal.

There are not many long-term experiments to quote. Barnett, Smart, and Widdowson (1971) kept 35-week-old rats in a residential maze for 12 days. Rats that had been half-starved from 4 to 12 weeks of age spent altogether more time out of this nest-box than either well-fed controls or rats fed on a low-protein, high-calorie diet, suggesting that among other effects their sleep may have been disturbed.

A few people involved in the pilot-scale manufacture of a systemic fungicide, ethirimol, complained of insomnia. The injection of 5 mg/kg ethirimol made a few rats (too few for statistical significance, but the apparatus was limited) slightly more active than controls the following night; they had been less active previously. In the daytime, when rats are mostly asleep, ethirimol clearly increased activity for 2, possibly 3 days. The short 'restless' periods suggested that the original complaints of insomnia were justified; steps were taken to minimise exposure in full-scale production and use.

Feeding

In conventional psychology the 'basic drives' are eating, drinking, and reproducing the species. We have already discussed drinking (Chapter 3).

The straightforward way of measuring food consumption is to offer the animals more than they are likely to eat, to weigh what you give them and weigh what is left at the same time next day. Thus, rats fed on a diet containing 0·01 or 0·02 per cent of the herbicide paraquat ate about 10 per cent less than those fed on an otherwise identical control diet (both paraquat groups averaged about 19 g/rat every day compared with 21 g/day in controls). There were no other behavioural effects, nor did lung fibrosis occur as it does at higher doses. The rats may well have been feeling mildly ill and off their food, but they had a slight preference for control diet if given the choice, so paraquat may have a slightly unpleasant taste.

There are some fairly obvious details to bear in mind when designing a food consumption experiment. There will usually be some wastage, even compressed cubes lose a little dust useful neither to man nor beast. If access to the food is too easy, rats drop and lose some on or through the floor. Especially if they have ever been starved, rats will take extra food and hide it near their sleeping quarters. Most rodents need to gnaw something abrasive, otherwise their incisor teeth grow too far. They might gnaw their normal diet plus the bars of the cage, a wooden plaything, or extra food gnawed but not swallowed. Either such non-nutritive losses of food should be minimised or they should be measured separately and exploited as new and distinct tests.

There are several alternative ways of measuring food consumption. Food can be given as a wet mash in a bowl on the floor of the cage. The rat would have to gnaw somewhere else and might overturn or soil a bowl left overnight. Rats prefer to urinate away from the sleeping place but (possibly to mark a territory) they commonly crawl over a hump on the floor and deposit a drop or two of urine.

If the rat is deprived of food for 23 hours every day and then offered the bowl of food for an hour, he will come to take all he needs in a restricted period.

Brief daily feeding requires a familiar situation. The procedure has to be carried out every day, including Sundays, and the food always offered in the same place, either at home or in a simple maze or alley. In a maze, the running time from the start-box to the food can make an extra measure of 'motivational strength'. Reynolds and Pavlik (1960) demonstrated predictably that rats ran faster if they had been deprived longer or had been conditioned to expect a larger amount of food.

Instrumental conditioning for food

When rats are trained to press a lever for a food reward, it is usually a means of obtaining an elaborate performance, but it can be used simply as a means of measuring food consumption. A 'constant reinforcement' schedule is sufficient, each lever-press delivering a standard pellet of food (e.g. commercial 45 mg tablets) or a drop (say 0·05 ml) of diluted sweetened condensed milk. Sweet milk (or chocolate) is taken both by hungry rats and rats fed up to the teeth with standard cubes and ravenous for variety.

The procedure has been useful in testing ideas about the control of food intake. Low blood sugar has long been thought to make one feel hungry. Balagura (1968) lowered blood sugar levels by daily injections of insulin; these were so effective that a dummy injection came to act as a conditioned stimulus to increase the rate of bar-pressing for food. Unfortunately the story is not so simple, since Lovett and Booth (1970) found small doses of insulin could accelerate satiation; larger doses could, later, elicit eating; and a flavouring in water (originally meaningless) could come to act as a 'negative conditioned stimulus', depressing drinking if it was usually followed by (presumably unpleasant?) insulin injections.

The lever-pressing technique has also been used to study something of what makes a rat end a meal as well as begin it (Davis, Gallagher, Ladove, and Turausky, 1969). If a rat was allowed to eat its fill, and some of its blood was then transfused into a hungry rat, the second animal ate less; consumption of milk fell by half, of pellets by 40 per cent. Since blood transfused from a hungry rat had no effect, the fall in consumption must have been due to something in the fed rat's blood. It could have been as simple a substance as glucose, or even insulin, or some other more subtle hormonal change.

Whatever the transfused substance was, it ought (in principle) to lead to a far better 'slimming pill' for those who need to lose weight. Since food intake was reduced but not totally suppressed, excessive dieting to the point of starvation is unlikely. Equally the fall in intake was probably not for such undesirable reasons as nausea or a pain in the guts, and not from fear or an overwhelming need to explore the surrounding countryside. Perhaps it worked by reducing the initial 'drive' to eat, whatever it is that starts and maintains eating, or perhaps by accelerating the satiation processes that normally bring a full meal to an end.

Two other simple methods of measuring food consumption were designed primarily as drug screens. Madinaveitia (unpublished) logically decided that the simplest measure is a linear one, and the nearest nutritional approach to length without breadth is a stick of dry spaghetti. Mice were deprived of food for 23 hours, dosed orally with the chemical on test, and an hour later offered a 20 cm stick of spaghetti, held in a vertical metal tube to allow gnawing only of the 0·5 cm at the bottom. Untreated mice ate a fairly uniform length, and quite small doses of standard appetite-depressant drugs like amphetamine or phenmetrazine drastically reduced the length eaten. Inert substances which still filled the stomach after an hour would inhibit eating too, of course, and so would anything causing pain or sickness.

Amphetamine reduces eating by at least two mechanisms simultaneously. There is varied evidence that it reduces all sorts of food-motivated behaviour, reducing appetite directly, and it often increases sheer motor activity, which competes with any specific behaviour including eating. Robert Clark (1969) followed standard procedure for measuring activity (see Chapter 7) with another ingenious measure of appetite. His mice had plenty of ordinary food, but were allowed one at a time into a cage containing a brass bar with ten 'cups' drilled into it. Each hole was 0·1 ml in volume, and was half full of sweetened condensed milk. Untreated mice soon lick up everything in the milk bar, and cups still containing milk after 45 minutes are easily visible.

Meal times

The quantity of food consumed is not an entirely satisfactory measure of hunger, if by 'hunger' we mean the tendency to do something to obtain food. Neal Miller and Herbert Barry (1960) point out how food consumption increases with deprivation for periods of up to 24 hours. Beyond 24 hours rats will continue to increase their readiness to work to obtain food, but will not eat any more when they get it.

It is perhaps necessary to know the spontaneous pattern of eating. Le Magnen and Tallon (1966) showed that a rat's nightly food consumption occurs in a regular number of meals at irregular intervals, each meal consisting of an irregular number of courses. The quantity eaten during a meal, surprisingly, did not depend significantly on the interval since the previous

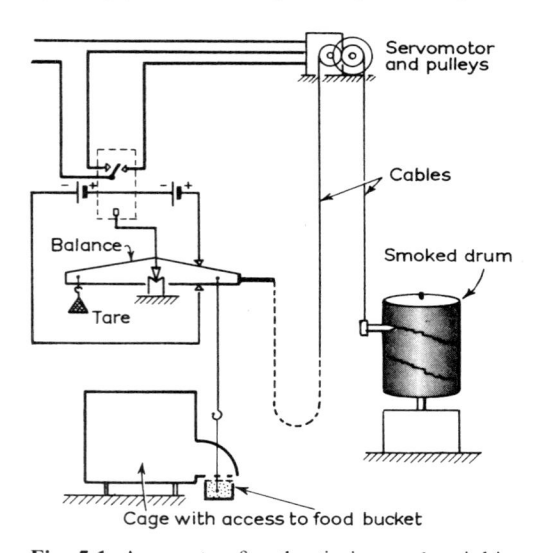

Fig. 5.1. Apparatus for the timing and weighing of food consumption by the rat (after Le Magnen and Tallon, 1966). The rat's cage gives access to a bucket containing powdered food, suspended from a balanced beam. Electrical contacts to the beam cause a servomotor to advance a cable until the extra weight just compensates for that of the food eaten; the other end of the cable raises the recording pen.

meal. Less surprisingly, it did govern the interval before the next one. A large meal was followed by a decent interval, a snack whetted the appetite for the next meal. Le Magnen and Tallon used an ingenious method (Fig. 5.1) which was claimed to record the time and quantity of food consumed, to an accuracy of 0·5 g and over a period of 200 days.

Harry Kissileff (1970) devised a 'pellet-detecting eatometer'. Rats were fed on 45 mg 'Noyes' pellets to give a digital measure, but they did not have to learn any elaborate lever pressing. A pellet was dropped into a trough, where it blocked a photocell beam. When the rat took the pellet, a very easy and congenial task, it unblocked the signal from the photoelectric cell and operated a counter and the mechanism for dropping the next pellet. Kissileff considered the distinction between bouts and meals to be arbitrary, but believed an interval between bouts of eating of less than 10 minutes to be a sign of definite inhibition – for example, short intervals were increased by the effort of pressing a Skinner box lever. Intervals of over 20 minutes were likely to be due to satiation.

Peter Wiepkema (1971) found a similar pattern of spontaneous feeding in mice by direct observation. Each meal contained a series of short bouts of feeding with longer intervals between meals. Deprivation of food increased consumption by lengthening bouts within a meal and shortening the intervals between them. Bouts were lengthened by highly palatable food and shortened by adding the bitter taste of quinine, without affecting bout intervals. Blood glucose rises a minute after the mouse starts to eat, but whatever the mechanism, Wiepkema suggests that there is an initial positive feedback

once a mouse starts to eat . . .

process. That is, once a mouse starts to eat, he makes a meal of it. Satiety, the negative feedback, sets in only later.

Specific appetites and conditioned taste aversions

Wild animals can only survive if they can select a balanced diet for themselves. The problem is worse for an omnivorous rodent than for an obligatory grass- or meat-eater that knows what it likes and can afford to like only what it knows. Rats have to be both ready to try a new kind of possible food, and to be extremely wary of it. Wild rats avoid any new bait until, overcome by curiosity, one bold rat cautiously approaches, sniffs, tastes a small sample – and waits a good long time before eating any more. Until it does, it is even said that other rats in the colony avoid the new bait (see Chapter 24). In the face of poisonous berries and rat-catchers, such bait-shyness must help them remain as successful pests.

Hunger is not necessarily a generalised desire for any food, but can quite rapidly become specific for (apparently) whatever constituent is especially lacking. Rats and mice achieve this partly by the way they eat. Barnett (1956) described how both captive wild rats and albinos sample anything available, both before settling down to the main meal and afterwards. They taste everything – grains of wheat, chopped liver, sugar, even wheat mixed with aniseed oil, whose smell deters them from anything more than a taste. A diet deficient in some essential vitamin is for practical purposes like a diet containing a slow-acting poison. Paul Rozin (1969) showed how laboratory rats on a diet lacking thiamin use their food-sampling technique to choose a better one. They will be ill and off their food, they eat no more than a sample from one dish at a time. If there are not too many to choose from, most rats can then select the food with the right physiological consequences, adequate in thiamin. Rats can even choose a nasty-tasting 'medicine' – temporarily – if it appears to act as an antidote. Lithium can produce toxic symptoms but is displaced from plasma by sodium. Rats usually drink tap water rather than 0.5 per cent saline, but if they were given nothing but lithium chloride solution to drink one day, they chose sodium chloride the next, and then reverted to water (Langham, Syme, and Syme, 1975).

The development of specific hungers to make up a particular dietary deficiency, the taking of antidotes to poison, and bait shyness or a Conditioned Taste Aversion are all essentially the same thing. They all depend on internal stimuli comparable to the human sensations of feeling ill, no doubt in several different ways (see the reviews by Revusky and Garcia, 1970; and by Rozin and Kalat, 1971). The phenomenon is remarkable because poisons and antidotes may take some hours to act, far longer than the longest delay between a conventional stimulus and reinforcement, so that for many years conventional theorists found it hard to believe.

A convenient procedure starts by putting rats on a schedule where they are deprived of water for 23.5 hours a day. Whether or not they are housed in groups, they are given access to water singly for 30 minutes daily and their consumption is measured (either by volume or simply by weight, using bottles with non-drip spouts). After a week or so when consumption stabilises, the water is replaced by a fluid with a distinctive taste that the animals have never encountered before but (after a timid 'neophobic' fall in intake on the first day) they find attractive. An 0.1 or 0.15 per cent solution of saccharin sodium (1 or 1.5 g/litre) is commonly used: it is excruciatingly sweet to man but rats may drink three times their normal fluid intake, with minimal nutritional consequences. A suitable time after the first sweet drink (say 15 minutes to 6 or 7 hours) the rats are injected with either saline or something (e.g. lithium or apomorphine) which would make a human being feel ill. The symptoms of 'poisoning' may be observable but need not: Marvin Nachman and Philip Hartley (1975) found little correlation between visible signs and subsequent aversion. At any rate on subsequent days, for a time said to be related to the logarithm of the dose, rats tend to avoid drinking saccharin solution. It is as if they attributed their sickness to something they ate.

Some experimenters offer the rats two bottles, both of water before dosing, both of saccharin on the day of dosing, and one of each (alternating right and left to minimise position preferences) subsequently, comparing the consumption from each. Green and John Garcia (1971) say that to offer two bottles confuses a preference for one with aversion to the other. They prefer to give water on alternate days (20 minutes once a day), and a single bottle of, say, milk on days 2 and 4, grape juice on days 6 and 8 and so on. Both preference and aversion can be demonstrated for long periods by comparison with previous consumption or with control animals.

The taste that is avoided is the most recent *novel* taste, for a familiar food offered between the saccharin and the apomorphine injection continues to be consumed; though there is also evidence that if two unfamiliar tastes are offered, e.g. condensed milk and grape juice, one may be preferred to the other, irrespective of which was offered first.

Conversely, if a rat is given apomorphine first and allowed to drink quinine solution while recovering from the consequent nausea, it acts as though the distastefully bitter quinine is a potent medicine.

Recovery from poisoning or conditioned aversions on account of poisoning lead to much more definite preferences than selection of diets to remedy deficiency, presumably because the symptoms (which may be different) appear and disappear so much more rapidly. If the poison acts over a matter of days, as anticoagulants like warfarin do, then the delay is too great even for rats to appreciate. Conditioned aversion is not a problem with warfarin.

Similarly, birds avoid eating certain distasteful caterpillars, poisonous berries, or stinging wasps more than once. In birds, the stimulus is clearly visual, for these insects and fruits advertise themselves with bright colours and bold patterns. Indeed various unrelated and quite harmless insects escape predation because of their close visual resemblance to the nasty ones, and mimicry could only work on the sense the predators are using (cf. p. 98).

In rats, however, conditioned aversion and dietary selection rely only on taste. Scott and Verney (1947) gave vitamin-deficient rats the choice of their familiar deficient diet and a flavoured supplement. When their preference for the adequate diet was established, the flavour was switched to the deficient diet – the rats' choice followed the flavour. Garcia and Koelling (1966) gave either electric shock or poison to rats, and presented light, noise, or taste cues. Shocked rats later avoided the light and the sound but not the taste, the poisoned rats avoided the taste but not the light or sound. It is curious that the ability to associate two sets of stimuli separated by several hours should be specific to taste. Theoreticians have invoked all sorts of complex mechanisms; Kalat and Rozin (1973) suggest that it is quite ordinary slow learning – only the rat has to learn that a novel taste is safe, not that it is dangerous. The rat, as it were, expects something new to be poisonous, but can learn that it is harmless. So that if it safely drinks an unfamiliar saccharin solution twice before being poisoned the rat avoids that taste *less* than if it drank only once (whereas learning that the taste meant danger would imply greater avoidance, since the animal has had more experience of the cue).

Drinking and other specific appetites

I am not sure how far drinking should be regarded as distinct from eating. True, we usually use a different word, but then we have no word in English that means both eating and drinking, except 'ingestion', and that is too clumsy even for scientists to say. True we usually treat two independent sets of movements as two different kinds of behaviour, and both rats and people use different actions for eating and drinking. Yet do we eat or drink a thick soup or jelly? Does a rat gnaw or lick a powder or wet mash? The movements are adapted to the physical form of the food.

Drinking, from one point of view, is a specific appetite. Thirsty rats eat water just as thiamin-deficient rats select thiamin-rich diets. There is some neurophysiological evidence both of the unity and the contrast. Grossman (1968) showed that both eating and drinking could follow stimulation of the ventromedial nucleus of the hypothalamus and various other sites in the brain. Grossman used a hollow electrode through which a tiny quantity of drug solution could be applied to a single neuron. At each site, both eating and drinking could be elicited in deprived rats: drinking by acetylcholine or other cholinergic or antiadrenergic drugs, eating by noradrenaline or other adrenergic or anticholinergic drugs.

David Margules *et al.*, (1972) gave ordinary food pellets and water, but put the rats for an hour, a few times a week, into a box with two calibrated burettes, one containing condensed milk, the other water. The Perspex spout of each bottle was wired to a contact-sensitive relay so that the number of licks was recorded – it did not correspond exactly with the volume consumed even allowing for the milk that dripped into the Petri dishes. Little water was taken. Milk consumption stabilised in a week or two, and was then used to demonstrate that noradrenaline applied to the lateral hypothalamus increased licking for milk in the daytime. At night, when the rats normally consumed most, the same dose of noradrenaline reduced feeding.

Even what we call eating is itself a complex of several specific appetites.

Grossman considers the ventromedial nucleus of the hypothalamus to be not, as usually assumed, a regulator of food intake in general so much as a 'glucostat' for calories as carbohydrate. There may be a 'lipostat' for fats somewhere else in the brain, possibly more than one for Baile (1968) found evidence for a separate acetate receptor in goats. The obvious gap is that there should be a 'proteostat' for nitrogen metabolism. And Rozin (1968) has evidence that rats adjusted their diet for protein (solutions of amino acids and peptides) independently of total calories. They even tolerated quinine in their protein but not in their sugar solution. However, there is some older work where rats were given a choice between diets rich and poor in protein. Many animals apparently failed to eat enough protein though all took enough calories.

In studies of food preference, appetite, and dietary habit, the method which gives the most evidence quickest is the 'cafeteria' popularised by Paul Thomas Young. It simply means offering the rat a choice of four or five foods which it can consume directly, without having to learn to press a lever or anything – just weigh or measure the amount consumed. The food could be given in solution and consumed in liquid form (as with Rozin's protein), or as powder, pellets, or grains of wheat, so long as the animal can make a measurable choice in familiar surroundings. Young himself (1945) showed with this method that new habits of food selection are acquired in relation to bodily needs, but that old ones tend to persist from habit, irrespective of need.

After all these wonders of rodent cleverness, it is surprising to learn that rats cannot, apparently, discriminate everything. They can select thiamin and other B vitamins much better than vitamins A and D which are absorbed too slowly. Melissa Lewis (1968) adrenalectomised rats, who developed a specific appetite for sodium as they lost the capacity to regulate the salt content of the urine and hence of the blood. She also removed the parathyroids from other rats who lost control of calcium. Rats offered the choice of calcium lactate and sodium chloride solutions pressed a lever more often for sodium than for calcium, the salt they needed more.

Excretion

Some other kinds of behaviour have been ignored as a source of tests by polite or prudish scientists. An exception is the urination and defecation of rats that appear to be frightened.

In his classic 'open field' experiments, Calvin Hall (1934 a, b) placed rats in a brightly-illuminated circular arena for daily 2-minute trials of the 'maze bright' and 'dull' Tryon strains of rats (Fig. 5.2). Among other things, he distinguished rats of greater or less 'emotionality'. He observed that some rats were more likely than others to walk in the outermost ring of the arena, under the lee of the wall. All rats walked faster if they had been deprived of food, but these remained reluctant to venture into the brightly-lit centre,

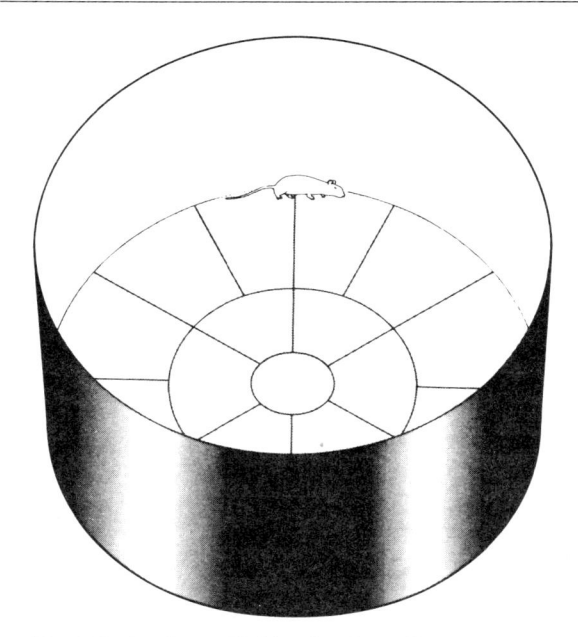

Fig. 5.2. An Open Field (after Broadhurst, 1965).

where the food was. If they collected food at all, they would not eat it on site, but hoarded it close to the wall. 'Emotional' rats sometimes defecated or urinated, though rarely on the days they ventured to collect food. Male rats, incidentally, were likely both to eat more and defecate more than females. Physiologically what goes in seems likely, eventually, to come out; I am not sure which sex is therefore supposed to be more emotional.

Hall specifically stated (1934a) that 'emotional' elimination was not quantitative: any individual either did, or did not, on any one trial. Nevertheless, the strain difference that Hall observed has led others to investigate the genetic background. The 'Reactive' and 'Non-Reactive' strains, originally bred at the Maudsley Hospital in London, were selected on the basis of the mean number of faecal boluses dropped in an 'open field', and Peter Broadhurst claimed (1965) that such defecation measures 'the extent to which fear has been aroused by experimental procedures. It can be shown that the more frightened the animal the more it will defecate.'

Moreover, these two strains also differ somewhat in various conditioned avoidance tests (Broadhurst, 1964).

Broadhurst and Giorgio Bignami (1965) and John Wilcock and Broadhurst (1967) measured conditioned avoidance in various ways in another seven strains of rats. Whether an increasing level of fear improves or retards the learning or performance of a conditioned avoidance task (see Chapter 16) is another matter. But in neither of these comparisons was there any correlation between defecation and avoidance; defecation did not turn out to measure anything but itself.

Incidentally I once observed rats venture forth from their home cage through a sliding door into a 2-m long enclosed runway. Although the rats defecated adequately in the corners of the home cage, and liberally if I picked them up bodily, they hardly ever defecated in the runways. In several trials of 30 to 90 minutes with each of twenty-seven rats, I found two boluses, both after at least an hour. Timid though many of the rats were, they left no hostages to fortune when they explored the runway or scurried back home of their own accord.

Robert Boice (1972) noted that captive wild rats appear more intensely emotional than albinos behaviourally – they fight more, they respond to (or even die from) levels of electroshock that albinos hardly notice. They show no 'emotional' defecation in open-field tests, an increase in defecation of wet boluses probably does mean something, but its absence does not.

'Reactivity' of one region of the autonomic system seems a thin euphemism for the fear presumably measured by conditioned avoidance. An obsessional need to avoid subjectivity hardly requires quite such solid evidence.

To call a person 'emotional' means, as I understand the word, that she or he oscillates wildly from the peak of one emotion to the peak of another, by turns exhilarated, furious, passionate, panic-stricken, miserable. Someone who was constantly fearful would more likely be called anxious, someone who oscillated less abruptly and intensely would be relatively placid. If animals have these personality types, and if these definitions are acceptable, why not be consistent in the use of words? To my mind the use of the general word for the specific emotion of fear seems bound to lead to confusion. It has. See the review by John Archer (1973).

Grooming or care of the body surface

Robert Bolles (1960) said an isolated laboratory rat spends 40 per cent of its waking time on grooming, mostly after eating, drinking, or exploring. Perhaps a rat in solitary confinement all its life is a special case, it has little else to do, but healthy wild lions (on safari travelogue films at least) also spend an inordinate time grooming their smooth, glossy fur.

In rats and other rodents the main units of self-grooming are (in the terminology of Grant and Mackintosh, 1963; and Draper, 1967): wash, groom, scratch, and lick penis. Wash refers to the alternation of licking the forepaws and wiping them over the sides of the head. Grooming means licking and combing the fur of the flanks, hindlegs, belly, and tail in the incisor teeth. Scratching is combing the flanks and back with the claws of the hind feet (Fig. 5.3). Licking of the penis/urinary papilla follows sexual mounting and often indicates ejaculation. Sometimes, out of the context of other grooming, a rat will briefly shake itself like a wet dog.

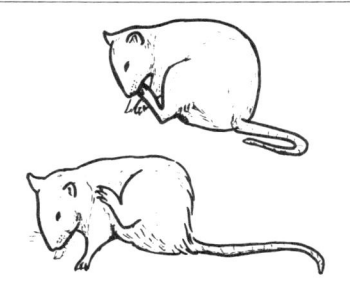

Fig. 5.3. Scratch and Self-groom.

Grooming has occasionally been used as an indicator of drug effects. Amphetamine notably reduces grooming as well as eating (Schiørring, 1971; Silverman, 1966a). I had the tentative impression that a rat given a fairly high dose of amphetamine seemed to avoid touching anything with his back, as though grooming it would hurt, and trotted round the cage, very near the walls but carefully not brushing against them. Rohte (1969) has used grooming to indicate effects of various drugs in mice. He used the ingeniously simple technique of brushing powdered charcoal into the fur of the flanks of albino mice, and observing the time taken to clean the charcoal off.

Interlude: Displacement activities – grooming as a tool to analyse the brain

The most effective use of grooming has been as an indicator of some fundamental processes in the central nervous system. It started when Niko Tinbergen and Adrian Kortlandt independently noticed what they called displacement activities. When an animal appears to 'want' to do something but cannot, because it is physically impossible (e.g. food is just out of reach) or because he also wants to do something else (e.g. both to attack a neighbour in a territorial boundary dispute and run away from him), the animal often displays an abbreviated but vigorous form of some third behaviour, commonly grooming, which seems quite irrelevant. Many kinds of behaviour can be selected, although in any one situation, the stimuli involved are frequently so consistent, that the displacement activity becomes ritualised in the course of evolution to act as a signal. Thus, many species of ducks preen a wing feather when they are stimulated both to peck an opponent and to turn away from him, and the preening has been 'ritualised' to be always of the same feather. The advantage that both ducks obtain when the opponent realises that the preening duck may well peck him is so great that the feather has evolved to be of a conspicuously different colour or pattern from the rest of the bird (Tinbergen, 1952).

Sometimes the displacement activity starts as a diversion from the original action. A herring gull in a boundary dispute may peck vigorously down at the ground, as if it meant to attack its opponent, but occasionally the gull seizes a blade of grass or other material and turns towards his nest as though to build on to it.

To cut a long and fruitful story short, one view of the phenomenon (van Iersel and Bol, 1958) is that the activity chosen is of a tendency active fairly continuously at the time (e.g. nest-building early in the reproductive season or grooming at any time). Daniel Lehrman (1956) noted that the developmental origin of the actual elements involved is relevant. Ring doves *Columba livia*) displacement preen when billing and cooing in courtship. Both billing and preening appear to originate from the same reflex in the new-hatched squab, to push the beak into a surface-with-projections – in the squab this action acts as food-begging, as it pecks into the parent's bill, and stimulates regurgitation of crop-milk.

The displacement activity and the inhibited tendency share at least one component. Grass-pulling in the herring gull starts from the downward peck meant for the opponent, wing-preening in ducks is both a modified peck and the beginnings of turning away and fleeing. The inhibited tendency is what gives the movement its characteristic vigour. In one sense, the displacement activity does not exist, it is the inhibited tendency redirected in a safe direction; it is abbreviated because the tendency itself is inhibited. Ian Duncan and Derek Wood-Gush (1972) let hungry hens feed in an experimental cage and then frustrated their feeding by putting a transparent Perspex cover over the food. The short, frantic bouts of preening suggested both rapid dis- and reinhibition and redirected pecking.

Rats can use many different kinds of behaviour as if they are displacement activities, often in the midst of social-dominance fighting (see Chapter 21). The commonest is an abbreviated single wash movement of the forepaws, sometimes missing the face altogether. The influence of the preceding activity is strong – an attack movement that occasionally leads to an inhibited bite (painful, no doubt, but not damaging) occasionally leads instead to eating. For a couple of seconds the crunching of food pellets reverberates significantly.

The influence of the stimuli presented at the crucial moment is also clear. If the rat ends up in an upright posture and happens to face the spout of the water-bottle, he drinks. Otherwise he explores the roof of the cage. If he is immobile but about to approach after either a crouch or an active retreat, he washes.

It is often uncertain what to call a displacement activity in rats, as what starts as typical frantic displacement turns into the real thing. A quick wipe of the paw near the nose turns into proper washing and grooming, and the rat may spend a leisurely minute or two carefully performing its toilet, carefully not getting on with the job. A quick sniff at something that catches the rat's attention when he seems ready both to retreat and approach, and the rat starts a long bout of exploration as if avoiding what an observer might think appropriate.

The sequences of such bouts of grooming or exploration in experimentally conditioned tasks are surprisingly regular (King, 1970; Morrison and Stephenson, 1973; see Chapters 12 and 17). People also show displacement activities very commonly; I do when I cannot think what to write next.

Grooming tends to occur, then, in the very short term of a second or two, in the transition from one kind of behaviour to another, and particularly from immobility to movement. The immobility can be relaxed or be a tense, fearful crouch. In the longer term also, grooming tends to occur in the transition between sleeping and waking.

One kind of behaviour can serve different functions in different animals and the same function can be served by different kinds of behaviour. Peter Slater and Janet Ollason (1972) watched sequences of actions in solitary Zebra finches, distinguished active and inactive phases of waking behaviour. The active phase comprised flying (of course), eating, etc., the inactive largely comprised grooming. The transition between them, provided other tendencies were at a low level, was marked by song.

Displacement activities can follow electrical stimulation of the brain of black-headed gulls (*Larus ridibundus*) at sites close to those eliciting sleep. Juan Delius (1967) argued from this and from spontaneous displacement activities that they act as a homeostatic mechanism, whose function is to reduce an excessive level of arousal. 'Excessive' in this context would mean a level too high for effective information transmission. Delius's speculation is interesting and could be extended. Grooming, etc., could serve not only to reduce intense excitement or even panic to normal alertness, but could also have the converse effect, awakening a sluggish, drowsy animal and stimulating satisfactory information transmission. Of course, arousal is not as simple as that, and Delius is as careful as anyone to distinguish the arousal of specific kinds of behaviour from arousal of all kinds in general. His main aim is to utilise the complex of actions I have called grooming (Delius prefers 'maintenance' or 'comfort' behaviour) as a very convenient one for studying the organisation of behaviour in the wild (for the example of skylarks, *Alauda arvensis*; see Delius, 1969), where the function may be easier to see. The elements are mostly easy to recognise and to distinguish from other behaviour. They occur in well-defined contexts and often in well-defined sequences. Moreover, they are influenced both by external stimuli (when you are tickled by a fly walking on your leg) and by central programming (among other things, when you only think there is a fly on your leg). There is a fair body of evidence on the relevant neurophysiology.

John Fentress and Frances Stilwell (1973) have observed some fine details of grooming in mice. Fentress is less explicitly concerned with the mathematical analysis than Delius, and more with the physiology. How far is grooming governed by central programming and how far by peripheral stimuli? And how far by central adjustments to sensory thresholds?

A mouse typically washes the head before grooming the body, but which parts of the head? There is an interesting tendency to retrace short subsequences. If we use the alphabet to designate, e.g. the side of the nose, the articulation of the jaws, behind the ears, etc., a typical sequence (this one is invented) might be *ABC, ABC, BCD, CDEFG, BCDC, DEF* ... Fentress has begun to experiment on such patterns, by cutting one of the branches of the facial nerve on one side, for example, or implanting an electrode just under the skin, to let him imitate an itch at some crucial point in the sequence and watch where the mouse scratches.

For all the detail and theory I have hinted at, these researches are still at an early stage. Similar analyses of how sequences of behavioural elements are built up into organic functional 'molecules' have been made on aspects of social behaviour, and will be described in Chapters 21 and 22.

Social behaviour

Social behaviour includes everything that individuals do in the presence of others of the same species that they will not do alone, or (to include displacement activities) not in the same way. It is, therefore, always likely to be complex, though perhaps other behaviour would seem equally complex if only we knew the details. Desmond Morris (1956) pointed out how courtship ceremonies of pair-formation and copulation involve more than sexual tendencies. Components of aggression and fleeing could invariably be discerned, and species could be classified according to the relative importance of Flight, Aggression, and Mating in each sex. The same may apply to other social behaviour — fighting includes aggression, by definition, but the animals are also 'frightened' and sometimes show sexual tendencies too.

It follows that to use any single aspect of social behaviour to assess an experimental treatment is almost certainly too simple. A single piece of behaviour may detect an effect but no single measure will permit proper interpretation. Nevertheless, there have been many attempts, using aggressive or sexual behaviour.

Aggression

The word 'aggression' is used to label behaviour induced in so many ways that they must surely be disparate — the behaviour of paired animals after social isolation, electroshock, or several different brain lesions, a cat's or rat's response to a mouse, a response to the frustration of previously conditioned behaviour. These will be described in Chapters 20–22 along with less-simplified analyses of social behaviour.

Sexual behaviour

'Sex-tests', by contrast, are usually exhaustively accurate as far as they go (and with the more obsessional experimenters they seem to go on and on and on). Their objectivity is attained by the use of clearly identifiable units: lordosis and mounting, intromission, pelvic thrusts, and ejaculation. Donald Dewsbury (1967) worried that rats spend less than 1 per cent of a sex-test in intromission, which is presumably their objective. He investigated what they were up to the remaining 99 per cent of the time, almost as if to help them to improve on this regrettable state of affairs (if Dewsbury will excuse the attempt at humour). Typically, the female sequence of run–crouch–lordosis is paralleled by the male pursue–mount, with mutual nosing, sniffing, and perhaps fighting, and both sexes showing post-ejaculatory genital grooming. One hopes for more simple fun in the report of the reproductive behaviour of the male guinea-pig by Grunt and Young (1953).

Sexual behaviour has mainly been used to indicate hormonal effects. Champlin, Blight, and McGill (1963) put a male mouse in a large, clear plastic cylinder for 4 hours; a female brought into heat by injections of oestrogen and progesterone was then introduced to the male and fifteen elements of the sexual behaviour (McGill, 1962) were observed. Males successful with ejaculation twice in 2 weeks were castrated. Of six mice given daily injections of 0·05 ml peanut oil, only one achieved even one intromission, and although in subsequent tests these mice showed some interest by sniffing and muzzling, only a few attempted to mount. Six other mice were given 32 μg of testosterone propionate, almost as much as their own testes would have produced, and these mice all copulated successfully. A gross excess of testosterone, 1024 μg daily, had no additional effect, not even the extra urgency, the shorter latency to mounting found by Beach and Holz Tucker (1949).

In most mammals, sexual attraction is, to say the least, strongly influenced by scent, and in the house mouse, *Mus musculus*, it is affected by the mouse's early upbringing. Mainardi, Marsan, and Pasquali (1965) reared female mice with or without their father present. Those that knew their own father chose mates of their own subspecies (*M.m. domesticus* or *bactrianus*) but of a different strain. To test whether these preferences involved odour, mice were reared with parents who were scented every day with a local perfume 'Violetta di Parma'. They were housed in small groups after weaning, unscented. At 3 months old, a male mouse's preference was tested by placing it in the middle of a three-compartment box. The compartments on either side each contained a female brought into heat with oestrogen but confined by wearing a collar too wide for the narrow door. One female was scented. The male could move, and his weight tipped the balance of the whole box on a central pivot so that a pen recorder revealed who he was with and for how long.

Male control mice ignored the perfume, and divided their time more or less equally between the two dear charmers. Males who had had perfumed parents stayed alone in the middle for 33 per cent of the total time instead of 24 per cent. Both males and females brought up by perfumed parents also

who he was with

spent about the same time with a scented male as with a control, but spent noticeably more time alone. Control females definitely preferred plain, manly males, and nearly all avoided perfumed males, behaving as if they were of a different subspecies. The analogy with certain human cultures is almost too tempting. Luckily humans do not show the corresponding Bruce effect. The smell of an unfamiliar male, particularly from a foreign strain, was found by Hilda Bruce (1960) to block pregnancy in mice and cause the embryos to be resorbed.

Frank Beach has studied sex experimentally for a lifetime, and early experience in dogs makes an interesting contrast with pharmacological experiments. Beach (1968) put pups into semi-isolation, into wire mesh cages where they could smell, hear, and see each other but not touch. Male puppies housed in this way, but allowed out to play with each other for 5 minutes a day were able to copulate as effectively as controls when they were adult. Semi-isolated pups, not allowed to play did not know one end of a bitch from the other and often attempted to mount her from the side or front. Children need to play together too.

Enriched childhood experience for rodents has not been much used as a test for anything, but must have potentialities. Rosenzweig, Bennett, and Diamond (1972) worked with David Krech on cholinesterase activity in brain tissue, especially the ratio between activity in the cerebral cortex and in subcortical structures. The ratio was higher in isolated rats than in those housed after weaning in groups of ten (which is rather too many for stable social relationships; see p. 67). But in groups which had had plenty of toys in the cage – running wheels, mirrors, climbing frames, etc. – the ratio was lower still. Maybe isolated rats could have used some toys too, to relieve the tedium. Behaviour therefore influences brain chemistry as well as vice versa. Levitsky and Barnes (1972) found enriched play to ameliorate the effects of a low-protein diet in infancy on later exploration in an open-field test and in fighting.

Parental behaviour

The suckling posture is the main parental element, the mother lying down somewhat on her side so that the pups can find her nipples. Other actions include licking the pups, building, or rather improving the nest, and retrieving errant infants back to the nest. Pups that are cold, hurt, or in other discomfort, emit hypersonic cries at about 35 kHz (rats) to 85 kHz (mice). They cry if they wander out of the nest and cannot find their way home; the mother leaves the nest, picks up the pup in her mouth (the cries redouble in frequency then and inhibit the biting that is otherwise likely), and takes the pup home by the scruff of the neck. [Allin and Banks (1972) give a nice description.]

Rodents sporadically but not uncommonly kill some of their young by a bite in the nape of the neck. Such deaths are commonest in the first 2 or 3 days, before pups begin to make hypersonic cries, or 2 weeks later, when they cease. The absence of such cries must play a part in these deaths (but only a part; after all most laboratory pups survive to achieve a role in scientific experimentation). A few laboratory rats kill mice (see p. 286) and it is tempting to suggest that they respond as to a pup which displayed neither a fighting–submissive posture nor distress crying. But in fact these rats do not usually kill pups (Myer and White, 1965), and regularly turn to the mouse when offered the choice in a T-maze where non-killing rats choose the pup.

Inexperienced golden hamsters (*Mesocricetus auratus*) nearly always killed any new-born pups they were offered, but responded parentally to older pups. Martin Richards (1966) related this to the shorter gestation period of golden hamsters, compared to other rodents. The adaptation enables them to breed in the arid climate of Syria with its irregular rainfall, and is evolutionarily recent; neither the stimuli from the pups nor the adult response has yet accelerated to catch up.

Eliane Noirot (1964a) regarded nest-building, retrieving, licking, and suckling in mice as independent responses to stimuli from the young, not indications of a unitary 'drive' determined by the hormonal state. Lactating mothers licked and suckled less as the litter grew up but their retrieving became more efficient (Carlier and Noirot, 1965). They picked up the pups near the centre of gravity, instead of by the extremities, and did not have to drop the pups on the way home. Experience with a 'strong' stimulus, a 1-day-old baby mouse. also increased the probability of a parental response to a subsequent 'weak' stimulus (the body of a drowned baby mouse), whether this was 1 minute or a few days later.

It is interesting that, at least in female mice, the increased 'parental responses' included nest-building. This involves carrying material to the nest, nibbling it into shape, and pushing it into position. These are related to suckling by function rather than by form, so that their occurrence in this experiment implies a 'parental drive' after all, a motivational relationship by which a stimulus for retrieving can evoke an otherwise unrelated response. But a simpler explanation may be that nest-building represents a displacement activity. The dead baby mouse is a stimulus for retrieving, carrying something to the nest, but is also unsuitable. The female mice perhaps carried something else, building material, to the nest as a substitute.

Except for being unable to actually give milk, male rats and mice show all the usual 'maternal' responses, and Noirot says (1964b) that they do so as much as females of equivalent experience. Communal nursing, the sharing of two litters by two mothers, lets the pups grow faster (Sayler and Salmon, 1971) and no doubt gives the mothers time to rest, or eat for themselves. I wonder about the selective advantage of parental responses by male mice or rats in the wild.

Parental behaviour must surely be involved in many 'multigeneration' toxicity studies, but I have not been able to find any examples where the possibility was explicitly tested. When methyl mercury hydroxide was injected to rats on day 8 of pregnancy (Hughes, Annau, and Goldberg, 1972), the pups were more subject to cannibalism than controls. This could be a 'eugenic'-like response to damage in the young (which as adults subsequently showed changes in open-field performance, shuttle avoidance, and so on), but it is possible that the poison had direct effects on the mother, leading to the cannibalism. It is also possible in principle that disturbed maternal behaviour could be sufficient to account for the low growth rate of the surviving young and their disturbed behaviour as adults.

SIX

Drug screening and brain pharmacology

Here are the flocks of geese – where's the golden egg?

The commonest practical use of behavioural tests is probably in the search for new drugs. The methods are very simple if somewhat specialised, but the pharmacology is relevant throughout this book.

Direct observation needs patience and something of a technique taught to actors and artists more often than scientists, namely to look at a quite complex situation and say what you actually see without interpreting it into what you think it means. Many 'hard' scientists reduce the question to something that can be put in a test-tube, crystallised, and weighed. A commercial CNS pharmacologist accepts that this latter approach can lose as much as it gains, but he may have no time for observation, literally as well as metaphorically, unless it takes an unambiguous form. A simple yes or no is better than complicated explanations.

The beginning of the problem is that the chemists of a fair-sized pharmaceutical company may well synthesise a thousand compounds a year. Even if only a proportion of these twenty compounds a week (four every working day) have to be tested for even a few well-known actions, the sheer organisational pressures become immense. Investigation of a single drug in depth is quite different from screening 1000 chemicals a year for signs of therapeutic effect.

Some of the therapeutic actions required are subjective, since severe pain or depression of mood are intensely personal to the individual, but success has an observable consequence when the patient is able to smile again. Others would be more directly behavioural if only there was a suitable animal model. Excessive anxiety for example: conditioned avoidance (see Chapter 16) has been suggested but makes an ambiguous model since drugs altering the observable behaviour need not act on 'anxiety' (however this may be defined). Finally, it is not yet realistic to expect a convincing model in animal behaviour of illnesses like schizophrenia.

Advances through side-effects

If it is to be useful, a screening test must be quick and easy to perform, the behaviour simple and unambiguous to recognise. There are many chemicals to be tested, preferably yesterday, and someone inexperienced may have to replace the person who left last week. A chemical altering behaviour may have side-effects, and if no suitable test of the behaviour is available, there is

Drug screening and brain pharmacology 59

often a change in body temperature, neuromuscular co-ordination, or the response to a second drug. It may be quite unrelated in principle to the desired therapeutic result, but if it occurs predictably in a series of drugs already known to be useful, it is just as good a marker.

Systems of screening

Screens usually operate in stages. The first must filter all the compounds to be tested, so it must be exceptionally quick, comprehensive, and reliable. It does not matter if it passes compounds which later turn out useless, but it must rarely miss anything likely to be useful. Once past the first screen, a compound is tested at progressively lower doses. Standard existing drugs are tested periodically as a check, since even at a dose as low as 1 mg/kg bodyweight, their effects should practically sit up and beg for attention. A compound still active at a dosage comparable to this, and whose toxic actions at higher doses are not considered unacceptable, is potentially a useful drug. It will then need much more individual consideration. What, more exactly, are its effects in a variety of possible situations? What is the behavioural mode of action, and the physiological and biochemical actions which the behaviour depends on? How does it differ from existing drugs? If there is no important difference in greater effectiveness or safety, then not only would it be difficult to persuade doctors to prescribe it, but the manufacturer would not get approval from government regulatory authorities to sell it. What are the toxic hazards to be expected if it is taken in small doses for a long period, or in a particularly vulnerable situation like early pregnancy? The screening process is only the first stage, reducing the number of compounds that need such extensive experimentation by a ratio of hundreds to one.

There are two approaches to the design of a screening system. The first is generalised, passing everything the chemists produce to a battery of simple tests for any pharmacological action of interest. The follow-up tests then specify what kind of effect it is and (taking the point to absurd extremes) show whether there is an illness for which it would be therapeutic. However, most compounds are synthesised for a definite target, by modifying an existing antidepressant or anticonvulsant for example. While a drug company may hedge its bets by having a generalised screen just in case an antiseptic or an antiallergic drug has a worthwhile CNS effect, most compounds go direct to the appropriate specialised test. The rather small chance of an action other than the one intended is ignored.

Some general screening batteries

'Considering the extensive use of mouse-screening techniques in most pharmaceutical industries,' commented Dag Campbell and Wolfgang Richter (1967), 'the scarcity of published material is astonishing.' They suggest no explanations, but describe the methods used by Pharmacia AB, Sweden, and the characteristic effects of 68 known drugs. Interestingly, a few well-known classes of CNS active drugs did not show a consistent pattern: various mild stimulants did not particularly resemble caffeine, nor were other mild analgesics (pain-killers) like codeine.

Campbell and Richter's procedure was to inject 200 mg/kg of the test compound into the peritoneal cavity of three mice and put them into a wide glass jar. After 15 to 30 minutes they looked for ptosis (half closed eyelids), piloerection (the hair of the back erected), Straub tail (the tail held almost vertically, characteristic of morphine-like drugs – 'opiates'), and a noticeable increase or reduction of motor activity. The mouse was then picked up by hand and examined under a low-power microscope for salivation, lachrymation, and dilated or contracted pupils ('mydriasis' or 'miosis'). Any of these four signs would suggest interference with the autonomic nervous system. When the mouse was placed on the table, the observer noted any bringing forward ('abduction') of the hindlegs, head drop, or partial or complete ataxia (i.e. staggering or a complete loss of muscular strength). However, neither these signs nor reduced motor activity mean anything if the mouse is then found to have lost its righting reflex, i.e. if it does not get up within half a minute after being placed on its back. The mouse's tail is then gripped in an artery clip to test for analgesia – a 'normal' mouse bites the painful clip within 30 seconds. Finally a thermistor was used to find the temperature of the rectum and of a paw, taking a rise or fall of 2° as significant. Several other signs were looked for (squeaking, bulging eyes, defecation, etc.), but were found to be either unreliable or trivial.

When all these tests had been done on one group of three mice, they were repeated on other groups. These were given either double or half the dose of the preceding group until the dose lethal to 50 per cent of a group (the LD_{50}) could be estimated and until a dose was found low enough to cause no mice, or only one, to 'react' to any test. The greater the number of doses causing mice to react without killing any of them, the more effective the drug. Known classes of drugs (sympathomimetics for example, or phenothiazine tranquillisers) share very similar signs, with rare exceptions that demonstrate how arbitrary pharmacological classification can be. A few drugs that usually show activity, were hardly detected at all.

Campbell and Richter's screen was partly derived from Samuel Irwin's (1962). However, their doses were spaced closer together than Irwin's (100–50–25– instead of 100–30–10–) and they looked for fewer signs, concentrating on those they thought most informative (even so, some turned out redundant). Campbell and Richter classified the mice as either reactors or not (strong reactors were sometimes distinguished from weak), whereas Irwin rated them on an elaborate 9-point scale but only used 3 or 4 points on some items. Normal mice would be rated either 0 (with 8 possible degrees of damage) or 4 (with reductions in whatever-it-is rated 3 to 0, and

Drug screening and brain pharmacology 61

increases 5 to 8). Irwin claimed good reliability for anything his assistants could see, and in some cases his diagrams (modified in Figs. 6.1 and 6.2) make the claim seem reasonable.

Irwin classified his mouse screen into behavioural, neurological, and autonomic groups of signs subdivided as shown in Table 6.1. Not all are always useful. Some of the words he described in fair detail, and others, including some used elsewhere in this chapter, are translated into English in standard pharmacology textbooks.

More promising compounds were then tested in groups of four cats,

Fig. 6.1. The assessment of drug effects in mice: rating scale for Struggle/Passivity (after Irwin, 1959).

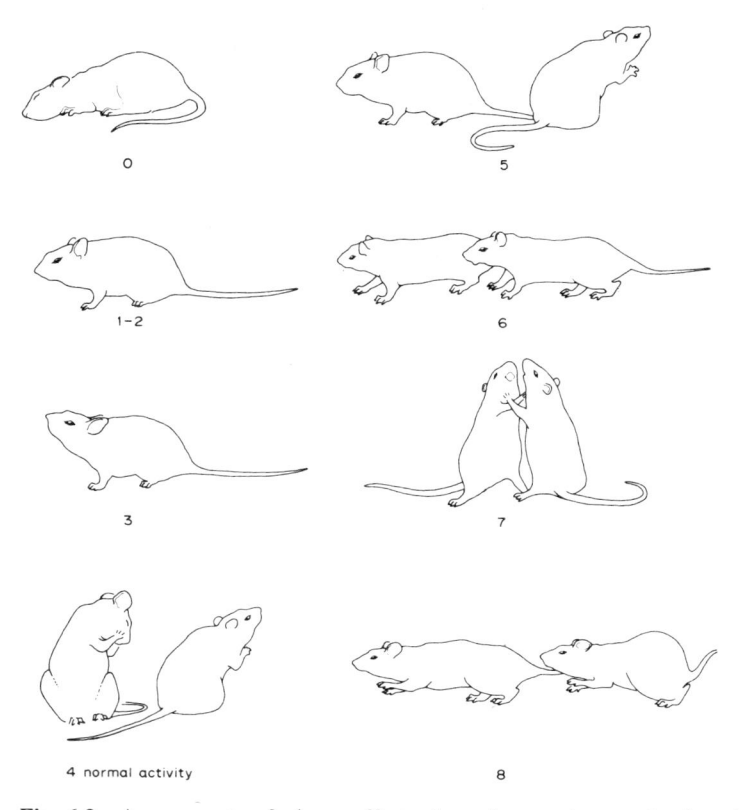

Fig. 6.2. Assessment of drug effects in mice: rating scale for Activity/Reactivity (after Irwin, 1959)

housed together and well known as individuals to the observer, with one cat per dose. The best compounds were given to several such groups, four cats on each dose, four on a standard reference drug and eight controls. Many of the cat signs were like those in mice. Irwin reckoned that his screens would allow at least a partial evaluation of a potential drug's specificity, side-effects, and approximate ED_{50} and therapeutic ratio (i.e. the ratio of the dose effective for 50 per cent of a population to that lethal to 50 per cent).

Many pharmaceutical companies interested in CNS-active drugs must operate comparable screens, but few have been published; the company gains no great advantage from publication. The screens change, they are improved in the light of experience, and the interests of the people operating them change from time to time. It may be useful, however, to describe another screen, also typical of many but orientated more to classical pharmacology than Irwin's more behavioural approach.

Drug screening and brain pharmacology 63

Table 6.1. Signs observed in Irwin's mouse screen (1959)

Behavioural	
Awareness:	alert/stupor, visual placing/spatial orientation, struggle/passivity, stereotypy
Motor activity:	spontaneous in wide glass jar, reactivity when let out on table, touch and pain responses
Mood:	grooming, vocalisation, restlessness, irritability, fearfulness
Neurological	
CNS excitation:	startle, Straub tail, dysmetria, opisthotonus, tremor, twitch, convulsions
Motor inco-ordination:	body and limb positions, staggering, unusual gait
Muscle tone:	grip strength, limb/body/abdominal tone, body sag
Reflexes:	on pinna, cornea, IFR, scratch, writhing, righting
Autonomic	
Eyes:	pupil size, palpebral opening, exophthalmos, opacity
Secretions/Excretions:	lachrymation, salivation, urination, defecation
General:	piloerection, hypothermia, skin colour, heart and respiration rates, arhythmia

The first generalised stage deals with some thirty compounds a week. Six mice are given 100 mg/kg by stomach tube and an hour allowed for absorption into the blood-stream. Various combinations of the first three tests detect the actions of barbiturate sedatives and major and minor tranquillisers. The first, *body temperature*, is measured with a thermocouple poked gently into the oesophagus, and a change of about 2 °C from controls is the criterion for following up the compound at lower doses. Next, a complex of skills labelled *agility* is assessed by placing each mouse on one end of a metal rod about 1·5 cm in diameter. If the mouse walks the 25 cm to the far end or clings on for a full 20 seconds on any one of four trials it is deemed 'normal'; if not, the mean time it managed to hang on is subtracted from 20 to make a score (I tried hard to avoid the pun!). Finally, any *anticonvulsant* action is tested by giving the mice a brief 20 mA a.c. shock between the ears. Antiepileptic drugs like phenobarbitone protect the mice from the tonic convulsion suffered by controls.

For *analgesia* a fresh group of mice are dosed and half an hour later are injected with acetic acid intraperitoneally (0.4 ml of a 0.25 per cent solution). This is just acid enough to make control mice compress their abdomens, lift up their heads, and generally squirm. If the number of squirms is less than 25 per cent of the controls' squirms, and the compound is not a muscle relaxant, it is followed up using a hot-plate test (p. 64).

The *motor activity* of six more mice is tested for half an hour in an activity box with a single photocell, within a darkened chamber. This seems oversimple, but in practice detects very small doses of such tranquillisers as chlorpromazine or haloperidol.

Depression. In man, reserpine can induce something resembling a depressive mood, so that antagonism to the more easily measured effects of reserpine is the best model available for *antidepressant* drugs. The day after an injection of 2 mg/kg of reserpine, among other effects, the mouse loses control of its body temperature, which falls to about 1° above that of the room. Both main groups of antidepressant drugs, tricyclics and monoamine oxidase inhibitors, antagonise this hypothermia, and a compound warming a reserpinised mouse by 2° is followed up.

Some specialised pharmacological tests

The hypothermia test for antidepressants is simple enough for use in a general screen, but could equally well have been classified among the following purpose-built tests with a relatively specific target.

Screens for analgesia

Some tests to find pain-killing drugs are behavioural, notably the hot-plate test. Mice are placed on a metal plate kept at 55 °C. This is slightly too hot to stand on, and normal mice promptly jump off and lick their paws. Mice given an analgesic drug, though apparently normal in every other way, remain standing on the plate. Eventually, of course, they realise the heat is on; but whereas nine out of ten untreated mice jump within 6–13 seconds (in the experiments of Nathan Eddy and Dorothy Leimbach, 1953), mice given various analgesic drugs were likely not to jump until 15–30 seconds after being put on the hot plate. Control mice were remarkably consistent in repeated tests, each mouse nearly always jumped within 3 seconds of its time in the first trial.

The hot-plate test has been especially useful with opiates (morphine and its relatives), but others were mentioned earlier. A rat will soon bite an artery clip pinching the base of its tail and 'squirms' after a small injection of acetic acid intraperitoneally.

Appetite reduction

Mice do not have the same problems in keeping their weight down as some of us do, though laboratory specimens can become quite obese. Some drugs, notably amphetamine and phenmetrazine include *anorexia* among their effects, i.e. the desire for food is reduced, which makes dieting easier. But as a motor stimulant, amphetamine has many side-effects and a safe and truly specific anorexic would be profitable. As a screen, the spaghetti test (p. 41) was ingenious, but food can be as easily measured by weight. Rats trained to be hungry on one meal a day eat a fairly regular amount. A drug limiting how much is eaten to a moderate proportion of the usual daily meal is either: (1) the anorexic that everyone has been looking for; (2) has made the animal feel sick (rats and mice cannot vomit but sometimes look as if they wish they could); or (3) maybe there is still 0·4 ml of sticky compound bloating the mouse's stomach. At least the compound is worth further study, especially if the animal did *not* make up the deficit next day.

Since most anorexic drugs stimulate motor activity, the two effects should be studied together. Clark (1969) dosed mice halfway through a 2-hour daylight session exploring an unfamiliar box, at the end of which controls had gone to sleep while mice given amphetamine or phenmetrazine were still actively exploring. Five minutes after being put singly into another box, controls were active, mice given sedatives or chlorpromazine were not. Controls were attracted to a 'milk bar' in the box (see p. 42) with cups half full of sweet condensed milk, and drank an average of 0·34 ml in 45 minutes. The combined system distinguished gross motor stimulation or sedation from a reduction in appetite.

A test like this, not trying to compel the mice to eat, but tempting them with a tasty morsel, seems useful, so long as novelty or conditioned taste

eating less and exploring more

aversion do not interfere too much. After all it is not that obese mice or people start eating earlier than others, for in many cases they are more 'finicky', but that once started they do not stop. The sensation of satiety which provides literally negative feedback, operates too slowly in the obese.

Barbiturate sleeping time

A conventional pharmacological test is to inject mice with a standard anaesthetic dose of a drug like hexobarbitone sodium. The length of time they 'sleep' can vary quite widely, for reasons of two main kinds, biochemical or neurophysiological.

First, the amount of the active drug in the brain depends partly on the rate of its conversion to an inactive metabolite, in the case of hexobarbitone and many other drugs by 'mixed function oxidases' in the liver. (The choice of barbiturate can make a difference however: barbitone, for instance, is slowly excreted by the kidney largely unchanged, while thiopentone is rapidly redistributed to other tissues before being metabolised in the liver). If the metabolic rate is slowed down, for instance by hypothermia in a cool, draughty laboratory (since an anaesthetised mouse cannot regulate its body temperature), the breakdown of the barbiturate is delayed and anaesthesia is prolonged. The same thing happens when other drugs like alcohol compete for the same enzymes. Conversely, pretreatment with these drugs (or with DDT, according to Wagstaff and Streets, 1971) induces the formation of extra enzyme, so that barbiturate metabolism is accelerated and anaesthesia shortened.

Secondly, the sensitivity of the brain can change. If the animal is already somewhat sedated by chlorpromazine, for example, then a standard dose of barbiturate will have a greater effect. On the other hand, a mouse stimulated by amphetamine will fall asleep later and awaken sooner than usual [as do mice infected with *Mycobacterium tuberculosis* and tested with alcohol (Venulet, 1967)].

Sleeping time after a barbiturate is therefore a convenient index of some pharmacological effects on the CNS. The distinction between the two types of action has practical importance. A drug depressing the CNS arousal system like chlorpromazine but without a barbiturate's side-effects on the respiratory centre can be used for surgical premedication. It allows a given depth of unconsciousness to be produced by a smaller and therefore safer dose of barbiturate. But if the drug depresses the metabolic breakdown of the barbiturate, then all its effects will be enhanced equally. Too many people have died from an otherwise reasonable dose of sleeping pills after a party, to allow alcohol to be considered as useful premedication.

Anaesthesia in mice is usually defined as the loss of the righting reflex, though this can itself be defined in several ways. Irwin (1962) tested it by flipping the mouse five times by the tail into a somersault, and counting how often it landed on its back or side instead of its feet. This is unnecessary with a dose big enough for anaesthesia, but the ability of a dosed mouse to regain its feet after being placed gently on its back is a convenient criterion. However, the phase when the animal is excitable and ataxic just before and after full anaesthesia makes testing the reflex tricky. The mouse might wake up, stagger to its feet, fall over, and go to sleep again before fully awakening.

Mackintosh (1962) devised a 'mouse-rolling' machine, where anaesthetised mice were placed in cylinders of wire mesh within a temperature-controlled cabinet, and the cylinders could be rotated about their axis. A mouse had to regain its feet three times at 2-minute intervals. I once saw another machine, a cabinet with twelve platforms projecting out of one wall. On each platform was an anaesthetised mouse whose weight kept a spring-loaded microswitch closed. When the mouse woke up, it would wriggle, roll over, and fall to a muslin safety-net, and the microswitch would open. Even though only the first wriggle can be timed, automatic timing is useful. If a large number of mice have to be injected with a test compound and, later, the barbiturate, the first mouse can wake up before the last has been dosed.

Diversion – uniformity of response

The interaction of genetic and environmental influences on this simple pharmacological measure makes Mackintosh's results interesting. The F_1 hybrids between CE and CBA mice were much less variable than either parental strain, although the mean sleeping time in all three cases was similar. This was thought to result from a lack of genetic homeostasis – homozygotes with only one kind of gene at a given locus will be as vulnerable to random environmental buffetings as a man standing on one leg in a high wind. What is not so well known is the equivalent effect of the social environment. Mackintosh housed his mice in groups of eight, in pairs, or singly, and tested them after 3 and 10 days. At 3 days, the pure-bred mice were more variable than the hybrids in any housing conditions, and those living alone or in large groups remained more variable at 10 days. However, pure-bred mice living in pairs became as consistent in their response to the anaesthetic at 10 days as the hybrids. Mackintosh thought the change was because the mice housed in pairs had had time to establish stable social relationships; mice in solitary confinement can obviously not form stable social groups but nor, apparently, do mice living in groups of more than five or six. Yet settled relationships can affect experimental reliability.

Motor inco-ordination and ataxia

'Agility' is commonly assessed with another old pharmacologist's warhorse, the rotating rod. Typically this consists of a cylinder with a roughened surface for the animals to grip, rotated on a horizontal axis by a motor and

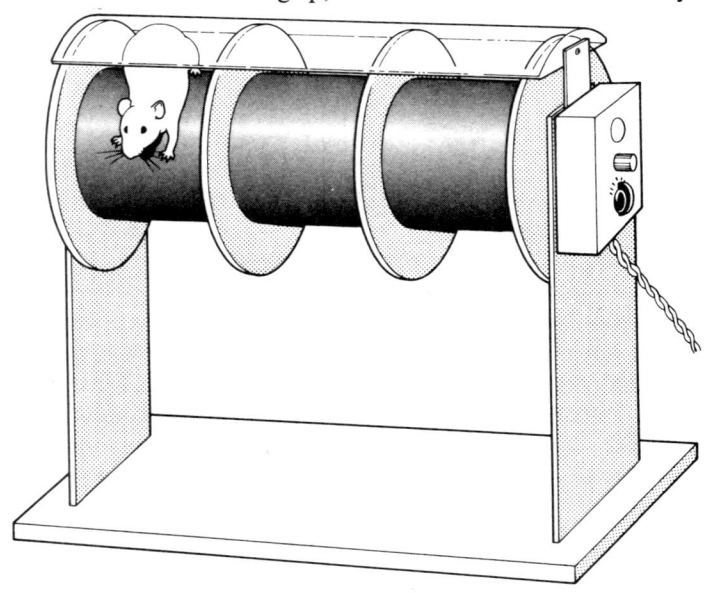

Fig. 6.3. A conventional Rotarod.

pulleys at various speeds (Fig. 6.3). The time that each animal manages to hang on the moving rod is timed in seconds until the mouse drops out, falling on to a platform mounted on a microswitch.

Rotarods depend on rats and mice having the right reflexes to run on a moving surface, and these must include a 'fear of heights'. In view of the height a mouse can fall from without injury, this is surprising. However, safety in a fall depends on the well-known falling-posture reflex (Fig. 6.4)

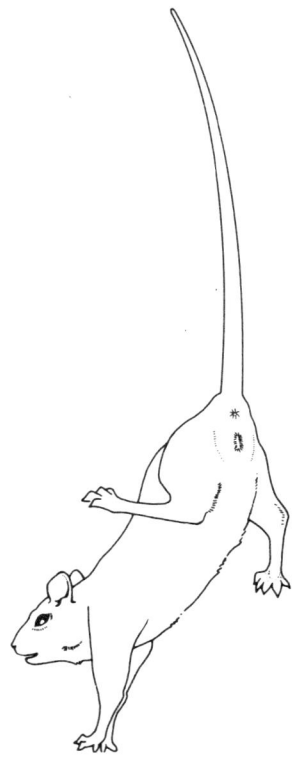

Fig. 6.4. The posture of a falling mouse (after photograph by Chance, 1953.)

and an anaesthetised mouse dropped from a height of 3 metres suffers haemorrhages on landing, sometimes fatally (Chance, 1953). Rats are clearly very cautious when climbing, and this no doubt explains their 'visual cliff' performance (Walk, 1965): half the undersurface of a piece of glass rests on paper with a pattern (e.g. like a chessboard), but there is a 20–30 cm vertical gap between glass and paper on the other half. In the light (but not the dark) a rat selectively avoids walking over the half of the glass lacking visible means of support (Fig. 6.5).

The abilities required in running on a moving rod, are much wider than the label 'co-ordination' or 'agility' would imply. They are interfered with, for

Drug screening and brain pharmacology 69

Fig. 6.5. A 'visual cliff'.

example, by drugs causing muscular relaxation, either centrally or at the neuromuscular junction. Barbiturates, mephenesin, tranquillisers like chlordiazepoxide, or curareform drugs all cause limpness and – at lower doses – staggering or milder signs of ataxia. Methyl mercury can have a similar apparent effect by damage in a different way to the long motor neurons. This effect has a delayed but remarkably sudden onset which can be tested by dangling the rat upside down by the tail: control rats splay the hindlegs outwards or parallel, severely poisoned rats clasp their hindlegs together across the abdomen.

When a rat or mouse is first placed on a rotating rod, he is quite likely to fall off quickly in sheer ignorance of what he is supposed to do, and needs several repetitions at slow and intermediate speeds before showing a stable pre-drug performance.

To minimise the tiresome training procedure, Jones and Roberts (1968) developed an automatic rotarod which accelerated smoothly from 2 to 50 rev/min over a period of 5.5 minutes. The mouse is less likely to fall or jump off unnecessarily as if it could never quite decide when a tolerable speed has become intolerable before the rod has gone even faster. The apparatus is claimed to use fewer mice to detect lower doses of standard drugs than the usual methods.

Even simpler is the 'rotacone' described by Christensen (1973). On a cone 1250 mm long, widening from 35 to 115 mm in diameter, a single flange is wound spirally. A mouse put on the cone at the sharp end therefore has to run ever faster, up to three times his original speed (i.e. from 3.7 to 10.0 m/min at 30 rev/min). When the mice eventually fall off, they drop into one of ten boxes. They are given four training runs a day (each taking about 20 seconds) at 18 rev/min on day 1 and 30 rev/min from day 2 onwards; after two or three runs on day 3, normal mice nearly all fall into boxes 5 to 8. There is no problem when a mouse clings on for a long time by determination rather than agility, as measurement is in terms of the position of the box the mouse falls into, not the time it can cling on.

Simpler methods than a rotarod have been described as tests for agility, etc., but seem to have few advantages over, say, the rotacone. One, as a rapid primary screen, is a simple horizontal metal rod (see p. 63). Another is a 'tilting plane', placing rats on a piece of fine wire gauze at 10° from the horizontal and steadily rotating it towards the vertical. When the rat is heard starting to slide, its claws scraping the mesh, rotation is stopped and the angle measured. Broadhurst and Wallgren (1964) found that alcohol increased the angle after doses of 0.25 and 0.75 g/kg; only after 2 g/kg was there a decline; but they considered this test less useful than a biochemical assay.

Trio-*ortho*-cresyl phosphate was once disastrously sold in Morocco as cut-price cooking oil. It causes severe damage to the axons of the long motor nerves in man and some other species (not, apparently, monkeys or rats). Glees (1967) described how in hens a single oral dose of 0.2 ml/kg caused gut disturbances, paroxysmal head-shaking, and paralysis of hindleg extensor muscles. As the hens became ill and later as they recovered, they 'goose-stepped'. To quantify this description, Glees made the hens climb a ladder at 30° to get their food from a platform about half a metre above the ground. Ataxia or paralysis was clearly visible and the hens took longer to climb it.

The problem of anxiety

In principle any method described in this book could be used as a screen. Conditioned Suppression, a learned response to electric shock (see p. 201), seems to work well enough for antianxiety drugs. However, anxiety illustrates a general point about even the best screening systems, that most major advances have been made by observing 'side-effects' in clinical practice, not in the pharmaceutical laboratory. Propranolol is a case in point, indeed it may be two cases for it appears as if it might possibly have two psychiatric uses quite different from its original purpose. Pharmacologically, propranolol blocks β-adrenergic receptors, particularly those which accelerate heart-rate, and is therefore useful in patients with tachycardia (i.e. whose heart beats too fast).

Now anxiety produces tachycardia, and propranolol was observed (Granville-Grossman and Turner, 1966) to reduce anxiety in man. One explanation might therefore be that there is a vicious circle, anxiety causing tachycardia and tachycardia acting as a conditioned stimulus for further anxiety. Propranolol breaks the circle by blocking tachycardia. However, once the question was raised, evidence was found that propranolol reduces anxiety in rats quite independently of its β-blocking action. For the dextroisomer is not a β-blocker, but is nearly as effective as racemic propranolol in reducing signs of experimentally-induced anxiety in rats (Bainbridge and Greenwood, 1971); in the open-field test (see p. 235) it is also more effective than practolol, which blocks β-receptors but does not cross the blood–brain barrier (Buxton, Verduyn, and Cox, in preparation).

A screening test that measures anxiety reliably in animals would obviously be preferable, for it would have discovered the effect several years earlier.

An excursion into brain pharmacology

One of the main reasons for research into either behaviour or the brain is to help in understanding the other. However, while a change in behaviour must depend on one in neuronal activity somewhere, attempts to find correlations between neuroanatomy, physiology, and behaviour have been less than universally successful. The experimenter wrestling with the complexities of one subject would naturally like to short-circuit the complexities of the others, and use simple, clearcut measures. So there was widespread interest in the discovery of a clear but limited behavioural sign of the activity of neurons using dopamine as a transmitter.

Dopamine (DA) is of practical as well as academic interest. Neuroleptic drugs (chlorpromazine, haloperidol, etc.) that relieve symptoms of schizophrenia also commonly antagonise dopamine, and are liable to have side-effects that resemble Parkinson's disease. Parkinsonism is thought to be due to degeneration of dopaminergic neurons and is alleviated by raising brain concentrations of dopamine (inhibiting its metabolic breakdown and administering its precursor, *l*-dopa). Conversely, one of amphetamine's many actions is to release dopamine from its neurons, and it can be hard for a psychiatrist to distinguish an amphetamine addict from a paranoid schizophrenic. Put crudely these arguments imply that schizophrenia is associated with too much dopamine, or too great a response to a normal amount of dopamine and indeed there is some direct evidence for both phenomena in different groups of schizophrenics, according to Rotrosen *et al.* (1976) those that respond or not, to neuroleptics.

Of course, things are not so simple. For instance Crow and Gillbe (1973) gave evidence that chlorpromazine and thioridazine were equally effective in treating schizophrenia and reduced motor activity equally well, but while chlorpromazine antagonised dopamine in rats, thioridazine did not. And then Kelly and Miller (1975) explained this with evidence that thioridazine does block dopamine, after all, but that it also has an antimuscarinic (anticholinergic) action which works in the opposite direction. The Parkinsonian symptoms depend on an imbalance between dopamine and other transmitters in the nigrostriatal system, the antischizophrenic action presumably on dopamine blockade somewhere else, the limbic system perhaps. Claims have been made recently that propranolol dramatically helps some long-term schizophrenic patients, far more than neuroleptics, but propranolol does not appear to block DA receptors in the brain. On the other hand, *l*-propranolol (the isomer that inhibits β-adrenergic receptors but not anxiety) also seems to block serotonin (5-HT) receptors in the brain. For treatments which raise 5-HT in the brain also greatly increase motor activity, and this increase is prevented or reversed by *l*-propranolol or another 5-HT blocker, but not by other β-blocking drugs (Green and Grahame-Smith, 1976). Propranolol's CNS actions are reviewed by Conway, Greenwood and Middlemiss (1978).

The dopamine story is therefore neither crudely simple nor likely to prove of unmanageable complexity, but it depends on a test simple enough to use as a screen in animals. The pharmacology depends on a careful mapping of where dopaminergic and noradrenergic neurones go in the brain (see Fig. 6.6), and on experiments using 6-hydroxydopamine (6-OHDA) to cause the selective degeneration of dopaminergic neurones.

The main dopaminergic and noradrenergic pathways run separately on each side of the brain but fairly close to each other. The traditional way of studying them is cutting surgically or electrolytically – and possibly destroying by mistake. Urban Ungerstedt (1971) found that such lesions imitate what are supposed to be lesions to the hypothalamic 'feeding centre' (see p. 46): the animals failed to eat, drink, or explore, and Ungerstedt wanted a more selective lesion. A small injection of 6-OHDA into the substantia nigra, where the cell-bodies of these dopaminergic neurons are, caused selective damage to these neurons only. To make the lesion

Drug screening and brain pharmacology 73

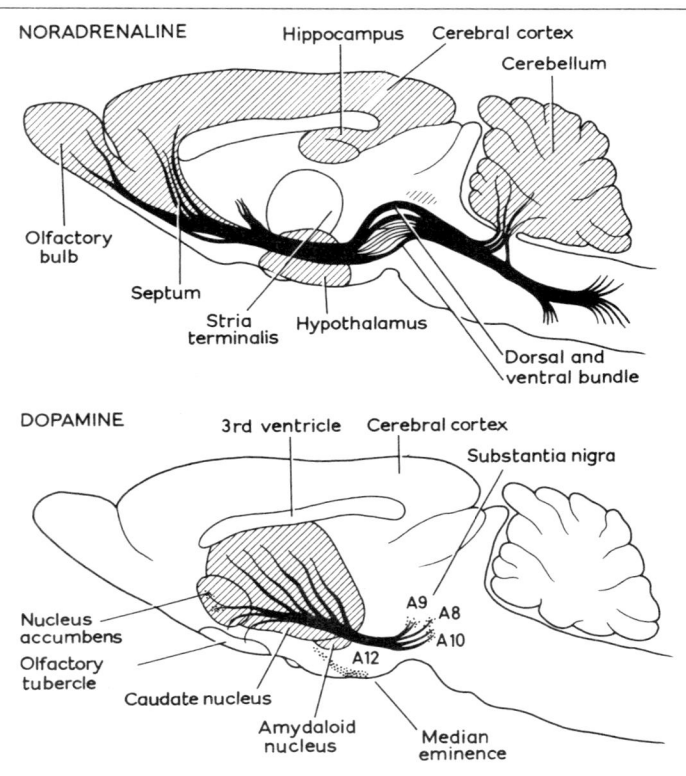

Fig. 6.6. Noradrenaline and dopamine in the brain: sagittal sections (after Ungerstedt, 1971) showing main ascending pathways and main terminal areas (hatched).

still more specific and informative, he made it to one side of the body only.

When rats wake up from anaesthetic, they usually run or stagger forward. Unilaterally lesioned rats ran in circles, and for the first day or two they stood in a C-shape, bending towards the side of the lesion. They otherwise recover but for the rest of their lives unilaterally-lesioned rats explore predominantly in one direction. It is this one-sidedness which provides the screening test.

Drugs like amphetamine or apomorphine cause 'stereotyped' behaviour. The dosed (but un-lesioned) animal appears to start something under the usual stimuli (exploring, grooming, fighting in a mutual upright sparring posture; see p. 283), but continues indefinitely as if locked in to the action, unable to stop. After the highest doses, grooming, biting, and gnawing can become irresistable and even self-mutilating. Stereotyped behaviour requires direct observation, and just because it is continuous it is hard to describe quantitatively. If the drugs are given to rats with unilateral lesions to the nigro-striatal pathway, the stereotyped exploration-like walking takes the form of going round in circles.

For convenience the rat is placed in a 'rotometer' (Fig. 6.7) wearing a light harness connected to apparatus for counting the number of turns in

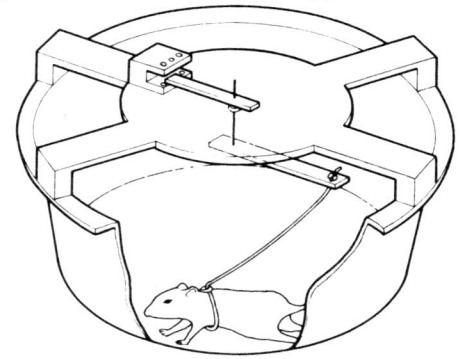

Fig. 6.7. 'Rotometer' to measure circling in each direction (after Barber, Blackburn, and Greenwood, 1973). The rat is placed in a Perspex bowl, wearing a harness attached to a pivoted vane. As the rat circles, the tip of the vane passes through a block of three photocells, and the sequence of their operation identifies the direction of circling.

each direction (Barber, Blackburn, and Greenwood, 1973). Without a drug the rat stops circling in a few minutes; after 1 mg/kg of apomorphine or 5 mg/kg d-amphetamine typical rats circled for 35 minutes and about 2 hours respectively.

The specificity of the test is shown by the fact that the two drugs cause circling in opposite directions. Amphetamine makes the rat turn towards the side of the lesion (1294 ipsilateral against 11 contralateral turns in a typical example), apomorphine away from it (4 against 256). Amphetamine probably works by releasing dopamine from the intact nigro-striatal neurons so that receptors are stimulated only on the intact side of the striatum. The evidence for this is that if dopamine synthesis is stopped with α-methyltyrosine, or if its post-synaptic receptor is blocked with pimozide, then amphetamine has no effect on circling. Its effect is reduced if the original 6-OHDA infusion is made slightly above or behind the substantia nigra, so that half the 6-OHDA misses its target and fewer neurones degenerate. Turning is elicited in normal rats by electro-stimulation in the same region.

Turning away from the lesion because of apomorphine is paradoxical. Apomorphine resembles dopamine structurally, and Ungerstedt (1971) suggested that receptors on the lesioned side, 'starved' of their normal supplies, become 'super-sensitive'. They respond more fully than the intact receptors to anything resembling dopamine that comes their way. Contralateral turning only develops gradually over 3 months or so, but at its peak doses as low as 0·05 to 0·1 mg/kg of apomorphine are effective whereas 1 mg/kg is about the lowest to cause stereotyped behaviour in intact animals. The receptor must be stimulated directly because contralateral turning is also caused by intraperitoneal injection of *l*-dopa. Dopa is converted to dopamine (a compound which prevents this conversion outside the brain has to be given at the same time, or else not enough dopa gets there) but again, there is no turning if the conversion to dopamine is blocked within the brain or if the receptors are blocked by haloperidol or pimozide.

Circling looks like a special case of stereotypy, at least when motor activity is also stimulated, but Jaton, Loew, and Vigouret (1976) describe a drug which causes circling without stimulation or stereotypy. Circling is a simple marker for some of the cogs of the brain machine, perhaps the first simple tool for its analysis, but of course it is only a beginning. Interactions are known with other transmitters, with noradrenaline, serotonin, and acetylcholine (does this balance dopamine only for Parkinsonian symptoms?). Circling due to amphetamine is potentiated by pre-treatment with reserpine, perhaps through super-sensitivity again, because reserpine empties the pre-synaptic stores of both dopamine and noradrenaline. But why does reserpine cause a good imitation of at least part of clinical depression and why is amphetamine not effective as an antidepressant?

Discussion: can you eat golden eggs when you have them? Hard-boiled or poached?

One characteristic of the pharmaceutical industry, according to critics and supporters alike, is the 'me-too-ism' of new drugs hardly different from other recent ones. One firm produced chlorpromazine and dozens of others produced their own phenothiazines, with just enough differences to get round the patent. Real improvements came late, in the form of slowly-metabolised versions where one injection replaces a month's tablets that were mostly dropped down the lavatory. Similarly with benzodiazepine tranquillisers and tricyclic antidepressants, when psychotropic drugs were a bandwagon worth climbing on to. One reason must be the obvious commercial one: if a drug is valuable medically, there must be a market. But part of the reason must also lie in the logic of the screening process.

Screens necessarily start with a target. Certain known drugs help in the treatment of a certain clinical problem – are there other drugs ripe for discovery which will do the same job more effectively or with fewer or milder side-effects? The screen must therefore be sure of detecting existing drugs.

Another requirement of a screening test is that besides being quick and simple, it must also be reliable and repeatable in the sense that all animals in a batch must respond, irrespective of differences in strain or even species, or in upbringing and previous handling.

Good routine laboratory care is not enough. The animals will be healthy but may be timid and therefore variable. Untouched by human hand since weaning, taken from stock-room to laboratory, grabbed by an immense human hand, lifted high as if by an owl taking them home for supper, and injected. No wonder some wee sleekit cowrin' tim'rous beasties do not acknowledge man's dominion and refuse to perform the experimenter's tricks. A technique which persuades even timid animals to do the same as bold ones – or which compels them – is essential. If, as is common, a new compound is screened in the first instance only by three or four mice, then one mouse going on strike can put the statistics right out. Either the whole test on this chemical is repeated, or another miracle is lost to modern science. But note that the more compulsory the method is, the greater the risk that it may become cruel.

There may not be a true animal equivalent of the therapeutic problem, especially with mental – i.e. behavioural – illness (a comment on how little we really know about either behaviour or psychiatry, perhaps). A model may exist, however, that can be accepted as a reasonably good analogy, without any commitment to the claim of absolute validity. In man, reserpine is said to produce the retardation of depressive mood but not the sadness. Yet it makes a reasonable predictive model in practice, for among the drugs that antagonise it are all the clinically useful antidepressants except the recent 'mianserin'.

When a model is available, it is not always possible to test it directly – a reserpine-treated rat may suffer from a depressive mood but sadness is difficult to measure. Even the observable consequences are not very specific to reserpine, and some are difficult to describe precisely. The rat moves slowly. It appears 'listless' with a hunched posture, half-closed eyes and a general lack of response to stimuli except for a rare burst of aggression.

Therefore, screens often measure a side-effect rather than the one believed closest to the therapeutic action. Campbell and Richter (1967) describe, for example, how the neuroleptics share 'a unique combination of signs at 4–11 dose levels: increased paw temperature, decreased rectal temperature, decreased motor activity, ptosis, abduced hindlegs, head drop, and loss of righting reflex'. There is nothing in this list, except just possibly motor activity, that suggests the slightest help to people suffering from mental illness. Yet if a new chemical were to show a similar profile of side-effects, it would certainly be worth examining its possible therapeutic usefulness.

Screening by side-effect, and by reflex action rather than by formal conditioned behaviour, is probably the only way a large screen can operate. With the many properties of the many compounds that have to be searched for, a test has to be quick, simple, economical of mice and money, and above all, reliable. It is inevitably a mass-production, assembly-line affair.

Nevertheless, it would be inaccurate to imply that a pharmaceutical screen is a rigid stereotyped affair through which all the test chemicals are squeezed. Each test is an independent mini-experiment, adapted in the light of results and directed at a specific target. To be commercially successful a company has to select a set of markets worth aiming at. There must be reasonable prospects both of finding an appropriate new drug, and of selling enough to recover the costs of all the safety-testing of the drug itself and of all the others that fall by the wayside. Tests are therefore directed towards the chosen market, and the company accepts the risk of missing a useful drug whose effect is very specifically on something else.

Most compounds are liable to turn out useless, having little effect in any of the screening tests, and many of the observed effects in screens may be secondary. For example, reduced motor activity or reduced food consumption could be genuine signs of useful sedative or anorexic action, or equally they could be consequences of pain or nausea. So the primary screen has to be followed up carefully, to find the dosage at which one effect occurs in relation to others. The pattern of effects must either resemble that of a useful known drug or suggest a new kind with a plausible appearance of potential usefulness. Any other actions, like tremor or convulsions, which could represent undesirable side-effects also need to be noted down and used in evidence against the compound. Since most test compounds are part of a series, the synthetic chemists need to know if they are getting nearer to the target. Nevertheless, it is important that the first stage of a screen should not be too selective. If a compound is accepted for further testing but turns out not to be sufficiently active, or to have undesirable side-effects, then no great harm has been done, but a compound rejected once is not likely to be tested again. It would be futile to speculate how many potentially useful drugs have in fact been missed.

Suppose that a compound takes substantially longer than usual to take effect (perhaps after conversion to an active metabolite). Though mice may be kept for several days to check for a delayed lethal effect, any behavioural change would have to be bizarre to be noticed as the mice doze in a corner of the cage. The first antidepressant drugs were not discovered in a screen, since their therapeutic effect in man takes 3 weeks to develop, but this is only the extreme of what could be a common enough case. A compound whose action appears and is finished before observation begins is less of a problem, since it would rarely be useful (cigarette smokers may care to dispute that point).

The drugs that conceivably might be missed because of the inevitable limitations to any system in an imperfect world are unfortunate. More important are those missed because of the inherent characteristics of the system we actually have. It is difficult to see how existing screens could be fundamentally improved at a stroke, though their continuous improvement in detail has in fact been considerable, yet radically new classes of drugs seem only to be discovered by the luck of someone shrewdly noticing effects in patients suffering from one illness that would help those suffering from another. After all, that is what screens are for. Yet we owe iproniazid, the first of the monoamine oxidase inhibiting antidepressants, to the euphoria it produced in patients suffering from tuberculosis. Chlorpromazine, the first neuroleptic tranquilliser was originally developed as an antihistamine. Imipramine, the first tricyclic antidepressant was then discovered in a trial for improved neuroleptics. The cardiovascular drug propranolol seems to relieve anxiety. Chlordiazepoxide was the first representative of the first new class of drugs to be deliberately discovered in the appropriate screen. The history of psychopharmacology is described by Anthony Hordern (1968).

Screens detect only the most reliable, uniform drug effects, the ones that tend to over-ride all other influences. It is surely no coincidence that drugs which show up well in screens, like chlorpromazine and amphetamine, are also thought to reduce the influence of external stimuli. Conversely, hallucinogens like LSD are thought to increase responsiveness to stimuli, to flood the organism with them. If true, this would itself partly explain why it is so hard to get consistent behavioural results from hallucinogens in animals, as they would be distracted by any random extraneous stimuli.

There is a contrast with the psychoactive drugs in the most widespread use. Ethanol, nicotine, the various extracts of *Cannabis sativa* are self-administered by millions of people, often in very small doses, but often also for very long periods. What the precise effects of these drugs are that induce people to dose themselves is a matter for debate, but it is not one that can at present be detected by a screening test. Screening tests would detect the nausea from a larger dose of nicotine, and the convulsions of near-lethal doses. Screens might detect the motor inco-ordination and loss of balance caused by alcohol, but few people drink for these.

Meanwhile screening tests select useful needles from a haystack of chemicals, quickly and remarkably economically in terms both of money and of mice.

SEVEN

Motor activity

Behaviour is movement. Any movement of the animal in relation to the surroundings, or any externally-observed movement of one part of the body in relation to the rest – these start an empirical definition of behaviour. It also seems reasonable to include the colour and pattern changes of cephalopods like the cuttle-fish, *Sepia officinalis*, since they are so varied and rapid that they reflect the animal's 'mood' and much of its likely next action (Holmes, 1940). But if this is behaviour, are not the seasonal colour changes of many birds and fishes, which signal whether they are in breeding condition and ready to mate? And the combination of immobility and anatomy which makes the camouflage of stick insects and leaf bugs so good? On the other hand, there are body movements too trivial to be useful (if that is not too dangerous a generalisation), and pathological movements like tremors or convulsions which are more the province of the physiologist.

To define behaviour as movement draws attention to the physical system, involving energy whose output can be measured by a suitable transducer. There have been many methods devised to detect and record 'motor activity', the acceleration of a mass resulting from the behaviour that we can see.

The more intense the behaviour the greater the output of physical energy, but only up to a point. The subjective intensity may be greatest when the animal is crouching, rigid, and motionless. If so, all the tense, mutually antagonistic muscles could burn up more chemical energy than when the animal is scampering lightheartedly round the cage, but the kinetic energy detectable as movement is less. In principle it should be possible to measure energy expenditure as heat output or carbon dioxide, but the apparatus necessary to do so accurately and fast enough would certainly stop the behaviour being shown in the first place.

Activity as a by-product of virtually all behaviour may, perhaps, be confused with motor activity as a specific tendency. Just as hunting in Carnivora has been emancipated, so that a well-fed cat may need to go hunting for its own sake, irrespective of any economic necessity (Tinbergen, 1951), so there may be an independent tendency to exercise. There is little convincing evidence, but the possibility should be borne in mind.

Methods of measuring activity

If there is an independent need for exercise, it is probably seen most clearly in the 'activity wheel' (Fig. 7.1), the earliest of the systematic measures to be widely used (reviewed by Curt Richter, 1927; and Mary Shirley, 1929), and still popular with pet hamsters.

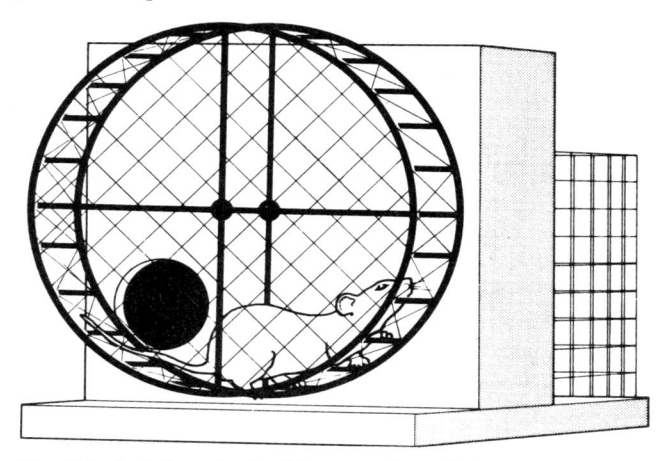

Fig. 7.1. Activity wheel with access from living cage (after Kreezer, 1949).

The rat or mouse has a living cage only just big enough to eat and sleep in, but there is free access into a large 'running wheel' which rotates under the animal's weight as it climbs in. There must surely be some positive feedback in this, since once started, rats and mice commonly continue running for hours. This is partly a reflex – any movement of the animal rotates the wheel and thereby upsets the animal's equilibrium, which it can only restore by rotating the wheel ... But this cannot be the whole story, since individuals manage to stop, and do so under defined conditions. Individual animals vary widely: some rotate the wheel enough to cover 15 or, exceptionally, up to 30 kilometres a night, some a few hundred metres, but any one individual is remarkably consistent.

Once they enter the wheel, the animals run; other activities – eating, sleeping, washing, exploring – all take place mainly in the living cage. Wheels allowed the first systematic studies of behavioural rhythms, for there is a daily cycle of wheel-running and rest. There are less well-marked rhythms every 2–4 hours, and in females every 4 or 5 days as well.

Activity wheels therefore measure a fairly specific kind of activity, when the animal, as it were, goes out for a walk. Another way of detecting walking, taking up less laboratory space, and not using noisy gears, is to use a photocell. An infrared light-beam is shone across the cage (infrared because visible light will be detected by the animal and might influence its

Motor activity

behaviour), so that when the animal walks the length of the cage it interrupts the beam and is detected. The animal that moves only at one end of the cage can be monitored by zig-zagging the light-beam through a delicately placed series of mirrors, or by using more than one beam. The possibility of interrupting two beams for the price of one is avoided by putting a block of glass where the beams cross. The possibility of an artificially high count if the rat washes his face where his nose or paws just break the beam several times a second, is fortunately somewhat remote.

If movement from end to end of a cage is sufficient, and movement from side to side can be ignored, two alternatives to photocells are the tilt cage and an electrified grid floor. The tilt cage, as you might guess, has a floor pivoted in the middle, and a microswitch at each end. Provided the rats are not reluctant to trust their weight on a floor that gives way slightly under them, and that mice do not play see-saw, then the tilt-cage is satisfactory enough.

An 'automatic maternal behaviour apparatus' (Holland, 1965) is an interesting variant of a tilt-cage to give more specific information. A low wall divides the cage into a small closed nest box and a larger area. The cage pivots so that, after adjustment for the weight of the mother rat, a counter and timer can record how long she spends nursing the litter and how often she makes excursions out of the nest. Several brief trips when the young rats are of an age to climb the wall indicate presumably that the mother rat has been retrieving the venturesome youngsters and carrying them home.

retrieving venturesome youngsters

On a grid cage, the floor consists of metal bars, alternate bars being electrically charged at a low voltage (ca 35 mV), too low for the animal to detect. A rat short-circuits some of the bars, and any change is made to activate a relay and the usual counters and timers. The grid can detect quite small movements, so long as the animal moves across the bars and not along them.

Activity is, of course, something more than walking or running, though these are necessary preliminaries to most other things. Barnett and Jim Smart (1970) used a 'plus maze' consisting of four alleyways in a cross with a sleeping cage at the centre. One or two alleys had different kinds of food or nesting material at the far end, one had water, and one was empty. Photocells showed that the number of visits to each alley is similar, but mice spend more time in the food or balsa wood alleys than in the water alley or the empty one.

However, while you may take a mouse to water, you can't make him drink, and many brief visits to retrieve a mouthful of food and hoard it are not necessarily equivalent to a single long drink of water. Something can be done with other sensors, arranged to detect when the animal actually licks the spout of the water-bottle. But in general there is no substitute for a human observer if you want to distinguish one kind of activity from another.

Vibration

Several methods detect activities other than walking even if they cannot distinguish one from another. Most depend on the animal's movements to cause vibrations transmitted through the floor. Perhaps the oldest established is the 'jiggle cage' (Richter, 1927) where the floor rests at each corner on, in effect, a rubber balloon. A skin is stretched across an air-tight drum, and a narrow tube leads to a pointed lever, which scratches a trace on a smoked drum. The pneumatic transmission is sensitive to eating and grooming and the response time is fast, so that, in their day, jiggle cages were very useful. The apparatus is tricky to set up, and the method is rarely used nowadays.

A complete cage can be suspended by a wire, and similar vibrations used to be recorded from the wire as from the pneumatic system, as the cage sways in the breeze.

Mechanical vibrations in the cage floor can be converted into electrical potentials. Even a Pied Piper would hardly think of a rat's running, scratching, or gnawing as music, but he can detect and distinguish them with a hi-fi record-player cartridge as if the cage floor is a disc. Ordinary plastic cages can be used, the stylus resting on the underside of the floor. Alternatively, a simple bar magnet can be allowed to vibrate within a coil. However, the strength of the signal depends not only on the vigour of the animal's movements but also on its body weight and its distance from the stylus. Some arrangement has to be made to insulate each cage from others and from vibrations due perhaps to people walking into the room. Knoll and Knoll (1961) used metal 'stepping stones' and claimed that the crystal under each one could distinguish oxotremorine-tremor from walking between plates.

More versatile and convenient is a capacitance method. The cage and animal are placed between two metal plates or (as in the 'Animex' version) on top of a box containing six coils mounted vertically. The animals can therefore be placed within the electromagnetic field of a tuned high-frequency (100 kHz) oscillator circuit where they act as part of the dielectric

Motor activity 83

of a capacitor. If any mass is moved into or within this field, it will de-tune the circuit. The discrepancy is used to provide a count of the animal's movements (Svensson and Thieme, 1969).

The sensitivity of the system can be varied, to measure either only large-scale movements of large animals, or movements as fine as those of a mouse's respiration. If the latter, then the mouse has to be asleep, insulated from noises which might disturb him, or anaesthetised – otherwise the larger-scale movements will swamp the fine ones. If the cage has a wire lid, as many plastic cages do, and the animal licks the metal spout of a water-bottle resting on it, then the capacitance changes are enormously greater. If the machine has two channels of independently-adjustable sensitivity, each kind of activity can be measured separately.

Given two channels for measuring strong and weak signals independently, it is also possible to measure the activity of two animals independently. Attaching a loop of copper wire to one of them, as a harness round the shoulders or (firmly but not tightly) round the neck, increases the capacitance greatly and therefore the strength of signal.

There is a comparable acoustic system where a hypersonic sound (about 40 kHz) is generated, a microphone detects it, and movement of animals in the space between disturbs reception. Since rodents are sensitive to, and use, high-frequency sounds up to at least 50 kHz, it is possible (though perhaps unlikely) that the detector could influence the activity it is supposed to measure. A tone of 39 kHz can inhibit shock-induced fighting in rats (Anderson, Murcurio, and Mahoney, 1970).

Activity in groups

Most methods, apart from the capacitance technique, will measure only one animal at a time. Several animals could, of course, be put into a cage. Even if they did not interfere with measurements, however, with two rats blocking one photocell, or one at each end of a tilt-cage, they would confuse the interpretation of the results. But whether or not social isolation is a distinct stress (see p. 272) rats clearly influence one another's activity.

influence one another's activity

Drugs can sometimes change the behaviour of animals *not* receiving them (Wilson and Mapes, 1964; Silverman, 1966a; Borgešová, Kadlecová, and Kršiak, 1971); the cage-mate of a dosed rat or mouse whose behaviour has changed, will respond differently to him. Animals receiving high doses of a stimulant – or an anaesthetic – may paradoxically be quite ignored. On the other hand, mice receiving high doses of amphetamine seem to exaggerate their reactions to each other, which in turn augments the effects of the drug. Doses of amphetamine which make solitary mice overactive and ill for an hour or two can kill grouped mice (Chance, 1946).

Measurement of the activity of one mouse in the presence of others might therefore help towards understanding the mechanism of group toxicity. The lethal dose of amphetamine (the LD_{50}) is smaller in grouped than solitary mice. It is intermediate when one dosed mouse is put into a group of untreated controls (Wang, Hasegawa, Peters, and Rimm, 1969). Do untreated mice respond more to an untreated intruder or one given a large dose of amphetamine? Does it matter if the mice are strangers or well known to each other? Are the bizarre long-lasting fighting postures produced by near-lethal doses of amphetamine and a few other compounds essential to group toxicity? At a pharmacological level, neurons using dopamine, noradrenaline, and serotonin respond to amphetamine: are some of these more closely related to motor activity and others to group toxicity?

This is not the book to go into the biochemical changes which underlie the behavioural effects. Let me just point out how quickly a question about an apparently simple measure of activity leads both to neurophysiological and biochemical topics and to the social organisation of mice. It is rarely useful to discuss 'activity' as if it is pure and simple. You have to ask what sort of activity exactly? And then, as like as not, what is its function? And (not the same thing) what causes it to happen in the individual?

The sounds of mice

The activity of a whole roomful of rats or mice is reflected by the noise they make. Anyone in an animal house early on a dark winter's evening will appreciate the method – while the lights are on and people are present and busy, the animals are silent. Within a few seconds of the lights going out there starts a gradually increasing din of rustlings, squeaking, and gnawing. John Mackintosh told me (1964) how he put a microphone into the room and tape-recorded the noise. Playing the recording back at a higher speed through a sound-level meter showed the mice to be silent all day, but with a peak noise intensity soon after people went home, continuing with a slight fall all night.

To identify these activities would need human observation, which could be tedious. A videotape recorder and closed-circuit television would minimise any interference by the observer, but would otherwise only postpone the hard work. Maybe a sound spectrograph and a computer could be used to analyse the different noises by the energy in different bands of frequencies (that is, loudness at different ranges of pitch). The gnawing of hard food pellets produces a noise whose peak energy must be at fairly low audible frequencies. The sound of scratching must have faster pulses of 'white' noise spread over a wide range of frequencies. Purer tones at high but audible frequency (4 kHz?) might represent the squeaks we can hear from fighting rodents. Rats emit hypersonic pulses when fighting, short ones at about 50 kHz associated with aggressive actions, longer cries (about 0·7 seconds) at around 22–25 kHz with submission or escape (Sales, 1972). The latter probably developed from the distress cries of infants. Francis (1977) says that the 22 kHz calls are also made – very loudly – by male rats just after copulating. He showed that rats regularly emit very similar 22 kHz calls while they are resting or asleep; these calls are of course very soft and quiet and have been associated with respiratory movements of the chest wall, and their occurrence is inversely related to motor activity. If all the sound of the rodents' daily life can be calibrated against the corresponding activities, it would make an interesting (if expensive) way of recording the times of day at which different kinds of behaviour occur without interference with the animals.

Rhythms of activity

Listening to a roomful of laboratory rodents is probably the most dramatic way of noticing that their activity varies according to the time of day. Its timing is largely governed by the day/night cycle of lighting, but to a lesser extent it is inhibited by the noise (or the smell?) of people. This can be shown by keeping the animals in a room with bright lighting controlled by a time switch, and dimmer red lighting at other times. Rats and mice seem to be relatively insensitive to red light (Halberg and Barnum, 1958), no doubt because in twilight or night they have to be relatively sensitive to blue, so that red must seem even darker to them than to us. The bright light can come on during the true night or at any convenient time. Figure 7.2 shows two days' activity measured by a capacitance method in a cage of two rats. A 2-hourly alternation of rest and activity is superimposed on a 24-hour cycle. On the Sunday, the most active period started when the white light went out at about 14.00. On the Monday this peak was much lower during working hours but business picked up again after people went home (by 17.30 or so), and with relatively short interruptions, stayed at a high level more or less until the lights came on again at 02.00 in the morning. Apart from a short burst of activity in response to light, and to noises, etc., from people after about 08.30, the animals were clearly asleep from then on. These records suggest that the light/dark cycle is the main influence on rats' activity, but that noise or other signs of human activity also affect them.

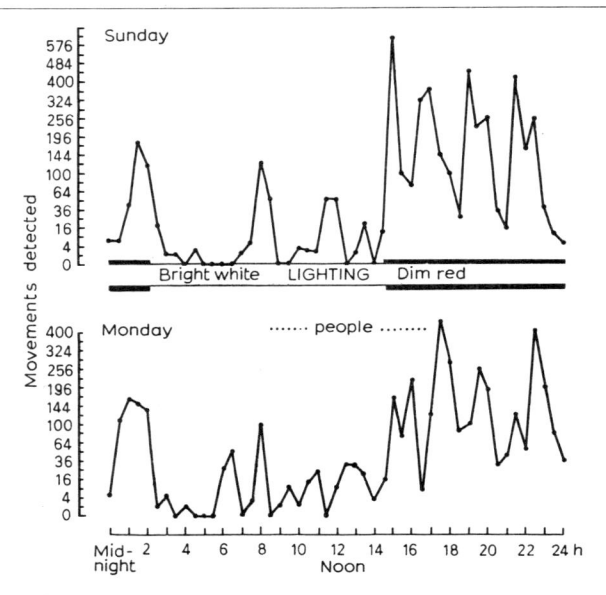

Fig. 7.2. Rats' daily activity cycle. The activity of a pair of male rats was monitored in their home cage about 2 weeks after arrival in the laboratory, using a machine detecting changes in capacitance near eight under-floor sensors. Counts were made every 30 minutes, note the square root vertical scale. Lighting on an approximately 12 hour light/12 hour dark cycle seems to be the main influence on activity, but the intermittent presence of people also has some effects (compare the scores at 15.00 hours on Sunday and Monday). An approximately 2-hour activity cycle seems to be superimposed.

Ever since rats and mice first shared human habitations, a caveman (or his wife) must have noticed that they are mainly nocturnal and avoid direct confrontation with man. In the first systematic modern study, Richter (1927) identified eating, drinking, and urination every 2–3 hours, and defecation every 5 hours or so. Using activity wheels he showed that although individuals differ widely, any one rat is surprisingly consistent in how many times he makes the wheel go round in 24 hours. Richter's records were mainly made at night and he discussed short (2 to 4 hour) and long-term (7 to 10 day) cycles, but does not actually mention the 24-hour rhythm.

On top of the basic nightly rhythm, female rats superimpose another, parallel with the oestrous cycle. For 3 or 4 nights, a female's activity in running wheels is fairly low, but is multiplied by two or three times on the night of oestrous (Wang, 1923). Her increase in running ends as you might expect, if she is allowed to mate. Running would be interrupted, of course, if any other animal is introduced into her cage, but a fertile or vasectomised male caused a much greater interruption than a castrate or another female.

One of the most interesting things about activity cycles is that they do not in fact depend on the stimulus which appears to control them. A rise in oestrogen may trigger the increase in wheel running every 4 days, but it is not strictly necessary; for spayed females show it, and so do males castrated and given one small dose of oestrogen at birth. The daily rise and fall in activity appears to depend on the alternation of light and dark, and certainly its timing can be altered experimentally by reversing the laboratory lighting schedule, and by changes in day-length in spring and autumn. But the rhythm continues indefinitely in a constant environment of continuous light or continuous darkness. The peak of activity continues at approximately 24-hour intervals: approximately, not exactly (hence the name 'circadian', 'around a day'), for some individuals start slightly early and some slightly late, as they would in spring and autumn. But it seems impossible to induce a rhythm conflicting with that of 24 hours; 12 hours possibly, but not 16, 22, or 27. Circadian rhythms are not confined to rats, but occur apparently in any animal or plant that has been studied. In man, circadian rhythms account for some of the difficulties that people find in shift work or in business negotiations immediately after flying between Europe and America. Of course the problems of shift work are partly a question of watching favourite TV programmes or of fitting social life into the timing of other people's, they are not purely a question of endogenous sleep rhythms in the individual. Again, some people are wide awake in the early morning but droopy in the evening when late risers are ready for their best work, and early risers are said to be worse affected by shift working. Living in a constant environment without clocks, perhaps early risers would be the ones whose circadian rhythm turns out to be a little less than 24 hours, the slugabeds might have a spontaneous rhythm of 24 hours and a bit.

Rodent social life is much simpler than human, but activity cycles are probably not as simple as they look in rodents either. Circadian rhythms are not confined to motor activity. There are circadian rhythms in cell division, in concentrations of insulin, or leucocytes or malarial trypanosomes in the blood, in stomach contractions, and so on, all adjusting at different rates if the light/dark cycle is reversed in phase.

Experiments on activity

Wheel-running experimental treatments may interact with circadian rhythms, so care is needed in timing. If the animals are asleep, they can show little further depression of activity, at their most vigorous they cannot show much increase. Jones (1943) gave rats a large (80 mg/kg) dose of phenobarbitone daily at noon. Wheel-running scores at 17.00 were normal, for neither sleeping nor anaesthetised rats run in wheels very much anyway; it was only the overnight score that was reduced. Bovet, Bovet-Nitti, and Oliverio (1967) found that large doses (0.2 or 1 mg/kg) of nicotine stimulated wheel-running in the daytime (controls mostly sleeping), but at night even the bigger dose could only reduce it. There is probably a 'ceiling', a physiological maximum which no drug can over-ride.

Food or water deprivation or small doses of amphetamine were equally able to increase 'general activity' from the levels of quiet times of day to those of peak times, according to Prescott (1970). He made direct observations of walking, rearing, and sniffing after placing rats for 10 minutes in an area away from the home cage and comparing these with wheel-running and activity in a kind of tilt-cage. He showed that these three components of what is often called 'general activity' are largely exploratory and that they are indeed equivalent. However, it would be unfortunate to think of them as the whole of 'activity', for while grooming, burrowing, and feeding are inversely related to exploration, they obviously occur regularly when the animals have settled down to live in a particular place. In fact, Raynaud, Ducrocq, and Raoul (1966) describe how an 'exploration' phase is followed in mice introduced into a new cage by an 'installation' phase where grooming is conspicuous, before the mice settle down to 'normal activity' and rest.

Exploration gets Chapter 18 to itself. Meanwhile, drug effects on motor activity are interesting. Cathleen Morrison and Jane Stephenson, finding (1972b) that amphetamine and nicotine had little stimulant action in running-wheels, put the same rats into grid cages for 30 minutes daily for 10 days. Amphetamine (1·6 mg/kg) consistently increased the activity recorded. As usual with a dose on the high side (0·6 mg/kg), nicotine depressed activity for the first day or two but the rats became tolerant to it, and in the last few days it stimulated them to increased exertions. Yet they were no more active than controls on return to the running-wheels each day.

Female rats show a 4-day peak of activity in the 6 hours before ovulation in running wheels but only slightly in tilt-cages and not at all on a grid floor (Eayrs, 1954). Perhaps they have no time while exploring to go running after Mr Right Rat or even to put their names on the waiting list for a nest-site. Flippantly put, this does raise the question of the functional reason for the oestrous peak in running: do wild rats copulate in individual nests or on common land within the colony area? Does the female in heat run round looking for males or do they smell her out? Wild hamsters are thought to defend individual territories, and female hamsters are active in running wheels during pro-oestrous as well as oestrous – do they have to search longer, or is there no connection?

Measures of activity have been used to relate drug effects to the concentration of possible synaptic transmitters in the brain. Saelens, Kovacsics, and Allen (1968) kept their animals for 24 hours in circular cages with six photocells. They used various drugs and showed that the amount, and timing, of changes in activity were related to changes in the concentration of brain noradrenaline, but not to that of serotonin to any great extent. Ahtee and Karki (1968) tested an amphetamine derivative in mice. The animals were placed for 5 minutes in a black plastic cage (since the laboratory was lit

Motor activity

by daylight), and in repeated observations, the drug reduced the activity recorded by photocells and also reduced brain noradrenaline, with smaller effects on serotonin. Chang and Webster (1971) tested rats in wire-mesh cages with two photocells and a Perspex block where the beams crossed. Tetrabenazine reduced brain noradrenaline and dopamine, and the activity count after 10 minutes in the cage; α-methyl-*m*-tyrosine given alone selectively reduced noradrenaline alone, but if followed by tetrabenazine, activity (but not dopamine) was also reduced. So although exploratory activity depends to some extent on noradrenaline, other transmitters are involved.

Costa, Grappetti, and Naimzada (1972) disagree about noradrenaline, but they altered activity with different drugs and measured it well after the time when initial exploration had finished. They used a most superior photocell apparatus, with 40 infrared photocells in the floor, said to detect grooming as well as walking, and with more photocells in the walls to detect rearing. They gave rats 30 minutes to explore before injection, and found in the next 60 minutes that 0.3 mg/kg of *d*-amphetamine intravenously or 3 mg/kg of cocaine selectively increased activity and the turnover of dopamine in the striatum.

The capacitance method was first used by Josef Lát (1965) to measure exploration (Fig. 7.3). Rats were housed for some time in a small compartment within a larger cage. When the intervening door was opened, a capacitance-type detector in the roof of the main cage recorded rearing as an exploratory movement. Lát was able to correlate rearing upright in five 3-minute tests a day, with both the time taken by the rat to emerge from the smaller home compartment, and the animals' speed of learning an operant discrimination task to open the intervening door. Both exploration and learning performance depended on the basic 'excitability' of the individual animal, which Lát related both to the effects of, and the preference for, a high carbohydrate/high sodium diet compared with a high protein/high potassium one.

Lát's technique is noteworthy as one of the few activity methods to measure exploration deliberately, and particularly in that he leaves it to the animal whether to explore or not. The rat is not compelled to explore a new environment by being dumped in it; it does not have to say anything, but anything it does say may be taken down and used in evidence.

Svensson and Thieme (1969) carefully evaluated the 'Animex' version of the capacitance method with coils beneath the cage floor. Mice were heavily sedated from 2 to 30 hours after the injection of 2 mg/kg of reserpine, and there was hardly any measurable activity. Twenty-minute samples of activity at 40 and 50 hours were almost up to control levels, indicating recovery. Conversely, 5 mg/kg of amphetamine increased activity, with the greatest increase between 15 to 25 minutes after injection; activity then slowly declined. Rats with iron-deficiency anaemia averaged less than half

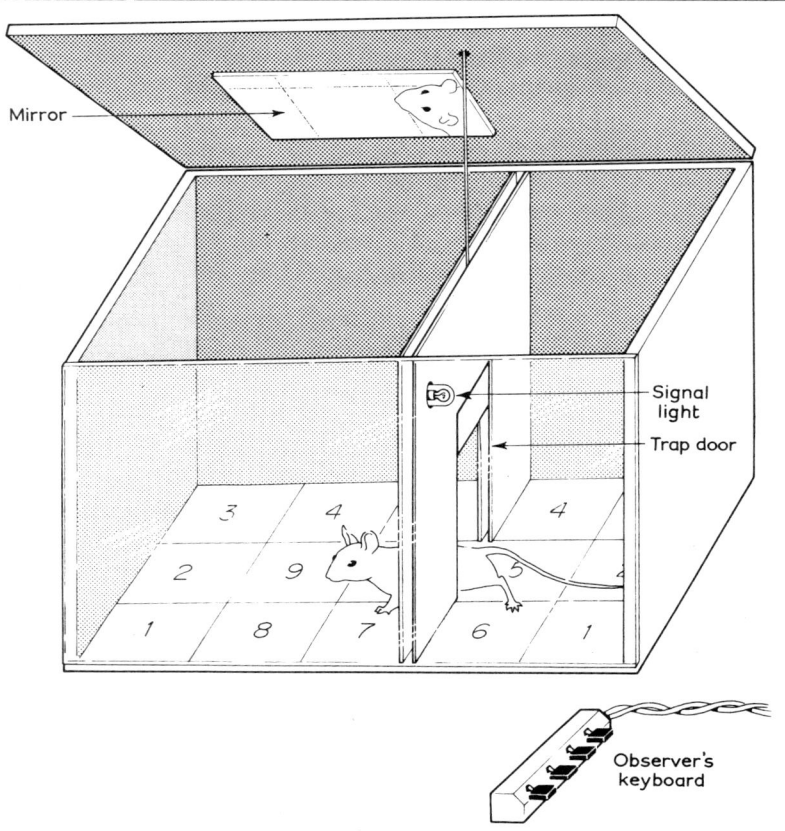

Fig. 7.3. Exploration/Activity box (after Lát, 1963). The figure shows an early model where the observer watches the animal through a mirror in the lid as well as through a window. In later models apparatus detecting capacitance changes monitored exploration automatically.

the daily activity of controls on an Animex meter (Glover and Jacobs, 1972), and what activity there was occurred erratically between about 15.00 to midnight (where controls were active from 18.00 to 06.00); anaemic patients complain of feeling tired and weak. Ferric ammonium sulphate, given for 2 days in the water increased the activity of anaemic rats but not of controls.

It is worth closing the chapter by emphasising how individual even inbred laboratory animals can be. Tremendous but stable individual differences in the distance travelled in running wheels have been known for many years. Lee Kavanau (1962) demonstrated this in two deermice, *Peromyscus maniculatus*. In separate cages they started and stopped running consistently at different times. When housed together, they started and stopped running by

Motor activity

mutual agreement at times intermediate between their former preferences, which they reverted to when separated again.

Further, this individuality includes the mouse's determination to control its activity cycle for itself. Kavanau (1963) studied the times and speeds that two other *Peromyscus* ran in their wheels. He then arranged for them to be locked into the wheels and turned round by an electric motor, at just those times and speeds. The mice were then able and willing to learn an operant response to stop the wheels and let them get off. (It is amusing to see Kavanau's photograph of the roomful of elaborate electronic apparatus to record and control a pair of 20 g mice.) Finally, the mice learned to press a

long live the revolution!

second lever in their home cage to give them access to the running wheels and to start the motors. They chose just the same times as they had originally chosen, but had rejected when the exercise was thrust upon them. Long live the revolutions and the dignity of Mouse.

Summary and comment

Motor activity can be described, for practical purposes, as the aspect of behaviour that does not need to be observed, the kinetic energy expended. Different methods are sensitive to different kinds of behaviour, though with considerable overlap, so it is useful to ask what kind of activity is being measured.

The commonest measures are:

(1) revolutions of a running wheel attached to a small living cage;
(2) mechanical vibrations in the floor of a cage, caused by the inhabitant walking, scratching, etc.;
(3) breaking a photocell beam, or short-circuiting a low voltage between the bars of a grid floor, caused by the animal walking past a given place;
(4) disturbances of electromagnetic, or acoustic, high frequency oscillations across a space (capacitance) caused by any movement within it.

Activity is commonly stimulated by putting the animal into the apparatus for a short time (say 5 to 30 minutes). In this case the activity detected is mainly exploration (see Chapter 18). Sometimes activity is not directly stimulated, the animal lives in the apparatus continuously for at least a few days. Activity detected in this situation is, so far as the experimenter is concerned, 'spontaneous'.

The running wheel appears to give a positive feedback, the activity is very specifically running, as if for its own sake. Some kinds of apparatus will detect almost anything: the 'capacitance' method can be set to detect any exercise from breathing upwards. Other apparatus will detect only movement of the whole animal from place to place, or movement plus eating, grooming, fighting or playing, and so on.

Units are rarely of a constant absolute size. Some vary according to the distance of the animal from the detector, and nearly all results depend critically on the timing and duration of the measurement in relation to what the animal is doing. Activity units have to be arbitrary or at best on an ordinal scale, they can rarely be of a fixed magnitude. Advantage can be taken of the different methods to measure different kinds of experimental effect. In particular, advantage can be taken of the animal's daily rhythm of activity to selectively test, for example, for 'stimulant' or 'depressant' drug effects.

EIGHT
Choice and self-administration
The customer is always right

We are apt to forget that wild animals look after themselves. Unless their habitat is destroyed by man, they can choose their own nest-site, their own food, their own mates. Their own survival depends on their own behaviour. These abilities can be utilised to tell us something about the organisation of behaviour not easily discovered otherwise.

Preference tests in temperature control

Golden hamsters (*Mesocricetus auratus*) kept in laboratories or as pets are all descended from a single female brought pregnant from Syria, and are adapted to cope with the blazing noonday sun and to hibernate through the freezing winter of the near-desert. Gumma and South (1970) studied their response to hypothermia. An arena maintained at $-2\,°C$ was surrounded by five boxes at temperatures up to $26°$. Hamsters chose the one at $26°$ as home, to store food and build a nest. Hamsters chilled to $0°$ or $10°$ as if they were hibernating for 3·5 hours and then allowed to warm themselves, went first to the $26°$ box. They then spent an hour or two in the cooler boxes, calling in briefly at the $26°$ box between visits, before returning home. Hypothermic hamsters warmed by the experimenters omitted the first stage, they explored and chose the cooler boxes for a while before returning to the warm home-box.

An operant method can be used similarly. Bernard Weiss and Victor Laties (1960) trained rats in a cold environment to switch on an infrared heater. The rate of lever pressing varied according to the power of the heater (125–375 watts) or the time it stayed on (usually 2 seconds), so that the rats maintained a constant preferred temperature. Gumma and South say their method is more sensitive, since it produces consistent results without the drastic need to shave the animals' hair off each day. But there is also a species difference, they chose hamsters rather than rats because of their rapid recovery from hibernation.

Strength of drive and companion preferences

In the good old days, it was thought useful to visualise a 'drive' making an animal do something, and people made lists: hunger, thirst, sex, hunting, maternal, exploratory, enclosed-space-seeking, sleep, aggression; the number soon became indefinitely large and arguable.

Now, there were two reasons for postulating the existence of drives. The first was to account for the obstinate fact that animals arrive at very constant goals but with enormous flexibility in the means of approach. The second was to explain why, by and large, the animal does one thing at a time. He is hunting for food or for a mate, or running away from a predator, but not all three at once. But why not? What determines the kind of activity the animal is pursuing at any one moment?

The first, naïve answer was that one drive might be stronger than another. The 'strength' of any one could be determined in the Columbia obstruction box (see p. 223). Or any two could be compared in a choice situation like that by Tsai (1925–6). (Fig. 8.1). Male rats were deprived of food for 24 hours and isolated from rodent companionship. They were then placed in

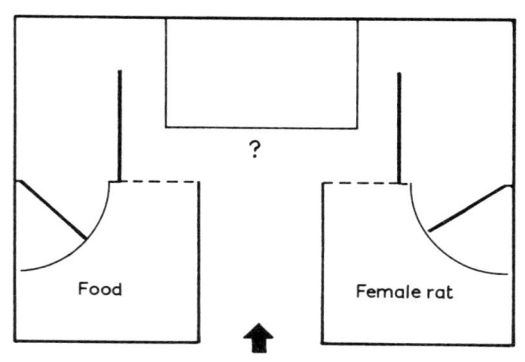

Fig. 8.1. Tsai's choice-box (after Tsai, 1925–6). The rat may smell, for example, food or a female in the two goals but has to make a detour to reach them.

the apparatus so that on one side they could smell their dinner and on the other a curvaceous female rat. In this experiment hunger was more powerful or at least more urgent than sex, the rats predominantly turned towards the food. But it only needs, perhaps, a shorter period of starvation or of isolation, or the incentive female to come into oestrous to get a different answer. The results allow no conclusions outside the particular experiment.

A curious preference test was used by Victor Denenberg and his colleagues (Anderson, Denenberg, and Zarrow, 1972) to discover if early handling of rabbits, as of other laboratory animals, improves their laboratory performance when they are adult.

Baby rabbits were either left undisturbed, or were handled daily by an experimenter. Half of the latter group were kept in isolation and fed by hand. This is probably less disturbing for rabbits than for rodents or other mammals, since it seems that rabbit mothers normally leave their litters in a separate burrow, and only visit them for suckling twice a day. Among other tests when they were adult, the rabbits were given four trials in an arena. In

Choice and self-administration

one corner sat the experimenter who had handled them, in the others were a caged rabbit, a caged rat from the room where the rabbits were housed, and a pile of wadding for nesting. Both handled groups made more visits of all kinds than the undisturbed rabbits. Visits were fairly uniform in duration, but the isolated rabbits spent longer with the experimenter. As might be expected, early handling produced a long-lasting habituation to being picked up and fondled, and the more handling the less timidity towards man. Nevertheless, rats learn an operant task to *avoid* being handled (Candland, Faulds, Thomas, and Candland, 1960).

A scent-preference test (Mainardi *et al.*, 1965) was described on p. 54, where mice chose between plain and perfumed sexual partners, tipping the balance of a see-saw to record their weighted preference.

Food preferences

Rats do not necessarily eat what is set in front of them, they prefer to take small samples of whatever is available before making a meal of what they like best (see Chapter 5). Rats deficient in thiamin can learn to choose the diet richest in thiamin, and can avoid a bait if previously they had taken a sub-lethal dose of poison from it. Either way, they react to a previously unfamiliar taste that later became associated with illness or recovery.

food preferences

Techniques for assessing food preference or avoidance are obviously much the same as those of measuring consumption in general; but simple weighing may not be enough for comparing preferences for liver versus wheat grains versus sugar in terms of calorific value or protein intake – weighing has to be followed by chemistry and complicated calculations. How does the food's calorific value, or the requirement for an essential amino acid, compare with the energy cost of obtaining it and the effort the animal will actually make?

You could therefore give the animal as many pots as there are diets or use a plus-maze with as many goal-boxes, and an extra pot or goal-box as a control for unrewarded exploration. The maze need not be for training to a particular route, it is enough if the animal locates the preferred food by smell.

It is better to change the positions around. It is probable that most animals classify mainly by location: here is home, there is the water, that damfool cat usually comes from over there. Particularly if the animal is warily exploring a new environment with strange smells lurking behind every object, the first place it finds food will seem promising. If it finds food there next time the animal is likely to develop a 'position habit' and you are likely to measure preferences not for food but for the second pot on the left. Encourage the animal to classify along the dimension you intend to test.

Observation of distinct trials day by day presupposes that the animal is deprived of food between trials, which does not necessarily give the same results as when the different kinds of food are continuously accessible.

Using a 'plus-maze', photocells could detect the number and duration of visits to each food source quite easily. A visit where the animal sniffed but did not eat could also be interesting, if it can be distinguished from an eating visit: Could a smell be ambivalent, both attractive and aversive?

In the end, food preferences are best discovered by the old, crude, but simple methods. Either leave the animal with access to two to four containers and weigh them, or watch the animal at some convenient and limited time and observe which containers are eaten from. In all cases, care is needed to measure what is intended and not, for example, the food in the favourite location in the cage, or the most familiar food, or the most novel one, or the food fortuitously with most salt or thiamin.

Statistics of preference

Like many of the authors quoted in this chapter, I would once have assumed that the appropriate statistical test of a preference would be Student's t. It is worth mentioning that, if I understand Siegel (1956) correctly, this test is neither strictly appropriate nor even the easiest to use. Within a given total consumption, the animal has to choose either one diet or another. Certain non-parametric tests are based on a more relevant model, for instance the Binomial test for two alternatives or the Kolmogorov–Smirnov test for three or more, and with care (for there can be pitfalls) these may be more sensitive too. Most methods imply, of course, that each animal has only one choice. On a single transferable vote, or some such system for expressing a rank order of preference, it would be worth knowing if all the rats chose a particular diet for their second best even though none did for their first.

Drug dosing by sugaring the pill

It is sometimes possible to persuade animals to take medicine directly, though they are as reluctant as anyone to swallow a bitter pill. Guile may work, or temptation. Cats are choosy about what they eat, but when grooming themselves, they lick their fur and swallow anything they lick off.

Choice and self-administration

An old trick for oral dosing of cats is said to be to mix the required dose in butter and spread it on the fur.

Rats and mice scratch more than they lick, and may not swallow. But omnivorous as they are, a tasty morsel tempts them to vary a monotonous diet. Herxheimer and Douglas (1963) offered rats a little paste made of two parts of chocolate to one part of starch. With due caution their rats would approach the wooden spatula, sniff the paste, lick it doubtfully, consume it voraciously, and return eagerly to lick the spatula clean as a whistle. Drugs could then be added.

Rats accepted paste with 3 mg/g of quinine mixed in, as a model of all bitter drugs, but 10 mg/g of quinine they rejected in no uncertain terms. Rats cannot spit or vomit, but push the bitter pill out of the mouth with the tongue, and they characteristically wipe clean the side of the snout against any convenient surface with a look of utter disgust. However, they accept 12 mg/g of hydrocortisone which tastes bitter to man, and reject 10 mg/g of stilboestrol which is acceptable to humans.

If you stick your finger or a pencil through the bars of a rat's cage, the animal will slowly approach curiously and snap at the intrusive projection, often quite sharply, and may hang on and worry it like a dog would. A sugar pill on a pair of forceps, the rat snaps, and once tasted, all eaten. Two or three rats in a cage encourage each other, but one rat may get both pills. After 2 or 3 minutes for the first pill, each rat only needs a few seconds.

Pills can be made exactly as pharmacists made them before tableting machines, except that sucrose is used as a sweet alternative to lactose filler. Icing sugar and gum acacia are mixed in a ratio of about 20 : 1 and water added drop by drop until the powder turns (surprisingly suddenly) into a slightly sticky dough. This is then rolled into a cylinder, chopped into segments, and dried.

Once trained on sugar pills, rats take drugged ones, so long as the concentration is not too high, and pills are convenient for the repeated oral administration of a small dose of a drug. An occasional sugar pill keeps the animal sweet. Rats took a pill containing 7–10 per cent of a chemical (2, 4-diamino-6-chloro-s-triazine) only a little slower than sugar, although it is irritant by intraperitoneal injection. The pills must have given the rats a mild stomach ache (though we saw no 'writhing' or abdominal contractions), for they selectively refused dosed pills next day. One rat took a dosed pill, slowly, all twelve readily took sugar. Well, it was a reasonable test of palatability . . . or conditioned aversion.

Hunting: seek and ye shall find

If you have dropped a penny on the ground, you do not search for just anything. You find it quicker if you form a 'specific searching image' and set your perceptual filters to screen out anything but a disc of a certain diameter and brown colour, ignoring such conspicuous but irrelevant stimuli such as a piece of white paper. The same is thought to be true of animal predators, and preference methods can test the hypothesis.

Marian Dawkins (1971) offered chicks the choice of 'conspicuous' or 'cryptic' food. Grains of rice dyed orange or green were spread on a floor made of small stones glued to hardboard and painted orange. Chicks fed in pairs (since lonely chicks tend not to eat), and the first 100 grains (out of 1000 of each colour) taken by one of the chicks was recorded. No chick chose either the cryptic orange or conspicuous green grains in random order, there were significantly long runs of each, in one example up to twenty-six successive choices of one colour and sixteen of the other. Dawkins suggested that the bird was attending to colour for a time, then to non-colour cues (shape, texture, etc.): if the chick is influenced in one choice by its own previous choice, there is probably a central switch governing the cues to which the chick is attending, or even capable of perceiving.

Dawkins backed up this experiment with a series of choice tests, where chicks were feeding on, say, green rice on a 60 cm^2 orange floor, and then she quietly placed a 7·5 cm^2 stoney orange-painted card in the middle of the floor. Two green and two orange grains were glued to the card, one at each corner, and she observed the first peck by one chick to one of these. She then repeated the choice test after preliminary sampling of cryptic orange grains. In one such experiment, the hypothesis was that chicks feeding on orange grains conspicuous on a green background would attend to colour-contrast cues. They would therefore tend to prefer conspicuous green grains to cryptic orange ones, even if they had never seen green grains of rice before. Conversely, after sampling cryptic orange grains, they should prefer cryptic green to conspicuous orange ones. Table 8.1 shows how Dawkins's prediction was justified.

Predators hunting by smell also prefer the scent they have been primed with, though 'priming' is not as strong a hypothesis as 'search image', and a

Table 8.1. (from Dawkins, 1971)

After sampling	No. of chicks pecking	
	conspicuous green grain	cryptic orange grain
conspicuous orange grains	11	1
cryptic orange grains	3	9

$p < 0.005$ by Fisher Exact Probability Test, 1-tailed

sort of toy experiment gives weaker evidence than Dawkins's. Soane and Clarke (1973) offered pastry pellets flavoured with either vanilla or peppermint to mice. Fearsome predatory mice consistently preferred timid little vanilla pastries but added a preference for the one they had been fed with previously, whether vanilla or peppermint. A diet exclusively of their favourite without any other food made them fed up with it, and they subsequently preferred the opposite flavour. As in real life, where a prey species exists in two or more forms each with a selective advantage in certain conditions, a balanced polymorphism helped the pastry population to survive severe predation.

Addiction to alcohol

If you ask a human what he or she wants to drink, you assume a choice of concentration of ethyl alcohol and of other contaminants. Laboratory animals are clean living and high thinking, and although some individuals like weak alcohol solutions, many never touch the stuff. Yet they *can* become addicted and then find it as hard to go on the wagon as any of us.

'What's your poison?'

Robert Myers and Warren Veale (1968) elaborately established a preference for alcohol in rats by repeatedly infusing tiny quantities of alcohol into the cerebral ventricles. If the rats were offered any two from a range of twelve concentrations of alcohol (from 3 to 30 per cent), a dose-dependent preference could be demonstrated. If they were then infused with saline their preference for alcohol increased. Myers and Veale thought that, whatever the situation in a human alcoholic, there were biochemical changes in the lining of the ventricles of the rats' brains, since the saline-induced increase was inhibited by α-methyl-p-tyrosine, which depletes catecholamines. A dose of p-chlorophenylalanine, which diminished brain serotonin, produced a long-lasting aversion to alcohol, reminiscent of a conditioned aversion to saccharin due to apomorphine. It is enough to drive rats to drink.

As a rule, laboratory animals only come to prefer alcohol after a period of compulsory exposure or of stress. They can hardly avoid alcohol infused into the brain. Similarly if mice are housed in a closed chamber, and alcohol is vaporised into it, they can hardly avoid breathing what they refuse to drink. Griffiths, Littleton, and Ortiz (1973) demonstrated that a fairly high atmospheric concentration of ethanol intoxicated mice (they staggered). Moreover, it produced tolerance (a higher concentration was required each day to keep the mice staggering) and even withdrawal symptoms when the alcohol was omitted after 10 days. The mice developed first 'locomotor excitement' then 'depression', with a fine tremor and piloerection, and characteristic convulsions when dangled by the tail. An actual preference for drinking alcohol was considered unnecessary as a criterion of dependence.

Animals subjected to fairly considerable stress can change their original aversion to alcohol to a preference. Masserman and Yum (1946) pioneered the study of this 'experimental neurosis'. They trained hungry cats to run an alley for a reward of fish, and when the habit was established, also gave them a blast of air in the face every time they took fish; not on every run but frequently and unpredictably. The cats were in a conflict of motivation, 'hunger' versus 'fear' and a conflict of expectations; they became neurotic. The word 'neurotic' begs the question, however, since it implies irrationality, whereas the cats' behaviour seems entirely logical and adaptive: they refused to enter the alley, struggled, they even forgot their manners so far as to bite the experimenter. Until they were consoled with a bottle or two, and drowned their sorrows.

A rather more subtle stress is to train rats to press a lever for food, and when the performance is well established, to reinforce it only intermittently (like a suddenly imposed Fixed Interval; see p. 150). One 45 mg pellet every 2 minutes in six 1-hour sessions was the schedule used by Falk, Samson, and Winger (1972). The continued arousal and frustration of the rat's tendency to eat causes it to drink enormous quantities of water ('polydipsia') if this is available. It is the licking rather than the water which is important since airlicking is equally well induced this way (Mendelson and Chillig, 1970), and it resembles displacement activities (I wonder if the animal grooms much?), supporting the view that drinking is a special case of eating. Anyway, if there is no water, the frustrated rat will drink a 5 or 6 per cent solution of alcohol. For the first few days, it gets drunk, becomes tolerant, and drinks more and more, ending (in Falk's experiment) at up to 13 g/kg a day, or 44 per cent of the total calorie intake.

There are strains of mice which voluntarily imbibe, but even these can treble their intake under stress (Brown, 1968), for example, if they are infested with mites or they are isolated (but not group-housed) and subjected to mild centrifuging in a merry-go-round.

Laboratory animals rarely drink alcohol spontaneously, but they are only

could they really prefer ... ?

offered pure ethanol solutions or (rarely) rough bourbon. One wonders – reluctantly – could they really prefer a dry burgundy or fine cognac?

Some comments on addiction

The Drug Problem is outside the scope of this book* and this section will be especially brief. There has been much debate on how to recognise the animal equivalent of human addiction. Among the suggested criteria are tolerance to a steadily increasing dose, withdrawal symptoms when the drug is stopped, and probably that the animal should come to administer the drug to itself. But there are no hard and fast lines between a severely damaging addiction, a mild dependence on a 'luxury' like nicotine, and something completely 'natural'. I believe it is not utterly flippant to suggest that we are all addicted to food, water, and oxygen. We are liable to very severe withdrawal symptoms if we are deprived of them, though with differing degrees of urgency. Less flippantly, someone habitually adding extra salt to his dinner becomes both relatively tolerant to high concentrations of sodium chloride and dependent on it, for the kidney and adrenal cortex become adapted to a relatively high intake and allow corresponding quantities to be excreted in the urine and the sweat. The habitual level of salt intake can therefore not be suddenly cut without causing withdrawal symptoms and/or salt-seeking behaviour.

There is of course a real distinction to be made. The 'normal', both in the sense of the usual, the mean, and 95 per cent confidence limits of a population, and in the sense of 'healthy', is one thing. The ingestion or injection of something on which you become dependent is quite another when it is demonstrably damaging. The interesting questions are why should anyone want to take a potentially harmful drug a *second* time, when neither initial curiosity nor ultimate dependence are relevant.

No doubt the reason is different for each drug, and each subject, but one experiment is interesting. Adams, Yeh, Wood, and Mitchell (1969) gave rats

* There are many good reviews elsewhere (e.g. Kumar and Stolerman, 1977).

weekly injections of morphine (5 mg/kg subcutaneously). After each injection, they tested the rats for analgesia, using the hot-plate test. As expected, the mice became tolerant to the drug and a dose which was an effective pain-killer after one injection was less effective by the fifth, for the rats came to jump off the hot-plate nearly as soon as controls. Now tolerance does not depend on the drug alone but also, as it were, on the use made of the drug. Many American soldiers on active service in Vietnam appeared to have become typical morphine addicts, but it was reported that on return home, many of them spontaneously stopped using the drug. Adams and his colleagues had a third group of rats also injected every week with 5 mg/kg morphine. Unlike the controls and the first morphine group, however, they were not subjected to the hot-plate test until the final day. Although this group had received the same dosage of morphine, they showed as slow a response to pain on the final day as the tolerant rats had on the first; they were not tolerant.

Self-administration of drugs

In a nice review of drugs, Charles Schuster and Travis Thompson (1969) quote Spragg (1940) as finding the first behavioural sign of addiction in animals: morphine-dependent chimpanzees would behave in the way demanded by the experimenter if he was to inject them with their daily 'fix'.

Headlee, Coppock, and Nichols (1955) harnessed rats into an apparatus where, if they turned their heads right, they triggered a photocell and obtained a little morphine through a needle implanted intraperitoneally. They turned their heads right.

With improved apparatus, a dog or a baboon can walk around fairly freely with a pack on his back (a monkey?), which allows intravenous injections to be made through a jugular cannula and is operated by radio telemetry. Smaller animals like rats can have a long lead of flexible tubing mounted from a swivel in the roof of the cage.

Morphine can certainly act as 'reward' and addicted rats can learn to press a lever if it leads to a morphine injection. Moreover, they come to take a fairly constant dose of the drug, and pretreatment with part of the daily dose reduces the number of self-regulated injections; withdrawal or a morphine-antagonist like naloxone increases them in proportion.

It would be simpler merely to offer the animal a choice of fluids to drink, but the bitter taste of morphine is an obstacle. However, an ingenious schedule of drinking overcomes both this and the need for prior injections. Ramesh Kumar, Hannah Steinberg, and Ian Stolerman (1968) deprived rats of water for 17 hours a day and on two days out of every three gave them 7 hours access to a weak (0·5 mg/l) morphine solution: the animals became thirsty enough to overcome their distaste and to drink. On the third

Choice and self-administration **103**

day they were offered the choice of morphine solution and water, with the dual aim of measuring how far the addiction had developed and of letting the rats discover that fresh water would lead to withdrawal symptoms which were ameliorated by morphine. This forced–forced–choice schedule led consistently to an increasing consumption of morphine, whether previous injections were of morphine or of saline; a quinine solution also tastes bitter but was consistently avoided. In some experiments, the rats drank more morphine solution than water, though Hill and Powell (1976) say that saccharine may have to be added to make such a positive preference reliable.

Schuster and Thompson also cite the preference thresholds for alcohol measured by Myers and Carey (1961). Rats had to press one lever to obtain water and another for ethanol, and could detect a concentration of 3 or 4 per cent. Other drugs have also been self-administered, notably nicotine, barbiturates, and dexamphetamine. Equally, various other drugs have been shown *not* to act as reinforcers at least under the conditions applied, notably chlorpromazine, pemoline, and – perhaps surprisingly – mescaline.

After a long series of experiments in rats, Neal Miller (1964) found that amylobarbitone specifically lessened avoidance of electric shock (cf. p. 220). The most economical explanation was that the drug genuinely reduced the rats' equivalent of fear. He tested this by arranging for rats to inject themselves with the drug. Two rats could each press a lever. One lever was a dummy, but each response on the other caused both rats to receive 2 mg of amylobarbitone sodium through a jugular vein. Both rats therefore received the same low dose of the drug at the same time and both pressed levers at the same rate. but only in one was there a connection between the lever and the drug. However, on days when both rats were subject to a shock a minute, the experimental rat responded three times as often as the yoked control, as if it were really using the lever-pressing to reduce fear of the shock.

Self-stimulation and unnatural vices

Analogies of the brain as a hydraulic machine, a telephone exchange, and a computer, have all been fruitful in their time. They have led to predictions about brain and behaviour never previously made so precisely. One consequence of the electrical theory of nerve conduction and of the analogy with an electrical machine was a belief in the usefulness of brain stimulation. In man, Penfield induced involuntary limb movements or sensations of light or sound, or complete integrated pictures or memories by mild stimulation in different regions of the cerebral cortex. In animals, Hess used hypothalamic stimulation to produce integrated sequences of instinctive behaviour. And James Olds discovered self-stimulation.

Olds's background was in operant conditioning, where the theoretical emphasis is on how the animal's performance of a 'response' (pressing a lever, or whatever) produces certain results (by the experimenter's arrangement) and the animal will only repeat the response if these consequences are 'reinforcing' (i.e. rewarding). This implies a pattern of nerve impulses in the brain matching the stimuli received with those to be expected, a means of detecting when a goal has been attained. Similarly the CNS needs some means of relating a variety of stimuli (representing pain, nausea, fear, etc.) to a mechanism which in effect says 'these stimuli are unpleasant' and switches on the motor patterns of avoidance or escape. There must, in short, be a functional switch associated with what we call pleasure and pain, serving to bring into play all the complicated relevant procedures.

Olds and his colleagues put Skinner's behavioural model and the electrical analogy together. They demonstrated that animals could be trained to press a lever giving a small electrical pulse to certain parts of the brain. Conversely they could also come to press a lever switching off a train of similar pulses elsewhere.

The obvious conclusion (possibly too good to be strictly true) is that these 'positive' and 'negative' regions of the brain correspond to the decision-making Go/No-Go switch, and contain the neurophysiological representations of pleasure and pain or unhappiness. Naturally there has to be a powerful computer to arrange the details of the contingency plans actually brought into operation, but stimulation of the appropriate regions tips the balance of the decision towards Go or No-Go.

Rats with 'positive' brain electrodes can press their lever two or three times a second for up to several hours at a time. Such extreme cases, where the animal must end up exhausted, seem ridiculous to me. Either the experimenter has found the site of paradise or merely a self re-exciting circuit, a case of feedback howl without emotional significance. Both could be true at different locations.

Olds, Travis, and Schwing (1960) mapped the areas of 'reward' and 'punishment' for self-stimulation in rats. There were two systems of reward in the brain, a dorsal club-shaped one from the caudate/septal area through the dorsal thalamus to the tectum, and a ventral cylindrical area, the median forebrain bundle, with a vertical projection, the anterior commissure. These more or less correspond to Hess's 'parasympathetic' region while the punishment region in the diencephalon and tegmentum corresponds to Hess's 'sympathetic' area, so that the self-stimulation sites at least seem related to other information on the functional organisation of the CNS. At some reward sites, the pleasure appears to be quite normal, but not particularly pure. Male rats that are self-stimulating have been observed to have penile erections and even to ejaculate.

Some interactions of drugs with self-stimulation were reported by Olds and Travis (1960). Chlorpromazine never increased stimulation of any site, but inhibited septal (positive) electrodes more than tegmental (negative) ones. So did morphine and meprobamate, but in some circumstances these drugs could stimulate responding. If they did so, tegmental (negative) electrodes were stimulated more than septal, presumably because of these drugs' analgesic and/or anxiety-reducing actions. Both morphine and meprobamate can reduce avoidance or escape in conditioned avoidance experiments, while tegmental stimulation can increase escape.

In a crafty development, Jeffrey Liebman and Larry Butcher (1973) trained rats to stimulate themselves in the lateral hypothalamus of periacqueductal mesencephalon, and then reduced the current to about half each animal's optimum. So when *l*-dopa or apomorphine (drugs transformed to or imitating dopamine) reduced self-stimulation rates the experimenters could show there was no interference with motor activity by simply restoring the original current and showing that the smaller doses (75 and 0·75 mg/kg respectively) were no longer effective.

Self-stimulation is more complex than we were originally led to imagine. Over-fashionable at one time, it now seems relatively neglected. Combined with detailed analysis of the associated behaviour, and the sensory as well as the electrical stimuli involved, self-stimulation could surely provide a limited but useful route into the organisation of the brain.

Summary

There are several useful techniques where the animal is allowed limited control over his own experimental treatment. Tests for preferences in food or drink are primarily of use in nutritional questions. They can also be used to demonstrate addiction, or conditioned aversion, but it is necessary to establish the addiction first either by direct dosing or by some form of stress.

Preference testing requires care to avoid confounding preferences for taste, with position habits or anything else only fortuitously associated. Like should also be compared with like, or at least a few doses compared with a constant control. Similarly, preference or addiction can only be demonstrated against a choice of alternatives. An apparent preference for alcohol over water has been shown to disappear when sugar was offered too.

Self-regulated brain stimulation remains a potentially powerful method for studying the CNS.

NINE
Interlude: Conditioned and unconditioned

In the next few chapters, 'conditioned' behaviour will be described in some detail and some preliminary comments will be useful. Traditionally behaviour has been classified as either 'innate' or 'learned': behaviour developing regardless of external conditions or behaviour conditioned by experience. In fact, a sharp distinction between one kind of behaviour and the other is now widely recognised to be wrong and seriously misleading, but it still leads to needless confusion.

One source of confusion is that 'conditioned behaviour' often refers, not to learning in general, but to behaviour deliberately conditioned by the experimenter. For instance, any adult dog secretes saliva when it smells meat, and Pavlov (see p. 121) called this an unconditioned reflex, using it as the basis for experimental conditioning. A newly-weaned puppy, though, that has never tasted anything but milk, does not salivate to the smell of meat until it has eaten some a few times. Pavlov himself pointed out that he did not use a truly unconditioned response, but a 'naturally conditioned reflex' that any healthy puppy could expect to achieve.

Behavioural elements that are probably innate in the strict sense are called reflexes. They may be simple, relatively isolated actions like shivering, yawning, or fluffing the fur, or they may be slightly more complicated patterns like swallowing (an elaborate chain of movements of the tongue and pharynx) that are yet controlled by a single on/off switch – it is not possible to stop swallowing half-way. Swallowing, like lordosis and ejaculation and like breathing in newts (see p. 19), is a reflex whose performance is part of the culmination and reward of a long sequence of appetitive behaviour.

Many other elements appear to be equally Fixed-Action-Patterns (to use Lorenz's term) in adults, and need very specific stimuli to be released. They are rigid in form, the experimenter cannot change them easily, he can merely sit and watch them happen. Yet they may not be strictly innate, springing fully formed from pre-existing neural circuits like Pallas Athene from Zeus' brow. They have a developmental history.

For instance one of the main preening movements in pigeons and doves, and the 'billing' of doves in courtship, are probably both derived from the way the newly-hatched squab begs for food (Lehrman, 1956). The squab pokes its bill into the parent's bill, opens the bill wide and makes the

Interlude: conditioned and unconditioned

parental bird regurgitate crop milk. Courtship billing is obviously similar, and so is the movement when the dove slides its bill under a feather to preen.

The classic example is the pecking of newly-hatched chickens. They peck, in a motor pattern that is complete from the beginning and needs virtually no training, at any visually contrasting stimulus below eye level, within reach and within a certain size range. Kuo (1932) claimed, nevertheless, that the action depends on a kind of passive embryonic experience when the embryo's head and neck are bounced up and down by the beating of the embryonic heart and, later, it opens the bill and swallows amniotic fluid. Whether Kuo is right or not, the form of the action is fixed at hatching, but the stimuli that release and guide it, i.e. what the chick pecks at, change greatly. Jerry Hogan (1973) described how unselective the chick is at first. It eats sand as readily as food for several days, though the mother hen draws the chick's attention away from pebbles or spots of paint by picking up suitable objects and dropping them. Chicks reject mealworms at first, because of the texture, and some may starve if there is no choice, but once a mealworm has been swallowed they become a favourite titbit. On the other hand, chicks rarely eat cinnabar moth caterpillars or bird droppings more than once: they fail to finish the peck, and retreat, uttering a trill, shaking the head and wiping the bill.

The second possible source of confusion is therefore whether the conditioning is supposed to be of the motor pattern of the behaviour itself or of the circumstances the behaviour occurs in, and the stimuli which release or inhibit it.

The third and most important cause of misunderstanding lies in the very attempt to contrast learned and unlearned behaviour in any absolute way. Even the patterns that are most fully complete at birth or hatching, like pecking, are subject to modification by experience. Newborn kittens share out the mother cat's teats and rapidly learn to suckle only on their own. Many birds that can walk as soon as they hatch have to learn what their mother looks like and, basically, they learn to follow the first moving object they see.

Conversely there are quite severe limitations on any animal's ability to learn, and the limitations are not necessarily a matter of its general 'intelligence' but of the ability to learn one thing in one context and something else in another.

Male three-spined sticklebacks (*Gasterosteus aculeatus*) take up a territory in spring, construct a tube-shaped nest attached to reeds in mid-water, and defend it against other sticklebacks. The response to an intruder is complex: it could be another male stickleback, a female, or another species of fish to be ignored or escaped from. The owner 'dances' in a zigzag path towards the intruder, the forward component being aggressive and ending if necessary in a bite, driving off a male or non-gravid female. The 'zag' component of the male's courtship response to a female bulging with eggs is to lead her to the nest and swim through it. She should follow, lay her eggs, and he then fertilises them. Piet Sevenster (1973) taught male fish to bite a rod and to swim through a plastic ring suspended in the water. Sticklebacks readily learned to swim through the ring if the reward was to gaze for 10 seconds at a curvaceous female in a glass tube. To glare at a red-bellied male they would readily bite a rod and, a little less readily, swim through the ring. But no chivalrous male stickleback could bite a rod again after gazing at the female, the courtship tendency inhibits biting.

Hamsters can be trained to scratch for food reinforcement (i.e. reward). Normally they groom themselves after meals rather than before, and grooming in an unfamiliar environment is mainly a displacement activity, a sign of frustration. Sara Shettleworth (1973) found it much easier to train them to scratch the cage floor for food than to scratch or wash themselves, although the movements are very similar. Wild hamsters looking for food would be expected to find grain or seeds to eat on or just under the surface of the soil.

Animals can adapt their behaviour by learning (assuming that these examples are typical) only if the response that is required does not conflict with the reward offered. Pavlov's dog does not salivate to the conditioned stimulus as such, rather it salivates because the conditioned stimulus signals that dinner is on the way, and (see p. 125) the timing of the salivation is related most closely to the time that dinner is expected to arrive. The stickleback treats the rod as if it were the other male, and would not bite a lady. He swims through the circle as if showing her the nest. One stickleback that had failed to bite a rod for sight of a female was shown the rod again, months afterwards; he courted the rod as if in his memory it really was the female. A Conditioned Stimulus is no more than a symbolic representation of the Unconditioned. A fixed action pattern may not be fixed rigidly, but it is on a short leash and cannot wander far.

The issue is really like one of embryology. Behaviour has to develop in the individual just as its body develops from the egg, and natural selection is likely to make sure that the process is efficient. Details that are common to

behaviour has to develop into the adult form

Interlude: conditioned and unconditioned

the whole species, especially in infancy, may be 'innate', those that vary from day to day or place to place may best be 'learned', and in most cases the genetic program causes the infant to behave in such a way as to present itself with stimuli appropriate to learn the next stage. An infant's behaviour must in the first place be adaptive for the infant, to let it survive to maturity. But it must also be capable of developing into the mature adult form; for a hen is the egg's only way of reproducing another egg.

TEN
Approach to a conditioned stimulus: mazes

At the bottom of the garden path

Behaviour does not consist entirely of fixed actions but is related in a flexible way to fixed locations. The burrow is in one place and the animal has a goal in another, bringing itself into a position to receive certain stimuli, e.g. food, or to avoid others, e.g. from a predator. The route to food can be widely flexible, and approach to or avoidance of a particular place is the oldest method in the laboratory for studying learning, and one of the easiest.

The first maze

A wild rat, like most animals, needs to be able to find its way from its burrow to the place where that nice rat-catcher put that tasty bait yesterday, and to find its way home again, to bring the goodies to its friends and relations. Steiniger (1950) noted that rats forage as much as 1 or 2 km from the burrow along a riverbank, though for much shorter distances, less than 100 m, inland. To navigate over such an area, rats must be able to generate the equivalent of a rudimentary map. In perhaps the earliest 'experimental study of the mental processes of the rat', Willard Small (1901) argued that a realistic model of this ability could be found in a maze like the one built for King William III in the 1690s at Hampton Court Palace. Small constructed a model of this in wood, with sawdust on the floor and a wire-mesh roof, and noted the resemblance to the burrows of wild mice.

Small was curious about the caution and carefulness of his pet albino rats, and still more of some domesticated wild rats, compared with the arrogant confidence of his cat. He first placed the home cage of his wild rats, a

Willard S. Small's experiment

Approach to a conditioned stimulus 111

male and two females, at the entrance to the maze, but they were too timid to demonstrate much to him. He was surprised, however, that although they were 'kept hungry enough that they would set about their task vigorously', they seemed to be motivated more by curiosity about the maze than by the food at its centre; also, they rarely followed each other about.

A pair of pet albino rats took 13 minutes to reach the centre of the maze on their first trial, and even then it seemed more by accident than by looking or smelling. Given the whole night to improve, they became a little quicker, with fewer pauses. As they became fully accustomed to the maze, they became bolder, and would eventually flash the complete path in 5 seconds, a distance of 4·9 m with sixteen right-angle corners. They often ventured to the central space to drink the milk provided there, and returned to their home cage carrying bread, or paper to nest with. Small noted that the main effect of hunger was indirect, to sensitise the rats to the effect of external stimuli (cf. Campbell and Sheffield, 1953). His description of his animals suggests that he knew as much as anyone ever has of the 'mental processes' of rats.

Subways and superstructures: wall rats and alley rats

The layman's idea of a psychologist is of a man who spends his life making rats race through ever more complicated mazes, and was probably not far off the truth between about 1920 and 1940 or even 1950. Everybody employed mazes, mostly to study the phenomena of learning, and by 1927 Warden and Warner estimated there were already over 100 different designs of maze in use.

A maze consists essentially of three things. A start-box to put the rat in, which can adjoin the animal's own home cage; a goal-box to put the food in, or whatever incentive is used to reinforce the animal's performance; and a set of runways with one or more decision points where the animal has to choose which way to go, to put the measurement in.

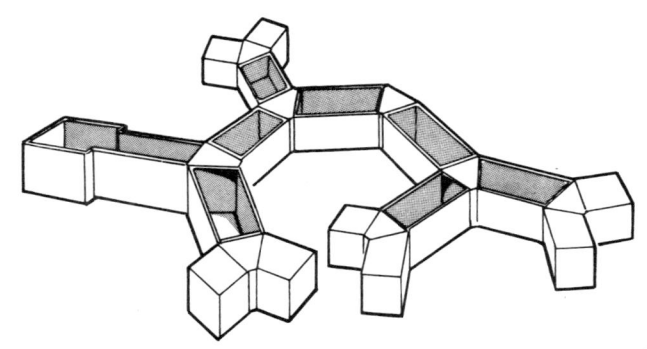

Fig. 10.1. Components for a multiple-Y maze (after Warden and Warner, 1927).

The runways of a maze can be enclosed tunnels, alleys with tall sides but no roof, or a wire-mesh for the experimenter to observe the animal through. Alternatives are elevated mazes where the rat walks along the top of a ridge or wall, temporal mazes, and water mazes in which the rat has to swim. Many of the techniques I would otherwise describe at length are included in an excellent and still widely available review by George Kreezer (1949).

The original Hampton Court maze was complicated but did not cater for all the complications required, and to standardise procedures (always the beginning of the end of a scientific band-wagon), Warden and Warner (1927) designed a modular maze (Fig. 10.1) whose junction and alley units can form a 'multiple-Y' leading anywhere or nowhere.

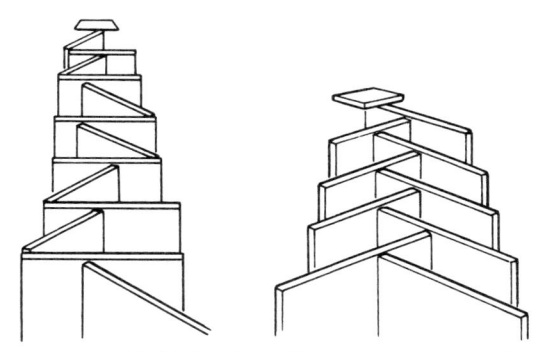

Fig. 10.2. Multiple Block Elevated maze (after Dennis, 1931).

An elevated maze was made by Dennis (1931) from blocks of wood 60 × 30 cm standing on edge to form a runway 4·5 cm wide; this too is modular, and Fig. 10.2 illustrates some arrangements. Surprisingly, rats seem to have a 'fear of heights' and not one of Dennis's 50 rats jumped down from the runway.

On an elevated runway, the rat presumably does not feel as secure as if he were scuttling along under the protective walls of an enclosed alley, but should be able to smell his way to food rather better and to see that blind turnings lead nowhere. In either maze, rats regularly venture down obvious blind alleys, and over a period will systematically visit the entire apparatus. As Small noted, rats seem mainly to be inquisitive even when they are hungry.

Procedure: 'All right, boys, we all turn left today'

The good experimenter starts by depriving the rat of food for 22 or up to 23·5 hours a day for a week or two: the rat has access to food for a limited time or in limited quantity, and both animal and food are checked daily until the animal weighs about 85 per cent of what it would have done if food had been freely available.

Approach to a conditioned stimulus **113**

Before the main training begins, the rat is given two or three sessions of half an hour in the goal-box, becoming conditioned to eat part of its daily mash or pot of powder there. At last the great day arrives when the rat is put into the start-box, the trapdoor is opened, and the time the rat takes to reach the goal and start to eat is recorded. The animal is allowed to eat for half a minute or so, then taken directly to Go and allowed to start all over again. A typical day's session includes ten such trials.

The start time, until the rat emerges through the trapdoor with all four feet into the first section of the runway, may also be recorded. An 'entry' into an alley is similarly defined by the position of all four feet, or by head and forepaws only. The interesting entries are the unnecessary extras not on the direct route to goal. They are usually called 'errors' with the curious implication that the rat has but one objective, food and nothing but food. Errors are also scored if the rat retraces its steps back towards the start along the correct route. These errors can be reduced by making the rat push through one-way doors along the direct route, but this seems unnecessary.

The experimenter knows that after all the food deprivation schedules, the rat is hungry; so does the rat. Nevertheless, it is important to distinguish the objectives of the two, and to imagine what the procedure must seem like to the animal. It is put into a strange and complex environment, and does not know at first that there is food waiting at the end of a long, tortuous and (for all it knows) perilous passage. When it arrives at the goal-box, the rat must be allowed a reasonably long time to eat there, otherwise it will associate the place not with eating, but with frustration, with finding food and being picked bodily up in a great big hand and dumped unceremoniously down in the start-box again. Equally it should not get so much food after one trial as to weaken its motivation to run the next.

Food deprivation is after all merely a means of persuading the animal to perform regularly at our convenience, and the maze is used to shape that performance into quantitative form – the time scores as a continuously variable analogue measure, errors as a digital one. Both are apt to decline from one trial to the next at first, and from one day to the next; and the speed-up of the start of eating is rapid at first, but reaches a relatively stable routine. Scores in the later trials on later days may fluctuate, as the rat explores again after it has assuaged the acutest pangs of hunger.

This decline in time and error scores is what we call learning. Maze learning for food is a shorthand description for the intake and registration of information, its filing and retention, and its retrieval and use. These may well be a dozen independent processes, and it is certainly too facile to take maze-learning as a model of all learning in rats, and still less in all mammals (cf. Chapter 19), although this was formerly often implied and sometimes stated.

There are at least two aspects of learning a maze for food to be distinguished: not only the obvious learning about where the food is to be found, but also the familiarisation with the maze as a whole. Whatever the reason, not only is the latter logically necessary before the animal can discover what the experimenter calls the goal, it also seems to be a biological necessity with a fairly high priority.

In most experiments several rats will be run through the maze, one after the other. They may influence one another. For instance, if rats are no longer rewarded, the conditioned response is 'extinguished'. In their frustration, rats appear to leave odours which delay the later rats. Edward Wasserman and Donald Jensen (1969) trained 20 rats to run a 1·2-m straight alley with a floor covered by paperstrip. After preliminary exploration, each rat was given 20 trials in 5 days, eating a 97-mg pellet in the goal-box and taken home to give the next rat its turn. The paper floor was changed each time. The ten rats running most uniformly became experimentals, the five fastest of the others became the extinction (E) group, the remainder the reward (R) group.

On test, Reinforced (R) rats were given two trials a day as in training, with food and with new paper that was returned for the experimental rat following. E rats ran, got no food, and were confined either for 30 seconds in the goal-box or 120 seconds in the alley. All E rats urinated, the R rats did not. Experimental rats had a warm-up trial each day, then three more (all reinforced) on new paper, following an E and an R rat (in a different order each day). As usual, starting speeds on the new paper became steadily quicker over the 12 test days in the experimental rats, and speeds on the trials where the rats ran on paper previously traversed by reinforced (R) rats were just as quick. But both start-latency and running speeds were significantly slower when the rats had to run on paper traversed by E rats. They must have left a smell with a message ('Abandon hope' or merely 'Look who was here'?). Some experimenters therefore wipe the apparatus with disinfectant after each rat. This has its own strong smell and its own problems. Chance and Mead tell the story of how rats became accustomed to this procedure on repeated testing – until one day, when each rat spent the whole time frenziedly sniffing the floor. The trouble was finally traced to

disinfectant ... has its own problems

a new bottle of disinfectant. Yes, replied the manufacturers, they had indeed changed the formulation, and would Dr Chance kindly stop his industrial espionage, for how else could he possibly know?

Technical reliability in the scores, as distinct from reliability of the experimenter's interpretation, has been given considerable emphasis (Kreezer, 1949). In the face of wide fluctuations from trial to trial of both time and error scores, a good measure seems to be to compare one block of, say, ten successive trials with another, the test–retest comparison. Better still, test for internal consistency: a positive correlation between odd- and even-numbered trials suggests that the same long-term changes must have taken place in both.

Temporal mazes: timing is all

Quite early in the history of experiments with mazes, interest began to centre on the processes of learning, rather than on the amazing fact that a rat could learn at all. The rat's exploration of the maze is not as random as it looks. If the rat has turned left at one point, it is likely to turn right on the next. The question then arises, how spontaneous is spontaneous alternation? Does the rat rely on apparently trivial cues at the choice-point, cracks or knots in the wood, and the like? If it comes to that, does the rat rely on physical cues to learn a maze? Or does it remember, 'two left turns, then a right, then a left', by tying suitable knots in its tail?

This problem was ingeniously tackled by Hunter (1920) in a 'temporal' maze, where the alleys were arranged in a sort of figure-of-eight and successive right or left turns all took place at the same choice-point. If the rat guessed wrong, it had to retrace its steps because the cunning experimenter had time to reposition the barrier. The rat may be required to alternate right and left turns, or be set a double alternation task, *RRLLRR* . . . and so on. Whatever the sequence, the physical cues at the choice-point are always exactly the same.

Alternation tasks turn out to be possible but difficult, because the animal needs a purely internal rule. If things get just too difficult, a sensible rat is likely to sit down and save his breath. Sol Evans (1937) forced the rat to keep moving, by making him swim to keep his whiskers dry. He used a temporal maze (Fig. 10.3) in warm water (20 °C) in a galvanised iron tank. A rat making the correct right–left alternation was allowed to climb up a ladder that Evans had thoughtfully put at the start of the centre alley. With trials morning and afternoon for 6 days a week, 12 of his 14 rats solved the problem in 36 to 173 trials, the other two were pensioned off after 200 trials, and eight rats went on to learn the *RLRL* sequence. The criterion was a sequence of three correct trials, without errors or retracing. Evans found, as you might expect, that excursions up a blind alley with the door closed, tended to become shorter and then rarer. Rats hesitated at the choice-point

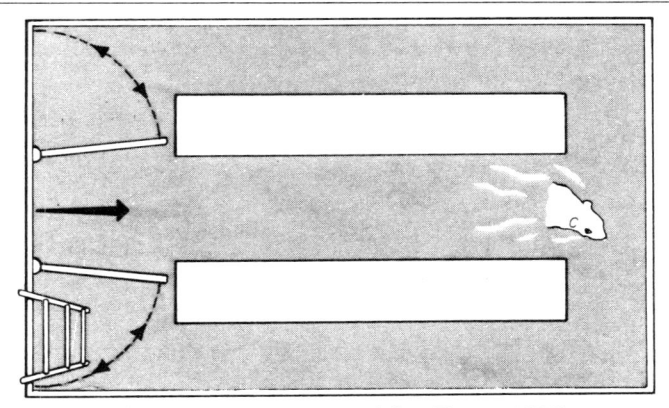

Fig. 10.3. A temporal water maze (after Evans, 1937).

for quite long periods, at first usually following the pause with an error, later with the correct choice.

Heredity, nutrition, and political relevance

Genetics was another fashionable band-wagon of science in the 1920s, and several painstaking experiments investigated maze-learning as a heritable character (e.g. Tolman, 1924). Eventually Robert Tryon (1931) succeeded in selecting the well-known maze-bright and maze-dull strains. It is perhaps needless to suggest that, in animals as in children, learning ability is not always what it seems: motivation, anxiety, and distractability are all relevant. In fact, Tryon's 'maze-bright' rats were so defined because they concentrated on running to food and explored less into side-alleys than the 'dull' ones.

There was considerable interest in the 1930s, as now, in whether malnutrition had any specific behavioural consequences. The experiments were politically admirable but many were scientifically naïve. Among others, Wentworth (1936) fed rats on limited quantities of the typical diet of Mexican immigrant workers in the south-western United States, chilli con carne, beans, and coffee. Small quantities were clearly inadequate for growth but our earnest scientist found no significant difference in the maze-running of these rats and those fed on unstated amounts of mash, fish-meal, and a generally varied and presumably middle-class diet.

Several inconclusive experiments would hardly make you consider nutrition to be important. But compare another experiment where the detailed description suggests careful attention to procedure (Koch and Warden, 1936). Fifteen control mice received 75 calories a week on average, from birth to the age of 13 months; 16 experimentals were restricted to 42 calories of cracked whole wheat, 'klim' with 1 per cent salt, unrestricted water and a weekly supplement of greens and egg. They were then given 2 days

Approach to a conditioned stimulus 117

pre-feeding in the goal-box of a multiple-Y maze (Fig. 10.4) of wooden alleys painted matt black with wire-mesh roofing. The next evening the mice were given two 2-minute trials in the maze, and then two 5-minute trials, five evenings a week until they achieved three errorless trials out of four.

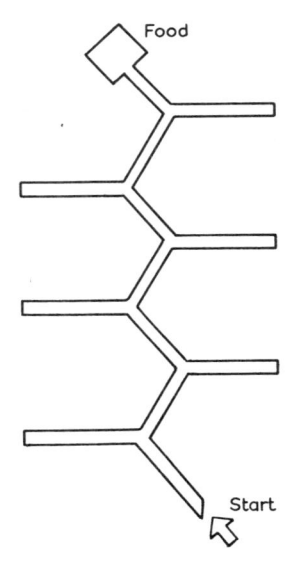

Fig. 10.4. Plan of the multiple-Y maze used by Koch and Warden (1936).

The maze was washed in alcohol every night, so that the later mice on each evening may have been able to follow a smell trail from the earlier ones.

The experimental mice were stunted in their growth and more active than the controls. As Table 10.1 shows, they ran the maze faster on each trial,

Table 10.1.

	Underfed	Well-fed
Trials to criterion	27·44	37·07
Running time (seconds)	37·99	50·79
Errors per trial	6·56	8·01

Data of Koch and Warden (1936)

made fewer errors, and needed fewer trials. Koch and Warden do not give results trial by trial, so that it is hard to judge whether undernutrition actually improves learning ability. More likely the underfed mice were hungrier, while the controls explored every last nook and cranny.

Straightforward simplicity

It is clear that the interpretation of the animal's performance does not particularly depend on how complex the maze is. Mazes were progressively simplified, from Small's original Hampton Court maze to the six units in line of Koch and Warden. It is obviously possible to simplify such a maze further. A single unit of a Y-maze can be used to measure only the 'errors' which constitute exploration as Steinberg and her colleagues do, for instance (see p. 238).

Alternatively, a single straight alley can measure running time. Miller and Miles (1935) made sure, however, that this highway was long enough to measure the rat at top speed; it was 8·5 m long with electrical timing devices. Not surprisingly the fastest rats were the hungry, but experienced, ones. Those fed beforehand, or those that had previously run the alley without reinforcement were both slower and more variable. Caffeine (50 mg/kg) reduced the variation, and increased a low speed (in the less highly motivated rats), particularly over the first 2·5 m where rats are usually slowest. It made no difference to rats already doing their best – please note before you try to stimulate a horse.

While mazes are no longer as fashionable as they used to be, for certain purposes they remain very useful. A straight runway gave Archer (1974) a simple way of testing Richard Andrew's suggestion that testosterone makes chicks persevere in trying to attain a goal. They should therefore pay more attention to relevant stimuli and less to others. After training 4-day-old male chicks for 3 days to run a straight runway for food, Archer injected 25 mg of testosterone oenanthate. This releases at least enough hormone to induce maximal sexual behaviour for a week or two, and also altered the chicks' runway performance more or less as predicted. Putting black and white panels half-way along the coloured sides of the runway delayed the dosed chicks' arrival at the goal, but not as much as it delayed controls. On the other hand changing the food-dish itself to black and white distracted the dosed animals far more than controls.

Running a maze for food gives two measures of 'motivation', speed, and amount eaten, and as they usually agree, one sometimes becomes redundant. Rats ran the fifth trial 70 per cent slower than the first if the eating was followed 10 minutes later by an injection of lithium chloride, and they ate 90 per cent less of the saccharine-sweetened food; obviously White, Sklar, and Amit (1977) had measured a conditioned taste aversion twice over. But if the injection was of morphine, while the rats ate a little less food, they ran in anticipation up to four times faster. The use of two separate measures of reinforcement let it be shown that morphine can in some way be simultaneously both aversive and rewarding.

Summary

One of an animal's fundamental abilities must be to find its way about its environment, to know where food, water, or in appropriate species, the nest or burrow are to be found. The laboratory model of this is to condition albino rats to approach a particular place, usually for food. Originally a highly complex maze was used. After years of enthusiasm, animals' ability to learn to run mazes rapidly for food became taken for granted. Interest was then centred on the process of learning, and the rats' ability in the maze came to be taken as a model for all learning in rats and even all learning in all animals including man. Mazes were somewhat simplified in form, and were made up in modular units. These facilitated the arrangement of choice-points – whether a right or left turn led into a blind alley or along to the next choice-point on the way to goal.

Measures taken in a maze are primarily of running time from start to goal, and of 'errors'. Errors are entries into a blind alley, or movements back towards the start. The word 'error' is revealing, in its implication that the animals' sole objectives are what the experimenter has prescribed, that all a hungry rat's behaviour is oriented towards eating. In fact it is likely that the animal also has to explore the maze, not only in order to discover the place where food is, but for its own sake or for reasons which, in a maze situation, can only be guessed at. Mazes have therefore become progressively simplified, into a simple runway to measure running time and a single Y-maze where 'errors' are observed overtly as exploration. Learning processes are more usually studied with operant methods.

ELEVEN

Conditioned reflexes

Spit summoned by bells

Responses are decided by the animal but stimuli by the environment, and stimuli are therefore easier for the experimenter to control and use in selecting a particular response.

Animal behaviour is in some ways the classic engineering 'black box' problem. You can manipulate the input, up to a point, and you can observe the output. Both can be complex, and poking around inside with an electrode is sometimes helpful, but not always. One of the most influential pioneers of the science was Pavlov, largely because he first realised that it is possible to simplify both input and output in a deliberately artificial laboratory situation. He traced the idea of 'brain reflexes' back to the early seventeenth-century philosopher Descartes: if behaviour can be regarded as mechanical it is at least predictable.

Pavlov's successors in the Soviet Union greatly modified his techniques and those they use nowadays are not very different from those used in the English-speaking part of the scientific world. However, even in English translation, much of Pavlov's language sounds arbitrary and unreal, but is much closer to what the animal does in a limited environment than it often seems. I will therefore try to summarise Pavlov's concepts, as he expressed them in his lectures on *Conditioned Reflexes* (1927). Quotations are all from this book.

Behaviour has been applied to toxicology in the Soviet Union more than elsewhere, as a sensitive indicator of the lowest dose of a substance to affect living organisms. An effect need not be harmful, of course, but harmfulness may be the safest working assumption and the issue needs to be debated on its merits in each case. Yet the experiments are often ambiguous in print, partly because the Pavlovian terminology is taken for granted. In the second part of the chapter, I will describe these experiments as far as I can.

Part 1. Pavlov and conditioned reflexes

In what is now Leningrad, the physiologist Ivan Petrovich Pavlov began (at the age of nearly 50) to study '. . . the activities of the digestive glands. I had to enquire into the so-called psychic secretion of some of the glands, a task which I attempted in conjunction with a collaborator. As a result of this investigation an unqualified conviction of the futility of subjective methods of enquiry was firmly stamped upon my mind.' Poor collaborator. To use strictly objective methods, Pavlov 'started to record all the external stimuli falling on the animal at the time its reflex reaction was manifested (in this particular case the secretion of saliva), at the same time recording all changes in the reaction of the animal'.

Salivary secretion enters into not one, but two kinds of behaviour. First is the obvious 'alimentary reflex' when food is put into the dog's mouth, the second a 'weak defence reflex' when something mildly unpleasant (5 ml of 0·25 per cent hydrochloric acid) is put there instead.

The secretion of saliva is an integral part of a complete behaviour sequence, but Pavlov isolated this component for all his formal study, because it is easy to make quantitative measurements by counting drops, and because tangible, liquid data minimise the temptation to interpret the behaviour anthropomorphically. So although Pavlov observed his dogs shrewdly, he used informal observations mainly to make his formal measures more vivid and convincing.

In the alimentary reflex, the dog turns to face the experimenter and divides its attention between him and the source of food, smacking its lips and (I suppose, for Pavlov did not mention it) wagging its tail. The saliva is thick and mucous. In the defence reflex, the dog turns away from the experimenter, whining and snorting, shaking its head and tongue, flooding away the acid in a copious flow of watery saliva.

In the original unconditioned reflex, salivation, chewing, and swallowing are themselves the entire pattern. One of Pavlov's pupils, Dr I. S. Zitovich, hand-reared some puppies himself and when they were old enough to wean, offered them bread or meat. They did not produce saliva at first, until the food was placed directly into their mouths, as one would expect of a simple reflex. When they had eaten a few times, however, the dogs salivated in response to the smell and sight of food. These stimuli had always been followed by taste and tactile stimuli and the saliva was produced in anticipation some time before it would be needed for mastication. This 'natural' conditioned reflex occurs in all normally brought-up dogs; experimental conditioned reflexes occur when an artificial stimulus (a bell or a light or anything the animal can detect) comes to act as a signal for the future smell of food just as the smell signals the future taste.

Pavlov seems to have called a 'reflex' what Macdougall called an 'instinct', a 'kind of behaviour' and he thought it possible to list all the inborn reflexes of both men and animals.

Thus, the first effect of a new stimulus is to elicit what Pavlov called the Investigatory (or 'what is it?') reflex. The dog raises its head, pricks up its ears, and orients all available sense organs to the source of the stimulus. With further information, the dog could then take appropriate action, but Pavlov was not greatly interested in this stage. He referred to a 'freedom reflex' in an otherwise quite docile dog that struggled when harnessed into the apparatus. A 'warding' reflex was strongly developed in a sheepdog that was tame and co-operative with Dr Besbokaya, but aggressive to Professor Pavlov himself when he came to visit. He was more worried while he was performing the experiment by the dog's excessive salivation. Only if he kept quite motionless did the dog calm down, gaze fixedly at Pavlov, and accept with little salivation that Dr Besbokaya was in no immediate danger from Professors.

Pavlov was well aware that inborn reflexes and a system to condition them to new stimuli, could only have evolved if they had survival value. He distinguished between active and passive defence reflexes, corresponding to counter-attacking a predator and hiding from one. Nevertheless, his procedures were deliberately artificial. Though stimuli can be linked to any reflex, some are inconvenient: the defence reflex to a powerful electric current makes the dog refractory to the procedure in future, the sexual reflex is too dependent on exigencies of age and season (or nowadays of hormone treatment). But feeding and the rejection of mildly noxious substances are everyday events, and, since business is business, the dogs co-operate. They stand patiently in their harnesses, give up hunting (unless unusually strongly tempted), and salivate.

Pavlov's procedure

To collect saliva from the sublingual or one maxillary gland, dogs underwent a minor operation. The end of the duct and a little of the mucous membrane was dissected free and led out to a small incision in the skin of the cheek or chin. Pavlov originally counted the drops as they fell. Later a hemispherical glass bulb ('A' in Fig. 11.1) was hermetically sealed over the

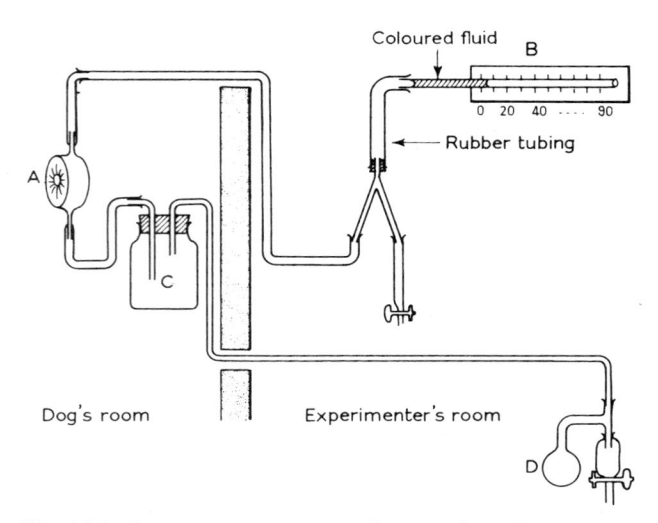

Fig. 11.1. Apparatus to measure the secretion of saliva (after Pavlov, 1927).

Conditioned reflexes 123

duct, where saliva would collect and displace air along the upper tubing to a horizontal graduated glass tube (B). This contained a coloured fluid, allowing the volume of saliva to be measured. The saliva could then be drawn off through the lower tube by vacuum and into the collecting bottle (C) – the experimenter in the next room compressed a rubber bulb (D) after each trial. Later still, Pavlov used electrical recording, but continued to describe the volume in terms of drops (0·01 ml).

On the sensory side, Pavlov had the same problem as everybody whose 'research deals with the ... cerebral cortex, a signalising apparatus of tremendous complexity and of most exquisite sensitivity through which the animal is influenced by countless stimuli from the outside world. Every one of those stimuli produces a certain effect upon the animal, and all of them taken together may clash and interfere with, or else reinforce, one another. Unless we are careful to take special precautions the success of the whole investigation may be jeopardized ... among so many and various influences, so intertwined and entangled ...' In short, the smells, sights, and sounds which the dog perceived had to be, so far as possible, only those which the experimenter provided. The dog was lightly restrained in a harness, if only to make it face the right way to see a signal light or a plate of food moving out from behind a screen – and to stop it hunting behind the screen too soon. In a purpose-built, nearly sound-proof laboratory even the experimenters (in 25 years Pavlov had over a hundred qualified assistants) had to be separated from their dogs. The slightest holding of breath, the batting of an eyelid, could distract the animal in those featureless surroundings or tell it what to do.

Nevertheless, Pavlov could use well-trained dogs to give live demonstrations at his lectures, in spite of the inhibitions caused by the presence of a large audience.

Concepts

(*1*) *Without any particular stimulus*, the dog secretes little or no saliva.

(*2*) *Unconditioned reflex.* If food is put into the dog's mouth secretion begins within a couple of seconds as a reflex response via taste and tactile receptors on the tongue and mucous membranes.

(*3*) *'Natural' conditioned reflex.* If an adult dog can smell or see the food, salivation begins about 5 seconds later and six drops can be collected in 15 seconds. The response is 'forced', the dog can hardly avoid salivating – provided it has previously experienced such stimuli before eating.

(*4*) *An 'artificial' conditioned reflex.* A metronome ticks, and after 9 seconds saliva starts to flow, eleven drops during 45 seconds, while the dog looks to where the food is due to appear and licks his lips. When it arrives, the dog is allowed to eat for a few seconds.

This was a well-trained dog in a lecture demonstration. A previously neutral, meaningless stimulus has preceded or accompanied the food on average about 20 occasions; the dog comes to secrete saliva in anticipation of the imminent arrival of the food. Once the first stimulus has been thoroughly conditioned, a second, third, and fourth can be established, later ones requiring as few as three or four trials.

(5) *Any sensory stimulus* that the dog can detect can become a conditioned stimulus. In fact, conditioning is nowadays the best way of discovering an animal's sensory capabilities, although dogs are more sensitive in many ways than Pavlov's apparatus was. Among the commonest stimuli he used, were the sounds of a metronome beating rhythmically, a whistle, a buzzer, the sight of a lamp, the touch of some object on various parts of the body, a fine point or a blunt one, a rough or smooth texture, the touch of a 'thermal stimulus' (an object kept at 0 °C or 45 °C), or the smell of camphor.

To form a conditioned reflex (CR), the potential conditioned stimulus (CS) must closely precede or overlap the unconditioned stimulus (US). Once the CR is established, then the interval between CS and US can be gradually lengthened (5–10 seconds a day) up to as much as 30 minutes. In principle, a CS could *follow* a US, but in long, wearying experiments, Pavlov failed to find an example (but see p. 130 since he revised this question later).

Conditioned reflexes based on responses to food and to dilute acid work in the same way. A dramatic case is the nausea, salivation, and vomiting caused by morphine. After five or six injections, V. A. Krylov (Pavlov, 1927) found the same symptoms if he merely approached the dogs. Electric shock or a pinprick deep enough to draw blood, stimuli which on their own would evoke a defence reflex, can nevertheless come to act a quite normal conditioned stimuli for food. On the other hand, a dog that has recently had its dinner will not condition any stimulus for food.

Pavlov nearly always gave food or acid after every stimulus, but sometimes inserted a delay between CS and US. On 18 February 1909, F. S. Grossman gave a dog one minute's tactile stimulation, followed by acid after a minute's pause. Table 11.1 shows the drops of saliva secreted in these 2 minutes in four successive trials.

Table 11.1

Time of day	12·40	12·50	13·15	13·27
Saliva, drops secreted				
during 1 min tactile stimulation	0	0	0	0
during 1 min pause	0·5	10	11	14

Conditioned reflexes **125**

If food is given every 30 minutes precisely, preceded by the sound of a metronome for 30 seconds, the metronome beating at shorter intervals will have little effect. I. Feokritova (Pavlov, 1927) produced a fantastic example (**bold type** marks the crucial observation) detailed in Table 11.2.

Table 11.2 (20 December 1911)

Time (after CS for 30 sec)	15·30	16·00	**16·29**	16·30
Saliva: drops in 30 sec	10	7	**0**	7

In one experiment a dog was reinforced first after every stimulus as usual, and then after every second stimulus, then after every fourth. Even after 60 reinforcements (where normally as few as three to five can be enough) the dog failed to learn the system. The time scale is slow, of course, so that in effect the dog was alternately learning and unlearning the CS.

(6) *Inhibition: external, or indirect inhibition.* An experiment may be proceeding smoothly and the dog salivating every time, when there is a sudden rustling as if a mouse is scurrying under the floor: the conditioned reflex is unobtainable for several minutes. Or the proud student wants to show Professor Pavlov himself how well the experiment is going, and when he comes, the CS fails, for the first time. Or a bitch in the next room is on heat.

an urgent inhibition . . . of conditioned reflexes

One reflex can thus inhibit another. An unusual noise or visitor evokes the 'What-is-it?-reflex', the dog listens and sniffs, and if the stimulus carries little information, the CR returns in a few minutes. If the hunting or sexual reflexes are evoked, however, the inhibition can be more complete and extend for several days. Conditioned reflexes may fail gradually one day, the dog takes on a glazed, preoccupied expression . . . the CRs only return after the dog is taken out of its harness and led away to urinate. If two incompatible reflexes are evoked simultaneously, the more urgent one inhibits the other competitively.

(7) *Internal inhibition: extinction.* A metronome clicks for 30 seconds every 2 minutes and is reinforced with meat powder every time. Ten drops of saliva are produced in 30 seconds, starting after a latent period of 3 seconds (Table 11.3). Then the reinforcement is omitted and the saliva production

Table 11.3

CS every 2 min	Latent period (sec)	3	7	5	4	5	9	13	pause of 23 min	5
	Drops of saliva in 30 sec	10	7	8	5	7	4	3		6

declines and is extinguished. Pavlov argued that this is active inhibition, not the mere waning of a reflex that is no longer useful, since it recovers spontaneously after an interval and the more unreinforced stimuli are applied, the later is the recovery. Extinction of one CR (e.g. the response to a buzzer) also reduces the response to other conditioned stimuli (e.g. metronome, touch, etc.) and even to acid reinforcement. Longer intervals between unreinforced stimuli make extinction slower and less complete – if the CR was passively waning through disuse, extinction should be quicker.

To my mind the crucial evidence for active inhibition is what happens to an extinguished CR (marked M in Table 11.4) when a second stimulus evokes a competing, investigatory reflex. On their own, the other stimuli (T, A in Table 11.4) had no effect. They would be expected to reduce saliva flow

Table 11.4

Time Stimulus (1 min)	Pre-experimental	13·53	13·58	14·03	14·08	14·13	14·18	14·20	14·23	14·28
	T	A	P	M	M	M	M + T	M + A	M	P	M	M
Saliva (drops in 1 min)	0	0	0	11	4	0	3	2	0	5	0

T = tactile stimulus to skin. A = auditory (knocks under table). P = Professor Pavlov enters room and talks for 2 minutes. M = Neat powder presented at a distance.

of an active reflex by external inhibition, or have no effect if extinction is a mere waning by disuse. In fact, 'the extinguished alimentary conditioned reflex is restored both by the actual presence of the extra stimulus (tactile and auditory), and by its after-effect (after-effect of stimulus of my entering the room)'.

(8) *Conditioned inhibition* (*differentiation*). Stimulus A is always reinforced by the food or acid. Stimulus B is added, but the combination A + B is not reinforced. Stimulus A continues to elicit saliva when alone, but not when the combination A + B is repeated.

The time relations of A and B are important. If B overlaps A, the dog can differentiate A from A + B. If B ends well before A starts, however, B can come to act as a secondary conditioned stimulus for A, and elicit saliva on its own account. But if B ends immediately before A starts, the conditioned inhibition is difficult and induces 'restlessness and various defence reactions'.

(9) Generalisation. Stimuli are subject to variation, like everything else, so that a dog will probably respond to a metronome beat of 76/min when it was trained at 80/min, or to a touch on the flank when trained to one on the shoulder. If the distinction is important, and if the dog can discriminate it, differentiation will occur. If it is not important, i.e. if both stimuli are reinforced equally, then generalisation occurs, the one stimulus is equivalent to the other.

At first there will be an investigatory reflex, transient if it appears of little importance. An extreme case of generalisation can be seen in the delay of a delayed CR, when almost any accidental stimulus can evoke a few drops of saliva – and unfortunately can easily form an accidental conditioned reflex.

Generalisation is a difficult phenomenon to work with. If you repeatedly test stimuli that 'ought' to have no effect, you either have to reinforce them (forming an independent conditioned reflex), or not (leading to differentiation and extinction). Pavlov either reinforced alternate stimuli or performed experiments only at 2- or 3-week intervals (which seems a bit slow).

(10) Differentiation. Conditioned inhibition (No. 8) is a special case of differentiation. Let *A* be a conditioned stimulus and *B* another stimulus similar enough to *A* to evoke saliva itself, at first, because of generalisation. *A* might be a tone of 1000 Hz, *B* a buzzer or a tone of 2000 Hz. If *B* is not reinforced, the response will be extinguished: quickly if the discrimination is easy for the dog, slowly if the stimuli are closer together. If the dog cannot distinguish them at all, the whole reflex disappears in the dog's 'extreme general excitation'.

A dog easily discriminated a white card from a dark grey one (No. 35 on a 50-point scale), but could not discriminate pale grey (No. 10) from white even after 75 trials. But when the dog was trained successively on Nos. 35, 25, and 15, it successfully discriminated No. 10 from white after a total of only 20 trials with all four cards, and with a correct choice on the first trial of the day.

Differentiation is by inhibition of unreinforced responses, and therefore tends to break down after an increase in 'general excitation' (compare an error-free training procedure, p. 186). M. P. Nikiforovsky (Pavlov, 1927) injected caffeine (5 ml of a 1 per cent solution subcutaneously) to a dog receiving food after tactile stimulation of the forepaw but not of the back. Caffeine increased the salivary response to both stimuli. (Could the drug have affected the salivary gland directly?) Deprivation of food for longer than the usual overnight fast, though less stressful for a carnivore than a continuously munching herbivore, was also thought to excite the dogs.

(11) Irradiation. Irradiation is most easily studied 'on the cutaneous analyser, with its extensive and easily accessible receptor surfaces ... Five small apparatuses for tactile stimulation of the skin were arranged along the hind leg of the dog. The first was fixed over the paw, and the remaining four ... at distances of 3, 9, 15, and 22 cm ... from the first.' One of these was conditioned as a stimulus for food. By generalisation, the others also elicited saliva, and were reinforced, except for the paw. By differentiation, therefore, the paw became an inhibitory stimulus when responding to it had been extinguished. Stimulation of the paw only once produced a trace of saliva; the site 3 cm away from the paw then produced no saliva or the merest trace, that at 9 cm fell to three drops, those at 15 or 22 cm gave a full or even enhanced response.

Since there is a point-to-point relationship between tactile receptors on the skin and their representation on the cerebral cortex, Pavlov concluded that whatever 'internal inhibition' consists of, it must have 'irradiated' outwards in space from the cortical projection of the paw. The cortical projections of the other sites were inhibited in proportion to distance. As you might expect, the site farthest from the paw was free from inhibition 0·5 minutes afterwards, the 9 cm site after 5 minutes, and the nearest after 10 minutes.

This irradiation of inhibition (also translated as 'spreading depression') was confirmed by Anrep, the translator of these lectures by Pavlov (1923;

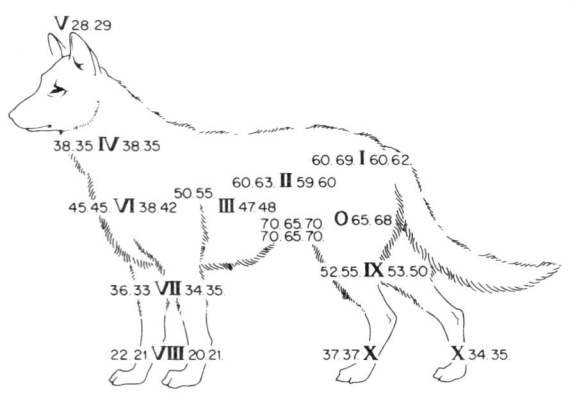

Fig. 11.2. The Irradiation of Inhibition ('Spreading Depression'). Percentage fall in output (arabic numerals) at left and right sides of body at various sites (roman numerals). Stimulation anywhere except at site 0 was reinforced with food, site 0 was extinguished and stimulation there became inhibitory: saliva produced after stimulation there was 65–70 per cent less than it had been originally; further away, for instance at the upper forelegs or on the left hindpaw, there was only a 34–35 per cent fall in output (from Anrep, 1923).

see Fig. 11.2). He also showed that the processes took time, measuring saliva output in the 30 seconds following stimulation and after intervals of 15, 30, 45, 60, 120, and 180 seconds. Inhibition was maximal after 30 seconds at all sites, so the process must be an active central one, not a purely local diffusion along the cortical surface.

(12) Concentration. With continued discrimination training, the inhibition ceases to irradiate but gradually concentrates exclusively on the unreinforced site. The process is very slow in some dogs.

(13) Positive and negative induction. Behavioural experiments are bedevilled by random variation, so when Pavlov found that a positive CS following a series of inhibitory stimuli evoked more saliva than usual, he originally attributed this 'positive induction' to '... various casual disturbing influences, the danger of which is so great in our investigation'. D. S. Foursikov (Pavlov, 1927) noticed how regular the phenomenon is when, for example, a metronome beat of 76/min was reinforced and one of 186/min differentiated from it (Table 11.5, induction marked in bold type).

Table 11.5

Time	17·05	17·15	17·24	17·24½	17·43	17·51
Stimulus (30 sec)	76	76	186	76	76	76
Saliva (drops/30 sec)	5·5	6	0	**8**	5·5	6
Latency (delay before CR)	5	5		**3**	5	5

Pavlov distinguished induction from disinhibition, because there was never any trace of an investigatory reflex, the appropriate response was evoked strongly from the very beginning.

Negative induction, inhibition intensified after excitation, was discovered when Kriikovsky (Pavlov, 1927) tried to eliminate a differentiation. A tone (T) signalled acid, a combination (C) of tone and touch was not reinforced and evoked no saliva. To restore the salivary response to C, Kriikovsky presented T and C stimuli alternately, ten times in 3 days, reinforcing both. The T stimuli evoked nine drops each, on average, yet in spite of reinforcement, the combination C not a single drop. Each T must have inhibited C by induction, for when the touch and tone were presented consecutively and reinforced, they rapidly came to elicit saliva.

Induction fluctuates in time and space. Pavlov quotes some elaborate and prolonged experiments with tactile stimuli all over the dog's back and legs, and responses measured immediately or from 15 seconds to 10 minutes afterwards. Since saliva flow had to be measured over periods of 30 seconds, the results were not very precise, but they suggested that waves of excitation and inhibition radiate out from the relevant cortical centre like ripples in a pond.

(14) Inhibition and some problems. Pavlov considered a negative after-effect to be very important. It is what leads to extinction. He even suggested that 'the function performed by the unconditioned reflex after the conditioned reflex has become established is merely to retard the development of inhibition'. If the conditioned stimulus is applied for 30 seconds, the latency before saliva starts to be produced eventually comes to approach 30 seconds; if the reinforcement is further delayed, the response can be, too. One of the practical disadvantages of Pavlov's methods is therefore that the response gradually diminishes as the dog learns to avoid wasting his spit prematurely.

Constancy of response can be maintained by occasionally presenting the reinforcement *sooner* than usual, and only gradually restoring the standard 30-second period; or by giving the dog a few days' holiday, or reducing the inhibition (boredom?) by teaching it some new conditioned reflexes.

A negative after-effect could explain why a conditioned stimulus can never follow reinforcement. In fact it can and in the early stages of conditioning it does. The small secretion which Pavlov originally overlooked or put down to experimental error, he later recognised; he argued that a few repetitions of the powerful inhibitory after-effect of reinforcement soon suppress it.

Occasionally, especially in delayed-response experiments, an experienced, docile middle-aged dog can develop an extreme inhibition. All conditioned responses gradually fail, it produces no saliva, even the unconditioned reflex fails and it refuses food in the laboratory. It becomes inert and listless, and this state of depression (which sounds quite analogous to the human state) can last a year or more. Teaching the old dog new tricks, and ignoring the old ones, sometimes helps to restore its spirits.

(15) Sleep. Inhibition, then, follows every stimulus but especially those that are prolonged or continually repeated. Pavlov regarded the inhibition as a 'protector of the cortical elements, preventing any excessive fatigue or dangerous functional destruction of this highly sensitive structure'. Repeated extinctions of a particular reflex lead to obvious drowsiness and even sleep. The dog droops in its harness, its eyes closing, its limbs sagging. Electric shock to the skin, surprisingly enough, can be used as a conditioned stimulus for food, if very weak currents are used to begin with. But shock used for many months leads to progressively increasing inhibition and sleep; and an attempt at generalising shock as CS for food caused a sudden reversion to a violent unconditioned defence reaction, and only one of three dogs could be used again.

Thermal stimuli were so likely to elicit sleep 'that in the early period of our research, I had real difficulty in finding collaborators who would agree to work with those stimuli'.

Pavlov makes a sad reference to '... the period of shortage in Russia a

Conditioned reflexes 131

few years ago'. (The famine of 1920–1. His bibliography is noticeably bimodal, with peaks around 1907–13 and 1923–6 when these lectures were first published in Russian.) 'The semi-starved animals could not be used for experiments with conditioned reflexes, since all positive conditioned stimuli assumed inhibitory properties, and the dogs invariably developed sleep exactly in conjunction with the application of the conditioned stimuli.'

In short, Pavlov identified sleep as inhibition irradiating throughout the cortex. In both, onset is gradual, over several minutes, and variable. There is often 'a fleeting phase of excitation, (the puppy) moved about uneasily, scratched itself and barked without any obvious reason, holding its nose up in the air. A similar state of general excitation preceding sleep, as is well known, often occurs in children.' (With feeling.)

A hypnotic or cataleptic state can also be observed between waking and sleep, fleetingly in most dogs, long-lasting in a few. The dog appears alert but is remarkably motionless, unresponsive to stimuli for many minutes. It occurs after weak but protracted stimuli (for example the monotony of months in laboratory harness) or short powerful ones, like being the subject of a lecture-demonstration to a large audience. It must have been an embarrassing lecture.

(16) Paradox. In one dog, some stimuli evoked more saliva than others, whistle > metronome > tactile > flashlamp. The tactile stimulus was a rhythmic touch at 24/minute, but a similar stimulus of 12/minute was differentiated from it. There was an extraordinary effect when 30 seconds at 12/minute (unreinforced) was followed by 30 seconds at 24/minute, given food. For nine days all the reflexes failed. On the tenth they reappeared, but in a paradoxical form, for the strong stimuli evoked no saliva, the weak ones a large volume. This paradoxical phase lasted for 14 days, and was followed by 7 days of equalisation, when all stimuli evoked similar volumes, then finally the original reflexes were restored. In extreme cases like the starving dogs of the famine period, positive and negative reflexes could even be reversed. In mild cases, paradoxical and equalisation phases can finish after a few minutes; they commonly occur in dogs made drowsy by too many inhibitory stimuli, but can be prevented with caffeine.

With the hypnotic drugs that Pavlov used, the transition between sleep and waking is smoother. Chloral hydrate (2 g in 150 ml water rectally) caused a gradual loss of reflexes, the weakest first, and after anaesthesia, a gradual recovery, the weakest reflex restored last. Abnormally exaggerated responses were rare.

(17) Individual differences. Personality types are discussed more often by the amateur psychologist than the professional, if only because they matter. Pavlov, a thorough professional, investigated the topic in relation to drowsiness. He tried choosing lively, vivacious dogs, those that sniff at everything,

alert to the slightest sounds, impossible to keep quiet, and slobberingly friendly. Since their excitability makes extinction slow, Pavlov thought they would be the dogs least likely to fall asleep on the job. Restrained in harness in a quiet uneventful room, they turned out to be the quickest dogs of all to fall asleep. They depend on a continual stimulus input, many reflexes conditioned concurrently but none tested more than once or twice a day. Pending a more scientific classification, Pavlov identified theirs with the classical 'sanguine' temperament.

Overinhibited dogs, those that slink close to the wall with their tail between their legs, are the opposite. They cower at the slightest disturbance, take a long time to habituate to laboratory conditions, but once acquired, their experimental reflexes are precise and reliable in a uniform environment. Theirs is the classic 'melancholic' temperament.

Dogs with a better balance include a lively and active group, often aggressive ('choleric'), whose inhibitory reflexes tend to be unstable.

Finally come 'phlegmatic' dogs with a moderate trend to inhibition. One such dog always seemed uninterested. Neither friendly nor hostile, its

a moderate trend to inhibition

reflexes were stable, it did not become drowsy, it kept its cool. But Pavlov 'succeeded in disturbing (its) placid calm ... by making most extraordinary sounds with a toy trumpet and having a frightful animal mask over my face. The dog ... began to bark determinedly and tried to get at me – a most "phlegmatic" but powerful type.' Pavlov's colleagues seem to have had some fun among the solemn, formal tests.

(18) Some 'pathological' reactions. Pavlov described some more stressful procedures, for instance, the violent defence reaction to electric shock as a generalised CS for food.

A dog was trained to discriminate a circle from an ellipse, at first one with axes in a 2:1 ratio, and by stages it almost managed a ratio of 9:8. After 3 weeks, the incomplete reflex degenerated, the once-quiet dog squealed, wriggled, and bit off chunks of the apparatus. It eventually relearned the discrimination, once, and promptly had another nervous breakdown into 'a state of extreme general excitation'.

That such 'clashing of excitation and inhibition' should lead to a 'neurosis' is not surprising. In the dogs, at least, the behaviour seems quite logical, and is often remarkably specific to the situation. A dog that lost its conditioned reflexes after a too-difficult discrimination, and then went through 5 weeks of paradoxical phases, was nevertheless entirely normal outside the laboratory, and had a healthy appetite.

Pavlov compared the loss of conditioned reflexes to the 'passive flight reaction', hiding from a predator when you cannot either run away or beat him off. His other conclusion is that the cortex is functionally a mosaic, where disturbance through 'overstrain' in one place can be encapsulated, and need not spread. The 77-year-old Pavlov encapsulated too: the book of these lectures is dedicated without comment to the memory of his son Victor.

(19) Temperaments tested. To investigate Pavlov's view of overexcitable or inhibitable temperaments, M. K. P. Petrova (Pavlov, 1927) trained two dogs on six conditioned reflexes, and then tried to convert them to delayed reflexes. One dog was chosen for its inhibited temperament, and mastered the task quite easily. The other dog, highly excitable, found the job of inhibiting six reflexes at once was just too difficult. It managed 2 minutes delay, but at 3 minutes went 'quite crazy, unceasingly and violently moving all parts of its body, howling, barking, and squealing intolerably ... an unceasing flow of saliva'. The dog eventually succeeded after Dr Petrova patiently reconditioned the original reflexes and then delayed one reflex at a time. She then upset both dogs with shock as a signal for food. This interfered with the inhibitory reflexes in the excitable dog, the excitatory reflexes in the inhibited one, so that two distinct types of 'neurosis' occurred for several months. Bromides (100 ml of 2 per cent KBr rectally, daily for 11 days) restored inhibition in the excitable dog; the dog that was already maximally inhibited eventually recovered on its own.

Comments

These lectures wonderfully convey Pavlov's common sense, even his sense of humour. He attempted a fully objective analysis of behavioural mechanisms, but he had little of the aridity and rigidity that this aim often entails.

In the final lectures, Pavlov questions some of his original assumptions. He wonders, although going beyond his evidence, if external inhibition from the investigatory reflex is not essentially the same as the internal inhibition found in extinction and differentiation. In either case, an unreinforced stimulus evokes inhibition. In fact, any stimulus paradoxically causes inhibition, but reinforcement or the prospect of reinforcement also produces excitation. Hence all inhibition is essentially the competitive inhibition of other reflexes. Yet equally, in some ways, inhibition resembles fear or caution.

Pavlov's approach is thoughtful, and his terminology – so arbitrary and theoretical in a textbook précis – seems much more convincing when applied to actual experiments. He concentrated on areas of behaviour only sketched by Western psychologists, and it should surely be possible to integrate the different approaches.

It is customary to draw a clear distinction between classical, Pavlovian conditioning, where a new stimulus is associated with an old response, and operant conditioning, where the next stimulus is a consequence of the response. Part of the distinction lies in the salivary glands. They are controlled by sympathetic and parasympathetic nerves, and it used to be thought that autonomic nerves were not subject to the same rules as the 'voluntary' nervous system – until reports from Miller and his colleagues (which they have regretfully been unable to confirm) suggested that heart rate, blood pressure, and other autonomic functions can sometimes be conditioned if there is 'biofeedback' of information about the results.

Tactile receptors in the mouth give this information for saliva anyway, and the distinction between types of conditioning can be overstated. Both methods lay almost as much emphasis on inhibition of responses as on their excitation. A fixed interval operant schedule and a Pavlovian delayed reflex lead to a similar type of response, in that output (saliva or lever-pressing) is low in the early phase of the interval, with a dramatic and easily measurable increase towards the end, when the animal can expect reinforcement.

A Pavlovian dog has to inhibit all responses except salivation; head-turning, barking, etc., are strictly unofficial, the dog has to stand patiently in its harness for a couple of hours a day and work off its energy in a frenzy afterwards.

Pavlov himself wondered uneasily whether the simple uniformity of reflexes is really due to the invariable structure of the nervous system, or whether it could possibly be to some extent an artefact. Could the uniform experimental procedures that are required to reveal the rules of conditioned reflexes be themselves responsible for shaping a rigid stereotyped pattern of cerebral functioning? It is surely an exaggerated worry, but a healthy one – I wonder if it has occurred to Skinner?

There are some awkward practical differences between Pavlovian and operant conditioning. In operant situations it is easy to attain a simple fixed ratio schedule where every fourth response is reinforced, although to put a rat straight from a 1:1 ratio to one of 1:50 or 1:100 leads straight to extinction. The Pavlovian reinforcement of every fourth *stimulus* is very difficult for dogs, although the analogy with the fixed response ratio does not seem too far-fetched. Perhaps the time-scale is too long, since an experienced dog can form a reflex after perhaps four or five stimuli, and can extinguish it just as fast.

When Pavlov used defensive reflexes, he was careful to use very mild stimuli, not for sentimental reasons but because excessively strong acid (as occasionally used by accident) or electric shock would not give him sufficiently consistent results.

Part 2. Motor–food conditioned reflexes

Conditioned reflex methods are widely used in the USSR in toxicology and pharmacology. For routine experiments dogs are less convenient than small rodents, but a rat's saliva is harder to measure, so Pavlov's successors developed the use of 'motor' conditioned reflexes for food or the avoidance of shock. The method most often cited is that of L. I. Kotliarevsky (1951).

Western scientists often justifiably complain that Soviet publications lack essential experimental detail, but Kotliarevsky's paper is reasonably explicit. He started by emphasising Pavlov's interest in new methods, including motor reflexes, tactfully supporting his director, Pavlov's pupil Ivanov-Smolensky, in his 'absolutely clear criticism of the idealist position held by certain of our scientists (Beritov, Orbeli, Anokhin)'. J. S. Beritashvili (Beritov is the Russian form of his name) later wrote an autobiographical essay (1966) giving an absorbing entry to quite a different literature.

Frolov's cross-feeding test

Kotliarevski actually describes four methods. Originally he used Iu. P. Frolov's cross-feeding test. This is analogous to shuttle-box avoidance: a wooden box is divided symmetrically into two, with a feeding trough and signal light at each end, a trapdoor in the central partition, and a mirror on the lid at 45° for watching the animal (Fig. 11.3). The rat or guinea-pig is allowed a day or two to explore the box, and to feed at troughs. A light or bell over the central partition signals that the experimenter is about to put in a piece of bread, meat, or carrot into the trough at the end where the animal is

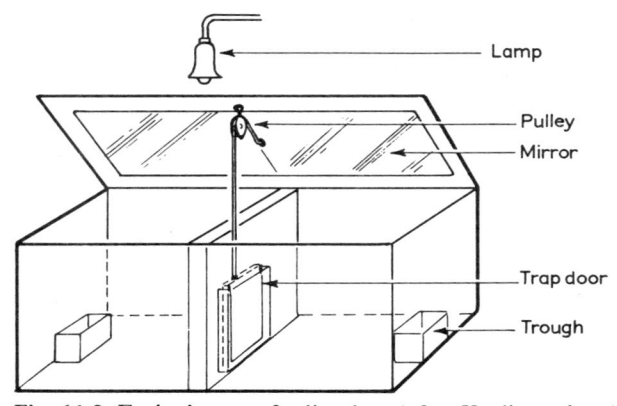

Fig. 11.3. Frolov's cross-feeding box (after Kotliarevsky, 1951).

not. *After* the animal has started moving towards it, the experimenter raises the trapdoor. An inhibitory conditioned reflex can be differentiated from the positive one by using an alternative stimulus (e.g. a buzzer) to signal that the trapdoor will remain closed.

Kotliarevsky found certain disadvantages in Frolov's method. Pavlov demanded that explanations should be both easily understood and biologically correct. But when the signal comes, the rat may have to leave one trough to approach the other. This is not simple, either to describe in (Pavlovian) physiological terms or for the animal to learn.

The experimenter might have to urge the animal towards the partition door, in case the conditioned stimulus becomes extinct for lack of reinforcement. On the other hand, if the animal is by the door, the experimenter cannot see when overt running begins. He has to start by pushing the animal away from the door, which hardly helps the rat to learn. The experimenter cannot observe the 'natural conditioned reflex' when the animal sees the food arrive, and the motor CR is 'all-or-nothing' and not easy to quantify.

One-cage motor–food reflex method

Kotliarevsky therefore tried using only one feeding trough. The trough is at one end of a long, brightly-lit box (see Fig. 7.3 on p. 90), but the rat spends most of its time in a small dark compartment at the other end. A small light over the trough becomes a signal that food is being put into it. The experimenter can see in the mirror how long the rat takes until it crosses the doorway of the compartment (the latency), runs to the trough and takes the food (running time). Rats generally snatch the food and carry it back to eat it in the compartment.

Kotliarevsky's method exploits the 'biological peculiarities' of nocturnal rodents to find a relatively constant starting position, without manhandling, and a straightforward run to a fixed goal is simpler both to learn and to explain. The approximate strength of the reflex can be estimated in terms of speed. Kotliarevsky was still not satisfied with the method. He still could not observe the 'natural' conditioned reflex to the first smell of food, and if the rat should hesitate at the trough, as it sometimes does, then does the reflex stop when the rat first reaches the trough or when it finally takes the food?

The inclined plane

Fadeyeva and Izergina (Kotliarevsky, 1951) therefore made the animal climb a slope of 30–35° to reach the trough (Fig. 11.4). The slope is made, presumably, of wire-mesh and is just uncomfortable enough for the animal to return to floor level to eat. The 'natural' reflex can be observed, and the latency of the CR is defined as the time from when the stimulus light goes on until the animal reaches the foot of the slope, and the running time until it reaches the top.

Conditioned reflexes 137

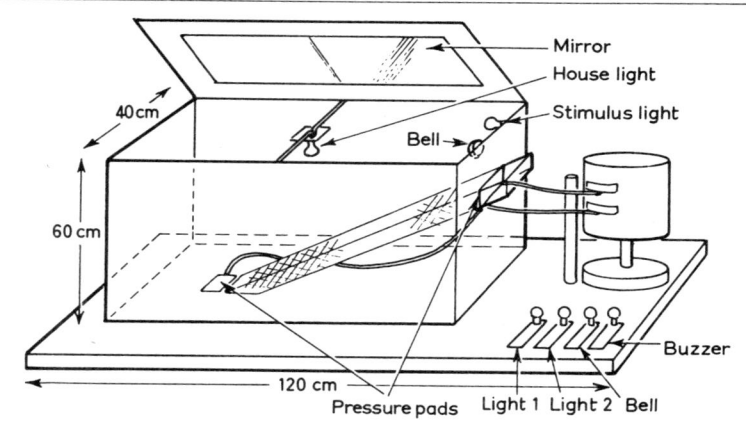

Fig. 11.4. Fadeyeva and Izergina's inclined plane (after Kotliarevsky, 1951).

The difficulty of climbing the slope should also allow any inco-ordination or slowing down of movement to be assessed (cf. p. 70), though this could occur without much harm to conditioned reflexes (in the sense that saliva output, for instance, would be unaltered), so that any toxic action could be misinterpreted.

In these last two methods, differentiation is achieved by an absence of reinforcement, an empty food trough.

The 'head-push' method

Kotliarevsky and his colleagues developed yet another method, putting an albino rat into a small wooden box with an even smaller compartment just big enough to hold a large rat. Presumably the rat enters the small compartment as the first part of the reflex. Once inside, its head rests against a glass door just in front of the food trough. The 'natural' reflex, when the experimenter puts food into the trough, is for the rat to push its head against the door, open it, and take the food. When the conditioned stimulus (a light) goes on, the house lights go off, and up to five auditory signals can also be given, including frequencies inaudible to man (rats squeak at up to 50–60 kHz). Any stimulus operates a 'reflex chronometer', giving times accurate to a few hundredths of a second.

As the rat pushes against the glass door the force of its push is recorded (in terms of the height of a column of coloured liquid), and therefore a crude but literal measure of the 'strength' of the reflex is obtained (cf. Conger's harnesses, 1951; p. 220). After the usual two or three half-hour periods, the conditioned reflex is formed and the rat pushes the door before the food is delivered.

Kotliarevsky summarises by saying that Frolov's cross-feeding method demonstrates the applicability of Pavlov's concepts to the motor behaviour of white rats. But to study '... the general motor conditioned reaction of the animal, especially in the ... tempo of movements and ... their coordination, the one can achieve the greatest effect with the aid of ... the one-cage method (variant of Kotliarevsky) and ... of Fadeyeva and Izergina. If the problem ... is ... the relatively local motor conditioned reflex of the animal normally and in pathological conditions, then the method most adequate ... is the last variant of Kotliarevsky ... a definite, relatively organic motor conditioned reaction ... in the form of the opening of the door ... with the head.'

Application of conditioned reflexes in toxicology

In the Soviet Union, a single scientist usually seems to become responsible for the entire toxicology of a given chemical, which must give an excellent education but may leave room for specialisation in standard histological and biochemical as well as behavioural techniques. However, 'the method of Kotliarevsky (1951)', presumably the one-chamber test, is straightforward enough, and it gets results.

Trichloroethylene is a useful solvent in engineering and dry-cleaning, and is also a useful anaesthetic 'gas' in childbirth. In the USA and Great Britain the highest concentration of the vapour that people can be exposed to for long periods at work is 535 mg/m^3 (100 parts per million), but this concentration is not completely without effects. N. V. Bannova (1961) was concerned to find the threshold of effect of trichloroethylene, and she exposed rats to 5 or 50 mg/m^3 for 5 hours a day for 6 months. At the lower concentration, rats kept within the range of variation of control rats. After 2 weeks at the higher level, there were changes in behaviour, in EEG patterns from chronically implanted extradural electrodes, and histologically in thickenings on the apical dendrites of many pyramidal neurons. Behaviourally, the latent period before a response was lengthened (perhaps the rats were drowsy after breathing an anaesthetic in a quiet exposure chamber?), with a weaker motor reaction to bell and to light, with certain reflexes lost, differentiation interrupted, and the appearance of equalising and paradoxical phases. These phenomena were as defined by Pavlov (see pp. 127 and 131), but Bannova did not describe any further details of her observations. On the other hand, Horváth and Formánek (1959) found exposed rats to respond more quickly to the stimulus. However, they too found impaired differentiation, for rats also responded more to the wrong stimulus or without any stimulus at all, especially the rat with the strongest excitatory and weakest inhibitory constitution.

The use of conditioned reflexes in toxicology (mainly of pesticides) was reviewed by L. I. Medved, Elizabeth Spynu, and Iuri Kagan (1964) in English. They found motor reflexes were more useful than salivation in small mammals, including cats (which are exceptionally sensitive). Motor defensive reflexes, in other words conditioned avoidance in a shuttle-box, were the

Conditioned reflexes 139

quickest. In rats, a motor–food reflex could take 4 months to become well established though Z. E. Grigoriev found that it was more sensitive to disruption by acetone when developing than when fully formed.

The organophosphorus pesticide parathion, like many others, inhibits the cholinesterase enzymes in blood and brain, so that cholinergic function can be exaggerated (in fact there seems to be a large functional reserve, since even Medved and his colleagues find enzyme action can be somewhat inhibited without behavioural effect).

Cats given 5 mg/kg of parathion by mouth or breathing it as dust delayed responding, especially to 'weak' stimuli such as a light for the 2 days after dosing, and running time was also slower. A blue light was differentiated from white (presumably by intensity rather than colour, since most mammals are colour-blind), but dosed cats continued to respond to both stimuli. However, since the positive response was delayed while its extinction was accelerated, parathion was said to increase internal inhibition. Parathion at 3 mg/kg only reduced the response to weak stimuli in cats with a 'strong' nervous system – these are individuals which are normally quick to develop conditioned reflexes in general and differentiations in particular.

In conclusion, despite the differences in terminology, and the lack of detail in the published results, it seems that Soviet investigators use methods that in practice are very similar to those used in the West. But their use of the methods is somewhat different. They tend to use low doses for extended periods. Until recently, at least, they seemed not to back up their subjective impressions with statistics (though here they are in good company), and they sometimes take systematic notice of differences in individual 'personality'.

Summary

Conditioned reflexes (CRs) and other forms of learned behaviour are largely similar phenomena, but the jargon (in *italic type*) is sufficiently different to require a separate chapter.

Pavlov's observation of behaviour was shrewd, but his formal analysis was confined to a single component, the secretion of saliva, because it is easy to measure quantitatively and unlikely to cause anthropomorphic misunderstanding. *Unconditioned reflexes* mean, strictly, innate salivation to food or dilute acid in the mouth, but usually refer to *'natural'* CRS, salivation evoked in adult dogs by the smell or sight of food. Any other detectable stimulus comes to elicit salivation if it regularly occurs before or during food or acid presentation (but not if it ends too long before, and only very temporarily if it occurs after), i.e. it becomes an *excitatory conditioned stimulus* (CS) for an *alimentary* or *defence* reflex. A stimulus for another reflex (investigatory, hunting, sexual, etc.) *inhibits* such salivation *externally*. If the positive CS is not *reinforced* by food (*extinction*), or if an additional or alternative stimulus is associated with non-reinforcement, salivation is inhibited *internally* (*differentiation*). If the dog cannot *discriminate* easily between the excitatory and inhibitory CS, pathological overexcitation is likely, and all CRs may be inhibited. The inhibition from a negative CS *irradiates* outwardly in time and space, best shown when a tactile inhibitory CS on, say, the dog's shoulder is *differentiated* from a series of excitory tactile CSs on other parts of the body. Excitatory stimuli have an inhibitory after-effect, and vice versa, causing the brief *induction* of increased response to a CS of opposite sign.

Animals have individual temperaments, corresponding quite well to the four classical humours, which can be ascribed to moderate or extreme tendencies to excitation or inhibition.

Nowadays it is usual to observe *conditioned motor reflexes* rather than salivation, using the movements of small laboratory animals to test drugs, or other chemicals (pesticides, solvents, heavy metals). A commonly used method is one of several described by Kotliarevsky (1951), and is similar in principle to many conventional Western methods. An illuminated box has a food trough, signal light, and buzzer at one end, and a small dark compartment at the other. A rat is likely to spend most of its time in the dark compartment. The response to the excitatory CS is to enter the illuminated part of the box, run to the trough, fetch the food, and return to the dark compartment. An inhibitory CR can be differentiated by not giving food.

TWELVE

Operant conditioning

For ha'pence and for kicks

Operant conditioning is a set of methods which, more than any others, allows precise experimental control of the stimuli that the animals respond to, and of the responses they make. For in the appetitive phase, behaviour is a flexible approach to definite objectives. 'Behaviour is governed by its consequences' (Skinner, 1966), and any action which is successful will therefore be reinforced, i.e. will reappear when the situation is repeated; other actions will disappear. Operant conditioning is a way of persuading an animal to perform behavioural units which are objective and unambiguous to record – the animal is trained to do something (press a lever, turn a wheel, peck a disc, and so on) which can conveniently be detected automatically so that an electrical pulse is used to record the response and trigger the reinforcement. The units can be made quantitative by being small in relation to the animal's total output, so small that it is their distribution in time that becomes the interesting variable.

Positive reinforcements can be anything the experimenter thinks the animal needs. Negative reinforcement includes anything (like shock) the experimenter expects the animal to escape from, or to avoid altogether if given the opportunity, and is described in Chapters 15–17. The use of operant methods for measuring discrimination between stimuli is included in Chapter 14. Some theoretical issues are discussed in Chapter 13.

Apparatus: the 'Skinner Box' and its control

Behaviour in an operant situation is moulded unusually closely to the surrounding apparatus. Fig. 12.1 represents this diagrammatically in a version typical of that used for rats. Pigeons are used equally commonly, and their apparatus is similar in its main features. The 'Skinner Box', named after B. F. Skinner who virtually invented the subject, is a box perhaps 40 × 20 × 20 cm. A side wall is hinged as a door and is of transparent Perspex, there is a house-light in the roof, and a grid floor wired to a scrambler for shock (apparatus for electroschock is described on p. 195).

The box itself is placed inside another, to insulate the animal as far as possible from external sights, sounds, and smells. There is a tinted window in the door, in case the experimenter should be so eccentric as to wish to observe the animal. A ventilating fan also provides a background masking

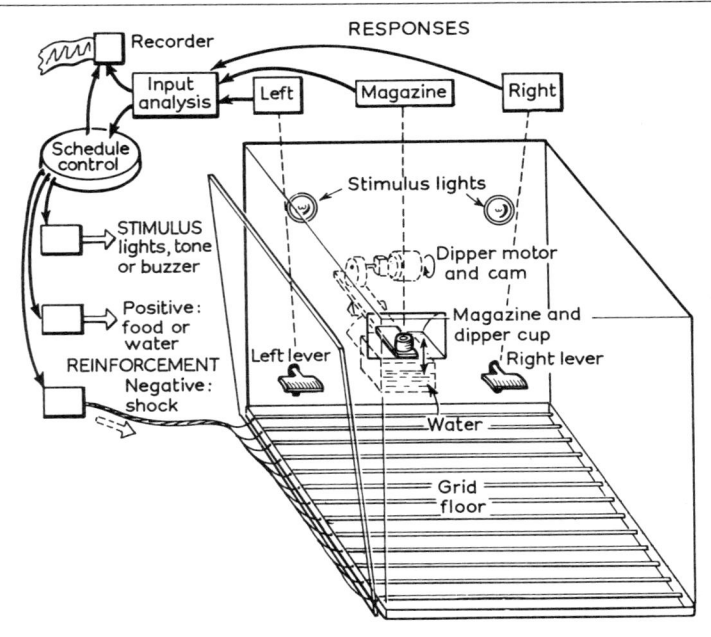

Fig. 12.1. Diagram of a Skinner box for rats and the main components of its control system.

noise. At the business end of the box, one wall contains a magazine, a small compartment where 'positive reinforcement' is delivered. Several devices are possible: a solenoid can deliver a food pellet with a slight clatter, or a small electric motor drives an eccentric cam through a single revolution, making just enough noise to act as a conditioned stimulus. The cam may dip a spoon into a tank of water or sweetened diluted condensed milk and then raise it to the animal, giving a rat from 0·01 to 0·1 ml of fluid. Alternatively a tray containing mash for a rat or grain for a pigeon may rise, give the animal a brief chance to take its reward, and be lowered out of reach again.

The magazine may have an access door which the animal can easily push aside to signal that it has come to collect its pay. On either side are two 'manipulanda' which operate microswitches and certify that the animal has performed its response. These may be levers pointing towards the rat or bars parallel to the wall or there may be one large wheel (see Fig. 16.2 on p. 214). Pigeons peck at a small disc or key set flush into the wall and operating a contact switch. Above each lever is a stimulus light, and the box may also be equipped to give audible stimuli, a pure tone and/or a buzzer.

The control of the relationship between all these inputs and outputs is a complex job. In principle, the experimenter could of course sit and watch through the peephole. He could count the lever-presses, time them on a

Operant conditioning 143

stopwatch, and press a button to deliver the reinforcement. In practice, this is just what he actually does. In the early stages, the first time the animal is put in the Skinner box, a person is still far more efficient than any computer at observing what the animal is doing and patiently channelling it towards the desired pattern.

Once the animal can press the lever adequately and take the appropriate reinforcement, the schedules become too laborious for a civilised human being to control (he would lack the uniformity and accuracy demanded in any case). Electromechanical and electronic systems have been made commercially, and recently mini-computers have been introduced for on-line control of several Skinner boxes, and to record the animals' responses and analyse them statistically.

In the old days, the only formal measures that were possible were total counts of reinforcements and of responses in each session. These give relatively trivial information. A complete record of the performance is obtained on a 'cumulative recorder' where a stepping motor moves a pen fractionally (<1 mm) across a strip of paper to mark each response by the animal. The paper is pulled along at a constant speed, so that the response

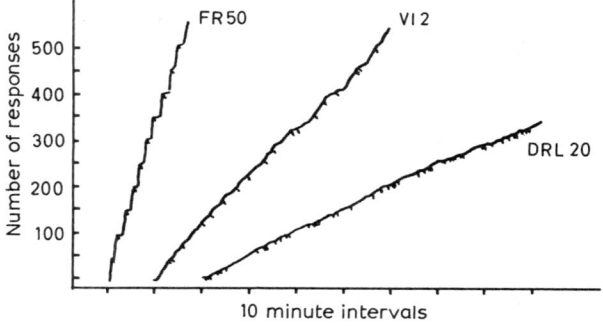

Fig. 12.2. Tracings of typical cumulative records on three operant schedules (from Morrison and Armitage, 1967). Each response moves the pen upwards on paper travelling across at a steady rate, so that the more frequent the response, the steeper the slope of the trace. Reinforcement (access to a drop of water) is indicated by a downward flick. FR 50 – every fiftieth response is reinforced. VI 2 – responses are reinforced at variable intervals averaging 2 minutes. DRL 20 – responses are reinforced only after an interval without responses of at least 20 seconds.

rate is shown by the slope of the line over an appropriate time – a horizontal line suggests that the rat is lying on its back having a quiet snooze. Reinforcements are recorded by a downward flick of the pen. Fig. 12.2 shows segments from the trace of rats' performance on three different schedules (defined later in this chapter).

On the FR50, for example, the rat responds very fast 50 times, then a little pen stroke downwards shows that it received its drop of water and a short horizontal line marks the pause while it drank and licked its lips before starting again. The other schedules led, on average, to lower rates of lever pressing, as shown by the average slope of the trace, but with bursts of faster responding that (on the DRL schedule) actually postponed the reinforcement. The interpretation of this kind of trace can be somewhat subjective, but it is still a most ingenious device for compressing the maximum information on to the minimum of paper.

What are the data required?

The cumulative record nevertheless remains raw data, and if each animal responds several thousand times a session every day for weeks or months, even an economical display produces an awful lot of paper to be carefully examined. A level of information is needed intermediate between this and the crude totals of responses per session. Statistics are the only way of summarising bulky information into a convenient form. If a rat had to press a lever 50 times for each pellet of food, you would want to know how long it took, in the form of the mean and standard deviation of the interval between reinforcements; the variation should become smaller as the animal learns the technique. A muscle relaxant drug making the animal feel slightly weak might either slow responding, or make it more variable as the rat alternately makes an effort or flops. Fifty responses are fairly hard work, it might be interesting to plot the graph of interreinforcement interval against time within sessions – intervals ought to lengthen as the animal gets tired. But they would also do so if the reinforcement is either too large or too small – the rat would either become less hungry with substantial meals, or it

fed-up with a tiny reward

would feel 'fed-up' at having to work so hard for such a tiny reward. In these cases there should be a longer pause after reinforcement, whereas fatigue should slow down responding once it has started. So pause-length and response-rate should be measured separately. There is another complication, for a rat rattling away at top speed might overshoot, and press an extra two or three times after reinforcement is delivered. So the post-reinforcement pause starts when the rat pushes aside the trapdoor into the food compartment and lasts until the first lever-press, while response rates are measured from then until reinforcement.

Skinner may be right when he says (1966) that an experimentally-induced change in a single animal's performance is still a change, and that there is therefore no need for statistics on large numbers of animals. But, even if you can be sure that a single animal is typical of all animals and not a freak, you still need to ensure that your change is a change and not a random fluctuation. So you must analyse the performance of even your selected individual.

The size of the prize: reinforcement

The layman thinks that operant conditioning by psychologists is for food. The layman is often right but for practical reasons solid rewards are less convenient than liquid. A rat might take half an hour to eat a large cube of diet 41B; while there must be a lower limit, a pittance too small to be worth the effort, a general rule is that the smaller the unit of reward, the more uniformly is the animal likely to respond through the session. Only uniform responses provide stable units for measuring behaviour. Commercial 45 mg tablets are often used, though inevitably somewhat expensive. Tablets could be made from sugar, for even well-fed rats (and children) work surprisingly hard for candy, but only up to the point where satiation sets in; they do not respond uniformly for long. Liquid reinforcement is more convenient, either water or condensed milk. The remainder of the animal's daily bread is weighed out as a square meal in the home cage after the training session.

Pigeons are usually reinforced with grains of corn or wheat, and rats can be fed on similarly irregular pellets or dry powder in the same way. A tray carrying the food is raised and lowered so that the animal is offered its prize briefly before it is whisked away like the drinks at a Scots laird's cocktail party.

If an animal is to work consistently for food, it has to be consistently hungry. Hunger cannot be measured directly, of course, but the difference between its actual bodyweight after restricting its diet and an estimate of the weight it would have attained without deprivation gives a fair idea. Adult rats or pigeons are fed a weighed amount of food, about half their normal consumption, once a day until they reach 80 per cent of their free-feeding weight. Although a stress at first, animals adapt well to the routine provided that on all 7 days a week the meals are properly related to bodyweight.

Water deprivation is easier to arrange, as the deficit occurs earlier. Rats may die after 2 or 3 days without water, but survive a couple of weeks without food. 'Dieting down' is therefore unnecessary, you merely remove the water-bottle every evening if the laboratory temperature and humidity – and the animal's state of dehydration and thirst – do not fluctuate too widely.

Other rewards have been used successfully, in fact, almost anything the animal needs or wants can in principle be used as reinforcement, if the experimenter can only think of it first. Weiss and Laties (1960; see p. 93) kept rats in the cold, and trained them to switch on an infrared heat lamp for 2 seconds at a time. Kavanau (1963: see p. 91) trained deermice (*Peromyscus maniculatus*) to switch off a motor that forced them to run in an activity wheel and later to switch it on again for themselves. Rats and monkeys have been trained to obtain drug injections or to stimulate their brains with sub-millivolt electric shocks. Monkeys in dark enclosed boxes work merely to open a window for a few seconds. They will work for peanuts, both directly and for tokens which they can cash for peanuts in a slot machine.

It is interesting that satiation does not set in for money as it does for the food that the money will buy. The monkeys will learn almost anything to earn a fast buck and make themselves millionaires. But tokens do not buy them their freedom.

Shaping the response: operant or classical?

Rats need time to explore the Skinner box. Once the rat is accustomed to the box, to eating the new pellets, and to the noise made by the motor or solenoid delivering them, the experimenter can 'shape' the desired operant response. Conventionally, the experimenter presses a button for reinforcement when the rat faces the lever ... approaches it ... touches it ... presses it tentatively ... until the rat can operate the lever for itself.

It is, of course, possible just to put the rat in the box, switch everything on, and let the animal discover for itself. Many will learn, eventually, but many will have to be discarded. If the box and food magazine have not yet become familiar, a step on a lever which suddenly gives way with a simultaneous sudden clatter from a solenoid can sometimes make a timid rat run to the back corner and crouch petrified for many minutes.

In pigeons, pecking is the response normally selected, a response used spontaneously for feeding and if necessary as an aggressive and antipredator weapon. In the Skinner box it is not directed at the ground but at a disc in the wall. To guide the bird to peck in this unusual position, a grain of corn is lightly cemented to the disc. By the time the pigeon has pecked it off, it has learned that a peck at the disc brings the tray of corn to the dispenser compartment. It is necessary to give the pigeon some previous experience in the Skinner box, to explore it, and to become accustomed to feeding from the dispenser.

In theory (Skinner, 1966), the response can, and indeed should be an artificial one, entirely conditioned by the experimenter. In practice of course, the experimenter has to start with something the animal does of its own accord, rather than wait weeks for a rat to peck with its nose, but in principle any action can be conditioned provided that action (and no other) is reinforced.

This hypothesis has been questioned. Sevenster's sticklebacks and Shettleworth's hamsters (p. 108) argue against it. Detailed observations of 'autoshaping' in pigeons by Bruce Moore (1973) and by H. M. Jenkins (1973) suggest overwhelmingly that the conditioned response is related to the reinforcement by classical Pavlovian, not operant, conditioning. If the pigeon is deprived of food, he opens the bill just before it hits the disc and snaps it shut when retracting it. If the bird is thirsty and expecting water, the bill is almost closed and stays longer on the disc while the bird makes swallowing movements. If the bird associates one stimulus with water reinforcement and another with food, he drinks at the first and pecks the second. If mated pairs are separated by a trapdoor, the male birds develop courtship movements which are directed at the stimulus light (bowing and cooing to it and, later, making the nest call to it) if this makes the trapdoor open and give access to the female. Hungry birds that have previously seen the light associated with food, peck at it the first time they are allowed close enough. Indeed, so little is the peck controlled by results and so strong is the Pavlovian conditioning, that pigeons pecked the stimulus light hundreds of times despite being on a schedule where the reward was delivered only if the bird did *not* peck it. Moore describes several experiments suggesting that operant conditioning in the strict sense does not really exist in the Skinner box. Pigeons can only use something like an element already existing in the species' repertoire and apply it to the stimulus symbolising the relevant reinforcement.

Rats certainly possess spontaneous responses which can be exploited for autoshaping. They bite and pull downwards on a string which the experimenter has thoughtfully tied to the lever ... Better, they examine and manipulate a new object. If the lever is removed from the Skinner box during the rat's first familiarisation sessions and is then replaced ... the rat autoshapes itself.

When the animal has responded a few times and has been rewarded every time, a start can be made on the desired schedule.

Continuous reinforcement (CRF)

Reinforcement with food (or whatever) on every single response is necessary as a stage in training, but is too simple to be very informative as a test. It might be used to detect satiation (which could be quite quick on CRF) or total anaesthesia, perhaps. Goldberg and Chappell (1967) used it to measure the effects of air pollution by carbon monoxide. After accustoming rats to food deprivation for 23 hours a day, they were trained on continuous reinforcement. A single 55-minute exposure to 250 parts per million (ppm) of carbon monoxide while the rats were earning and eating their daily bread caused a slight, temporary increase in response rate, but a reduction after three sessions. A carbon monoxide concentration of 500 ppm caused only a deeper depression of responding, but on subsequent pollution-free days, consumption went up beyond control levels; no doubt the rats might have been hungrier than usual.

Schedules sometimes leave room for differences in the pattern of responding, and individual animals may characteristically adopt one of the alternatives and stick to it indefinitely. Continuous reinforcement is commonly used with the variation that a discrimination is required in addition. Will (1974) trained rats on a schedule where a 1 kHz tone sounded for 5 seconds every minute, and during the tone each lever-press delivered a food pellet until the supply was exhausted. Fig. 12.3 shows the 'strategies' that can be

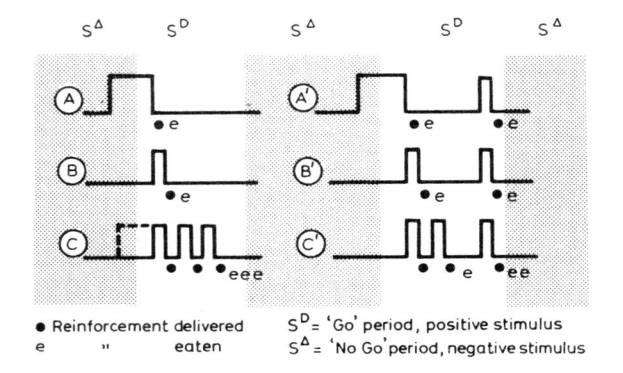

• Reinforcement delivered S^D = 'Go' period, positive stimulus
e " eaten S^Δ = 'No Go' period, negative stimulus

Fig. 12.3. Strategies of operant responding on a simple discrimination schedule (after Will, 1974). A sugar pellet is delivered (●) every time the rat lets go the lever while a tone sounds (5 seconds in every minute). Rats may hold the lever down in anticipation (A) or wait before pressing the lever (B), in either case consuming (E) the pellet before responding again. Alternatively, the rat may press twice or more and then consume both or all pellets at leisure (C). Some rats manage a further response within the 5 seconds 'Go' (S^D) period (A', B', C').

adopted. In A, the rat starts to press the lever during the silent period, and uses the stimulus as a signal to let go, obtaining one pellet which is then eaten. In B the rat waits until the tone sounds before pressing briefly. In C, whenever the response begins, several responses are made in rapid succession, collecting several pellets to be consumed at leisure. On any strategy the more experienced rats may respond a second time (A', B', C',) during the tone and a few change from A or B to C, but in general the strategies were remarkably stable once started. With a fixed number of pellets to be obtained, the only consequence of the different strategies is the length of session, so that although there is no great incentive to change, neither is there any to stay. The relationship between these strategies and Pavlovian 'temperaments' (p. 132) might be interesting.

Extinction

If constant reinforcement is followed by a period when lever-pressing, etc., is suddenly not reinforced at all, then eventually lever-pressing will be extinguished: that is, the rat eventually gives up. But the first response to the non-arrival of reinforcement is to press the lever faster and faster, just like a person who suspects that the (expletive) contraption has broken down again (perhaps the human reaction is as automatic as the animal's but we can rationalise it in words).

Adult rats that had been treated with reserpine in infancy did not adapt to the extinction situation as well as controls. Kulkarni, Thompson, and Shideman (1966) injected rats with 0·1 mg/kg of reserpine every day from 11 to 30 days of age. Catecholamine concentrations in the brain fell to about 30 per cent of control levels within a couple of days, and returned to normal 10 days after dosing stopped. When the rats were about 3 months old, they were dieted to 80 per cent of their free-feeding weight, and trained on constant reinforcement for 45-mg food pellets; sessions lasted until they obtained 100 pellets, and each rat's time for this stabilised after 4 to 6 days. In the next 3 days, the number of lever-presses in the 30 seconds before and after the seventy-fifth pellet was compared (the 30-seconds-before score was actually averaged from a 2-minute period) – the ratio should be 1 : 1. On each of the final 3 days, each rat received 75 pellets, followed by 2 minutes' extinction. As expected, the response rate in the first 30 seconds of non-reward more than doubled in all rats, but in control rats it rose little on the second day, and by the third, response rates started to fall within 30 seconds. The brain chemistry of rats that had been reserpinised in youth had long returned to normal, but they made this burst of frustrated responding as much on the second and third days of extinction as the controls had on the first. They were unable to learn efficiently to inhibit a response that had become unproductive.

The method sounds attractive as a quick and simple way of testing for some kinds of drug effects but (for what this is worth) a colleague of mine has not found it easy to replicate.

Fixed ratio (FR)

Continuous reinforcement is a poor bargain for the experimenter, the animal is overpaid for too little work, and various expedients have been developed to improve productivity. The simplest is to make the animal respond not once but many times for each unit of reinforcement; 50 times is common (labelled FR50 in the jargon).

A large ratio should not be started abruptly, for it would look to the animal like extinction, but should be introduced over one or two sessions. For a few times, the animal gets only one pellet for two presses ... for 4 ... 8 ... 16 ... until it is rattling away as fast as its little legs will carry it. In effect the unit of behaviour on FR is not the single lever-press but the series, and FR characteristically induces a very fast rate of response. The animal may not count precisely the right number of responses but respond, perhaps, for about the right length of time; nevertheless, if reinforcement fails to arrive, the animal stops after making only slightly too many responses.

Harbans Lal and Roger Brown (1969) used short FR schedules (they could have used others) to find an equivalent to what happens when we 'feel ill'. Rats were trained on FR4 for food or FR5 for water and then injected with a bacterial endotoxin from *Escherichia coli*. It almost completely suppressed responding even at low doses where the rats' body temperature did not go up. After a second injection responding was no longer so greatly affected. However, the rats ate and drank nearly as much as usual in their home-cage immediately after the operant session, and there was little change in lever-pressing to avoid shock. So it looks as if rats lose their 'initiative' and 'energy' as a result of some infections rather than their appetite, or their ability to work if they really have to.

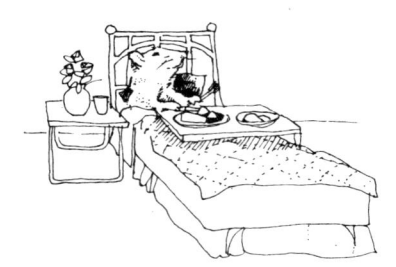

losing energy rather than appetite from an infection

Fixed interval (FI)

Instead of scheduling a set number of responses before reinforcement, the experimenter can set a time. In fixed interval (FI) a clock is set at, say, 1 minute, so that in the first 60 seconds after reinforcement, any responses will be ineffective, but the first response from the sixty-first second onwards will be rewarded. This schedule is conventionally labelled FI 1; the number can refer to minutes or seconds.

Starting from CRF, only the longer interval schedules need be introduced in stages. 'Frustration-responding' will interfere less than extinction after a long interval. In the first half of a typical well-learned fixed interval, response rates are low and intermittent, but accelerate up to a very high rate by the time that reinforcement is due. The trace on a cumulative recorder therefore takes on a characteristically 'scalloped' appearance – horizontal at first but curving round almost to the vertical towards the end of the interval.

Mescaline and LSD illustrate drug effects on FI. They are both hallucinogenic drugs but their physiological effects are not quite the same and they seem not to induce the same subjective experiences. H. A. Tilson and Sheldon Sparber (1973) trained three rats thoroughly on intervals of FI 15 ... 30 ... 45 ... 60 ... and eventually 75 seconds. At the fairly low dose, for animals, of 15 µg/kg, LSD increased responding in all parts of the interval. At lower doses (5 µg/kg) LSD had no consistent effect; at higher doses up to 150 µg/kg, it tended to reduce responding (presumably the rats were freaked out). On the other hand, mescaline caused dose-related (3–12 mg/kg) increases in responding in the first 15 seconds of each interval (where responding is normally almost non-existent), but nevertheless reduced the (normally high) rates in the final 15 seconds, and generally flattened the usual Fixed Interval scalloping. Dexamphetamine acted a little like LSD: low doses of 0.15 to 0.48 mg/kg increased response rates throughout (the stimulant action outweighing the appetite suppression), while a dose of 0.96 mg/kg increased the low and reduced the high response rates of the first and final 15 seconds respectively, so that the average rate was not much changed. However, the pharmacological mechanism of this action must be different from that of LSD, since rats tolerant to one drug were not tolerant to the other, and dexamphetamine is not hallucinogenic (some related drugs are). Rats tolerant to mescaline, however, were slightly tolerant to both the other drugs.

Variable ratio (VR)

In real life, the cat does not catch the mouse after a set number of jumps, or at a set time after the previous mouse. The precise schedule will vary pseudo-randomly: there may well be regularities in the ratio or interval actually required, but the pattern is too complex for the cat to predict. A similarly pseudo-random operant schedule is not likely to represent real life, but it can provide a useful laboratory model where reinforcements may come predictably on average, but unpredictably in detail.

A variable ratio of 6 responses (VR 6), therefore, will require an average of 6 responses for each reinforcement, but successive single pellets of food might follow 4, 9, 2, 6, and 9 responses respectively. Unfortunately, VR schedules turn out not to be very useful, since animals tend to respond at high rates interspersed with sporadic pauses (but see p. 189).

Variable interval (VI)

Variable intervals are far more useful. In a variable interval of 1 minute (VI 1) the average interval between reinforcements is 60 seconds, but the actual successive intervals may be e.g. 72, 96, 20, and 52 seconds. The animal cannot easily follow such a rhythm as this, so it cannot predict when any response may bring reinforcement, but there is no penalty for trying your luck and animals tend to respond at a fairly steady rate, neither fast nor slow, but whenever something might turn up.

In operant experiments in animals, nicotine often acts as a stimulant somewhat like amphetamine, although the former is thought to act partly by imitating acetylcholine in parts of the brain, and the latter by releasing noradrenaline. Morrison (1968) tested the cholinergic mechanism behind changes in VI performance. Four rats were deprived of water 21 hours a day for 5 days a week, and given access to water for 90 minutes in a Skinner box, 90 minutes in their home cage, and from Friday to Sunday afternoon. The first two sessions were on CRF, 0·1 ml water for each lever-press, the next seven sessions served to train the rats on a 2-minute variable interval schedule, and then testing could begin. Subcutaneous saline injections were given just before the sessions on Tuesdays and Thursdays, drugs on Wednesdays and Fridays, and the total number of responses counted every 10 minutes. A dose of 200 μg/kg of nicotine hydrogen tartrate increased the rate of responding by as much as 80 per cent at its peak, smaller doses (50–100 μg/kg) somewhat less. At 400 μg/kg nicotine reduced responding in the first 10 minutes: perhaps even rats accustomed to nicotine suffered the equivalent of nausea or other cholinergic side-effects. The fall was followed by a rise as high as after the 200-μg/kg dose, and a final fall back to control levels by 90 minutes after injection.

Physostigmine, in a dose just enough to inhibit the enzymes metabolising acetylcholine, made little change in response rates by itself but inhibited nicotine's increases in response rates, and potentiated the initial fall from the 400-μg/kg dose. Neostigmine, a quaternary anticholinesterase which does not penetrate into the brain, had no effect. So it seems that part of nicotine's effect depends on the acetylcholine it releases in the brain.

Differential reinforcement of low rates of response (DRL)

On interval schedules reinforcement is not given until a set time has passed, but although the animal gains no advantage from responding before this, there is no penalty either. A harder task for an animal to learn is one where premature responses set the clock back to zero. If the schedule is DRL 10, the animal has to wait at least 10 seconds after reinforcement before pressing the lever again. A response after 8 seconds starts the count all over again, so the animal has to wait 18 seconds in all – and more if it should respond prematurely again.

DRL is not difficult to learn in principle, but it is difficult in practice because the animal has to learn both to respond and not to respond. The animal is in a state of mild but steadily increasing conflict – to press or not yet to press – without external cues to guide it. A useful way of analysing DRL performance is therefore to classify the responses by the delay since the previous reinforcement. There might be two classes of success, one for a direct hit on a 20-second target (say 20–23 seconds delay); and the other for responses delayed longer than necessary (more than 23 seconds). Premature responses might be classified as near misses, where the animal had the patience to wait 17 seconds, but not quite long enough to meet the

20-second criterion, and as two very premature classes, say 0 to 10 and 10 to 17 seconds.

A classification like this helped Keith Extance (unpublished) to a sensitive measure of small doses of scopolamine. After a fairly high dose of 0·4 mg/kg, DRL performance was badly disrupted, but after lower doses, the total response rate was not greatly altered, and the rats obtained nearly as many reinforcements as usual. However, there was a significantly lower ratio of direct hits to near misses, and this was dose-related down to as low as 0·05 mg/kg. It seems that scopolamine, and perhaps other cholinergic blocking drugs, may interfere with a rat's ability to withhold a response, or with whatever a rat does to mark the passage of time.

Some kinds of operant experiment are still best appreciated by simple inspection of the cumulative record. One example concerns hallucinogenic drugs. By definition, hallucinations are subjective and curiously intangible. Experiments to understand the phenomenon therefore have to be carried out in man. These have severe limitations, not only to minimise the obvious dangers, but because the mere suggestion that the research concerns subjective effects will itself help to provoke them, even if the next tablet is a placebo. Animal experiments could be useful: it is not unethical if you forget to tell them what you are giving them, you can give higher doses, and so on. But you need a way of telling whether the drug that the animal has had is hallucinogenic or not.

Maybe rats do not have enough brains to have hallucinations, but there might be a behavioural or neurophysiological test which would be diagnostic: an effect produced by all hallucinogenic drugs and by no others. John Smythies and his colleagues have looked for years for such a test or combination of tests, and Smythies, Johnson, and Bradley (1967) found one possibility in a characteristic effect of mescaline on a DRL 15 schedule. On a fairly low dose, 12·5 mg/kg, a rat behaves quite as usual for a while, with a low but steady rate of lever-pressing. Then quite suddenly it ceases to press the lever at all. After a period without a single response, or the odd one or two followed by another fit of absent-mindedness, the rat returns to typically accurate responding as suddenly and completely as it stopped.

The same pattern was found with mescaline by Webster, Willinsky, Herring, and Walters (1971), but not often when they extended the investigation to another supposed hallucinogen. They gave various doses of an extract from marihuana, Δ^1-tetrahydrocannabinol (Δ^1-THC) but only twenty-two of their forty-nine records showed any disruption of DRL 10 performance, and of these only four were like mescaline with an abrupt halt to responding and an equally abrupt return. This stop-start effect is not as characteristic of THC as it is of mescaline: fourteen cases may represent an extra-powerful effect (see Fig. 12.4), as the rats stopped responding and did not start within the hour, two others represent a weak one, as the rats merely slowed down, and two more represented an amphetamine-like rise in

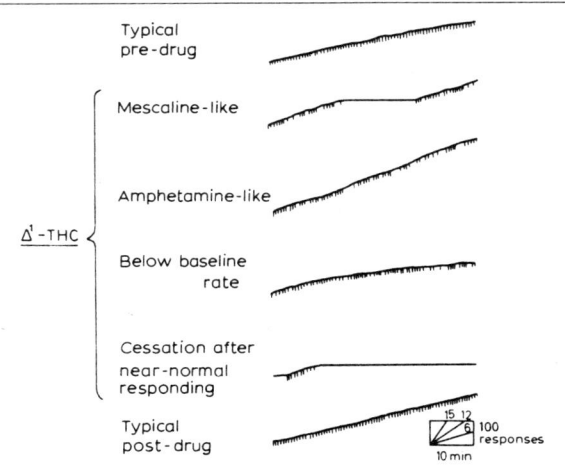

Fig. 12.4. Response patterns in four rats given various doses of Δ^1-Tetrahydrocannabinol (THC) (after Webster *et al.*, 1971). Effects of THC in different individuals mimic those typical of other drugs.

response rate without reinforcement. Either stop-start on DRL is too sporadic to be a reliable test of anything (although people also differ widely in liability to hallucinations), or Δ^1-THC is only a feeble hallucinogen.

Comparison of some simple schedules

Different schedules are obviously suited to reveal different effects. On fixed ratio, the animal will be reinforced most by responding as fast as possible, so there is little room for a rise in rate, and several possible causes of a fall (direct motor effects, appetite, diversion to other kinds of behaviour, and so on). A high response rate would be a waste of effort on interval schedules. On fixed interval, it would be difficult to detect or interpret a general rise or fall in response rates, since they vary so widely between early and late parts of the interval anyway. FI is probably the schedule best adapted to measuring time discriminations, possibly better in some respects even than DRL because of the lesser constraints imposed. DRL calls for more precision in timing, and its most sensitive aspect might be the ability to inhibit responding. The schedule with most room for revealing both rises and falls in general activity is probably a variable interval, since the animal's best option on this is to respond at a moderate rate – too few responses would risk missing opportunities for reinforcement; too many would be a waste of effort. But these penalties are minimal, and quite large changes in response rates, in either direction, make surprisingly little difference to the number of reinforcements received. On all schedules, the most interesting questions are usually in the fine detail.

A straightforward comparison of drug effects on three schedules was

Operant conditioning **155**

made by Morrison and Armitage (1967). Fig. 12.2 shows the baseline pattern on VI 2, FR 50, and DRL 20 in their rats, and Fig. 12.5 compares the effects of nicotine and *d*-amphetamine from 20 to 60 minutes after injection. Larger doses of nicotine tended to have a biphasic effect, a fall in response rates followed by a rise; *d*-amphetamine (0·2–0·8 mg/kg) and smaller doses of nicotine increased rates, but the extent of such changes varied with the

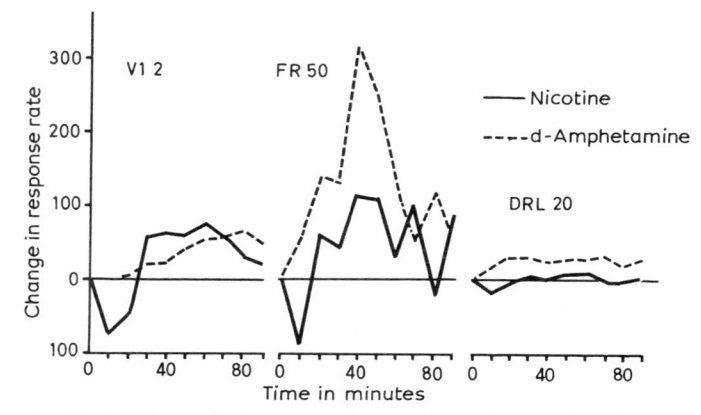

Fig. 12.5. Effects of nicotine and *d*-amphetamine (both at 0·4 mg/kg) on three schedules of operant performance (after Morrison and Armitage, 1967). Changes in number of responses in 10 minutes compared with pre-drug performance.

schedule. On a 2-minute variable interval, nicotine increased response rate from 20 to 60 per cent over the same rats' control performance, amphetamine by a fairly steady 30 per cent. On a fixed ratio of fifty responses, nicotine had a rather sporadic effect, amphetamine increased responding by 70 to 140 per cent by shortening the unusually long pauses after reinforcement – it did not let the rats relax, they had to be up and doing. Perhaps for the same reason, amphetamine increased response rates on DRL, though the anorexic action could mean that the rats did not worry too much about losing their reward. Nicotine had little effect on DRL, which is often the most sensitive of schedules; the authors thought that perhaps the initial fall in response rates showed the rats that slower responding on DRL brings more water reinforcement, maybe learning was improved.

The important influence of schedules on behaviour is shown when they make the same individual animals respond differently to the same dose of the same drug. Peter Dews (1955) trained four pigeons on both fixed ratio and fixed interval schedules. In both cases the birds were injected with pentobarbitone or saline after a warm-up period, put back in the box for 15 minutes in the dark, and the schedules started when the stimulus-light came on. FR 50 led, as usual, to high rates of pecking and the three lower doses made the birds peck even faster, while the top two doses slowed them considerably, no doubt because of ataxia (see Fig. 12.6). A 15-minute FI led to the usual low but accelerating rate of pecking, so that the birds won a few seconds feeding every quarter of an hour. Pecking became a little faster after the smallest dose but was depressed by all others. Drowsy from prolonged waiting, perhaps, the birds must have become more sensitive to sedation. In

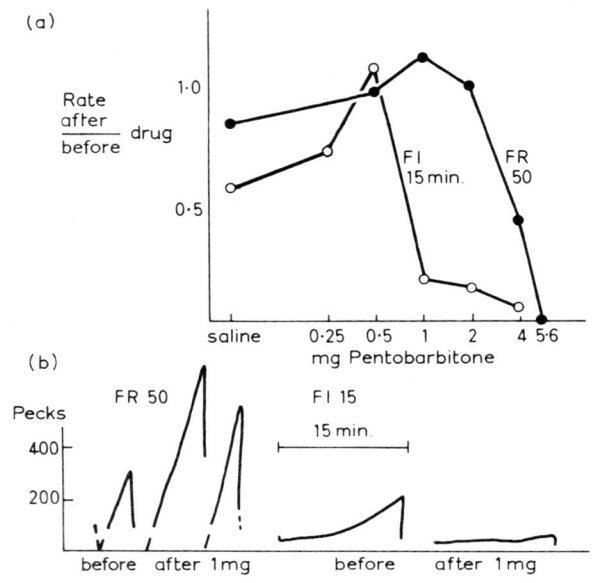

Fig. 12.6. Pentobarbitone's effect depends on the schedule. Four pigeons were trained on two schedules: (a) log dose-effect curves for pentobarbitone, pecking rates as the ratio of drug to control rates; (b) Typical cumulative records before 1 mg pentobarbitone and 15 minutes afterwards on Fixed Ratio 50 and Fixed Interval 15 minute schedules (after Dews, 1955).

short, the dose–response curve was shifted according to the schedule, and the middle dose exaggerated the difference, further raising high rates on FR and lowering low ones on FI.

Timing and superstition

In principle the animal's only stimuli should come from the all-important schedule cues chosen by the experimenter. In practice, the animal depends partly on feedback stimuli from the apparatus: the lever's resistance to displacement, perhaps a faint click as the switch closes, a quiet whirr as the dipper dips or a clatter as the solenoid delivers. These cues become classically conditioned stimuli, in a sense, to the correct performance of the animal and of the machinery. Although the animal would, no doubt, learn to do without such cues if it were possible to eliminate them, the cues undoubtedly help.

However, these cues are little help in the schedule itself, so how does the animal manage? On fixed ratio the problem is probably simple enough, the conditioned response merely has to be repeated until the effective unit may not be one lever-press but the series. But on a fixed interval, the animal tends to pause first and to respond faster later. On DRL this pattern is even more marked since it is a reinforced aspect of the schedule. How does the animal know when to act?

Consider again the basic concept of operant conditioning – whatever a water-deprived animal is doing when water becomes accessible to it (or just before), will tend to occur again in the same circumstances. In the early stages of operant-training, the experimenter goes to great lengths to ensure that the animal performs as officially authorised. But if reinforcement is presented without the experimenter shaping any particular behaviour, then whatever the animal happens by accident to be doing at the time will be reinforced in the same way. From the animal's point of view, it must seem that the response required is a whole sequence of behaviour in which lever-pressing is but one step.

A pattern of behaviour accidentally reinforced once and then repeated was called 'superstitious' by Skinner, by analogy with human rituals (these too may once have been fortuitously reinforced). There is more to the question, of course, for the 'superstitions' are not entirely accidental and unique to the individual, they are also characteristic of the schedule. Just as each schedule imposes certain constraints on the pattern of formal responses, so does it influence all that the animal does. Morrison and Stephenson (1973) found that on DRL some rats would lie down flat with the nose pressed into the dipper compartment, waiting; most rats spent most of the time restlessly grooming and walking. On interval schedules, rats were likely to remain immobile for a while, then to groom and then tentatively touch the dipper or the lever. Superstitious behaviour is said (Herrnstein, 1966) first to increase and then decline as the parts really useful in timing the schedule are selectively reinforced and the remainder extinguished and discarded. In effect, if external cues are not available, the animal has to invent them.

'Collateral' behaviour really does help the animals to perform effectively on a DRL schedule (Laties, Weiss, and Weiss, 1969). After about thirty daily sessions, five rats had all developed 'collateral' behaviour, which was accompanied by a dramatic increase in the number of condensed-milk reinforcements obtained. The behaviour nearly always consisted of gnawing a piece of wood or a projecting piece of the apparatus or the animal groomed its own tail. One rat licked the wall if gnawing was prevented. None of the animals passed the time by running through alleys, the action had to be related to those of eating. If gnawing was prevented, DRL performance deteriorated; if the DRL schedule was allowed to extinguish, gnawing disappeared.

Laties and Weiss (1966) also argued that operant performance should become less sensitive to interference by drugs if external stimuli are made available. On a 5-minute fixed interval, various drugs flattened the scallop: early in the interval, pigeons tended to peck more, but later less, than they did without drugs. However, the birds were also trained and tested on a version of FI 5 when successive minutes were marked by changes in symbols (X, O, etc.) projected on to the illuminated response key. As expected, most of the drugs had much less effect on the distribution of response rates when there was a visible clock to watch.

The same phenomenon occurred when pigeons had to peck eight times on one key before a peck on another key brought reinforcement (Laties, 1972). If the bird switched keys too soon, it had to start again with eight more pecks on the first key. As before, a stimulus to mark the eighth peck made the birds more efficient. They switched less often after too few or unnecessarily many responses. All five of the drugs Laties used tended to alter response rates and if the birds had no help from external stimuli, four of the drugs also caused them to make mistakes, to switch prematurely. The addition of the discriminative cue greatly reduced the errors made under the influence of scopolamine and *d*-amphetamine, but the phenothiazine neuroleptics, chlorpromazine and promazine, caused as many mistakes with the cue as without. Haloperidol slowed response rates as much as the other neuroleptics but caused fewer mistakes, with or without cues. Perhaps it does not interfere with sensitivity to stimuli, or the attention paid to the world outside, as phenothiazines are said to do.

Discriminative stimuli and time out

Discriminative stimuli are commonly used more crudely. If a certain stimulus is present, then responding on the appropriate schedule brings reinforcement; if absent, or if the converse signal is present, then it does not.

The clearest example lies in the unwillingness of pigeons to eat in the dark. They can be trained to do so if necessary (see p. 188), but as a rule they eat in the daylight and roost and sleep at night. Without conditioning, switching off the light switches off a pigeon's operant responding, a procedure known as Time Out. The pigeon resumes where it left off when the light comes on again. In an experiment with alternate 1-minute periods of Time Out and Time In (Azrin and Holz, 1966), the paper on the cumulative recorder did not travel forward while the lights were out, and the trace showed uniform responding on the VI schedule quite unaffected by the interruptions. Provided it is without scheduled causes or consequences for operant responding, Time Out is ignored as irrelevant. But if Time Out bears some systematic relationship to reinforcement, it can become a conditioned inhibitory stimulus.

Rats do not seem to have an exact unconditioned equivalent to Time Out, unless of course they are literally carried out of the Skinner box, which can

Operant conditioning **159**

have some curious results. Rats perform quite as usual on FR 30 for 10 minutes or so after the injection of mescaline but very erratically for the following 25 minutes (when they stop DRL responding altogether, see p. 153) and then return to normal. Sparber and Tilson (1971) found, however, that if they took the rats out of the Skinner box 2 minutes after the drug effect started and put them back 2·5 or 5 minutes later, the rats resumed normal service almost immediately, 20 minutes earlier than expected. If the rats were left in their home cages for 10 minutes after injection until the drug ought to start taking effect, they performed the FR 30 nearly as well as usual; the drug had some effect but not much.

The phenomenon must depend on the stimulation involved in handling the rats as much as on whether they were in or out of the Skinner box. Perhaps Time Out in pigeons can be regarded as a neat way of removing them from the Skinner box without disturbance. It is unfortunate that rats are predominantly nocturnal. I wonder what an owl would do.

Meanwhile, rats perform regularly in hundreds of brightly-lit Skinner boxes; indeed light can be used as a reward in its own right, and also as a discriminative stimulus. If responses bring reinforcement only when a light is shining, then it becomes a positive conditioned stimulus (conventionally labelled S^D or $S+$), and darkness becomes the negative inhibitory stimulus (labelled with the Greek delta as $S\Delta$ or $S-$). The use of operant methods in experiments on discrimination is described further in Chapter 14.

Not all operant experiments involve lever-pressing. One example concerns the trichloroethylene vapour as an industrial hygiene problem (see p. 138). Etienne Grandjean (1960) trained three rats to climb a rope to reach a pellet of sugar. They were given a total of eighteen 3-hour sessions exposed to clean air or trichloroethylene at concentrations of 200 or 800 parts per million. Immediately after exposure 'optical and acoustic signals' occurred at variable intervals during a 25-minute test: a light shone in the chamber and a dextrose pellet was dropped down a little tube on to a tray at the top of the rope. The rats always climbed the rope after receiving the signal, and the

training with optical and acoustic signals

time they took was not altered by the solvent. But occasionally they climbed the rope spontaneously, without a signal and without getting their sweet. In the control sessions, the three rats did this a total of 4, 5, and 5 times each. after 800 ppm trichloroethylene the number was 5, 7, and 18 times respectively, but after 200 ppm, 13, 14, and 12 times.

Stimulant drugs like amphetamine and caffeine had similar effects, but higher doses of trichloroethylene are clearly not stimulant. Grandjean could not decide whether the solvent increased hunger or curiosity, or weakened fear or the memory that there would be no pellet without a signal, or if it generally increased excitability. Certainly when rats were exposed to 200 ppm they were not quite in a normal state.

Combinations of schedules

A single schedule is often not informative enough. A lowered response rate on FR does not mean the same as on DRL. One answer is to train two groups of animals on two different schedules, and compare results. Another is to train each animal on both schedules in turn. Still better, is to use both schedules in the same session. The training of each animal is more complicated, of course, but each schedule can then act as a better control for treatment effects on the other.

There are at least a dozen different ways of putting two or more schedules together, listed exhaustively by Ferster and Skinner (1957) and by Morse (1966). The three most commonly used are called tandem, chained, and multiple schedules. In a tandem (*tand*), one simple schedule is followed immediately by another. Thus, *tand* FR 15 FI 2 means that a fixed ratio of fifteen responses is followed without reinforcement by a 2-minute fixed interval. Or you could have three successive FI 2, where the animal has to respond three times at 2-minute intervals, without stimuli to help it time the responses, but (unlike DRL) with superfluous responses not carrying any penalty.

A chained schedule is the same as a tandem, except that a stimulus is added to tell the animal when the next component of the schedule has started. In both schedules, however, the animal has to go through all the components successively to obtain a single reinforcement. In a multiple (*mult*) schedule, two or more components occur successively, but each is reinforced separately and an appropriate stimulus tells a pigeon what to do. Thus *mult* (FI 2 FR 15) might have a red light signalling a 2-minute fixed interval while a green one indicates that fifteen quick pecks will also be reinforced.

Tandem schedules

Tandem schedules can sometimes be responded to in a simple manner. Cook (1964) trained squirrel monkeys (*Saimiri sciureus*) on *tand* VI–DRL.

In this example, food reinforcement was given after a variable interval averaging 90 seconds, but to be reinforced, the successful response had to occur at least 7·5 seconds after the previous response. So where a standard VI 90 induces a rate of about twenty responses a minute, on average, the DRL component lowers the rate to about eight a minute. Neuroleptics like chlorpromazine lowered the rate still further and ultimately the monkeys stopped bothering at all. Effective doses of tranquillisers like meprobamate and chlordiazepoxide increased response rates considerably, although the animals were therefore rewarded less often.

Chained schedules

Rhesus monkeys (*Macaca mulatta*) became addicted to morphine after infusions through an intravenous catheter (Thompson and Schuster, 1964) and learned a chain FI–FR schedule to obtain further morphine infusions. Once every 6 hours a tone sounded and the first response after at least 2 minutes switched a white light on and the tone off. After twenty-five responses in the white light, a red light came on, at the same time as the monkey was given his fix.

The chained (discriminated) FI–FR schedule became a useful measure of the monkey's dependence. After 24 hours deprivation of morphine, or after 1 mg of the morphine antagonist nalorphine, they responded more often than usual in the interval and even faster on the ratio, as if hurrying. On two other schedules, discriminated shock avoidance and a series of five fixed ratios in tandem for food, performance was stable, unless the monkey had been deprived of morphine or given nalorphine. If a trick was played on the monkey, as it were, and he was only given a saline infusion instead of morphine when the red light shone, a placebo effect occurred: the monkey happily returned to food and avoidance responding; but performance deteriorated early and remained poor until the next maintenance dose.

A note of caution

Monkeys are born free and everywhere are in chains. This paper of Thompson and Schuster is a clear example of the need for common sense when you read about procedure. Authors do not always describe details of the procedure which seem trivial, especially when journal editors press for brevity. But the reader should not always take the outline of procedure too literally. 'Rhesus monkeys seated in restraining chairs obtain all of their food and avoid painful electric shocks by pressing levers under specific visual or auditory stimulus conditions ... The animals are in the experiment for 24 hours a day, so that large and continuous samples of the animal's behaviour can be brought under experimental control ... from day to day over a period of 6 months.' In 24 hours, there were four 6-hour cycles of four food periods (5 times FR 35, up to 8 minutes), four shock-avoidance periods (maximum 8 minutes) and one FI–FR drug period, with intervals between periods of between 8 and 32 minutes. A monkey in a restraining chair for 6 months continuously would surely get friction or pressure sores where it sat down, where the leather waist-belt delivered the shocks, and wherever else a harness was necessary. It would get no more than half an hour's sleep at a time, it would get no exercise, it would be largely unable to groom itself – and the experimenters would get several hundred metres of cumulative-record paper to be inspected, analysed, and interpreted. This is clearly absurd and therefore did not happen.

Multiple schedules

Multiple schedules seem complex. Thompson and Schuster's monkeys had to remember that a yellow light signalled FR for food, that 10 seconds clicking signalled shock unless the lever was pressed, and a tone signalled the start of the chained schedule for morphine. You might think that only a primate, with plenty of time, could manage it. In fact, multiple schedules are child's play for chickens only 3 days out of the egg.

Since the blood–brain barrier is incompletely developed, young chicks are useful not only as cheap subjects for teaching purposes but for studies on drugs insoluble in lipid which would otherwise not reach the brain. Marley and Morse (1966) trained chicks cheaply in a cardboard box with a panel to carry the response key, stimulus light, and a food magazine. Chicks are not greatly disturbed by occasional noises around the lab; but the box has to have a mirror behind the feeding aperture. Newly-hatched chicks spend most of their time close to each other and the hen. If they cannot see another chick in the mirror they search for company or crouch timidly in a corner emitting 'distress' cheeps.

Groups of ten chicks, 1 day old, are put into a cardboard box like the test-box, with a feeding aperture in the floor. At this age, chicks do not yet feed properly, and still have a little yolk, so they are not fed on the first day, but fed on the second, deprived overnight, and then start training at 3 days of age. They can only eat small quantities of the chicken starter-diet, can be fed to satiation several times a day, and need not be deprived very long to be hungry, while still weighing 20–40 per cent less than their fully-fed broodmates.

Chicks mostly face the mirror at first, but can be easily shaped to the illuminated response key. If trained on a white key, they often fail to respond at first to a red one, or vice versa. This stimulus control at 3 days old can be used to start a multiple schedule on day four. One colour signals a fixed ratio, extended over a few sessions from FR 1 to 3 to 10 to FR 30, the other a 3-minute fixed interval. Characteristic performance can be evident in 2 or 3 days, high rates of pecking on FR, a pause and acceleration giving a typical scallop on FI. As a rule, although they can cheep and peck at the same time, young chicks emit most cheeps in the early part of the interval, and very few while pecking rapidly.

Summary

Operant conditioning can be complicated in practice. Because so much of the animal's behaviour is under experimental control, there are innumerable unexpected details of apparatus, of sequences of stimuli provided both deliberately and inadvertently, or of the animal's previous experience, that turn out to be relevant to the animal's performance and have to be taken care of. Nevertheless, the principle of operant conditioning is simple. In the long run, an animal only repeats a response to a given set of circumstances that has previously brought about the consequences required – only those actions which lead to the built-in goal are reinforced.

Operant conditioning is a way of turning this approach into a flexible laboratory technique, by conditioning both the stimuli presented to the animal and the response which it makes. The response that is utilised is developed from a pre-existing action (pecking in birds, manipulating a projection in rats). It is shaped into something that is both easily recorded automatically and objectively, and is essentially artificial, so that it is not performed in the absence of the stimuli chosen by the experimenter. The response is small in relation to the animal's total output, so that many hundreds of units can be recorded in each day's session. The reinforcement can be 'positive', food, warmth, or anything else the animal needs but has been deprived of, or 'negative', the avoidance of something potentially harmful like electric shock (see Chapter 16).

Each unit of reinforcement is small in relation to the total intake – the animal must work hard to take several bites at each cherry. The animal must therefore be hungry at the start of the session and still hungry enough at the end to keep responding, provided it gets enough at each nibble to find it worthwhile working.

Continuous reinforcement (CRF) of each response is useful mainly in early training, but repeated extinction after CRF has provided an unusually rapid test of drug effects. Schedules with a fixed and relatively high ratio of responses to reinforcement, up to 50 or 100 (FR), generate high rates of responding. Where there is a fixed time interval (FI), animals typically respond very little in the early parts of the interval after reinforcement but accelerate as the next reinforcement becomes due. Where the animal cannot predict how long it will have to wait (Variable Interval, VI), the rate is moderate and steady. Where the animal is penalised for not waiting a set interval (20 seconds is a delay commonly used on this DRL schedule), the rate of responding is of course low. These schedules can be combined in innumerable permutations and combinations, especially when one or more of the components is signalled to the animal by a specific stimulus.

THIRTEEN
Comments on operant and other behaviour
Adventures in the Skinner trade

The study of behaviour in the twentieth century has been both blessed and cursed by great men. Expert shepherds and circus trainers have always understood their animals' behaviour in practice, if patchily. But academic theories which will explain laboratory experiments, naturalists' observations, and above all, medical attempts to help the desperately unhappy or control the excessively bizarre, inevitably start from widely different viewpoints. It needs a great man to inspire a genuinely fruitful new way of looking at behaviour. The trouble is that the new insight demands new words and a genuine insight has comprehensive implications, so that the same phenomena can be described on different assumptions in mutually incomprehensible languages. The great man himself is usually perfectly well aware of this and is quite capable of discussing his views objectively. But some of his followers become Hero-worshippers *plus royalistes que le roi* and turn a technique or a way of thinking into a school or even a religion. There is no theory but operant conditioning or psychoanalysis or ethology, and Skinner or Freud or Jung or even Lorenz is its prophet.

Operant conditioning is at present perhaps the most fashionable of these schools, and certainly it is among the more useful of techniques. Two particularly useful specialist books are the collections of essays edited by Werner Honig (1966) (referred to briefly as 'Honig') and Robert Hinde and Joan Stevenson-Hinde (1973). However, many 'experts' in psychopharmacology in particular, persist in mistaking the part for the whole. Operant conditioning is an extremely useful set of techniques but is by no means the only such set, and in any case has the limitations of its virtues. The following comments may of course show that I have misunderstood the issues; several comments apply to all methods in animal behaviour in any case; and some will best be understood after reading the ethological chapters (20–23); but I hope they will assist you to consider the issues for yourself.

Operant origins
The origin of the theory lies in a useful distinction between two types of conditioning. 'Classical' conditioning is said to occur when the animal does something (e.g. salivates) in response not only to the usual stimulus but also to a quite different one that formerly had no effect. If a noise precedes the

smell as predictably as the smell precedes the dinner, then the dog salivates in response to the artificial stimulus as a symbol of the real thing.

However, although the conditioned stimulus causes the dog to produce saliva, the saliva does not cause the production of the meat. Skinner's crucial contribution was to draw attention to the fact that in real life, the dog depends on its behaviour to obtain its food. By definition only those parts of its behaviour which help the dog to get his meat will be reinforced. If only some actions are reinforced, others will gradually be extinguished, on a principle analogous to natural selection, as a waste of effort.

Choice of response – the experimenter's and the rat's

Operant conditioning converts this process into a useful set of laboratory techniques. In operant writing, however, some of the most fundamental aspects of the conversion are often passed over rapidly as if they are mere technical details of apparatus. One such detail is that it is the experimenter who selects which response will be functionally successful, and the process is of interest.

In the first place, the experimenter chooses the stimuli which will be presented to the animal. The animal is put into a Skinner box, where only a few things are allowed to happen. Visually it is opaque except for a dark glass window. Sound transmission is damped, and a fan creates background noise as well as a flow of air of uniform temperature. The box itself or the detergents used for cleaning it may smell. There may be deliberately chosen discriminative stimuli, lights flashing, buzzers buzzing. When the lever is depressed, the animal will receive tactile and proprioceptive stimuli and perhaps an audible click. As far as possible, other stimuli are excluded lest they become accidentally associated with reinforcement or lest they distract the animal from its work.

Secondly, the experimenter selects what he wants from the animal's behavioural repertoire, or from so much of it as the animal will perform in the apparatus, or from so much of that as the experimenter perceives. Even the reinforcements (manufactured food pellets in a shape that fits the machinery, or dilute condensed milk sweetened with sucrose, or electric shock) are all man-made. When the animal is accustomed to taking what the experimenter offers, then either by gluing corn or illuminating the response key to attract a pigeon's attention, or by shaping the most generalised nod of a rat's head towards the lever successively to approaching, touching, and pressing it just hard and long enough, the experimenter channels the behaviour towards the one thing he wishes to record.

In theory, this has to be essentially artificial. It should not be something the animal performs spontaneously, because, if it were, the relevant stimuli would be unknown, difficult to eliminate or make allowances for, and would therefore interfere with the proper results. Moreover, spontaneous responses inevitably have a history of reinforcement of some kind, and an attempt at extinguishing them would be necessary. Extinction cannot be made complete, especially as there is an innate component, so the experimenter can never start with a clean slate.

Therefore the operant must start from something which the animal has a low but finite probability of performing – just high enough to make it possible to train the animal to perform it regularly (weeks could be wasted conditioning a rat to peck a disc like a pigeon). The final version must be altered in form so that it would virtually never be performed spontaneously (which would confuse the results of the officially authorised performance). The animal will then show the operant response as often as circumstances and the experimenter require, but no more.

Apart from special demonstrations like hamsters scratching, the response must be something that is easy to record automatically, so the rat's lever and the pigeon's disc open or close a microswitch.

What is the animal actually doing?

So far, I have emphasised how artificial the response is, on Skinner's claim that it is an 'operant' governed solely by results. However, although the lever is certainly artificial and pigeons rarely find grain stuck on a brick wall, it is necessary to ask what pressing the lever or the disc means to the animal.

The question arises because, while Skinnerians recognise that animals of a given species can make one movement more easily than another, the pure theory suggests that any movement that the animal is capable of making should be applicable equally easily to any kind of reinforcement. There are many cases where this does not happen. Sevenster's sticklebacks could swim through a ring for the opportunity to fight a male or court a female and they could bite a rod to fight, but courtship inhibits biting (see p. 108). Shettleworth's hamsters could not groom themselves for a food reward. Chaffinches can peck for food and perch in a special perch to hear another chaffinch sing, but very few can also peck for singing unless they have also

a special perch to hear a chaffinch sing

been deprived of food (Stevenson-Hinde, 1973). Rats seem to find pressing a lever harder to learn than other kinds of avoidance response or than this response for positive reinforcement. Pigeons, however, seem to peck for food or tread on a lever to avoid shock rather more easily than the other way round. In 'autoshaping' (see p. 147) it is clear that the pigeon does to the disc what it is stimulated to do to the food or water shortly afterwards. The conditioned stimulus is a symbol of the unconditioned and is treated the same way, with an action from the animal's repertoire appropriate to that particular kind of behaviour. If this view is correct in general, what movements does a wild rat make which can be, and on this theory must have been, adapted for pressing a lever?

Repetition and ritual

In spontaneous behaviour it is surprisingly uncommon to repeat the same response over and over again. There are a few but not many examples: a cow chewing the cud or a sheep grazing; some birds' territorial song can be monotonously repeated even without a neighbour's competition; many sessile marine animals – mussels, barnacles, brachiopods, and so on – use their cilia to maintain a constant current of sea-water carrying oxygen and delicious plankton over their gills and mucous membranes. In few cases does the functional need for the behaviour continue for far longer than the component unit. More often, one action takes the animal into a situation where it receives the stimuli for the next response. In principle (though things are rarely so simple) all the units functionally related to a single goal occur in a chain, one after the other. The use in operant conditioning of repetitions of a single unit has, of course, both advantages and disadvantages.

One advantage is the practical convenience of only having to train the animal to a single response. Another is that you can study rates of response. A maze experiment has to run a series of separate trials with at least half a minute's wait in the goal-box, and rather few trials a day, operant conditioning can have thousands of responses an hour. The rate of responding can be seen to change over a time scale of minutes or seconds, and performance can be monitored a few seconds after injecting a drug, continuing for days or months afterwards. You do not have to accept Skinner's grandiloquent claim (1966) that response rates are to behaviour what combining weights were to chemistry in the days of Dalton and Avogadro, to realise that rates are important.

However, the chosen action is a largely secondhand measure of what the animal is really doing. Consider how the responses are generated. For instance, on a DRL schedule the animal is under pressure to wait for perhaps 20 seconds, yet equally it must not wait too long if it is to maximise the reinforcements per session. What the animal does while waiting is as interesting as how far it succeeds. The experimenter presumably does not particularly mind whether it sits on its bottom or dances twenty bars of a jig, while for its part the animal does not at first know what it is supposed to be doing.

In practice just enough is known of 'superstitious' or 'collateral' behaviour to show that the pattern is characteristic of the schedule (see pp. 147 and 228) and so is partly under its control. If the animal grooms itself while waiting in frustration before making the correct response, then grooming will be repeated both for the original reasons and because it has been reinforced.

The process is similar in discrimination experiments, where it looks as though the animal makes a series of hypotheses, which it tests – it may choose always the left-hand goal-box, or alternate from right to left, and the experimenter's task is to enable the animal to falsify quickly each wrong hypothesis until it arrives at the discrimination that he intends it to make. If the wrong hypothesis is not disproved quickly, the animal may persist in it, since it may well be reinforced by up to 50 per cent.

Skinner's analogy with supersition is reasonable (does it imply that the correct ritual is analogous with the one true religion?). Herrnstein's analogy (1966) with the pathological rituals of an obsession is closer, if the rituals of both rat and patient are derived from the pacing of a set route like a lion or an elephant in solitary zoo confinement, and from 'displacement' grooming exaggerated by frustration or conflict. However, superstitious operant behaviour tends to drop out in time whereas obsessive rituals in human patients seem to increase if they are not treated, because they are reinforcing to the extent that they succeed in keeping the bogy-man at bay. Ferster (1967) makes a superficial but fascinating classification of mental illness in operant terms. The resemblance should not distract us from trying to understand the real determinants of each.

Fins, fingers, and functional resemblances

The theory of operant conditioning as a sort of natural selection is striking and intuitively plausible. An individual's successful actions are repeated because the unsuccessful ones are forgotten and lost. It must surely apply to all species of animals with the capacity for more than simple reflexes. Certainly the cumulative record of an individual operant performance shows readily enough what the schedule was, but you can seldom guess the species of the performer. Within limits, all animals that have been tested, from goldfish to man, perform any given schedule in a similar manner if they can perform it at all. The apparatus has to be a little different of course: humans find it a little inconvenient to get inside a goldfish bowl, and goldfish have no spare fingers to press buttons. The reinforcements are different: people do not find rat pellets very appetising and a rat could not spend a penny if it was paid one. But the fundamental pattern of response to a given schedule is the same, and in Honig's book, human performance is treated in exactly the same terms as animals'.

However, it does not follow that the resemblance between species necessarily reflects a uniform structure of behaviour. There may be convergence to a common pattern because of similar constraints, in the same way as insects' legs and wings resemble those of birds. I believe that fundamental behavioural mechanisms must be common throughout the vertebrates, but this is unprovable. Uniform performance on an operant schedule shows that

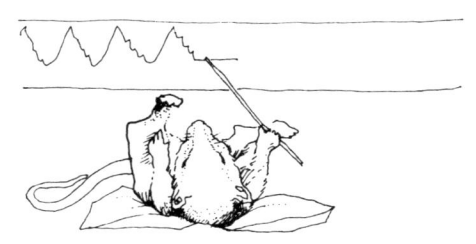

how the performance is achieved

all surviving species can successfully make a cost–benefit analysis of the situation they are faced with. It tells you little about the mechanism of how that performance is achieved.

Individuality and population samples

Nevertheless, it would be a fault on the other side to overemphasise the similarities between species. Performance is not as rigidly determined by the schedule as I may have implied. To suggest that schedules 'control' behaviour [as Dews (1964) implies, for example] would be an exaggeration if it were claimed to be 100 per cent true, for there would then be no room for drugs or genes or anything else to alter the behaviour at all. Within the limits of quite an ordinary schedule, Will showed (1974) (see p. 148) there was room for several patterns of responding which different individuals could adopt and stick to indefinitely, since they were equally effective.

Operant conditioning has always claimed the extra virtue of concern for individuals. The average of a group cannot accurately represent any one of its members, but operant conditioning deals directly with the individual. This is true, of course, but is perhaps a case of making a virtue of necessity. The earlier experimenters seldom possessed apparatus that could cope with the control of more than one Skinner box at a time. Furthermore, until computers became cheap enough to be almost within reach, it was not possible to apply statistics routinely to the interesting parts of the behaviour. The interpretation of the trace on a cumulative recorder has to be a matter of judgement and experience. This is reasonable in itself, but unfortunately puts back into the interpretation all the subjectivity which the performance was supposed to take out.

Skinner has ridiculed what he claims to be a fashionable emphasis on statistics (1966). Before the twentieth century, scientific discoveries were still discoveries without a probability level being attached; Newton only needed a single apple to fall on his head to discover the law of gravity, his experience was sufficient to tell him that it was a representative sample of the whole population of heavenly objects. However, Skinner overstates the case. Just because he deals directly with individual animals, it is necessary to establish objectively how far you can take one as typical of all.

Considering the emphasis on individuality, it is a little curious that there has been so little concern to specify what it consists of. Operant experimenters frequently mention a genetic strain of rat but leave it at that. Pavlov described a typology of nervous systems in which a dog may have a 'strong excitatory process in his nervous system' with only 'weak inhibition', or 'strong and well-balanced higher nervous activities'. It is sometimes difficult for the Western reader to understand (and for some Soviet scientists too, I believe), but it is curious that it has not been examined further in the land of the free operant.

Non-specified operants

One of the difficulties with the use of operant conditioning as an experimental method is that precisely because the behaviour is controlled so closely, it becomes resistant to interference by external stimuli. 'Give a rat an anaesthetic, and if pressing the lever has been made very important, then that will be the last thing he struggles to do before falling asleep, and the first on waking up, no matter how groggy and ataxic he is. So it has been suggested that the most sensitive measure is something *not* seeming to be a crucial part of the schedule (King, 1970). Milan Horváth and Emiel Frantik (1970) used conditioned avoidance of noise, where 30 seconds of a quiet noise (about 45 dB) was followed by 30 seconds of a louder one (70 dB) unless the rat pressed one of two pedals. The noise was therefore controlled by how often the rats responded to the warning and how quickly; these parameters were the least variable, either between rats or within any individual, and were hardly affected by four assorted drugs. Discrimination between the two pedals was less important, more variable from time to time spontaneously, and more sensitive to drugs. The duration of pressing the pedals was totally irrelevant to the schedule, was the most sensitive measure of drug effects and fatigue within sessions, and was the only one of seven operant measures to be altered when the rats had inhaled enough trichloroethylene or carbon disulphide to reduce their spontaneous motor activity by half. Similarly the only difference between human control subjects and 'workers who had been exposed to toxic substances for a long time' was that the workers pressed the signal button for longer. They had not been told that it would be measured.

Schedules at home and abroad

The principle of operant conditioning, that an animal uses its behaviour as a tool to obtain the reinforcements which enable it to survive, is so fundamental and so obviously true that it must surely apply universally. Yet after all, it is only an assumption, and while operant conditioning works well within deliberate limitations in the controlled conditions of the laboratory, it is important to try to discover how far it really applies in real life. Before uncritical attempts at 'behaviour therapy' to human beings in captivity in prisons or hospitals or schools for the maladjusted, its assumptions should be tested in free-living animals in less rigidly controlled conditions. After all, the aim of behaviour therapy is to enable the patient to cope with a relatively open society.

In a sense, the various laboratory operant schedules based on fixed or variable ratios and intervals represent all the logical possibilities, so it ought to be easy to find comparable schedules operating in the wild. In practice the parallels do not often seem to be close. It is true that reinforcement is more-or-less continuous for a suckling infant and also a grazing sheep gets grass on nearly every bite, for large herbivores, cattle, horses, elephants, hippopotami, are adapted to eating for long continuous periods on large quantities of low-grade food.

Reinforcement programs approaching the standard laboratory schedules are harder to find. A lion does not make a kill after every fifth or fiftieth ambush. I suppose he could be on a variable ratio schedule, which might explain why he lets his lionesses or the neighbouring hyenas do most of the actual hunting. A camel swaying through the desert is hardly on a fixed interval schedule for water reinforcement; the caravan drivers may try to reach the next oasis regularly before nightfall, but an acceleration as the camel gets closer probably depends on the smell of the water more than a typical FI scallop. A small animal may not get the opportunity to condition an avoidance response to a predator – if it does not respond without conditioning it may not get a second chance.

A proper study of response-reinforcement relationships in a variety of animals in natural or semi-natural conditions is important. The flippant speculations above are, I hope, useful in setting your imagination going; but all they can really point out is that standard schedules of reinforcement are laboratory models. They provide a vocabulary which a real study of the timing of a wild animal's responses can use. But what is the real relationship between stimuli, responses, and reinforcements in a variety of wild animals? How do these relationships vary with the animals' way of life? And are they imposed by experience or internally generated?

More studies are needed like the test of Optimal Foraging Theory by John Krebs, John Ryan, and Eric Charnov (1974). They found the hunting pattern of some hand-reared chickadees (*Parus atricapillus*) in the laboratory was not based on learning to expect a fixed number of prey in each patch of model pine-cones, nor did the birds spend a fixed time on each patch. They left the patch a set time after the last capture, the time being set according to the average capture rate in that environment.

The drive concept

How are we to explain why an animal performs a particular action? Tinbergen (1951) points out that this is actually two questions. What is the animal's immediate motivation? And what survival value does the action have?

In human terms, as a rule we do not eat because we would otherwise starve to death, but because we feel hungry; we do not usually copulate in order to reproduce the species, but because of what we feel for another human being, and because we desire certain physical sensations. But to explain an animal's behaviour, it does not help to postulate a conscious emotion or sensation. Animals may well feel emotions, but we cannot appeal to these for an explanation. If it comes to that, we need to analyse accurately the precise sensations a human being feels when he is 'hungry' or 'in love', but this is another question and a surprisingly difficult one.

So to avoid postulating a conscious purpose, we can postulate a reflex in the central nervous system to relate one stimulus, or one set of stimuli, with one response. Where several responses are functionally related, like going to the larder, picking up a knife and a loaf of bread, cutting a slice, spreading it with butter..., then we can postulate an internal drive state. At a certain level of analysis a drive concept is useful. It provides a useful description of the fact that, after a certain point when the stomach walls are slightly stretched and glucose, fatty acids, and amino acids begin to enter the hepatic portal vein, a set of functionally related actions cease to occur. The cycle raise hand to mouth, bite, lower hand and chew, swallow, raise hand ... stops. Hearing a baby crying starts a very different set of actions, related to quite a different function.

However, when you come to analyse the causation of any single action, Hinde (1959) demonstrates that a concept of 'drive' is positively misleading. Skinner put it simply (1966): 'The term is little more than a synonym for cause, and various relations between cause and effect are usually not distinguished.' When you analyse the stimuli involved in pushing the breadknife backwards and forwards, pressing downwards on the handle with just sufficient force to move the cutting edge obliquely down as well as back and forth, in a plane parallel with the cut edge of the loaf and at a distance both from this and your other thumb ... the drive concept is no longer useful even as mere description. Though the whole sequence of actions would not start without the 'hunger drive' in the first place, the stimuli necessary for bread-cutting to start are rather different: in one hand an object of a certain volume, consistency, appearance, and smell, coming from the bread-bin, in the other hand a knife of a certain size and type of cutting edge, and in front of you a table at a certain height to rest the bread on. Even the drive might not be your own present hunger, but the anticipated future hunger of your guests – and what is the name of your own motivation for that?

The human terms clarify the problem, but it applies to animals too. Certainly there must be something, some pattern of neural activity somewhere in the brain, which relates all these actions to the goal of taking in essential (or superfluous) nutrients. It is affected by body chemistry, by anorexic drugs, by infection, by 'habit strength', and by a past history of severe deprivation of food or of parental love. But these complexities, even if we could analyse them properly, would only tell us about neurophysiology and not yet about behaviour, although ultimately neurophysiological and behavioural theories and descriptions will have to be mutually compatible.

In the meantime, both operant conditioners and ethologists prefer in principle not to postulate anything at all about the nervous system, though both are tempted to accept a little cautious 'neurologising' on occasion, as a temporary conceptual crutch. Both groups see the solution as the careful analysis of the behaviour we can actually watch, 'the topography of a response without identifying or manipulating any anterior stimulus ... analysis of the conditions which govern the probability that a given response will occur at a given time'. Both groups appeal to natural selection, ethologists primarily in the ordinary sense, Skinnerians applying the principle within the individual's lifetime.

The similarities between the followers of Skinner and of Tinbergen highlight the differences. Where one group uses deliberately artificial responses, the other attempts to recognise units in spontaneous behaviour. It is an amusing irony, if I have summarised their positions fairly, that the name of the doyen of the hard-line engineers should start so biologically, while that of the most biological of scientific naturalists should start like a metallic machine.

Why is a reinforcement?

Ethologists try to recognise a goal where one whole class of actions stops and is succeeded by another (see p. 304 for an example). Most Skinnerians take conventional reinforcements for granted, which limits the method's scope for advancing our understanding.

Consider the operant definition of reinforcement, in the beautifully clear formulation by Honig (1966). He discusses punishment but it would be easy to convert his three model definitions into their positive equivalents: '(1) punishment occurs when a response is immediately and consistently followed by a painful or unpleasant stimulus; (2) punishment occurs when bar presses made by a white rat in a Model 7690 B operant behaviour apparatus are followed by a footshock of at least 0·75 mA lasting not less than 0·5 seconds; (3) punishment is a reduction of the future probability or rate of a specific response as the result of the immediate delivery of a stimulus contingent upon that response.'

Honig rejects the first definition, quite rightly, because of the subjective words 'painful or unpleasant'. We cannot know what a rat is feeling, we can only see what it is doing (or in this case, has stopped doing). Honig also rejects the second, again rightly, because although it is objective and shows exactly what the experimenter should do, it is too particular. It confuses means for ends. Maybe 0·6 mA for 0·4 seconds would be sufficient in another manufacturer's apparatus. So Honig chooses definition No. 3. It is functional, specifying the principle of the concept in general terms, without getting bogged down in details of the means.

Yet there is more to be said. Honig's first definition is frankly subjective but it is by far the most informative. He quoted it first for the good reason that the instant we read it we understand what the question is about. If the second question came first, we might worry so much about whether a hooded rat or a model 7689 apparatus would fit the definition that we might forget that while a mild electric shock gives no more than a tingling or tickling sensation, the severer levels *are* painful and unpleasant. And he deliberately avoids indicating a mechanism, or even suggesting the need for one. Because there is no implication of pain or discomfort, the reader can only memorise a theoretical definition, not gain a vivid understanding.

True, we cannot know if anything is painful or unpleasant for the animal, and so we have to define our terms operationally. We have to use Honig's chosen definition about the animal ceasing to make a particular response as an objective criterion. But we should not throw out the baby with the bathwater. Because we cannot see inside the black box, we cannot conclude that there is nothing there.

Where Honig is careful not to imply any particular mechanism in the CNS, Skinner (1966) goes further. Whereas other psychologies have to construct 'some mental, physiological or merely conceptual inner system' to find 'orderly, continuous and significant processes ... there is no comparable inner system in operant conditioning. Changes in rates of responding are directly observed.'

Leaving aside the assumption that the only useful measurement is the rate at which the animal makes a single specified response, this starts out as a valuable approach. Skinner is not tempted to postulate a genie in the bottle, not to identify an area where we are ignorant, give it a name like 'Instinct' and unconsciously consider the name to be an explanation. Nevertheless, there must exist some neural mechanism to control these rates of response and to match the stimuli received against a built-in specification. For Skinner's definition of reinforcement (1966) is 'simply the strengthening of a response'. Without some sort of very specific mechanism, this definition becomes circular: in effect, reinforcement is a stimulus which reinforces.

White-coated operant conditioners therefore tend to ignore the question so long as their white-coated rats continue to work successfully. It may be possible to argue in any given case that a particular reinforcement is secondary, conditioned by association with primary reinforcement – but what makes the latter primary?

Theories of reinforcement, drive, and motivation are discussed by Peter Milner (1977). He arrives at a position similar to mine, but takes a much more solidly argued route.

Not all operant conditioners take Skinner's rigorous line in avoiding 'neurologising'. Larry Stein (1968) centres a review of the 'chemistry of reward and punishment' on the unabashed comment that 'organisms seek to repeat pleasurable experiences and to avoid repeating painful ones'. He proceeds to a fascinating account of self-stimulation experiments, correlating positive and negative results with the tracts of the brain and adrenergic/cholinergic mechanisms involved. Stein also takes reinforcements for granted.

Observation and the interpretation of laboratory experiments

When McDougall tried to list the basic Instincts, half a century ago, he started with eating, drinking, the need to reproduce, and to escape enemies, and he hardly knew where to stop; or how to check how far this list was accurate. Yet 'eating' may consist of several specific, relatively independent appetites. Tinbergen suggested (1951) that in many ground-living birds, anti-predator behaviour may well be of two distinct kinds (with internal 'drives' to match?), for they have two distinct kinds of overt escape, including separate alarm calls, to stimuli from the air (as from hawk or an owl) and to stimuli from the ground (as from a fox or a man). It was the armchair postulation of what an animal's goals ought to be that made it so difficult up to the 1950s to recognise that a rat needs to explore quite as much as to eat, indeed to explore first.

In testing discrimination abilities, for instance, the type of reinforcement does not seem to matter so long as it is convenient (in mammals – it matters in bees), and in many operant experiments you can hardly tell which was actually used. But observable behaviour cannot be understood by guesswork beforehand. Hunting in Carnivora is not only their predictable method of catching food, it can be seen to be an independent kind of behaviour: cats play at catching mice *after* they have been fed. Kittens may need to practise tying their hunting movements together into a coherent sequence, presumably reinforced by mice, but they play at each movement many times without any reinforcement being apparent. Without having seen it, who would predict both that cats would go so far as to dig a hole in the ground to defecate and bury the results by scraping more earth over, and yet that despite her fastidious nose, it is quite sufficient for the cat to go through the motions? For a domestic cat may scratch a hole in an earth-covered tray, or a sheet of paper, miss her aim, make a few scrabbling movements on the hard floor around the mess, and stalk off satisfied, leaving the mess to evolve its characteristic aroma. The movement pattern is apparently self-reinforcing and sensory feedback control is presumably unnecessary. Again, who would predict both that rats submit to aggression by a familiar cagemate – but less often to a stranger – by lying flat on the back (and respond to this submission by another rat) and that mice do not?

Only after observing these patterns of behaviour and the differences between species do we realise how complex are the selective forces operating, and how animals have goals (unconscious but effective) that we could not imagine beforehand.

Before it is possible to make and test a realistic hypothesis about behaviour, it is therefore necessary to define the problem. Karl Popper's description of science as a cycle of hypothesis, test, disproof, and new hypothesis misses the essential first step.

Certainly we all have misleading preconceptions, but we are more likely to minimise the damage they can do if we are aware of them while observing, than by prematurely confining ourselves within a rigorous scientific test of a half-baked hypothesis. Operant experts, like their Journal, rightly aim at the Experimental Analysis of Behavior but – like all of us – tend to ask not 'What techniques do I need to analyse this behaviour?' but 'What behaviour can I analyse with this technique?'

Personally I confess to a subjective difficulty which I seem to meet in operant conditioning more than in other areas. Many experiments seem so utterly abstract; perfectly competent, quite rigorous, but just meaningless by comparison with those experiments (operant or otherwise) that strike me intuitively as fresh and fruitful. This is of course a very personal response and others might not recognise a problem. But is there any means of testing an emotional judgement in a rational manner?

Consider some drug experiments in which Boren and Navarro (1959) trained rats to a multiple FI–FR schedule. The results were not especially complicated, but my point is that they were apparently open to two contradictory interpretations. Dews (1964) concluded that scopolamine selectively affected the FR 26 component, because the mean rate of responding on FR was reduced very much more than that on FI 4. Boren himself said (1966) that the Fixed Interval was more sensitive because the lowest doses interfered with the pause-acceleration 'scallop' typical of FI, without altering the mean rate of response on either schedule at all.

The Boren and Navarro experiment is actually not so bad, because you can distinguish two distinct effects fairly clearly. I rather prefer Boren's interpretation, because he was looking closely at the actual data, and might have been able to show something statistically with an 'index of curvature' (the ratio between responses in the first segment of the interval and the last). Dews, on this occasion, took the hard line. If the drug effect could not be described in terms of the rate of response then it was not an effect. It is this attitude, superficially objective and reliable, that I find abstract, formal and, for all its virtues, fundamentally sterile.

On the other hand, both the neuroleptic chlorpromazine and the stimulant methylphenidate reduced the rate of operant responding for water, and the patterns on the cumulative recorder were fairly similar. However, Dalbir Bindra and Joseph Mendelson (1962) also watched what the rats were actually doing. Chlorpromazine slowed down all

insufficient time to . . . press the lever

movements, more or less uniformly. Methylphenidate stimulated exploration and grooming, and the rat was so busy walking round the Skinner box and washing its face that it had insufficient time to do its duty and press the lever. Naturally, these observations are, so far, merely another description of the drug's effects rather than an explanation. Nevertheless, the main point is clear: if you relied on the objective operant data, you would think these two drugs had the same effect instead of pretty well opposite ones. Not only were the effects easily visible, they hardly needed an operant test at all.

Operant conditioning must be used with common sense, like all the most powerful tools. If the same results can legitimately be interpreted in two contradictory ways, or can be obtained by two contradictory means, then they are purely formal. Conditioning methods at their best can be both highly sensitive and tailored to answer a specific question. Schedules are highly repetitive, both within a session and from day to day, and the animal adapts to the schedule as well as it can so as to optimise the reward/effort ratio. Operant conditioning is therefore especially suitable for effects on timing – the time of onset of a treatment's effect and of recovery, over a period of minutes with a brief-acting drug or of days and weeks following a single injection of lead or mercury. Above all, the flexibility of operant conditioning allows its use to test a precise hypothesis about a drug effect, once the problem has been analysed with more open methods.

In an applied science it is necessary to use whichever techniques promise the most information for an acceptable effort. To distinguish spontaneous from artificial units is to suggest that the best results are likely to come by approaching the target from both sides in turn. One approach runs the risk of subjectivity where you see whatever you want to see, the other of chopping the behaviour up into predetermined units. The animal cannot tell you anything you do not know because you have put the words into his mouth. To the extent you can avoid these risks, it is worthwhile to discover both what the animal does of its own accord in specified conditions and the limits of what it can be trained to achieve.

Operant conditioning provides an extremely useful set of techniques. It does not provide a guide to the solution of all the world's problems, and the grandiose claims of some of its more passionate adherents are counter-productive.

FOURTEEN
Discrimination

Can you tell black from white?

The ability to make fine distinctions between complex stimuli that differ only in some subtle manner is regarded as a mark of intelligence. It is interesting that we should also use the word Discrimination crudely with an unfavourable emotional load. For when we speak of racial discrimination we mean a crude division in black and white terms, without really discriminating between genuine differences and imaginary ones, which are rarely relevant to the action taken on them anyway.

A stimulus does two things to an animal – it tells him to do something, and it tells him where to do it. The experimenter must discriminate clearly between these functions of arousal and orientation. Any one stimulus need only have one function or the other, although most have both. A sudden noise, for instance, is likely to arouse anti-predator responses and to inhibit all others. In the absence of directional information, the animal is likely to freeze. He will, however, tune his receptors to the appropriate stimuli, and a second noise will arouse a further response oriented quickly to the nearest stimulus-complex signalling safety – a rat runs to a dark corner with a protective roof, or a child to mother.

Discriminative abilities

Whenever the animal is offered a choice, it must be able to discriminate between the alternatives. In a food-preference test, the rat must be able to distinguish (by smell, taste, shape, etc.) wheat grains from chopped liver or sugar. A thiamin- or sodium-deficient rat somehow detects a difference in taste between the deficient and the adequate diet. A rat in a maze must know right from left; if not in the abstract, then at least from the previous choice in a sequence, or from minute cues in the maze itself. A male mouse alone in his cage behaves differently towards a recent male cage-mate than to one separated two weeks previously, and a female can distinguish a male of the strain she has mated with from one of another strain. A rat can learn to press a lever to obtain an intravenous injection of a very small dose of morphine, amylobarbitone, or nicotine, but does not bother for saline.

For all I know, these are not the most impressive examples of discriminations that could be found, but the discrimination was incidental to the main object of the research, so that the cues involved are not known, at least in

a female can distinguish

detail. Formal tests of discrimination work the other way round. Rather than see what the animal can do, and then trying to see how, formal tests take the less rewarding but simpler and more practical route. Starting with deliberately chosen cues, which may not use the animal's favourite sense-modality, they try to find the limits to what it can be trained to distinguish, employing a relatively simple and standardised form of behaviour as a measure.

Analyses of the stimuli actually used in the wild are difficult. Newly-hatched herring gull and black-headed gull chicks are among the best-studied of the relatively few examples (Tinbergen and Perdeck, 1950; Weidmann and Weidmann, 1958). The chicks are fed by both parents, and when they are aroused by a slight shaking as the adult arrives at the nest, they peck at the parents' bill. In herring gulls (*Larus argentatus*) the exact orientation of the peck is at a red spot near the tip of the yellow bill. The parent then regurgitates some fish on to the ground, picks some up, and holds it out to the chicks. The chicks peck again and get some of the partly digested pieces of fish.

Tinbergen and Perdeck observed this response sequence in detail, and used models to establish by experiment what cues the herring gull chicks respond to. Conveniently the gulls nest in large colonies on the ground, with sufficient space between nests to allow a small tent to be used as a hide. Chicks were in their own nests and were tested by raising a model of an adult gull's head over the rim of the nest. Models were cut out of cardboard and painted, and each chick was shown a short series, not more than five or six, in order to minimise both positive conditioning and habituation. The proportion of a large group of chicks that responded to each kind of model was taken to measure the model's effectiveness as a stimulus.

The best models were placed fairly low, just over the nest rim. There had to be a long, thin projection from the roughly-circular head, pointing obliquely down. The whole model had to be moving. The colour of the 'bill', or of the 'head', made little difference so long as the bill colour

Discrimination

contrasted with a definitely red spot near the tip. It is interesting that these stimuli could be provided better by a cardboard head disc and a red plastic knitting needle with three white stripes near the tip, than by a realistic coloured plaster model of an adult gull's head.

These experiments are unusual in the simplicity of the behaviour studied and in being possible on a large scale in wild animals. The conclusions are not unusual in requiring a little modification in the light of further work (Hailman, 1969).

Tests for discrimination – conditioned reflexes

Laboratory studies of the different kinds of stimuli which animals can be trained to utilise began, perhaps, with Pavlov (see Chapter 11). If a sound of a certain pitch and timbre regularly precedes food or weak acid in the mouth, a dog will produce saliva in response to the stimulus alone. If a second stimulus (say, a touch on the shoulder) occurs at the same time as the first, and the combination is not reinforced, the dog soon ceases to salivate. Pavlov (1927, c.f. p. 127) began by demonstrating that any such stimuli that the dog could perceive and that Pavlov thought of testing, could come to consistently excite or inhibit salivation. For most purposes Pavlov used stimuli of different modalities, light contrasted with touch, for example, but to test discrimination he had of course to use just one. With tactile stimuli, he contrasted rough textures with smooth, or either kind brushed against different parts of the body, far apart or close together. He contrasted objects of different temperatures. Visual stimuli were various shades of grey, or ellipses with various ratios between the lengths of the two axes, from 2:1 approaching 1:1, a circle. Auditory stimuli were noises of differing tone qualities (a buzzer compared with a toy trumpet), or pure tones of differing pitch. He found that if the stimuli were widely different at first and easy to distinguish, they could be brought gradually closer together, till the dog could quite easily discriminate between stimuli that confused it at first. But eventually the dog would have to try to discriminate between two stimuli that seem to him to be identical, and therefore both to salivate and not to salivate to the 'same' conditioned stimulus. Faced with an impossible task, the dog would refuse to perform at all and try to struggle out of his harness and the laboratory. Such behaviour seemed to Pavlov, as to Masserman 20 years later, to be a fair model of neurosis.

At about the same time as Pavlov, Yerkes (1907) started testing visual discrimination in a sort of simplified maze; Fig. 14.1 shows a later version. The hungry rat is given two or three exploratory sessions to find his way from the start-box into a choice area, across one side or other of an electrifiable grid floor, through a door into an alley with food at the far end. In later sessions he has to observe two stimulus panels illuminated from behind. If the rat chooses the correct one, say a white triangle on a dark

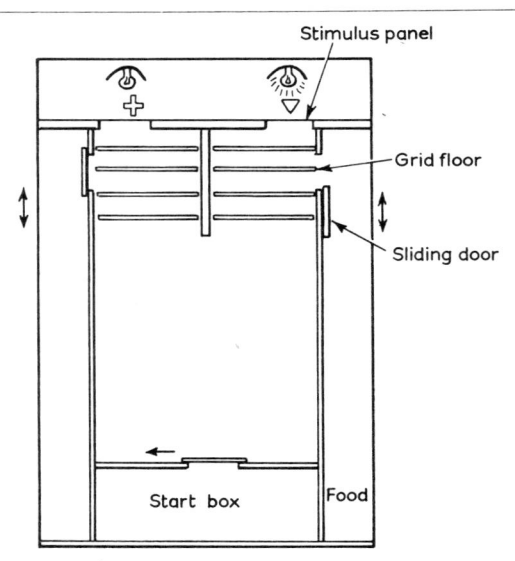

Fig. 14.1. Yerkes's Discrimination Box (Yerkes and Watson, 1911; after Kreezer, 1949).

ground, the door is opened and all is well. If wrong (say a dark triangle), the door is closed and he may also be subjected to shock. Either way, he is soon picked up, put into the start-box again, and given perhaps ten such trials daily. The position of the correct stimulus has to be changed in some random sequence, such as one of those arranged by Gellerman (1933). Otherwise, the rat may always choose the left-hand alley, or systematically alternate, or follow the smell of his own trail. When he has achieved, say, forty correct runs out of any consecutive fifty trials, he is deemed to have acquired the discrimination.

Even a simple light/dark discrimination required an average of about 125 trials in a Yerkes's box, and that seems a lot of hard work for a simple problem. Various people improved the box by removing the partition between the stimulus panels and the shock-grid, both of them unnecessary, and bringing the food reinforcement closer to the stimulus. A full redesign is the jumping platform of Karl Lashley (1938). Fig. 14.2 shows the improved version. The two patterns to be distinguished are painted on pieces of cardboard 15 cm square and placed behind windows in a vertical wall. One is held in place by a latch, the other is easy to knock over to get to the food on the platform behind. At first, the hungry rat is placed on a movable stand just in front of the empty windows, to become accustomed to stepping through them. The stand is moved, day by day, a few centimetres further back, so that the rat has to step across a gap and eventually jump across 25 cm and through the windows. He may need 'encouragement' to jump – shock has been tried, or tail pinching, or a blast of air from behind. Then

Discrimination 183

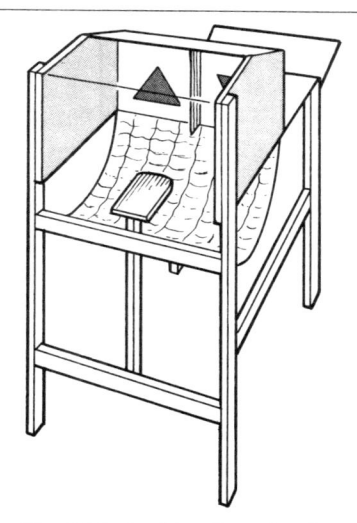

Fig. 14.2. Lashley Jumping Stand (after Lashley, 1938).

the cards can be placed across the windows, varying the fixed card's position from left to right in the usual randomised sequence. If the rat jumps against the fixed card, he does not get the food, but bumps his nose and falls a few centimetres into a net and is returned to the jumping stand. (I would have expected it to be easier to train the rat with two knock-down cards at an early stage, before training him to jump; but apparently not.)

On a criterion of 20 or 30 all-correct trials at ten a day, black can apparently be discriminated from white after a mere 4·3 trials, on average, horizontal from vertical lines after 27 and north- and south-pointed triangles after 28·6 trials.

Lashley (e.g. 1938) made a long series of experiments on 'the mechanism of vision', working out how much detail a rat could be conditioned to look at – squares, triangles, crosses in various orientations, singly or in groups, or singly against a confusing background of miscellaneous complex shapes common to both cards. The results gave Lashley evidence of a 'law of mass action' in the cerebral cortex. It appears (1939) that rats' ability to retain well-learned discriminations after surgical ablation of part of the cortex depends on how much is taken, but not which part is taken. Any milligram of cortex, on this view, plays just the same role as any other milligram, and the total quantity, from whatever region, is what is important.

Lashley's method still makes the experimenter spend considerable time and trouble in patiently teaching rats to jump through hoops. Even then, if the rat unfortunately chooses to jump at the wrong card a couple of times too often, he might refuse to risk falling into the trough again.

Norman, Munn and Marjorie Collins (1936) reverted to something like Yerkes's system when testing for colour vision in rats. Most mammals are thought not to distinguish colours as such, seeing colours as various shades of grey. Rats, being predominantly nocturnal animals, are in any case relatively more sensitive to blue and less to red than a diurnal animal like man, so that red should appear definitely darker to them than us. Hence the use of red light rather than merely very dim light in laboratories, for observing rodents' activity.

Anyway, some suggestive evidence led to a suspicion that rats could actually distinguish red from any shade of grey. After several graded training trials, the rat chose which way to go after leaving the start down a 16° slope, by the two stimulus panels (Fig. 14.3). If he chose correctly, the

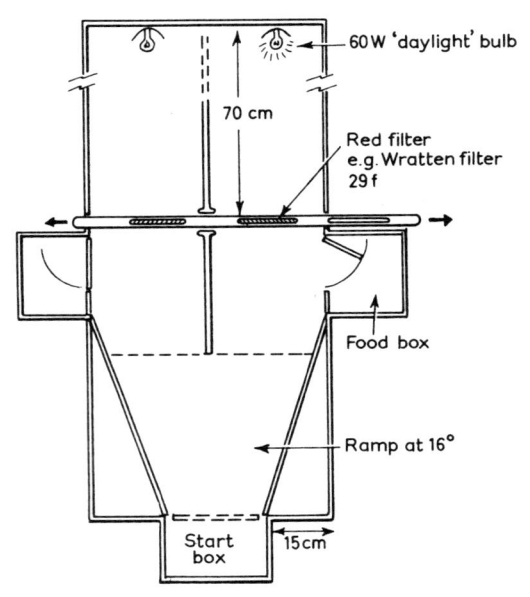

Fig. 14.3. Colour discrimination box (Munn and Collins; after Kreezer, 1949).

experimenter would pull a string to open a door into the goal-box for some Purina chow and lettuce. If wrong, another string would close a door behind him until he was put back into the start-box. The cabinet was wooden, lined with black velvet, and the stimulus panels carried Wratten filters illuminated from behind by 60 W bulbs whose brightness could be matched by sliding one away from the window and by using sheets of paper as additional filters.

Three filters were placed in a sliding panel. The red one (Wratten 29f) was in the centre so that it could be shifted to appear randomly left or right. Six albino rats were given ten trials a day discriminating red from black and a further ten from white. Comparing red with both darker and lighter shades of grey every day enabled the rats to discriminate it from both with virtually

100 per cent accuracy. Only against one particular shade of grey did accuracy decline to a mere 80 per cent, itself usually taken as a satisfactory criterion. Hence the possibility that the rats were selecting the absolute brightness of one shade of grey is the only alternative to a limited degree of colour vision.

Internal discrimination: do you know when you are high or tight?

Subjective feelings can influence the effects of drugs. Human beings often (but not always!) know what the drugs they take make them feel like: dreamily dizzy when drunk, drowsy, and dry-nosed on antihistamines, and so on. Δ^9-tetrahydrocannabinol (THC) is one of the most active components of cannabis and is supposed to give experienced smokers a fine emotional feeling. Sally Caswell and D. Marks (1973) gave ten naïve and ten experienced marihuana smokers cigarettes containing 3·3 or 6·6 mg of Δ^9-THC, and set them a monotonous vigilance task. They had to detect when one

naïve and experienced smokers

regularly flashing light failed to flash, and when any one of ten other lights did flash. THC impaired their performance, but neither group of smokers was able to distinguish the THC cigarettes from placebo dummy cigarettes.

Still, it is important if mental patients know the difference. If somebody suffering from schizophrenia or depression improves on regular treatment with phenothiazines or tricyclics, what happens when she stops taking her tablets? Is her pattern of expectations dependent on a conditioned cue from the sensations she obtained in the drug state? Conversely (whether she is conscious of the fact or not) is the drug-free state a cue for feeling depressed?

A nice example of the animal equivalent is a demonstration that rats can distinguish nicotine from saline and indeed from related drugs. Martin Schechter and John Rosecrans (1972) trained rats in a T-maze. After 0·4 mg/kg of nicotine the rat learned to turn right for 15 seconds access to condensed milk and to avoid a hefty 1·5 mA shock; after a saline injection the rat had to turn left for the same reinforcements. After injections of various other drugs – isomethonium diiodide, lobeline (which people have used to help them give up smoking because it blocks nicotine receptors), d-amphetamine, arecotine – they did not know which way to turn. Although the dose was fairly high, perhaps fifteen times what a person gets from a cigarette, the cues from nicotine were remarkably specific and reliable.

There are cases where the rat has to make a similar discrimination, but where experimental attempts to imitate the drug's internal cues fail. This 'state-dependent learning' is discussed on p. 255.

Discrimination without errors

Nowadays it is usual to use operant methods. To persuade a rat to press a lever for a little food or water, and in particular to stabilise the animal to get a uniform performance from day to day, requires patient conditioning. But once achieved, the response can be so finely adjusted to the animal's capacity that for this purpose operant conditioning is unrivalled. As it happens, most of the interesting experiments have used pigeons rather than rats, but this should make little difference.

One great advantage of the operant method for discrimination testing is that it facilitates an 'errorless' training procedure, with some differences in final behaviour from the conventional product. Conventionally, the animal has the choice of two stimuli and has to choose one. It must necessarily choose wrongly sometimes, and suffer – for otherwise it would never have the opportunity to discover that one curious stimulus card conveys information to its advantage and the other carries a government health warning. At best the animal will be confined and go back to square one without a bite to eat, at worst it will fall into a tangly net or suffer a painful shock. Some individuals will lose too much confidence to continue and may have to be discarded.

H. S. Terrace pointed out (1963a, b) that when the pigeon is shown with the positive stimulus right from the start of operant responding, the distinction lies between whether the pigeon pecks at the disc or whether it does not. It need never peck at the disc in response to the wrong stimulus. However, to learn the discrimination, the negative stimulus has to be present. It is not associated with punishment, it is merely never associated with reward.

The technique of errorless training is best shown by Terrace's first example. The pigeons were first conditioned until they were capable of a variable interval schedule. They were trained to peck at an illuminated red key, and their task was not to peck at a green one. In the first session, the red light was on for 30 seconds at a time, correlated with a variable interval 30-second schedule of reinforcement. The green key was dimly illuminated in the intervening 30-seconds, at first for 5 seconds, then for 10, 15 ... 30 seconds. Then, for 5-second periods, the illumination was gradually intensified till it was as bright as the red. Finally, the brightly lit green key was illuminated for periods increasing from 5 to 30 seconds. In the second and third sessions, the red, positive stimulus was on for alternate periods of 3 minutes, with a VI 1-minute schedule, the green negative one was gradually increased from 30 seconds to 3 minutes also.

Pigeons trained on this scheme hardly ever pecked when the green light was on. The rare mistakes were in the last few seconds of the 3-minute green light period, or the very first few seconds when the bird could not stop in time after a burst of pecking for the red light. Otherwise, the pigeons waited calmly for the correct stimulus.

Pigeons which were abruptly shown the green negative stimulus at full brightness, or which received gradual negative training only after some weeks of successful responding to red, or both, made many responses to the negative stimulus. If pigeons trained without errors to a red–green discrimination are then gradually introduced to the harder one between horizontal and vertical lines, they again learn without errors. But if the lines directly replace the coloured lights instead of being superimposed over them as they gradually fade, then the birds make errors. They also show signs of ambivalent arousal, stretching the neck as high as possible, or facing away from the stimulus or flapping the wings – the negative key appears to be both attractive and aversive.

Terrace also showed (1963c) that drugs like chlorpromazine and imipramine do not necessarily interfere with discrimination. True, pigeons given a perfect but conventional discrimination training would respond, to an extent related to dose, to the negative stimulus. But pigeons trained without errors still made none when drugged, so that the drugs cannot be said to interfere directly with sensory discrimination. Terrace suggests, as a possible explanation, that after errorless training, the negative stimulus is not aversive, it is no more than a cue that the positive stimulus is not yet available. In conventional training the negative stimulus has to be responded to, but is not reinforced and the pigeon is therefore conditioned actively to avoid it. The drugs reduce conditioned avoidance.

Operant thresholds

A very elegant procedure was used by Donald Blough (1958) to establish the light intensity a bird can just see. Though it is beautifully simple in principle, there are reasons for great complexities in practice. Basically the pigeon has to peck at one response key (key A) when an illuminated window is visible and another (key B) when it is not. The first key makes the window go dimmer, the second makes it brighter, so that its brightness oscillates just above and below the bird's threshold.

The apparatus is shown diagrammatically in Fig. 14.4. The pigeon has to put its head through a 45-mm aperture in the light-proof Skinner box, to

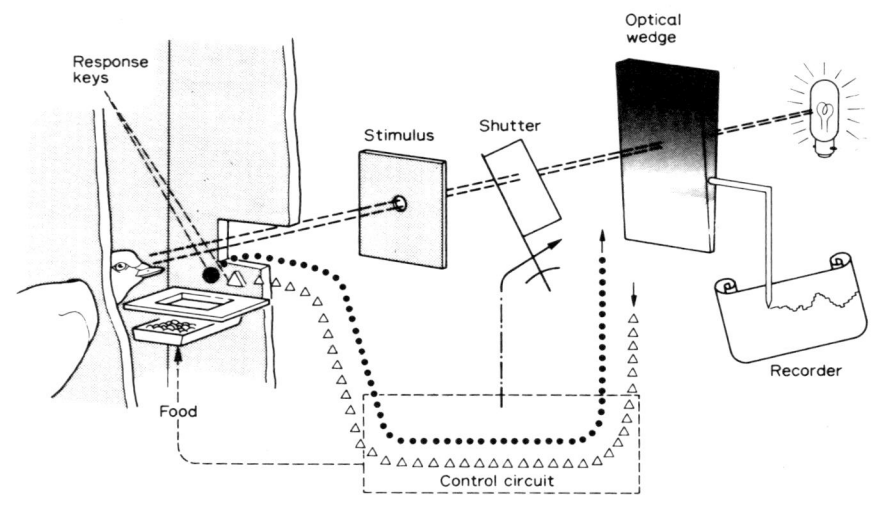

Fig. 14.4. Operant apparatus to find visual intensity thresholds in pigeons (after Blough, 1958).

keep its position constant in relation to the window above and behind the response keys. A silent shutter can shut off the light entirely, and an optical wedge of smoked glass is driven by a motor to change the stimulus intensity in steps of about 0·02 log unit, taking about 0·3 seconds to change. These values can be adjusted to suit the individual pigeon.

The pigeon is starved to about 70 per cent of its free-feeding weight, otherwise it would roost and go to sleep in the darkened Skinner box. The food magazine is brightly lit at first, and the bird can eat grain from it. Then the magazine is lifted within reach for 5 seconds only if the bird approaches and, later, if it pecks at either of the two keys with a grain of wheat glued to each. After the pigeon has pecked successfully for about fifty grains, the stimulus panel is brightly lit. A peck on key A turns the light off, a peck on key B when the light is off produces the grain for 5 seconds. The light then usually comes on again, but about one time in five it stays off and another peck on B brings more food. Otherwise the bird would always peck A first, whether the stimulus is on or not.

At this stage, all the lights are made gradually dimmer, and the house- and magazine-lights are turned off. After two or three pecks on each key, key A is made to shut off the light and B to summon the food; short variable ratio schedules are brought on, to prevent the bird getting too much food too soon, and to stop it pecking A and B alternately. To prevent bursts of responding on alternate keys, 'punishment' contingencies are applied – a false peck (e.g. on B if the light is on) subtracts 1 from its own ratio of responses. Thus if the ratio on B has 5 to go and the bird pecks A when the light is off and it ought to peck B, then the count on B is increased to 6, delaying reinforcement. To make sure the pigeon looks at the stimulus light, a peck on B is ineffective if it occurs too soon, less than 0·25 seconds after a peck on A. A variable interval of 15–30 seconds on average precedes the variable ratio of 4–8 on key A to prevent a discrimination based on time after reinforcement.

This textbook is not supposed to become too detailed, but it is worth listing these complications here, I think, to show the care which is needed. You must make sure you are actually testing what you think you are. It would be simpler if only animals would or could communicate with us without the need to superimpose food reinforcement schedules on the performance. Anyway, after about sixteen daily sessions of 0·5–2 hours, the stimulus intensity is finally put under the control of the bird's responses. The onset of darkness is now a reinforcer for the pigeon. If the light is really on but is too dim for the pigeon to see, it will peck B and increase the brightness until it is above threshold (meanwhile adding to the pecks required on B's VR schedule). If the bird can see the light it will peck on A, dimming the stimulus, until the ratio on A has been achieved. This will close the shutter and allow pecks on B to be reinforced with access to grain.

Blough confirmed that one pigeon was in fact responding to the light intensity by adding a filter which dimmed it by 0·7 log unit. The bird promptly increased the brightness by 0·7 log unit. Another bird aroused Blough's suspicion by the variability of its apparent threshold. It ignored the filter, so it must have been responding to something else until one of the complications was introduced to stop it.

There was evidence that, just as in man, the threshold is at a slightly brighter level going from darkness to light than from light to dark. And dark adaptation could be nicely illustrated. The threshold is quite high when the pigeon is first moved from daylight into a darkened Skinner box, and remains fairly stable for perhaps 20–30 minutes. Then the threshold falls quite rapidly to a new, low level, also quite stable. A fairly large dose of LSD, 300 μg/kg by mouth, also affected the threshold (by about half the amount that light adaptation would). Perhaps unexpectedly the drug did not lower the threshold, but raised it. Pigeons, like humans, seem to be most sensitive to a green light, of about 550-nm wavelength.

Discrimination as an indicator of concepts

Animals' abilities are often much more acute than we expect. I do not mean merely that, since threshold discriminations must be difficult almost by definition, Blough's pigeons were able to resort to so many subterfuges to get their grain easily. And I mean more than the ability of some animals to make amazingly fine discriminations, remarkable though some can be – perhaps the finest is the ability of some dogs to distinguish between the odour traces left by pairs of human twins and yet recognise the similarity by accepting either trace in the absence of its pair (Kalmus, 1955).

The most revealing discrimination experiment is surely one showing that pigeons can form concepts, and can recognise Man by his artefacts. Herrnstein and Loveland (1964) showed colour slides to some pigeons caught wild in Boston city streets. To get their corn they had to distinguish between photographs containing one or more human beings and those that were definitely non-human – animals, mountains, trees. The people could be in any part of the picture, in varied postures, clothed or nude (that must have been interesting – cornography?), adults or children, black or white, yellow

colour slides for pigeons

or brown. The pigeons clearly had a generalised concept of the human species, the task was too complex for simple recognition of individual people or pictures. Crucially, the pigeons treated such non-human artefacts as automobiles or houses as if they were human.

Go/No-Go discrimination

In the end the animal is required to respond when, but only when, a certain stimulus is present. The decision whether or not to go and collect the reward could be a question of the ability to distinguish one stimulus from another or of the balance between excitation and inhibition.

'Errors' can therefore be of two kinds, a failure to respond in the presence of the correct stimulus, and a failure to inhibit a response in its absence. An experimental treatment that increases the number of errors of either kind is often said to interfere with the ability to make correct discriminations. If the mechanism of the interference is pursued it often seems more likely that the relevant change is in the excitation, or the inhibition, or (though this is a difficult one to prove) a change in how much attention the animal pays to external rather than internal stimuli.

The point is worth mentioning here because of the 'discrimination' label attached, though some examples were discussed on p. 138. The trichloroethylene case is interesting, because the evidence on whether the vapour

Discrimination　　　　　　　　　　　　　　　　　　　　　　　　　　　　　**191**

causes the first type of error is conflicting, but is unanimous about the second. Using 'motor–food conditioned reflexes', Bannova (1961) and Horváth and Formánek (1959) found exposed rats to retard or to accelerate the positive response, respectively, and Grandjean (1960) found no difference. Using a pole-climbing avoidance technique (see p. 205), Goldberg, Johnson, Pozzani, and Smyth (1964a and b) found that some rats failed to respond to the stimulus in time, and they commented on the absence of a dose–response relationship and on individual variations between rats. But in all these reports it is mentioned, almost casually, that the animals were more likely to make spontaneous responses even when the traffic signal said stop.

Note, however, that a stimulus effective in one situation may not even be available in another. An extreme example is shown by honey bees which have good colour vision for flowers when gathering nectar, but seem to be unable to use colours in an escape response (Tinbergen, 1951).

Summary

Almost any reliable method of testing behaviour can show whether the animal can distinguish between a given pair of stimuli. Remarkably acute examples are scattered throughout this book. To demonstrate that an animal is able to discriminate, however, is far easier than to discover what features of the stimuli are actually used. Formal testing of discriminative ability therefore has to ask the less rewarding but more practical question: not what stimuli is the animal using in this situation, but how far is it capable of utilising these particular stimuli at all?

When an animal's performance in some experiment has been impaired one of the first explanations to be suggested is nearly always that the drug, or whatever it is, has interfered with sensory discrimination. Yet there are remarkably few cases where this ability really seems to have been affected; possibly only when a recent conditioning of some especially difficult distinction is involved. Nearly always an apparent failure of sensory discrimination turns out to be the inability to make a Go/No-Go decision accurately, usually an inability to inhibit a response when the 'Go' tendency is highly aroused. For when drugs seem to impair discrimination, the animals turn out to have been trained by presentation of both reinforced and non-rewarded stimuli. Discrimination after 'errorless' training, not being based on an inhibition or conflict, is not affected experimentally by drugs in the same way as the conventional product.

FIFTEEN
Behaviour after aversive stimuli: suppression, punishment, and withdrawal

Even in Utopia, children are going to trip and cut a knee, prick a finger on a rose bush or scald it on a cooking pot. Sometimes one human being inflicts pain on another, at least ostensibly in the hope of changing the recipients' future behaviour. It is possible that a distinction can be made in man that has not been made in animals, between stimuli inevitably received from the physical environment and emotionally loaded punishment from man. The question is whether both forms of retribution change behaviour equally well in the appropriate direction.

Behaviour in response to stimuli that are at least nominally painful is therefore a subject well worth study. The methods used are non-emotional, despite the use of words like 'punishment' which carry a heavy emotional loading to the layman (see the discussion on pp. 173–4), and do not of course attempt to distinguish social from physical retribution in experimental animals. In fact most of these experiments are not particularly concerned with academic models of human behavioural development, but merely with a useful set of techniques.

The usual stimulus is electric shock, mainly because it can be accurately and reliably controlled. As a result, the stimuli involved need not involve actual pain. In the majority of experiments, perhaps, the current intensity is below that causing pain, at least to a human being; your hand jumps away from the grid floor of the cage before you are aware of being startled. The shock would be tolerable if there were anything to be gained by it, and in some circumstances, rats also accept shock. However, severe shock is undoubtedly cruel, and some experimenters use intensities which seem quite unnecessarily high. While a method so easily misused requires special care, it is not the use of shock that matters in itself, but the intensity.

In this chapter, methods are described which mainly involve behaviour following the electrical stimulus. The next chapter describes how the animal can be conditioned to avoid the stimulus altogether, and Chapter 17 sets conditioned approach and avoidance tendencies into conflict.

Definitions

Aversive stimuli are those which the animal is likely to withdraw from, if given the opportunity, and not expose itself to again. The immense variety of methods where experimentally conditioned responses to such stimuli are used, are best classified in terms of the most commonly used such stimulus, electric shock.

(1) The simplest procedure is to *inflict shock directly* and observe results. Without knowing what these are, the results of more complex procedures could not be interpreted, but direct responses to shock are too difficult to measure for experimental purposes. Direct responses to heat, to pinching the tail or the injection of weak acid are useful in screens for potential pain-killing drugs, and swimming in lukewarm water may be healthy exercise.

(2) A conditioning stimulus can be made to regularly precede the shock. Some of the responses to shock will then be shown in anticipation, in response to the previously meaningless stimulus. This is the original *Conditional Emotional Response*, a term later applied to what is better known as *Conditioned suppression*.

(3) Conditioned suppression. The animal is trained to perform some other response, and the effect of shock or the conditioned warning of shock is measured by the interruption of the otherwise continuous performance.

(4) Punishment. The shock may not merely interrupt the other behaviour as if by chance, it may be inflicted as a direct consequence of the animal's response. The animal may be punished by shock every time it takes food, for example. Scalding hot coffee or neat whisky can (occasionally!) punish as much as reward.

(5) Conflict. Conditioned suppression or punishment may involve a shock so mild that the approach behaviour may not be entirely inhibited, but merely diminished. Tendencies to approach and avoid will then be visibly in conflict.

(6) Escape. If you can't beat them, join them. If animals persist in climbing out of the cage and escaping the shock, then let them. Take advantage of the behaviour by utilising it as a formal test.

(7) Avoidance. In practice, escape from shock after it has started is always tested with avoidance, the same response made before shock begins. If officially authorised by the experimenter, avoidance is usually in response to a specific conditioned stimulus; if the animal bites the experimenter and thus avoids being put into the apparatus, it is said to suffer from experimental neurosis. An established avoidance response may be tested with or without actual shock (Fear only or Fear plus Pain, in Neal Miller's phrase).

There are several versions of avoidance tests:

(8) *Active avoidance*. The animal has to do something specific in response to the warning signal. Many active avoidance tests adapt and reinforce one of the rat's unconditioned responses to shock, e.g. running, jumping, or climbing. Running does not have to be a one-way process, the animal can be trained to shuttle alternately from one end of a box to the other. Active avoidance may also utilise an artificial response like lever-pressing.

(9) *Free-operant* (*or Sidman*) *avoidance*. This is distinguished from ordinary active avoidance by utilising responses in the absence of a specific signal. With or without the additional discrimination of a conditioned stimulus, free-operant responses postpone shock for, say, 20 seconds.

(10) *Passive avoidance – one-trial learning*. One possible response to shock is to freeze, immobile, and this can be utilised to contrast with active avoidance. Instead of having to respond to avoid shock, the animal merely has to refrain from responding, for instance to refrain from leaving a brightly illuminated chamber to enter a dark one where it had previously been shocked. Passive avoidance depends on a conflict between the conditioned avoidance of shock and Unconditioned avoidance.

(11) *Unconditioned avoidance*, e.g. of light. Most rodents are largely nocturnal, and vulnerable to predators in the light. Their tendency to avoid such exposure is the background response against which passive conditioned avoidance can be measured; it can also be used as a test in its own right.

Stimuli which lead to withdrawal

Intense stimulation in any modality is likely to damage tissues: extremes of heat or cold, of bright light or loud noise ultimately cause damage visible under the microscope. But first they activate the fine 'C' nerve fibres and behavioural withdrawal.

A stimulus can be too weak to be detected at all. If it is just strong enough for the animal to detect, the stimulus evokes Pavlov's 'orientation reflex', i.e. exploration. The ordinary senses receive information. Stimuli for actions are carried by the pattern and only excessive intensity causes withdrawal. Electroshock normally carries little information, and there is no intermediate range of intensities between the thresholds for detection and for pain (except in those coastal fish which possess electric organs for social signalling and radar navigation).

Communication by sound is fundamental to humans in speech and music and could mislead us about the importance of sound to other animals. In rats ordinary sounds do not appear to carry a great deal of unconditioned information at frequencies we can hear, but they are remarkably easily conditioned as signals of approaching predators or food. Rats may become readier to flee, but otherwise seem largely to ignore another rat's squeal. At hypersonic frequences (around 35 kHz) baby rats emit calls which evoke retrieving and inhibit biting by adults, and Gillian Sales (1972) reported that adults submitting in dominance fighting call at similar frequencies. Arnold Myers (1959) found correspondingly that pure tones at audible frequencies were not aversive at intensities of up to at least 100 dB; a buzzer (including very high harmonics) increasingly causes withdrawal above about 70 dB.

As a stimulus for withdrawal, noise has been well investigated (Azrin and Holz, 1966). Its intensity can be controlled reasonably closely, it is pretty well inescapable (as anyone living near an airport can tell), and in experiments it is observably capable of altering behaviour without inhibiting it entirely (as anyone who continues to live near a motorway manages to prove). If you make the noise yourself, with a pneumatic drill or a motorbike or if other inducements are given at a disco, noise can be positively reinforcing to human beings – amazing as it may seem – at intensities which damage the sense of hearing.

noise can be reinforcing

Horváth and Frantík (1970), used noise as the negative reinforcement and a quieter noise (45 dB instead of 70) as the conditioned warning stimulus. Other aversive stimuli have been used: deep water, a blast of air (see p. 100), dilute hydrochloric acid for Pavlov's dogs, etc.

The engineering of electric shock

Electroshock is the most commonly used stimulus. Besides the technical reasons, so much work has been done with it already that the details of how to use it are well known, including its limitations, sophisticated apparatus is commercially available, and the experimenter can easily compare his results with others.

Azrin and Holz list some criteria for the ideal experimentally-aversive stimulus. It should be specified in physical terms (i.e. amperes or watts) rather than behavioural, measured as received by the animal so far as possible, and it should be delivered uniformly.

The electrical resistance between rat and apparatus is somewhat variable. Shock is usually administered through a grid floor of parallel metal bars, set 20–25 mm apart. Defecation and urination are among the responses to shock, and if the bars were set much closer, excreta might not fall between them, causing a risk of short-circuits; set much farther apart, a small rat might slip through the gap. The current, and hence shock-intensity, will depend partly on the area of contact between the rat's skin and the floor bars (and on how clean these are), and partly on the skin's conductivity. It will increase further if the stress is so great as to cause a moistening of the skin and fur. The original way of minimising the effect of such variation in conductivity was to use a high voltage and a high resistance in series with the rat, so that variation due to the rat formed a small part of the total resistance. Nowadays there are constant-current and even constant-power devices. I am not sure whether the relevant parameter is the electrical potential across the nerve endings themselves or the heating effect of the current across the skin as a whole. Fortunately, small variations in shock intensity are usually of small importance.

The third criterion of Azrin and Holz is how far the animal is able to control the intensity of the stimulus. After all, it has a strong incentive to escape altogether by climbing out, or biting through the wires and breaking the circuit. So the cage has to be rat-proof and the bars of stainless steel. If the bars are alternately positive and negative, the rat will avoid shock by straddling every second bar. So a 'scrambler' system is used, to make each bar in turn momentarily negative to all the others.

The rat can still win. It will climb the wall if it can, or jump and at least shorten the duration of shock. To the extent that such responses reduce the shock, they will tend to be reinforcing; the animal will have less incentive or opportunity to learn any other desired response. The experimenter will either underestimate the animal's performance by measuring only an officially authorised response, or will discard the rat; either would seem to be an unfortunate waste. Azrin and Holz show a delightful photograph of a rat which seemed not to respond to shock at all. In fact it lay down on its back so that it was completely insulated from shock by its fur, and calmly pulled the lever down, letting manna from the food dispenser drop gently into its mouth.

An aversive stimulus may have to be painful, but should not cause physical damage. A rat with a painful burn might be physically unable to perform its task, and currents above perhaps 5 mA can cause tetanus so that the rat cannot move. Nevertheless, the ideal stimulus would be easy to vary smoothly from the barely detectable to the total inhibition of alternative behaviour – by behavioural means, so far as this can be logically distinguished from physiological trauma like tetanus.

Is this precision really necessary? For conditioned suppression or punishment apparently it is, for conditioned avoidance apparently not. Where the animal has to overcome the shock-barrier to perform some other action, the height of the barrier is continuously important. Hake and Azrin (1963) found that a 20 per cent increase from 50 to 60 volts caused a 50 per cent fall in monkeys' response rates. There are other factors, of course, since extra deprivation of food can sometimes restore food-reinforced responses almost totally suppressed by shock. For conditioned avoidance, on the other hand, the shock only needs to be sufficiently intense to give the rat an incentive. Rats can detect about 0·1 mA but a higher current is required to induce avoidance, about 0·5 mA according to Hoffman (1966), though King (1970) found 0·1 mA quite effective for his rats in his apparatus. Once the rat is efficiently avoiding, of course, the shock that it is *not* getting hardly matters. In practice the rat does not avoid every shock even when well trained, but Stone (1960) found 0·5 mA as effective as 1·0 mA; if rats fail to learn, it is not surprising that increasing the shock does not help (Hoffman, Fleshler, and Chorny, 1961). You cannot knock sense *in*.

Direct responses to shock

Responses to shock depend on its intensity and duration, from an orienting reflex ('what is it?') upwards. A slightly greater current makes the rat run for shelter with a roof over its back or up the nearest wall or tree. If two rats are shocked together, they may momentarily attack each other (see Chapter 20). They may jump unpredictably hither and thither. In the extreme case there may be tonic or clonic convulsions. Convulsions are surprisingly effective in confusing predators, who give up the hunt in frustration, and this may be their evolutionary function (Humphries and Driver, 1970). In short, some aspects of behaviour following shock resemble anti-predator behaviour, and the belief that avoidance is accompanied by the rats' equivalent of fear is therefore plausible, though not necessarily true.

Direct responses to shock have rarely been used as indicators of drug effects. An occasional example is enough to explain why many people have a conditioned emotional response. Mallov and Witt (1961) wished to test whether tranquillisers protected against atherosclerosis which was thought to result from stress. They exposed rats to 1-second electric shocks at irregular (1·25 or 2·5 minute) intervals for 0·5 to 7 hours at a time. The shock intensity was chosen to produce 'subjectively maximal' responses. After 20 minutes, control rats showed signs of stress or fear that were clearly well-observed: bristling, a form of crouching with the back arched and the tail raised tensely, an upright posture (maybe with the lower spine vertical, the upper spine subsiding to the horizontal) and of course defecation. The main measure, however, was the plasma concentration of free fatty acids (FFA) which were thought to cause deposits in the coronary arteries, and which gradually rose from 0·36 mEq/l before shock to 0·78 mEq/l 7 hours later. Chlorpromazine injected 5 minutes before shock in the fairly substantial doses of

4 or 8 mg/kg was not effective, but the larger dose an hour beforehand kept plasma FFA almost down to normal. Rats given chlorpromazine were relaxed and sleepy and seemed not to worry about the shocks they still seemed to feel. Since the drug without shock did not alter FFA and since jumping and dancing induced by shock without drugs tend rather to lower FFA. It was concluded that it was probably the 'tranquillising' action that protected the rats.

Now there are good reasons for investigating the relief of stress and I may not have properly understood this particular experiment. Yet with hindsight I wonder if its rather small results really brought enough benefit to man to justify 'subjectively maximal' responses for 7 hours at a time. Witt won his high reputation by his subsequent analyses (e.g. Reed and Witt, 1968) of drug-induced disturbances to spiders' webs.

To the deep blue sea

Most animals swim as innately as they walk, but the fur of small land animals like rats gets bedraggled in water and they rarely swim spontaneously. So to dunk a rat in water produces a reliable performance and if the water is warm and the rat is dried off afterwards it need only be a mild stress.

Swimming to exhaustion has been used but seems as open to misuse as long periods of shock, and in any case the end-point is difficult to judge. Uyeno and Graham (1966) took as their criterion that a rat should sink for at least 20 seconds, and showed that rats' stamina ranged from 70 to 1156 seconds, more than a fifteen-fold difference (do you have to wait superstitiously for it to sink three times?). Repeated swim-testing makes an unusual method because you condition the rat's muscles and respiratory system as well as its behaviour. However, rats are uninterested in the rat race, the hope of an Olympic gold medal does not reinforce a drowning rat as much as the prospect of getting out of the water.

not interested in the rat race

Evans (1937) demonstrated that rats can swim a temporal maze, and Bättig and Grandjean (1963) that swimming a 4-metre channel was impaired by trichloroethylene: rats were exposed to 400 ppm for five 7-hour days a week. On Thursdays and Fridays they had to swim the 4 metres ten times, wearing a harness on five of the trials so as to pull a 27-g weight. Exposed rats swam slower than controls after 6 weeks with a load and after 13 weeks when unencumbered.

A Czechoslovak–German team has extended the method into a kind of 'shuttle-bath' (cf. p. 206). Tušl, Stolin, Wagner, and Ast (1973), put a rat on a platform which gradually submerged under water. The animal had to swim to another platform 4 metres away and back when, after a time to rest, the second platform submerged in its turn. Swims were timed with the aid of photocells, and control equipment set the number of swims automatically, stopping the test if a swim took longer than a predetermined 'exhaustion-time'.

The tank could be sealed in order to test the animals while exposed to a gas or vapour, in this case nitrogen dioxide (NO_2). Fig. 15.1 shows that control rats breathing clean air improved after the first month's testing, and

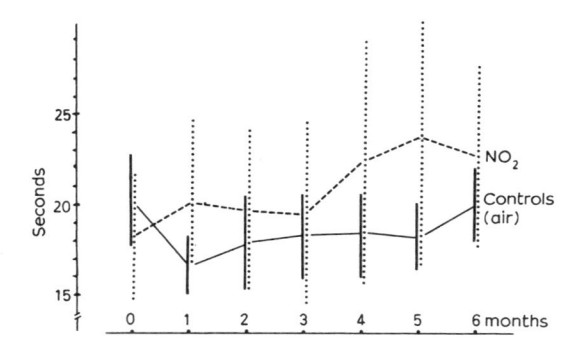

Fig. 15.1. Swimming times in rats exposed to nitrogen dioxide (after Tušl *et al.*, 1973). Rats were exposed to 20 ppm NO_2 for 6 hours a day and tested monthly for their ability to swim twenty trials in a 4 m water tank. The graph shows mean swimming times and 99 per cent confidence limits: some rats are affected by NO_2, some rats seem unharmed.

kept their fitness until middle-age crept upon them at 6 months. Rats exposed to 1 ppm of NO_2 tended not to improve, those exposed to 5 ppm swam about 25 per cent slower and as the figure shows, 20 ppm made them swim much slower. An interesting point is the wide variance in the 20-ppm group, suggesting that some rats were affected quite badly, others not at all. Another group of rats was first tested after 8 weeks of daily exposures to 3·5 ppm. Controls steadily improved over twenty trials, exposed rats deteriorated and swam the last five trials slower than the first. Presumably these are signs of lung damage otherwise detected only by elaborate lung-function tests, and shows that concentrations thought to be without significant risk (the Threshold Limit Value is 5 ppm) are not quite harmless.

Conditioned emotional response

Rats first respond to irregular electric shocks by jumping or freezing briefly (p. 197), but later stand continuously immobile. Such postures occur between shocks rather than during them, notably in response to a light or buzzer that always switches on 10 seconds before the shock . . . the 'emotional' response has become conditioned. With relatively mild and brief shocks this 'conditioned emotional response' (CER) is likely to be tied fairly closely to the specific stimulus, but with severer shocks to the situation as a whole, making the animals difficult to work with.

The word 'emotional' in psychologese is curiously subjective and curiously limited. If animals feel any emotion they must surely feel all.

Now it may be reasonable to suppose that animals do feel emotions, because human emotions must have evolved from some precursors. Furthermore a plausible function can be postulated. For whole classes of heterogeneous stimuli have to be connected with whole classes of responses, and the heterogeneous stimuli have to be added together. They must operate by sharing a single set of control systems and a conscious emotion might be the simplest means of achieving this with limited computing power.

However, we must be careful about the evidence. Seward and Raskin (1960) gave rats intense electroshock in the goal-box of an alley and the rats promptly learned not to run the alley, but remained immobile at the starting gate. This was claimed in a flash of the blindingly obvious to give '. . . evidence of an inhibitory factor [supporting] the usefulness of the fear construct in the theory of avoidance behaviour'. Emotions may exist, but by definition they are unobservable and cannot logically be used as explanations.

Fear was also postulated when rats showed a conditioned emotional response to a buzzer associated with unavoidable shock. If the rats could do something to avoid the shock, or if they were given the neuroleptic drug thioridazine (related to chlorpromazine), or both, they did not show the CER. Torres (1961) argued therefore that an effective avoidance response and the drug both reduce fear.

Howard Hunt (1956) attempted to quantify CERs by grading the postures in intensity, but appears to have concluded (1961) that the results were not worth the effort.

Nevertheless, detailed observations of responses in a CER situation are useful. John Bainbridge and David Greenwood (1971) inflicted twenty 4-second bursts of noise on rats. Every fourth buzz ended in mild shock (0·1 mA for 0·6 seconds), so that a CER was produced. Saline-injected rats never groomed themselves more than once, but propranolol, chlorpromazine, haloperidol, and phenobarbitone all let the rats groom themselves three to four times out of twenty. In a further experiment, grooming and movements of whiskers, ears, or head occurred as an interruption of immobility rather than of activity, and propranolol and phenobarbitone both permitted exploration by reducing freezing. Since grooming usually occurs at the point of balance between one kind of behaviour and another, the drugs may have reduced anxiety, they certainly hastened extinction of the CER.

Conditioned suppression

A conditioned emotional response is more easily measured indirectly. The animal is first conditioned to perform some action continually and reliably; commonly a rat presses a bar for sweetened condensed milk on a schedule that generates a steady rate of responding, neither fast nor slow. A light or sound is then conditioned to act as a signal of impending shock. If the rat develops a CER it becomes immobile, and ceases to respond on the milk schedule. If the shock is only mild, the responding might slow down but not be altogether suppressed, so that response rates can be quite a sensitive measure of the inhibition. Tranquillising drugs like the benzodiazapines, which are clinically useful in the treatment of anxiety, are quite effective in restoring bar-pressing (Lauener, 1963).

Such disinhibition is not necessarily a sign of reduced anxiety. Cappell, Ginsburg, and Webster (1972) found that while amphetamine tended to slow down responding on a Variable Interval schedule for food, it partly restored responding suppressed by the threat of shock: during the 1-hour sessions, lights shone for two 3-minute periods ending in a 0·5-second shock and few responses were made after saline injections during these periods. The increased responding in these periods after amphetamine was dose-related and while it was greatest in respect of mild or moderate shock (0·5 or 1·5 mA) there was some indication of an increase under threat of a 2-mA shock.

Now amphetamine could be expected, as a stimulant, to accelerate responding under both baseline and suppression conditions; as a drug reducing food consumption, to depress responding under both conditions. To depress baseline responding and increase it during the warning stimulus is what would be expected of a tranquilliser, which this drug is not. All results are worth examining, interpretations can only be tentative.

Klaus Miczek agrees (1973). A typical conditioned suppression experiment showed that a stimulus signalling shock inhibited responding on a VI schedule for food, and that chlordiazepoxide, but not scopolamine or amphetamine (unlike Cappell and colleagues!), restored the lost responding. But in another similar experiment, the conditioned stimulus signalled an extra ration of food, not shock, and again lever-pressing for food was suppressed – after all, why work for your food if you are going to get a free handout? In this case, however, amphetamine was the only drug to restore responding on the VI schedule – the rats ate no more, either of the free food or of their wages, but they went back to work anyway!

Conditioned suppression can be a sensitive indicator of sensory thresholds. Birds are commonly thought to have a very poor sense of smell, but Wendon Henton (1969) showed that pigeons can detect and distinguish amyl acetate, butyl acetate, and butyric acid by odour at about 0·1 per cent, a sensitivity similar to man's. The birds were trained to peck for grain on a 2-minute Variable Interval schedule in a 'breathing chamber' where a controlled flow of air passed, saturated with water vapour. A little air saturated with the test vapour was added occasionally to the main airstream for 18 seconds, ending in brief shock. The birds pecked in air control trials but almost stopped during the amyl acetate stimulus. Assuming that a 50 per cent fall in response rate marks the concentration that a bird could just smell, Henton varied the small additions of saturated stimulus air into the main airstream in falling, rising, or irregular sequences very much as Donald Blough did for visual thresholds (see p. 187).

Punishment

Punishment means just what you would expect, but without the implication that the animal is morally wicked. The animal does something, punishment is a shock applied when and only when that action is performed; it is a stimulus that inhibits repetition of the action in future (see p. 174). There are, of course, several ways of stopping an action associated with feeding. You can give the animal sufficient food to satisfy its appetite, as Azrin and Holz point out (1966) (see Table 15.1) or you can extinguish the response (or even the animal) by not giving it any food at all. The definition of punishment therefore implies a situation which would otherwise stimulate that action's

Table 15.1 (adapted from Azrin and Holz, 1966)

Procedure	Effect, suppression is:			
	Immediate	Enduring	Total	Irreversible
Stimulus change. = external inhibition				
Extinction = internal inhibition		+		
Satiation	+	+		
Physical restraint	+	+	+	
Punishment	+	+	+	+

+ = Yes

performance (e.g. food deprivation plus the chance of obtaining food). There is also a difference from the everyday meaning of the word. In real life, the parent, teacher, or judge is supposed to aim mainly at redirecting the offender's behaviour into more socially-acceptable channels. The theory may not always be stated, and practice may be far from theory – and equally far from suppressing the unacceptable behaviour, for that matter – but in the human case we are concerned with the behaviour that increases to fill the gap left by the punished action's absence. In the laboratory, the experimenter aims merely at suppressing the animal's response and punishment need cause no more signs of distress than extinction.

The most absurdly simple punishment experiment was a 'cat-and-mouse' test by Sacra, Rice, and McColl (1957). They selected cats that readily pounced on mice under their experimental conditions. Then they gave the cats a shock every time they touched a mouse. The cats stopped. Fairly large doses of meprobamate, chlorpromazine, or benactyzine let them start pouncing again. It was not stated what sort of anxiety-reducing drugs they gave the mice. More conventionally, Leonard Cook (1964) used a schedule where, when a tone sounded, every response brought food and alternate responses also brought strong shock (1·6 mA for 1 second). Squirrel monkeys understandably stopped responding, unless they were given meprobamate or chlordiazepoxide, but chlorpromazine did not restore punished responding even at a dose (2 mg/kg) which interferes with non-shocked Variable Interval responding.

Conflict

Punishment need not entirely suppress the response. Mild or less frequent shock need only reduce the rate when every response is reinforced by both shock and a drop of milk: it need not totally inhibit it. The animal is subject to two conflicting tendencies. To press or not to press? That is the question for Chapter 17. It only remains to suggest here that conflict techniques are likely to be more informative than punishment or complete suppression, because both tendencies are observable, and because room is left for both rises and falls in two kinds of behaviour.

The next chapter describes methods where the animal is less likely to continue receiving shock.

SIXTEEN
Conditioned avoidance of aversive stimuli
Where rodents fear to tread

Animals have anti-predator tactics: active running, passive immobile concealment, and if necessary counter-attack. Some of these have been exploited as laboratory tests.

Escape

Any response which results in escape from shock will naturally be reinforced. Flaws in the construction of the apparatus or the procedure are discovered when rats climb over walls or bite through wires. The behaviour can be utilised by officially providing and recording a means of escape.

A simple route is a wooden pole projecting vertically down from the lid of the cage (Cook and Weidley, 1957). Wood is an insulator of course and rats can readily climb in response to predators or shock, so it is likely to occur and be reinforced readily. Hecht (1967) described a chamber with a series of such escape routes: the rat can climb a wooden pole, jump up on to a shelf high on the wall, run to a safe part of the floor, or up a sloping string net, or jump through one of three windows to safety (discriminating the correct one on the way), or he can run 40 cm to a lever which switches the current off when pressed. Hecht confirmed that these measures are affected the same way by any given treatment, and therefore that they measure the same thing. Climbing a pole for food was, fortunately, altered differently.

Escape responses are often called 'unconditioned', since by definition they are responses which follow shock rather than some arbitrary signal. The fact that a response exists is certainly not conditioned but to find the one which works needs practice and learning.

Pole-climbing avoidance

Escape is not very interesting on its own, but it makes an informative contrast with avoidance. If the animal can predict the imminent onset of shock it soon comes to cry before it is hurt. Or rather, instead of a CER, it avoids the shock by making what would be called the escape response if it was made later. Avoidance is scarcely a matter for surprise either, but is useful because it can be prevented by treatments which do not interfere with escape.

Pole climbing was at one time a favourite procedure. In one version (Goldberg, Haun, and Smyth, 1962) a rat was placed in a plastic chamber and after a generous 15 seconds for exploration, was given a series of shocks through the grid floor. In this experiment, they were very intense, averaging 8 mA for ten 20-msec pulses per second for 30 seconds. At the same time as the shock, a buzzer sounded, with the whole cage surrounded by a soundproof shell so that other rats waiting their turn, would not hear the buzzer without reinforcement. After a few trials, rats discovered the benefits of climbing on to the roughened wooden pole. When a rat escaped consistently, the shock was only applied during the final 15 seconds. Rats climbing in the first 15 seconds of buzzer would therefore avoid the shock altogether, the so-called conditioned response (CR). As Maffii (1959) first noticed, over-responsive rats tend to develop a 'secondary' conditioned response: they climb the pole without waiting for the buzz. If they climb down again, the 'primary' CR is very fast.

Generally, a small dose of an effective drug selectively inhibits the secondary CR, an intermediate dose the primary CR to the buzzer, but very large doses are needed to inhibit escape. Goldberg and his colleagues, investigating methyl cellosolve (the monomethyl ether of ethylene glycol) after a few daily 4-hour exposures estimated that 150 parts of the vapour per million would inhibit the secondary and 500 ppm the primary response to the buzzer, but rats only lost the response to the shock itself at concentrations which would later kill them. A concentration of 500 ppm did not interfere with the ability to ride a rotating rod but potentiated barbiturate sleeping time. In factory workers exposed to moderate concentrations, methyl cellosolve can cause 'headache, drowsiness, forgetfulness, and disorientation amounting to a temporary incapacity'. Yet ethyl alcohol only inhibited conditioned avoidance at 32 000 ppm, where the rats were staggering drunk and could not escape either.

Conditioned avoidance by pole-climbing is clearly a useful measure of some sorts of behavioural effect. The difficulties come, as usual, in the interpretation. Cook and Weidley's original experiment with chlorpromazine illustrates the issue very well. The median effective doses inhibiting avoidance and escape were 10·5 and 40 mg/kg respectively. Now if the animal is still capable of responding to the shock, the drug has not drastically impaired its physical capabilities. If it can still detect the stimulus, it is obviously tempting to say that the drug has diminished the animal's fear of the shock, as Cook and Weidley implied quite strongly. Yet diminished fear does not seem a good explanation of the symptoms of temporary 'toxic encephalopathy' from over-exposure to methyl cellosolve. And there is considerable evidence (Miller and Barry, 1960), that alcohol can reduce experimentally evoked fear in rats as well as giving Dutch courage to humans, yet it did not selectively reduce conditioned avoidance.

Now we could leave the result as it stands. A valuable drug inhibits conditioned avoidance, selectively, and we can look for similar drugs without enquiring how far the screen explains their clinical usefulness. However, even on the test's own terms, Irwin and his colleagues (1959) found that, using milder shock in a shuttle-box, the effective doses of chlorpromazine were several times smaller than in Cook and Weidley's experiment, 1·4 and 16·7 mg/kg for avoidance and escape instead of 10·5 and 40. If the important variable turns out to be the strength of the shock, then how specific is the inhibition of avoidance?

Other forms of conditioned avoidance test are equally subject to this difficulty, but they are less liable to the problem of the secondary conditioned response: you cannot easily describe pole-climbing as a response to the buzzer if the animal clings to the pole as soon as it enters the cage and has to be encouraged to let go.

Shuttle-avoidance

Instead of climbing a pole, you could train the rat to escape by merely running to a safe place, perhaps at the other end of the cage. But after a couple of unhappy experiences, the rat would stay at the safe end. You could carry him back to the shocking end of the cage and he would promptly run back. You could put a barrier say about 20 cm high, that the rat would have to jump over. The effort involved would be a mild deterrent but he might nevertheless jump before the signal, just to be literally on the safe side. To get him back again, you might have to give him a shock on that side too . . . with a warning signal . . . and you end with a double cage, the grid floors on each side of a barrier electrifiable separately, a buzzer or light providing the conditioned stimulus on each side. With mild shock the rat can be made to shuttle back and forth for hours at a time.

Stein (1964) used shuttle avoidance to support one of his usual stimulating ideas. He argued that amphetamine facilitates reward mechanisms in the brain, specifically that it lowers the threshold of neurones in the median forebrain bundle, so that electrodes implanted there should reinforce self-stimulation with lower currents. Stein's theory was admittedly and cheerfully 'fanciful . . . it nevertheless has the dual advantage of comporting with the data and contradicting common sense'.

He first distinguished between the process of learning a response and performing it when fully established. Stein argued that on the first few trials, the stimulus buzzer warning of shock activates the 'brain mechanisms for punishment' (that in man would be accompanied by subjective fear) and suppresses the mechanisms for reward by reciprocal inhibition. When the animal escapes, and still more after the first successful avoidance, the fear mechanisms will be switched off, releasing the reward processes and indeed letting them overshoot. This rebound phenomenon, no doubt the process responsible for our subjective sense of relief and thankfulness (cf. p. 10), is the positive reinforcement mechanism for avoiding shock.

It follows that, once the avoidance response has been conditioned, it can be maintained without fear. And if avoidance really works by increasing positive reward, then you have a single explanation of amphetamine's facilitation of avoidance behaviour and its inhibition of food consumption, as a substitute for actually eating.

Stein tested this ingenious idea in a shuttle-box. Warning lights at both ends told the rat to run to the other end within 7·5 seconds and get 15 seconds peace and quiet or else receive a brief series of shocks through electrodes implanted into the periventricular region of the brain.

Avoidance learning is slow in a shuttle-box, for the rat finds it difficult to run towards a place where it had previously been shocked and perhaps towards a stimulus warning of shock still to come, but escape is usually prompt and so is an established avoidance response. When the performance of Stein's rats was reasonably stable, they were given brief (0·2 second) and weak 'priming' shocks through a different electrode aimed at one of the 'reward' areas of the brain. They were given fifty trials when the priming stimulus occurred just as the warning light switched on and fifty ordinary trials without priming, and each electrode was later tested to see if it would reinforce self-stimulation. Seven of the eleven electrodes which proved rewarding were also electrodes where the priming stimulus improved conditioned avoidance (from 10 to 60 per cent). The thirteen electrodes which did not reinforce self-stimulation did not improve avoidance either, in fact one clearly made it worse. Injection of 1 mg/kg of amphetamine made a similar improvement to avoidance performance (up to 65 per cent better than after saline). So Stein thought that amphetamine and rewarding primary stimuli probably work by the same means.

It is an attractive theory, especially as some conceivable alternative explanations can be excluded. The primary stimulus could have acted as an extra warning stimulus, but surely no better in the regions where it rewarded self-stimulation than where it did not. It did not bring any other reward. Amphetamine and the priming stimulus both increased spontaneous intertrial responses, and to a similar extent. Both self-stimulation and avoidance were increased in parallel with increasing current, steeply from 0 to 200 μA and to a small extent from 200 to 700 μA.

It seems correct that continued performance of an established avoidance response is a routine, like crossing a busy road at the official pedestrian crossing place, and does not depend on the 'punishment mechanism' and also that the first successful avoidance response gains a rewarding sense of achievement and so reduces fear secondarily. The priming stimulus could therefore help to give the rat confidence. But while Stein is right that amphetamine *may* lower the threshold of this 'reward' mechanism, I am not convinced that he has excluded the possibility that it lowers the threshold of the 'punishment' mechanism instead – it remains possible that an *increase* in avoidance is due to an increase in 'fear' and that it is the sense of reward which is secondary.

At least some of amphetamine's effect could also be simply explained by a direct effect on motor activity. A rat perceiving signs of a predator has two possible responses, either to run for shelter faster than the cat can reach it or to freeze motionless and avoid attracting the cat's attention. A shuttle-box with the warning light at both ends is like having to run towards the cat to reach safety. So the rat tends to freeze, and irrespective of reward or fear, amphetamine may improve shuttle performance merely by switching the rat towards activity. Conversely chlorpromazine reduces both pole-climbing and shuttle-box avoidance (Oliverio, Renzi, and Sansone, 1973) and may do so merely by switching the animal towards immobility, even though more shocks are received. Chlordiazepoxide is a tranquilliser clinically useful in relieving apparently excessive anxiety, but has little effect in either kind of conditioned avoidance. It does, however, disinhibit behaviour that had been suppressed by shock. Interestingly it also restores behaviour inhibited by satiation or extinction or even by the bitter taste of quinine (Margules and Stein, 1967). Perhaps Pavlov was right in classifying all these as internal inhibition.

A one-way avoidance task was used to test the interaction of alcohol with five drugs thought to be tranquillisers. Hughes and Rountree (1961) used intense shock (10 mA for 5 seconds) in a main chamber with two smaller compartments. They argued that a drug can only be called a tranquilliser (i.e. antianxiety) if, besides reducing conditioned avoidance, it also lets the rat select the correct one of two excape routes. On this definition, alcohol and pentobarbitone are not tranquillisers, because after doses sufficient to inhibit avoidance but not making the animals too limp to walk and escape from shock, rats did not discriminate between the two exits. Rats receiving reserpine, chlorpromazine, hydroxyzine, or meprobamate in suitable doses still chose correctly. [However, on the same criterion, Doty and Doty (1963)

selecting the correct route

would call chlorpromazine a tranquilliser only if the task was easy. The harder the problem, the greater the inhibition of avoidance and the more errors the drug caused.] A dose of alcohol (0·5 g/kg) giving blood–alcohol levels thought to be safe enough in man, had no particular effect on its own, but added to any of the other drugs converted 'tranquillisers' into 'general depressants' where both avoidance and discrimination deteriorated. Take care.

Instrumental avoidance

Avoidance can be conditioned with any of the usual operant responses – lever-pressing, key-pecking, wheel-turning, and so on. It can take two forms (which can be combined). The first is Discrete-trial avoidance, the direct analogue of pole-climbing, etc. The animal has to respond to a conditioned stimulus within a set time, or else receive a shock; the same response permits escape. The animal may also have to discriminate the correct one of two stimuli or two levers. The second is the free-operant technique popularised by Murray Sidman (see p. 211); shock is inflicted at regular intervals, without any obvious signal, but whereas in many methods a response between trials has no effect whatsoever, in Sidman avoidance it postpones the shock for a set period. Regular spontaneous responding (if this is not a contradiction in terms) lets the animal avoid shock altogether. A combination schedule where spontaneous responses postpone shock, but where, in their absence, a signal of impending shock is given, will be labelled as discriminated free-operant avoidance.

Discrete-trial avoidance

Pole-climbing is, of course, a perfectly good operant response in principle, if a little too close to a spontaneous response and a little too cumbersome to be convenient. The precise equivalent, where instead of climbing the rat was required to turn a long cylindrical 'wheel' (Verhave, Owen, and Robbins, 1958), gave the expected results with chlorpromazine. A buzzer sounded for 7 seconds alone, and could be turned off by rotating the wheel. If the rat did not avoid, then the buzzer continued with shock added until the rat did turn the wheel. When the rats responded with 95 per cent accuracy, i.e. when they received only one shock for every twenty buzzes, they were given chlorpromazine. As usual, fairly low doses greatly inhibited avoidance while leaving intact the response to shock. Morphine did the same (Verhave et al., 1959).

A wheel takes up far more space in a cage than a lever, but it does help to avert a problem. With a lever, rats try to turn the schedule into free-operant avoidance by holding the lever down (just as they climb a pole without the official stimulus if the shock is too strong). Howard Hoffman (1966) became worried by this, without actually saying why 'such behaviour... is considered undesirable', and suggested ways of reducing it. None were altogether effective. The lever might provide the electrical control pulse, not when it is pressed but when it is released; if it is fairly inaccessible, holding it down becomes too much like hard work. The lever could be withdrawn between trials, but the loss of all spontaneous responses would lose information. Giving a shock for undesired responses would cause unnecessary complications to the main experiment. Even Verhave's wheel could be whizzed round and round.

What seems like a straightforward example of the method led to some disturbing results. Casterline, Brodie, and Sobotka (1971) were worried about the interaction of pesticides and malnutrition. Carbamate and organo-phosphorus insecticides act by inhibiting cholinesterases in the insects' nervous system, as they do to some extent in ours. Inadequate diet in the first 2 or 3 years in human children can apparently lead to irreversible deficiencies in brain development. What happens if a mal- or undernourished child can only obtain food containing appreciable residues of pesticides?

After weaning, rats were housed singly and fed on diets containing either low or adequate protein (5 or 18 per cent casein), with or without 1000 ppm banol (a carbamate) or 4 ppm of the organophosphorus parathion. In an hour's avoidance conditioning each weekday, animals had to learn to switch off a light and noise stimulus (5 seconds) followed by stimulus plus shock (5 seconds) followed by 10 seconds peace and quiet; the animals were left to discover the use of the lever for themselves. The curious result was how often rats failed to respond at all, even to escape. Rats eating sufficient protein, with or without added pesticide, learned fairly rapidly and those on inadequate but pesticide-free diet learned more slowly. But in nearly every week, rats fed on low-protein contaminated diets more often failed even to escape than others, indeed the low-protein/banol group deteriorated from 49 per cent failure in week 1 to 84 per cent failure in week 10. Their brain enzymes seemed normal. Direct observations were not reported, nor was the strength of shock, but a plausible guess is that the shock was too strong (or too weak); the half-starved rats might have overreacted to shock with a CER. It remains worrying that malnutrition and pesticides should interact to interfere so severely in a situation that other animals could cope with.

The interpretation of drug effects is helped most by direct observation. Stone (1960) watched rats in their first 2 or 3 hour avoidance-learning session, 15 minutes after drug-injection. Pipradol, a stimulant thought to cause less disorientation than amphetamine, tended to prevent freezing after shock and enabled the rats to run round the Skinner box faster than controls. They were therefore more likely to brush against the lever and discover that it would switch off the shock. Conversely, thiopropazate slowed down all walking so that the rats had less opportunity to discover the operation of the lever and avoid. When shock came, thiopropazate-dosed rats went into tetanus, even after only 0·5 mg/kg, and could not move to the lever anyway. Rats given benactyzine, a tranquilliser, could still walk after shock; in fact they pressed the lever often enough to escape, but appeared unable to learn from escape-reinforcement and therefore failed to avoid.

Free operant avoidance

A common problem in lever-pressing avoidance is that rats are apt to hold the lever down in the absence of the signal. They may even bite the lever (a phenomenon whose motivation would be interesting to analyse), which could explain bursts of responses *after* the shock. If spontaneous responding interferes with efficient avoidance, why not make use of the behaviour that exists?

Murray Sidman (1953) is credited with the first use of what he prefers to call free-operant avoidance. It is also called continuous avoidance, because a rat that spontaneously and regularly presses a lever which postpones the shock need never be shocked at all; also because Sidman used sessions of 8 hours continuously, which is a long stretch for a little animal.

A typical free-operant schedule might program a shock every 15 seconds. It is a relatively mild and brief shock, say 0·4 mA for 0·5 sec, but comes without any special warning. Escape is hardly relevant from such a brief shock, but any lever-press re-sets the timer, so that shock is postponed. The interval between the response and the next shock may be the same as between shocks (as they are in Fig. 16.1) but need not. If the response–shock interval is 30 seconds, two perfectly-timed responses every minute would let the rat avoid the shock altogether.

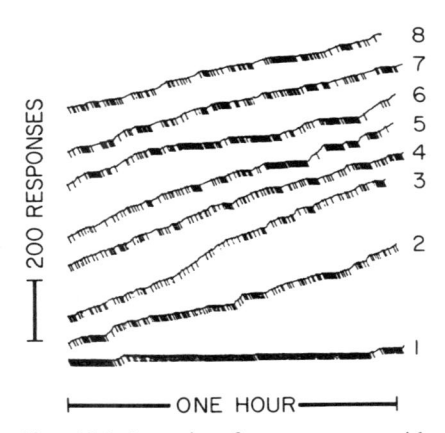

Fig. 16.1. Learning free-operant avoidance (from Sidman, 1966 by permission). The cumulative record of the responses of one rat on its first 8-hour session where a mild shock was delivered every 15 seconds unless postponed by a lever-press. The slope of the continuous line shows responses, oblique 'flicks' indicate shocks.

Sidman gives several illustrations (1966) of how rats perform on their first 8-hour session. The bottom line of Fig. 16.1 shows how a typical rat seemed to have begun to learn what to do with the lever by the end of the first hour. The response rate rose quite high later, as the steeper slope shows for the third hour, but declined later so that by the eighth hour the rat was performing quite efficiently. Nevertheless it never managed to avoid shock for more than 4 minutes at a time. Another rat, despite pressing the lever a total of 253 times, clearly failed to grasp that pressing postponed the shock, and must have received close to the maximum number of shocks in the session. At an interval of 15 seconds, this means nearly $4 \times 60 \times 8 = 1920$ shocks. The performance of the official response, as Sidman comments drily, is a necessary but not a sufficient condition for learning, and this particular rat needed four 8-hour sessions. A third rat seemed to begin avoiding after only half an hour. In the fifth and sixth hours it successfully avoided all but twenty-eight shocks, by responding at an unnecessarily high rate.

Individual variability in either response rate or learning ability is not surprising, as Sidman remarks, but it is relevant to experimental results. Bignami, de Acetis, and Gatti (1971) were interested, because some tranquillising drugs have been reported both to improve acquisition of conditioned avoidance and either improve or impair its performance. They used a form of discriminated free-operant avoidance, with an interval between shocks of 30 seconds, and a warning light after 10 seconds. Responses before the light came on were ineffective, but afterwards would postpone the shock (2 mA for 2 seconds) by 20 seconds. The drugs (pentobarbitone, chlordiazepoxide, diazepam) all acted in much the same way, but the effect of all three depended on the animals' pre-drug performance. Rats which were usually efficient received more shocks than usual: they increased their rates of response, but mainly because of ineffectual bursts (particularly before the warning light). Rats which usually received many shocks improved their performance: maybe the drugs raised the previously low response rates, just possibly they made the rats more receptive to the stimuli from light, lever, and shock, and so helped them learn. Or maybe the drugs ameliorated the state of dithering conflict that rats are in before pressing an avoidance lever (see p. 228) and so let the animals respond more promptly.

Executives, ulcers, and how to cope

Free-operant avoidance, indeed avoidance generally, can undoubtedly be stressful and sometimes causes gastric ulcers, duodenal ulcers, and colitis. But the stress is not related simply to the shock or the great length of the sessions. Joseph Brady (1966) described some necessary conditions using 'yoked pairs' of animals, where one performs the avoidance but both receive the same shocks. In one experiment, eight Rhesus monkeys were restrained by the waist and neck in 'primate chairs' for 6 or 7 weeks at a time. Each pair of monkeys received identical shocks (5 mA for 0·5 seconds) every 20

Conditioned avoidance

seconds on a 6-hour on, 6-hour off schedule. Each monkey had a lever, one lever did nothing, the other postponed the shock by 20 seconds for both animals. During the 6-hour avoidance periods a red light shone and the active monkey pressed the lever fifteen to twenty times a minute, dropping to less than once an hour when the light was off; the yoked control never pressed more than twice an hour. After 3 or 4 weeks, four of the monkeys had 'developed extensive gastrointestinal lesions with ulceration . . .' But the yoked control monkeys, exposed to fairly unpredictable shocks showed no signs of lesions, indeed the one shown in Brady's photograph looked remarkably relaxed and alert. It was the monkey with the responsibility for controlling the shocks that suffered.

Curiously, the phenomenon occurred much more on a 6-hour on, 6-hour off cycle than on others. Monkeys with 30 minutes on/30 minutes off, or rats on 1/1 or 12/12 hour cycles showed a far lower incidence of ulcers, rising at intermediate periods, 3/3 or 9/9 to a peak at 5 or 6 hours (cf. the 'Kamin effect' p. 216). Even more curiously, the fact that it was the 'executive' monkey that got most ulcers seems to have been a special case. Jay Weiss found precisely the opposite in rats, and pointed out that Brady had decided which monkey should be the executive and which the yoked partner after a preliminary training session. The executive was the one that could learn the avoidance schedule best. On Weiss's theory, the animal readiest to learn free-operant avoidance is most likely to get ulcers anyway.

Weiss based his theory on a linked series of experiments (1971). The rat was placed in a plastic cage for 48 hours with water available but no food, and was loosely restrained by fixing an aluminium disc and taping electrodes to his tail (Fig. 16.2). One rat randomly chosen from a matched set of three was trained to turn a wheel to escape or avoid shock. Control rats developed ulcers from close confinement and food deprivation. Executive rats, receiving shocks but being able to escape or avoid them, developed more and worse ulcers, but not so badly as the helpless yoked partners. In all groups, there was wide variation, but the degree of ulceration was correlated with plasma corticosteroid levels.

Being able to do something about the shocks, therefore was half way to not getting hurt. Superimposed on this, however, was the question of warning and feedback signals. On a pure free-operant schedule, the rat neither knows exactly when the shock is coming nor, very often, whether his response has been received by the apparatus. He just has to wait and see. If the shock-train was preceded by 20 seconds of a loud 'bleeping' noise silenced by a response, both executives and yoked partners developed fewer ulcers than the corresponding unsignalled free-operant rats. If a quiet low tone became higher and louder every 30 seconds for 3 minutes before the bleep, then the crescendo acted as an audible clock, the rats knew more exactly where they were and suffered less ulceration still. Finally Weiss added a punishment contingency. The executive rat, in conflict because the

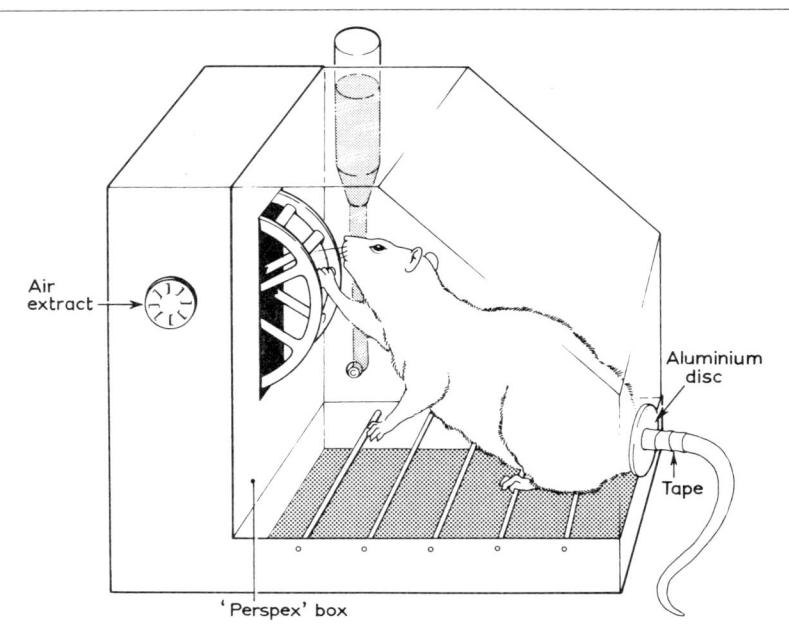

Fig. 16.2. Apparatus used in an experiment on yoked conditioned avoidance (after Weiss, 1971).

avoidance response nevertheless incurred a brief shock penalty, suffered far worse ulcers than the helpless yoked partner receiving the same shock unpredictably. Conversely, if a response was followed by a brief audible tone, the executive rat was in the best position of all, and developed hardly more ulceration than the unshocked control.

Part of the stress caused by free-operant avoidance must lie in the relatively long delays. Except in the special case of conditioned aversions to novel tastes (see p. 245), 20–30 seconds is a long time for a rat to wait for the consequences of his action. Learning should be faster if the interval between shocks is reduced (Sidman, 1966) and so it is. When the shock–shock interval was only 5 seconds instead of 30, while a response postponed shock for 20 seconds, acquisition of the response was quicker. Some rats develop a temporal discrimination, responding after quite long pauses, others respond at a needlessly high rate. On an 'adjusting' schedule, each response only postpones the shock a short time, say 5 seconds, but the animal can build up a cumulative credit instead of the response merely setting the timer to zero. Shock intervals are therefore irregular and temporal discriminations are not made.

An interesting logical point is that extinction must be very slow. There is no burst of responding as there is after constant positive reinforcement. The more effective the free-operant avoidance, the longer it will be before the rat discovers that there is nothing to avoid. Rats behave almost as if they use the occasional shock to check if that boring old lever-pressing is still a necessary chore.

Discriminated free-operant avoidance

Discrete-trial and free-operant avoidance were nicely combined by Webster and his colleagues (1971) to test for hallucinogenic drugs. In their version, the first phase was a pause of 32 seconds, then a light came on accompanied by a clicking noise for 8 seconds, and lastly came a shock (1 mA for 0·5 seconds) every 4 seconds until the rat responded. A lever-press at any stage re-started the 32-second interval. After extensive training, rats responded mainly during the signal. Webster *et al.*, predicted that hallucinogens like *l*-Δ^1-tetrahydrocannabinol (THC) would increase both 'premature' responding before the signal, as amphetamine does, and delay responding to escape after the shocks have started, as chlorpromazine does.

During the 5 days of the experimental week, the rats had a 30-minute warm-up, and were then handled, injected with solvent (alcohol and Tween 80, but not enough to alter the behaviour), or THC solution. The cannabis ingredient did just what was expected: the rats definitely received a few more shocks and greatly increased premature responses. Webster and his colleagues thought that this schedule is more sensitive and perhaps more specific than the DRL approach they also tried.

Passive or one-trial avoidance

For all the differences between pole-climbing, shuttle-box, and free-operant avoidance, these methods of conditioned avoidance share their most important characteristic. The animal has to actively avoid the shock. When the time or the signal comes, it has to do something specific. It is also possible to condition an inhibition, and treatments may well have opposite effects on active and passive avoidance.

A typical passive avoidance apparatus consists of a small transparent brightly illuminated chamber with a small doorway into a second, dark chamber with a grid floor. In the single training session, the rat is either placed in the dark chamber and confined there for a severe shock, or allowed to find its own way in. Frank Holloway and Richard Wansley (1973) put the rat into the light chamber, and timed it until it found the opening to the dark chamber clambering through (in 1·2 to 46·9 seconds in this experiment). Once in the dark chamber, a 5-second shock was started (0·1 watt constant power) – and surprise, surprise, all the animals returned to the bright chamber well within the 5 seconds. Within 20 seconds of making their escape, all the rats had been returned to the home cage.

Learning need be tested only once. The rat is put back, always into the illuminated chamber, and the time it takes to enter the dark chamber again is measured without further shock. Control rats do not re-enter the place where they were hurt. For practical purposes, learning is assumed if the rat fails to enter the dark chamber within a convenient arbitrary time of, say, 3 minutes.

Holloway and Wansley were investigating the 'Kamin' effect (Kamin, 1957) where it looked as though rats had remembered less 6 hours after the shock than 12 hours after, and found that the 'learning' and partial 'forgetting' were repeated rhythmically. Holloway and Wansley tested different batches of rats at various times after shock. Rats tested after an interval of 15 minutes or 12, 24, 36 . . . 72 hours nearly all waited the full 5 minutes in the light. But at 6, 18, 30 . . . 54 hours only 25 per cent of the rats stayed in the light, and 50 per cent at 66 hours; the median rat clambered into the dark shock chamber about half-way through the trial. Since the cycle takes 12 not 24 hours, it does not look like the usual circadian rhythm, especially as rats trained in the late morning or the afternoon and tested strictly on schedule showed no difference. However, the highest circadian activity peaks occur around dawn and dusk. Holloway and Wansley do not give the raw data but it looks as if the rats 'failing to remember' might have been tested closer to 08.00 and 20.00 hours than the possibly sleepier rats tested at intermediate times.

Discussion of passive avoidance in terms of 'learning' is curious, since it is defined by whether or not the animal leaves the brightly lit part of the apparatus. It is assumed that the rat ought to avoid utterly entering the place where it has suffered. As a practical measure, passive avoidance is reasonable, but it is not necessarily, or not only, a measure of learning. For this obscures the test's dependence on the rat's unconditioned avoidance of light. If non-shocked rats could not be relied on to enter the dark chamber in the first place, there would be no reason to compare this with avoidance of the place of shock. While fluctuations in the balance between avoidance of light and of shock might certainly be due to changes in conditioning or remembering, they might equally be due to a decline in 'fear of shock' or an exaggerated 'fear of light' or an increase in curiosity or sheer blind motor activity. Passive avoidance is no simpler to interpret than any other test (cf. p. 257).

Height can be used as the basis of a passive avoidance test, 'step-down' passive avoidance, in the same way as light. The rat is placed on a small platform a few centimetres above a grid floor, where it is given a shock as soon as it steps down. Control rats generally remain on the platform, in slight discomfort from the apparently precarious and exposed position, throughout the subsequent trial.

Passive avoidance in a Y-maze

One good reason for being tentative in interpreting Holloway and Wansley's cyclical data is that the evidence is conflicting. Ramesh Kumar (1970a) gave rats a shock in one arm of a Y-maze at a time chosen to allow the rats

Conditioned avoidance 217

to be tested between 11.00 and 14.00 hours, after an interval from 0·5 to 120 hours. Avoidance increased to a maximum at 6 hours and declined by about half from 30 to 120 hours, yet when these same rats were tested again after a week even the early-tested rats (which originally had hardly avoided at all) avoided as completely as the rest. There was no evidence of a repeated rise and fall in avoidance; but Kumar's rats were all *tested* at the same time of day, where the others were *trained* more uniformly. Nevertheless, there was evidence that the avoidance took some time to develop, was complete by about 6 hours, and premature testing would neither reveal nor interfere with the developing avoidance.

In Kumar's Y-maze one arm was white and could be closed off from the others. Each rat was confined there for 3 minutes and subjected to two 10-second periods of inescapable shock (0·5 mA) at the end of the first and second minutes. For testing, rats were placed at the central point and observed for 3 minutes. Entries into the white arm and each of the two black-painted arms were counted and timed, white being used more for discrimination than to provide the usual degree of sheer light avoidance; control rats, previously in the white box but not shocked, averaged about 20 seconds in the white arm in the first test and about 16 seconds in the second. Shocked rats spent less time in the white arm (Fig. 16.3) but were as active in exploring the other two arms as controls were in three.

In a standard passive avoidance test (Bovet, Robustelli, and Bignami, 1965) amphetamine can appear to diminish avoidance of the shock. Kumar

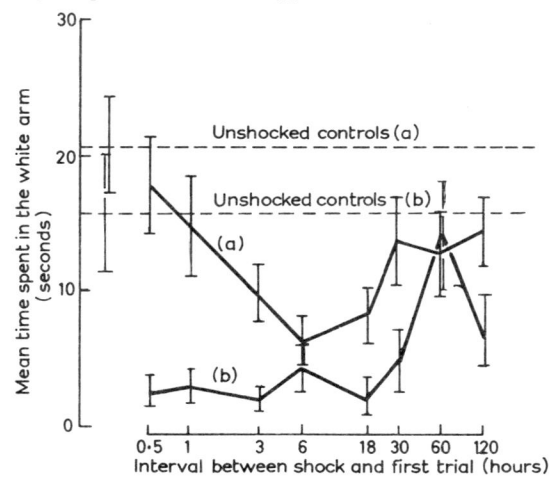

Fig. 16.3. Passive avoidance in a Y-maze (after Kumar, 1970a). The rats were confined in the white arm of a Y-maze for 3 minutes and given a painful shock. They were then given two trials, the first after an interval of 0·5 to 120 hours after shock; rats tested early avoided the white arm little more than the un-shocked controls (a), but when re-tested a week later (b) avoided it as completely as those whose first trial avoidance had been significant.

(1971a and b) found that dexamphetamine increased entries into the two dark arms of his Y-maze (while reducing the time spent sniffing at a disused food trough at the end of each arm), but amphetamine-injected rats did not enter the white arm where they had been shocked any more than saline controls. The drug increased motor activity, but while it may not have actually increased avoidance it certainly blocked its extinction.

Amylobarbitone also increased activity but in addition it reduced avoidance, for rats given 4–15 mg/kg spent more time in the white arm than saline controls did. In this case, Kumar believed that the drug overcame a still-active fear, i.e. gave courage, for if the fear had been extinguished the difference from controls should have widened in repeated trials as the rats learned safety; in fact the performance paralleled that of the controls.

Chlorpromazine reduced activity. More surprisingly, most of these few entries were into the dark arms: chlorpromazine usually reduces avoidance, but in this passive situation increased it.

Unconditioned avoidance

If passive avoidance depends on a spontaneous tendency in rats and mice to prefer dim illumination, it should be possible to measure and use this specifically as a test. Note that light-preferences can change according to the time of day. Kavanau, Ramos, and Havenhill (1973) found that various weasels and other small carnivores have a preference for bright or dim illumination related to their activity in running wheels, and largely depending on whether the species normally comes out of doors to hunt or just to bask in the sun.

Another test can be the unconditioned avoidance of heights. For instance Montgomery (1955) found that rats delay entering a maze if it is open and elevated well above ground level. Morrison and Stephenson (1970, 1972a) used a Y-maze. One arm was 61 cm long, the walls 10 cm high and painted matt-black, and black paper covered the wire-mesh roof. The second arm was painted gloss white, and the roof was open to the overhead fluorescent strip lighting. The third arm was sometimes black like the first, and sometimes the rat found it was merely a runway, without walls and elevated 1·2 m from the floor. Control rats spent little time in the light arm; different groups averaged from 18 to 46 out of 180 seconds. Albino rats invariably preferred both of the dark arms to the white one, a few hooded rats treated the white arm as second best. The open arm was avoided even more, groups averaging from 4 to 14 seconds, and many rats did not enter it at all. Nicotine (0·4 mg/kg) had no effect, d-amphetamine had little, but tended to increase avoidance of the light arm. However, amylobarbitone and the tranquillisers chlordiazepoxide and diazepam all increased both activity in general and the previously-minimal time spent in the open arm while mild avoidance of the light arm continued unchanged.

It is relevant that most rodents avoid predation partly by being nocturnal;

Conditioned avoidance **219**

but if they are alarmed in the open, they are quite likely to climb trees or walls to escape. In fact, black rats (*Rattus rattus*) are more likely to climb than common rats (*R. norvegicus*), they run cautiously but without undue circumspection along ledges or branches. They might well show less avoidance of elevated runways in the laboratory than common rats, but comparable levels of light avoidance. Both forms of unconditioned avoidance undoubtedly share characteristics with the various versions of conditioned avoidance of shock, but seem distinct.

Summary of Chapters 15 and 16

There is a general class of behaviour where the animal moves away from a particular stimulus, or where a set of stimuli cause the animal to inhibit the action it would otherwise make. At the lowest detectable intensity, any stimulus evokes exploration. At the highest intensities, any stimulus causes pain and withdrawal, and heat or cold, noise, or immersion in water can be used experimentally. Because its physical parameters can be fairly precisely controlled, and because there is no 'natural' use of intermediate intensities to carry information, the best experimental aversive stimulus is electric shock. At low intensities, this is still aversive but probably due to startle rather than pain.

The direct responses of an animal to painful shock are observable but not easy to quantify. Similar responses occur to stimuli conditioned to signal inescapable shock, but remain hard to measure, unless they are superimposed on a positive response, e.g. for food. Responses to shock can then be measured in terms of the behaviour that they inhibit, whether shock merely interrupts on-going responses or is so directly related to their performance that it 'punishes' them.

The most widely used measures are instrumental, where the animal can do something to escape from a shock or to avoid it altogether, by responding to a conditioned stimulus beforehand. Avoidance can be active, either by direct movement to a place insulated from shock or by pressing a lever to postpone shock that is otherwise unsignalled. Avoidance can also be passive, where the rat ceases to enter a place where it had previously been shocked. Passive conditioned avoidance depends in practice on the existence of a spontaneous preference for conditions such as those chosen for the place of shock, e.g. a preference for dim rather than bright illumination. Avoidance of bright light can itself be used as an independent test method.

SEVENTEEN
Conditioned conflict with aversive stimuli
Coming or going or dither

Behaviour is always liable to be complex, even in situations the experimenter considers simple. This chapter considers certain stylised procedures where competition between two kinds of behaviour is experimentally conditioned.

Approach–avoidance conflict
When a hungry rat is put into the start-box of a maze for the first time and the trapdoor is opened, the rat does not immediately gallop at top speed. It may take a long time to leave, stretching a tentative nose out and suddenly withdrawing it and washing, taking a cautious step or two and rushing back. Even in a late stage when the rat is fully familiar with its environment, Miller and Miles (1935) showed that running speed was slowest in the first 2·5 m of an 8·5-m runway. A rat is capable of far too high an acceleration for the constraint to be merely physical.

We commonly label this inhibition fear, anxiety, or caution. The label is reasonable but open to objection, and indeed the inhibition may not be a single unitary factor requiring a single all-embracing name. But the inhibition, or set of inhibitory factors, exists and has to be considered.

To bring the inhibition under better control, it is usually thought necessary to set up a deliberate conflict between the tendency to approach the goal (usually food) and the tendency to avoid it (usually due to shock). Miller and Herbert Barry (1960) give a stimulating review. One way is to add quinine to the food, to make the fruits of victory turn bitter in the mouth In a maze, food adulterated with quinine is analogous to food that is not there: less is consumed and in future, frustrated rats approach the goal more slowly and with more 'errors'. It suggests a reduction in approach more than inhibition by what we call fear.

Conflict provides ways of testing, among other things, for 'Dutch courage'. Conger (1951) among several ingenious experiments, tested the effect of alcohol almost literally on the strength of approach and avoidance. He put rats into little harnesses and made them pull on a spring balance so as to measure 'drive' in grams. Alcohol reduced the pull away from a place where the rats had been shocked, without affecting the pull towards food. Not only, therefore, did the drug alter the motivational tendencies selectively, but the inebriated rat's inability to walk straight was not the explanation. It is a pity that nobody since Conger's time seems to have succeeded in repeating this delightful technique.

A straightforward conflict began when twelve young cats were deprived of food 22 hours a day, and set to run a 1·6-m alley. On a shelf at one end, hidden behind a door the cats could easily push open, was a tasty pellet of fish. After sixty-three trials in 8 days, Bailey and Miller (1952) found the cats reached the fish in less than 3 seconds. After two warm-up trials on day 9, a conflict was set up by giving the cat a 0·1-mA shock when it touched the cover door. Shock was progressively intensified in steps of about 0·05 mA until the cats hissed, arched their backs, scratched at the door cover, and three times refused to run down the alley. They were then injected with saline or sodium amylobarbitone (18 mg/kg intraperitoneally), and in four trials over the next 20 minutes only one control cat ran the alley even once. The seven drugged cats were inco-ordinated but active, and all staggered as directly as they could to push at the dreaded door and took the fish. The drug therefore seems to have reduced experimentally-conditioned fear.

Satisfactory experiments with rats seem to have needed a telescopic alley of adjustable length, for rats readily learned to run quickly down a short safe alley and slowly on longer, more dangerous trips, but not apparently the other way round when the safe journey was the longer one. On the first trial they ran 0·3 m without shock. Each trial was 0·3 m longer than the last and occasionally the rats were given shock when they reached the goal. The longer the alley, the more frequent and the more intense the shock. Very reasonably, the rats ran slower, the higher the risk and the penalty.

Miller and Barry emphasise the distinction between trials when the rat is actually subjected to shock, and trials when the trained rat runs without shock. In commonsense terms, they distinguish Fear alone from Fear plus Pain. In the telescope alley, a substantial dose of alcohol (15 ml/kg of a 10 per cent solution intraperitoneally) but not amytal, made the rats run faster in the short safe alley. In the longer, dangerous, alley in the fear-only condition, intoxicated or drugged rats still ran faster than controls though slower than the controls in the short alley. Actual shock made all rats stop, drunk, drugged, or sober.

shocked rats stopped, drunk, drugged, or sober

One of Miller's strengths is the way he looks at alternative hypotheses, which, if true, would undermine his favourite motivational explanation. For example, rats were trained in one telescopic alley and tested in another one. Both approach and avoidance were reduced, but especially avoidance, so that the novelty had the same effect in this respect as alcohol or amytal. (Pavlov would not have been surprised. He had often noticed that external inhibition of an inhibitory conditioned reflex by a novel stimulus, would disinhibit the original excitatory reflex.) Miller thought that the drug might have reduced fear, not directly, but by somehow changing the stimulus situation.

He therefore trained four groups of rats, two after amylobarbitone injections and two after saline. One group of each pair was then tested under the drug, the other under saline, so that for half the rats the internal stimuli had changed and for half they had not. As usual, rats given the drug ran the final, most dangerous section faster, but amylobarbitone given previously in training had much less effect than when actually present during the test. It therefore did not act merely by changing internal stimuli.

In all these experiments, animals had first been trained to run for food, and shock avoidance was added later. Miller (1964) then developed a shuttle alley to test whether amylobarbitone primarily reduced fear or disrupted merely the most recently-learned habit. The alley was 2·4 m long. Five seconds after a light started flashing at one end, the grid floor was electrified, but the sections further from the light delivered a progressively weaker shock. Since there was a light at each end, rats could be trained to shuttle repeatedly to the end furthest from the light, the place free of shock altogether.

When the rats had learned this, they were deprived of food, and placed in the alley alternately at each end, finding a pellet of food in a tiny cup at the end of every 0·3-m section. Next, the light flickered at the far end of the alley as soon as the rat was put in. Shocks were delivered at unpredictable intervals, getting more intense nearer the light – which the rats had to approach to get the food. Tested in the fear-only condition without actual shock, rats given 20 mg/kg amylobarbitone approached closer to the light to eat pellets than saline controls. So once again Miller concluded that, irrespective of which response has been conditioned first, amylobarbitone reduces Fear much more than Hunger.

Measurement of drives

Some classic psychologists of the 1920s and 1930s made great efforts to list the distinct Drives that a rat possesses to enable it to satisfy specific needs, and to attempt to measure the strength of each. Not all of them had the naïve and over-simplified view of behaviour that this statement implies (though some to them did). Kreezer (1949) for example, defines drive as 'a condition in the animal which leads to activity directed toward a particular end-result . . . in the sense that persistent and varied activity of the animal takes place until that end-result occurs . . . [it] may be regarded as analogous to the potential difference of electromotive force of the electric circuit . . . a condition of disequilibrium in the organism which tends to produce activity of the organism in a given direction . . . possessing both direction and magnitude'.

Kreezer then spoils an intelligent expression of the concept with an uncritical review of methods supposed to measure 'drive'. The most popular involved approach–avoidance conflict. The animal was deprived of food, water, a social or sexual partner, etc., which was then offered beyond a barrier whose 'height' gave a rough measure of the incentive's value. For instance Moss (1924) used a short alley with a electrifiable grid whose voltage was progressively raised until the rat refused to cross. Unfortunately this assumes that the tendency to approach, the 'drive-strength', remains constant; which is now known not to be true. Wiepkema (1971) found first a rise and then a fall in a mouse's tendency to continue eating within a meal. It cannot be assumed that shock will have no effect on the value of the incentive (see p. 227). When Aesop's fox found the obstacle between him and the grapes to be insurmountable, he realised that they were sour anyway.

Similarly, in the 'Columbia obstruction-box' (Warden, 1931) the test was to see how often a rat would run through a tunnel where it was liable to a shock (of constant voltage). Locke (1936) looked for a social drive in general. He attached the rat's own home cage to the goal-box end of the tunnel, with a familiar cage-mate still living in it. After controls to exclude various specific drives, and after varying periods of deprivation of rodent companionship in solitary confinement, Locke found rats were not particularly willing to put up with shock to meet their mates. Perhaps they reacted aggressively to foot-shock as paired rats often do.

Operant conflict: anything mazes can do, levers do better?

The conflict between an animal's tendency to press a lever associated with some reward and its tendency not to press because of shock, needs care. If the 'punishment' is too severe or is introduced too soon, then the result is conditioned suppression or passive avoidance. The word 'conflict' is usually applied when the inhibition is only partial and some overt approach behaviour remains.

Irving Geller and Joseph Seifter (1960) trained rats on a rather slow VI schedule where they obtained a drop of sweet condensed milk on average every 2 minutes. Five times in a 75-minute session, a tone sounded for 3 minutes, and every lever-press summoned its drop of nectar; needless to say, the rate of lever-pressing jumped when the tone sounded. But after seven sessions, the tone signalled that each lever-press would bring a shock as well as a drop of milk. If the shock intensity was low (0·35–0·5 mA), the response rate remained pretty high, but at higher intensities (0·6–0·75 mA), lever-pressing was nearly suppressed.

On this conflict schedule, meprobamate and low doses of phenobarbitone and pentobarbitone (5–15 mg/kg) increased response rates when the shock intensity was high; which is just what you would expect after reading about barbiturates reducing fear in Miller's telescope-alley conflict situation. d-Amphetamine (0·5 mg/kg) reduced the number of mild shocks that rats would accept, surprisingly for a drug known as a stimulant, not surprising in one reducing appetite and possibly increasing avoidance.

Chlorpromazine usually reduces conditioned avoidance, so in a conflict situation you would expect it to resemble barbiturates and to increase responding suppressed by the threat of shock. In fact it and a similar neuroleptic, promazine; actually reduced response rates where controls accepted mild shocks (Geller, Kulak, and Seifter, 1962; Ray, 1964). Responding on the intervening VI schedule was slower but not enough to reduce the amount of milk the rat obtained, and so was unlikely to account for the rats' unwillingness to accept shock. Of course, a lot depends on how much milk and how much shock, but it remains possible that chlorpromazine exaggerated the avoidance due to an ambivalent stimulus.

Conflict of response but not of stimulus

Sebastian Grossman (1961) used a technique with lever-pressing for food on a constant schedule, but where increasingly intense shock was signalled by increasingly loud sound. The effects of chlorpromazine were different from those of Geller's method, and perhaps it is relevant that the audible stimulus signalled shock only, not shock plus extra supplies of milk.

The rats started on a Variable Interval schedule, where they were given a food pellet at about 1-minute intervals (actually 20, 76, 92, and 52 seconds). Then came avoidance training. Thirteen 12-minute sessions were divided into six periods of 2 minutes; the first and last were on the food schedule alone. Then, between 2 and 10 minutes a buzzer sounded, quietly for the second period, 20 per cent louder for the third, and so on. At the same time, another variable interval schedule started, where the lever was electrified for 7 seconds in each 2 minutes, at a voltage rising from 20 to 200 V parallel to the crescendo on the buzzer. The last 2 minutes were silent.

Thus the hungry rat was persuaded to press a lever for food at a fairly steady rate. The buzzer acted as a signal of the risk (no more) of shock when the lever was touched, and its loudness signalled the intensity of any shock which might occur. Two sessions were run each day, one without shock (to avoid confusing anti-anxiety effects with analgesia), one with (to remind the rat).

Both chlorpromazine and perphenazine reduced response rates in the first and last shock-free 2-minute periods, but whereas the buzzer brought the rate down quite steeply in saline control sessions, it had little effect when the rats were drugged. The net result was that the drugs increased total responding while the buzzer sounded. This sounds as if the rats paid less attention to sensory stimuli, but Grossman argued that they must have been listening because they recovered much less in the final buzz-free period after actual shock than in the Fear-only condition. He therefore interpreted the drug's action as a general depression plus a specific reduction in fear – or was there an after effect of the shock related more to pain than to fear?

Two-lever approach and avoidance. Experiments on the interpretation of drug effects

In conflict situations, the rat has to press one lever, bringing both food and shock. An interesting comparison is made when the rat has to press two levers, where one stimulus signals that one lever will summon liquid refreshment, and another stimulus spells trouble which may be postponed by pressing the other.

This scheme is intended to separate the approach and avoidance types of behaviour that are combined in a conflict type of experiment. Oakley Ray (1963) pointed out that tranquillisers are given in clinical practice to reduce the patient's anxiety without affecting other aspects of behaviour.

tranquillisers in clinical practice

Further, anxiety in clinical practice is usually not the valuable fear of a real threat, but in most cases a general worry, anxiety that has persisted longer than the situation where it was functional. An animal model of true tranquillisation should therefore separate avoidance behaviour from other kinds, and should include avoidance in the 'Fear-only' condition, without actual shock.

Unfortunately, rats had some difficulty in learning the two tasks Ray chose, and after an enormous amount of training (instructive to follow in some detail) he was left with 40 successful rats out of 100. The difficult part was the avoidance training. A buzzer or a 1000-Hz tone sounded for 20 seconds until it was switched off by pressing a lever and it sounded again about a minute (35–85 seconds) later. The second half of the sound was accompanied by fairly intense shock, individually adjusted between 1 and 2 mA to be just below the intensity making the rat freeze or dance with pain. There were five 2-hour sessions a week, but less than half the rats could press one of two levers, three times out of four, soon enough to escape the shock.

These rats graduated to 'positive' training. If they approached the dipper they were given 0·1 ml of condensed milk. After 100 drops (far more than rats usually need) they were shaped to press the lever they had not used for shock avoidance. After 200 drops on continuous reinforcement the milk lever only supplied while a tone of 500 Hz (an octave below the warning signal) sounded for 20 seconds. After the first 2 days, pressing the other (avoidance) lever switched off the milk-stimulus.

When the rats responded adequately to the dinner-bell, avoidance training was gradually reinserted until half the stimuli were for shock and half for milk and the rats responded at least 90 per cent correctly.

Drugs were injected after half an hour's warm-up and sessions lasted 4–5 hours, twice a week. Shock itself was not given (though milk was), and Ray emphasised that even when avoidance responding was inhibited by a drug, it always returned next day without shock, despite the animal's opportunity to learn safety.

Pentobarbitone (10 mg/kg), chlorpromazine (2 mg/kg), and two other drugs all made the rats temporarily stop responding to either stimulus. However, when the rat started to respond after pentobarbitone, it did so to both stimuli. After the other three drugs, avoidance-responding was inhibited for quite a long time after milk-responding returned. Since both kinds of lever-pressing demanded the same kind of motor activity and the same attention to stimuli, Ray concluded that he had evidence that the last three drugs reduced fear specifically.

It is curious that pentobarbitone did not inhibit fear in this situation as it did in alleys. However, as Hurwitz and Dillow (1969) point out, Freud's concept of Defence could apply (cf. Stein, p. 206) – fear is responsible for learning avoidance but then subsides and only arises again if the avoidance is prevented. If true, this argument makes Ray's results a bit harder to explain.

It is also relevant that Ray used only one level of deprivation and of shock. Nigro (1967) and King (1970) varied both, and found that chlorpromazine could inhibit either food- or avoidance-responding separately, depending on the values of the parameters.

Alan King trained rats on two stimuli and two levers, as Ray did one for water after 22 hours deprivation, the other to avoid shock. But 40 minutes before one session, he let the rats drink either 25 or 12·5 ml of water or he

Conditioned conflict

left them thirsty. In another session, where the rats were all thirsty, he varied the shock intensity, using currents of 0·1, 0·2, or 0·4 mA.

King concluded from the results (Figs. 17.1a and b) that you cannot predict the interactions of drug effects with the parameters of a complex experiment. The thirstier the rats were, the more likely that they would respond to a water stimulus, without altering the avoidance of mild shock, and chlorpromazine merely set all the probabilities lower. On the other hand, thirsty rats would respond equally to all the levels of mild shock after

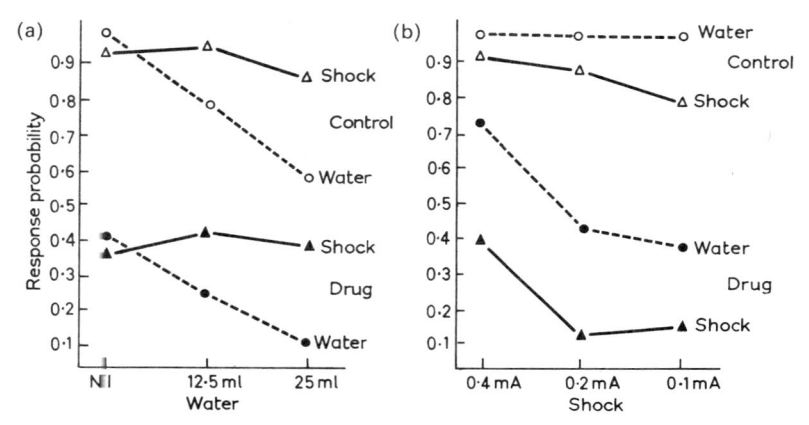

Fig. 17.1. Effect of chlorpromazine on the occurrence of water-approach or shock-avoidance responses (a) as a function of water-deprivation; (b) as a function of shock intensity (after King, 1970).

saline injections, and constantly for water. But chlorpromazine made them reluctant to respond at all unless the strongest of the weak shock levels galvanised them into activity. Presumably, if they tended not to avoid the shock because of chlorpromazine, they found out the hard way which shocks were strong enough to need a response and which were too trivial to bother with. The important point is that the stronger the shock, the more the chlorpromazine-treated rats also responded for water.

The generalisation between different kinds of behaviour suggests an interesting point about Ray's results. Ray used a larger dose of chlorpromazine than King (2 mg/kg instead of 0·4–0·8 mg/kg) and far higher shock intensities. While the threat of shock increased the probability of a response, perhaps the drug delayed an already slow response beyond the 5-second time limit. For King actually watched the rats' behaviour and found that avoidance responses could take nearly twice as long as the nominally identical responses for water.

What the rats did after the water-stimulus started was fairly simple (Fig. 17.2a). They would either walk or crouch and then approach the lever or the water fountain. They might then scratch or look around, and might

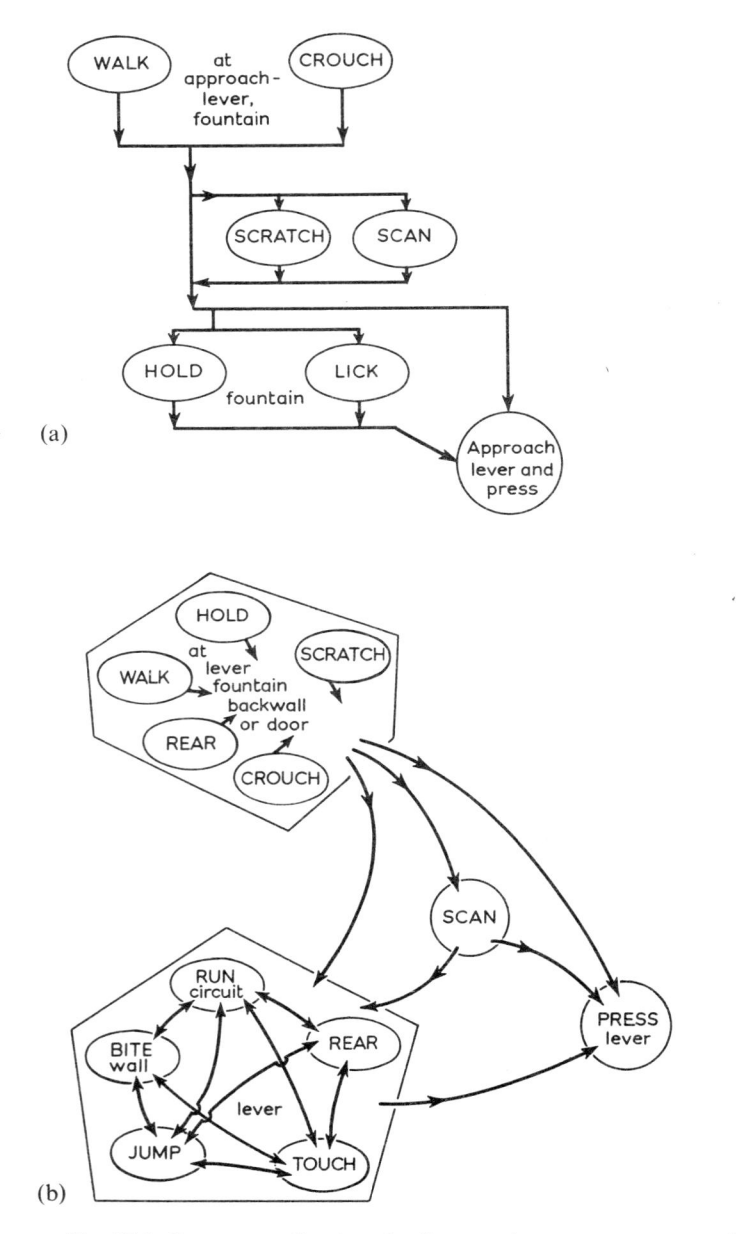

Fig. 17.2. Sequences of actions leading to a lever-press response: (a) for water; (b) to avoid shock (after King, 1970).

Conditioned conflict

hold or lick the fountain before approaching the lever and pressing it. The sequence took about 1 to 5 seconds. But the time from the start of the avoidance stimulus until the rat actually pressed the lever ranged from about 2 to 8 seconds. Rats could go through a complicated series of contortions. (Fig. 17.2b) They could rear, crouch, or walk all round the cage. They might touch the avoidance lever or jump over it.

Pressing a lever to prevent shock seems a simple and straightforward response, but rats take a remarkably long time to work themselves up to do it, and give every appearance of being in a state of conflict. Drugs might inhibit avoidance merely by delaying the response beyond the 5-second dead-line.

Note that this chapter is concerned with conditioned conflict as an experimental method, not with the analysis of motivational conflict in itself. This is better observed, for instance, in territorial boundary disputes or in courtship, but has rarely been exploited experimentally as a measure of drug effects.

Summary

Animal behaviour is never as simple as a psychologist's mind, if rarely as convoluted as his language. Even when a hungry rat has to run straight down a well-learned alley for its supper, the changes in its speed suggest that there is an inhibitory factor. In this chapter, methods are described to exploit or exaggerate this ambivalence experimentally. Animals are trained to run an alley or press a lever for food or water, and a tendency to avoid shock is deliberately set up in opposition – the animal has to retreat from shock and food, or has to press a second lever which may be independent and nominally not in conflict. The complexities involved in interpreting the effects of drugs like chlorpromazine or pentobarbitone suggest that these procedural details have surprisingly far-reaching consequences. Direct observation suggests that lever-pressing to avoid shock is itself a source of motivational conflict.

EIGHTEEN
Exploration

The old Stimulus–Response idea that animals lie passively waiting for a stimulus to come along and tell them what to do was never more than a working hypothesis, and is obviously inadequate when you observe the first actual response an animal makes to most identifiable stimuli. Each stimulus does not summon its own separate response, like an automatic vending machine responding to each button with a different kind of hot soup or cold coffee. Nor is a stimulus an isolated event, a flash of light in the darkness. Rather, a quantitative change occurs along a continuum, a change in the intensity or especially the pattern of a continuing input. All sense organs – nose, eyes, ears, paws, and whiskers – are directed towards the source of the arousal of any one of them. Before the animal can decide whether a stimulus demands that he stop what he was doing and busy himself with something else, he has to find out what the stimulus means, what caused it, and what future stimuli may be expected.

This orientation (or 'what is it?') reflex, as Pavlov called it, may not be the most important thing the animal does, but it is urgent and takes priority over practically everything else. Even without external stimulation, the animal has to be constantly aware of what goes on in its environment and it is noticeable how rats, in particular, spend any otherwise-unoccupied waking moment in exploration. Man is an animal too, and though we commonly explore only with our eyes briefly and inconspicuously, the orientation reflex is remarkably difficult to inhibit. Try to suppress a quick glance round a room when you enter it, or try not listening to the casual noises going on around you at this moment.

Because the orientation response takes so high a priority, it is highly predictable and can be utilised as perhaps the most reliable of all behavioural measures. Whenever a rat is put into a new cage, a Skinner box, a maze, or even a balance for weighing, the stimulation is of exploratory activity. Laboratory rats are unusual animals in making it easy to see that exploration is not limited to the immediate stimulus. A minimally-effective stimulus makes the animal turn its head for a moment, anything more makes it scamper systematically round the whole accessible environment. It pauses every few steps to sniff at some discontinuity in the floor, walls, or roof, or to sample smells floated in on air currents from greater distances.

The longer bouts of exploration, for instance in a new cage, may be

Exploration　　　　　　　　　　　　　　　　　　　　　　　　　　231

interrupted by pauses for rest, as if the tendency to explore is subject to relaxation oscillations of which only half appear above threshold (diagrammatically shown in Fig. 18.1).

A disturbance that is in some way excessive, inhibits exploration. The rat crouches immobile, before or after a sudden dash for the nearest cover with

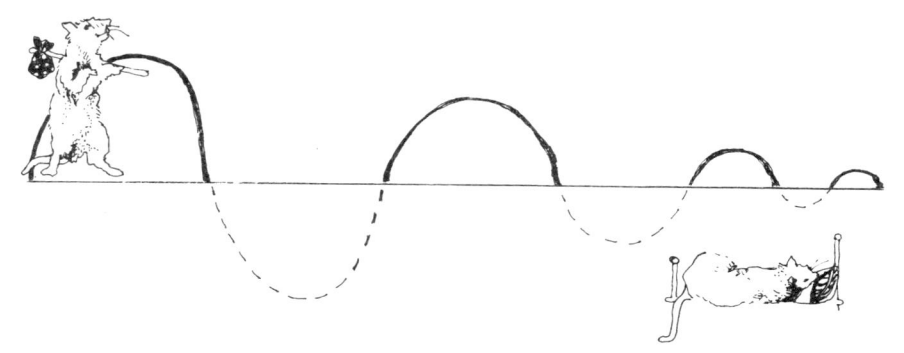

Fig. 18.1. Hypothetical time-course of exploration. Observable exploration (above the mid-line) is interspersed with apparent resting. In practice this pattern is superimposed on a daily activity cycle like that of Fig. 7.2: moving the cage to a new location may have effects detectable for 2 or 3 days.

burrow-like tactile stimuli over its back, and waits until the passage of time or minimal exploration from a safe distance has reduced the apparent intensity of the stimulus to manageable levels.

What distinguishes large stimulus-changes from small is not just a question of physical magnitude. It seems to be more a matter of information in terms of its meaning to the animal. Unfortunately this can only be inferred from the exploration it causes or because one kind of behaviour changes to another thought to be relevant to the stimulus. Between the minimal stimulus which the animal can only just perceive and the potentially damaging stimulus of high intensity, lies a broad band of olfactory, auditory, visual, and tactile stimuli that may carry useful information.

Novelty is certainly important, but the rate of habituation to repeated stimuli depends on the response as well as the stimulus, and this depends on what the animal was doing in the first place. Scourse and Hinde (1973) (cf. p. 266) exposed mice to a tone or a click twice a minute, and found the orienting response disappeared after about 5 minutes. However, the mice remained more likely than controls to get up and explore the cage for about 3 hours, and twitches during sleep did not revert to normal frequency for at least 49 hours. The stimulus does not altogether cease to have an effect, but it remains below the threshold of a visible response if this has become a waste of effort. You cease to hear the clock ticking, unless you are reminded to listen to it, or unless it stops.

Match and mismatch. Some physiology of motor control

In general, it seems likely that the animal scans and integrates the sensory stimuli from moment to moment, and compares them with what they were previously and with what might be expected. If event B has always followed A, its absence would cause just as great a discrepancy between Observed and Expected as the arrival of new event C. The discrepancy would release exploration, until the new situation is known well enough to make the new pattern of stimulation the future Expected state in its turn. An excessive discrepancy, or perhaps one of a particular kind, would cause avoidance. The animal would retreat until the new stimuli would no longer be received at all, or only at a low rate which the animal could assimilate more easily. Chance (1962) showed that animals can literally close their eyes to certain stimuli or turn the head away, if they would otherwise tend both to approach and to retreat. If one class of stimuli is 'cut-off' near a territorial boundary, for instance, the animal can act on the other and approach.

A mismatch is not the same as a totally new set of stimuli. Captive wild rats (cf. Chapter 24) placed in a new environment explore it vigorously but show every sign of fear if a new object is placed into a familiar home cage. Exploration and feeding can be delayed for hours. Monkeys are said to be greatly disturbed by odd but *nearly* normal stimuli: a puppet or an almost life-like mask. The combination of familiar and unfamiliar, the expected and the not-quite-right creates a greater discrepancy between observed and expected than a completely new environment. Being picked up and transported by human hand must make the animal expect some fairly unfamiliar stimuli.

The result of exploration, as Robert Hinde pointed out (1970), is to change the expected pattern to bring it into line with the newly-observed. The same principle is used in reverse by chaffinches building a nest. They match the half-built construction with the 'expected' for the completed nest, but a discrepancy is resolved by adding a few more twigs on to the observed pattern until it matches the bird's concept. No other model of the process accounts for the bird's flexibility of approach to a constant goal or its ability to make repairs.

The idea of a process of matching observed and expected stimuli is an extension of the 're-afference principle' of Erich von Holst and Mittelstaedt (1950; see Hinde, 1970). They pointed out the demands of engineering logic, that everything an animal does must be preceded by a pattern of neuron firing formally equivalent to a decision to perform the action. The decision must obviously generate a sequence of instructions to muscles to contract in the right order, but it must also produce an 'output copy' of these instructions, transformed into a prediction of the internal and external sensory stimuli to be expected in consequence. Expected and observed must be compared in order to correct any deviations, and the action would only end when they match closely enough to constitute the attaining of a goal.

A comparable principle is known to operate at the level of 'voluntary' muscle movements. The instruction to contract is not sent directly to the powerful myofibrils (B and C in Fig. 18.2) but to the weak modified 'muscle spindle' A. This contracts but all it achieves directly is to stimulate the

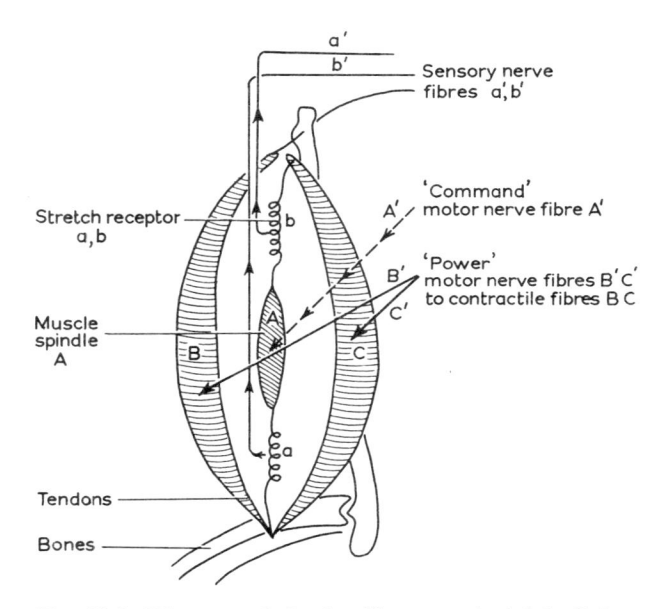

Fig. 18.2. Diagram of the 'reafference principle' of the control of skeletal muscle movement (see text).

receptors that measure the length of the whole muscle. These stretch-receptors stimulate a reflex arc via the sensory neurones (a, b), the spinal cord and the motor neurons (B', C'). Only then does the muscle contract as a whole, just enough to relax the stretch receptors again. This indirect procedure takes a little extra time but simplifies the problem of making the movement smooth and controlled. It simplifies the integration of all the muscles flexing the same leg, of relaxing the antagonistic muscles that would otherwise extend it, and of adjusting other muscles elsewhere to compensate for changes in balance. The entire movement is made, not by programming all the muscle contractions directly, but by initiating a series of relatively simple local reflexes, each causing the discrepancy between the expected rate of firing of the stretch receptors and the actual to be eliminated.

By a simple extension of the principle, repetitive movements like walking could be switched on by activating a self-re-exciting cycle of reflexes rather than by controlling each muscle directly from the centre, provided that the results are monitored – an unseen step down surprises you as your foot continues downwards into a rain puddle.

By a further simple extension, you must hold something analogous to a map of your route, and monitor the observed landmarks against those expected, both in the sequence in which they appear (are you going in the right direction?) and in the approximate time since you started. In an unfamiliar area you will have fewer clues beyond a sense of time and of direction and what you have been told about it. To let you make future journeys over the same route as economically and semi-automatically as over your usual routes, you have to build up a detailed representation of the area in your own mind; you have to explore.

The basis of practical tests. Exploration the route of all learning

Many tests utilise exploration, some of them deliberately and explicitly, some of them inadvertently by relying on exploration to generate motor activity or to start the process of learning.

exploration seems clearly systematic

To summarise this chapter, then, there seem to be three independent factors relevant in the measurements made in tests of exploration: the systematic motor activity of the animal wandering round the new environment, the inhibition on this that is often observed at the beginning, called fear or anxiety, and exploration in the strict sense of curiosity. This is variously measured by the number of places visited, by the number of *different* places visited and so by a preference to visit new unfamiliar places. It is also measured indirectly in terms of the time taken before the animal can do something else, like eating, in the presence of novel stimuli. And it is measured in terms of the intake and utilisation of information, i.e. of learning, by changes in exploratory activity in a second trial in the same previously unfamiliar environment.

Commonly only a single measure is taken of behaviour in unfamiliar surroundings, usually of motor activity. Much of this chapter nevertheless concerns the ways people have sought to distinguish activity, information-intake and fear.

The first explorer

The first explicit description of exploration was by Small (1901) (see p. 110) telling of his rats' cautious ventures from their home cage into a model Hampton Court maze, slow advances alternating with sudden scuttles back to home and safety. Despite their hunger, he thought they eventually found their dinner more by general curiosity than by searching for food. After a few hours in the maze the caution disappeared, rats racing at top speed from cage to centre and back, along the correct path, carrying supplies for feeding and nesting.

The open field

For 30 years psychologists extended one side of Small's work, marvelling at how clever rats are to learn such complicated puzzles, studying how they learned mazes, simplifying the mazes while complicating the theories. Until Hall (1934a and b) cut straight to an 'open field' as featureless as possible, to contrast with the complicated stimuli of mazes. He gave rats repeated trials, but his main interest (like Small's) was their adjustment to a new environment. The 'open field' was a circular arena of about 1·2 m radius bounded by a sheet-metal wall 0·45 m high, standing on a washable linoleum floor marked out in radial lines and concentric circles (see Fig. 5.2 on p. 48). After placing a rat in the outer ring of the arena, just under the lee of the wall, Hall observed its movements for 2 minutes, sketching its movements with pencil and a plan of the arena and estimating the distance with a map-measurer. The method was reliable, for day-to-day variability was small.

There was little unnecessary cleaning; Hall merely picked up food or faecal pellets, mopped up urine, and swept out every few days, so that the smell of the arena must have become increasingly homely.

On some days, food was placed in the centre of the arena, and rats were tested either fully fed or deprived for 24 or 48 hours. When deprived of food, rats walked further than when well fed, but they did not necessarily eat while in the arena. Hall called those that did not eat 'emotional' and described how they stayed at the edge of the open field, under the shelter of the wall. Non-emotional rats ventured into the centre, so that activity in the central zone was inversely related to that on the periphery. Emotional rats were likely to defecate in the open field, a mildly stressful situation, and (see p. 48) defecation has been used as a sign of fear. The evidence for the sign's validity is not solid.

The open-field test has been widely used, often simplified to a single trial. The distance walked is estimated by counting the gridlines on the floor that the animal crosses with all four feet. Sometimes the number of times the rat rears on its hindlegs is added, with little difference to results. Broadhurst (1957) has described a meticulously standardised procedure, including the breeding of the animals, diet, temperature, daily light/dark timing, and general husbandry in the ways most laboratories take good care of. He handled his rats as rarely as possible, however, weighing them as a litter soon after birth, and singly on weaning at 21 days, before housing them in single-sex groups of four, preferably litter-mates. They were marked for individual recognition at 50 days of age and used at 100 days.

In a typical experiment, Broadhurst and Watson (1964) looked for relationships between brain cholinesterase concentrations, body build (the ratio of hindleg length to shoulder-blade width), and emotionality in five strains of rats. As it turned out, there were strain differences in each parameter, but not correlated. The test arena was much smaller than Hall's, 42 cm in radius with white-painted plywood walls 32 cm high and a chipboard floor marked into a central circle, six inner and twelve outer segments – the number of segments entered worked out at 4·63 times the distance in metres. A single light-bulb illuminated it from directly overhead, at 1·65 foot candles (approximately 18 lux) at floor level, with moderately loud background noise (78 dB) provided by an electric motor. The rats were tested one at a time for 2 minutes on each of 4 days starting precisely at 101.4 ± 1.98 days of age. Presumably the moment of each animal's birth was timed with a stopwatch.

Measurement of exploration: the eye or the photoelectric cell

Activity in the open field is observed very simply as the number of squares traversed. There seems no good reason not to measure this automatically, and several possible techniques were described in Chapter 7. The question is whether automatic recording and direct observation obtain the same information, for what human beings lose in precision they may gain in selectivity. Kršiak, Steinberg, and Stolerman (1970) made a direct comparison. They placed one rat at a time in a photocell activity cage, a 27-cm cube with two infrared beams crossing 4 cm above floor level and a Perspex pillar in the centre of the cage to prevent double counts where the beams crossed. An observer counted 'walks' of a distance the photocells should be able to detect, i.e. half-way along a side of the cage. They also counted 'rears' which photocells may fail to detect, and grooming which they would certainly ignore, and timed the duration of each activity. Two observers achieved correlations of $r = 0.97$ on counts of walks and rears in control rats and correlations were nearly as good with photocell counts, with other groups of rats, and with other observers, including untrained students in a practical class.

Unfortunately the correlation of observed walks and rears with photocell counts was not so good in rats given dexamphetamine. The photocells counted twice as often for drugged rats as for controls, especially in the second half of the 10-minute trial when controls' activity declined. The response was broadly related to dose from 0·25 to 2 mg/kg, and was seen whether the counters were capable of 10 counts/second or only 2 or 3. But walks, as observed, increased much less, especially at the higher doses and rears hardly rose at all. The discrepancy was thought to arise because observers looked for integrated walks half-way across the cage, the photocells may have detected stereotyped sniffing when amphetamine makes the rat continually sway its head from side to side (it is curious that this phenomenon was quoted from the literature rather than directly observed). Photocells could not, of course, detect the dose-related decline in grooming seen by direct observation. Amylobarbitone increased all observed measures at low doses but high doses depressed them all when ataxia followed an early low dose-like, stimulant phase; and the photocell counts agreed very well with a composite of walks and rears. Automatic recording can therefore be safely used, but only if the drug effect is one that the machine happens to be suited for. Equally, observation can often be as accurate as one of the more practical automatic methods.

Observation can be hard work if it is to be reliable, and Kršiak and Janků (1971) investigated how to observe most easily and economically whether a drug reduces exploratory activity. They considered the size of the arena, illumination, and the duration of observation that made their mice (strain H males of 19–21 g) show about 70 per cent of their maximum activity. Three enclosures were 8 × 24, 16 × 48, and 32 × 96 cm in area with a white plastic floor marked in 8-cm squares and cardboard walls 15 cm high were painted grey. Two light-bulbs were suspended at two heights over the arenas at 36, 72, or 114 V to give illuminations of 2, 200, or 2000 lux: the lights glowed rather red at low voltages (making them effectively even dimmer to the mice), and the brighter lights also warmed the arena from 20° to a maximum of 27°. These variations were thought acceptable in a practical test of the conditions obtainable in a working laboratory. The observer pressed levers attached to the arms of his chair to record walks from one square to another and rears with both forepaws off the ground. Grooming did not occur regularly. Mice were placed one at a time in the centre of the arena and observed for 1 minute. This is brief but reliable, and each mouse was tested five times at hourly intervals starting half an hour after being brought into the laboratory. (Transporting the mice from the stock room must itself have stimulated exploration.)

The larger the enclosure, the fewer the rears and the more squares were crossed, so that the total time spent walking and rearing was the same in all three enclosures. The brighter the light, the fewer walks and rears, and mice were mobile for about 57 seconds out of 60 in the dimmest light, 50 in the moderate and 40 seconds in the brightest light, in the first trial. In dim and moderate lighting, rearing/walking time declined linearly over the five trials, especially quickly in the smallest arena where there was least to explore. In the brightest light, rearing/walking time actually increased on the second trial as if exploration had been actively inhibited in the first, but then declined, and in pilot experiments a small dark chamber accessible from the arena was occupied mostly in bright light. So to induce the maximum exploratory activity in mice but the fastest decline on repeated trials, a small, dimly illuminated arena is best.

This conclusion was tested with two drugs. Chlorpromazine was injected after the first trial and reduced the rearing and walking time 30 minutes later at a dose of as little as 0.3 mg/kg. At 0.9 and 2.7 mg/kg activity remained even lower for longer, and the top dose of sodium barbitone (10 mg/kg) reduced activity for 4.5 hours. In previously habituated mice, the same drugs acted at 0.44 and 5 mg/kg respectively. These low doses show how effective the 'tuning' of the test was for finding sedatives, since small doses of barbiturates can be stimulants for a short time under bright lights. The end result of tailoring the test to the target is to obtain more information for less work: injecting and observing each mouse took 65–70 seconds.

Why mazes?

It could be that a physical structure to the arena might shape the animal's exploration differently, and a simple Y-maze makes it convenient to record exploration as the number of times a rat enters an arm with all four feet. Hannah Steinberg and her colleagues have used a Y-maze extensively. Their maze has arms about 38 cm long and 13 cm wide with plywood walls 38 cm high and a 75-watt light-bulb suspended 75 cm above the central triangle. They use female rats housed sixteen to a cage from weaning at 21 days to testing at about 120. Drugs are injected subcutaneously in the flank, allowing the rat to turn its head and watch, and 35 minutes later the rat is placed in the central triangle. Tentative entries when only the head enters an arm are observed as well as complete entries, but seem less consistent.

Some parameters affecting Y-maze exploration were investigated by David Williams (1971). He gave male hooded rats four 3-minute trials on successive days in a maze made of transparent Perspex. Entries from the centre to the end of an arm declined from the first minute to the second to the third, but if the maze was only dimly lit by a 15-watt red bulb the decline was slight, and there was little change from day to day. In bright white light from a 150-watt bulb, the first day's entries were like those under the red light, but declined steeply from one day to the next and from minute to minute, without the temporary increase found by Kršiak and Janků. This was the only discrepancy between their results and Williams'. It might be due to the difference between Y-mazes and boxes, or mice and rats, but some other possibilities might not be trivial. Williams' maze was transparent and enclosed and he wiped it after each rat and cleaned it properly each day. He brought each rat into the room immediately before each trial, whereas Kršiak and Janků brought their mice 30 minutes early, allowing considerable exploration in the home cage, but only 1 minute for each trial instead of 3.

Under the bright light, rats defecated more, as Broadhurst has found, but Williams did not see this as strong evidence for fear since the rats kept moving and did not freeze. Since entries decline faster in bright than dim light, he thought they represent true exploration, implying that the rats absorbed information quicker under bright light – or did bright light inhibit all but the most urgent exploration?

Circadian rhythms could affect exploration, it may matter whether animals are woken from sleep, and Davies, Navaratnam, and Redfern (1974) tested rats' performance throughout the day and night. They were housed for at least 10 days in a soundproof room on a 12-hour light/dark cycle and taken for testing at 4-hour intervals; excessive interference with the experimenters' own circadian rhythm and observational efficiency was avoided by adjusting the experimental room's lighting without reference to real time outside. Entries into the arms of the Y-maze (which was always brightly lit) were more frequent when rats were taken from the light phase than from the dark, 17.2 ± 1.7 entries in 3 minutes at one extreme, 12.7 ± 1.8 at the other. Rats reared upright most often in trials near the beginning and end of the dark phase when entries were particularly low and when brain noradrenaline concentrations are apparently at their highest. Entries and rears were both increased by 1·25 mg/kg of amphetamine, especially at the end of the light period; 100 μg/kg LSD and 12·5 mg/kg mescaline reduced both and all three drugs reduced defecation.

The Y-maze: activity and conditioned fear

Although intense fear inhibits exploration, it has been suggested that mild fear may increase it, that exploration may even be a means of reducing mild fear (Halliday, 1967). Kumar tested the idea (1970b) in the same Y-maze as he had used for drugs (p. 217). He confined rats in a white-painted arm for 3 minutes with or without two 7-second periods of 0·5-mA shock. When put in the complete Y-maze for six 3-minute trials, shocked rats predictably entered the white arm less often than controls, delayed entries longer, and spent less time there (typically one 12-second visit on the first trial instead of three 9-second visits). But the initial avoidance extinguished by the sixth trial without any extra exploration, either of the white arm or indeed of the black ones. When the former control group were confined and shocked, they avoided the white arm more than the first group had done; perhaps by that time there was less need to explore. Further experiments with even milder shock for shorter times or at longer intervals, etc., all produced the same result – shock led to avoidance of the stimuli associated with it (e.g. of *both* black arms if the rat was shocked in one of them). The avoidance was more complete and lasted longer the stronger had been the shock. There was no evidence that even the mildest degree of fear, as conditioned in this way, could increase exploration.

Exploration and unconditioned caution

Fear is, in the end, a label for some factor internal to the animal, which inhibits other behaviour like exploration.

The most direct way of demonstrating curiosity in a rat is to show that the animal will leave a comfortable living cage and enter an unfamiliar area of its own accord – and then return to the cage again. Yet there are inhibitions to this exploration obvious to anyone who watches. Small showed this in 1901, Montgomery (1955) measured it. When a rat had lived a few days in a cage, long enough to regard it as home, a trapdoor was opened, giving access to a simple maze. The rats were immediately interested, approached the doorway and looked out, but did not emerge instantly; it took time before the rats scampered freely about the maze. Before ever they did, Montgomery counted 'retreats' from the doorway to the opposite side of the cage and the number of times the rat 'looked away' towards the back half of the cage immediately after looking out into the maze. Eventually the rats cautiously emerged, meanwhile elevated mazes (simulating the branches of a tree or the top of a wall) elicited more fear-responses than the burrow-like tunnel of an enclosed maze. Such fear declined steadily while the rats were exposed to the novel stimulus, and subsequently revived in proportion to the time without access to it.

Activity and exploration

If entries into the arms of a maze constitute exploration as well as motor activity, we cannot tell what information they are seeking; but a decline in the rate of entries can help tell us if they have obtained it (assuming that sheer fatigue is not likely).

Neuroleptic drugs reduce motor activity, and Shillito (1967) showed that both chlorpromazine and thioridazine reduced entries in a Y-maze. It was interesting that on a second trial without dosing, rats previously given low doses (1 or 2 mg/kg) of chlorpromazine made as few entries as controls and so did rats given up to 32 mg/kg of thioridazine. Despite their reduced activity on the first trial, they must have obtained sufficient information. Rats given higher doses of chlorpromazine had been extremely inactive and explored as much in the second trial as controls had in the first, as though the maze was still unfamiliar.

One way of investigating the information that should come from exploration is to look for latent learning (see p. 261 for an example).

Hole boards and tunnel boards

Curiosity implies a search for novelty, so it would be possible to use a complex maze instead of the three arms of a Y-maze and consider exploration in terms of the number of different places visited at least once. This view has not been applied to mazes, however, so much as to the response to holes in the ground. Presumably related to burrow-dwelling, holes a little wider than their own bodies tempt rats and mice to crawl through.

A tunnel-board was made for mice, a square with twelve tunnels made from strips of plastic bent round and screwed in, as in Fig. 18.3 (Shillito, 1970b). The tunnels were 7·5 cm long and 4 cm in diameter, a size suitable for mice 15–20 g in weight. On its first trial, a mouse was apt to walk slowly, approaching a tunnel and touching it with paws and whiskers: one or two of

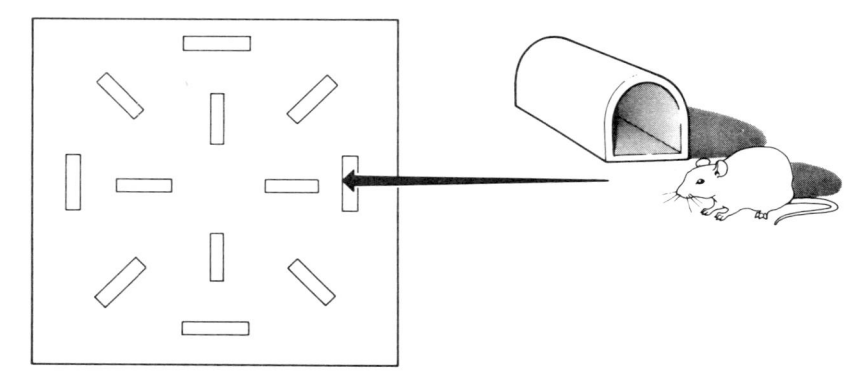

Fig. 18.3. Tunnel-board (after Shillito, 1970).

the central tunnels might be entered in a minute. Mostly the mice walked around and between tunnels, occasionally remaining inside instead of crawling right through. Batches of mice differed, averaging from 12 to 25 visits to 6 or 8 different tunnels in 5 minutes. In the second trial next day, mice typically scampered through 3–5 tunnels in the first minute, less hesitantly than before, and the number of different tunnels visited in 5 minutes was clearly related more to exploration (even if the response was not in itself strictly exploratory) than to motor activity.

Most drugs had effects like those seen in a Y-maze. Amphetamine (4 or 8 mg/kg) seemed to confuse the mice; they repeatedly entered the same tunnel and seemed to increase activity, though no formal measure was taken of trotting between tunnels. Antidepressant drugs were especially interesting as various monoamine oxidase inhibitors given 24 hours before testing all actually increased the number of different tunnels entered. Imipramine, a tricyclic antidepressant did the same on day 2, after some sedation on the day of injection. These were the only drugs Shillito tested which did so, and selectivity for antidepressants is unusual. But for general purposes the test is difficult to operate because the relationship of tunnel size to mouse size is so critical. Tunnels that were too short were sniffed at but not entered, but mice never emerged from those that were too long; too wide and the mice ran through without stopping, too narrow and they never entered. Bigger mice or rats presumably need bigger tunnels.

Another hole-test relies on a similar response in rats. Krnjević and Videk (1967) built a box with a 5-cm hole in the lid. The procedure was to swing a male rat gently by the tail on to some wire netting about 8–12 cm away from the hole and facing it (Fig. 18.4). The rat sees the hole, approaches, sniffs, and climbs through into the dark box below. Rats were given two or three

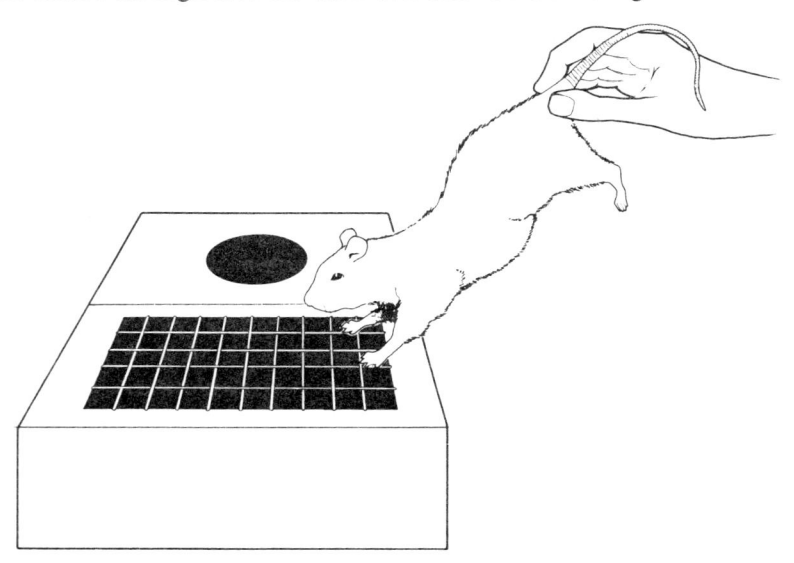

Fig. 18.4. Hole-test (after Krnjević and Videk, 1967).

training trials and the few rats (about 1 in 20) that took longer than 2 seconds to climb down through the hole were discarded. Most drugs could then be tested next day for delaying the response, but after longer training (say thirty trials) the control response is slower (8–20 seconds).

The size of the box, the darkness within it, and other such details did not matter so long as the floor was within reach (about 9 cm) of the rat standing on the roof. The size of the hole was critical, for a diameter of less than about 5 cm was too narrow for a 150-g rat but wider holes were less effective as stimuli and above about 12 cm the response appeared no faster or more direct than ordinary exploration.

Saline injections tended to delay the response a little, five of fifty control

Exploration

rats took longer than the 2-second training criterion. Chlorpromazine delayed it more: fifteen rats took up to 10 seconds and five stood staring into the dark hole for up to 30 seconds before climbing through. A moderate dose of amphetamine (1 mg/kg) also slowed the response a little but tiny doses (0·05 and 0·01 mg/kg) accelerated it and some rats were timed through the hole in less than half a second (a remarkable piece of stopwatch expertise). Imipramine (0·01 mg/kg an hour previously) delayed rats given the usual two or three trials in training, but accelerated the response of overtrained rats given thirty trials from an average of 7·75 to 1·71 seconds. So, although the hole-test requires rather a large number of animals, it joins Shillito's tunnel-test as one of the simplest methods claiming to discriminate antidepressants.

The hole-board of Jaques Boissier and Pierre Simon (1962) is the best-known method involving holes. It is hard to say if these present a specific stimulus to burrow-dwelling animals or if they are merely conspicuous excuses for general exploration, for in this case the animals (mice) merely sniff. A wooden board has, say, sixteen large holes (3 cm diameter) drilled through and is placed about 50 cm above the floor of the room. The mouse sniffs at the holes and dips its head into them but does not climb through, as if from fear of heights (Fig. 18.5).

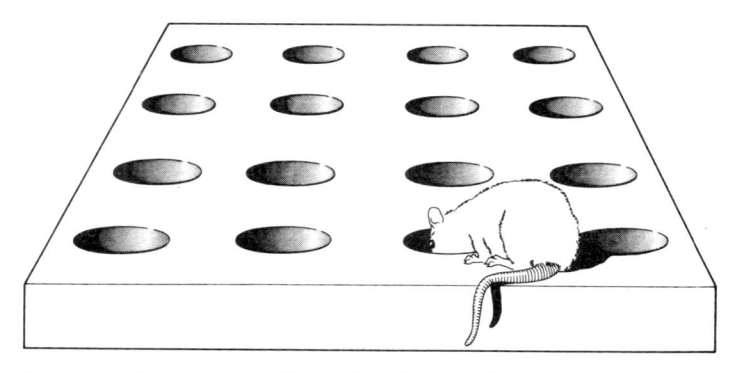

Fig. 18.5. Hole board (refer to Boissier and Simon).

There is some variation between batches of mice. In an experiment by Bradley and six colleagues (1968) male mice averaged a total of 19·1 dips (deep enough for their eyes to disappear into the hole) in 3 minutes on their first trial, females averaged 18·5 dips, and both sexes averaged nine on their second trial next day. The mice of Boissier and Simon made 41·2 ± 1·15 dips in 5 minutes, declining steadily but slightly from 9·0 in the first minute to 7·9 in the fifth. In a second trial an hour later they dipped at little more than half this rate, but declined again at a steady rate from minute to minute. The board, incidentally, was not cleaned between trials, and though the observers kept rigorously quiet and still, no attempt was made to introduce a background noise to mask minor disturbance. Marian Dorr and her five colleagues, some of whom were also Bradley's (Dorr et al., 1971) found mice to average about thirty-two dips in 3 minutes and about twelve in trial 2 a week later. Sandra File (1973) gave rats three 3-minute trials at 1-minute intervals while the board was wiped clean. Even in the first trial they only averaged six head-dips, declining to two or three in the second trial and one in the third (including repeat visits to the same hole). Maybe the method is not well-suited to rats under these conditions.

For the most part, head-dips conveniently measure much the same thing as walking. Dorr and her colleagues, for instance, found that dexamphetamine led to a moderate increase in head-dips; the interesting point was that this concealed a much larger increase in repeat visits and in dips over the outside edge of the board. Chlordiazepoxide made no difference to the total (3 minutes) but concentrated most head-dips into the first minute: the mouse rushed madly round and then stood quietly. The mixture of the two drugs dramatically increased the total count, presumably because the amphetamine maintained the high rate of dipping begun by the chlordiazepoxide. Again, the large proportion of repeat visits suggests that the drug(s) either stimulated activity rather than exploration or interfered with the uptake of information. On the second trial, most mice walked and dipped about half as fast as they had done when given drugs the week before, so that, remarkably enough, the original dose–response curves reappeared at a lower absolute level. Only the mice given the highest dose of dexamphetamine walked faster than previously; those given the top dose of the mixture, originally too ataxic to rush dramatically round like those on lower doses, nevertheless also walked more slowly on the second trial. The mice almost seemed to recall how they had behaved previously.

Exploration as a search for novelty

After a monotonous life in the laboratory rats seek out novelty, as Willard Small's original maze experiment demonstrated. The force of this tendency

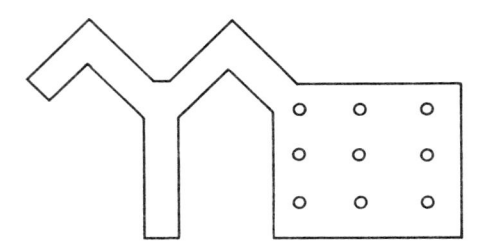

Fig. 18.6. Linking of Y- and Dashiell mazes (after Montgomery, 1954).

to explore was demonstrated when Nissen (1930; cited by Hinde, 1970) showed that rats learned to cross an electrified grid for the opportunity to examine a maze containing a variety of objects. Montgomery (1954) pointed out the implication that novel stimuli not only stimulate exploratory 'drive', they also reinforce it. Montgomery dispensed with the objects and merely placed a fairly complex 'Dashiell' maze as the goal-box of a Y-maze. The Y-maze had bent arms (Fig. 18.6) to stop the rat seeing the goal from the choice-point. Nevertheless, rats put into the stem of the Y-maze came in twenty-four trials to choose the arm leading to the Dashiell maze sooner and more often, just as if for food, and they changed direction in the same way when the Dashiell maze was switched to the other arm. You must explore before you can learn: you can learn in order to explore.

Exploration into a novel environment can be used as a test for drugs and, more interestingly, as a measure of various differences in nutrition. Lát developed Kotliarevsky's two-compartment box originally used for 'motor-food conditioned reflexes' (see p. 136) into a form shown in Fig. 7.3 (see p. 90). The room had subdued lighting and the noise of a fan masked any slight disturbance. A rat was put into the smaller compartment for 8 minutes, then the trapdoor was opened (originally the experimenter pulled a string, later the rat pressed a pedal) and for 7 minutes the experimenter (or a capacitance-change detector in the roof) counted how often the rat reared on its hindlegs, how often it groomed itself, how long it waited before first passing through the trapdoor and how often it did so.

Lát, Widdowson, and McCance (1960) wondered whether fast-growing, overfed rats behaved differently from underfed slow-growing ones, since physically well-developed children also seem to score higher in mental tests than smaller children of the same age. They reared male rats in litters of 3 pups or of 15–20 pups, weaned at 21 days. Despite free access to food, the slow-growing rats from the large litters remained puny all their lives. Tested at 21, 39, or 49 days the fat rats reared more than the thin ones, groomed briefly but more often and were generally more active. They emerged into the large compartment marginally sooner and passed through the door more often. They also defecated more. Tested again as old codgers at 500 days of age, they were still heavier but behavioural differences had gone. Another group of rats were tested repeatedly between 21 and 49 days of age, through puberty. They anticipated the opening of the trapdoor and emerged steadily sooner. Otherwise, they behaved very uniformly except for a few days between 30 and 37 days, when they became restless and fidgety, bouncing round the cage with superabundant energy, occasionally interrupted by a few seconds of tense powerful trembling and then immobility. This hyperactive phase occurred sooner in the faster-growing rats, at a constant weight rather than a constant age.

Another test of a search for novelty is much more prosaic but seems practical. Hughes (1972) used an 'exploration-box' divided, like Lát's, into two compartments, each subdivided into two cells 20 × 20 cm. A rat was placed in one half of the box and left to explore it for an hour, then injected, put back into its home cage, and left undisturbed for half an hour. Then at last it was put again into the familiar part of the exploration box, but with access to the unfamiliar half also.

As is commonly found after low doses of chlordiazepoxide (2·5–3·75 mg/kg) rats made more entries into the four cells in 10 minutes. Rats given 5 mg/kg were no more active than controls, though this dose is still small (Dorr et al., gave 12·5–50 mg/kg). Curiously though, they explored less – in the later minutes of the 10-minute observation, they entered the cells mainly in the familiar half of the box where controls preferred cells in the novel part. Activity can therefore be distinguished from exploration by the proportion of entries or of time spent in the unfamiliar area. (It is arguable that a timid animal might similarly confine its exploratory activity to the area it knows something about already.)

Exploration as behaviour with high priority

A hungry rat in an unfamiliar environment cannot eat until it has found out where the food is, and an obvious function of exploration is to allow the animal to do this. Yet there must be other functions too, because exploration can be so reliably elicited by any change in the environment irrespective of hunger.

In fact eating can be delayed or interrupted by exploration, and Chance and Mead (1955) studied the competition between them. Rats were housed singly in wire cages (Fig. 18.7) for 5 days, long enough to settle down and call them 'home', and were deprived of food for 24 hours. The rat was removed from the cage, while various changes were made, and was then returned after 10 minutes or 1, 3, or 5 days with food available. Once started, the rat usually ate for at least 30 seconds continuously – a few rats made some preliminary brief bites, but these were disregarded, as were scanning movements of the head if the rat continued chewing; walking or grooming were counted as interruptions.

Control rats, deprived of food but remaining at home, started to eat 48 seconds after food was presented, on average, and ate 1·63 g in 10 minutes. Rats removed for 10 minutes and returned to the familiar cage started their continuous meal after 75 seconds (eating 1·25 g). Clean fresh sawdust bedding on the tray delayed eating for 125 seconds (0·67 g). Removing a familiar food container (a wire hopper suspended from hooks) made little difference but a new one (whether a replacement or an extra), changing the cage itself while retaining the container, tray, and bedding, or changing the bedding for a rough or smooth metal tray, all presented new sights, smells, and tactile stimuli. The greater the stimulus change, the longer the delay before the rat started eating and the less he ate in 10 minutes. Increasing the

Exploration

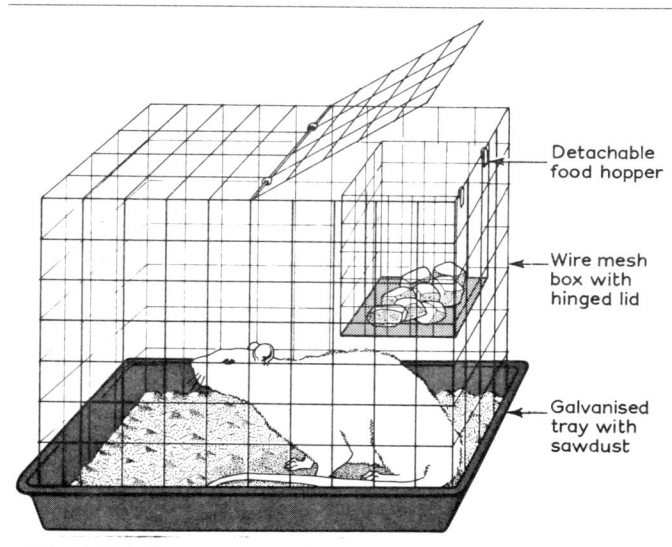

Fig. 18.7. Components of a modular wire cage (after Chance and Mead, 1955).

time away from home had the same effect as unfamiliar stimuli at home, though 5 days' absence had no more effect than 3. However, increasing deprivation of food from 1 to 2 or 3 days hardly changed the delay, as the hungriest rats still had to explore but ate without interruption once they had started. Latency and rate are therefore independent measures of feeding and presumably of other kinds of behaviour too.

In effect, Chance and Mead were using feeding as an indirect measure of exploration, and Stephens (1973) applied this principle as a drug screen. Mice were deprived of food overnight, when they usually eat most, and after dosing were offered unfamiliar food (wet mash) in an unfamiliar plastic box. If the mouse had been habituated to the mash on the previous 4 days at home, it ate 70–100 per cent more in 30 minutes in the novel test-box, and so did mice habituated to the test-box by four previous visits. Mice familiar with both box and mash ate more still. Using naïve mice, to which both box and mash were new, chlordiazepoxide and other tranquillisers and phenobarbitone all increased consumption over a wide range of doses. As expected, amphetamine and fenfluramine reduced food intake, but other drugs did so only as part of a general motor depression.

Stephens's test is neat but loses some easily accessible information. Peter Carlton (1968) used the principle in two stages. He gave rats a moderate dose (0·5 mg/kg) of scopolamine and then put half of them and half the controls singly into an unfamiliar chamber for 15 minutes. Two days later, after deprivation of water overnight, rats that were new to the chamber started drinking there after about 2 minutes, and so did experienced rats that had previously been dosed. Control rats that were familiar with the chamber started to drink much sooner, with a mean latency of about 35 seconds. In effect, scopolamine interfered with latent learning.

An 'exploration–thirst' test of chemicals' effects on behaviour

It seems logical to try to extend this approach. If you put a rat into an unfamiliar environment and watch him scamper round, you get a measure which is closest to being one of motor activity. The function of this activity seems to be largely the gain of some kind of information (as latent learning experiments demonstrate, see p. 261), even if we cannot know what kind. If the rat has some other specific need, e.g. for food, and if food is available, then the start of eating shows indirectly that the necessary information has been obtained. In addition to finding out where the food is, Chance and Mead showed that the latency to eating is related to the amount of novelty elsewhere in the environment and can therefore, within limits, be used to measure the animal's exploration. If the procedure is repeated next day, the animal is likely to start eating sooner, and the difference is (again within limits) a measure of the information the animal has taken in on the first trial, retained, and utilised on the second. In effect we have the first two trials of a maze-learning situation.

In practice it is easier to measure drinking than eating, since it is easier to watch the rat licking a water-bottle spout or to detect licking electronically than to distinguish between gnawing, chewing, and merely holding a chunk of food in the forepaws. Drinking can be induced after a shorter period of deprivation than eating or, if necessary, by oral dosing with hypertonic saline.

So in the 'exploration–thirst' test (briefly described by Silverman, 1973) a rat is placed in an unfamiliar environment (usually another cage) after deprivation of water overnight. Water is available, but whether or not the rat drinks, it is returned to the home cage after 5 minutes, offered water, deprived again overnight, and given a second trial in the same formerly-unfamiliar cage.

The main measures are the rat's motor activity and the latency until it starts to drink. There is an interesting complication. On the first trial, most rats drink continuously for half a minute or more once they start, but a few – perhaps a majority on trial 2 – only take two or three licks at first, and resume exploration for a while before returning to drink. Separate measures are therefore made if necessary of the time to the first lick and the time until the rat starts drinking for at least 10 seconds continuously. (Brief pauses of about 1 second are ignored, and for the few rats that take many brief drinks, the time when they have accumulated a total of say 30 seconds drinking can be treated as equivalent.) These criteria are arbitrary but convenient for timing by observation and a stopwatch; with automatic recording (the capacitance of a metal spout changes when a wet tongue licks it) the

Exploration 249

conventional equivalents are the time to the first lick and the time between the first lick and the hundredth, which will clearly be longer if the rat interrupts drinking by further exploration. Rats that fail to drink in 5 minutes are credited with a time of 300 seconds; times are transformed to the square root for statistical analysis, to normalise variance.

The other major measure is of exploratory movements, in order to measure motor activity separately and (as it turns out) independently of drink-latency. Any of the usual automatic measures would work satisfactorily (photocells, capacitance, etc.), as would observation of crossing squares or entering alleys if the method is applied in an open field or Y-maze (Fig. 18.8).

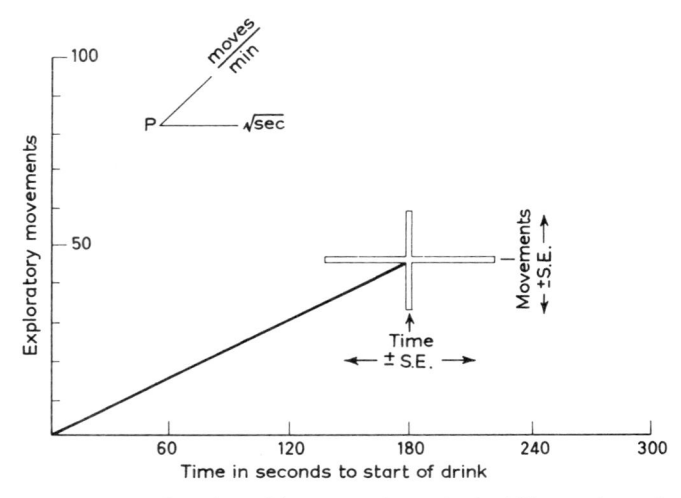

Fig. 18.8. Exploration–thirst test – hypothetical illustration of method.

However, these measures tend to define the animal's behaviour by human criteria for the sake of objectivity. One can also attempt to observe the rat's own units a little more directly as pauses in exploration: whenever the rat stops walking to sniff or stops sniffing at one place on the floor, wall, or roof to start at another. Observers can differ in what they recognise as a new and distinct place, but need not: correlations between observers are high ($r > 0.9$), often high enough for there to be no significant difference between them. Differential drug effects on different exploratory movements (walking, rearing, etc.) have rarely been observed. Since the movements are defined by the animal not the apparatus, any convenient environment can be used (I have used a transparent plastic living cage, 50 × 30 × 25 cm including the wire lid with sawdust on the floor), provided it is not one where control rats crouch or 'freeze' for long periods.

Chlorpromazine (4 mg/kg injected just before trial 1) made rats explore much more slowly and most of the four rats failed to drink in the 5-minute trial, but a 1 mg/kg dose had no apparent effect. On the second trial next day, without further drug treatment, rats previously given chlorpromazine walked as fast as controls, and took their first lick of water as soon. However, unlike controls, rats given either dose of chlorpromazine delayed the 10-second drink. Since they found the water-bottle on day 2 as quickly as

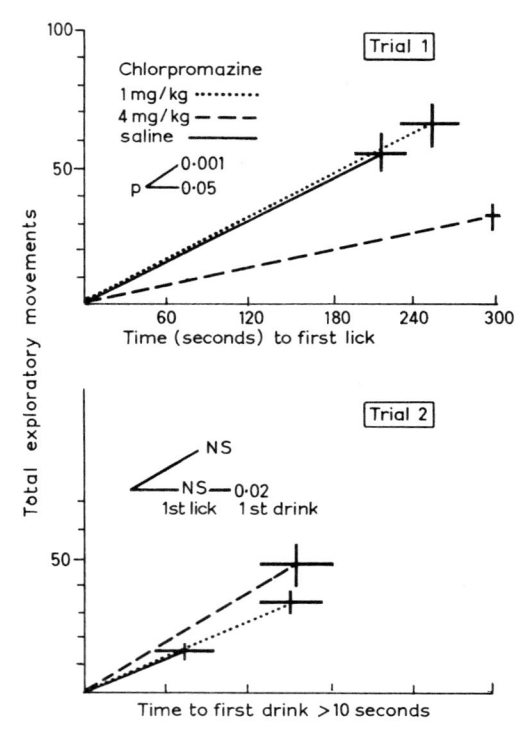

Fig. 18.9. Exploration–thirst test – effect of chlorpromazine given just before trial 1. A dose of 4 mg/kg intraperitoneally caused four rats to explore at half the control rate, and they failed to find the water-bottle in 5 minutes. A dose of 1 mg/kg appeared to have no effect. On trial 2, 24 hours later, the time to the first lick was unaffected, i.e. even dosed rats retained enough information from trial 1 to find the water-bottle as fast as controls. However, rats from both dosed groups had to explore further before drinking for 10 seconds or more.

controls, dosed rats must have obtained the important information about it on day 1 even though they may not have used it at the time. Since they had to break off drinking on day 2 for further exploration, they appear to have failed to obtain or retain other information they needed about the cage in general (Fig. 18.9). Both motor and sensory-input effects of the drug are well known (cf. p. 325) but are not usually separable in one simple test.

In modern toxicology, in the safety-testing of chemicals to which human

Exploration

beings may be exposed, the lowest dose with a reliably-detectable effect is the most important. The exploration–thirst test appears to be more sensitive than all conventional toxicological measures in a substantial number of cases (50 per cent of a small series of compounds for screening). At concentrations of trichloroethylene down to the 'threshold limit value' of 100 ppm, exposed rats were not usually different from controls on trial 1 but were consistently quicker to either the first lick or the first long drink on trial 2 (Silverman and Williams, 1975). They probably took no more water than controls and certainly walked no faster, so that the effect was shown to be selective.

Methyl mercury is a poison largely of the nervous system and can cause a scatter of sensory, motor, or 'psychological' symptoms in man. In rats, a diet containing 30 ppm causes gross motor damage in a few weeks, but this is not seen after 9 months on 15 ppm, nor was any behavioural change noticed (Magos and Butler, 1972). The exploration–thirst test indicated an early effect in rats fed on only 5 ppm (a dose believed toxic in man, of course) of the same methyl mercury compound (Extance, Silverman, and Williams, 1976). After 9 days on the diet, rats made their first lick (but not their first long drink) sooner than controls on both trials. Four rats given 50 ppm also made their first lick early on trial 2 but two of them delayed the long drink and at 3 weeks became obviously very ill. The high-dose effects could well be due to kidney damage, but this is unlikely at 5 ppm because there was no effect in animals tested until the diet had continued for over a year. An early stimulation, apparent tolerance, and a delayed return of the effect was also shown in the same rats by a social behaviour method (Chapter 22).

Some sources of variation in tests of exploration

Behaviour is variable, and this book is above all a discussion of ways to find the underlying regularities. Nevertheless, behavioural tests are all still subject to a relatively high variance, which may be why the art of statistics has been developed so much by psychologists. Exploration tests are simple and show the variation clearly (see the reports of open field, Y-maze, and hole-board tests quoted earlier); Hoffman (1966) discusses the same question in discriminated operant conditioning. I have more experience of the exploration–thirst test.

Some fluctuation is hard to account for. Helen Williams (unpublished) ran the same rats daily for 21 days; as in the original open-field (see p. 235) or in any maze-learning experiment, 'learning' was obvious in that the first lick came gradually sooner, especially between days 1 and 2; but the actual time fluctuated from day to day for no apparent reason. The chemical under test was not responsible, for controls fluctuated in parallel.

Some possible sources of variation turn out to be not important. Within single experiments there is sometimes a difference between the sexes, but in a long series this cancels out. I thought that females might fluctuate more widely because of the oestrous cycle, but the variance of the sexes turned out equal. Observers, as mentioned earlier, may differ in what they recognise as exploratory movements, but need not do so and are self-consistent in any case.

A surprising real influence is the order of observation. Suppose rats are housed in groups of four and randomly allocated as individuals. Every time one rat is removed from the group and again when it is returned, the disturbance is a stimulus for the others to explore. The first rat is tested fresh but the fourth is tired out. When two observers tested one cage at a time, first one pair of rats and then the other, the variance was less and the mean rate of exploration higher.

Another influence is probably the smell left behind by one rat which can apparently either accelerate or retard the next. Air-currents through the wire lid of the cage can be distracting, but using a transparent plastic dome instead of the wire only made things worse: the rats were apt to crouch for long periods or to run fast and not to drink at all. I once saw instant avoidance of a box painted gloss black (Silverman, 1966b), the rats jumped straight out of it. In both box and dome I could see shadowy internal reflections, and can only suppose the rats had seen a ghost.

Precisely because exploration is a sensitive measure, it is affected by environmental influences as well as experimental treatments. Although the fluctuations are fairly minor, they entail a trade-off between sensitivity and either dose or sample size.

Summary

Animals have to be constantly aware of their environment and to investigate any change in it. For a human being, it is enough to look, listen, and occasionally to touch. A rat has to walk around periodically or in response to stimuli, sniffing at what it can touch or at air-currents from elsewhere. The greater the stimulus change, the more complete the exploration and the longer it lasts – with two limiting factors. First, fatigue can interrupt a really long sequence into a series of diminishing bouts. The second is that the more intense the stimulus, the greater the inhibition (fear?) it also arouses, so that any on-going behaviour is postponed.

The intensity of a stimulus depends partly on its physical energy but mainly on the discrepancy between the observed environment and the expected. Expectation depends in turn both on past experience and the stimuli that ought to follow from the animal's present behaviour.

The most reliable way of eliciting predictable behaviour from a laboratory animal is therefore to place it bodily in an unfamiliar environment. This is the basis of short-term tests of spontaneous motor activity. Exploration is also an essential preliminary to conditioned behaviour which relies on the animal to discover food in the maze or how to use a Skinner box.

It seems possible to distinguish between experimental treatments (e.g. drugs) that act relatively specifically in this context on motor activity, fear, and on curiosity itself. Attempts have been made to distinguish fear from activity by defecation, by avoidance of the central area of an open field (even when that is the only source of food for hungry rats), by passive avoidance of the arm of a Y-maze previously associated with shock, and most directly by comparing approach and avoidance responses when the animal is offered access from its home cage to an unfamiliar area. Exploration is information-seeking independent of the associated motor activity. It has been measured by the visits to or time spent in the more unfamiliar or more complex places in an arena, by the inhibition of eating or drinking in deprived rats due to the presence of novel stimuli, and by a simple two-trial learning task.

NINETEEN
Some aspects of learning
To travel hopefully

'Learning' has traditionally carried high prestige even if the man of learning has been respected for what he possesses, however useless, rather than for the process of acquiring it, and even if on both counts the man of learning comes a poor second to the man of property. Similarly, tests of animal learning seem generally to be thought somehow superior. The subconscious logic is probably something like this. Man (we claim) is the highest of animals; much more of our behaviour is learned than in any other animal; therefore the learned aspects of animal behaviour are, if not the highest, at least the most suitable as models of human behaviour.

Fortunately it is not necessary to accept the assumptions behind this logic to agree that many conditioning methods are informative and model some aspects of human behaviour very well. In this chapter a miscellaneous collection of topics will be outlined which share a concern with the process of learning, the development of a conditioned response of one sort or another, as distinct from its final performance. It remains an untidy chapter because some of the experiments could have been discussed in the chapter concerned with the particular technique – the one on development of maze-running in Chapter 10, and so forth. The chapter would also be tidier, no doubt, if it were built around formal learning theories, but it nevertheless illustrates some of the more important principles and a more comprehensive view can be obtained from suitable textbooks.

Some definitions

Learning is not a single process. It is not obvious that the effort of learning a poem by heart shares very much with the recall of a visual image from a childhood seaside holiday, of the incoming tide slowly washing away the crumbling sand-castle. There is a little more in common between a pigeon learning to peck at a red disc on the wall instead of a yellow grain on the floor and my learning how to form the letter 'A' with a pen or on a typewriter. Even here there is a difference between the shaping of a rat's leverpress by successive approximations and verbal shaping by a teacher.

Wilfred Thorpe (1963) gave a working definition of Learning as 'that process which manifests itself by *adaptive* change in *individual* behaviour as a result of experience'. For theoreticians, this is oversimplified but it draws attention to two points which I have emphasised. Learning must be adaptive; the definition must exclude the direct consequences of breaking a leg, like being unable to walk, but include behavioural changes which compensate for the damage like, as it were, using a crutch. Individual experience is included to avoid confusion due to changes as a result of maturation and natural selection: sexual behaviour appears spontaneously at puberty in animals and can appear fairly complete without experience but not without hormones.

Thorpe classifies several types of learning, for convenience rather than theoretical correctness. *Habituation* is the waning of response to a continuous or repetitive stimulus. *Classical conditioning*, the increase of response to a repeated stimulus as it comes to convey information. *Trial-and-error* learning, the first of several versions of operant conditioning, in effect, where the animal exposes itself actively and systematically to a variety of stimuli so that classical conditioning or habituation are given the opportunity to occur. In *Intuition* where (if it occurs in animals at all), any trial-and-error occurs purely in internal rehearsal, and to all appearances the animal puts together the solution to a problem from several sets of otherwise unrelated information.

There must be several distinct stages in learning, and perhaps the processes can be experimentally interfered with separately. The sensory information has to be detected and taken in by the animal, it has to be encoded into some form of storage, the store has to be maintained without serious leakage, and finally when the time comes, the information has to be searched for, taken out of the store without either loss or contamination from irrelevant information, and utilised. In brief, the information has to be registered, retained, and retrieved.

State dependence

Before it is possible to say that some drug or experimental treatment has altered conditioned behaviour, you have to exclude alternative explanations of the observed facts, and one of the most interesting possibilities is state-dependent learning. This is not a school financed through government taxes, but the possibility that when a drug makes an animal perform differently from usual, it might not be a physiological process but a case of learning, as if the drug is acting as a conditioned stimulus. A human being often knows when he has had a drug, he feels dopy, drunk, or dizzy. The phenomenon is said to be more specific than this. Donald Overton (1964) trained rats on a T-maze, dropping them from about 40 cm on to the grid floor of the centre arm with a 1·6-mA shock already on, giving them a few seconds rest when they reached a goal-box in one of the other arms, and a minute after lifting them out, dropping them in again until they reached criterion. They learned equally well after injections of 25 mg/kg pentobarbitone or saline, but could not repeat the performance except after the injection they had been trained on. Trained or tested after smaller doses, there was some transfer, but attempts to mimic the drug's internal stimuli with a curare-like drug to cause limpness, and so on, or even to distinguish between food- and water-deprivation, all failed. The drug's effect is not so easily explained; various hypotheses are discussed by Bliss (1974). While state-dependence must often be a possibility, it has seldom been demonstrated. For the novelty of an unfamiliar injection could interfere with a conditioned response to the familiar one. Repeated tests, perhaps alternately under drug and control conditions might help, but would have conditioning effects of their own, obscuring any state-dependence.

Chemical transfer of learning: ghosts that go bump in the dark

Given the choice between a brightly lit arena and a dark enclosed compartment, rats usually choose the dark unless they have previously been given a fairly hefty electric shock there. Much depends on the details of the training procedure. Rats showed better passive avoidance if they had walked spontaneously into the dark compartment before shock than if they had been placed there directly by the experimenters (Mellgren, Willison, and Dickson, 1973). Presumably exploration had allowed the rats to recognise the entrance.

Genetic differences can also be relevant (Sprott, 1972). DBA/2J mice performed best if the shock had been at least 1 mA whereas $C_{57}Bl/6J$ and $B_6D_2F_1$ mice learned better at a near-threshold current of 0·1 mA. In one strain, it mattered how old the mice were, but not in the others. This does not make cowards of the C57 mice, nor are the DBAs necessarily heroic, tough, or intellectually 'thick'; it might be that the skin of their paws is less electrically conductive.

It is usually thought that there are two phases within the registration stage of 'memory', first a short-term buffer-store to hold the information until the second phase of permanent filing can be organised for items needing storage. Much of the experimentation described in this chapter concerns efforts to decipher the details of these processes.

If memories are to be coded chemically, polypeptides or proteins are the chemicals most likely to have the necessary complexity and to be synthesised at a more or less suitable rate. Moreover, inhibitors of protein synthesis such as cycloheximide block learning in the passive avoidance test. Unfortunately, when Randt, Barnett, McEwen, and Quartermain (1971) injected mice 30 minutes before training and tested them at times from 5 minutes to 72 hours afterwards, cycloheximide's greatest effect was at 5 minutes when the memory trace should have been in short-term storage, not long; so learning and protein effects seem separate.

The most dramatic attempt at validating the protein hypothesis of long-term memory is the 'scotophobin' story. G. Ungar and his colleagues have argued that there should be a chemical difference between mice that have or have not learned some simple behavioural response. They set themselves to extract and identify such a substance (Ungar, Galvan, and Clark, 1968; Ungar, Desiderio, and Parr, 1972) and to look for its effects in naïve mice, using passive avoidance as the measure. They put Swiss-strain mice for 3 minutes in a bright arena – the mice that went for at least half this time into a dark compartment (how many mice failed this criterion is not stated) were selected as 'donors'. They were given a 2-mA shock for 5 seconds before being allowed to escape, and were given five shocks at 10- or 15-second intervals every day for 6 or 8 days. Again, it is not stated whether the mice returned voluntarily to the dark cell or whether they had to be persuaded to help the experimenters with their enquiries. In fact, as Stewart drily commented (1972) Ungar and his colleagues had published over 100 printed pages of preliminary reports without ever describing their procedures in detail.

Anyway, a substance was extracted from the brains of trained mice which was claimed to 'transfer the learned fear' to other mice, though its effectiveness seems to have been more closely related to the duration of shock endured. It was even synthesised as a short peptide named 'scotophobin'. Injected into unshocked mice which had previously spent 130 ± 15 seconds out of a possible 180 in the dark compartment, it caused them to average only 52 ± 17 seconds over four trials in 2 days. Mice receiving the equivalent extract from untrained donors averaged 120 ± 20 seconds.

The difference between mice receiving extracts from trained and untrained donors is statistically highly significant, but as Stewart and others have suggested, there is some doubt about what it means. Assume for the sake of the argument that scotophobin is chemically one well-characterised substance (and apparently there are some doubts about an ambitious chemical procedure). Ungar may be right in claiming that scotophobin carries the message 'it is dangerous to enter and remain in dark places', but there are too many alternative explanations that fit the available facts. Electric shock might itself cause the formation of the substance and the place where the shock was given would be irrelevant: a second control group is required, given the same shocks but in the home cage. If scotophobin is specific, the comparable extract from such shocked controls should not inhibit recipients from entering the dark chamber. On the other hand, the extract from mice not selected as donors should also be effective, because they avoided the dark chamber quite spontaneously.

What is the actual behaviour of mice receiving scotophobin, and how do control mice differ? As so often, if the behaviour was even observed it was not described. Did the mice peacefully explore the illuminated arena, did they crouch timidly where they were put, or did they rush abruptly from corner to corner? Did those mice that entered the tunnel to the dark chamber at all explore it systematically, and did they show any extra hesitation, any tentative half-entries to the dark chamber itself before finally entering it?

In other words, was there any evidence that scotophobin had reduced the unconditioned avoidance of the light compartment, or increased the conditioned avoidance of the dark one specifically? Or had the severe shocking procedure produced a substance which merely inhibited any activity at all? Since the interval between training mice and testing them for passive avoidance – or at least the time of day – influences the results, what were the time intervals between training the donors and killing them? And when were the recipients tested? Finally, to take the speculations to absurd extremes, did Ungar use the same apparatus for donors and recipients? Could the shocked mice have left an aversive smell behind to which scotophobin sensitised recipients?

Not to throw the baby out with the bathwater, Ungar and his colleagues certainly report an interesting difference between brain extracts from shocked and unshocked mice. But dramatic claims, using a method which is decidedly crude when used on its own, inevitably provoke critical attention. Less pretentious work might not withstand this criticism either, but does not ask for it. Ungar may yet be right, but he needs better evidence.

Learning pills. Can a drug improve short-term learning?

It seems to be agreed that there is a distinction between short- and long-term phases of registration, but not where one ends and the other begins, whether the short-term buffer fades out in seconds, minutes, or hours.

Historically the distinction presumably arose in man from the amnesia that mercifully follows concussion from a knock on the head. The victim can rarely remember what happened immediately before the accident, but his memory is otherwise unimpaired. The classic, storybook loss of memory for your name and all your past life, is rare and not just a simple accident. At any rate, although a knock on the head with a hammer is not a fashionable experimental procedure, it has stimulated some useful research.

Needless to say, it is easier to harm learning than to help it; too hard a knock inhibits both short- and long-term memory very permanently. Nevertheless, certain drug treatments actually seem to facilitate learning: if only it were always so easy! There seem to be some undeniable successes, however, reviewed by James McGaugh (1973).

The time of dosing in relation to training and testing is critical. One possibility is to give a drug chronically for some weeks before training begins, to see if this improves a rat's (or a child's) educability. Bauer (1972) gave twenty once-daily injections of the convulsant drug pentylenetetrazol, in a very small dose of course, and Bauer and Duncan (1971) gave amphetamine. Both drugs improved both shuttle-avoidance learning and discrimination learning and performance, even though dosing stopped 24 hours before training started.

Drugs given just before training can either improve or impair conditioning. There are many examples, so that the fact has become less interesting than the possible mechanisms behind it. Many people believe that a small dose of amphetamine, for instance, increases 'arousal' from low to moderate levels, which should increase the attention the animal pays to the problem and therefore improve its learning. But arousal increased to an intense level would so greatly increase the need to do something that the animal becomes as it were, unable to stop to think what it is best to do. A large dose would therefore impair learning by increasing arousal too far.

An alternative suggestion is that a drug could improve learning by either sensitising the animal to sensory stimuli or, in other circumstances, insulating it. McGaugh quotes experiments where the convulsant drug strychnine improved maze-learning an hour or two afterwards, perhaps by minimising excessive exploration, or accelerated habituation, perhaps by attenuating responses to all stimuli (surely two ways of expressing the same idea). McGaugh finds this inconsistent with reports that strychnine can improve retention when given soon after training, but surely the same explanation could apply: the drug reduces the input of potentially distracting stimuli.

It might be difficult to distinguish true learning from 'state-dependence' if the drug is given before training, so it is sometimes administered just afterwards. If the drug reduces distractions or somehow facilitates a transfer of information from short- to long-term storage, an improvement in learning could be more convincingly demonstrated – provided that the drug administration itself is neither reward nor punishment.

McGaugh (1973) quotes experiments where d-amphetamine can improve appetitively-motivated discrimination learning in mice if given before or up to 15 minutes after training; effective doses were from 0·5 to 2 mg/kg, but not 2·5 mg/kg which approaches the dose causing 'stereotyped' repetitive exploration, etc. Racemic amphetamine (1 to 5 mg/kg) facilitated maze-learning if given after the first few trials in the maze, but impaired it after later trials (Breda, Carlini, and Sader, 1969). The impairment was not produced by injecting amphetamine before training or saline afterwards.

Getting over the shock

An important way of interfering with learning is by electroconvulsive shock (ECS), which seems to produce amnesia like a knock on the head. It should otherwise be just as aversive as shock in avoidance conditioning. The precise form of the deficit caused by ECS is uncertain, but the obvious possibility is that it breaks up a newly-formed short-term memory trace or prevents its transfer to long-term storage.

The timing of ECS is relevant, as usual, and Kral and Beggerly (1973) found an ingenious way to expand the time-scale in order to experiment on it more accurately. They used conditioned taste aversion, an interesting learning phenomenon in itself (see pp. 43–46), giving rats some nice saccharin-sweetened water, and followed this with an injection of nauseous lithium chloride. If they also gave ECS at any time during the 4 hours between saccharin and lithium, the rats later drank as much saccharin solution as controls never given lithium at all. ECS given immediately after lithium was the same, but if it was delayed only an extra 5 minutes the lithium had time to act, and the rats subsequently avoided saccharin. ECS therefore seems to prevent the association between a potential conditioned stimulus (sweet taste) and the unconditioned ('sick') reinforcement, without disrupting a pattern established only 5 minutes previously.

ECS itself has some characteristics of a learning process. ECS takes time to consolidate and disruption of another association is only partial if tested 2 hours after ECS but complete after 24 hours. It can itself be antagonised (Duncan and Hunt, 1972), for strychnine given up to 2 hours after ECS partly restored the conditioned performance, implying that ECS may not interfere with the short- or long-term traces themselves (whatever these are) but with the connection between them. And if the original conditioning is strengthened with a reminder, then that is when ECS has the greatest effect. Lewis, Bregman, and Mahan (1972) trained rats thoroughly in a maze, gave them a week's rest, and then ECS. The maze performance next time was actually worse in rats given an extra trial in the maze just before the shock. You might prefer to call ECS aversive, a punishment for running mazes.

Other experiments quoted by McGaugh (1973) fail to confirm that strychnine antagonises ECS, and in any case it may act by strengthening the original learning rather than directly on ECS. Strychnine given daily to trained mice during a 10-day retention period improved their subsequent performance, the drug reduced the 'loss of memory' due to the passage of time as well as to ECS.

It is paradoxical, though, that a drug which causes convulsions (by *lowering* synaptic barriers to nervous transmission) should antagonise the effect of convulsions produced electrically, and that it might act by reducing the flow of sensory information. Of course the memory-protecting doses of strychnine are far below convulsant doses, and memory-disruption by ECS may not actually be because of the convulsions either – Gold and McGaugh (1973) found that electrical stimulation in some regions of the brain caused seizures without amnesia. Moreover, the shock did not have to be electric. Jacobs and Sorenson (1969) put mice on a platform and let them climb through a hole on to a grid floor. The hole then closed and they were given 1 second of 0·7-mA shock. The grid then folded smartly out of the way, and the mice were dropped into water for 10 seconds, either ice-cold or hot (48 °C). If there had been a pause of 10 or 30 seconds or 6 hours between the electroshock and the bath, or if they were dropped immediately after the shock on to sawdust, the mice learned passive avoidance: 24 hours later they refused to crawl through the hole. But a sudden hot or cold bath within 2 seconds after electroshock and the mice seemed happy to repeat the process next day.

Exploration and latent learning – Ye know not what ye seek

Exploration is an essential preliminary to learning. A hungry rat put into a maze for the first time has no reason to suspect that food is available (except perhaps by smell), and part of its 'learning' to start eating sooner is the declining need to explore elsewhere. Similarly the early stages of operant conditioning depend on the animal's tendency to sniff every scent and manipulate anything movable; 'shaping' largely depends on guiding the animal's exploration to the food magazine and the lever.

Exploration could therefore explain 'latent learning', the fact that a rat placed in a maze for a time without conventional reward subsequently learns more quickly when it has to run the maze for food. (To demonstrate true latent learning a second control group may be useful with experience of unfamiliar environments in general but not of the particular maze.)

Kumar (1969) used his modified Y-maze. All three arms had a trough at the end, partly covered so that rats could smell food but not eat. Female rats explored the maze for 3 minutes daily for 10 days, one group with all troughs empty, one with mash in both black troughs, and one with the food in the white trough (since rats tended to avoid the white arm, a fourth group were habituated to it for 20 days). All the rats were fully fed and the groups did not differ, but entries to the arms and time sniffing the food were correlated in individual rats, as if measuring the same thing. On the eleventh (or twenty-first) day, the rats had been left hungry for 24 hours but the troughs were left empty. The rats did not increase general activity (i.e. entries) but did increase the time spent sniffing the trough(s) where food had previously been, especially the white-arm groups, and more especially the group with twenty previous trials instead of ten. Since the rats behaved as if they knew where to find food when (but only when) they needed it, there must have been latent learning.

Dexamphetamine increased entries and especially half-entries of head and shoulders only, but even the smallest dose halved the time spent sniffing. Kumar concluded that the drug increased activity but reduced exploration and, by implication, latent learning. In spite of anorexia, McGaugh reviewed evidence that small doses of amphetamine can improve appetitively-motivated learning, which would argue against Kumar's conclusion.

Exploration as a one-trial learning

In the exploration-thirst test (p. 248) rats given various drugs that changed their speed of exploration on trial 1 generally walked neither faster nor slower than controls on the second trial without injection next day. A curious phenomenon has occurred in some other experiments (Rushton, Steinberg, and Tinson, 1963; Rushton, Steinberg, and Tomkiewicz, 1968) where corresponding differences appear in a second trial as much as 3 months after the first.

Rats given a mixed injection of 0·75 mg/kg of amphetamine plus 15 mg/kg of amylobarbitone (group M) made nearly twice as many entries into the arms of a Y-maze as saline controls (group S). Controls given saline again (group SS) before a second trial 3 days later showed the usual decline in the number of entries into a now-familiar maze. Group MS (given the mixture before the first trial and saline before the second), though they showed a similar decline from their first-trial activity, still made twice as many entries on the second trial as group SS. Group MM, given the mixture on both trials, maintained the original high activity and group SM maintained the original moderate activity, with neither a decline to SS levels nor a rise to the MM peak. Hence the drug effect on activity on the second trial depended on the previous activity in the same environment. The interval between trials could range from 3 days to 13 weeks, and mice showed similar results from a chlordiazepoxide/amphetamine mixture on a holeboard (Dorr *et al.*, 1971; see p. 244).

The phenomenon is curious and unexplained; it is in a sense the opposite of state-dependent learning, for instead of the learned performance depending on the presence of stimuli from the drug, the drugs in effect cause the

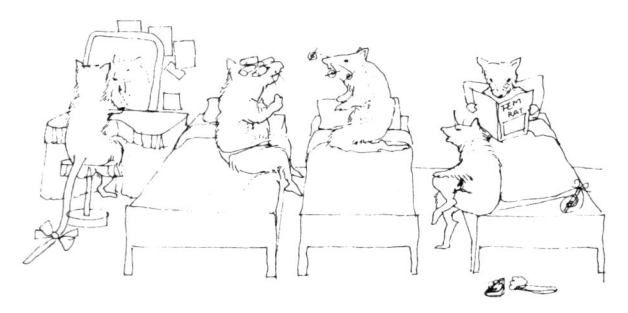

quiet undisturbed lives

learning of a response to the situation. It would be interesting to know how specific the response is to the particular apparatus – would animals persistently more active in a Y-maze transfer the increase to an open-field? Rushton *et al.*, comment that their rats had led sheltered lives undisturbed during the interval (if herds of sixteen females housed together can ever remain undisturbed). The test was the first dramatic event of their lives.

Imprinting

As it clambers out of the broken shell, the first moving object that a greylag gosling should see is mother goose. The little birds follow their mother and are kept warm and safe under her wing, are guided to where appropriate pecks pick up nutritious grain, and so on. Birds and mammals can be classified either as nidicolous, where the young are brought up safe and warm in a nest, or nidifugous where there is no nest. A new duckling, guinea-pig, sheep, or horse has to be able to run after the mother, indeed after the herd if mother and offspring are not to become vulnerable in isolation to predators. The lamb must therefore have some means of knowing which ewe is the one able and willing to give suckle, and the ewe also has to know her own lamb. They need a rapidly effective recognition system.

The first object (fulfilling certain minimal conditions) that a chick sees, the chick follows. If it should not be the mother hen, then the chick will follow the wrong object, not the hen. Douglas Spalding was the first to describe this accurately, in a lecture to the British Association in 1872 (reprinted 1954), but it was Lorenz who really publicised the phenomenon (1937) and still better in *King Solomon's Ring* (1953). He brought up greylag geese by hand, almost as pets, and they followed him around, not mother goose, although older and more sophisticated goslings might oblige only if he squatted on his heels and hopped across the garden flapping his arms and honking. A little more mature still, and the young geese even started sexual advances to Frau Lorenz or to visitors. The goslings not only treated Lorenz as if he was their mother, they generalised to other human beings and took his species-specific characteristics as the stimuli for courtship behaviour later on. But imprinted geese would only fly with other geese, and showed parental responses to goslings, not to human babies.

Lorenz claimed that four characteristics make this 'imprinting' quite different from ordinary learning. It is remarkably fast and in the extreme case a few seconds exposure to a stimulus is sufficient (compare the numerous trials a rat needs to learn a maze or an operant schedule). It seemed irreversible – once learned never forgotten. It occurs in a brief sensitive period, geese more than a few days old can no longer be imprinted. It is transferable from the response (following the mother) for which it was originally developed to a different kind of behaviour (courtship) which is not in the chick's repertoire at the time the stimulus is conditioned.

Lorenz was of course being deliberately provocative to armchair psychologists. They responded characteristically with 20 years of earnest laboratory experimentation, transmuting the golden romance of fresh insights into the base metal of a thousand dreary scientific papers. But the study of imprinting has done more than anything to weld two approaches to the common set of problems of animal behaviour into a single integral science. It has shown ethologists how to conduct laboratory experiments to test hypotheses based on observation (and just as often, how *not* to). It has revealed to psychologists how dusty and meaningless are laboratory experiments unless they arise out of an appreciation that behaviour is adapted to help the wild animal earn its living.

The upshot is that imprinting is no longer thought of as unique in kind, but as an essentially ordinary kind of learning extensively developed. It is certainly unusually fast. It is also fairly permanent compared with most laboratory conditioning; it is not strictly irreversible but it is difficult to change, for in the wild there would hardly be the need. When Salzen and Meyer (1968) show that chicks can be trained to change the object they follow, a reply might be that a flashing light does not give the reinforcement of warmth and contact which Spalding showed is usual. Peter Driver (1960) printed wild Eider ducklings on to himself but only when rewarded by gentle pressure on three specific places, the back of the head and on each side of the upper edge of the base of the bill.

The development of the following response in domestic chicks closely parallels that of an operant response – Peter Bateson and Ellen Reese (1969) found that day-old chicks would learn to step on a pedal to switch on a coloured flashing light, and when later offered a choice, preferred the colour they had been trained with. Yet there were some apparently innate preferences – seventeen of twenty naïve chicks followed an orange flashing light when offered the choice, rather than a green one that was equally attractive when offered alone. On the whole, however, Bateson and Reese believe that imprinting does not positively associate one stimulus with the following response, it eliminates the others. An older chick fails to follow any stimulus that it is not familiar with.

Spalding originally recognised a critical period – a young bird that has not been imprinted by a certain age never will be. A chick kept in the dark for 3 days was then imprinted, one kept for 4 showed fear and flew away. Eckhard Hess (1959) rediscovered this. Mallard ducklings were imprinted when they became able to walk. Their ability (or need) to follow did not end, but while younger ducklings showed no fear, older ones made avoidance responses and 'distress' calls to unfamiliar stimuli in a standard situation. Hess used a circular runway, mounting a stimulus-object on a toy railway engine which could be trundled round. Young ducklings followed it, older ones followed only if they were given meprobamate, a muscle-relaxant drug then commonly used as a tranquilliser: the ducklings became ataxic but staggered bravely towards the train. Hess concluded that the critical period ends because fear of unfamiliarity begins.

However, older birds have been successfully imprinted without anxiolytic drugs in several experiments, so casting doubt on whether critical periods exist. Alan Ratner and Howard Hoffman (1974) solved the problem on noticing that older birds became imprinted on a stimulus only when compulsorily exposed to it for much longer than usual: a bird that runs away

Some aspects of learning 265

from a stimulus has no time to become imprinted on it, but fear can be overcome by habituation as well as by drugs. They tested the hypothesis on twenty common ducklings (*Anas platyrhynchos*) hatched in a dark incubator and then housed singly in white translucent plastic containers. The test was in a box divided by a fine wire-mesh screen into two compartments (Fig. 19.1). In one, a foam-rubber object was mounted on a toy railway engine which

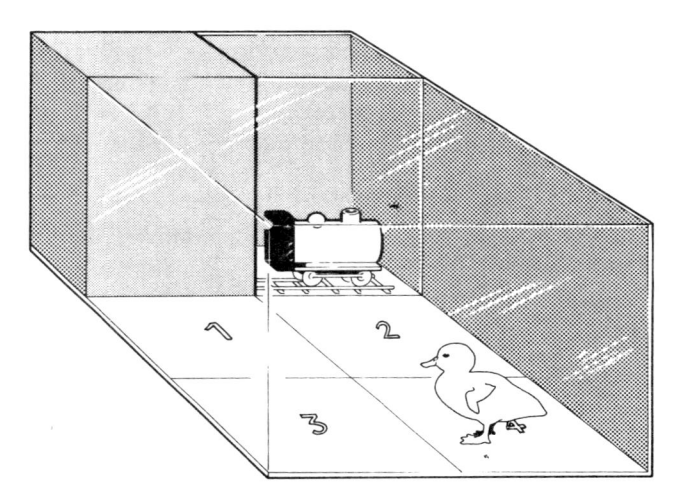

Fig. 19.1. Imprinting of ducklings (after Ratner and Hoffman, 1974). A toy engine is trundled in and out of its shed, and the ducklings' tendency to approach or avoid the engine when it is visible out of the station can be observed.

shuttled back and forth from hiding in its shed out to where the duckling could see it. If the duckling was detected by photocells in the area closest to where the engine was visible (i.e. square '2' in Fig. 19.1), the train shuttled; if the duckling moved elsewhere, the train remained in its shed. The train was therefore under the bird's control for two 30-minute sessions a day for 3 days, either days 1–3 or 5–7. Young ducklings spent longer in square 2 if they could see the stimulus; they tried to catch the train. The older ducklings entered the square less than controls not exposed to the train on day 5 and less still on days 6 and 7; the moving, perhaps noisy train is still the dominant stimulus which these birds switched off almost as much as possible. Then some 8-day-old ducklings were used: half could switch off the train as before, but the others had to look and listen to the train trundling back and forth no matter what they did. This group retreated at first, like the others, but approached increasingly, eventually staying 80 per cent of the time in quarter No. 2.

Therefore, there is no absolute critical period, for habituation can overcome the fear whose onset usually terminates it; nevertheless, the concept of a critical period accurately describes the natural situation. Stevens drew the same conclusion in 1955 from a wild gosling that lost its flock at 1–2 weeks old. It gradually ceased to hiss at and avoid Stevens, and then called to him to be let out to graze. Eventually it followed him and his friends but continued to hiss at strangers and other animals.

Habituation

A continued or repetitive stimulus soon ceases to convey any fresh information. However, this depends on the animal as well as the stimulus – 8-day-old ducklings interpreted the model train as conveying two kinds of information, whereas the 1-day ducklings only recognised one. The fear-response in the older ducklings nevertheless habituated faster than the following response.

Scourse and Hinde (1973) subjected mice to various audible stimuli and showed again that habituation is specific to the response as much as to the stimulus. Every 30 seconds either a short tone sounded, or clicks which included hypersonic frequencies, or both. The mice turned to listen to the noises at first, but this initial orienting response faded in 5 minutes. Readiness to explore, climbing all over the cage, was increased for 3 hours. The jerks, twitches, and restless changes of position seen after stimulation during non-REM sleep, or after intense stimulation at other times, did not habituate for at least 49 hours. While there is no need to exaggerate the complexity of an essentially simple process, it is not completely monolithic.

Reversal learning – Comparative 'intelligence'

If 'intelligence' is defined as learning ability, it is tempting to compare different species or phyla. Earthworms could be called unintelligent because although they can be trained to turn left in a T-maze, they need hundreds of trials, but the ciliate Protozoan *Paramecium* is even poorer at learning tasks devised by man. Paramecia have essentially a single response: they swim forwards on a spiral trajectory until they meet conditions unsuitable for them, outside certain limits of pH, salinity, or temperature. Then they retreat a short way, turn through about 30°, and advance again until they next come to some unfavourable stimulus. Apparently they can 'learn' nothing harder than a temperature preference. A paramecium swimming happily at 15–18° recoils if it encounters colder or warmer water. If it is kept at 18° for a while its tolerance changes, and it may recoil at about 16° and 20° instead.

Unrelated animals may therefore have next to nothing in common in what they can learn. At one time it was thought that a fairly quantitative index of intelligence would be a delayed response – a cat could wait longer than a rat after the end of a conditioned stimulus before starting the response; a monkey could wait longer than a cat, and (most gratifying of all) a man can wait very much longer still, language lets us wait most of a lifetime for the opportunity if we have to. Gerard Baerends (1941; see 1976) put an end to that idea with studies on the digger wasp *Ammophila pubescens*. Even an 'intelligent' insect could hardly delay a conventional conditioned response by more than a couple of seconds. *Ammophila* digs a burrow, kills a caterpillar, puts it in the burrow, lays an egg in the caterpillar, seals the burrow, and goes away. Each morning she visits up to three such burrows with offspring at different stages of development to see if more caterpillars are needed. She then provisions each one as required (as shown by the experimenter discreetly pre-loading or emptying the burrow in her absence), so that by the time the last hungry mouth has been provided for it may be as much as 15 hours since her dawn visit. Now a machine with the electronic logic to control such a system would not be especially complex, but the delay is still impressive enough to discourage anybody who feels a mere insect should not be so clever.

Clearly each species may have its own specialised learning abilities, which are as likely to be related to ecological niche as phylogenetic status. Given an appropriate task, a woodlouse can apparently learn a discrimination task as quickly as a rat and faster than an elephant, and a well-trained rat can learn a new discrimination quicker than an 8-year-old child.

These results led Rajalakshmi and Jeeves (1965) to doubt that discrimination (Chapter 14) is a good basis for comparative psychology either, but they suggested that discrimination reversal might be a fairer one. However difficult a particular species finds it to distinguish black from white or stars from stripes, once the animal responds to one and ignores the other, the task of reversing the discrimination, so that B is the stimulus to approach instead of A, should be of much more nearly constant difficulty. In rats, the ratio between the number of trials (or errors) to criterion on the original learning and on the reversal, was remarkably consistent on a series of tasks of varying difficulty. Literature on chicks, monkeys, octopus, showed this ratio to be sensitive to age and development, brain surgery, X-irradiation, or upbringing in bare or enriched environments, and in children it correlated with performance on intelligence tests. Rajalakshmi and Jeeves considered that valid comparisons come only if the index is computed: (1) on the first discrimination and the first reversal, to minimise bias due to overtraining; (2) on the same kind of task (e.g. discriminations on shape, brightness, and position are not equally difficult); (3) on the same kind of reinforcement (shock teaches faster than hunger); (4) on the same criteria; (5) on a large sample of animals; and (6) reversal should not be more difficult than the original learning.

Reversal learning can test concepts a little less academic. In electrophysiological experiments (Bradley, 1964), LSD made neurones of the reticular formation respond to a meaningless sound (normally ignored) when it was almost as quiet as the quietest audible conditioned stimulus, and also made it easier to distract rats from running down an alley for fish. If LSD makes meaningless stimuli appear to carry information, King, Martin, and Arabella Seymour (1974) thought it should facilitate reversal learning.

Rats were trained in daily 10-minute sessions for 8 days to run down one of two parallel alleys. On each run, one randomly chosen alley was illuminated, the other was left dark as black Perspex and the rats shuttled from one end to the other for an 0·2-ml drop of water. Half the rats were rewarded for choosing the light alley, half for the dark, and after 3 days' rest they had to reverse their preference. They were given 120 trials, irrespective of how many rewards they earned, starting 15 minutes after an injection of saline or from 6 to 50 µg/kg LSD. Rats formerly given water for running down the dark alley were now rewarded only after seeing the light, and vice versa. LSD (at all but the lowest dose) helped them learn the change: in the block of trials seventy-one to eighty, LSD-rats were already choosing correctly more often. Rats given bromlysergide, a chemically-related drug not causing hallucinations in man, did not.

Anything which makes the animal persevere at the original conditioned performance (and therefore improve the first learning) would be expected to interfere with reversal learning. Kendler and Lachman (1958) pointed out that intensified motivation, from prolonged deprivation of food, should make the animal try harder to find food where it used to be. Similarly if the original training was only intermittently reinforced, the rat would expect not to find food on some trials, as it were, and should therefore take longer to realise that something was amiss. Their experiment became complicated but supported the hypothesis. However, Kendler and Lachman say that when the rats noticed something wrong, they did not actually reverse their conditioned preference at first. They started with the hypothesis that rats usually begin with, on position. Some rats consistently turned right, some left, before starting to make the correct discrimination.

In fact, some discriminations are much easier than others. Rats trained on a series of ten reversals in a T-maze were shown by Weyant (1966) to learn the reversal progressively more easily if the discrimination was right from left. In effect they learned that if food was exhausted in one place, it would become available in the other. If the discrimination was of light from dark, there was no 'learning to learn'; each reversal took as long as the original training. Even after ten reversals, the rats had to learn the discrimination anew.

Maze learning and cholinesterase

Carlton (1968) and others have suggested that drugs interfering with cholinergic function affect behaviour only in the very early stages, before tolerance sets in. Among neurotoxicological studies of two carbamate insecticides, Dési, Gönczi, Simon, Farkos, and Kneffel (1974) investigated this point with both the learning and the final performance of a maze-running task.

Some aspects of learning

Adult male rats were fed on meals small enough (100 g/kg bodyweight daily) to make sure that they ate everything. The insecticides were mixed in with the diet to calculate the dose by the animals' bodyweight: 100 and 200 ppm of carbaryl gave doses of 10 and 20 mg/kg daily, and arprocarb (12·5 and 25 ppm) gave 1·25 and 2·5 mg/kg, enough to inhibit cholinesterases in brain and red blood cells but not plasma. Each rat was allowed to explore a four-unit T-maze until he reached the far end where his dinner was waiting, ready dosed.

All groups averaged about 28 seconds to reach the food on the first day, and entered an average of nearly 2·5 blind alleys along the way. With one trial a day, control rats gradually shortened the running time to about 10 seconds by day 20, and then fairly consistently ran directly to the food with few 'errors' until day 50. All the dosed rats learned significantly more quickly. Most groups averaged about 10 seconds from day 2 onwards, but by day 25 they started to dilly-dally on the way, especially the 25-ppm arprocarb rats: running times and visits to blind alleys increased.

Dési and his colleagues believe the apparent changes in 'learning' were in fact a consequence of increased 'irritability', a sensitivity to stimuli which first helped the rats explore the maze and then (despite their hunger) compelled them. It is interesting that Tryon's maze-bright and -dull strains of rats (see p. 116) differ along the same dimension, the maze-bright rats are distracted less from food and make fewer 'errors'.

Discussion

Learning is only that part of the development of behaviour that depends on the individual's experience. And, to put it provocatively, it is now becoming obvious that in an otherwise genetically programmed development, the gaps left open to be filled by individual experience, are themselves programmed as a result of natural selection. Expressed in black-and-white terms, the bits which are most economically developed by genetic programming are innate, the bits which fluctuate most according to circumstances are left open for learning, and most bits are developed after an intricate interaction of the two types of process.

Human language illustrates the argument best. The details of any language are clearly learned, but some of the basic grammatical rules are thought to be innate, and the child's *capacity* to learn can only develop under genetic guidance. Indeed watching babies babbling and listening suggests that 'drive' is not too strong a word for their development of all the necessary skills in oral/aural communication.

It is important not to fall into traps posed by the very words themselves. The ordinary-language use of words like 'learning' and 'memory' is legitimate in a rapid survey of relevant experiments but they skate lightly over some problems. It is hard to see how a change in behaviour called passive avoidance could be carried specifically on a particulate lump of matter to be called a memory. For the information is only accessible in the right context. A section of computer tape may carry the pattern of magnetisation that codes for my name, address, and my family's electricity consumption for the last 3 months. It would only be meaningful if it could be physically inserted into exact alignment on the right kind of computer file, and even then it could only be correctly interpreted with the correct programs. Inserted into the wrong reel of magnetic tape, it would not cause an invoice to be printed to demand my money, it would be transcribed as an unusually noisy squawk of music.

Consider also the logical processes involved. Taking the passive avoidance example again, the animal has to see and smell the light and dark chambers, build a mental map of the apparatus, associate one place with shock, and change the flag which says 'keep out of here' from the code for one place to that for the other. Logically if not physiologically, these are distinct stages; which one is to be called 'learning'? It may not be necessary actually to answer such questions, but it is essential to be aware that a concept like 'learning' is as vague as one like 'drive'; both are useful in their limited place, but when analysed in sufficient detail (Hinde, 1959) both break down into a whirlpool of specific questions.

Summary

The development of behaviour conditioned by the experimenter is as interesting and as good a source of methods as the performance of the finished product.

Learning is only a part of the development of behaviour, the part which it is not efficient to pre-program genetically, because it involves stable adaptations of the individual to unpredictable details of the environment. Learning includes widely varied phenomena, from the waning of response to a stimulus which has ceased to convey new information, to imprinting, to the timing of operant responses. Consideration of the logical steps involved makes it seem unlikely that the physiological processes can be the same in all cases. A few interesting topics involving learning in various ways are briefly discussed.

Most learning processes include three main stages, though no doubt each is itself a conglomerate – the reception of the relevant information and the registration of what is needed, its retention in a long-term store, and its subsequent retrieval and use.

It is emphasised how learning is an active process by the animal. A stimulus provokes exploration, and it is the search for new stimuli and for their relationship to the old which allows the learning of mazes and other experimental procedures.

TWENTY
Tests of behaviour in groups and of stimulated aggression
No rat is an island entire of itself

Animals behave differently when they are alone. Pharmacologists first realised this, uncomfortably, during the World War of 1939–45, when air pilots used a stimulant drug, benzedrine, to keep awake on long flights. The effective dose was, according to some reports, disturbingly close to the dose that would kill half of a group of mice (the LD_{50}), but other reports gave it a wide margin of safety. Systematic work by Chance (1946–7; see p. 84) identified the reason – some tests had used grouped mice, some solitary mice, and the LD_{50} is different. High doses of amphetamine, as the drug is known nowadays, exaggerate the animals' responses to each other in a way that exacerbates the physiological effect of raising body temperature.

A mouse given a very high dose runs continually round and round the cage or continually gnaws the bars of the cage or even its own tail. Two mice meeting rise into a mutual upright posture, pushing at each other with their forepaws. Normal mice do this a dozen times a day, but briefly and without having to prop each other up. Heavily drugged mice seem somehow to be locked into the posture for minutes at a time; and they die at doses causing no more than stereotyped, repetitive gnawing or walking in solitary mice.

Group toxicity has been a happy hunting ground for pharmacologists ever since. It happens with several compounds (though with thiourea and Λ-THC there seems to be safety in numbers) and some strains of mice show it at lower ambient temperatures than others, as if they more easily boil with rage. More seriously, stereotyped actions have been shown to depend on overstimulation of dopamine receptors, directly by drugs like apomorphine, but indirectly via the release of dopamine by amphetamine. Littleton (1974) distinguished one toxic mechanism independent of group stress and associated with noradrenaline release, another one via dopamine and potentiated by stress causing group toxicity.

Animals can perform in groups everything they do alone; but a solitary animal of a group-living species is only half an animal. This chapter contains descriptions of some differences between grouped and solitary rats or mice, and something of the social structure they adopt in groups. It also describes methods utilising fighting stimulated in various ways – fighting often resembling that shown by mice given a heavy dose of amphetamine.

In this chapter, 'fighting' is treated as a single, easily-recognisable kind of behaviour without internal structure. In Chapter 21 some analyses of social behaviour will be described, in which fighting is conspicuously a part with its own complex structure. The distinction between 'stimulated fighting' and the analysis of social behaviour is a little arbitrary, and entails some repetition but is convenient for a complicated subject.

Some differences between grouped and solitary rats and mice

Rats isolated for 3–16 weeks were more highly aroused than rats in groups of ten – their tails stuck straight out instead of drooping, they fell asleep later after a standard dose of pentobarbitone and they woke up sooner (Wiberg and Grice, 1965), and the lethal dose of pentobarbitone was higher. Rotarod performance differs: solitary mice drop off a rotating rod at lower doses of several drugs than group-housed (Kršiak, 1975), but not by falling limply, they actively jump. Isolated mice were more greatly stressed by mild centrifugation on a record-player turntable, for in a strain that voluntarily drinks alcohol, isolated mice drank more than grouped mice (Brown, 1968), companionship made the drink go round further.

isolated mice drank more

Solitary deermice (*Peromyscus*) consumed more food, sugar solution, and water than when they were housed in pairs, but Cooper and Levine (1973) suggested that this did not mean that social behaviour interferes with consumption (nor that lonely mice compensate with food), but that even in a laboratory kept at 20 °C, deermice could not otherwise keep warm without huddling together.

Sexual behaviour is disrupted by isolation in male rats. Gerall, Ward, and Gerall (1967) found that twenty-six of thirty rats, isolated at the early age of 14 days, were unable to copulate properly at 90 days. They circled and sniffed the females, jumped and seemed generally overexcited, but were unable to mount or achieve intromission. Only after living with a female for 3 weeks or so did their performance improve and even this practice did not make perfect – they were the only animals the authors saw which ejaculated before intromission. Males housed in groups of six until the age of 16 months were also clumsy with females, however (Drori and Folman, 1967) but were easily and completely cured by a few months cohabitation.

Social relationships form part of the environment that guides growth and development, and there is evidence that in many ways isolated rats and mice are more *variable* than group-housed animals. Even some physical characters like ovary weights or the number of tail vertebrae vary more widely in isolated animals. Probably the absence of genetic and social–environmental buffering leaves some characteristics vulnerable to other external vagaries. F_1 hybrids always responded uniformly to a standard dose of pentobarbitone (Mackintosh, 1962), but mice of the parental strains 'slept' for widely varying times when first tested. A week afterwards pure-bred mice housed in pairs or fours were now as uniform as the hybrids, but solitary mice or those in groups of eight remained variable. It seems likely that mice set up stable social relationships if numbers are small enough for individuals to recognise each other.

It does not follow that grouping rats and mice must necessarily be 'better' than isolating them. Much depends on how it is done, on your purpose in testing the animals at all, and on the species. Hamsters, for instance, seem to be naturally more solitary than rats, though even hamsters have to come together to reproduce. And groups differ: with up to four or five in a cage, rats and mice can form some form of social structure. larger groups appear not to do so.

Group toxicity with amphetamine reinforces this point – a stable small group is under far less stress than a larger one newly formed of strangers, especially if a dying mouse is immediately replaced by another stranger to keep the numbers up (as in one experiment I read some years ago).

Ziporah Speizer and Marta Weinstock (1973, 1974; Weinstock and Speizer, 1973) believe that prolonged isolation of rats can provide a model for human mania. Rats isolated 6–8 weeks from weaning are abnormally active in an open field. β-Blocking drugs with or without sedative activity (*dl-* or *d-*propranolol or practolol) reduce the activity of isolates to that of group-housed rats at doses of 0·2–0·5 mg/kg, whereas the latter were reduced only by 20 mg/kg.

The deterioration in isolation can be intellectual as well as emotional. Rats isolated from weaning were as tame during periodic handling as group-housed rats, and as quick to learn two tasks where they had to remove or overcome an obstacle. Morgan (1973) found however that isolated rats could not cope so well when the task was made more difficult, or even when it was merely changed. They tended to persevere with the original solution whereas group-housed rats – especially if brought up with plenty of 'toys' to play with – could change their strategy quickly. Isolated rats were less likely to enter an open-field arena of their own accord, but would run faster round it or along an alley for food than grouped rats; they ate more too. Altogether, Morgan thought, isolates resembled rats with non-specific cortical lesions, in their perseverance and preoccupation with food. An isolated rat is not a whole animal.

The opposite concept of an 'enriched environment' started when Donald Hebb (1949) kept some rats at home as pets for his tolerant wife and family. Back in the laboratory, these privileged rats were far superior to their disadvantaged lab-housed relatives in the transfer-learning of a series of maze problems. Krech and his colleagues (Rosenzweig, Bennet, and Diamond, 1972) followed this up by housing young rats in rather large groups of ten, with or without 'toys', a selection from twenty-five varied objects changed

with and without toys

every day. Comparing these rats' brains with those of isolated rats without toys, they found a greater ratio of cortical to subcortical cholinesterase activity, larger synaptic junctions, more glial cells, and more cholinesterase in them. The technical difficulties in answering the more specific and interesting questions about brain structure are formidable; but if you need evidence on the anatomy of rats before you provide a stimulating, varied environment for children then topics well worth pursuing include whether small groups (say of four) differ from large, and whether toys are any use to isolated rats.

Dominance by fighting

What is the social organisation of small groups which is both stimulating and yet enables unstable pure-bred mice to settle down together? The standard answer has been a rank-order, a dominance hierarchy: one domestic hen in a flock can peck all the others without being pecked at in return, another can peck all but the first, and so on. The first bird grows sleek and portly, and rarely needs to do more than stalk towards another bird and glare. The second- and third-ranking birds may be more obviously aggressive, but although not every individual bothers to exercise its rights on every other bird, a flock of perhaps twenty or thirty hens, turkeys, or geese can be ranked into a single linear order. Only rarely might there be a circular relationship in the middle of the line, K pecking L pecking M pecking both N and K. Only the 'omega' bird at the end of the line has nobody to peck at, and flutters off anxiously if any of its tormentors comes too close.

In poultry (outside intensive battery systems) the hierarchy is very obvious when a flock is newly formed of strangers. Even after settling down and when crude pecks are comparatively rare, and when everyone scuttles away from her superiors, the social structure is apparent enough, and farmers often go to considerable trouble to discourage hierarchies. Certainly in flocks with a floating population, the poor runt at the end of the line gets thin and scrawny, she gets all the kicks and the farmer gets no ha'pence. Whole flocks have even been supplied with pink plastic contact lenses: if all is red, then the red comb ceases to provide an adequate colour-stimulus to provoke aggression.

Rank-orders therefore made at one time a fine bandwagon for research. Every species had one, wherever two or three were gathered together. One of the more interesting observations, by Konrad Lorenz, of course (1953), was that a flock of jackdaws has two rank-orders, one for each sex; when a high-ranking cock married beneath him, the happy bride took on his status and lorded it over her erstwhile superiors.

Evans and Abramson (1958) with Fremont-Smith (1958) described the actions used in setting-up dominance hierarchies in newts (*Triturus viridescens*) and Siamese fighting-fish (*Betta splendens*). In both species, LSD enabled low-ranking individuals to rise in the hierarchy, apparently by lowering the threshold for aggression. The criteria were threats and displays as well as obvious chases and bites, and the other animals in the group recognised them as well as the experimenters; for although the dominant newt or fish did not allow itself to be displaced the omega individual could rise and remain promoted for long after treatment had stopped and the drug metabolised.

A linear rank-order is an abstraction, a simplification so that the observer can make sense of a potentially complex set of relationships. A true rank-order is more than one highly aggressive animal and a few abject cowards, and implies some surprisingly complex abilities. The alpha and the omega individuals at top and bottom can easily be recognised by their sleek or runted appearance. The omega animal must have been conditioned to flee from any other animal, the alpha to expect all his subjects to make way before him as he strolls round his estate. But how does animal number 3 distinguish number 2 from number 4, and vice versa? There is a distinction between a stable group whose members recognise each other as individuals, and the relative aggressiveness of strangers who meet each other for no more than a few minutes at a time.

Rank-orders in rats and mice

Rats, our usual example, may differ both from animals that defend individual territories, and those living in flocks. It is obvious that for most of any 24 hours, rats and mice are not oriented to each other except when they huddle together in sleep. If the stimuli involved in rank-order formation are visible, and not merely a long-continued smell, then they must be shown for only brief periods.

Margaret Warne (1947) made 'a time analysis of certain aspects of the behaviour of small groups of caged mice'. She kept four C57 Black or C Bagg albino mice to a cage, under reversed lighting so that they would be active in the daytime, and she probably increased the activity by moving a cage to a convenient place before observing it. She therefore seldom saw the mice apparently asleep or huddled together in one corner of the cage, but the small size of the cage meant that, equally, they were seldom dispersed by more than a body-length. Overt fighting, when one mouse submitted, or inhibited the attack by standing upright with one forepaw flexed, was very conspicuous and could be seen fairly frequently without needing any special procedure, but it took up only 0·24 per cent of the observed time. A simple rank-order could be observed, in that one mouse attacked the others with little retaliation, sometimes apparently at random, sometimes picking on one or two particular targets. Nevertheless, Warne thought there was some group cohesion, in the time the mice were awake but aggregated; her small groups never had more than one dominant male, unlike the larger groups of Uhrich (1938). Warne's mice also indulged in so-called non-fighting aggression, where one mouse would stretch out, grab the shoulder of another in its teeth and drag it back to the corner of the cage where the mice slept. In its complete form this action resembles a mother mouse retrieving an errant infant and is shown by one mouse of either sex more than others in the group, not the one that attacks most.

Rank-orders were described in male albino rats by Grant and Chance (1958) on the criterion of who shows a 'submissive posture' to whom, by lying flat on his back (see p. 304). The dominant rat sits over the submissive one and may groom him quite fiercely for a moment, but the initiative is actually taken by the one who finally decides to lie down and thus decide which rat is which. The ranking was statistical, in that few dominate/submit relationships were 100 per cent one way, but it was always significantly non-random in any pairs of rats living in groups of up to six, but no more; most relationships were stable over an interval of 6 weeks. I too found rank-orders in the strain of rats that Grant and Chance used, but not in three others (another albino, a brown, and a black-hooded strain): either a given combination of rats from the three or four in each cage did not perform often enough to give a significant score or, occasionally, what looked like a definite relationship one week was reversed the next. Fairly stable relationships were usual but might well be a non-aggression pact.

The main problem in looking for rank-orders is being there at the right time. On Warne's estimate, the odds are 400 : 1 against. In the long term, such behaviour probably represents the maintenance and testing of a dominant–subordinate relationship which might have been established by a single decisive battle soon after the animals first met. If this were to be observed, it might be recognised intuitively, but it is hard to demonstrate that a single event is statistically significant.

The numbers can be increased by looking for more than a single pair of postures, by including all the mainly-aggressive and mainly-submissive elements associated with the main criterion and described in the next chapter. This makes you interested in the details of behaviour but does not always establish the existence of rank-orders.

The traditional solution is to isolate male rats for a few days and then introduce one to another. If rats are starved of rodent companionship, they

starved of rodent companionship

make a meal of it when they meet, and introducing a dozen rats to each other in all possible pairs allows them to be ranked. Unfortunately a ranking in terms of initial aggressiveness and timidity is not necessarily the same as one determined by a group social structure. A neutral arena might be expected to be useful, since introducing one rat into the home cage of another might give the home owner a territorial advantage. In practice the home rat starts investigating the intruder and may attack him while the latter is still exploring the cage, but as Hall and Klein (1942) first demonstrated, has no more than an even chance of winning. In a neutral arena, Seward (1945b) failed to find a rank-order of any sort.

I had the impression, for what it is worth, that only Grant and Chance's albino strain were ready to settle for a given balance of dominance and submission. The hooded rats seemed too 'emotional' in the sense that they were more likely to fly to extremes, while the brown rats seemed calmer, less rigidly conditioned but readier to come back and challenge again. The structure of behaviour within the individuals must govern the organisation rigidly conditioned but readier to come back and challenge again. The structure of behaviour within the individuals must govern the organisation between them. Social relationships need not be as simple as dominance in any case, and as Seward pointed out, there is a conflict between the conditions required for the formation of a social structure and those enabling someone to observe it.

Rank-order measured by feeding

Dominance may be established by some form of fighting, but it could be measured experimentally in other ways. Dominant hens get priority of access to food, they merely approach the food and the subordinate withdraws to a safe distance. In Rhesus monkeys, too, status gives the right of first refusal, and it is possible to see in this a likely evolutionary function of dominance. If there is plenty of food for everybody, then all can feed; if not, then at least some individuals get enough to eat, instead of postponing starvation for everyone. Itani and his colleagues observed a troop of originally wild Japanese monkeys (*Macaca fusca*) by providing food at a convenient place. The troop came out of the jungle every day, and sat down to eat – a central core of six males with a linear rank-order among themselves, females and infants sitting round them, and a periphery of proletarian and juvenile males. They took their provisions more or less in this sequence. In a few years the troop grew from 25 or 30 individuals to over 200 – with the same inner council of six dominant males growing grey in the service of the community in the best democratic tradition. Yet an unfamiliar food was first tasted, not by the dominant animals but by a juvenile, more adventurous than the rest, then his mother, then her friends and their offspring, and only then the adult males.

Dominance as priority of access

The boss Rhesus or Japanese monkey has priority when a female comes into oestrus, and she associates with him more than with her usual grooming companions or even a handsome young Romeo. But this too is related to the social structure of the species. Many monkeys do not live in large troops but in small bands of a male with two or three females and their infants; the older and subordinate males roam separately. Gibbons live in 'nuclear families' of a couple and their kids. Baboons live in rather complex small groups or larger bands in different areas, perhaps reflecting resources in food or in shelter from leopards. The most dramatic illustration of the irrelevance of dominance comes from gamebirds. Cocks of the Ruff (*Philomachus pugnax*) stake out small territories of a couple of square metres within a traditional communal 'lek' in spring. The breeding plumage of the competing territory owners is largely black, but each has a hanger-on, who literally shows the white feather and avoids being driven off his chosen master's territory. When the hens arrive there is so much competition between the territory owners, that the cock who actually succeeds in copulating is not the aggressive owner but the devout coward who squats in his shadow.

Rank orders have been described for eating and drinking in rats, though you have to contrive apparatus which will permit access to only one animal at a time since they usually eat peacefully side by side, and two or three rats can lick the same water-bottle spout simultaneously, their little pink tongues lapping neatly out of phase. A tug of war over food is not common.

Tomkiewicz (1972) deprived groups of four male albino rats for 21 hours a day, making them compete for water for 3 minutes before giving them 3 hours free access. While competing, a consistent rank-order emerged in the time that each rat possessed the spout. Daily injections of amylobarbitone (7·5 mg/kg 20 minutes before the competition) abolished the hierarchy, all rats obtained more-or-less equal possession, but it re-emerged subsequently. The drug presumably reduced any 'fear' the subordinates had of the dominants, although barbiturates have also been reported (e.g. Schmidt and Dry, 1963) to increase water consumption.

Norman Heimstra (1961) deprived solitary rats of food for 22 hours daily and fed them in pairs for 5 minutes before their main meal at home on each of 5 days. Dominance was defined as being 'in control of' the food-box in the test cage. An hour before testing on the second 5 days, one rat or the other, or neither or both, was injected with 0·5 mg/kg chlorpromazine. The drug seemed to make the rats hungry and though they consumed no more food, they increased possession. The group with most reversals of dominance was that where the subordinate rat alone was injected. Nevertheless, increased dominance was accompanied by an actual reduction in an undefined form of fighting, because the drugged rat completely ignored its partner except to 'tenaciously resist efforts ... at displacement'.

Both male and female rats can be ranked by this method. Edward Uyeno (1960) mated rats of known rank and fostered some of their offspring to mothers of the same or opposite ranks. Other things being equal, offspring of dominant parents were more dominant – unless they were fostered on to a dominant stepmother. Dominance was not related to bodyweight, to timidity (in terms of the time taken to explore out of the cage when the door was left open), to activity in an open-field test, or to 'intelligence' in a learning task.

A note of warning. Syme, Pollard, Syme, and Reid (1974) point out that dominance in terms of time spent in control of a source of food or water implies that both rats should spend as much time as they can guzzling, and that they are equally efficient in obtaining refreshment. Neither assumption is true. Rats can take turns in feeding, for example, one taking his food ration while the other chews. In neither eating nor drinking is the time the animals spend at the source of supply particularly highly correlated with the weight they gain, so that individuals must differ in their skill in obtaining their reward. Social facilitation might also complicate the issue by encouraging an animal fed to satiety to eat more when his sparring partner feeds.

The Frustration–Aggression hypothesis – is fighting frustrated feeding?

Greediness is not the same as bossiness and there is surprisingly little evidence on whether dominance in terms of aggression is the same as in competition for food or water, i.e. whether the same individuals obey the same ranking in both. In poultry and in Rhesus monkeys (Richards, 1974) they correlated highly enough to justify a single concept of dominance, in rats (Syme, 1974) it ain't necessarily so. Seward (1945c) found no correlation in hungry isolated rats between eating or controlling the access to food and winning or losing an encounter in a neutral arena. Losing rats could eat much less than the winners and grow thin or eat far more in Freudian compensation and grow fat. Hall and Klein (1942) found that water-deprivation did not affect male rats introduced into each other's home cage.

Now much of this work was to test the alternative hypotheses: (1) that aggression is innate, an original sin which we cannot control and which leads inevitably to world wars; and (2) that aggression is a response to frustration, that if you are starving and somebody else is present (whether or not he possesses all the food), you will attack him. The answer is not necessarily the same for all species, of course, but the evidence supports the compromise view, I believe, that an aggressive tendency is as innate as one to eat or to reproduce; yet it is nevertheless open to changes in intensity or target in the light of experience. 'Fortunately', as John Seward commented, a little naïvely perhaps, 'to conclude from the existence of dominance pugnacity that war is inevitable, is even less justified than to argue from the existence of a sex-drive to the necessity for free love.'

Most of the evidence – in rats – is that feeding and fighting are independent. Hall and Klein found wide individual differences in behaviour despite the most uniform environment they could devise, which they could only interpret as hereditary. The only frustration–aggression that Seward could find (1945a) occurred when a female approached a male and solicited him to groom her, crouching broadside on as he was peacefully grooming himself. When he failed to oblige, she attacked him and then resumed soliciting, successfully. Female rats also sometimes appear to use aggression as if to attract attention when they are on heat.

Nevertheless, there are a few hints that fighting and feeding are linked. Rats seldom bite each other and hardly ever draw blood, yet I have seen a typical attack with the teeth exposed and slightly parted in readiness, abruptly displaced on to the energetic gnawing of a pellet of food. Chlorpromazine usually inhibits aggression as well as reducing activity, but in drugged rats deprived of food for 12 (but not 24) hours, aggression formed the same percentage of total activity as in controls. They ignored the food for 7 or 8 minutes, then ate for a long time (Silverman, 1966a). Davis (1933) repeatedly introduced rats from a group of four to four isolated rats – after

24-hours deprivation of food, the home rats investigated the intruders but there was little or no fighting; after 48 hours they shared a meal amicably, and then fought vigorously (but without biting) for an hour or more.

Wild rats may be different from albinos, but the evidence is still conflicting. Boice (1972) found a rank-order in captive wild rats, applying both to status and for access to water, but Boreman and Price (1972) did not, though albinos were usually dominant to others (see p. 360). Pay your penny and take your choice.

Finally, moderate deprivation of food combined with moderate doses of marihuana also provokes a bizarre form of fighting. Carlini, Hamaqui, and Märtz (1972) housed rats in pairs. Depriving them of food for 20 hours a day did not lead to an unusual amount of fighting, nor did extracts of *Cannabis sativa* or Δ^9-tetrahydrocannabinol. However, hungry rats given either of these injections vigorously attacked their cage-mate. They reacted

response to marijuana

violently to sudden noises or puffs of air, and stood in mutual upright boxing postures, seeming to try to bite each other, for periods long enough to be worth timing on a stopwatch. The curious point is how specific the phenomenon was. It followed moderate deprivation of food and marihuana derivatives but not hallucinogens like mescaline or LSD or other common drugs like amphetamine, amylobarbitone, or caffeine, nor injections of lactic acid or ammonium chloride sufficient to alter barbiturate sleeping time. The fighting appeared if the rats were injected with a glucose solution but not if they were allowed to drink it. Rats fed on protein-free diets or on maize (deficient in a single amino acid) showed all the usual signs of malnutrition, but not the fighting response to marihuana. It is the actual eating and swallowing that appears to be crucial – I wonder if rats with a gastric fistula, so that food never reaches the stomach, would show the phenomenon?

It now seems that lack of REM sleep (one of the results of starvation) is involved, and the physiological mechanism is interesting. The combination of marihuana or Δ^9-THC and deprivation of REM sleep causes this fighting and also increases the rate of dopamine (DA) production in the brain

(Carlini, Lindsey and Tufik, 1977). Apomorphine, which acts on DA receptors, could be used instead of sleep deprivation, and drugs preventing the conversion of DA to noradrenaline could replace the cannabinoids, supporting the idea that this fighting might depend on an excess of dopamine over noradrenaline.

The aggressions induced by drugs: and some definitions

Carlini and his colleagues give a characteristic description of mutual upright fighting postures, and it is time to discuss the difficult problem of how to recognise fighting in laboratory rodents when you see it. Paradoxically, it is difficult largely because fighting is so dramatically clear and conspicuous that it seems unnecessary to describe it in visible detail. I suspect that there may be several distinct kinds of behaviour covered by the same umbrella label. Some of these obviously confuse the issue. In 'extinction' in operant conditioning, when reinforcement suddenly fails to appear every time a rat presses the lever, the frustrated animal responds much faster than usual for a time, before giving it up as a bad job. Thompson (1961) called this acceleration 'aggression' but (until the connection can be proved) the phenomenon seems different enough from fighting for the use of the same name to be confusing.

Other ways of eliciting aggression were reviewed by Luigi Valzelli (1967): by some drugs, by electric shock, or other painful stimuli, by introducing one mouse into the home cage of another or of a 'killer' rat. At least, these procedures all elicit behaviour called 'aggression' but I am quite uncertain whether they all refer to essentially the same kind of behaviour. Differences between them may be of kind, or merely of degree so that it could be just as misleading to give them several names as one. The evidence is not sufficient, because few pharmacologists and indeed not all psychologists realise the need to give adequate descriptions of what they actually observe.

To begin with there is the spontaneous 'agonistic' behaviour which can be observed at certain times of day and season in undisturbed animals. Typically a *variety* of actions and postures are used and they often occur with great speed. The observer gets the subjective impression of great emotional intensity but it is surprisingly uncommon to see physical damage. Agonistic behaviour is complex, for besides an 'aggressive' tendency there is the understandable tendency to run away (conventionally named 'flight'), and some of the actions have been shown to act as signals to the other animal of the balance and the absolute levels of these tendencies.

Agonistic behaviour is not the same as competition for food, for the actions are quite different. A feeding rat pushes a competitor away with one forepaw and even a highly dominant rat holding a titbit in his forepaws will turn to face away from an approaching competitor, a movement which in agonistic behaviour reveals a slight excess of the tendency to run away.

Consider now the 'bizarre social behaviour' nicely described by Lammers and Van Rossum (1968). They gave rats l-dopa, together with a peripheral dopa-decarboxylase inhibitor to ensure that the dopa was metabolised to dopamine only within the central nervous system. The rats became excited, they salivated with bulging eyes and clicking tongues. After any sudden noise, the rats stood upright in pairs facing each other, but often standing so far apart that it was hard to tell if they were using the forepaws to fend each other off or prop each other up. They might stand there as much as 20 minutes, until they tired, slowly subsiding into an inverted L-shape.

Now a mutual upright posture like this certainly appears frequently in spontaneous fighting, where it signals that each animal is more or less equally likely to attack and to retreat (words defined in Table 21.2 on pp. 302–3). It lasts a second or two at most before one rat breaks off and runs away or submits. I have seen two or three episodes where 'bizarre' mutual uprights can occur spontaneously, and disappear a week or two later. Perhaps one older male in a thousand comes to attack his cage-mate excessively. Both rats become hypersensitive, and superficially hard to tell apart. They are easily startled by trivial stimuli and immediately take up mutual uprights lasting 10 or 15 seconds. They become difficult to handle. It is interesting that the hyper-aggressive rat seems as frightened as his cagemate, though it is the latter that loses weight and hides in a corner. The influence of one rat on the other is not surprising but has implications for mental health.

Lammers and Van Rossum said their rats appeared to be trying to bite each other; nevertheless, they thought the rats were frightened, because of their hypersensitivity to slight noise and because they did not in fact bite, not even when one experimenter put his finger into the rat's mouth. Yet it may not have been pure 'fear' either, since the rats did not run away.

In many ways, 'bizarre fighting' seems comparable to stereotyped gnawing or walking, an essentially 'normal' action which the animal gets locked inescapably into. It too seems dependent on an excess of dopamine, since l-dopa alone did not cause bizarre fighting, the decarboxylase inhibitor allowed rats to respond to other rats but not to start the quarrel, and it was abolished by low (0·4 mg/kg) doses of haloperidol, a dopamine antagonist. Bizarre fighting occurs after apomorphine (which stimulates dopamine receptors), p-chlororesorcinol, 2,4-diamino-6-chloro-s-triazine, and of course amphetamine, at doses not far below the LD_{50}. At low doses, the triazine reduces aggression because a local irritant action causes some pain. According to some reports, but not all (see Borgen, Khalsa, King, and Davis, 1970) rats addicted to morphine are lethally aggressive when the drug is withdrawn. The crimes that human addicts are alleged to commit could therefore be a more physiological response to shortage of supplies than merely the shortest way to get the money for a 'fix'.

It would be surprising if all drug-induced 'fighting' is the same. p-Chlorophenylalanine (pCPA), given in a dose of 500 mg/kg for a few days, reduces the brain concentration of another transmitter, 5-hydroxytryptamine (5-HT or serotonin) by 90 per cent for long periods. Shillito (1970a) gave it to groups of young male rats. She observed them without further disturbance soon after 'nightfall' under red light, when most spontaneous play-fighting occurs, and saw an increase in cages where some animals had been given pCPA. She also saw more untreated rats than usual with one shoulder bare of hair as if they had been aggressively groomed (see p. 303) to excess. pCPA also increased sexual behaviour in adult and adolescent (10-week-old) males but not females. Mouret, Bobillier, and Jouvet (1968; see p. 38) found that pCPA exaggerates various other kinds of normal behaviour non-specifically.

Defensive fighting induced by shock

If two rats are given a small electric shock in the same cage (O'Kelly and Steckle, 1939), they turn and attack each other, they stand briefly in mutual upright postures and push each other in the chest with the forepaws. Since the response occurs under the experimenter's control, it is a favourite model of supposedly spontaneous human aggression.

Defensive fighting induced by shock closely resembles bizarre fighting induced by dopaminergic drugs, except that it typically lasts for no more than a couple of seconds; bizarre fighting characteristically lasts much longer. Both forms utilise only one or two of the actions and postures visible in agonistic behaviour, as a rule, though Adams (1971) says that 'at high intensities the rats sometimes ... rolled over together biting and kicking'. He could not use rats experienced in shock-induced fighting subsequently for 'isolation-induced fighting' because they seemed to regard another rat as a conditioned stimulus for pain, to be avoided rather than approached.

Shock-induced fighting was described in ugly detail (see p. 28) by Ulrich and Azrin (1962) for rats, with P. C. Wolff (1964) for other species. In their laboratory, cats ignored rats before shock, but attacked and injured them after it; two of the six rats provoked them by attacking first. Shock is the

'Take that, you rat!'

most convenient stimulus for defensive fighting, but a sudden tail-pinch, flash of light, or clap of sound can startle rats into it. I once squirted a rat with cold water from a syringe, he threatened his cage-mate and the cage-mate retaliated; the response rapidly habituated but seemed as reflex as a swear word.

Shock releases defensive fighting in the same way as conditioned avoidance (Ulrich, Stachnik, Brierton, and Mabry, 1966). Logan and Boice (1969) confirmed how rodents of several species learn free-operant avoidance (p. 211) very effectively when trained singly but not in pairs (or after training in pairs). If one animal was trained and a second introduced, it was, surprisingly, the newcomer that performed any wheel-turning. The experienced animal would squeal in fear when the warning signal came, and threatened, using a gesture characteristic of the species. Wild rats and house-mice turned the head towards the newcomer and 'lunged', albino rats adopted upright postures, Florida pack-rats thumped their feet, deermice (*Peromyscus*) squealed in threat. After shock, all species nearly always fought, but albino rats remained so close together that the dominant would occasionally mount. Enforced proximity in a small Skinner box, suggest Logan and Boice, may be why paired rodents fail to learn free-operant avoidance; they are successful enough in shuttle-avoidance, where two rats can learn to run away from threatened shock as easily as one.

Defensive fighting has been used as a pharmacological test, notably by Tedeschi, Tedeschi, Mucha, Cook, Mattis, and Fellows (1959). They counted the number of episodes of fighting in pairs of male mice elicited by shocks to the feet. They used bursts of five shocks a second, 3 mA at 400 V, as greater intensities prevented the mice from standing upright [sic]. The drug that was most selective at inhibiting fighting was the mildly muscle-relaxant meprobamate. Other drugs inhibited it at lower doses on a weight-for-weight basis, but only if they also reduced all kinds of motor activity like reserpine or chlorpromazine, or at doses greater than those protecting the mouse against electroconvulsive seizures, like diphenylhydantoin or pheno-barbitone. (Low doses of barbiturates can in some circumstances stimulate fighting.) Narcotic analgesics presumably stop the stimulus hurting enough to be worth fighting about. But selectivity is an arguable concept, as Janssen and his colleagues pointed out (1960) since it depends on which alternative tests you choose for comparison. Meprobamate does not show up so advantageously if you include a test of motor strength and co-ordination such as a rotating-rod test (see p. 67).

Mouse-killing

Aggression provoked by painful shock seems an unnecessary way of testing a half-defined kind of behaviour. The next sort of 'aggression' (Karli, 1955; see Valzelli, 1967) seems worse.

If a mouse is put into the home cage of a rat, most rats investigate it a little and take no further notice. A few rats turn out to be killers, and the mouse dies from bites in the back of the neck. Now cats and other predators kill their prey in this way, and when an experienced and hungry cat, well-trained by its mother, is hunting for food it can kill very quickly, and probably far more humanely than the average experimenter with a jar of chloroform. Steiniger (1950) found a colony of wild rats which stalk and kill small birds in a similar, if clumsier way, and says that a very few female rats occasionally kill a rat or mouse intruding on the colony territory – while in one case a family of voles was tolerated undisturbed. But inexperienced albino killers are few in number, tentative and clumsy, and need far more training than most kittens to become efficient. There is certainly a case for laboratory studies of true predatory behaviour (Leyhausen, 1955). There is even some case for studying this 'muricide' behaviour in its own right: it is clearly a phenomenon which exists. I see no case for using the technique to study 'aggression' since the results are either doubtfully interpretable or equally well obtained in other ways.

Mouse-killing may represent either hunting or aggression (assuming these are truly distinct; cf. Huntingford, 1976a). If aggression, it may start by mistake. One may imagine a rat responds to a mouse as an intruder, but mice do not possess the rat's submissive posture and if they cannot retreat out of the cage, they crouch . . . the rat aggressively grooms a bit too hard for the mouse's tender skin, and once it has tasted blood the rat is forever a killer. However, I have seen two male mice fostered by a rat with two sons of her own; as they grew up, the poor little mice tried desperately to play-fight with their huge foster-brothers and were continually and comically ignored.

Infanticide could possibly be relevant, since occasionally an adult rat kills pups in the same way with a bite through the skull (see p. 56), but infanticide is even less well-understood.

Aggression induced by brain lesions

Not surprisingly if various small parts of the brain are destroyed – or stimulated electrically – there are changes in behaviour. This is not the place to describe them in detail but a few examples are relevant. In general, they emphasise that the problems of interpreting behavioural effects are the same whether the cause is chemical or physical interference with the animal. In particular they emphasise similarities and differences in what is called aggression.

Lesions in the septum classically produce 'sham rage'. For some weeks after recovery from the operation a rat or cat is highly irritable, and the slightest stimulus makes it attack, bite, and grimly hang on to any suitably shaped object (like your finger). Eventually the hypersensitivity fades, but while it lasts, fighting is also facilitated, or at least biting. Keith Michal (1973) found fairly subtle changes in the pre-copulatory behaviour of male rats after ablating the septal area to varying degrees. In five, but only five, of the ten operated rats, sexual behaviour was overridden by crude 'rage' and attempts to bite the female. Otherwise, as with lesions in most of the other areas he tried, septal rats became restricted to rather stereotyped routines, and lost much of their flexibility of response.

Amygdaloid lesions left the rats with their usual adaptability, but made them avoid the female rather than pursue her. Despite this increased Flight, there is some excuse for the traditional view that amygdaloid lesions increase a form of aggression, for lesioned rats bit females who came too close. Counter-attack is not aggression in the usual sense, but the female whose advances are spurned might be forgiven for not appreciating the difference. After all, the function of courtship behaviour is partly to overcome 'individual distance', the reluctance of one animal to let any other get too close; an apparent predator gets bitten if simple avoidance is not effective.

Perhaps the amygdala are involved in regulating the balance between social and non-social behaviour as a whole. Bunnell, Sodetz, and Shalloway (1970) tried to model territory-formation in hamsters by isolating them for a month in cages arranged round the edge of a wide arena. The hamsters were allowed to explore the arena in pairs and meet for 5-minute periods. Bilateral amygdaloid lesions reduced aggression in dominant hamsters and flight in subordinates, with no change in rank order nor, apparently, in the detailed pattern of which led to which. The hamsters merely devoted themselves to gathering food and nesting materials.

The brain is complex and any one nucleus may be involved in many details of many kinds of behaviour. A series of nuclei may be links in a chain or a few dozen neurons may inhibit a complete nucleus nearby or far away. While the names of several kinds of aggression can cause confusion, the nuclei controlling them might overlap. It is not surprising if experimenters disagree about the role of a given structure. A lesion half a millimetre forward or to the side might cut an inhibitory tract and reverse the previous results. So disagreement on whether amygdaloid lesions increase a form of aggression or a form of flight or merely blind the male to the ulterior motive of the female's advances could be a question of the precision either of anatomy or observation.

Olfactory bulb lesions similarly are said to cause aggression, and Malick (1970) found them the only ones to increase 'territorial' fighting in rats, whereas hypothalamic and septal lesions induced 'hyper-sensitive' or 'defensive' biting of the prudent experimenter's glove, or they induced the killing of mice. Yet on slightly different criteria, Albert and Friedman (1972) found lesions to the bulb provoke defensive biting, mouse-killing, and defecation in the open field. However, the lesions do not act merely by destroying the animal's sense of smell: while olfaction is important in releasing and inhibiting aggression in mice and probably rats, rats made anosmic by packing the nostrils with cottonwool soaked in zinc sulphate showed no changes in aggression. In the mice of Denenberg, Gaulin-Kremer, Gandelman, and Zarrow (1973) olfactory bulbectomy did not increase aggression but suppressed it. Operated mice placed in another mouse's cage presented all the right stimuli for the territory owner and were nearly always attacked but rarely fought back and never started the quarrel; they ran away or crouched immobile.

The region of the brain thought most likely to 'control' the minute-to-minute organisation of behaviour is the hypothalamus, but this is still complex. Adams (1971) watched for 'offensive sideways' and 'dominate' postures (pp. 302-3) shown by isolated male rats and intruders. Bilateral lesions to the lateral hypothalamus (including the medial forebrain bundle) abolished feeding so that the rats had to be fed by stomach tube, and also abolished 'territorial' fighting; owners were docile and investigated intruders but turned away without attacking. But these rats showed just as much defensive fighting after shock as unoperated controls. Comparable currents were required, found by 'titration': the current was lowered if the rats fought in response to twenty half-second shocks in 20 seconds, increased if they failed. Lesions in the medial and posterior hypothalamus, on the other hand, had no effect on territorial fighting, but exaggerated defensive fighting: only a tenth of the usual current was needed for the operated rats and mutual upright postures often continued after the shocks ceased.

Electrical stimulation in the brain

In general, stimulation of appropriately low intensity produces effects opposite to those of a lesion at the same site. Lesions of the amygdala abolish some forms of aggression. Stimulation produces the classical sham rage, though this primarily makes a cat hypersensitive to the experimenter's touch. Yet the effects of electrical brain stimulation depend also on ordinary sensory stimuli, which have often been neglected. If visual stimuli from a live or anaesthetised mouse are present, amygdaloid stimulation makes the cat pounce.

Stimulation of the brain requires specialist knowledge and all I can usefully do is call attention to some less well-known ethological work. Ethologists have traditionally plotted agonistic actions on a graph whose axes represent aggression and flight. This 'ethogram' is a description, not an explanation, but the suspicion lurks that behind two or more actions with a common function, there really is a system of patterns of neuronal activity corresponding to 'drive'. When stimulation in the hypothalamus produces short but integrated sequences of actions fitting the ethogram, you have no proof but some tempting support. Juan Delius (1973) remarked how often brain stimulation (like lesions and shock) produces threat postures, representing aggression and flight simultaneously. Using juvenile black-headed gulls instead of the usual well-worn laboratory mammals, he found that stimulation at many locations often evoked threat postures, and sometimes pure flight. Pure aggression occurred even more rarely than it appears in the wild birds' behaviour. The orthodox concept is that any appropriate stimulus (visual–external or electrical–internal) stimulates both tendencies together, but independently. Alternatively, the relevant neurons are close together so that in a sense the animal gets frightened of its own aggression. Delius provocatively suggests that maybe the basic unit is not the pure tendency but the ambivalent threat itself. The juvenile gulls are timid, and there are many sites where stimulation evokes pure escape movements. Immediately after stimulating these, stimulation of sites which usually evoke threat now evoke pure aggression. The formula is Flight + Threat = Aggression, not the conventional A + F = Threat. After all, 'only cornered animals attack'. The conventional view is still easier to understand since it is additive where Delius postulates in effect that Flight subtracts itself from Threat. But he does account for the curious fact that electrical or chemical overstimulation leads to a stereotyped *ambivalent* posture. He might have provocatively added that aggression appears only out of frustration, when threat has failed to chase away a certain class of flight-inducing stimuli.

Tests of territorial aggression in mice

Artificial fighting stimulated with fearsome pharmacology, surgery, or shock is unnecessary. Animals are perfectly capable of responding appropriately to stimuli: an isolated male mouse is likely to attack a stranger introduced into his cage. Now if the behaviour we call aggressive exists in animals, as it does in all higher species where it has been looked for, it must have survival value. Whatever this function may be (see Chapter 23), it would presumably be outweighed if fighting often caused one or more contestants to die. So an animal should be able to inhibit another's aggression or to escape it – in normal conditions (i.e. unless confined in a laboratory cage?). It is important to bear in mind the circumstances to which the behaviour is adapted. A male mouse may attack an intruder, spontaneously and without training, but attack is not the only response possible. Not all resident mice attack intruders, in one study only 10 per cent did so after 24 hours isolation. Miloš Kršiak (1975) found that after 3 to 5 weeks isolation, 40 per cent attacked, 15 per cent were sociable (following and investigating the intruder) and 45 per cent were consistently timid – they watched and avoided the intruder, even though he never attacked them, and reared into defensive postures. Such timidity could be selectively reduced by drugs thought to reduce anxiety in man.

Isolation-induced aggression is worth detailed attention. It is an important method of testing and attempts to improve its reliability even further are instructive about how behaviour is controlled. Stimuli from the intruding mouse are one important source of variance. Fighting seems to be associated with a smell in the urine of unfamiliar males (see p. 335), but the intruder's behaviour is variable: he will certainly start by exploring but may or may not fight back if attacked. Scott (1947) arranged preliminary fights and selected clear winners and losers. A losing mouse, if used again, is likely to crouch or run away without fighting back and is therefore relatively uniform in response, while so prompt are some eager experienced residents to attack that they may not wait for the experimenter to finish putting the intruder into the cage. So Scott dangled intruders by the tail and counted the number of residents that attacked at all, or the time (up to 1 minute) that they took to do so. In fact he mainly observed the resident's conflict between weak tendencies to attack and to run away revealed by tail-beating, fluffing, and grooming.

Immobile mice seem not to present the appropriate stimuli, for they are not often attacked. Cairns and Scholz (1973) showed this quantitatively by using the activity-reducing effect of chlorpromazine. All control mice were attacked by residents isolated for 35 days, but the probability of attack fell according to the dose (4, 8, or 16 mg/kg) received by the intruder; those given a lethal overdose were not attacked at all. Still trying to get the ideal stimulus for unprovoked aggression, Denenberg and his colleagues (1973) ablated the olfactory bulb of their intruders – such mice walked round the cage quite freely, were uniformly attacked but did not themselves attack, nor did they fight back. Kršiak's intruders had been housed in groups of twenty, were observed under bright light in clean cages for 4 minutes and did not attack at all.

Aggression depends partly on genetic constitution and strains differ; male mice attack and are attacked, females usually do not and are not. A more rewarding question is their past history. There is some evidence that mice handled as infants are more likely to attack intruders when they grow up, not from greater aggression but perhaps because they are tamer in the experimenter's presence, they are less likely to 'freeze'.

The length of isolation alters the probability of attack but not in as simple a way as is sometimes assumed. The longer a mouse lives in a particular cage, alone or in company, the more his smell gets attached to it, and he to the smell; other mice respect this. The longer a mouse is isolated, presumably, the more aggressive he gets; but the rate of increase may not be linear, and the mouse starved of rodent companionship may also accumulate other tendencies, sex or shyness, also at different rates. Mice give the impression of increasing aggressiveness, on the whole, where rats eventually seem more anxious and depressed, but I do not know of any systematic comparisons of isolation for different periods of time, of introduction to the home cage and to a neutral arena, or of mice and rats. Eleven weeks seems excessive when in the right conditions (see p. 335) 10 minutes can be enough.

Edwin Banks (1962) isolated C57 Black mice on weaning at 25 days old. At 60–100 days old, i.e. after 5–11 weeks, he observed them in a neutral arena after each mouse had explored his own half for 5 minutes. Four of ten mice were 'biters' and not only bit the opponent but were likely to investigate, fight, and mount him (however, Banks seems to have included in 'mounting' what Grant and Mackintosh, see p. 303, called attack and aggressive groom). Three of Banks's five males that met a female, bit her. Recording the behaviour on 1200 m of cine film, Banks failed to find a pattern to the aggression, but then he considered only biting as fighting.

In the first use of fighting as a pharmacological test, Yen, Stanger, and Millman (1958) isolated mice for 2 or 3 weeks and introduced strangers. Home mice given 'ataractic' drugs like reserpine, serotonin, etc., but not phenobarbitone, showed 30–90 per cent less hyper-excitability, anxiety, and aggression than controls. In a one-page publication they could not describe how to distinguish these kinds of behaviour but they rejoiced that fighting is easily recognised without ambiguity or special apparatus.

While this apparently territorial attack needs no previous training, it is not thereby immune from conditioning. Janssen, Jageneau, and Niemegeers (1960) found that 102 out of 1000 home mice attacked an intruder within 1 minute after 16 hours' isolation, and again 6 hours later. In the next six daily trials, three of these 102 mice failed to attack a total of only eight times, after the injection of inert solvents, a reliability of about 98 per cent. The selection was pretty rigorous, too, for the numbers involved meant that trials had to be limited to 1 minute, and many of the discarded mice might have plucked up their courage if given a little longer. Nevertheless, reliability probably depends on the frequent repetition of the test. If aggression is not strictly self-reinforcing, it must be reinforced by the prompt removal of the intruding stimulus by the obliging experimenter.

Once Janssen's mice were proven, they could be tested. Once a day they were injected with saline or with one of at least three doses of twenty-nine different drugs, and presented with another mouse at 1, 4, and 25 hours after dosing. The dose that suppressed fighting in at least one trial for five of a group of ten mice was calculated by the usual quantal log-probit method. The three most effective drugs were the anticholinergic scopolamine, at 'doses producing maximal mydriasis but far below those inhibiting ... co-ordinated motor activity'; the phenothiazine neuroleptic acetopromazine 'at doses producing a marked ... motor depression' but no mydriasis; and the morphine-like analgesic dextromoramide. Although all the drugs had some other observable effect, it was considered unlikely that these were responsible for inhibiting attack, for each drug had different side-effects, while other related drugs had the side-effect more strongly and the anti-aggressive effect less.

Paul Janssen's method is the classic pharmacologist's approach. A quick and simple method was developed as a screen for drugs suppressing fighting, using a simple yes/no classification. Effectiveness on this screen was compared with that on other standard screens representing a reasonable but not exhaustive list of possible pharmacological mechanisms – anticholinergic signs in the pupil of the eye, suppression of foot-licking after escape from a slightly painful 55° hot-plate, and loss of righting reflex and co-ordinated motor control on a rotating rod. And the specificity of the effect was assessed by screening a large number of drugs and drawing conclusions from a comparison of dose–response curves.

This is admirably objective and practical, but like anything else worth considering seriously it has disadvantages which are by no means obvious. There are inevitably several possible mechanisms behind the fall in aggression. At a behavioural level some possibilities (each, no doubt, with a biochemical or physiological counterpart) are a rise in fear, or in friendliness, or in apathy. We should not altogether rule out the possibility that a mouse has its diminutive equivalent of these. A rapid screen is unlikely to distinguish these tendencies easily, but behavioural methods are available that go a little further than Janssen's. What his method gains in simplicity of procedure it loses in discrimination. It assumes fighting to be a single coherent unit without internal structure. Within the test's own terms of reference, a drug that increased aggression instead of suppressing it, could not be detected – you cannot increase much over 98 per cent of a maximum, nor test for much less than a minute. And in mice so thoroughly conditioned, even the suppression of aggression might well require a crude and powerful blocking action.

Summary

In group-living species like rats and probably mice, there are differences between animals housed singly and in groups. Isolated animals seem more highly aroused than grouped ones and less able to reverse a previously-learned task. Some drugs are more toxic in grouped mice, a few are safer, and isolated rats and mice are often more *variable*. Groups are only more uniform, however, if they are small enough for individuals to establish stable social relationships. In the crudest case these take the form of a dominance hierarchy involving recognisable dominant, sub-dominant, and subordinate animals, but rank-orders are not found as consistently in laboratory rodents as they are in poultry. In poultry and in primates, a ranking based on fighting and maintained by submission is likely to show the same individuals getting access to food or water in the same order; in rodents, any rank-orders that can be found may be independent. There may be a link between not-feeding and fighting but it is more complex than mere frustration.

Repeated testing of isolated strangers conditions a stereotyped aggressive/submissive performance; the ranking is not based on the same kind of responses as those conditioned to familiar individuals of a stable group.

Some tentative distinctions are made between different kinds of fighting. 'Bizarre' fighting is evoked by very high doses of some drugs, consisting of mutual upright postures and boxing, held for long periods. 'Defensive' fighting is similar, but is brief; it is typically evoked by startle or by painful electroshock, apparently as an alternative to conditioned avoidance. Lesions in various parts of the brain can evoke or suppress 'sham rage', a form of defensive fighting where the animal is unusually ready to bite in counter-attack. All these forms of aggression can be distinguished from the behaviour used to establish or defend a territory or dominance, because they are stereotyped, a selection of one or two elements from a varied repertoire, and because they can be differentially affected by electrical stimuli in various parts of the hypothalamus. Other behaviours have also been called aggressive but have not been shown to be related.

In mice, territorial fighting can be conspicuous and unambiguous, and is widely used as a test for drugs as if it were a single, simple unit without internal structure. Olfactory stimuli can be enough to release it, but prolonged isolation or repeated tests are usually used. These minimise the inherent complexities of tendencies to investigate, copulate with, perhaps remain near to, or run away from the intruder which real animals possess in addition.

TWENTY-ONE
Analysis of behaviour in a social situation
The paradox of aggression

Paradoxically the behaviour that gives a social group its structure is aggression. You have to approach somebody before you can attack him, he has to approach you before you have any interest in doing so.

Aggression is very conspicuous and attractive to human beings. We have a strong desire to observe it and to exaggerate what we have seen. It is not only its genuine importance that makes fighting a favourite subject in applied behavioural tests. However, it is not very easy for an experimenter to control. Feeding can be elicited almost at will by depriving an animal of food and then offering it. If you deprive a rat of rodent companionship and then introduce it to another rat, you may or may not see fighting. Hence the technology of 'stimulated' aggression described in Chapter 20.

The reason is that aggression is only one part of one animal's behaviour to another, and the part most easily inhibited. Consider a species holding solitary territories: a territory owner has to drive off an intruder but in turn has to withdraw if the intruder is a predator or if he is himself the intruder on someone else's territory. The sexes have to come together to mate, and the territory owner has first to investigate any intruder to discover which response is appropriate, and this varies with the season and situation. One individual provides stimuli releasing various kinds of social behaviour in others, but these are internally regulated too. Isolating a rat increases the probability that he will attack an intruder, but in practice the probability of overt fighting rises and then falls. Other tendencies also change, and if 'flight' also increases with time it will eventually inhibit aggression, sexual behaviour, and even investigation of another rat. Whatever the reason, a rat isolated a long time gives the subjective impression of depressive mood. Experimenters are therefore tempted to compel fighting with brain lesions or shock, though the results may not, perhaps, resemble the human behaviour they wish to model. Even behaviour that does seem to be related appropriately is often used uncritically as a single unit in the search for experimental simplicity. In this chapter, social behaviour will be described as it appears under detailed observation.

Checklist observation
First mention goes to the first pharmacological test explicitly to recognise that social behaviour has several independent components. Stata Norton's

Analysis of behaviour in a social situation **295**

main observations were on cats, especially their response as she entered their cages (Norton and de Beer, 1956), though she also observed Rhesus monkeys and golden hamsters (Norton, 1957). In all three species she identified five categories of behaviour each comprising five elements (a suspiciously square set of numbers) grouped on the basis that they occurred in the same trial. For instance, a cat jumped up at her approach, mewed, erected its tail, came forward as she entered the cage or was at least alert, watching her and pricking its ears; these were all classed as signs of Sociability. They occurred less often in cats given any of the drugs she used. Signs of Contentment were, she thought, washing, kneading the forepaws up and down or unsheathing and sheathing the claws, purring, rubbing the top of the head against the cage-bars or Norton's legs, or resting. Reserpine reduced contentment. Excitement was recognised in a cat yowling, lashing its tail, erecting its fur, dilating the pupils, or pacing up and down away from Norton, and was increased by chlorpromazine, morphine, and pentobarbitone. Hostility was the 'expression of fear, and defensive behaviour', and not the same as aggression: the cat would growl, hiss, withdraw with flattened ears, and crouch. Hostility was reduced by chlorpromazine and meprobamate.

Norton's approach is interesting in making a virtue of what most experimenters go to great lengths to minimise or ignore, the animal's response to herself. Her observation was clearly careful, nevertheless, her description of elements was inadequate and their classification quite arbitrary. While anyone can recognise when a cat rubs her head on his legs, there are several sorts of mew with differing meanings. No doubt Norton had adequate criteria for distinguishing them but her readers have not. Head-rubbing has been described as part of the female's courtship, would it not be better classified as Sociability? And unsheathing the claws as Hostility? Why did Norton classify both of these as Contentment? Her recognition of the importance of the animal's own behaviour and of the need to look at several kinds at the same time are too valuable to waste.

Objective observation

If we wish to obtain reliable results from behaviour that cannot be measured by machinery, it is necessary to observe objectively. This means more than just naming an element ('attack', 'rub', 'washing', etc.) and assuming that the reader can identify the correct pattern. You have to describe the pattern in physical terms as precisely as you can. 'Rubbing' might be described as pressing the occipital surface of the head between and behind the ears, against the observer's leg or other animate column, and moving it rhythmically backwards and forwards for a few seconds. Obviously there is a limit to how pedantically you have to explain the meaning of every word, but you have to describe what you see, not what you think it is for. There is always the temptation to guess at function prematurely. An attempt at interpretation can only follow an accurate description of what you are trying to understand, it cannot substitute for it.

To take the argument of Chapters 2 and 3 a stage further, the steps are: (1) identify by observation what seem to you to be natural units; (2) name them – the name might as well be picturesque and memorable so long as it suggests the appearance and not the function; (3) write a description of what you can see or hear, as precisely as possible without unnecessary pedantry. Ask a colleague to read the descriptions, observe the animals, and see whether he sees what you did; (4) observe as much as possible of the animal's behaviour to discover when the elements occur, in what context, what other elements occur before and after; (5) redefine the elements you have named, since you may want to subdivide what you first thought of as one unit, or two units you thought separate may now appear to be essentially the same; (6) observe similar behaviour in related species – the comparison will illuminate both the well known and the newly observed; (7) make a hypothesis about function or rather (since you have inevitably had one from the beginning), make it explicit and attempt to make predictions which can be tested experimentally. This last stage, of course, involves reintegrating each element into the complete pattern.

Early studies of aggressive behaviour in laboratory rats

The stages I have suggested seem logical enough with hindsight, but it was not until Tinbergen wrote *The Study of Instinct* (1951) that this approach was adopted by laboratory-bound scientists. Earlier observers of social behaviour in rats were content with rating scales. They observed and sometimes named elements, but not enough for their readers to identify them; and without giving evidence to justify their grading by intensity. We have to rely on intuition.

Apart from a brief note by Higginson (1930), the first description was by Frank Davis (1933). He isolated four male albino rats for 2 days and then, every couple of days introduced members of a group of four into the isolates' home cages. The rats were fed once a day and approached and sniffed the intruders without fighting. If they were starved for 2 days and fed when their visitor came, they would share a meal amicably – and fight afterwards. Davis noted how rats might bite human beings, but rarely other rats. He named elements as Push, Crowd, Sidle, Puff, Snort, Bristle, and so on, but described few; his rating scale is given in Table 21.1. Sherwin Klein thought it inadequate and wrote his own which does not seem very different [the published paper Hall and Klein, 1942 was actually written by Hall; Klein only did most of the work!].

Rating scales are introduced when you want to be objective but do not

Analysis of behaviour in a social situation

Table 21.1 Rating-scales for aggression in rats

Davis (1933)		Hall–Klein (1942)
No overt attention	0	No interest, rare nosing
Intermittent approach, snort, bristle	1	Frequent vigorous nosing, no other interest
More continuous approach, snort and bristle	2	Occasional blocking, shoving, crowding
'Crowding against other rat, standing over him when latter lies flat on his back, but not biting him'	3	Frequent blocking, shoving, and following
As 3 – with occasional bites	4	Slight wrestling or dancing
Bites causing other rat to squeal	5	Fierce wrestling; jump, roll, turn rapidly
As 5 – and draw blood or separated by experimenter	6	Fierce wrestling; bite to draw blood

know how. Davis is slightly less ambiguous, but Hall and Klein were able to compare each other's observations. Their records of the frequency of aggressive elements had a correlation of about 0·9, and their assessment of severity of about 0·5.

Both Davis, and Hall and Klein reported attempts to change the intensity of aggression: comparing a neutral arena with one contestant's home cage, being housed with a female before the 5 days' isolation, deprivation of food or water. None of these made much difference except prolonged (48 hour) deprivation of food. Hall and Klein, who had taken care to equalise the previous history of their rats as much as possible, concluded that the wide and consistent differences between individuals probably reflect differences in genotype.

establishing relationships on introduction

Genetic differences certainly exist, but if rats fight in order to establish dominance/submission relationships, overt aggression could hardly fail to differ between individuals. Repeated introductions condition a stable, indeed stereotyped, pattern of behaviour, some individuals becoming predominantly aggressive, most becoming timid.

Rats' social encounters portrayed as drama

Seward must have spent many a fascinated hour watching rats (1945a; b; and c). He usually observed isolated rats in a neutral arena for 10 minutes at a time, noticing how rats 45 or 50 days old seemed to be playing, while the same pattern of movements nevertheless seemed quite serious at 90 or 100 days. But even when two 14-month males struggled fiercely for dominance, he commented how rare it is to see blood drawn. I have only seen bites to draw blood in two situations. First, in rare episodes with older males (see p. 283); second, when six males were put into the same cage after living with females as breeding pairs, fighting was intense and in an albino (but not a brown) strain frequently ended with the last of five terrified losers receiving bites on the rump.

Although Seward distrusted rating-scales, he did not achieve the objective definitions he wanted. Lacking formal measures, he settled for deliberately impressionistic descriptions; but he so greatly enjoyed dramatic writing that he conveys a more vivid idea of the shape of an encounter than a dozen ordinary scientists can do in a book.

'... Two males or two females may attack each other and roll about with great abandon, till suddenly there is a flurry and a squeal, a moment of strenuous scuffling – then the two stand apart, perhaps pawing at each other like boxers, then separate. From that point there is a distinct change. One rat, or both, is wary, cautious, rising defensively at the other's approach. "The fun is over".'

An encounter starts slowly. After anything between 25 seconds and 19 minutes in Seward's observations, and usually after a distinct nip, 'the cage suddenly seems filled with leaping, rolling, bouncing white bodies. Then the turmoil resolves itself into two rats, one on his back in a corner fending off attack with all four feet, the other standing over him on his hindlegs, forcing him down by repeated jabs with his forepaws.'

Seward noted that hair erection usually denotes aggression more than escape. Soft defecation usually shows escape, though he saw clear instances of the opposite. Hops, feints, rumpings, sparring (I *think* I recognise what Seward meant...) indicate motivational conflict. As signs of a predominantly aggressive tendency, he listed Maul, Rump, Attack, and Bully; as submission, he recognised Crouch, Freeze, Withdraw, and Fall over. If only he had helped us recognise them, and explained why he thought they mean what they do ...

A rat very dominant after previous clear victories can either ignore his erstwhile opponent, or bully and make him squeal. Sometimes the dominant can become curiously defensive, standing in a fairly rigid, arched posture broadside on to the other 'until finally he turns on his hesitant companion and crushes him under a furious attack'. A submissive rat can be passive, standing upright in a corner or crouching, or climbing the wall of the cage and hanging on grimly. Or he can actively follow the other rat, perhaps mounting him repeatedly, or he may yet be aggressive. 'One rat . . . beaten in two fights the day before, started several attacks only to break off . . . and crouch frozen or fall over on his back . . . spontaneous (without the other rat attacking) . . . conditioned . . . by the rat's own aggression.'

Behaviour in a social situation

A rat wakes up, stretches himself, walks round the cage sniffing in and outside it as if to make sure he is in the same place as he was yesterday, washes his face, and settles down to breakfast. These actions occur in both solitary and group-housed animals but not necessarily in the same way. Grouped rats may possibly gnaw less in long bouts than solitary animals, but more often in an abbreviated but intensive way, suggesting displacement activities. If aggression, for example, is frustrated by the equally urgent need to run away, a third kind of behaviour, often non-social, may briefly occur to reveal the conflict (see p. 50). It is interesting that displacement acts cannot always be distinguished from the same kind of behaviour occurring for their own sake. What starts as a cursory half-wash can turn into a short real wash and then into a long grooming session. A single lick of water at a convenient spout can turn into a long drink as if the rat suddenly remembered an urgent thirst. Even a brief scan of an interesting smell can lead to meticulous exploration everywhere but where the other animal happens to be standing.

Watching a group of rats for long periods, the first thing to become obvious is how little time they spend in social behaviour. They sleep huddled together, one may be attracted to the particular piece of food that another rat happens to be eating, one occasionally grooms another . . . It is remarkable, however, how intense the few minutes a day they spend actively oriented to each other should seem. Perhaps the intensity is in the eye of the beholder; yet if you can imagine behaviour as a quantity, weighed out in grams – as much behaviour occurs in those few minutes as in the whole of the rest of the day.

At first social behaviour seems amorphous, a heterogeneous jumble of miscellaneous movements, interspersed with pauses while the animals separate and return to the fray. Gradually, as you watch, certain regularities emerge. One animal may approach another and either may then depart. Many approaches lead to nothing more than investigation of the other animal, some to clearly sex-related behaviour, and even in groups of one sex you can sometimes see nearly-complete mounts. Gradually it becomes apparent that while investigation of most of the other rat's body can lead to any other kind of social behaviour (including departure), sniffing of the ano-genital region leads disproportionately to mounting. Although many sniffs lead elsewhere, yet nearly all mounts are preceded closely by sniffs. It

Fig. 21.1. Attend and Investigate.

Fig. 21.2. Genital sniff by male of female.

Fig. 21.3. Mounting of one male rat by another.

follows that sniffing in the genital region indicates not only general curiosity about the other animal but also some sexual motivation. One can imagine either that sniffing represents a low 'level' of 'sexual energy' and that a high enough level for mounting has to be reached through a low level, or simply that one kind of information has to be obtained to provide for the next stage.

A technical interlude: recording the data

Familiarise yourself informally with the behaviour by just watching, for as long as anything is going on. For formal tests, each animal needs its own observer, and for simplicity this generally means two people each watching one of a pair of animals. Individual rats can be identified with a small patch of hair-dye on head, shoulders, or rump.

Analysis of behaviour in a social situation 301

The obvious method of recording the data, after recognising and naming the elements, is to write. But writing even a one- or two-letter code is slow, and you tend to watch what you are writing while the rat performs two or more actions unobserved. Method 2 is therefore to type, either on an ordinary typewriter, a piano-like keyboard, or preferably on a teletype for direct computer input. The latter has the great advantage that you do not waste time transcribing the data again, and White (1971) and Dawkins (1971) independently designed cheap and simple apparatus for this purpose. The disadvantage is that touch-typing demands a skill too demanding for scientists interested in higher matters.

At an average rate of perhaps an element per second, and a peak rate of up to two or three elements a second for up to 5 or 10 seconds at a time, there is a premium on both speed and accuracy. Direct typing on a keyboard leaves no room to correct mistakes either of observation or typing, nor is it easy to add an informal comment to interpret some formal sequence or to record a new element which you have never recognised before.

For these reasons the best method is to speak the names of the elements into a microphone and record them on a tape recorder. The main advantage is the human speed of response. Most people have to 'think' a word before typing it, but can speak the name quickly and can add a comment when the animals pause for a moment's rest. The record then has to be transcribed, unfortunately, and this is the boring part whether you type for computer input what you hear your recorded self saying or merely tally the numbers of each element on a checklist. The sound quality for recording when you mumble very fast, combined with the possibility of inching back if you have missed a word or two when transcribing are best provided at present by reel-to-reel recorders or cassette recorders with a 'Review' facility.

There are some advantages to filming behaviour, preferably on videotape because you can use a low light intensity camera and amplify the brightness electronically on playback: the bright lights necessary for ciné-film can inhibit the rats' performance. But since you still have to observe the behaviour (and definition and depth of focus are poorer on a TV screen than in the naked eye), videotape recording merely postpones the effort of analysing what you see. It is useful mainly for demonstrations to visitors to your laboratory, for the animals do seem to be somewhat inhibited by strangers, and it helps in teaching new observers, and in calibrating how well two observers correlate on the same behaviour. Two people cannot observe the same animal directly, because they influence one another by speaking the elements aloud.

Elements in the social behaviour of laboratory rats

Seward gives a vivid and highly dramatised impression. Ewan Grant and

Table 21.2. Elements in the behaviour of *Rattus norvegicus*

NON-SOCIAL	**Exploration**	ex — *explore* (= walk)	Locomotion, a few steps and a pause, nose and whiskers oriented to physical environment
		sc — *scan* (= rear)	Pause, often in an upright posture oriented to physical (distant) environment
	Maintenance	wa — *wash* (= preen)	Wipe face with licked forepaws
		sg — *self-groom*	Lick and comb body fur with teeth
		sr — *scratch*	with claws of hind feet
		sh — *shake*	shiver like a wet dog
		li — *lick penis*	typically after ejaculation (could be in Sex category)
		ea — *eat*	
		df — *defecate*	
		sf — *scan food*	exploration clearly oriented to food
		dr — *drink*	
		ur — *urinate*	
		fp — *gnaw faecal pellet*	
	Residual	dg — *dig*	(may show some Escape)
		pd — *push dig*	burrows with forepaws, kick material back with hindlegs (could represent Maintenance or even Escape)
		co — *crawl-over or jump over*	kick material forward with back of forepaws other rat (2 elements?)
		cu — *crawl under*	other rat. Said to be friendly gesture in wild rats, rare in lab
		bo — *bounce*	sudden vertical jump, apparently not oriented to other rat
		hu — *head-up*	raising of head, intention movement of sc or du
		st — *stagger*	possible sign of (drug-induced) ataxia
		tr — *tremor*	
SOCIAL APPROACH		Approach-avoidance ambivalence (investigation and escape?) x = other rat	
		tf — *to-fro*	rapid *rt* and *ap* x ↷
		sa — *stretched attend*	head approaches, rump remains behind
		wr — *walk-round*	x ↻
		o — *circle*	x ↺
		ts — *tailswitch*	side-to-side movement of tail
		at — *attend*	orientation to other rat from a distance (often superimposed on *cr* or

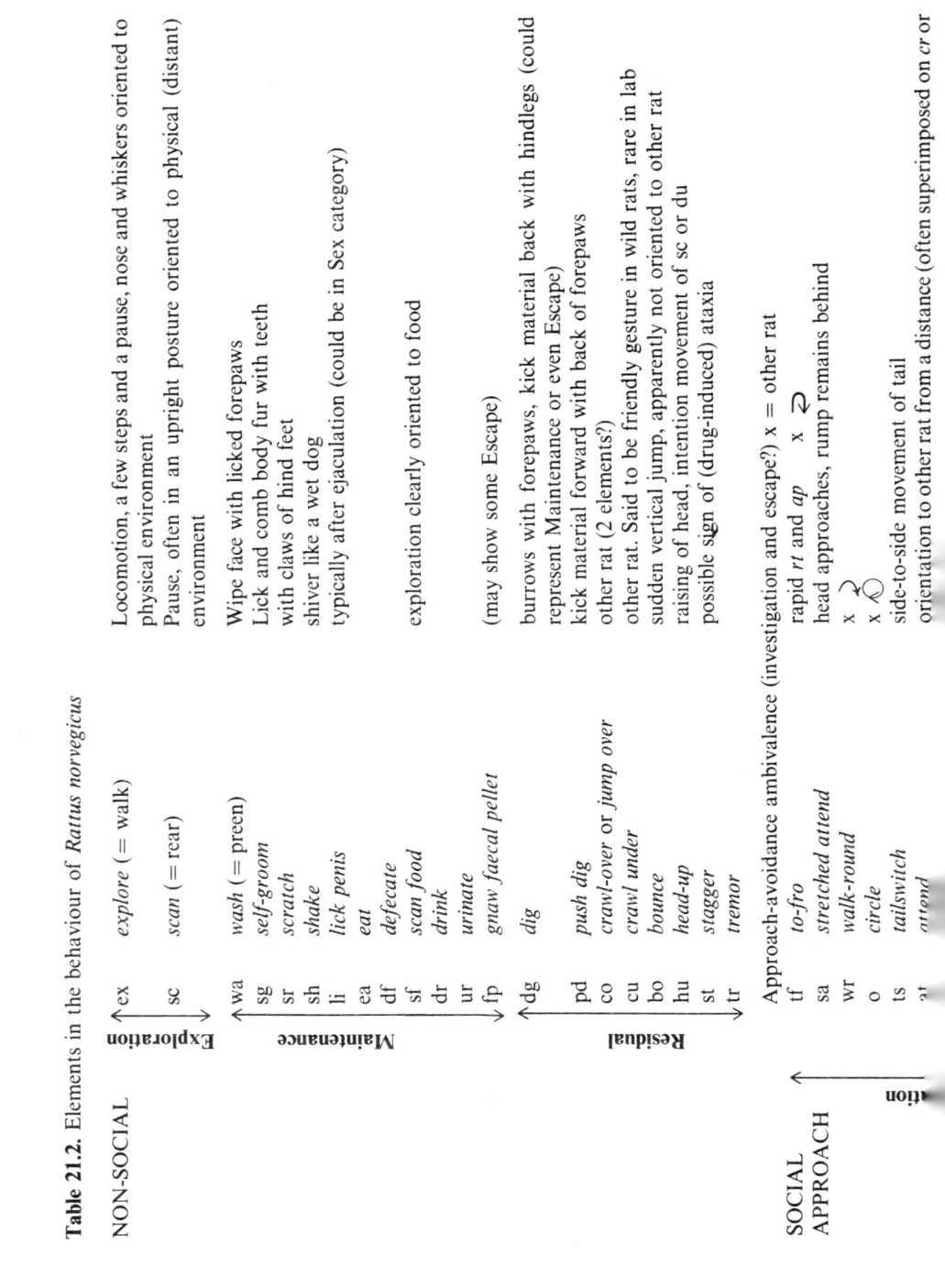

Sex-related beh.	in	investigate	by nose and whiskers to body of other rat
	sn	sniff	by nose and whiskers to genital area of other rat
	fo	follow	approach when other rat moves away
	pw	paw	pat other rat's flank with forepaw
	m	mount	full male sexual pattern: climb on back, palpate other rat's flank with forepaws, pelvic thrusts, and (if other rat is in oestrus) intromission
	am	attempt mount	incomplete or disoriented mount
	li	lick penis (qv)	
	lo	lordosis	(if female in oestrus)
Aggression	bi	bite	rare and inhibited from penetrating skin
	ag	aggressive groom	hard nibbling of other rat's fur (seems to combine groom and bite)
	pu	pull	inhibited bite leads to backward walk, pulling other rat sideways, similar to retrieval of pup to nest by its mother
	th	threat	sudden turn of head towards other rat, teeth partly exposed
	ak	attack	rapid approach, teeth partly exposed, ends with head over far side of other rat's shoulder. A still photograph would resemble *do* and *ou*
	do	dominate (= aggressive posture)	head over and at 90° to other rat in *sb*
	ou	offensive upright	on hindlegs, leaning forward, eyes, ears, whiskers oriented to other rat
	os	offensive sideways	broadside approach, head turned towards other rat, back arched
	du	defensive upright	on hindlegs, leaning back, eyes closed, or lower back vertical and upper body subsiding to horizontal, eyes round and attend other rat
Submission	ds	defensive sideways	broadside to other rat, body partly rotated away from him
	sb	submit	lies flat on back, ventral surface exposed to other rat, may kick
	p,k,b	push, kick, box	fend off other rat with fore- or hind-paws, may be in *du*
	rt	retreat	directed movement away from other rat *flee* very fast, may jump
	on	on bars	climb wall of cage
FLIGHT Escape	sq	squeal	squeal when bitten or ag. groomed
	fl	flag	head turns away from other rat
	ev	evade	head and forebody turn away from other rat
	cr	crouch	on all 4 paws, or with 1 forepaw raised. Shoulders low, back straight or arched (2 elements?)
	ec	elevated crouch	as *cr* but legs extended and back arched In extreme Escape, some postures (du, sb, cr) can be held for long periods in absence of other rat.

John Mackintosh write simply, describe the elements that can actually be seen, and give evidence for their interpretations. The (mobile) acts and (static) postures Grant and Mackintosh recognised (1963) are listed in Table 21.2 for rats; those for mice, hamsters, and guinea-pigs are closely similar. There is some direct evidence that these are real units and some theoretical support but no proof, and ultimately they are valid if they work. The classification of Table 21.2 is based on analysis by Grant (1963) of the relationships between the elements, the frequency with which each element led to each other element, in the way outlined above for investigate, sniff, and mount. Analysis of course is never complete. The grouping is similar to that I found useful in the interpretation of drug effects (Silverman, 1965), but has been amended in the light of experience.

Grant first noticed that the play-fighting of young rats seemed to stop for a moment when one lay down flat on his back. Preceding this there was always obvious fighting, like play in young rats around the age of weaning, but more serious in older males meeting after a few days' isolation. The other rat would stand over the one on his back and maybe groom him. And

Figs. 21.4 and 21.5. Dominate (full aggressive posture) and Submit. Note how 'submissive' rat fends off other.

then, as like as not, the rats would separate and proceed to exploration or eating or self-grooming.

In formal terms, Grant assumed some sort of motivational relationship between elements if they occur closely enough in time: Grant assumed 3 seconds. On this basis, in his experiments a total of 454 social elements preceded the flat-on-back posture but only 195 followed it. In nearly all other social elements, the ratio of preceding and following is nearly 1:1. Similarly the other rat moves away after 'standing-over' for a few seconds, just as you would expect if these two elements, the end-points of distinct sequences of social actions, were the consummatory acts of two drives.

Analysis of behaviour in a social situation

Assuming 'drive' to be a useful concept, which ones? A rat that lies down on its back does so spontaneously. The other one does not usually push, he may have approached rapidly with his teeth bared, but the rats may not even touch. The one lying down actively avoids being bitten, in fact the immediately preceding element may be Retreat, 'a directed movement away

Fig. 21.6. Attack, and Defensive Sideways turning to Submit.

from the other rat'. The other preceding elements are most commonly those that also lead to Retreat. Equally, although bites are rare in rats and in normal circumstances never damaging, the elements that precede the standing-over-a-supine-rat are most commonly those that lead to Bite when it

Fig. 21.7. Aggressive Groom or Pull, and Paw by one rat, Defensive Upright by another.

does occur. Grant's objective evidence, then, suggests that lying-down-flat-on-the-back is an act of submission, motivated by a flight drive; like a small boy in a school playground, crying, 'I give in'. If this is called 'submit', then the standing-over element is an aggressive posture, an expression of dominance.

A note on nomenclature and on what is being named

Elements have to have clear and unambiguous names, both as written and spoken, but these can be more than the code-letters BX or PO or nonsense syllables, Brobdingnag or Laputa. If they illustrate some essential characteristic, names help an inexperienced observer to visualise and recognise the elements they refer to. 'Flat-on-back' is suitable for this purpose but is a bit too clumsy to speak rapidly into a tape-recorder. At one time Grant used 'crab' as a vivid and memorable metaphor for the characteristic movement of Offensive Sideways, and 'ferret' to suggest the long-necked elongated sausage posture now known as Stretched Attend. I still think it a pity these names were replaced in the interests of scientific solemnity.

A name summarising a physical description does not encourage the observer to prejudge the element's meaning. We all inevitably have the impression that a rat doing so-and-so is being aggressive but in such-and-such a posture is frightened. No matter how hard we try, the subjective interpretation is continually likely to creep back, and the danger is that a functional name like 'win' or 'lose' will reinforce it. Even if we do not deceive ourselves, we run the risk of deceiving the readers of our imperishable publications for years to come. Nevertheless, a functional name is sometimes justified: we have seen the evidence that the posture labelled 'submit' means to a rat just what we should expect. We should cautiously question the evidence sometimes, but it will probably continue to support the same interpretation it always has. To continue pedantically to say 'flat-on-back' or to use initials SB or a nonsense-word like 'jabberwocky' would not change our interpretation but only hide it. A functional name, if it is valid, also helps to trace homologies between species. If to submit, to explore or, for that matter, to eat mean in any real sense the same thing in rats, gulls, sticklebacks, and men, then attention can be drawn to the fact by using the same name.

Nevertheless, the evidence must be found independently in each species. Mice do not submit. They occasionally roll over in fighting just as rats do, but they continue rolling and end up on their feet again. Moreover, and this is crucial, the other mouse does not recognise Flat-on-back: where a rat adopts a stereotyped posture ('Dominate') an aggressive mouse continues trying to bite. It is its signal value that gives 'Submit' its survival value, and if it is not recognised – i.e. if there is no detectable change in the responding animal's behaviour – then it is not a true unit of social behaviour. Hamsters may go 'flat-on-back', but this is the equivalent not of the rat's Submit but of Offensive Sideways, and can mislead a human observer until he notices the other hamster's response. Young hamsters play-fighting try to seize one another by the jaw (Payne and Swanson, 1970); as a first step towards a Defensive Upright, one hamster raises its head, so that the other one rotates on to its back to get a better grip of the jaw. It would be interesting to

Fig. 21.8. Upright postures. Note rotation of body.

Analysis of behaviour in a social situation

Fig. 21.9. Intermediates between Upright and Sideways postures, Offensive and Defensive.

discover how far individual 'learning' is involved in the development of Offensive Sideways and Submit in young rats and hamsters.

Incidentally, Grant's original name for the 'full aggressive posture' seems clumsy, and the term Dominate used by Louise Baenninger (1966) follows the logic of the word Submit.

Sequences of elements

The elements described in Table 21.2 are grouped into categories which are named in functional terms. The names are purely stick-on labels, of course, but should mean what they say. 'Maintenance' is a collective name for anything which a solitary animal could do in caring for itself: eating, drinking, grooming, and so on. Primarily non-social, most elements can also occur as apparent displacement activities, vigorous, abbreviated, and so closely following one or more other kinds of behaviour as to suggest motivational conflict. 'Exploration' refers to movement round the cage not oriented to the other animal but apparently seeking information from the physical environment. Non-specific 'motor activity' takes the same form and Kršiak (1975) refers simply to Walking.

In determining what the rat's social postures represent, it is assumed that two elements with related functions will probably need to occur close together in time, for instance as successive steps towards a particular goal. Now we must not confuse function with motivation (I do not eat to live but because I enjoy it, my sexual behaviour is not always directly in order to reproduce the species), but two elements contributing to the same functional end-point will be most efficient if they also share something of the same causative mechanism, i.e. 'motivation'. So we can provisionally take proximity in time to indicate related motivation. Two elements that are not consecutive, but separated by a third, may still be motivationally and functionally related, but to demonstrate this statistically needs a huge sample size.

What Grant did (1963) was to count the number of times in a series of experiments that each element was followed by each other element. Table 21.3 shows part of his table. Reading from left to right, there were 131 Threats in all, 12 of them leading to Attack, 44 directly to Dominate and 75

Table 21.3. From Grant (1963) (modified)

	Th	Ak	Do	Ag	Total
Th	/	12	44	75	131
Ak	0	/	52	14	66
Do	0	0	/	19	19
Ag	14	1	15	/	30
Total	14	13	111	108	246

to Aggressive Groom. There were some other Threats, leading to a few of the thirty or forty other elements not shown in this sample. Similarly the columns show which elements preceded which. Thus Attack was preceded by all others in this table thirteen times.

Now if there is no (motivational) relationship between elements, they would follow one another at random. If so, Attack, Dominate, and Aggressive Groom would be expected to lead to Threat in the ratio 66:19:30, the ratio in which they lead to all other elements. The observed ratio was very different, 0 : 0 : 14. In this way the formula (row total) (column total)/(grand total) gives an expected value (E) for each transition (strictly the grand total should exclude the element itself, but with forty-two elements the correction can be neglected).

The significance of any difference between what is expected on a random basis and what was actually observed (O) can then be calculated from the χ^2 formula (O − E) /E. Various other statistical methods have been used, most of them theoretically superior, but the conclusions they lead to do not seem very different in practice. The recent survey of cluster-analysis methods by Brian Morgan, M. J. A. Simpson, Jeannette Hanby, and Joan Hall-Craggs (1976) shows how valuable these modern methods can be in visualising complex sequential patterns. The complete table, with forty-two elements appearing with a grand total of over 9000, does not give quite the same expected values as the small part shown here, but it is clear that Attack and Dominate lead to Threat less often than they should on a chance basis, and Aggressive Groom does so rather more. In the other direction, Threat is the precursor of 12 of the 13 Attacks, of only 44 of 111 Dominates (which is not quite significantly less than expected), and of 75 of 108 Aggressive Grooms (which is just significantly more).

In the complete table, relatively few possible transitions occur with about

Fig. 21.10. Aggressive Groom and Defensive Sideways.

the frequency expected on a random distribution. Many occur only very rarely, as if by accident, or not at all. Attack is never followed directly by Submit or vice versa (although rapid juvenile play is recognised partly because a sequence with few intermediates like Attack–Dominate–Evade–Retreat–Submit–Attend–Attack–Dominate is so common). It follows that such pairs of elements share nothing in their immediate motivation or in function, except so far as the two sides of a coin are related just by being opposites. Some pairs of elements are significantly associated. By hypothesis they are therefore said to share something in their motivation. Threat leads to Aggressive Groom, and Aggressive Groom to Threat, for example, and by both appearance and the relation of one of them to Dominate, the common factor is one which we can label Aggression. Note, however, that some significant transitions are one-way and not reciprocal. Threat is the commonest of all elements before Attack, but never follows it. The reason is partly one of definition, for in Threat the rat turns his head and shoulders rapidly towards the other rat but then stops; if he continues, we call it Attack. It is quite common for the movement to begin, pause, and continue from there – or for the observer to start by naming Threat and then realise the rat is making a full Attack.

Such artefacts aside, a one-way association implies a sequence. The function of one element is to bring the rat into a position to perform the next step in the chain. You can strike a match to light a cigarette, or to light a fire to boil some water for tea. You smoke a cigarette or drink tea for some further reason, you rarely use a cigarette to light a match. The sequences in a rat's behaviour form a number of distinct pathways.

The cross-correlation sequence, analysing what one rat does following a given element shown by the other rat, is also interesting. Dominate, for example, can by definition only exist if the other rat has just Submitted; although the posture is characteristic it would otherwise certainly be called an Offensive Upright. If the other rat were to Crouch instead, the frustrated dominant rat Aggressive Grooms, again taking up nearly the same posture. A rat can submit, however, without the other rat adopting a Dominate position; it is rare, but shows once more how Submit is an active initiative, not a passive fall under the physical weight of the other rat's Attack.

In general, there are fewer significant transitions in the cross-correlations than in within-rat sequences, yet some elements in one rat definitely alter the behaviour of the other. Submit leads to Dominate by the other rat, and then often ends social activity for a time. Attack by one rat is followed by Submit in the other and so on. These elements must therefore be acting as signals to the other animal, stimuli to which the other animal makes a relatively specific response.

It is very common in animals for a postural behavioural signal to be reinforced morphologically, as when ducks preen their coloured wing feather. Golden hamsters are counter-shaded a light grey underneath, but there are two dark patches on the chest. In the Offensive Upright and Offensive Sideways postures the hamster holds its forepaws well apart, keeping the patches visible; in the Defensive versions they are hidden by folding the paws across the chest. Colin Lerwill cunningly suggested enlarging and intensifying the patches with black hair-dye. Marked hamsters (Grant, Mackintosh, and Lerwill, 1970) were in fact dominant to unmarked when either was introduced to the home cage of the other. Unmarked hamsters showed less aggression and more flight, especially the more intense elements.

The organisation of social behaviour

Fuller analysis is needed to interpret these results. Submit was considered as the end-point of a Flight tendency in rats (p. 305), partly on the evidence of its association with Retreat. If Retreat is the criterion, elements leading to or from it must also be largely flight-motivated, and Defensive Sideways and Defensive Upright can lead either to Retreat or to Submit. One rat cannot retreat far from another in a small cage, so he then crouches. Flag and Evade are incomplete (intention) movements of Retreat and can both precede and follow Crouch. Fig. 21.11 shows what a predominantly aggressive rat is likely to do and Fig. 21.12 the options open to one motivated mainly by flight. The arrows show the main transitions and their width is roughly proportional to their frequency in Grant's (1963) experiments. Attend and Approach lead either through the Upright and Sideways group to Submit, or through Retreat, Flag, and Evade to Crouch. Although there is some crossing over between these pathways, they seem fairly distinct. There is some evidence that crouch is more common in encounters between strangers: a rat entering someone else's territory is more likely to run away home, crouching only if the retreat is blocked. Rats living in the same colony are more likely to have stable relationships, the fight is more equal; one rat

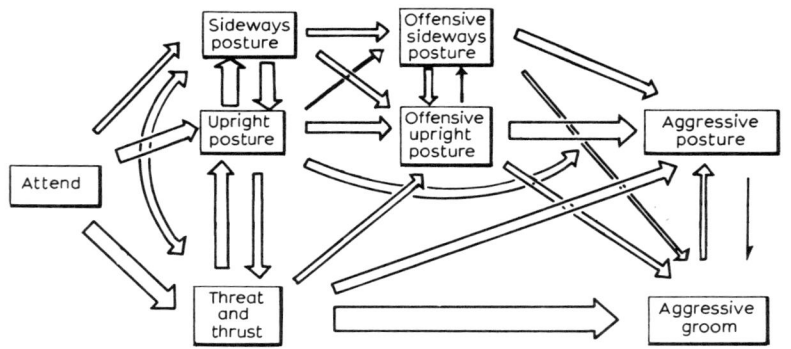

Fig. 21.11. Aggressive pathways in the rat. 'Thrust is virtually synonymous with attack. The probabilities with which each element led to each other are represented approximately by the breadth of the arrows (after Grant, 1963 by permission).

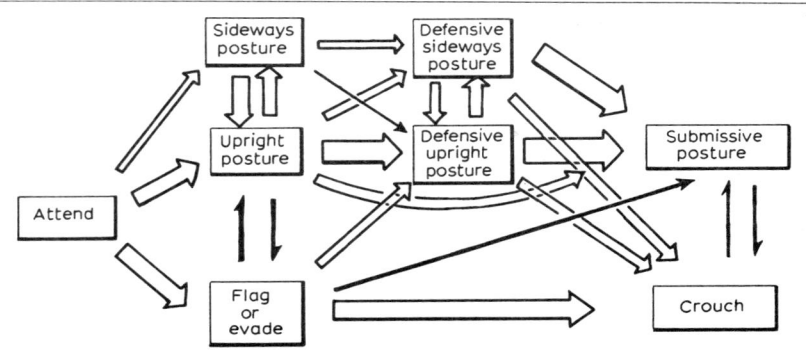

Analysis of behaviour in a social situation 311

Fig.21.12. Flight pathway in the rat (after Grant, 1963 by permission). Grant distinguished fully ambivalent Upright and Sideways postures from those where aggression or flight predominates.

submits yet stays in close proximity (next time it may be the other rat's turn).

Mice and hamsters have no submissive posture and face the alternatives of fight or flight out of the territory. They are much more likely to defend iindividual territories than rats. A Defensive Upright in these species therefore signals not submission but that the animal is on the way out anyway, and had better not be intimidated on the way, otherwise he might get desperate and counter-attack.

In all the species, the Upright and Sideways postures are ambivalent and probably lead either to aggressive or flight-motivated elements, e.g. in rats either to Dominate or to Submit. The distinction between offensive and defensive is one of proportion. In a Defensive Upright, the head is held vertically upright, the eyes may be half-closed, the ears and whiskers retracted. This is most likely to lead to Submit. The more the rat leans forward, with eyes, ears, and teeth directed to the other animal, and perhaps

Fig. 21.13. Upright postures. Note rotation of body.

Fig. 21.14. Offensive and Defensive Sideways postures.

advancing towards him, the more likely is the upright to lead to Dominate. However, even an Offensive Upright can lead to Submit, a Defensive Upright (rarely) directly to Dominate.

Fig. 21.15. Crouch–Attend and Offensive Sideways. Note erection of hair on the back in the Offensive Sideways posture.

Similarly in Sideways postures, the more the head curves inwards towards the other rat the more probable is Dominate, the more it is rotated away, the more likely is he to submit. There is some evidence that, although both uprights and sideways are ambivalent, they do not represent precisely the same thing. The sideways postures represent a balance of tendencies which are relatively more aggressive than the Uprights and at a more intense level. The relationships are plotted graphically in Fig. 21.16, which shows the rank-order correlations of various elements with attack in the mouse.

Upright postures perhaps represent more than one kind of approach–avoidance ambivalence. A male is sometimes seen in what looks like an Offensive Upright but follows it most often with Attempt Mount rather than Dominate, and sometimes with Submit (so may the object of his desires); the ambivalence is between Sex and Flight. Similarly a rat may gradually sag from an ordinary Defensive Upright into a right-angled pos-

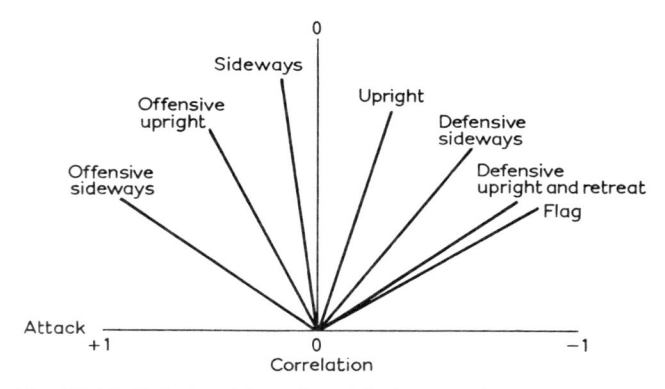

Fig. 21.16. Relationships of social elements in the mouse. The figure shows rank-order correlation of selected elements, with Attack: elements thought predominantly aggressive turn out to be positively correlated, those thought to represent flight are negatively correlated and ambivalent elements are intermediate. Note how sideways postures are relatively more aggressive than uprights (after Mackintosh as quoted by Chance, 1968).

ture with the lower back vertical but the upper back and head horizontal, eyes wide and all attention on the other rat for a minute or two at a time. This occasionally occurs after intense territorial-type fighting or after large doses of some drugs and seems to represent intense flight blocked by the inability to run far in a small cage or the need to keep a wary eye on what the other rat is doing. In a similar general way, a flight-motivated rat that is running away rather than submitting will crouch. If some tendency to approach the other rat, usually aggression, is still present, the crouch will be elevated: the legs are extended, the back arched like an angry cat, and an aggressive element occasionally follows.

Fig. 21.17. Varieties of Crouch (and Attend) and walk-round.

Most of these elements are at close range, but the animals also move towards or away from each other and several actions reveal approach–avoidance ambivalence. At the shortest range, one rat can simply Walk Round the other with a radius of about half a body length. At the far end of the cage or in a larger arena, several elements can be grouped as 'distance

Fig. 21.18. Varieties of Elevated Crouch.

ambivalence'. Typically a rat retreats to a safe distance from the other, turns, pauses, and then approaches again. During the pause, when the two opposite tendencies are nicely balanced, the animal washes its face briefly, scratches, switches the tail, or walks in a circle or figure-of-eight. The rapid alternation of retreat and approach, dominate and submit is characteristic of young rats playing. Older rats change their mood more slowly, and show ambivalent postures. In fact, an intensely aggressive older rat seems to frighten himself with his own aggression, for even without retaliation from the other rat, pure Attack is very quickly replaced with Offensive Sideways (put less vividly, a stimulus for aggression is also one for flight).

In a large arena the approach tendency can be puzzling. A rat well-beaten retreats but usually approaches again, very cautiously and with no visible trace of aggression or sexual motivation. Curiosity/Investigation could be a factor, but Grant was led to wonder if such a reluctant approach may not be evidence of a true social drive.

Summary of the argument

In conclusion, most elements visible in a social situation occur in characteristic places in the pattern, some apparently representing single tendencies, others more than one, some in contexts which suggest conflict. The regularities are great enough, even in such a complex and unpredictable situation, to allow a human observer to interpret them in relatively simple terms with a fair degree of confidence. In this, we copy the animals themselves, for several elements act as signals. Not all do: so conspicuous an element in

Fig. 21.19. When the signals don't work: one rat has just bitten the other, who jumps and then retreats.

mice as Tail Switch seems to be ignored by other mice, and to make no difference to their behaviour. However, an Offensive Upright is the classical threat signal: 'I want you to run away and get out of my sight, and if you don't, I may bite you. But if you stand up for your rights I may run away myself.'

Laboratories and species compared

Wild rats in captivity display many of the same elements, although they have not been observed in such detail. Barnett (1963) has described how intense their fighting may be, so that a stranger introduced to an established group can be found dead in the morning apparently from heart failure; there are no signs of bites or other injuries. Wild rats (*R. norvegicus* and *R. rattus*) are described more fully in Chapter 24, but it is relevant here to discuss Barnett's belief that laboratory rats do not fight. His photographs are very like the illustrations in this chapter, yet he and his colleagues do not appear to have seen these elements in albinos.

Davis (1933) and Seward (1945a) both described Submit, Hall and Klein (1942) did not, though it is quite conspicuous. I have watched rats of five strains (two albinos, two black-hooded, and one with brown, wild-type colour), all with the same repertoire and only minor differences in the way they use it. Unless intensely-aroused captive wild animals emit hypersonic cries or urinary pheromones which inhibited the albinos in the same laboratory, the discrepancy seems hard to account for. Perhaps, as so often, the problem concerns the use of words – if laboratory rats go through the same motions at (usually) lower intensity, Barnett may call it playing, not fighting.

Comparing four laboratory species, Grant and Mackintosh (1963) found, predictably, that the closer the taxonomic relationship the more similar the behaviour. Different strains of *Mus musculus* were closer to each other than any of them were to rats; golden hamsters were less like either species, but all the myomid rodents resembled each other more than the guinea-pig (*Cavia porcellata*). The black rat (*Rattus rattus*) is closely related to the common wild rat (*R. norvegicus*) and has been observed under semi-natural conditions by Ewer in Ghana (1971; see p. 358). She was interested in ecology as much as behaviour and while not describing the elements in great detail, her outline suggests surprisingly wide differences between species. Many of the differences can be related to the black rat's preference for climbing rather than burrowing. A rat up a tree would fall off if it lay down on its back, and Submit is replaced by an appeasement gesture. This is mouth-to-mouth contact, virtually a kiss, and may have evolved in the same way: infant black rats are weaned as human babies used to be, by the mother chewing a tasty morsel and pushing it into the infant's open mouth with her tongue.

Black rats defend a group territory, expelling all but determined intruders. The group had a dominant male and two or three more tolerant top females, then a group of subordinates and juveniles. The dominant male chased his victim as far as the territory boundary but not beyond. The boundary was marked by rubbing with the belly, as laboratory rats do occasionally, but Ewer did not see the expected drop of urine. Both black rats and albinos seem to ignore the tail-switching that is so conspicuous to a human observer, and albinos also seem to ignore the fur erected on the back of an aggressive rat; Ewer thought that black rats used piloerection as a ritualised threat signal.

Another threat Ewer called 'stegosauring' which sounds like either Elevated Crouch (probably showing aggression and escape) or Offensive Sideways (showing aggression and submission); since she mentions no rotation of the body or movement broadside towards the other rat, the description fits Elevated Crouch best. Perhaps the Norway rat's submissive posture has influenced the neighbouring ambivalent elements, so that the semi-rotated Sideways postures are as unique to the species as the flat-on-back Submit. The black rat's social organisation seems similar, perhaps with more emphasis on the chase-flee pattern of juvenile laboratory rats than on the slower-moving ambivalence typical of adults.

Territory in the laboratory

Hamsters are not rats, and even littermates may not remain peacefully in groups as adults. Females are particularly aggressive and are believed to hold territories in the wild. Now territory, by definition, is an area where one individual is dominant to all others. If others of the same sex, age, and species do not withdraw from it of their own free will, the territory owner attacks them and can enforce their removal. Equally important is the implication that others recognise territory when they see it and territory owners away from home are defeated as easily as anyone else. So that laboratory tests of so-called 'territorial' fighting between isolated rats or mice may be confusing the issue. In the uncertain period when ownership is still being established, the boundary between two territories can be the scene of much to-and-fro battling which the introduction of two isolated albinos certainly resembles. But the home mouse can be aggressive without being territorial and in any case 'loses' as often as it 'wins'. In an established territorial situation, overt aggression could be brief and of low intensity.

Wild house mice (*Mus musculus*) can form territories in certain conditions, but these territories are only a part of the social organisation. Peter Crowcroft and Fred Rowe (1963) released mice into a large room (40 m^2). After a few hours tentative, timid but systematic exploration first in the lee of the walls and then into the centre of the room, a mouse can flee to the shelter of the nearest nest-box when disturbed. After 24 hours, a solitary mouse invariably rushed into headlong attack on any intruder. Mice of opposite sexes or two females soon settled down amicably but two males would fight savagely until one established dominance. The subordinate, chased at every opportunity, would roam actively only when the dominant was asleep. A third mouse would retreat headlong the first time it encountered the subordinate, stimulating dominant behaviour in the latter.

Family groups showed little fighting among themselves; the father occasionally chased one of his offspring away from a food tray. All would attack an intruder of either sex, but the adult male (or pregnant female) attacked by far the most. Juveniles sniffed but usually avoided the intruder, yet very small mice that hardly ever left the nest alone, were observed to rush at a stranger who entered the nest and successfully cause its retreat. Interactions between whole families resembled the response to single intruders, and families remained separate. A family member removed for a week and then returned would be accepted with little fighting, but after 2 or 3 weeks a long-lost relative was treated the same way as a stranger. Not all such encounters were aggressive but a few mice (usually an adult male) could be vicious and the intruder bitten. Such intruders might be found dead after a few days (Rowe and Redfern, 1969).

These mice sound very like Steiniger's rats (p. 353) and the behaviour strongly suggests territory. True territory, where several mice are dominant but each in his own small area, could only be found in certain conditions. Since one mouse can tyrannise over many others over a wide area, geographical complexity is more important than sheer space, giving cover with obstacles, hay, and large nest-boxes. Usually an adult male slept in one box alone or with his wife (until she became pregnant and chased him out), while two or three females and their growing litters all shared another box, and left several others vacant. Short-sighted mice can easily lose sight of the quarry round a corner and fleeing intruders often escaped in a crowd of residents attracted to the excitement. Most within-family fighting seemed due to mistaken identity, and occasionally three resident mice could be seen chasing each other in circles round an obstacle while the intruder walked away whistling with his hands in his pockets. The obstacles, and the large two-door nest-boxes allowed individual males or pregnant females to defend particular small areas against others, while tolerating members of their own extended family. Crowcroft and Rowe thought such territories within a large colony help to restrict the movement of individuals, and to adapt mice to exploiting the huge sources of food represented by corn-ricks and warehouses.

If captive wild mice can form true territories, what about their laboratory relatives? According to Mackintosh (1970; 1973) they can, but only if four requirements are met. There must be adequate stimuli for the boundaries to be recognised, which must operate both at near and distant range; visual cues are surprisingly more important than olfactory ones. There must be cover to retreat to in emergency. The territories might be defended primarily by single adult males, but they must be occupied by a group, probably of mixed sexes and ages, and two territories can be developed only if they are formed separately before the mice are allowed to meet. Mackintosh used two groups at a time, each consisting of two males and two females. Without somebody to boss, the one male would not feel proprietorial rights; without initial separation one male would dominate all the mice he meets; and if the groups are not then allowed to mingle, you could not demonstrate that the defended areas are true territories. Each dominant male defends his area against the other, and after initial attempts and violent fighting, no longer ventures into the other's territory. The females, juveniles, and to a limited extent the subordinate males (if they dare) can wander fairly freely over the other group's territory as well as their own; nevertheless as in Crowcroft's experiments the groups remain distinct. The subordinate who wanders is the one most likely to set up his own new territory or to take over the home territory if anything happens to the dominant.

It is still fairly difficult to demonstrate territory formation in laboratory mice, but it does show that the fighting when one mouse is placed in another's cage is, after all, related to territory. Mice are likely to go to extremes in this situation, one mouse is either extremely aggressive or excessively timid – or if he meets another irresistible force he might be first one and then the other. This makes it reasonable to take mouse fighting as a single simple unit in pharmacological testing, and to ignore its internal structure. Without details of flight and non-social behaviour you still lose much information relevant to the mechanisms behind any experimental effect, but for a crude first approximation, the all-or-none character of mouse fighting makes it easy to observe. Rats have a true submissive posture, allowing a defeated colony member to stay in the group, while a stranger escapes. Their social behaviour seems adapted to maintaining an organisation in colonial groups, and is consequently more subtly balanced within the individual. It is therefore even more worthwhile to observe in detail.

TWENTY-TWO
Social behaviour as an experimental method

If the ethological analysis of behaviour is valid, then an experimental treatment known to affect behaviour in general ought to alter the pattern of social behaviour systematically. It should be possible to make a convincing story of the effects of, say, a drug known to be useful in treating mental illness. There should be some advantages over conventional methods: (1) taken at face value, the behaviour would be one stage closer to the therapeutic target, i.e. the behaviour of the patient to (or away from) other people; (2) if the units observed have not been stabilised by elaborate conditioning, they may often be sensitive to lower doses; (3) less speculatively,

the therapeutic target?

behaviour in a social situation is complex. Many kinds of behaviour are observable within the same few minutes. While they are by no means fully independent of one another, neither are they so highly correlated that a change in one is necessarily reflected in all the others. In short, we can take measures of different kinds of behaviour, aggression, flight, grooming, etc., and assess the relative importance of multiple effects of a drug in the same animals at the same time; (4) at the most mundane and practical level, the behaviour is spontaneously present in all animals, and does not have to be conditioned by the experimenter. While the normal upbringing of the infant almost certainly involved conditioning, all the experimenter has to do is to provide conditions in which the results can be demonstrated; (5) in a social situation animals can be remarkably highly active.

Introduction of isolated male rats

To use social behaviour as a test, one problem is to persuade the animals to perform at an adequate rate at a time when the experimenter is ready. I started with the traditional method of isolating the animals and introducing one into another's home cage (Silverman, 1965). Male rats, usually of a brown strain, were housed at weaning in groups of four under reversed lighting conditions. When they reached about 200–250 g in weight, they were separated one to a cage, usually for 7 days, as this seemed to maximise activity on introduction. Isolation was sometimes for 3 days only, to leave room for drug-induced increases in social activity. To reduce any stress from isolation and particularly from being picked up, gripped, and turned upside down for intraperitoneal injection, rats were handled after 24 hours isolation.

Observations were made at the time of day that rats are most active, in the first hour or two after the white lights went out. Six rats were designated as 'partners', not to be injected themselves, but to be introduced three times on successive days into the home cages of strangers, meeting a saline-control, a low-dose and a high-dose rat in a suitably counter-balanced order. One observer watched the experimental rats (injected a minute or so beforehand), another watched the partners, speaking the names of the elements on to a stereo tape-recorder. Behaviour of all kinds was recorded – exploration, maintenance, social behaviour, and all – so as to approach as closely as possible to a complete description.

Since Grant (1963) originally analysed sequences of elements, the first hypothesis was that drugs would alter the transitional probability of one element leading to another. For example, an Upright posture is called ambivalent when it normally leads equally to aggressive and submissive elements; if, in a drug-injected animal, it leads invariably to submission, we infer that the drug has reduced aggression or increased flight. However, direct computation of the transitions is both tedious and unnecessary. In a standard time, such a drug would increase the total number of flight elements or reduce the number of aggressive ones, or both.

A simple count of totals would underestimate the importance of elements lasting a relatively long time. Crouch and Explore, for instance, often last for many seconds, whereas Attack and Retreat occupy less than half a second. In practice this is not a serious problem because the longer one element lasts, the less time is available for anything else and the slow element occupies a greater proportion of the whole. A direct, if approximate, estimate of the durations of different elements is possible but I am not sure that it yields much more information.

Taking an experiment with chlorpromazine as an example (Silverman, 1965), six rats were injected at 1 mg/kg, six at 4 mg/kg, and six were saline controls. The three observations on the partners let us assess the indirect effect of the drug on the behaviour of the animals *not* receiving it. For each rat, the data consisted of the total score in a 10-minute introduction for each of up to forty or forty-five elements (some occur only rarely).

Statistical analysis of such complex data presents a formidable problem, and there is no perfect solution, certainly none that will satisfy the purist statistician and yet be practical as a routine. The clearest way of explaining some of the relevant issues will be to show the development of my own understanding (so far).

In the chlorpromazine example, the total number of elements of all kinds (henceforward called the Total Activity, for convenience) shown by the six rats given 1 mg/kg averaged about 12 per cent less than controls, but since nearly all methods show that chlorpromazine reduces activity, this did not seem of dramatic significance. I was more interested in changes in the distribution of this activity between different kinds of behaviour.

The most straightforward statistical method would be to take each element in turn and apply a *t*-test. I preferred a method that corrected for the drug's reduction of total activity and looked for changes in any one element relative to this reduced expectation. So I assiduously read Sidney Siegel's (1956) *Non-Parametric Statistics for the Behavioural Sciences*, though he is scarcely to be blamed for any misconceptions I still retain. An interim solution was to apply the chi-squared test to the whole of the data, on the basis that χ^2 does not rely on the data being normally distributed, could be computed fairly easily on an electromechanical calculator (computers were less accessible in 1960), and is very effective at picking out where any differences in pattern lie.

Unfortunately, the χ^2 test is not strictly valid for this purpose, since by taking the total count of an element for all six rats in a group it ignored the variation between individual rats. The test can assess how many rats in a group performed some action but not how many times the average rat performed it. Moreover, it treats all elements as independent, whereas in fact the occurrence of a Submit implies that a Defensive Upright or Sideways has just occurred too. Consequently the χ^2 accurately locates in what kind of behaviour two groups of animals differ, if they differ at all, but nearly always overstates the significance of such a difference. As I later learned, a multi-variate parametric test like discriminant analysis using many more animals and a large computer gives a much more reliable result. However, the answers obtained by the χ^2 technique were so consistent that they are almost certainly correct.

Observer reliability was also high. Before the era of videotape recorders, two observers could only be compared when watching different samples of rats, because of the influence of one spoken commentary on the other if they watched the same animal at the same time. Including sampling effects, therefore, the difference between two observers (measured by χ^2) was about as great as from a fairly large drug effect; but this difference was concentrated into two or three single elements rather than in complete categories. Thus Offensive Upright differs from Attack mainly in the speed of approach towards the other rat, and people differ mainly in where they draw the line. Note that looking for a difference between observers is a remarkably severe test. On the conventional null hypothesis that they are different, a Spearman rank–order correlation on the same data showed that the observers were extremely similar, $r_s = 0.922$ at 40 degrees of freedom (well beyond the 0·1 per cent level of probability).

Interpreting drug effects: chlorpromazine

In the illustrative experiment the six control rats totalled 2170 elements of all kinds, the six injected with 1 mg/kg chlorpromazine 1898. We would expect, if the drug had no effect, that all the elements making up that total would be distributed in the same way. Some were. The ratio between drug-injected and control rats for Approach was 100 : 117 and for Retreat 55 : 60. The observed being so close to the expected for these elements, they contributed nothing to the overall difference in pattern. On the other hand, Offensive Sideways occurred in the ratio 11 : 57 and a statistical test is hardly needed to show that this is far less than expected. The bigger an element's contribution to χ^2, the more likely it is to have been altered by the drug. Although one element in twenty would appear significant at the 5 per cent probability level by definition, it is interesting to see how many there are, and which ones.

The elements that were disproportionately reduced were Follow, Attempt-Mount and Walk-round, representing sexual behaviour and approach–avoidance conflict, together with six of the seven elements in which aggression predominates: Threat, Attack, Dominate, Offensive Upright, and Offensive Sideways. Some elements (Crouch, Attend, and Wash) were increased by chlorpromazine. Rats given the drug crouched twice as often as controls and were more often seen sheltering under the food hopper ('uh' in Table 22.1) as if in a burrow with a roof over their backs. In this position they would fix their attention on the other rat and warily observe his every move. It appears therefore that chlorpromazine mainly reduced aggression and sexual behaviour, and increased escape away from the other rat.

Now a motivational interpretation is not the only one possible. The drug might conceivably have interfered with the animal's sensory input in some way. But if that were the case, why was only one of the elements affected that represent exploration of the cage or of the other rat? Again, the drug could have caused ataxia or some comparable functional weakness of the muscular system. Postures where the rat stands upright on his hindlegs all make similar demands on muscular strength, yet they were not affected in the same way: the drug reduced Offensive Upright, had no effect on Scan, and actually increased Wash and (not significantly) Defensive Upright.

Social behaviour as an experimental method

Table 22.1. [Adapted from Table 2 of Silverman (1965)]

Category	Element	Saline	Chlorpromazine 1 mg/kg	χ^2
Exploration	ex	146	134	0·2
	sc	173	167	0·8
Investigation	ap	117	100	0
	no	245	233	0·8
	tf	3	3 ⎫	14·0 ***
	wr	79	31 ⎭	
Sex-related	fo	84	37	12·6 ***
	sn	79	51	2·9
	am	26	3 ⎫	17·4 ***
	m	5	1 ⎭	
Aggression	do	46	24	4·3 *
	ag	8	6	0
	th	15	3	6·5 *
	ak	15	2	8·2 **
	ou	162	108	4·8 *
	os	57	11	25·3 ***
Submission	du	139	145	2·2
	ds	141	115	0·3
	sb	102	85	0·1
Escape	rt	60	55	0
	fl	14	20	2·0
	ev	17	18	0·4
	cr	22	46	12·1 ***
	ec	14	7	1·5
	uh	48	73	9·0 **
	ob	43	36	0
	at	85	144	24·3 ***
Maintenance	wa	56	76	6·3 *
	sg	27	17	0·9
	dg	7	7 ⎫	1·3
	dr	8	1 ⎭	
Residual	various			(4·9 in all)
Total		2170	1898	$\chi^2 = 163·1$

The elements are described and classified on pp. 302–3 (Table 21.2)
  *$p < 0·05$; **$p < 0·01$; ***$p < 0·001$.

Another kind of motor effect was certainly present, for fast acts were often reduced and long-lasting postures like Crouch and Attend increased, probably enough to account for the reduction in total activity. But a slow-down in movement is not the whole story, for a slow-moving posture like Offensive Upright could be reduced if it was predominantly aggressive, while fast energetic actions like Retreat or Climb On Bars could remain frequent if they involve escaping from the other rat. The decline in motor activity so commonly found in experiments on chlorpromazine could be as much a consequence of the change in motivation as a cause of it.

If the drug has really changed motivation, then all the elements representing related tendencies should be changed in parallel. Now no two elements have identical motivation – there is presumably no selective advantage in evolving two signals for a single message – but they can be grouped approximately according to the tendency predominating. A useful arrangement is shown in Tables 21.2 and 22.1 though other groupings are also valid. For instance while Attend, Follow and Sniff all represent Investigation in themselves, Attend so commonly followed Crouch and preceded Evade that I took it as evidence of a tendency to escape from the other rat, while Follow and Sniff precede mounting and so suggest sexual motivation. All the ambivalent Upright and Sideways postures could well be placed in a group of their own. Alternatively the classification could be reduced to three categories: exploration and maintenance fall into a non-social class; investigation, sexual behaviour, aggression, and to some extent submission all involve approach to the other rat; and escape represents social behaviour with a negative orientation.

So, comparing the sum of elements in one category with all other behaviour, we should detect specific drug effects. In the example, rats given chlorpromazine showed a total of 158 predominantly aggressive elements and (1898 – 158) others, whereas controls showed 308 aggressive elements to the same partner rats and (2170–308) others. Conversely, the chlorpromazine-injected rats showed 403 escape elements on the classification of Table 22.1 but the controls showed 306, confirming that chlorpromazine disproportionately reduced aggression, investigation, and sexual behaviour, but actually increased escape (Fig. 22.1). Yet the non-social categories occurred more or less in proportion to total activity, and so did submission which simultaneously represents both approach and avoidance. The χ^2 test was repeated within each category, and though I now doubt how useful this was, it tended to confirm how uniformly the drug acted on all the elements of a category. The experiment was repeatable. In fact, there were nineteen groups of rats given doses from 0·5 to 4 mg/kg chlorpromazine in twelve experiments; only two did not lead to the same conclusions and even these two could be plausibly explained (Silverman, 1966a). Thus, total activity was consistently reduced by about 10 per cent, but this did not account for the disproportionate reduction in behaviour involving approach to the other

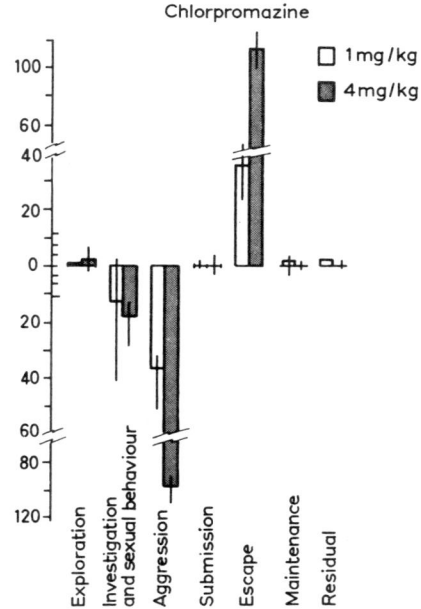

Social behaviour as an experimental method 325

Fig. 22.1. Effect of chlorpromazine on behaviour of isolated rats, one introduced to the home cage of another (from Silverman, 1965). Bars represent the value of χ^2 for the difference between dosed and control rats, meeting the same untreated partners, for the sum of all elements within each behavioural category, above the line the behaviour was increased by the drug, below the line it was reduced. Vertical lines represent the value of χ^2 for the elements within each category as a measure of variation.

rat and the increase in Escape. In any case amphetamine (5 mg/kg) increased total activity but had a surprisingly similar effect on the pattern of activity, reducing most aggressive elements and increasing many that represent submission and escape (Silverman, 1966a).

The reduction in approach would be neatly explained if chlorpromazine reduced all responses to external stimuli, as Dews and Morse suggested (1961). It is a difficult concept to test critically, but would also account for two other phenomena. In one experiment, chlorpromazine was injected immediately before observation; a week later the rats were reallocated to new experimental groups (to equalise their past experience) and observed again an hour after injection (a delay common in behavioural experiments). The saline controls of the second half of the experiment differed quite widely from those in the first, presumably because they had spent much of the hour's delay in exploration, but stimuli during the delay made no difference to rats given chlorpromazine. Secondly, deprivation of food is said (Campbell and Sheffield, 1953) to increase responsiveness. Rats deprived of food for 12 or 18 hours before introduction behaved socially for the first 7–8 minutes before starting to eat. While those given chlorpromazine were, as usual, less active than controls, all kinds of behaviour were reduced equally. It is conceivable that increased responsiveness through hunger antagonised the drug's reduction of responsiveness but not that of motor activity. Neither responsiveness nor activity account for the surprising increase in escape. Benactyzine in the same series of experiments reduced aggression more than chlorpromazine but hardly altered escape (Silverman, 1966a). Perhaps what we called escape does not represent a retreat from the other animal in particular but an attempt to withdraw from the whole situation. Behaviourally, however, this distinction is not nearly as clear as it should be if it was important to the animals, and the implication remains that chlorpromazine and amphetamine increase the rat's equivalent of fear. An increase in fear (also postulated for these drugs by Kumar 1971a and b) would also account for the otherwise paradoxical increases in response rate quoted by Dews and Morse for some conditioned avoidance schedules, and for the reduced rate in a 'conflict' situation (Geller *et al.*, 1962; Ray, 1964) where a response brings both food and shock. A rat is also an ambivalent stimulus for both approach and avoidance and it could be the uncertainty that makes the drug increase the latter.

Chlorpromazine therefore had a clear and repeatable effect on behaviour in a social situation and one that makes a plausible story. The partner rats detected it too, for they showed less submission and escape to subdued, unaggressive chlorpromazine-injected rats than to controls, but more unambiguous attacks. Perhaps out of frustration at the doped rats' lack of response, they also showed more exploration and maintenance.

Multi-variate analysis

The χ^2 test therefore allowed some interesting interpretations which, in spite of the theoretical shortcomings, were so consistent that I believe the conclusions to be broadly correct. But there are better statistical methods.

Observing more animals for a shorter time, say sixteen rats per group for 3 minutes each, reduces the variance. To analyse each element separately, a t-test (perhaps using a log transformation) or the non-parametric Mann–Whitney U-test would be obvious, but both have disadvantages. Besides being laborious even to enter all the data on a computer, there is too great a risk of zero scores. If two rats are equally aggressive, but one shows it entirely by Attack and Dominate while the other (meeting a partner that defends itself) shows Offensive Sideways and Upright, we might fail to detect a genuine effect because each element is too variable when considered on its own.

So we could apply the U- or t- test to whole categories. If the final interpretation of the results is going to be clearest in the motivational terms of these categories, it seems as useful to add the elements together before the statistics as after. An additional classification would also be useful, sorting elements into fast and slow categories, upright postures and horizontal ones. Classification along a motor dimension as well as by motivation should discriminate different types of drug effect.

However, even complete categories are not likely to be independent, and may therefore suggest several effects where there is really no more than one. An extreme case is trichloroethylene (Silverman and Williams, 1975), since the vapour caused a flat reduction in all categories more or less equally. At the highest concentration used, nearly all these reductions were significant by the t-test, but it would be absurd to discuss them separately when the most likely explanation is that the vapour made the animals feel drowsy.

Again, suppose you were to find a pure aphrodisiac for the rats. Its direct action would only be to increase sexual behaviour, but there would be all sorts of consequential changes. Approach and investigate would increase in males, the come-hither pattern of retreat and crouch would increase in females. Neither sex would waste much time in exploration of the cage. Much would depend on the other rat, of course, on its sex, its age, and state of oestrous – but it could co-operate joyfully, or run away in terror or counter-attack in annoyance, or merely complain of a headache and opt out, and each of these would call forth a suitable response in the sexually aroused rat.

So a truly multivariate test is needed and Discriminant Analysis and Multivariate Analysis of Variance ('Manova') are said to be suitable (Hope, 1968). Both need a large computer. One form of discriminant analysis starts, in effect, with a t-test or simple analysis of variance on each variable, i.e. each kind of behaviour, but uses analysis of covariance to relate two variables together, another analysis of covariance to relate a third to the combination of the first two, and so on until a single equation finds the clearest discrimination between the two (or more) groups of animals. Meanwhile, each category's value of t (or F) is scaled in proportion to the information it gives not already available from all the other categories.

To illustrate one use of these tests, suppose you want to see whether two football teams occupy different areas of the pitch. You might take a series of photographs and plot the positions of the corresponding players on each side (the two halves of the match are of course the original crossover experiment). The two goalkeepers constitute variable No. 1, and you hardly need a statistical test to notice that they are consistently at opposite ends of the pitch. Backs are highly likely to be found at positions near their own goalkeepers, but they are mobile in modern football and may come forward to score goals: the positions of the two left backs would be significantly different over the whole match, but not in every photograph. Midfield players roam everywhere, and although United's forwards are often in their own half of the pitch, they often overlap City's forwards and may even be caught offside beyond City's backs. The variance may be too great for a statistically significant difference in position. Note that the line joining the mean position of United's No. 11 and City's No. 11 will not lie parallel to the line between the two goals: it will certainly be oblique and may be more or less reversed. So a t-test could well be significant and yet add little (if the line is oblique) or nothing to the overall discrimination between the two teams. A single variable, if the players overlap, could be significant and yet actually detract from the overall discrimination. There will also be a strong correlation between a City forward and the United defender whose job is to mark him. 'Manova' detects a difference between the teams, discriminant analysis is analogous to walking round the pitch to find the place where such photographs will best distinguish them. The values of t correspond to the true distance between the average positions of the two players wearing their club's No. 11 shirt, but the line joining them will not be perpendicular to the photographer's line of sight, i.e. the perspective reduces their apparent distance from each other and the scaling factor corresponds to this.

Observation of selected elements

The attempt to observe everything the animal does has great advantages. It minimises how far you prejudge what kind of behaviour will be affected by the treatment and lets you treat one kind of behaviour as a built-in control for treatment effects on another. But the disadvantages can seem more formidable than they really are: the effort of transcribing data on to paper and the elaborate statistics. As an alternative if the background to the problem is well-enough known, a rational prediction may be possible about the kind of behaviour that is relevant, so that only a preselected set of elements need be observed and analysed; other information is regarded as not relevant.

This approach was taken by van der Poel and Remmelts (1971) in studying scopolamine. They isolated male rats for 10 days and then tested them six times at 3-day intervals, giving the drug at 3, 1, 0·3, 0·1, and 0·03 mg/kg and saline or, in a second experiment, 0·01 mg/kg as a dose believed to be too small to have any effect. Rats were first placed singly in a chamber for 5 minutes and observed on videotape. Exploration was not consistently changed by scopolamine and changes in maintenance elements were complex. Then an untreated partner was introduced for 5 minutes.

For each of the chosen elements, the regression was computed for occurrence (as a percentage of the control score) at each dose. The regression line for Attend was fairly flat, suggesting that scopolamine had little effect on this element. The line for Approach declined more steeply while Attack, Aggressive Groom, Dominate, and Bite were virtually absent at the highest dose. Retreat, Kick, and Submit were reduced in parallel with the aggressive elements, but Crouch was not. Scopolamine therefore seems to have reduced agonistic behaviour at very small doses fairly specifically, leaving

Crouch as a sign either of escape or of discomfort. The drug must have acted within the central nervous system because methylscopolamine, which does not get into the brain, had no effect at less than 10 mg/kg. Because these elements were more greatly affected the later they occur in Grant's sequences, van der Poel and Remmelts argue, the drug's action was not on the individual elements but on the pattern as a whole; to put a word into their mouths, on 'drive'.

This approach is attractive and pharmacologically careful, but its validity depends on every rat showing all the selected elements often enough in the control observations to make percentage changes meaningful. A fall from 2 to 1 is a fall of 50 per cent, which sounds a lot bigger than it is. In this particular experiment, van der Poel and Remmelts make no mention of the upright and sideways postures so common in other experiments, and I wonder why.

Repeated observations on rats – introducing isolates and parting pairs

If the differences between individuals are large, it is often helpful to observe the same animals several times under control and experimental conditions. Even a small experimental effect should then emerge clearly without being swamped by the variation between individuals. But for this to work, the successive observations must be independent. What you see must not depend on what the animal did on previous occasions.

Unfortunately, from this point of view, experience also has an effect – there is such a thing as conditioning. A single trial of exploration (see p. 262) influenced a repeat trial as much as 3 months later. In 'aggression tests' of isolated mice (Janssen et al., 1960; Kršiak, 1975) repeated introductions make the aggressive or timid response more reliable, in other words rigid. While there is only a little evidence to justify the impression, repeated introductions of rats seemed to make their performance progressively more stereotyped, as if the rats became conditioned to act in a particular way, and therefore less sensitive to the effects of small doses of drugs. Note that there is no reason to believe that the sequences of behaviour change. Grant originally calculated the transition probabilities between elements on data from repeated introductions, but he compared it with sequences observed in small undisturbed groups of rats, The findings were closely similar. What becomes stereotyped with repeated introductions is not the pathways available but the pathways actually followed.

Unfortunately, the timing of social behaviour in small groups is not under the experimenter's control. You can influence it a little by the light/dark cycle. The problem is to persuade the animals somehow to perform their normal ration of social behaviour, whatever that may be, at a convenient time. The behaviour of newly-introduced isolated rats seems too intense to be flexible.

social behaviour not under the experimenter's control

One possible solution appeared serendipitously in an experiment with vinyl acetate vapour. The vapour turned out to have only the slightest of effects (Silverman, 1970), but it happened that the exposure chamber was divided into individual compartments. Rats housed in pairs were therefore separated for 6 hours per day, 5 days a week, and were returned together to the home cage early in the daily dark period. After a few uneventful days of this routine, it became very noticeable how remarkably active they were in the first few minutes after their return home before settling down to breakfast and tranquillity. Even control rats looked as if they concentrated into a few hectic minutes the social behaviour normally spread over several hours. It would be wrong to overstate the 'normality' but the procedure ensures a high level of social activity which turns out to permit repeated observations on the same rat and which remains sensitive to delicate drug effects.

Separation and return: nicotine

It was thought that nicotine would provide a critical test of the sensitivity and accuracy of this revised rat social behaviour test. It appears that people smoke tobacco in order to give themselves a precisely regulated dose of nicotine, about 1–2 μg/kg per puff or about 15–30 μg/kg in a cigarette (Armitage, Hall, and Morrison, 1968). Monkeys and perhaps rats can learn an operant response to inject themselves with nicotine, but in no species is it altogether clear why. Rather mixed cardiovascular and EEG changes have been seen after puff-sized doses in animals and many a smoker remembers nausea and sweating after his first cigarette. People might start smoking out of curiosity or to feel grown up, and maintain smoking in the long run to ward off withdrawal symptoms, but why does anyone ever smoke a *second* time? Some people say that smoking helps them wake up, and nicotine accordingly stimulates rats' performance on several operant schedules (Morrison and Armitage, 1967) after at least 40 μg/kg. Other people find it 'calms their nerves' but tranquillising effects have not been reported in animals.

In the social behaviour experiment (Silverman, 1971) there were sixteen pairs of male rats, one albino and one hooded rat in each pair so that I could tell them apart. One rat (each strain alternately) was removed from

Social behaviour as an experimental method

the cage for a few hours every weekday, returning home soon after the laboratory lighting had switched to dim red (at about 15.00 hours). Observations were on Thursdays and Fridays, watching the home rat for 6 minutes after the return of his uninjected cage-mate.

The first observation was only a warm-up to accustom the rats to being observed (if the home and holding cages are put on the observation table a few minutes beforehand, extra exploration is reduced). The second, a week later, provided a baseline comparison of the rats that were later to be injected: as it turned out, there was a slight difference (just short of the 5 per cent probability level by discriminant analysis) since the randomly-allocated pre-nicotine rats showed a little less aggression and submission than controls (see Fig. 22.2).

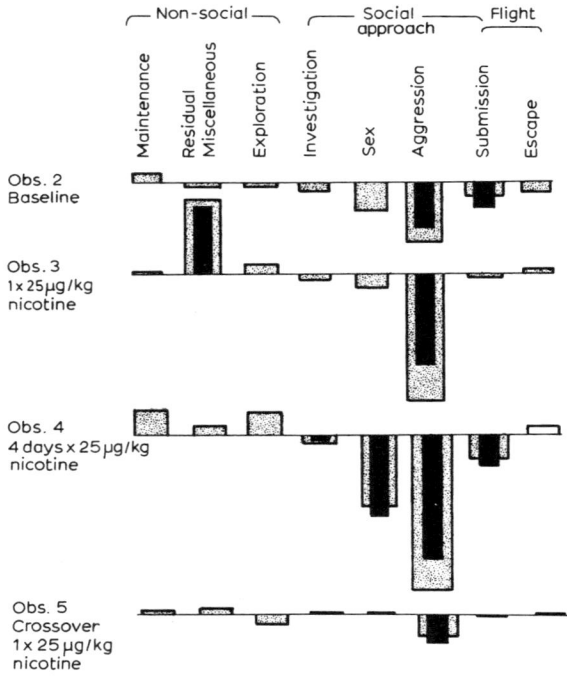

Fig. 22.2. Effect of a 'smoking dose' of nicotine on categories of behaviour in paired male rats returned after daily separation. Observation 1 had been a 'warm-up'; Observation 2 shows the baseline differences between the future experimental and control rats; Observation 3 immediately followed a single subcutaneous injection of nicotine (25 μg/kg) or saline to one rat of the pair. Observation 4 followed the last of four once-daily injections; and in Observation 5 the former control rats were given a single dose of nicotine. Differences were assessed by Discriminant Analysis. Outer hatched bars represent the contribution of each category to the overall discriminant function. Solid black bars represent the re-computed contribution after the stepwise elimination of categories not contributing significantly (after Silverman, 1971).

Immediately (i.e. about 30 seconds) before the third observation, the rats were injected subcutaneously, either with saline or a dose of 25 g/kg nicotine base, about what a person gets from a cigarette. The previous discrimination between the groups was doubled, mostly because aggression was reduced in the rats of both strains after nicotine. The residual category was also increased, mainly because the hooded rats, especially, repeatedly lifted their heads (as rats do in circumstances where other species might vomit) and occasionally staggered.

If nicotine made the rats 'feel sick' they would be expected to show less of any behaviour such as aggression, requiring initiative and activity. So after a week's pause, the rats were again separated and injected on 4 days in the hope of inducing some tolerance. Nevertheless, the difference between the groups after the series of doses was greater still, and was again due mainly to a decline in aggression. Other behaviour involving approach to the other rat (investigation, sex-related behaviour, and submission) was also slightly but significantly reduced by nicotine, but this time there were no signs of nausea. Aggression therefore could not have fallen as a consequence of nausea nor was there an increased tendency to escape nor any change in total activity to explain it. It was therefore reduced either specifically or as the kind of social behaviour most easily affected in this situation – sexual behaviour is fairly infrequent between males in any case, investigation is a necessary preliminary to anything else and submission a response to aggression.

The final observation was a crossover experiment, where the former controls received a single 25-μg/kg injection of nicotine, the former experimentals received saline. The overall difference between the groups faded to insignificance, but the ex-control rats that had formerly shown more aggression now showed less. They showed no signs of nausea or other autonomic effects.

The crossover design allows the animals to be considered as their own controls, and discriminant analysis showed the same results as before, with the addition that the ex-nicotine rats showed a little less escape in the final saline observation than they had previously – does nicotine slightly increase anxiety, or at least maintain it in susceptible individuals?

It appears therefore that there are stable differences between individual rats which can sometimes be detected in randomly selected groups, and that these differences mainly lie in the aggressive and submissive behaviour involved in social relationships. More interestingly as far as drugs are concerned, nicotine acted fairly specifically on just that aspect of behaviour which controls relationships, so that it added to or subtracted from the differences between individual animals.

One can argue that nicotine, like chlorpromazine (p. 322), probably did not affect sensory mechanisms in any simple way because there was no change in exploration or investigation; nor did it cause a simple motor change because upright postures or fast acts in several categories (had they been affected) would not have caused a significant fall only in one.

The near specificity of the drug's apparent effect on aggression is interesting. But suppose that aggression merely reflected a fall in total activity ... Or if escape was really increased, as one comparison suggested it might be, that would itself inhibit aggression. However, multiple linear regression equations showed that while albinos were more active than hooded rats and showed less escape, nicotine-injected rats of either strain were neither more nor less active than saline controls, and escape formed a virtually constant 16 ± 0.7 per cent of total activity; the effect of nicotine on escape turned out

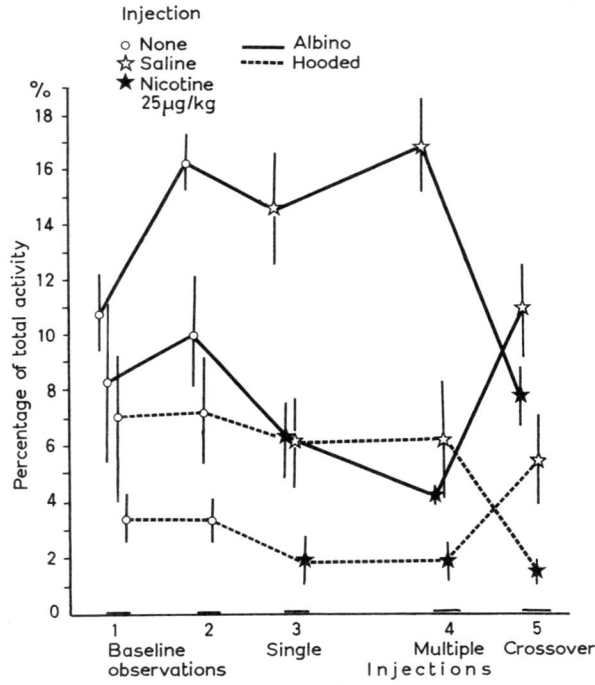

Fig. 22.3. Aggression as a proportion of total activity is reduced by nicotine. Data from the same experiment as Fig. 22.2. Continuous lines show albino rats, experimental and control, dashed lines show hooded rats (one of each strain was in each cage). Mean and standard error for groups of eight rats. Stars represent observations after an injection (after Silverman, 1971).

to be quite insignificant. On the other hand, aggression was reduced by half in every group (Fig. 22.3). Nausea, had that been the cause, would more likely have inhibited aggression altogether, if only in certain affected individuals. Since the correlation between aggression and escape, though significant, was fairly low ($r = -0.374$), it looks as if the drug's effect on aggression was fairly specific.

In behaviour, of course, specificity is not absolute, if only because a change in one kind of behaviour is always likely to have consequences on other kinds. Nor can you have a behavioural effect without a physiological cause, a change in the pattern of firing of neurones, and this in turn depends on a biochemical change somewhere. But nicotine's effect on aggression does not seem to have been secondary to anything else at a behavioural level; and for that matter the known cardiovascular or electroencephalographic changes cannot easily be related to it. It seems a reasonable model in animal terms for the calming effect of tobacco.

It might be interesting to try to adapt the social behaviour test to look for the stimulation suggested by operant methods. Maybe nicotine should be given when the rate of activity is likely to be lower, perhaps on Mondays after a weekend off. In the present experiment, the animals were fairly active, about two elements were observed every 3 seconds. While higher rates have been observed, up to 127 in 1 minute or 315 in 3, there is clearly a limit both to the animal's ability to perform and to the observer's ability to record, and stimulant effects can only be revealed when controls are well below the ceiling. 'Arousal', as neurophysiologists sometimes discuss it, compares sleeping and waking rather than what, on an ordinary-language scale, is called 'drowsy–alert–excited'. Maybe nicotine has a centralising action, bringing drowsy or over-excited animals towards the middle of the waking range.

Aggression is not reduced by all drugs. Certainly many drugs reduce it, either fairly specifically or as a secondary consequence of a wide variety of other actions some of which depend on environmental circumstances more than others (e.g. perhaps the drowsiness from trichloroethylene). But in some circumstances, low doses of barbiturates can increase aggression (Silverman, 1966b; Kršiak, 1975), and so can apomorphine (Senault, 1977).

Development of the social behaviour test – male chauvinist rats?

We have begun to use 'cross-introductions' of paired rats, by returning separated rats to somebody else's cage. Present impressions are that social approach is reduced, partly because one rat has to explore the unfamiliar cage, but the rats may be more wary with strangers. The procedure may be worth testing as a mild stress.

In long-term experiments, where frequent full-scale observations of the details of social behaviour are too laborious, it might be worth while to use a machine of the 'animex' type (see p. 82) to monitor the gross activity of the separated rats on return home daily. Detailed observation could then be used at intervals as a check, or if the gross activity indicated something interesting.

Daily separation and return might be useful with female rats too. Females have been unduly neglected, partly because their agonistic behaviour is thought to be sporadic or related to the oestrous cycle, so that the experimenter has less control or more work. Females possess all the male's repertoire – is it true that they fight less than males? That they fight more at oestrous, and that in effect they use aggression to attract attention, to attack, then retreat, stop, crouch, and be mounted? Is there any pattern of behaviour characteristic of any other stage of the cycle? Could female or breeding pairs provide a more useful model for drug effects than all-male pairs? For example, changes in aggression were tentatively attributed to changes in responsiveness to stimuli by introducing isolated males to females (Silverman, 1966b), since sexual behaviour was then changed instead.

Cross-introductions of paired mice

Mackintosh and Grant (1966) housed mice in pairs, and found that aggression increased in proportion to the unfamiliarity of an intruder's smell. Aggression was least if a mouse was removed from its cage, rubbed on the anal region with a bit of wet cotton wool and returned 10 minutes later. Aggressive elements were more frequent, on average, if the mouse was rubbed with cotton wool soaked in urine from a mouse in another cage, were further increased if the unfamiliar mouse was put into the waiting home-mouse's cage after being rubbed in urine from the familiar ex-cage mate and were maximal if the stranger was just dabbed in wet cottonwool. No doubt the unfamiliar mouse's responses also play a part, but most of the aggression was shown by the home mouse, most of the escape by the intruder. The technique is an ingenious way of investigating some stimuli involved in social behaviour.

Mackintosh also noticed that territory-owning male mice attacked male but not female inhabitants (1970). Keith Dixon and Mackintosh (1975) used the soaked-cottonwool technique to confirm this. Urine was collected from a female mouse simply by holding her by the scruff of the neck over a funnel, and the urine from several females was pooled. Some were in oestrous, some in the unreceptive stage of the cycle, and some had been ovariectomised, but urine from all groups greatly reduced aggression in male mice, whether they were cage-mates or strangers. Aggression was not inhibited by fear since the duration of flight was also reduced. Since it is the intruder who carries the smell, it must be (and nearly always is) the home mouse that starts the quarrel, and he was affected most. You might not be surprised that a lusty male mouse fails to attack another who carries a female smell on top of his own – he would be puzzled even if he was not tempted in other directions, and certainly social investigation and sex-related elements increased. However, sexual behaviour rose mostly in response to 'oestrous' urine and otherwise did not increase much more than exploration and self-grooming: Dixon and Mackintosh did not distinguish these (in print) so that it is not

arousing sexual interest

clear whether urine-damped mice spend longer than merely wet ones in cleaning themselves up. They argued that all female urine contains a factor directly inhibiting aggression, or at least nothing that provokes it as male urine does. The chivalry-factor can thus be found throughout the oestrous cycle and in females without ovaries; the factor arousing sexual interest seems to be separate, occurring only at the appropriate stage.

Margaret Cutler, Mackintosh and Chance (1975a, b) used a variant of the cross-introduction procedure to examine the effects of cannabis (a mixture of Δ^9-THC and other cannabinols) either injected at 4 to 100 mg/kg or fed at 0·4 per cent in the diet for 2 weeks. Male mice were paired for a week, the dominant identified, marked with hair-dye, and introduced for 10 minutes to the subordinate from another pair in a neutral observation cage. Introductions were of one cannabis-injected mouse to a control or of two mice from the same diet-group. In both cases, the drug produced a characteristic immobility, the mouse flopping weakly on to the floor to an extent proportional to the log of the dose, and non-social behaviour was reduced in parallel. Aggression was not changed but Flight by the dominant mouse was increased as a function of dose, but only as an exaggeration of the response to any aggression by the partner. Submissive mice did not change their behaviour. It is interesting that people taking Δ^9-THC are said to feel paranoid, to feel that they are being stared at, and also that these mice showed intensified fighting when the cannabis diet was withdrawn.

Summary

In a social situation, it is more than usually obvious that behaviour is complex, and therefore that it offers more information, particularly on the balance between different kinds of behaviour. Fighting is the most conspicuous kind but is not a single, simple unit. It has an internal structure, by definition involving at least aggression and a tendency to flee from the other animal.

The variety of information available requires observational methods. To

Social behaviour as an experimental method

be objective, it is assumed that behaviour is composed of pre-existing units not conditioned by the experimenter, and that the sequence in which the animal selects units from this repertoire contains relevant information. These elements can be recognised and used as a basis for interpretation, provided that they are explicitly described as accurately and unambiguously as possible.

To obtain a high rate of social activity at a time under the experimenter's control, there are two main techniques. The first is to isolate rats or mice for no more than a few days and then introduce one into the home cage of another, inducing a fairly intense form of all social tendencies, including Flight, as if the animals had been starved of rodent companionship. Alternatively, the animals are housed in pairs: with mice, one mouse is removed and replaced for some minutes with an unfamiliar mouse from another pair or with the smell of an unfamiliar mouse's urine added. With rats, a pair is separated for a few hours every weekday, and after a few days a brief period of high activity occurs on return to the home cage. This technique has been shown to be exceptionally sensitive to low doses of drugs and to allow repeated observations which remain drug-sensitive.

Since behaviour of several kinds can be observed, a lack of effect on one kind of behaviour can be exploited as an internal control for the effects of a treatment on another. Although social behaviour involves some laborious transcription of the spoken record of the data, and although attention has to be given to the appropriate statistical methods of analysis, the technique therefore saves time in the long run. Since there are measures of several kinds of behaviour, the hypotheses which can possibly explain a given result are few, and so fewer follow-up experiments are necessary to distinguish between them.

TWENTY-THREE
Sociobiology: ecology and the function of social aggression

Behaviour which can plausibly be compared with human aggression is probably universal in higher animals, certainly in all vertebrates and some invertebrates where it has been looked for. Because of this and because it is elaborately ritualised in a context of behaviour related to investigation, sex, and flight, it does not seem likely that aggression is necessarily pathological in itself. No doubt aggression can be exaggerated to a pathological degree, like any other breakdown in the system, but in the right context it must have evolutionary value. Considering how destructive human aggression can often be, a positive selection pressure is surprising – what is its function?

Apart from its intrinsic interest, the question is worth discussing because it helps us to evaluate practical laboratory methods and to interpret the results. Tests of aggression were described in Chapter 20 and tentative distinctions were drawn between different kinds. Several of those induced experimentally (by drugs, shock, prolonged isolation, etc.) were thought to be in one way or another caricatures of 'normal' agonistic behaviour – caricatures in the sense that in order to isolate one aspect of behaviour for practical laboratory work, they are both exaggerated and oversimplified. Any such abnormality, of course, may yet be found to be much like that of human behaviour in mental illness, and therefore a valid model to test therapeutic drugs. But a resemblance between experimental distortions of animal behaviour and pathological distortions of human needs direct investigation.

Spontaneous behaviour observable every day in an intact group of animals is much more flexible within a complex but easily-understood system, and in Chapter 22 it was claimed to provide, as a rule, a generally superior measure of the effects of drugs and other treatments. The advantages claimed are mainly practical, in sensitivity over repeated tests to low doses, in sensitivity to several kinds of drug effects, and especially in the ability to discriminate between various behavioural modes of action. I also believe that this more flexible complex pattern is closer to the 'normal' behaviour of animals outside captivity and is therefore more likely to be homologous in its fundamental features to human behaviour. The belief is not easily subject to experimental test, but the reasons for it will become apparent from a discussion of the survival value of the social behaviour of which aggression is a part.

Population explosions

Thomas Malthus (1798, revised 1803) pointed out that any human population is liable to expand but food and other resources are in the long run limited. There must therefore be increasing competition for food in which the strong will grab all they need and the weak will get what is left. The population ends up in a steady state because the 'surplus' starves. Malthus was wrong in fact, at least for the first century and a half, because the agricultural and industrial revolutions that started in his lifetime increased the resources on the other side of the equation. Nevertheless, he must be right in principle. The fact is not altered by the unpleasant misinterpretation put upon his theory by people with socioeconomic power in his time: acting as if what is inevitable is also morally right, as if Malthus made it a social duty to grind the faces of the poor.

Charles Darwin saw that competition for resources applies to all living things. A tree produces millions of seeds a year, many fish produce thousands of eggs. If two survive to reproduce themselves instead of one, the population doubles at the price of an infinitesimal change to the food supply of seed- or egg-eaters. The seeds inevitably compete (in effect) for a safe niche in the warm earth, and seed-eaters compete to find the last available seed that failed. Darwin saw how normal variations between seed-eaters could lead to specialisation. If one individual is a little cleverer at detecting half-buried seeds, another has to move a little quicker to get to those left exposed. In the face of competition, variation leads to specialisation and then, so far as the variation is genetic, to speciation because it allows a higher standard of living.

Yet animal populations are much more nearly stable in numbers, up to a point, than you might expect. Of course species whose life-span is very short are strictly opportunistic: aphids are adapted to population explosions every summer and crashes every autumn. Severe weather – drought, flood, or frost – can cause havoc in any species. Nevertheless, boom-and-bust population crises like those of lemmings or aphids are conspicuous just because they are exceptional. Nor is nature really 'red in tooth and claw', the law of the jungle is obeyed without obvious policemen. You seldom see sick or starving animals (some of the exceptions are due to man, e.g. in overcrowded wildlife reserves or where pollution is heavy). Starving animals would be most vulnerable to predators and would disappear for that reason, of course. Nevertheless, malnutrition is much less conspicuous and seems to be less common in animals than in some human societies.

The population problem and social behaviour

These subjects are related to social behaviour by the suggestion that behaviour provides mechanisms which limit reproduction as much as they promote it, that the limitation is related to food supply, and that the selective value of the system is to stabilise population numbers.

related to food supply

Factors controlling numbers can be considered under two headings – those that are not particularly related to the size or density of the population (accidents, bad weather, etc.), and those that are density-dependent. Thus, the bigger the population in a given area, the harder it will be for all individuals to find enough food, and the easier it will be for predators or parasites to find and feed on them. In the test-tube, protozoan or yeast populations are inhibited in density-dependent fashion by pollution from the organisms' own metabolic products. However, although density-dependent factors must exist, their importance has been questioned, notably by H. C. Andrewartha. For example, lions, eagles, and other predators are not themselves preyed upon, they are rarely diseased, yet they maintain a population that is both very stable and very low. In wild animals, population density is closely correlated with food supply. Man and his cattle frequently suffer from overgrazing or overfishing: the former huge populations of passenger pigeon or American buffalo have been hunted to death. The herring in the Baltic and North seas and whales everywhere are not far from extinction because man cannot, or does not, limit his exploitation to cropping a sustainable yield. V. C. Wynne-Edwards pointed out (1964) 'that animals face precisely this danger with respect to their food supply, and they generally handle it more prudently than man does'.

Consider birds that feed on seeds and berries over the winter. If there is 6 months' supply for ten birds it must look in autumn as if there is plenty – enough for sixty, except that they would all starve after a month. In fact, small passerine birds are capable of living at least 3 or 4 years, and annual mortality is 'only' 50 per cent.

In man, faced with a clear-cut threat of overfishing, the first thought is a straightforward agreement to limit catches, but in practice there are difficulties. The present whaling agreement makes one blue whale equal to 3·5 fin whales, I believe, which is fine for the accountants but unhelpful to a blue whale looking for a mate. And there is always the suspicion that somebody else is not obeying the rules. So the more practical method used in fisheries, human nature being what it is, is to allow each group of people its own area. In each country's territorial waters, only its nationals are allowed to fish.

Enforcement is easier through national courts, and above all, those who restrain themselves now have some confidence that they themselves will reap the benefit next season, not some thieving foreigners. In short, competition is diverted, disputes are no longer directly for the desired resource, but for an area of sea, useless in itself except in giving access to the resource. Man has also evolved a stage further still; we compete for something even more symbolic, money.

Wynne-Edwards argued that social behaviour in animals provides just such a set of conventional, symbolic substitutes. Instead of a free-for-all scramble to compete for a fluctuating and limited food supply, animals compete for territory or hierarchical status. In the simplest form, each territory contains within its boundaries the resources for one breeding pair to bring up their family. Alternatively, a population of sea-birds, gulls for example, compete on land for nesting sites within a restricted colony area − there may be plenty of suitable nest sites which the colony could expand into but they do not. Otherwise they would deplete the stocks of fish they feed on far away. The actual nest site bears no direct relationship to the food supply, but the total number of birds permitted to breed is correlated with the food resources within range. Some animals compete merely for status in a group. Only those accepted into the group, or achieving a certain status within it, are able to breed.

In many species, sexual differentiation is related to this, in that the female has the hard work of gathering food to supply the eggs, or giving milk to the young, while the male concentrates on achieving and defending a territory or rank in a group. The extra males excluded from a herd of deer or wild cattle, the extra birds that fail to win a territory, act in effect as a reserve. Should the more successful breeder-leader or territory owner meet with an accident, or lose his grip, there are enough and to spare to take his place. The actual population that can be supported is bigger than the number able to breed.

In the long run food supply must obviously set limits to population size, but it is clearly not the only factor, and the mechanism is by no means clear. Wynne-Edwards (1964) quotes a population of red grouse (*Lagopus scoticus*) near Aberdeen. In the year when the heather they fed on was poorest, there were only sixteen large territories. Two years previously there had been forty, and 1 year later there were twenty-eight, some of them occupied by cocks who had once insisted on much larger territories. In all years, cocks occupying a few of the smaller territories remained unmated. Presumably in a good year, there are more birds vigorous enough to compete. Equally, if each grouse finds its food on or near its territory, the area it fights for might be related to the effort of finding enough to eat. It is the time-lag I find hard to understand. Many species establish their territories in early spring or late winter − do they have to predict the weather next summer when the young will require most feeding?

When a change in the size of a breeding colony is accompanied by a change in food resources, you cannot tell which came first. Colonies of gulls which have been carefully watched, for example at Ravenglass and at Bass Rock, have grown substantially larger over the last 20 years or so. In the same period, gulls which at one time obtained most of their food by fishing at sea, greatly increased a habit of scavenging from man, from rubbish thrown overboard from ships and later from rubbish dumps on land. I do not know if these phenomena are really related, but on the face of it you could equally well argue that the exploitation of a new source of supply has allowed the breeding colony to grow, or that the growing population pressure has forced a versatile group of birds to eat whatever they can get.

The question of how animals *estimate* their population size seems easier. Wynne-Edwards drew attention to the conspicuous noisy aggregations of many species at certain times of day or season: the dawn chorus of birds, the swarms of starlings and of midges on summer evenings, the mating-flight of ants, the croaking of frogs, the annual congress of the Palolo worm. Most of the time is left free for the individual to eat and sleep, but the whole population of a locality meets regularly for short periods at times synchronised by dawn or dusk or the tide, at the season when it is important to know how big the breeding population is. The dense visual packing of the swarm, the noisy singing, should give sensory stimuli proportional to the aggregate numbers of animals present.

The argument is that this information is translated into competition for dominance or territory so that ultimately the denser the population, the lower the proportion that breeds successfully. Hence, while death rates are under the control of external agencies, some dependent on density and some not, birth rates are partly under the animals' own control.

This is not to say that the method is comfortable and painless, for all that physical damage is rare in animal fighting, but it is better than starving. The heartache of the old maid, the gloom of the unemployed have their animal analogies. John Price (1967) wondered if depressive mood could have an adaptive function. An old incapable and dispossessed dominant male, an ambitious second-rater or would-be territory owner who failed, would be disruptive to the group if they continued to struggle in vain. Depression takes them quietly right out of the rat race, miserable but out of harm's way. There is little experimental support for the idea but it is intuitively attractive.

The genetics of 'altruism'

A serious difficulty is the question of how social behaviour ever evolved if its function is primarily to *limit* reproduction. An animal which failed to breed because it could not become dominant would be unable to pass on its genes to future generations despite the long-term advantage to the population as a whole. For an otherwise identical population whose members reproduced to the maximum allowed by the immediate physical conditions would obviously have a great short-term advantage. But when winter comes, they could die out entirely. The self-limiting population would have husbanded its resources, in effect, and a nucleus will survive the seven lean months till better times come round.

However, when a mutation first arises, it can only occur in one individual at a time, and if it is to reach a future generation it must confer a selective advantage on that individual. However small the advantage may be, a mutation cannot last if it can only confer an advantage by preventing its own passage to future generations. So how did the mechanism begin?

The details of the answer have not been worked out but the principle is well known to any self-made businessman or peasant – keep it in the family. A parent feeds its young because the young pass on its genes to grandchildren or, more accurately in diploid species, an average of 50 per cent of its genes. But the parent's brother or sister is also likely to carry 50 per cent of the same genes, so any help given to a sister will contribute to their spread through the population in future. Hamilton (1964) expressed this formally by saying that the 'inclusive fitness' of a gene depends not only on what it does to the reproductive success of the individual carrying it, but also on indirect help or harm to the individual's relatives; the latter is, however, scaled down in proportion to how distant the relationship is. Thus the benefit to your sister has to be more than twice its cost to you; investment in a nephew is only worthwhile if he gets more than four times what you give, since he only carries 25 per cent of your genes. Conversely an individual is selected to avoid a selfish act if its cost to a relative (discounted by the degree of relatedness) is greater than the benefit.

Hamilton's theory of altruism has been worked out most fully in social insects like ants and bees, because their extremes of social behaviour have been shown to result from their peculiar genetic system. Since males develop from unfertilised eggs with a half set of genes, sisters turn out to share not half but three-quarters of their genes, and it is advantageous for the gene if they invest in their mother's offspring rather than their own in most circumstances. Robert Trivers and Hope Hare (1976) are fascinating about the details of demographic structure and social behaviour to be explained by the theory.

In principle the theory also explains why populations remain in one geographical area, why birds may migrate across continents to mate and breed where they were hatched. For in an outbred but essentially immobile population most of your neighbours are likely to be also your cousins. If the whole breeding population competes for territories, even those that fail and therefore do not breed nevertheless benefit from their self-denial. For the winners carry some of the non-breeders' genes, and their benefit from the altruism is in the long run, enormous.

The winners are still likely to insist on the territorial system and to try to prevent the proletariat from breeding, however, because landowners are more closely related to their offspring than to their landless cousins. Charity is only an investment when it begins at home.

A mechanism for refraining from breeding is not difficult to imagine in principle, provided we do not let our human awareness of what we are doing mislead us about animals. We can deliberately choose to behave sexually, animals probably cannot imagine things in advance. It is only necessary to postulate that before sexual behaviour can start, the animals must have achieved the necessary status: a territory, a nest, or whatever qualifications the species has evolved. The right form of aggression might be almost as important a preliminary, perhaps, as the presence of a partner.

Aggression as a means of obtaining status and a licence to breed is therefore quite distinct from self-defence against a predator (including an experimenter), and even from the mobbing of an owl by a screaming, wheeling flock of chaffinches. Both are distinct from the predator's own hunting and killing for food. The weak and sporadic squabbling directly over food that can sometimes be seen in laboratory rodents and in winter flocks of starlings is something else again. It is premature to say that these forms of 'aggression' have nothing in common or that those induced by shock, lesions, etc. (Chapter 20) are merely artefacts. They may yet turn out to represent the same physiological system, but it seems safer at this stage to consider them separately.

Behaviour, nutrition, and ecology

The integration of anatomy and sociology with the ways in which animals earn their living is beautifully illustrated by Jarman (1974). Antelopes are all herbivores but their social organisation varies widely. Jarman explained this by their nutrition. Grasses grow with about 4 per cent protein throughout the plant but concentrate the growth in time, whereas dicotyledonous plants may be woody and inedible as a whole but continuously grow fresh leaves and buds containing 15 per cent protein. Herbivorous animals can therefore be tissue-selective, browsing on highly-nutritious growing-points, or they can be plant-selective for the species they feed on, or they can be relatively unselective. Jarman classified antelopes loosely into five classes on this basis.

Extremely tissue-selective animals have to be quite small to select a young leaf off a small bush in open woodland. The leaves are nutritious so they need to eat relatively small amounts, but they will in effect remove all the food from one plant at a time. The food will be therefore dispersed, and so will the animals feeding on it, but if they know a small area thoroughly, a pair can find enough to support them for years at a time. Yet being small, they are vulnerable to predators and in any case cannot afford to run far from the area they know. Tissue-selective antelope therefore are small and shy, secretive, and nocturnal. If surprised, they freeze; if detected, they run a short way and hide. To their own species, they are strongly territorial, solitary, or paired for life. Their eyes are lateral to see predators coming from all directions and they mark their territories inconspicuously by scent.

Class B animals (reedbuck, lesser kudu, etc.) are a little less selective in drier country, with food more scattered. Males hold solitary territories, females wander more freely through the territories rather than sharing in defence, because they have to travel further to feed the young. At the opposite extreme are the largest (type E) antelopes, buffalo, and eland, which eat grass. They have to eat large quantities since the nutritional value is lower and is spread throughout the plant, but since they eat so much of the plant, the whole of a herd grazing close together can still obtain enough. However, the herds have to migrate to follow the growth spurt of the grass over wide areas, so that there is no opportunity to hold a spatial territory. In open grassland, there is not much chance to hide from a predator, but the large size needed to deal with large quantities of low energy food also means that only the largest predators need apply. Even the biggest can regret it, for buffalo defend themselves and will defend even a single attacked young. They rely on numbers to detect a predator, to distract him from selecting a single victim, and to counter-attack safely. So they live in quite large herds, with a fixed female membership as well as a dominance rank-order of several reproductive males, and there are bachelor herds that separate from and merge with the reproductive ones. Since no spatial territory is possible with visible or olfactory boundary-signs, the hierarchical males need flamboyant displays of spectacular shadow-boxing to establish dominance. Herds wander over a fairly fixed range. There is little obvious competition between herds, but remarkably little overlap either.

Typical antelope like Grant's and Thomson's gazelles, impala, and so on are intermediate in tissue- and species-selectivity, and intermediate in size (type C). They live in woodland or open country, some of them in both, according to season. They freeze if they spot a predator, or in open country move towards him, watching. If alarmed, they run fast and far with eyes directly forward to detect obstacles. Only a mother might attempt to defend her young. Males may take solitary territories for a season, rich enough to attract females for a time, insufficient to support even one animal throughout the year. Territorial males nevertheless tolerate bachelor bands and the larger, fluctuating female herds wander freely. Territory owners may try to capture a female but fail, the females choose where to stay. Bachelor herds have a dominance order, and only the top rankers try to obtain a territory. Displays can be audible: Uganda kob whistle and impala roar, they have characteristic gaits and postures, they dig horns symbolically into the earth. Kob form a lek like grouse, with miniature territories for breeding in, while non-territorial but randy males have to try to drive a female long distances. At the end of the rut, territories collapse when their resources are exhausted, and large migrating herds may form.

Larger species like wildebeest (Jarman's class D) may have seasonal territories or may form mobile ones, one male driving off others from round the place where some females have gathered during a temporary pause in migration.

A correlation exists, Jarman points out, between diet, body size, anti-predator tactics, social organisation, and quite small details of the social behaviour maintaining that organisation. In an evolutionary sense, the diet that a species chooses to exploit goes a long way towards dictating even such details as whether a pair bonds throughout at least one season and whether the young are rejected by the mother after they are fully weaned or retain membership of a stable herd.

The essential point is that behaviour is an integrated whole. When you come down to detail, you can only separate social behaviour from feeding or anti-predator behaviour as an aid to analysis; in real life they are all at one with each other, with anatomy (body size, the position of the eyes in the head, the length of the gut, the presence of scent glands), with diet, habitat, ecological niche, and evolutionary history, in short with biology as a whole.

Social behaviour disrupted

If social behaviour's function is to act as an automated homeostatic governor of population size in relation to food supply, it should be possible to test this function by experimentally manipulating food supply.

Population studies have been made in laboratory cages, but from the husbandry point of view, where artificial emigration solves the population crisis, and you have a steady supply of rats for experiment. On a larger scale, population studies have been made in enclosures with plenty of nest sites and with excess food supplied (e.g. Crowcroft and Rowe, 1963).

There are also some studies full of apocalyptic rhetoric from the Book of Revelation about the doom of mankind; and though new enclosure is but old cage writ large, there are some uncomfortable parallels between mouse and man.

John Calhoun (1973) built a galvanised iron 'universe' 2·57 m square by 1·37 m high. The top 43 cm was left sheer to prevent the mice climbing out, but the rest of the walls were covered with vertical mesh tubes that the mice could climb into at floor level and up to nest boxes – a total of 256 high-rise apartments, each big enough for fifteen mice. If the mice climbed up the outside of the wall, they could reach a food hopper half-way up, with water-bottles higher still, and an excess of food, water, and paper strips for nesting always available. The place was kept warm, 20 °C up to 30 °C in summer, and infections were kept at too low a level for disease to have been important.

Four pairs of Balb-C mice were isolated 21 days from weaning and introduced into the enclosure amid considerable turmoil, and the first litters were born as long as 104 days later. The population grew exponentially for the next 6–7 months and then more slowly, doubling only every 145 days. Censuses showed an unequal number of young in each segment of the enclosure wall; each segment contained four 'walk-up apartments' with sixteen nest-boxes containing from 13 to 111 young.

In the early stages, the young were well-cared for and healthy. The 'universe' provided ample space, and was notably well-structured in terms of nest-boxes, tubes to climb, and so on. There were no predators, and there was constant replenishment of an ample food supply. At first, therefore, there were no limits to growth, at least none external to the mice, for the number of young in a group was related to the degree of dominance of the dominant male in the area. The territorial boundaries were determined more or less by the physical structure of the enclosure, one segment of the wall defining a social unit of population, the group inhabiting one defended territory. At the point of change in population growth-rate, there were about 150 adults in all and 470 young.

In the wild state any young that survive healthily to maturity but can find no room to live at home, emigrate. That was how all the segments of the enclosure came to be occupied. Once the preferred places in the enclosure were occupied, these mice could emigrate no further, nor were they picked up and eaten by cats or owls or by bacterial infections for that matter. The excess mice who failed in the competition tended to withdraw. Females retired to the upper, less-preferred nest-boxes, males gathered glumly in the centre of the floor. The syndrome irresistibly provokes a facile comparison with human cities and with human depression. The 'excess' mice did not initiate interactions with other mice, particularly the territorial ones, and they were themselves ignored. However, when a couple of males returned to the crowd after eating or drinking, the resulting disturbance often precipitated one of the quiescent, apparently withdrawn males into sudden vicious attack. The immobile mice did not try to escape, nor did they fight back, but received some nasty wounds; and an attacked mouse would itself attack others at some later stage. The females, withdrawn into their high-rise nests and without offspring, were not vicious.

With huge numbers of mice wandering about, the territorially dominant males were increasingly hard put to repel invaders, or expel obstreperous young whipper-snappers from their own group. As time went on they defended smaller territories and patrolled less meticulously, with the result that wandering mice more often blundered through the nests. The lactating females, who previously could remain peaceable, had to take over the role of territorial defence; but their aggressiveness generalised to their own older young, who were attacked, wounded, and forced to leave home before normal weaning, presumably to join the layabouts roaming the central area. Fewer conceptions took place, more foetuses were resorbed, young were more often injured during birth, and whole litters disappeared between censuses. Females restlessly transported their litters from one nest-box to another, and sometimes abandoned them in the process.

Population increase stopped 'abruptly' 560 days after the colony was founded, and the last surviving infants died about day 600. Older mice survived, but the conception rate declined and there were no births. The last conception was about day 920, and though some mice lived 2 years longer, the population was (at the time Calhoun wrote this) not expected to continue.

From about half-way through the phase of slower population growth, nearly all the young were badly brought up – they were rejected before normal weaning, they had not formed 'adequate affective bonds', and the sheer numbers of mice moving about physically prevented coherent social interactions. In a sample of females nearly a year old, only 18 per cent had ever conceived, only 2 per cent were actually pregnant, and all three of these females had but a single foetus. Their male counterparts, 'the beautiful ones', never fought, but confined themselves to eating, drinking, sleeping, and grooming their healthy fur. Such mice of either sex could be picked up and transported into other enclosures at low densities, but even with well brought-up partners were unable to interact socially. Calhoun went so far as to call them autistic-like. His model universe – if valid – is a frightening one.

'This is the way the world ends, not with a bang but a whimper.'

TWENTY-FOUR

A comparison of laboratory and wild rodents

'There be land rats and water rats, I mean pirates.'

Laboratory animals lead pampered lives within their confined cages. They are kept warm but not too hot, in air-conditioned comfort. They toil not for their daily bread, neither do they spin, their house is rent- and mortgage-free. And in consequence they are idle and maybe bored, they have neither materials nor opportunity for anything but to grow fat and lazy. In Chapter 20, some experiments were summarised on solitary laboratory rats, group-housed rats, and those brought up in 'enriched' environments with toys to play with, and how they differ in behaviour and learning ability. It is easy to extrapolate to the view that even the best laboratory animals are soft, degenerate creatures compared to their tough, hard-bitten wild cousins. (Similarly 'civilised' urban man?) Laboratory selection is for fecundity and docility, in order to raise dense populations rapidly from small numbers of parents, amenable to handling by the experimenter, and crowding by each other without stress. And indeed laboratory rats have smaller adrenals and a lower output of corticosteroid hormones than wild rats, or the descendants of confined wild rats, bred and brought up in the laboratory and accustomed to the conditions.

Are all behavioural experiments on laboratory rats a waste of time then? At best restricted to models of civilisation, at worst mere academic exercises? For this reason alone, laboratory-bred and wild animals have to be compared, for if they are really very different in important ways, then we had better stop breeding the one and catch some more of the other.

The rat-catchers' stories

Like electronics, ergonomics, and nuclear physics the scientific study of the behaviour of wild rats received its greatest impetus during the Second World War, when the political authorities, a practical problem, and the people who had, or could take, an interest in the topic for its own sake, came together. And in the years around 1950 the fruits were published of a concern to make pest-control more efficient, more scientifically based, and less crafty.

The respect which wild rats evoke is apparent in Harry V. Thompson's observations (1953) of rats in traps, or rather not in them. With the simplest trap, he had to watch for hours nearby and then pull a string to close the door when he judged the time ripe. He caught twenty-three rats in four pulls in 4·5 hours – but 14–16 hours later very few rats entered the trap although at least ten raked out some of the bait through its wire sides. Perhaps the first trial catches the more reckless rats so that only the more cautious are left for later attempts. Later observations, when still fewer rats entered the cage, supported the idea of 'trap shyness', as if an active warning spread through the population in a few hours.

Thompson made most observations with the 'Wonder' trap patented by Henri Marty in 1883 (Fig. 24·1). He pre-baited for a few days first, leaving wheat grains in the rear compartment with the rear access door left open.

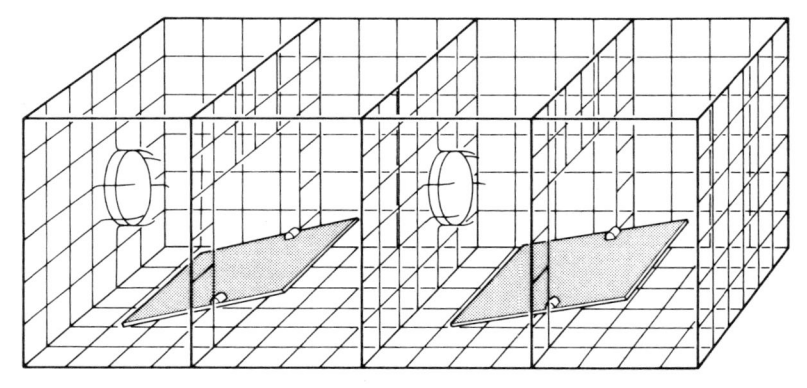

Fig. 24.1. Sketch of a double 'Wonder' trap (after Thompson, 1953). Four chambers have entrances that rats are intended to pass one way only, through a lobster-pot entrance or over a tip-up platform.

Thompson then watched for 20 minutes daily. The rats were very timid at first, scuttling home at the least sound, notably the squeak of one rat trodden on by another. Gradually more of the visits ended with a rat taking the bait, but only two rats passed into the front compartment, even though the tip-up platform was held open. On a normal day there were 100–300 visits in all, but there were far fewer on the day or two after a different food was offered as bait, and only seven visits on a day of heavy rain. When the traps were finally set and the back door closed, many rats scratched food through the wire, but it took 25 minutes before the first rat entered the front compartment. He stepped gingerly on the tip-up platform twice, fled out through the lobster-pot entrance, came slowly back 2 minutes later, and stepped timidly on the platform three times before stretching through to take some of the bait – but holding the platform down with his hindlegs and withdrawing to eat in the front room. A minute later, he was finally caught, struggling vainly for 12 minutes before being removed. Next day, five rats were caught, after which no rats were seen at all for 3 days, though some food was taken from the upset trap overnight. With further pre-baiting and setting the platforms to wobble but not tip up, rats began to visit. However, when rats were later caught, they mostly escaped again. Small rats squeezed between the wires, larger ones either made partial visits by holding the platform steady with their hindlegs or escaped by climbing over the back of the next partial visitor. And their frenzied struggles scattered free gifts of bait outside the trap.

Thompson then made a double Wonder cage from two in series (see Fig. 24.1), set the platforms to wobble without tipping, and prebaited in com-

'But the nurse said – "I will buy a mouse trap!"' (*after Beatrix Potter, 1904*).

partment 3. Ten minutes after the trap was finally set, the first visitor calmly walked in, helped himself to a mouthful of wheat, and let himself out by operating the tip-up from inside. He did this repeatedly, pulling it down with a forepaw, sometimes after first pushing it from the top. In 9 days, at least five rats from a farm population became experts in this way, presumably after 'partial visits'. Remarkably enough, though, each rat had to learn for itself and trapped rats could not learn to escape by imitating the experts. But once some rats had been truly caught, fewer and fewer other rats even visited the trap.

Feeding patterns, neophobia, and the division of labour

Thompson never succeeded in catching more than about half a colony, to judge from the amounts of bait taken. Trap-shyness seemed to spread even though few rats directly observed their mates in the trap and could not copy escape techniques. A belief in this cultural transmission is widespread but the evidence is not solid, nor is it known how it might work. A conditioned taste aversion to poisoned bait seems likely, but Nachman and Hartley (1975) found that taste aversions developed after rats ate some poisons commonly used as rodenticides, yet not after others – whether observable signs of toxicity appeared or not. Anyway, the story goes that once one rat recovers from a sublethal dose of poison, not only does it avoid the relevant bait in future, so do all other members of its colony and their descendents after them.

Both wild and albino rats are omnivorous feeders, and in the laboratory will eat whole grains of wheat, flour, chopped raw liver, sugar, and so on. They can be cannibals, though probably only if the usual diet is deficient in some way. A dead laboratory rat is usually ignored by his cage-mates but is occasionally eaten, starting with the testes and the brain. Rats can generally select a nutritionally adequate diet (Chapters 5 and 8).

Given a choice of foods, rats start by sampling, taking a small bite or two from everything available and gradually concentrate for the main meal on one preferred food, sampling again as they become satiated. They sample even from foods they dislike, wheat mixed with arachis oil or butyric acid which they otherwise avoid unless they are extremely hungry. Indeed, even the smell of peppermint oil or n-butyl mercaptan are sufficient to cause increasing avoidance after a couple of samples (Barnett and Spencer, 1953). These preferences can only be shown if the foods are thoroughly familiar. Wild rats in the laboratory, or those feeding from baited traps, avoid an unfamiliar food or even a favourite in an unfamiliar place. Wild rats confined in the laboratory, which may of course be under an extra stress, may even stop feeding altogether. Barnett (1963) describes how wild rats or their laboratory-bred descendants will not touch food offered to them in a tin at the front of their cage if they are accustomed to taking the same kind of food from a wire basket at the back, and may not eat anything at all for several days. The rats can hardly fail to recognise the food just because of the unfamiliar context, and even if the food is put in its usual place in the basket, as usual the mere presence of an unfamiliar tin at the front is enough. The rats do not explore the tin, it is completely avoided, just as Thompson reports wild rats stop using a favoured pathway if a new object is put on to it. Albino rats under the same conditions may inhibit feeding and exploration in precisely the same way but only for a matter of seconds or minutes, not for hours or days. They soon come out to examine the new object, and a new food may very soon be preferred to the old for sheer novelty.

Barnett emphasises three points about this 'new object reaction' ('neophobia'). First, it is only temporary, the animals habituate to the new object. Whereas a distasteful food is sampled and then avoided, the unfamiliar food is first avoided, then cautiously sampled and, after delaying long enough to recognise the samples as safe, eaten. It seems preferable to regard neophobia as vestigial in albinos rather than absent. Second, neophobia is a response to new stimuli, only in familiar surroundings, to the contrast between unknown and known. In a completely new environment, wild rats explore as soon as albinos, if only to discover where the hiding places might be. Conditioned aversion to a 'poisonous' taste is probably developed from neophobia. Rats avoid any taste that is unfamiliar except for a sample. If the food turns out kosher, it is then eaten, if not, then that taste is avoided in future.

Barnett's third and most important point is the value of neophobia to survival. A species which eats a wide variety of any food available cannot rely, as some insects can, on a single innate or imprinted recognition mechanism for the one species of plant it can live on; a rat has to be highly inquisitive and taste everything, but also needs an inhibition on its curiosity. Neophobia is in any case only an exaggeration of the caution of most small animals and may be weaker on small islands or, as Boice (1972) points out, on municipal rubbish dumps where new objects with a human smell arrive daily. Rats on small islands are not subject to such heavy predation as those on a farm with a couple of terriers.

Variation between individuals might explain another of the species' adaptations. Not all wild rats are excessively timid. Thompson describes one that sat cheekily in the front compartment of a Wonder trap under his gaze for 19 minutes 'and only moved when coughed at very loudly at the expiration of the watching period'. Rat societies may have no formal organisation or written constitution, but there could be an effective functional division of labour. The neophobia of most individuals means that they wait for one bold fool to sample any unfamiliar potential food. When a food is accepted, some rats eat it on the spot, some carry it off a little way to a safer spot, and some carry it back to their burrows. Some rats virtually never emerge from the burrow, but snatch their food from the stores or indeed the mouths of the more venturesome. Parasitic as this seems, it is adaptive, for if the bolder rats all get carried off by owls or Harry V. Thompson, then the colony has a reserve population. When they get hungry enough they emerge and forage in their turn, but when others find a surplus there is no need.

If the first rat's decision is really conveyed to others, the method is not known. Presumably other rats accept a new food carrying something of the first rat's scent. A clue to a method of rejection was observed by Steiniger (1950): if the first rat decides not to eat a new bait, he climbs over it and urinates and defecates on it; other members of the colony then express a similar picturesque opinion.

The sociology and biology of the Norway rat

Fritz Steiniger backed experiments on wild rats in large enclosures with 20 years' experience of free-living rats throughout northern Germany from the Friesian Islands to the Baltic, and as far north as Latvia. He emphasises the importance of local traditions, and he quite expected south German rats to behave somewhat differently.

Observations of rats confined in cages or in cellars Steiniger rejected as useless, and he constructed enclosures of 64 m^2. These were surrounded by slate or concrete walls 1 m high (which rats do not bother to jump over) and extending 60 cm underground (which they do not dig under). The rats must have found these enclosures almost adequate, for some rats found a rusty underground hole in the corrugated iron of an early version, and habitually emerged to play in the field outside, yet were always found at home when Steiniger conducted a census. Wire netting enclosures were not so suitable because the rats climbed them and, occasionally, clung on upside down from the roof for hours at a time. One wall of the enclosure was always next to his laboratory, so that Steiniger could observe the rats through the window without his smell or movements disturbing them.

The rats could be watched because, it turns out, they are not truly nocturnal. The main activity periods are on the daylight side of dawn and dusk, so that in the far north at midwinter they are most active around noon. Rats are inhibited by human activity (cf. pp. 85–6) so that although most rats tend to pause around midnight, those infesting a house delay their peak activity until after the people go to bed.

Rats which are well known to each other as individuals can be confined together with fair safety even in quite a small box, and so can young strangers. Furthermore, Steiniger was sure that when colonies of rats migrate to the countryside for the summer, some of the aggregations at the more popular lakeside or seaside resorts include several town colonies. But it is a different story when adult rats captured from several different colonies are confined in the same large enclosure.

When first released, the rats explore rapidly and though they fight briefly on encountering each other and may bite, they give the impression of being more defensive than aggressive. Each rat finds somewhere to hide or digs a burrow. When food is laid out, only one animal feeds at a time, dashing back and forth to its own burrow until it has what it wants and lets the next take its turn. The rank-order is fairly rigid and needs no further fighting, a brief nose-to-nose greeting is enough. Nevertheless, the dominant respects the other's burrow, unless he is himself being chased by Steiniger; he might then flee down the wrong burrow, a few squeals are heard, and the subordinate ex-owner emerges disconsolately. When a female comes into heat the males all attempt to enter her burrow, but only the dominant can stay there. A persistent subordinate is repeatedly bitten and driven out. Courting males may take gifts of food and nesting material, the dominant may take his gift home again.

Once a pair have mated the situation becomes serious. They take the whole enclosure as their territory and drive off all the other rats one by one. Free-living victims would normally flee, but are vulnerable to predators, for in densely-infested localities Steiniger sometimes found exhausted rats clinging for hours to shrubs or branches of trees, where they were taken by goshawks or owls. In the enclosure, they could not escape and were chased and bitten on the back near the base of the tail, males by the male, females by the female [just as ex-breeding males are almost the only albinos to draw blood (see p. 298)]. In the enclosures such bites could turn septic so that the victims died one by one until only the mated pair were left. A very few rats, all females and only in the territory-forming situation, sometimes killed directly, sneaking up to the victim, jumping on its back, and biting through the back of the neck to kill in a few seconds.

Once the mated pair have their enclosure to themselves, the situation again changes utterly. In all the excitement, the first copulations turn out infertile, for the first litter is not born for a month or two, but from then on the picture is of domestic bliss. The parents, their offspring, and further generations in due course form an extended family of the utmost tolerance. There is no apparent dominance hierarchy. Youngsters can take food out of the mouths of adults and can enter and remain in anybody's burrow. Steiniger regularly found pups in the same burrow that must have been 2 weeks apart in age, so that litters are most probably nursed communally. In laboratory mice, Sayler and Salmon (1971) also found shared nursing of mixed litters to be quite common, irrespective of maternal age or experience. The young can suckle more continuously while the mothers have more time off to recuperate and feed themselves.

Young rats approach and crawl under older rats, as if for reassurance and emotional security. Steiniger doubts if it is merely attempted suckling, since the young rats may crawl under an adult male from the rear, nor is it the same as the genital sniffing of courtship. Both Steiniger and Barnett call it a gesture of friendship. Crawling under, incidentally, is rare and inconspicuous in laboratory rats, though it does occur and is easily distinguished from huddling to sleep in warmth and comfort. Older wild rats may crawl over young ones when they meet, and the two can remain one on top of the other for 5 or 10 seconds, quivering and slowly lashing their tails (usually a sign of frustration or conflict). Infants trying to crawl under can be a bit too intrusive, and older rats may gently kick them away with a hindleg; if necessary, the adult, fed up, may threaten with the teeth or advance in an Offensive Sideways posture (see Fig. 24.2 and p. 303), the young miscreant adopting a Defensive Upright or Submitting. Youngsters play-fight repeatedly and adult rats may join in.

Steiniger, like Barnett, makes a clear distinction between the play-fighting of juveniles and the real fighting of adults, both the defensive aggression of strangers meeting in a strange environment, and territoriality. To me, it seems that there is a real distinction of degree but not of kind. The daily dominance-testing that albino adults show a couple of times a day clearly grades into play on one side and a territorial type of fighting on the other (no doubt less intense than in wild rats). But then play-fighting can seem just as serious to human children, even between best friends, as anything in adult life. Steiniger once saw one rat bite his litter-mate after being refused entry into his burrow – a quarrel resolved only when both joined in the colony's attack on an intruder.

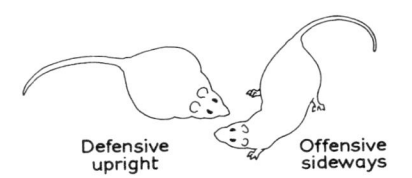

Fig. 24.2. A sudden stop in flight, and Offensive Sideways and Defensive Upright postures in wild rats (after Steiniger, 1950).

Rats recognise each other by smell; colony members touch noses briefly on meeting, but could be jumpy (literally they nervously jumped) if Steiniger introduced a strange rat, or a dead one, into the enclosure. The older rats, especially the founding pair, are mainly responsible for defence of the family territory against intruders, and take less part in sexual activities, tolerantly letting the lads and lasses have their fun.

Wild females seem not to come into heat as frequently as albinos, and the winter decline in birth rate is much greater. Oestrus causes intense excitement throughout the colony. As a female comes into pro-oestrus, the males become restless and sniff and crawl under her. At the peak of oestrus, the female keeps running but stops for 2–3 seconds in lordosis if a male touches her with a paw or leaps on her back, which is quite long enough for a spry male. In this way she may mate with many males, up to 200 or 300 times in all in 6 to 10 hours, snapping at the male after each mount, or at any other male who gets in the way (an intruding foreigner may even be killed), and making a faint whistling noise – Steiniger wondered at the origin of the Pied Piper of Hamelin story. Next day the colony is peaceful – exhausted.

Burrows

Rats make burrows to sleep in, to store food in, and to hide from predators in. In human habitations, they make use of any warm, dark, secure crevice of suitable size, a half-open drawer is ideal, but they dig in the ground in any case. In Steiniger's enclosures, a sleeping burrow has three to five entrances, tunnels 7–12 cm in diameter and 0·5 to 1·5 m long, meeting about 30 cm below the surface. Nearby is a larger cavity where one or several rats may sleep huddled together, and Barnett measured nest temperatures as 5–7

A comparison of laboratory and wild rodents

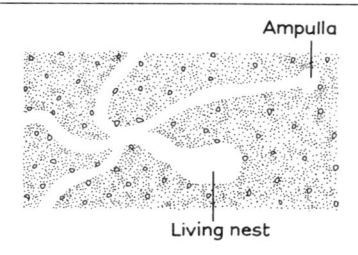

Fig. 24.3. Diagram of a simple living burrow in sandy soil (after Steiniger, 1950).

°C above those in the rest of the burrow. There is also a tunnel several metres long ending in a slightly enlarged ampulla. This is where the rat will be found if the burrow is dug up, head and shoulders in the ampulla, back arched and braced as in one form of a laboratory rat's crouch (Fig. 21.18), so as to block the tunnel as tightly as a cork. It is extremely difficult to pull the rat out, even for a weasel or a farmer and his dog, and Steiniger quotes stories that a rat can survive flooding or poison gas this way, using its back as a plug to keep out the water, breathing air filtered through the earth.

There is continual digging of new tunnels, for exits and to connect with other burrows. Old exits, which may have discarded food scattered round or be partly filled with debris, are allowed to collapse through disrepair. I wonder, incidentally, if laboratory rats' curious habit of biting a pencil or a finger poked into their cage, could originate from a response to clear away roots projecting into a burrow. Juvenile rats dig their own narrow little tunnels, where they can escape from adults. Food-storage burrows have a larger chamber than sleeping burrows but no escape tunnel. They are kept fully stocked, especially by rats who have suffered a period of starvation, but food may be left to rot or be thrown out. The reserves in the larder must help sometimes however. In the hard winter of 1946–7, Steiniger saw burrows covered with ice for seven weeks, but the rats eventually emerged not much thinner than they went in.

Rats also dig short blind tunnels as temporary shelters near a source of food. They are liable to sudden panics when out in the open, at the mere fluttering of a bird, and dive for the nearest shelter, from which a cautious nose emerges 10 seconds later. If a cat is really prowling, they dash to the emergency shelter and after a pause to draw breath, emerge to make another dash for home.

One colony went hunting. These rats could prey on birds up to the size of small ducks. They walked up to the birds as if unconcerned, managing to inhibit both their tendency to panic at the sudden hopping of small birds and their own bouncy lolloping; they could not achieve the stealthy slinking of a cat, but made a creditable attempt at a steady smooth approach, then jumped on the bird's back and bit through the neck. Steiniger found no other rats that could do what most if not all the rats in this particular colony did. It is reminiscent of mouse-killing 'aggression' by a few laboratory rats, and in Steiniger's experimental enclosure, mice, guinea-pigs, and occasionally intruding rats could also be killed – yet a family of voles could live with the rats quite peacefully.

Rats are cunning beasties in popular tradition. Not only do they steal eggs from poultry farmers but around Birmingham, where of course the eggs are all bigger and better than one rat can carry by itself, everybody knows that they co-operate. One rat is supposed to lie on its back holding a large egg firmly in four paws, another grips the first rat's tail in its teeth and drags it triumphantly backwards home. Unfortunately the only person I ever met who had seen this with his own eyes was being treated in a mental hospital at the time.

The Black rat (*Rattus rattus*)

To compare free-living and laboratory strains of one species usefully, it helps to compare two species. *R. rattus* the black or ship rat is very similar to the brown *R. norvegicus* in most respects – the differences mostly seem related to its greater tendency to climb rather than burrow, while both species can have both black and quite light brown strains. Jirsik (1955) says that the brown strains of *R. rattus* resemble Norway rats in habits like fruit-picking, and tend to displace the black strains much as the Norway species has displaced the black from most parts of Europe since the fourteenth century. However, *R. rattus* seems to displace *R. exulans* on Pacific islands, taking over their globular nests of leaves inside rotten logs. They sometimes gnaw at, and waste, unripe green coconuts which *R. exulans* wait for until they fall ripe on the beach. Black rats climb trees and run along the tops of walls more than Norway rats, the long tail grows much faster in infancy for use as a balancing organ and they also develop clinging responses and avoidance of cliff edges earlier, according to Ewer (1971). She observed a colony in West Africa by laying out a little food. Numbers increased as a result and then stabilised, partly by balancing a little immigration and emigration, partly by the limiting of breeding. As the colony was free-living she could not experiment as much as Steiniger, but the responses to immigrants were probably more normal since they had not been introduced over an impassable barrier by the experimenter. The colony defended a group territory, marked by rubbing the belly on suitable stones. They explored outside the boundary but did not chase exploring visitors beyond it, and the occasional determined intruder remained and became accepted.

There appear to be a few other differences between black and Norway rats' social signals (see p. 315), but not many. Black rats also eat a wide variety of foods, mostly vegetable, but whatever is available and fairly familiar. They prey on small vertebrates or large insects when they can catch them. Small pieces of food are eaten on the spot, larger pieces are taken

A comparison of laboratory and wild rodents

home and presumably hoarded and shared out. They do not, however, seem to warn other individuals about a trap for Thompson (1953) did not see the same extreme decline in the number of black rats visiting a trap from one night to the next as he did in trap-shy Norway rats.

Confirmation of laboratory conclusions

Detailed studies of the behaviour of small animals in the wild are not possible, and are limited in large animals, whether free-living or in the laboratory, or, in practice, on the farm. There have been some attempts to check whether the behaviour observed in detail in the laboratory is consistent with what can be seen in free-living animals.

The courtship behaviour of three-spined sticklebacks is far more comfortable to watch in glass fish tanks than in streams and ditches in the late winter of Northern Europe. But, except when raindrops spoiled visibility,

watching in streams and ditches

Wootton (1972) put his rubber boots on, and while his quantitative descriptions would not rival laboratory experiments for clarity and detail, they were quite adequate to confirm the experiments' validity. Dallas Colvin (1973) staged encounters in the laboratory between pairs of male voles of five species of *Microtus* living in the same areas. Some pairs fought and could be seen to win and lose, other pairs evaded the issue by mutual avoidance. Colvin was a little worried by the artificiality of such staged encounters, until by chance he heard squeals and squeaks in the long grass one day and saw one vole chasing another of a different species, biting its rump in a way precisely comparable to his laboratory experience. As incidents these are reassuring, if hardly adequate.

The difference between laboratory and wild rats

Laboratory albino rats, according to Barnett, lack neophobia and 'some components of fighting and of amicable behaviour have been totally lost'

(1963). There must be both natural and artificial selection for tameness: experimental animals are not much use unless they put up with handling, and quarrelsome or over-timid animals would be at some disadvantage, while feeding or in cage-cleaning, and thrive less well. The process threatens degeneration – Barnett emphasises the absence of selection for characters promoting survival in the wild, more than positive selection for docility.

Now Barnett is an experienced observer, and his book *A Study in Behaviour* (1963) is one of the best introductions to the subject, so his views are worth great respect. But I believe he exaggerates. It is curious that he quotes Seward's failure to find dominance hierarchies in albino rats but omits his vivid description of their fighting (Seward, 1945a and b; and see Chapter 21). Perhaps the difference is merely semantic, of course. Barnett recognises play-fighting in albinos but does not think it amounts to fighting. It is certainly untrue that the 'components ... have been totally lost' but it is interesting that what he and Steiniger describe as a gesture of friendliness, crawling under, should also be comparatively uncommon in laboratory rats, in view of Lorenz's idea (1968) that animals are capable of love in direct proportion to their capacity for intense aggression.

Wistar albinos were compared with grey Norway rats by Edmond Farris and Eleanor Yenkel (1945). Despite 55 generations of laboratory breeding, the grey rats remained more nervous and excitable. Picking up and handling infants before weaning made albinos easier to handle as adults; it was essential for picking up adult grey rats at all. Repeated handling did not make them tamer, like albinos, but more likely to squeal and bite. The greys were more active in the open field than albinos, but from courage, since they defecated more too. After fifty-five generations the direct stress of captivity must have been minimal, and so must any maternal effect through behaviour or corticosteroids in the milk. The difference is probably genetic, therefore, presumably due originally to the albino gene (though modern black, brown, or hooded laboratory strains are tame), lowering the wild rats' heightened arousal of fear.

Laboratory rats were dominant to wild rats, and hybrids intermediate, in both submissive postures and access to water. John Boreman and Edward Price (1972) put groups of four laboratory-bred wild rats, two of each sex, into a large experimental room for 2 weeks, together with four laboratory rats (from a mixed-up colony of four common strains) and four hybrids between wild males and domestic females. There were twelve nest-boxes, each occupied for 2 or 3 days at a time by two or three rats of any strain, and no competition was seen for the two food baskets. But rank-orders were formed for access to the single water-bottle when the supply was restricted, and the same order was apparent between the strains in terms of submitting flat-on-back. The two kinds of dominance were not correlated for individuals within strains, however, and so they might be two different phenomena. The wild rats, Boreman and Price suggest, were only submissive to albinos because they misinterpreted as aggression what the albinos intended as play. Given that the groups were made up of adult rats (and strangers) the experimenters might have misinterpreted as play what the albinos intended seriously enough. The wild rats were definitely more territorial and became dominant if they were put into the room as little as 10 minutes before the others. Boreman and Price conclude that laboratory rats are not degenerate but have adapted to a different environment.

The reputation that wild rats are difficult to breed in the laboratory, is a myth according to Robert Boice (1972). He distinguished between rats with wounds round the base of the tail or their healed scars, and rats without signs of injury, arguing that traps round a settled rat community on a farm or an inner-city ghetto would catch mainly peripheral, surplus, or low-ranking rats, bearing scars and unlikely to breed anywhere. So he set traps in a city's landfill rubbish dump, where new objects would arrive and be bulldozed from place to place every day, and high-status rats would be less likely to avoid new objects carrying a human scent. Unscarred rats turned out to breed almost as well as albinos. Even when first introduced after a week's solitary confinement, unscarred males and females rarely fought, had nearly as many litters as albinos, and nearly as many pups survived till weaning in each litter. They built good nests, kept them clean of faeces and retrieved wandering infants. Scarred pairs of wild rats, by contrast, fought and bit each other, had few litters and were likely to kill or neglect the infants. Their nests were filthy and tumbledown, and many of them drank excessively – a daily consumption of their own bodyweight seems a lot even if it is only water.

Groups of four wild (but not albino) rats given water for only an hour a day formed well-marked dominance orders; unlike Boreman and Price, Boice found that submissive postures gave the same rankings. Scarred rats were nearly always subordinate and in low temperatures (3°) were liable to adopt stereotyped 'catatonic' postures. Hybrids crawled under and over each other so actively that no ranking was possible.

Boice commented on how little evidence there is for the common belief that wild rats are cleverer than albinos. Because wild rats do not always respond well on laboratory learning tasks, he could only test the hypothesis by compelling them to show what they could do. He therefore started with Escape, learning to turn a wheel to switch off shock for 18 seconds. He was careful to start at a moderate intensity (0·5 mA), since two wild rats died after as little as 1·5 mA.

The wild rats were the first to achieve the criterion of keeping the shock switched off for 80 per cent of a 1-hour session, and at the minimal shock intensity, because they continually bit the grid floor during shock, transferred the biting quite easily to the wheel, and thus moved it the necessary one-tenth of a revolution. Their laboratory-bred offspring were slower and the albinos came last (but had been left untamed, unhandled and in isolation since weaning).

The schedule was then modified to free-operant avoidance. A response between shocks, previously without effect, now postponed the next one for 18 seconds. At first the wild and F_1 rats received fewer shocks but came to freeze more, and did not seem to learn by results; by day 15 the albinos were the better. Next, the shocks were signalled by a light 3·5 seconds beforehand, and (as expected) the albinos improved further, responding increasingly while the light shone. The wild and F_1 rats developed a Pavlovian rather than a Skinnerian response – they froze, so that the light stimulus inhibited wheel-turning instead of eliciting it.

Boice thought the wild rats were superior at passive avoidance, but his evidence that experienced wild rats never made an active avoidance response in a kind of one-way shuttle-box, and untrained ones only did so as if by accident in the course of exploration, hardly meets the usual criterion. He argued that wild rats appear so poor at these artificial laboratory tests not from an inability to learn but from rigidity of response, and he tested this. Both wild and laboratory rats drink predominantly at night time, and both strains learned to press a bar for a drop of water (0·05 ml), obtaining about 40 ml a night if every response was rewarded (constant reinforcement, CRF). Then for 15 days the schedule was changed – at night, a fixed ratio of sixteen responses for each drop of water (FR16) while CRF was continued by day. The albino rats switched to getting their water the easy way in the daytime, and after about 5 days were obtaining 30 ml/day.

water reward

The wild rats retained their nocturnal habit, but obtained only about 10 ml/night on FR16. When the original CRF schedule was restored full-time, the albinos readjusted quicker, but all rats returned to a nightly intake of 40 ml. The lighting cycle was then reversed, i.e. dim red lights came on in the daytime. The albinos reduced their total intake only for a day or two, the wild rats did so until their entire activity cycle had been reversed in about 2 weeks. So while free-living rats can adjust their activity to match daylength or avoid human activity, they are less flexible than albinos in the laboratory.

They were not avoiding Boice, by the way, for he read the meters at 5 o'clock in the morning; he suggests that inflexibility might itself be an advantageous learned response in some circumstances.

Strain-specific behaviour in mice

With all the emphasis in the literature on adaptation and genetic selection in the laboratory, Farris and Yenkel's evidence that wild rats were still wild after fifty-five generations of domestication comes as a surprise. Even more surprising after more than half a century of selection, it seems that the behaviour of highly inbred strains of mice remains characteristic of their wild ancestors.

C. C. Little started the DBA inbred line in 1909, and the similar C57 Black strain from the stock of Miss Lathrop, a mouse fancier, in 1921. H. J. Bagg started various albino strains, the CPBs from a dealer's stock in 1913, and the CBA line, though now treated as inbred, started as a hybrid between DBAs and one of the Bagg albinos. Because they started from so few individuals and are so highly inbred (at least forty-seven generations of brother–sister mating), these strains are generally assumed to be genetically homogeneous, and degenerate, not real mice, but toys. Van Oortmersson (1971) studied four of these strains and is not so sure.

CPBs mice were highly territorial. Resident males attacked intruders more readily than the other strains and fought harder even when losing, but once they had lost they fled further and were less likely to come back. They were also wilder and more likely to bite humans. The C57 Black males were not territorial, resident males approached and investigated an intruder but rarely attacked him. CPBs and C57 males seemed to misunderstand each other's signals, because if a C57 were attacked he crouched on the spot instead of running away, even if he elicited severe biting by the CPBs. But C57 males actually fought more as a defence in a strange environment than they did as residents. CBA mice from the originally hybrid strain were mixed, some more like CPBs, some like C57 mice. CBA mice losing a fight were more likely to flee a short way and then adopt a 'submissive upright posture', an extreme defensive upright with some intimidatory effect.

Sexual behaviour differed in consequence. The unaggressive C57 males showed little courtship of a female in heat but mounted almost immediately. CPBs males needed to overcome both their own tendency to attack and the resulting wariness of the female, and therefore spent longer following, sniffing, and crawling under her before attempting to mount. Again, the CBA males were intermediate.

All the strains explored an equal amount, but in different ways. CPBs mice reared upright, looking and sniffing for distant objects whereas the C57 and CBA mice directed their attention more to smells on the floor. The

C57 mice were expert in digging holes in the sawdust floor, especially when given paper strips or grass to nest with. The CPBs mice did not dig much but built elaborate spherical nests which could stand up even without support from the walls of the cage. They did this by fraying the edges of the paper strips so that they became tangled up and supported each other. The CBA mice dug in an undirected, scattered manner and could not build proper nests; either they did not try, or they bit and chopped the material so small that the pieces fell flat on the floor.

Efficient fraying therefore depends on a balance, biting the material neither too little nor too much. Fraying appeared to be genetically controlled as it was inherited but not altered by cross-fostering pups with fraying parents on to non-fraying step-mothers or vice versa. The CPBs varied in the amount they frayed, but the most efficient medium frayers were both heterozygous and more viable in general. Van Oortmerssen tried selective breeding for high and low fraying, but the lines either failed to change or died out.

These differences are not, as they must seem, a ragbag of miscellaneous characteristics arising from small samples, genetic drift, and inbreeding. On the contrary, van Oortmerssen shows them to be integrated functional adaptations to two different habitats by the CPBs and C57 mice, while CBA mice are mixed up hybrids not properly adapted to either. The CPBs mice are adapted to living on the surface of the ground. They are territorial, with strong tendencies both to attack and to flee a long way out of another mouse's territory, and therefore require pre-copulatory courtship. They are more likely to bite a (human) predator. Their mainly upright exploration gathers information from a distance, and their elaborate nests can be freestanding. The C57 mice, on the other hand, are adapted to living underground in burrows. They dig efficiently and line the holes with nesting material, choosing the darkest place available to sleep if they are not allowed to dig. In the confined space of a burrow, a high level of aggression would be counter-productive, elaborate courtship unnecessary, and active fleeing impossible. If attacked, they crouch, preferably with a roof over their backs. They explore mainly by examining the floor for traces of their own smell or of other passing mice.

In a suitably designed cage it was possible to demonstrate preferences for habitats consistent with these adaptations, including the unpredictability of CBA mice. Since at least one of the relevant patterns is genetically controlled, it seems likely that these integrated behavioural differences are not adaptations to laboratory life, where they are largely irrelevant (CBAs are perfectly good laboratory animals even though they would be unsuccessful if free-living). They must have bred true from different wild ancestors. *Mus musculus* may have as many as seven fairly distinct subspecies and is adapted to living in small populations descended from a single pair, to exploit a corn-rick, an island, or a laboratory colony. The genetic control of fraying may be typical of many adaptations to maintain heterozygosity. It is not, therefore, surprising that inbred strains have retained their character in the laboratory for so long.

Summary

If experiments on laboratory animals are not to be academic exercises but relevant to real life, it is important to know if, and how far, their behaviour differs from that of their wild relatives.

Differences could be either because the comfortable life of the laboratory has removed the selection pressures bearing down on free-living rodents and made albinos decadent, or they could be positive adaptations to different (not absent) pressures. Probably all the differences between wild and laboratory rats can be interpreted in terms of the chronic arousal of behaviour suggesting anxiety and stress in the wild form. Wild rats have enlarged adrenal glands, show an almost excessive avoidance of new objects in a familiar environment, an inflexibility of response in conditioning experiments, and intense fighting when one is put into the home cage of another without being able to escape. However, fighting and neophobia are greatly weakened in laboratory rats rather than absent. In any case, wild rats do not necessarily fight intensely: there is nothing more than play-fighting within a stable colony consisting of a single extended family, and wild rats caught without scars of old wounds (and so probably of high status) fight little even in captivity. Nevertheless, there does seem to be a genetic difference between wild and albino rats, the latter operating at a lower 'arousal' level. A study of inbred strains of laboratory mice suggests that they have retained integrated patterns of behaviour adapted to the surface- or burrow-dwelling habitats of different sub-species of their wild ancestors.

TWENTY-FIVE
Finale

The belief is still surprisingly common that behavioural studies are neither rigorous nor relevant. Because behaviour varies to relate the animal to the fluctuations of the environment, its study is assumed to be subjective. Other sciences can also be handicapped, of course, and a pathologist may not be able to define precisely how he knows that certain cells are undergoing a malignant transformation. But the microscope slide is fixed and stained, and one pathologist can call in another for an independent – if equally subjective – opinion. Behaviour is further handicapped by changing from moment to moment, so the suspicion arises that even an accurate observation does not matter very much, the behaviour can always change back again.

We can acknowledge the problem, ironic though it seems after all the evidence summarised in this book. Indeed conditioning methods may over-react to the difficulty by imposing predictability from outside. The animal may still have several options, it can even bite the experimenter, but usually co-operates. When it is made very important to behave in a proper manner, animals can be as conformist as the rest of us.

However, on balance, observation suggests that it is the animal that takes the initiative. Behaviour consists in choosing the appropriate environment or even modifying it as much as in reacting to it. If you look carefully, regularities appear which are related more closely to the animal than to its surroundings.

as conformist as the rest of us

It has been a fruitful assumption of ethology that behaviour is not infinitely variable but is constructed in modular fashion of distinct elements. In principle, these units must be identifiable and recognisable, though they will always require disciplined observation. While the assumption remains unproved, the concept of a finite number of building blocks has been fruitful above all as a tool for careful observation, in the wild as in the laboratory. Lorenz and Tinbergen have done for behaviour what Mendel did for genetics. Neither science has been greatly advanced, incidentally, by too great an emphasis on acquired characters.

Even in laboratory strains of rodents there exist a rich variety of actions and postures which occur reliably in the right conditions. This is not to say that these elements are strictly innate – some may be innate in form, most will have a complex developmental history, and all will be subject to conditioning in the extent to which the frequency of their use is reinforced. But they exist in the repertoire of all individuals brought up in the way usual for the species, and we can observe and make use of them.

In most cases personal observation is necessary; you have to believe your own eyes. However inexperienced, observers can recognise elements from the written description, even in exploration where apparently natural units are less clearly marked than in grooming or social behaviour. Experienced observers commonly achieve rank-order correlations of well above $r_s = 0.9$, and in some cases there is no significant difference between observers in the same analysis of variance used to assess drug effects. Maybe this means only that people can condition themselves to bias their observation according to the same rules, but at least the observation need be no more subjective than, say, a chemical titration.

It is both as possible and as necessary to study biology on the behavioural level as on the physiological.

An end and a beginning

The last piece of behaviour I will describe is the development of a quite new response by some laboratory rodents. If not taken too seriously it amusingly summarises much of the argument of the book.

In a study of the inhalation toxicity of tobacco some years ago, various rodents were exposed singly in glass cylinders (Fig. 25.1) to cigarette smoke diluted 1:100 in clean air. They were exposed for 4 hours a day for 2 weeks – the experiment should have continued longer but the method had to be changed, for the animals plainly disliked even the very dilute smoke, and from the second day onwards they started to do something about it. Tony Riley (personal communication) observed faecal pellets deposited in the 1-cm inlet piping to some of the exposure cylinders. Many of the animals repeated this every day, and 6 of the 8 rats, 10 of the 12 hamsters and 10 of the 16 mice were observed to show the response at one time or another. Guinea-pigs did not, but characteristically stood with their backs to the airflow at the downstream end, acquiring a brown stain on their white fur

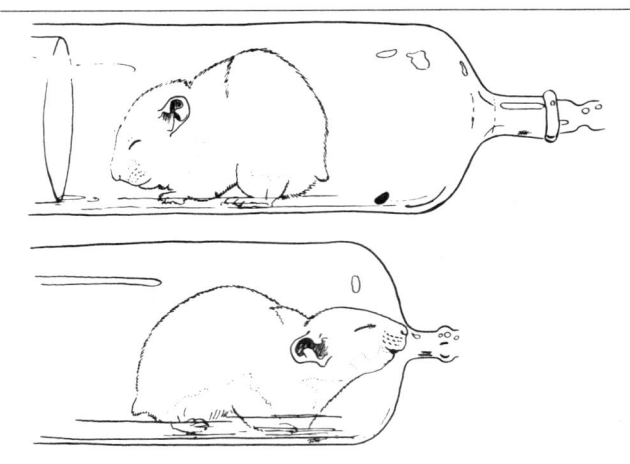

Fig. 25.1. Hamsters exposed to cigarette smoke (traced from photographs). Mostly the rodents crouch, cough, sniff the incoming air, or just sit it out. They defecate or tear chips off the rubber bung.

and looking miserable. The response became very quick – one rat stuffed the inlet pipe only 10 seconds after being put in the cylinder for the third day, before the first cigarette had even been lit. And in one case it was very effective: a poor hamster stuffed the inlet so thoroughly that it suffocated. The method of exposure was promptly changed to prevent the cure becoming worse than the unpleasant stimulus, but the behaviour seemed worth investigation in its own right.

Blocking of the inlet pipe turns out to result from the integration of several pre-existing elements of behaviour, some of them occurring every day in the home cage, and all of them in the apparatus long before exposure to cigarette smoke. The rodents scrabbled, scraping up the glass floor with the forepaws, kicking backwards with the hindleg like a dog digging, and push-digging forwards, flipping sawdust or a faecal pellet with the back of the forepaws. They carried food or a faecal pellet in the mouth, and rats occasionally carried their tails. The animals were quite willing to enter the glass cylinder a second time. One rat once put a strip of tissue paper into the inlet, and took it away again. A faecal pellet carried in the mouth could be thrown forward by a sudden raising of the head, and I once saw a hamster toss a pellet that it had been carrying balanced on the tip of its nose.

However, these actions occurred singly or in brief bouts, little more often when confined in a cylinder than in the home cage. They were not integrated into a pattern until after experience of tobacco smoke. A cold draught caused by sometimes increasing the flow of air from about 0·7 litres/minute (leaving the inlet tube slowly at about 0·6 km/hour) to 15 litres/minute did not persuade them to block the tube, nor did brief whiffs of ammonia. Yet tube-blocking was not a direct response to the smoke either.

Finale

When rats or hamsters were first exposed to cigarette smoke (for 3–4 minutes at a dilution of about 10 : 1) they coughed and lifted the head repeatedly as if retching. Occasionally an animal put its nose into the inlet for a moment, mostly they faced away from the smoke, enduring it immobile but for an occasional twitch. They defecated and urinated much more than before exposure. These responses were predictable side-effects of a relatively large dose of nicotine, and were milder after later cigarettes, although on the second and third days (three or four cigarettes were smoked a day in about 4 hours), one rat refused to enter the cyclinder until the air-supply was temporarily turned off; there was a persistent faint smell of cigarettes in the apparatus, not unpleasant to me. Suddenly in intervals between cigarettes on the third and fourth days, all three rats filled their inlet tubes. They scrabbled and kicked material until it was under or in the inlet, lifting it up by mouth or the back of the hands and patted and plastered it in with the palms (Fig. 25.2). On subsequent days, the rats

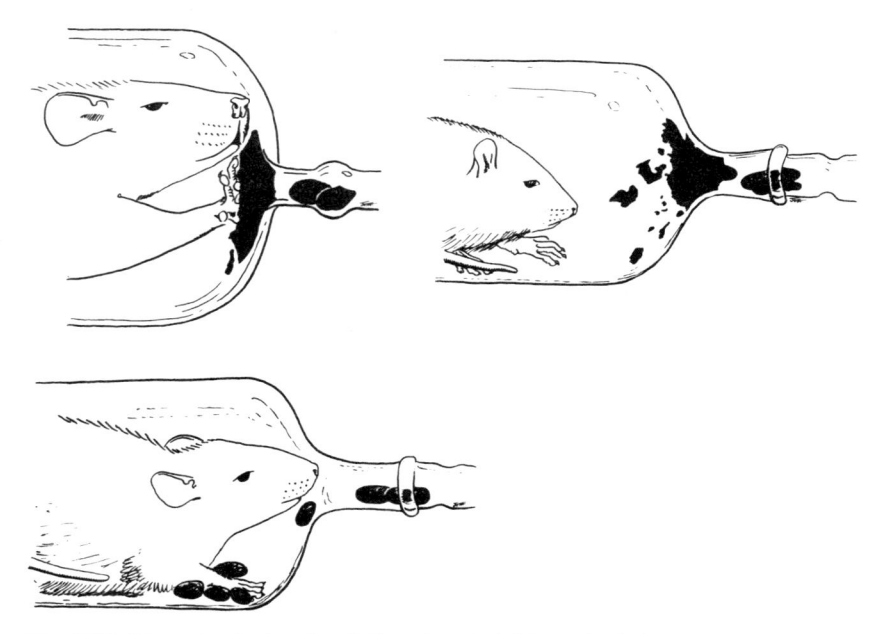

Fig. 25.2. The rats plastered soft faecal material into the inlet spout.

did not wait for the cigarettes, but put material into the inlets as soon as they were placed in the cylinder.

The response is therefore 'learned', almost certainly using the apparatus and the residual smell of old cigarettes in particular as discriminative stimuli. It is also 'innate', constructed from a series of movements that all individuals show in other contexts. Significantly the three species concerned, rats, mice, and hamsters, are all species that often live in burrows. Guinea-pigs probably live under surface vegetation and did not show the response. I once saw a film of a European hamster (*Cricetus cricetus*) in an artificial burrow, blocking the entrance with leaves before settling down to sleep.

The response looks in principle very like tool-using, as if the animals had an insight into cause and effect, and it would be difficult to prove they did not. But especially at first, the separate movements were not integrated; one would follow another only after a pause, or the rat would kick material first in one direction and then the other. The scrabbling and digging suggested that earth would have been used if it had been available, rather than faeces. Chips of rubber bitten off the bung were included, and the hamsters included grain from their cheek pouches. But the animals did not use strips of tissue paper, with one tentative exception, although some made nests from it.

The diameter of the cylinder may also be critical. Mostly they were of a size comparable with a burrow, just wide enough for flexible animals to turn round in. Hamsters exposed in cylinders wide enough for adult rats of twice their size went through all the separate motions, including sniffing the incoming air with the nose right in the inlet, and they lifted faecal material half-way up. They did not achieve the complete pattern, which suggests its rigid 'innate' nature.

In fact the flow of air was not often reduced, so it is uncertain whether the tube-blocking response was actually reinforced. The material may have absorbed or filtered some of the irritant smoke particles, but to my nose seemed to add a scent rather than subtract one. This also suggests that the actions were more or less 'automatic', performed with little understanding but possibly needing specific stimuli before they can form a coherent pattern. Reproductive behaviour is said to mature in a similar manner in adolescent birds, developing in most individuals in the relevant situation without tuition, any reinforcement coming afterwards.

The function of the response in the wild, if it occurs, is uncertain. If the response functions to defend the animals against smoke from prairie fires, for instance, they ought to respond during the actual exposure to smoke. In fact they endured the noxious smoke quietly, sitting facing downstream, motionless or occasionally twitching. Tube-blocking occurred before or between cigarettes.

Tube-blocking was only one of several sets of elements. Animals also put their nose into the inlet pipe and sniffed, no doubt partly out of curiosity. It was interesting however, how long the male mice in the original experiment seemed to sniff. Spot checks showed all eight guinea-pigs standing as far from the smoke as possible, and only one or two of the eight rats and hamsters sampled the incoming air at any one time. But in the second week four of the eight female mice and seven males persistently jammed their noses far into the inlet for long periods (instead of the faecal pellets formerly inserted). Perhaps the mice liked smoking.

So even a simple piece of behaviour is set into a complex framework. The animals' responses to a single stimulus include signs of possible toxicity (coughing, etc.), then simple avoidance, curiosity, a rather more subtle positive (but presumably avoidance) response, and lastly maybe an addictive approach. While an experimenter should concentrate attention on whatever he finds interesting, it should never be forgotten that it is but one aspect among several, whose importance to the animal can change with time and circumstances.

The smoke-blocking response is a refreshing reminder, too, that even such an intensively-studied animal as the albino rat can still surprise us.

Comparing animals and man

Can we learn about man from animal behaviour? And can we extrapolate conclusions from experimental treatments on animals to man? Caution is called for first, simply because so many people have looked at animal behaviour and seen so many different things. The conclusions that have been drawn from animals, indeed from albino rats alone, are so contradictory as to suggest that we might all begin with the conclusions and look for supporting evidence afterwards. Or if we are not so crude as that, nevertheless what we think determines how we look, and that in itself determines what we can see. The holes in the net largely determine the fish that can be caught. But not entirely, or we would never learn anything new. If we cast a variety of nets, we can hope for a realistic sample of sea creatures.

a framework to study ourselves

If the 'proper study of mankind is Man' nevertheless we cannot understand ourselves fully unless we compare ourselves with animals. It is too simple to say that man is 'only' an animal, but since man evolved from animals, human behaviour must be a development from that of animals. No doubt we are far more complex in detail, but if the behaviour of all vertebrates, at least, follows a common set of ground rules, then we have a framework around which we can study ourselves.

Behaviour is functional, however, and it may be that behavioural organisation depends entirely on the demands it has to meet. While the similarities of a bird's wing and a bee's represent convergence to solve similar problems, the differences may represent different problems, as well as historical differences in the structures the wings evolved from. So we also need to know how closely related species differ, and why.

The classic study is of the gulls and other Laridae. Gulls are typically birds which nest in colonies near the sea-shore, in sand dunes or marshes. Pairs defend a small territory round the nest, partly to stop cannibalism by other gulls, but locate the territory inside the colony, partly as a defence against foxes and falcons. Kittiwakes are closely related to gulls, with one important difference. They nest on cliff-ledges, and Esther Cullen (1957) showed how this one factor implies a whole series of changes in behaviour. On ledges the eggs and chicks are safe from ground predators, but chicks cannot run away from birds of prey without tumbling into the sea. Gull chicks run to a bush and hide, kittiwakes crouch. All the birds regurgitate fish for their chicks: gulls call their chicks, which recognise the individual parent's voice and come running for the parent to regurgitate on to the ground. Kittiwakes and their chicks do not need to recognise each other as individuals. The parents fly back to the nest and regurgitate directly into the chick's open mouth. The main organisation of the behaviour can be seen to remain the same but once you appreciate the reason for the differences, innumerable small unnoticed details become significant.

Every species is a study in its own right, but if we know how and why kittiwakes and gulls differ, three- and ten-spined sticklebacks, rats, and mice, and also how far and why they are the same, then we have a peg to hang our studies of ourselves on.

Trends in the study of behaviour, and the four questions of biology

While nobody can keep up with more than a small sector of a science nowadays, some parts of the science of behaviour seem to me to be developing very fast and others at a very pedestrian pace.

Tinbergen (1963) asked four questions about a behaviour, as he would about anything in biology. What is its survival value? How is it caused and controlled within the animal? How does it develop in the individual? And how did it evolve in the species?

Laboratory scientists tend to concentrate on the second of these questions, on at least two levels. Behaviourally we can ask about the animal's situation, what internal and external stimuli start, guide, and terminate the behaviour. We can also ask about the underlying physiology, ultimately the relevant pattern of nerve impulses. More realistically at present we can ask for 'brain research' on the pharmacology of neurotransmitters, on localised electrical or chemical lesions or stimulation, on any treatment specifically changing the behaviour.

Brain research has recently been developing very fast. One area of great excitement is the neurophysiology of vision, tracing the response to specific elements of visual stimuli from the retina through successive areas of the visual cortex. There is equal excitement over the localisation of neurotransmitters, both anatomically and chemically, on their metabolic pathways. Some of this was discussed in Chapter 6 in relation to dopamine, and this is already out of date: two dopaminergic tracts now appear to be distinct, the nigrostriatal and the mesolimbic, and Susan Iversen and her colleagues have begun to distinguish their behavioural functions. However, the behavioural methods used until recently have been crude – the chemical and anatomical complexities are quite enough to cope with – and the time is ripe to disentangle the behaviour as elegantly as the physiology.

To an open-air biologist like Tinbergen, the other three questions are at least as interesting and important, though they have attracted less academic attention. The question where progress is fastest at present is that of survival value, the function of the behaviour. This 'why' question should not be confused with that of motivation, a question of mechanism: human sexual behaviour is not always performed consciously to reproduce the species, and animals too may respond to internal and external stimuli without considering the long-term benefit.

Function is more complicated than it may seem, for once a behaviour is performed for one reason it becomes subject to further selection pressures, and may therefore come to fulfil secondary functions also. Displacement preening in birds comes to act as a social signal, mutual grooming by monkeys promotes the cohesion of the group. The survival value may be negative, as when an animal comes out to feed and becomes a predator's dinner. The final pattern therefore becomes an optimal compromise: rats tend to snatch their food and carry the booty home, cattle graze in herds whose peripheral members act partly as sentinels.

The function of behaviour relates in the end to ecology, the way the animal earns its living, and the progress comes from Edward O. Wilson's concept of *Sociobiology: the New Synthesis* (1975; see also 1976). However, since it is rarely possible to calculate survival value empirically, the subject at present has a somewhat soft centre. On the one hand come theoretical calculations like those of Trivers and Hare (1976) of why it is usually advantageous for worker ants to care for their sisters rather than their brothers or even their own offspring – they also show that their theory correctly 'predicts' sex ratios in various species of ants with different ways of life. On the other hand come empirical studies of real animals like the fine one of Jarman (1974) on antelopes, identifying in gross terms what look like selection pressures and the solutions adopted; the answers are very believable but not yet provable.

Studies on the development of behaviour in the individual seem somewhat lop-sided. There is a vast literature on the learning of deliberately artificial associations of stimulus and response, and to a lesser extent on the imprinting of the following response in new-hatched chicks and some interesting physiological studies on the development of vision in kittens. I have seen relatively little on the lines of Lehrman's hint (1956) about the origin of an adult dove's preening and courtship billing from the new-hatched squab's begging for food.

Tinbergen has done so much to develop the objective analysis of behaviour that he now takes it for granted. Yet for a long time there has been little progress in method; Grant's study in rats, for example (1963, see Chapter 21), was technically little more advanced than the pioneering analysis by Baerends and Baerends-van Roon (1950). The problem is to analyse associations or sequences of behavioural elements in a way which is at the same time mathematically rigorous, technically feasible, and instructive. Only recently have statistical methods come into general use, like the set of cluster-analyses and the principal-components analysis (Morgan *et al.*, 1976; Huntingford, 1976b), which seem to add up to useful advances in ways of visualising such sequences objectively.

Behavioural toxicology is, to me, one of the most interesting developments on the borders between behaviour and other sciences. Modern toxicology is largely a matter of the safety-testing of new chemicals, or of old ones where a problem is known or suspected. It is not quite the impossible art of proving a chemical is utterly safe, but aims to discover, as early as possible, if the lowest dose at which any harmful effect occurs is one to which human beings are at all likely to be exposed. With some chemicals, but not all, behaviour can provide a uniquely sensitive set of measures – now that the right methods are being developed. For to detect the threshold of an effect when it is not known which effect should be looked for, is not at all the same problem as the screening of candidate tranquillisers at a high dose.

Methyl mercury compounds have had a tragic variety of sensory or motor or 'psychological' effects in people exposed to excessive quantities, but conventional behavioural tests in animals showed no sign before the sudden onset of gross poisoning. If the very fine detail of operant performance or sensory discrimination tests is examined, however, the precise equivalents of human clinical symptoms can be detected (Evans, Laties, and Weiss, 1975; Extance, Silverman, and Williams, 1976). By contrast, some chemicals have a very simple, non-specific action. Touching or inhaling nitroglycerine can give you a headache even when it does not explode, besides or because of its hypotensive action. By analogy with a human being suffering from a headache, I predicted that rats treated with nitroglycerine would show a non-specific reduction in all spontaneous social behaviour (though they might continue to perform an operant task conditioned to be important to them); they should also avoid drinking a newly-presented and otherwise attractive saccharin solution (since rats given drugs like lithium with other 'unpleasant' consequences also show a conditioned taste aversion). Preliminary evidence (Silverman, 1976) was consistent with the prediction.

Some 'toxic' effects indicate greater damage than others and indeed there could be effects which in another context would be considered beneficial. After all, a toxic action is (up to a point) only a pharmacological effect in the wrong place. It may be a price that is considered to be worth paying for the sake of the other benefits that the chemical concerned can bring. The question is the severity of the effect, how likely it is to occur and whether it is reversible if it does occur, and above all whether the people who undertake the risk are the same as those who get the benefit.

Fundamentally, scientific experiments are only the first step. Science can obtain factual evidence; it can set the facts in their context so that we can understand them; but this is no more than the essential basis for a value judgement. To take the example of toxicology, the scientist can detect the point at which a chemical begins to have an effect and can specify what the effect is. The decision on what should be done about that effect is in the broad sense a political one. The scientist must play his part in the decision, but in his role as a citizen.

In this book I have tried to show how changes in animal behaviour can be measured, and to evaluate what these techniques can tell us and what they do not. In the process, I hope also to have conveyed an understanding of behaviour for its own sake, and the feeling that if something is worth doing, it is worth enjoying.

what animal behaviour can tell us

References

Adams, D. B. (1971). *Nature*, **232**, 573–574.
Adams, W. J., Yeh, S. Y., Wood, L. A., & Mitchell, C. L. (1969). *J. Pharmac. exp. Ther.*, **168**, 251–257.
Ahtee, L. & Karki, N. (1968). *Acta Pharmac. Tox.*, **26**, 55–63.
Albert, J. R. & Friedman, M. I. (1972). *Nature*, **238**, 454–455.
Allin, J. T. & Banks, E. M. (1972). *Anim. Behav.*, **20**, 175–185.
Anderson, C. O., Denenberg, V. H., & Zarrow, M. X. (1972). *Behaviour*, **43**, 165–175.
Anderson, D. C., Murcurio, J., & Mahoney, P. (1970). *Physiol. Behav.*, **5**, 577–581.
Anrep, G. V. (1923). *Proc. R. Soc.*, B, **94**, 404–426.
Archer, J. (1973). *Anim. Behav.*, **21**, 205–235.
Archer, J. (1974). *Anim. Behav.*, **22**, 397–404.
Armitage, A. K., Hall, G. H., & Morrison, C. F. (1968). *Nature*, **217**, 331–334.
Azrin, N. H. & Holz, W. C. (1966). In *Operant Behavior: areas of research and application.* (ed. W. K. Honig). New York: Appleton–Century–Croft, pp. 380–447.

Baenninger, L. (1966). *Anim Behav.*, **14**, 367–371.
Baerends, G. P. (1941). (*See* 1976, *Anim. Behav.*, **24**, 726–738).
Baerends, G. P. & Baerends-van Roon, J. M. (1950). *Behaviour Suppl.* **1**, 1–242.
Baile, C. A. (1968). *Fedn. Proc.*, **27**, 1361–1366.
Bailey, C. J. & Miller, N. E. (1952). *J. Comp. physiol. Psychol.*, **45**, 205–208.
Bainbridge, J. G. & Greenwood, D. T. (1971). *Neuropharmacology*, **10**, 453–458.
Balagura, S. (1968). *J. Comp. physiol. Psychol.*, **65**, 30–32.
Banks, E. M. (1962). *J. genet. Psychol.*, **101**, 165–183.
Bannova, N. V. (1961). *Gigiena Truda*, **3**, 9–13.
Barber, D. L., Blackburn, T. P., & Greenwood, D. T. (1973), *Physiol. Behav.*, **11**, 117–120.
Barnett, S. A., (1956). *Behaviour*, **9**, 24–00.
Barnett, S. A. (1963). *The Rat, a Study of Behaviour.* London: Methuen.
Barnett, S. A. & Smart, J. L. (1970). *Q. Jl. exp. Psychol.*, **22**, 494–502.
Barnett, S. A. & Spencer, M. M. (1953). *Br. J. Anim. Behav.*, **1**, 32–37.
Barnett, S. A., Smart, J. L., & Widdowson, E. (1971). *Devl. Psychobiol.*, **4**, 1–15.
Bateson, P. P. G. & Reese, E. (1969). *Anim. Behav.*, **17**, 692–699.
Battig, K. & Grandjean E. (1963). *Archs environ. Hlth.*, **7**, 694–699.
Bauer, R. H. (1972). *Psychopharmacologia*, **24**, 275–295.
Bauer, R. H. & Duncan, N. G. (1971). *J. comp. physiol. Psychol.*, **77**, 521–527.
Beach, F. A. (1968). *Behaviour*, **30**, 218–238.
Beach, F. A. & Holz-Tucker, A. M. (1949). *J. comp. physiol. Psychol.*, **42**, 433–453.
Beritashvili, J. S. (1966). *A Rev. Physiol.*, **28**, 1–16.

Bignami, G., Acetis, L. de, & Gatti, G. L. (1971). *J. Pharmac. exp. Ther.*, **176**, 725–732.
Bindra, D. & Mendelson, J. (1962). *J. exp. Psychol.*, **63**, 505–509.
Bliss, D. K. (1974). *Fedn. Proc.*, **33**, 1787–1796.
Blough, D. S. (1958). *J. exp. Analysis Behav.*, **1**, 31–43.
Boice, R. (1972). *Behaviour*, **42**, 198–231.
Boissier, J. R. & Simon, P. (1962). *Thérapie*, **17**, 1225–1232.
Bolles, R. C. (1960), *J. comp. physiol. Psychol.*, **53**, 306–310.
Bolles, R. C. (1961), *J. comp. physiol. Psychol.*, **54**, 580–584
Boreman, J. & Price, E. (1972). *Anim. Behav.*, **20**, 534–542.
Boren, J. J. (1966). In *Operant Behavior; areas of research and application.* (ed. W. K. Honig). New York: Appleton–Century–Croft, pp. 531–564.
Boren, J. J. & Navarro, A. P. (1959). *J. exp. Analysis Behav.*, **2**, 107–115.
Borgen, L. A., Khalsa, J. H., King, W. T., & Davis, W. M. (1970). *Psychonomic Sci.*, **21**, 35–37.
Borgešová, M., Kadlecová, O., & Kršiak, M. (1971). *Activitas nervosa superior*, **13**, 206–207.
Bovet, D., Bovet-Nitti, F., & Oliverio, A. (1967). *Ann. N.Y. Acad. Sci.*, **142**, 261–267.
Bovet, D., Robustelli, F., & Bignami, G. (1965). *C. r. Acad. Sci. Paris*, **260**, 4641–4645.
Bradley, D. W. M., Joyce, D., Murphy, E. M., Nash, B. M., Porsolt, R. D., Summerfield, A., and Twyman, W. A. (1968). *Nature*, **220**, 187–188.
Bradley, P. B. (1964). In *Animal Behaviour and Drug Action.* (ed. H. Steinberg *et. al.*) Ciba Foundation. London: Churchill, pp. 119–131.
Brady, J. V. (1966). In *Operant Behavior: areas of research and application.* (ed. W. K. Honig). New York: Appleton–Century–Croft. pp. 609–633.
Breda, J. B., Carlini, E. A., & Sader, N. F. A. (1969). *Br. J. Pharmac.*, **37**, 79–86.
Broadhurst, P. L. (1957), *Br. J. Psychol.*, **48**, 1–12.
Broadhurst, P. L. (1964). In *Animal Behaviour and Drug Action.* (eds. Steinberg *et al.*). Ciba. London: Churchill, pp. 224–236.
Broadhurst, P. L. (1965). *Sci. J.*, (June), 39–43.
Broadhurst, P. L. & Bignami G. (1965). *Behav. Res. Ther.*, **2**, 273–280.
Broadhurst, P. L. & Wallgren, H. (1964). *Q. Jl. Stud. Alcohol*, **25**, 476–489.
Broadhurst, P. L. & Watson, R. H. J. (1964). *Anim. Behav.*, **12**, 42–51.
Brown, R. V. (1968). *Q. Jl. Stud. Alcohol*, **29**, 49–53.
Bruce, H. (1960). *J. Reprod. Fert.*, **1**, 96–103.
Bunnel, B. N., Sodetz, F. J., & Shalloway, D. I. (1970), *Physiol. Behav.*, **5**, 153–61.
Buxton, D. A., Verduyn, C., & Cox, T. (in prep.)

Cairns, R. B. & Scholz, S. D. (1973). *J. comp. physiol. Psychol.*, **85**, 540–550.
Calhoun, J. B. (1973). *Proc. Roy. Soc. Med.*, **66**, 80–86.
Campbell, B. A. & Misanin, J. R. (1969). *A. Rev. Psychol.*, **20**, 57–84.
Campbell, B. A. & Sheffield, F. D. (1953). *J. comp. physiol. Psychol.*, **46**, 320–322.
Campbell, D. & Richter, W. (1967). *Acta Pharmac. Tox.*, **25**, 345–363.
Candland, D. K., Faulds, B., Thomas, D. B., & Candland, M. H. (1960). *J. comp. physiol. Psychol.*, **53**, 55–58.
Cappell, H., Ginsburg, R., & Webster, C. D. (1972). *Br. J. Pharmac.*, **45**, 525–531.
Carlier, C. & Noirot, E. (1965). *Anim. Behav.*, **13**, 423–426.

Carlini, E. A., Hamaqui, A., & Märtz, R. M. W. (1972). *Br. J. Pharmac.*, **44**, 794–804.
Carlini, E. A., Lindsey, C. J., & Tufik, S. (1977). *Br. J. Pharmac.*, **61**, 371–379.
Carlton, P. L. (1968). In *Anticholinergic Drugs. Progress in Brain Research*, **28**, (eds. Bradley & Fink). Amsterdam: Elsevier, pp. 48–60.
Casterline, J. L., Brodie, R. E., & Sobotka, T. J. (1971). *Bull. Environ. Contam. Tox.*, **6**, 297–303.
Caswell, S. & Marks, D. (1973). *Nature*, **241**, 60–61.
Champlin, K., Blight, W. C., & McGill, T. E. (1963). *Anim. Behav.*, **11**, 244–245.
Chance, M. R. A. (1946). *J. Pharmac. exp. Ther.*, **87**, 214–219.
Chance, M. R. A. (1947). *J. Pharmac. exp. Ther.*, **89**, 289–296.
Chance, M. R. A. (1953). *Br. J. Anim. Behav.*, **1**, 118–119.
Chance, M. R. A. (1962). *Symp. zool. Soc. Lond.*, **8**, 71–89.
Chance, M. R. A. & Humphries, D. A. (1967). *Brit. J. med. Educ.*, **1**, 131–134.
Chance, M. R. A. & Mead, A. P. (1955). *Behaviour*, **8**, 174–182.
Chang, O. L. & Webster, C. D. (1971). *Br. J. Pharmac.*, **41**, 691–699.
Christensen, J. D. (1973). *Acta Pharmac. Tox.*, **33**, 255–261.
Clark, R. (1969). *Toxic. appl. Pharmac.*, **15**, 212–215.
Colvin, D. V. (1973). *Anim. Behav.*, **21**, 471–480.
Conger, J. J. (1951). *Q. Jl. Stud. Alcohol.*, **12**, 1–29.
Conway, F. J., Greenwood, D. T., & Middlemiss, D. N. (1978). *Clin. Sci. & Molec. Med.*, **54**, 1–8.
Cook, L. (1964). In *Animal Behaviour and Drug Action.* (ed. H. Steinberg *et al.*) Ciba Foundation. London: Churchill, pp. 23–40.
Cook, L. & Weidley, L. E. (1957). *Ann. N.Y. Acad. Sci.*, **66**, 740–752.
Cooper, J. & Levine, R. (1973). *Anim. Behav.*, **21**, 421–428.
Corbit, J. D. & Luschei, E. S. (1969). *J. comp. physiol. Psychol.*, **69**, 119–125.
Costa, E., Grappetti, A., & Naimzada, M. K. (1972). *Br. J. Pharmac.*, **44**, 742–751.
Crow, T. J. & Gillbe, C. (1973). *Nature, New Biol.*, **245**, 27–28.
Crowcroft, P. & Rowe, F. P. (1963). *Proc. zool. Soc. Lond.*, **140**, 517–531.
Cullen, E. (1957). *Ibis*, **99**, 275–302, cited by Hinde (1970).
Cutler, M., Mackintosh, J. H., & Chance, M. R. A. (1975a). *Psychopharmacologia*, **41**, 271–276.
Cutler, M., Mackintosh, J. H., & Chance, M. R. A. (1975b). *Psychopharmacologia*, **44**, 173–177.

Davies, J. A., Navaratnam, V., & Redfern, P. H. (1974). *Br. J. Pharmac.*, **51**, 447–451.
Davis, F. C. (1933). *J. Genet. Psychol.*, **43**, 213–217.
Davis, J. D., Gallagher, R. J., Ladove, R. E., & Turausky, A. J. (1969). *J. comp. physiol. Psychol.*, **67**, 407–414.
Dawkins, M. (1971). *Anim. Behav.*, **19**, 575–582.
Dawkins, R. (1971). *Behaviour*, **40**, 162–173.
Delius, J. D. (1967). *Nature*, **214**, 1259–1260.
Delius, J. D. (1969). *Behaviour*, **33**, 137–178.
Delius, J. D. (1973). *Anim. Behav.*, **21**, 236–246.
Denenberg, V. H., Gaulin-Kremer, E., Gandelman, R., & Zarrow, M. X. (1973). *Anim. Behav.*, **21**, 590–598.
Dennis, W. (1931). *J. comp. Psychol.*, **12**, 429–432.

Dési, I., Gönczi, L., Simon, G., Farkos, I., & Kneffel, Z. (1974). *Toxic appl. Pharmac.*, **27**, 465–476.
Dews, P. B. (1955). *J. Pharmac. exp. Ther.*, **113**, 393–401.
Dews, P. B. (1964). In *Animal Behaviour and Drug Action.* (ed. H. Steinberg *et al.*) Ciba Foundation. London: Churchill, pp. 191–201.
Dews, P. B. & Morse, W. H. (1961). *A. Rev. Pharmac.*, **1**, 145–174.
Dewsbury, D. A. (1967). *Behaviour*, **29**, 154–178.
Dixon, A. K. & Mackintosh, J. H. (1975). *Anim. Behav.*, **23**, 513–520.
Domino, E. F., Yamamoto, K., & Dren, T. (1968). *Prog. Brain. Res.*, **28**, 113–133.
Dorr, M., Steinberg, H., Tomkiewicz, M., Joyce, D., Porsolt, R. D., & Summerfield, A. (1971). *Nature*, **231**, 121–123.
Doty, L. A. & Doty, B. A. (1963). *J. comp. physiol. Psychol.*, **56**, 740–745.
Draper, W. A. (1967). *Behaviour*, **28**, 280–306.
Driver, P. M. (1960). Ph.D. Thesis. McGill Univ.
Drori, D. & Folman, Y. (1967). *Anim. Behav.*, **15**, 20–24.
Duncan, I. J. H. & Wood-Gush, D. G. M. (1972). *Anim. Behav.*, **20**, 68–71.
Duncan, N. G. & Hunt, E. (1972). *Physiol. Behav.*, **9**, 295–300.

Eayrs, J. T. (1954). *Br. J. Anim. Behav.*, **2**, 25–30.
Eddy, N. B. & Leimbach, D. (1953). *J. Pharmac. exp. Ther.*, **107**, 385–393.
Ericksson, K. (1967). *Nature*, **213**, 1316–1317.
Evans, H. L., Laties, V. G., & Weiss, B. (1975). *Fedn. Proc.*, **34**, 1858–1867.
Evans, L. T. & Abramson, H. A. (1958). *J. Psychol.*, **45**, 153–169.
Evans, L. T., Abramson, H. A., & Fremont-Smith, N. (1958). *J. Psychol.*, **45**, 263–273.
Evans, S. (1937). *J. genet. Psychol.*, **50**, 243–275.
Ewer, R. F. (1971). *Anim. Behav. Monogr.*, **4**, 127–174.
Extance, K., Silverman, A. P., & Williams, H. (1976). In *Adverse Effects of Environmental Chemicals and Drugs.* (ed. M. Horváth & E. Frantík). **2**, Amsterdam: Elsevier. pp. 197–200.

Falk, J. L., Samson H. H., & Winger, G. (1972). *Science*, **177**, 811–813.
Farris, E. J. & Yenkel, E. H. (1945). *J. Comp. Psychol.*, **38**, 109.
Fentress, J. C. & Stilwell, F. P. (1973). *Nature*, **244**, 52–53.
Ferster, C. B. (1967). In *Neuropsychopharmacology.* (ed. H. Brill *et al.*). **5**, Excerpta Medica Foundation, pp. 749–756.
Ferster, C. B. & Skinner, B. F. (1957). *Schedules of Reinforcement.* New York: Appleton–Century–Croft.
File, S. E. (1973). *Br. J. Pharmac.*, **49**, 303–310.
Fitzsimons J. T. (1966). *J. Physiol.*, **186**, 130–131 P.
Francis, R. L. (1977). *Nature*, **265**, 236–238.

Garcia, J. & Koelling, R. A. (1966). *Psychon. Sci.*, **4**, 123–124.
Geller, I. & Seifter, J. (1960). *Psychopharmacologia*, **1**, 482–492.
Geller, I., Kulak, J. F., & Seifter J. (1962). *Psychopharmacologia*, **3**, 374–385.
Gellerman, L. W. (1933). *J. genet. Psychol.*, **42**, 207–208.
Gerald, M. C. & Maickel, R. P. (1972). *Br. J. Pharmac.*, **44**, 462–471.
Gerall H., Ward, I. L., & Gerall, A. A. (1967) *Anim. Behav.*, **15**, 54–58.
Glees, P. (1967). *Proc. Europ. Soc. Study Drug Tox.*, **8**, 136–148.
Glick, S. D. & Jarvik, M. E. (1969). *J. Pharmac. exp. Ther.*, **169**, 1–6.

Glover, J. & Jacobs, A. (1972). *Br. med. J.*, **2**, 627–628.
Gold, P. E. & McGaugh, J. L. (1973). *Physiol. Behav.*, **10**, 41–46.
Goldberg, H. D. & Chappell, M. N. (1967). *Archs. environ. Hlth.*, **14**, 671–677.
Goldberg, M. E., Haun, C., & Smyth, H. F. (1962). *Toxic. appl. Pharmac.*, **4**, 148-164.
Goldberg, M. E., Johnson H. E., Pozzani, V. C., & Smyth H. F. (1964a). *Acta pharmac. tox.*, **21**, 36–44.
Goldberg, M. E., Johnson, H. E., Pozzani, V. C., & Smyth, H. F. (1964b). *Amer. ind. Hyg. Assoc. J.*, **25**, 369–375.
Grandjean, E. (1960). *Arch. environ. Hlth.*, **1**, 106–108.
Grant, E. C. (1963). *Behaviour*, **21**, 260–281.
Grant, E. C. & Chance, M. R. A. (1958). *Anim. Behav.*, **6**, 183–194.
Grant, E. C. & Mackintosh, J. H. (1963). *Behaviour*, **21**, 246–259.
Grant, E. C., Mackintosh, J. H., & Lerwill, C. J. (1970). *Z. Tierpsychol.*, **27**, 73–77.
Granville-Grossman, K. L. & Turner, P. (1966). *Lancet*, **1**, 788–790.
Green, A. R. & Grahame-Smith, D. G. (1976). *Nature*, **262**, 594–596.
Green, K. F. & Garcia, J. (1971). *Science*, **173**, 749–751.
Griffiths, P. J., Littleton, J. M., & Ortiz, A. (1973). *Br. J. Pharmac.*, **47**, 669–670P.
Grossman, S. P. (1961). *J. comp. physiol. Psychol.*, **54**, 514–521.
Grossman, S. P. (1968). *Fedn. Proc.*, **27** (6), 1359–1360.
Grunt, J. A. & Young, W. C. (1953). *J. comp. physiol. Psychol.*, **46**, 138–144.
Gumma, M. R. & South, F. E. (1970). *Anim. Behav.*, **18**, 504–511.

Haeusler, G., Gerold, M., & Thoenen, H. (1972). *Archs. Pharmac.*, **274**, 211–228.
Hailman, J. P. (1969). *Scient. Am.*, **221**, 98–106.
Hake, D. F. & Azrin, N. H. (1963). *J. exp. Analysis Behav.*, **6**, 297–298.
Halberg, F. & Barnum, C. P. (1958). *Proc. Soc. exp. Biol. Med.*, **97**, 897–900.
Hall, C. S. (1934a). *J. comp. physiol. Psychol.*, **17**, 89–108.
Hall, C. S. (1934b). *J. comp. physiol. Psychol.*, **18**, 385–403.
Hall, C. S. & Klein, N. (1942). *J. comp. Psychol.*, **33**, 371–383.
Halliday, M. S. (1967). *Q. Jl. exp. Psychol.*, **19**, 254–263.
Halliday, T. R. (1977). *Anim. Behav.*, **25**, 39–45.
Halliday, T. R. & Sweatman, H. P. A. (1976). *Anim. Behav.*, **24**, 551–561.
Hamilton, W. D. (1964). *J. theor. Biol.*, **7**, 1–52.
Headlee, C. P., Coppock, H. W., & Nichols, J. R. (1955). *J. Am. pharm. Ass. Sci. Edn.*, **44**, 229–231.
Hebb. D. O. (1949). *The Organisation of Behavior.* New York: Wiley.
Hecht, K. (1967). In *Neuropsychopharmacology.* (ed. H. Brill *et al.*), **5**, Excerpta Medica Foundation, pp. 848–856.
Heimstra, N. W. (1961). *Behaviour*, **18**, 313–321.
Henton, W. W. (1969). *J. exp. Analysis Behav.*, **12**, 175–185.
Herrnstein, R. J. (1966). In *Operant Behavior: areas of research & application.* (ed. W. K. Honig). New York: Appleton–Century–Croft, pp. 33–51.
Herrnstein, R. J. & Loveland, D. H. (1964). *Science*, **146**, 549–551.
Herxheimer, A. & Douglas, M. B. (1963). *J. Pharm. Pharmac.*, **15**, 849–850.
Hess, E. H. (1959). *Science*, **130**, 133–141.
Higginson, G. D. (1930). *J. comp. Psychol.*, **10**, 1.
Hill, S. Y. & Powell, B. J. (1976). *Psychopharmacology*, **50**, 309–312.
Hinde, R. A. (1959). *Anim. Behav.*, **7**, 130–141.
Hinde, R. A. (1970). *Animal Behaviour.* (2nd edn). New York: McGraw-Hill.

Hinde. R. A. & Stevenson-Hinde, J. (1973) eds. *Constraints on Learning*. London: Academic Press.
Hoffman, H. S. (1966). In *Operant Behavior: areas of research and application*. (ed. W. K. Honig). New York: Appleton–Century–Croft, pp. 499–530.
Hoffman, H. S. Fleshler, M., & Chorny, H. (1961). *J. exp. Analysis Behav.*, **4**, 309–316.
Hogan, J. A. (1973). In *Constraints on Learning*. (eds R. A. Hinde & J. Stevenson-Hinde). London: Academic Press, pp. 119–139.
Holland, H. C. (1965). *Anim. Behav.*, **13**, 201–202.
Holloway, F. A. & Wansley, R. (1973). *Science*, **180**, 208–210.
Holmes, W. (1940). *Proc. zool, Soc. Lond.*, A., **110**, 17–36.
Honig, W. K. (1966). *Operant Behavior: areas of research and application*. (ed. W. K. Honig). New York: Appleton–Century–Croft, p. 9.
Hope, K. (1968). *Methods of Multivariate Analysis*. University of London Press.
Hordern, A. (1968). In *Psychopharmacology, Dimensions and Perspectives*, (ed. C. R. B. Joyce). London: Tavistock, pp. 95–148.
Horváth, M. & Formánek, J. (1959). *Zh. Vyssh. nervn. deiatel.*, **9**, 916–921 (English translation in *Pavlov J. Higher Nervous Activity*, **9**, 829–835).
Horváth, M. & Frantík, E. (1970). In *Chemical Influences on Behaviour*. Ciba Study Group No. 35. London: Churchill, pp. 171–187.
Hughes, F. W. & Rountree, C. B. (1961). *Archs. int. Pharmacodyn. Ther.*, **133**, 418–432.
Hughes, J., Annau, Z., & Goldberg, A. M. (1972). *Fedn. Proc.*, Abs. 1906.
Hughes, R. N. (1972). *Psychopharmacologia*, **24**, 462–469.
Humphries, D. A. & Driver, P. M. (1970). *Oecologia*, **5**, 285–302.
Hunt, H. F. (1956). *Ann. N.Y. Acad. Sci.*, **65**, 258–267.
Hunt, H. F. (1961). *A. Rev. Pharmac.*, **1**, 125–144.
Hunter, W. S. (1920). *Psychobiology*, **2**, 1–18.
Huntingford, F. A. (1976a). *Anim. Behav.*, **24**, 485–497.
Huntingford, F. A. (1976b) *Anim. Behav.*, **24**, 822–834.
Hurwitz, H. M. B. & Dillow, P. V. (1969). In *Animal Discrimination Learning*. (eds R. M. Gilbert & N. S. Sutherland). London: Academic Press.

Iersel, J. J. A. van & Bol, A. C. A. (1958). *Behaviour*, **13**, 1–88.
Irwin, S. (1959). Paper presented to Gordon Research Conference.
Irwin, S., Slabok, M., Debiase, P. L., & Govier, W. M. (1959). *Archs. int. Pharmacodyn. Thér.*, **188**, 358–374.
Irwin, S. (1962). *Science*, **136**, 123–128.
Iversen, L. L., Iversen, S. D., & Snyder, S. H. (eds) (1977). *Handbook of Psychopharmacology*, **7**, *Principles of Behavioral Pharmacology*. New York: Plenum.

Jacobs, B. L. & Sorenson, C. A. (1969). *J. comp. physiol. Psychol.*, **68**, 239–244.
Janssen, P. A. J., Jageneau, A. H., & Niemegeers, C. J. E. (1960). *J. Pharmac. exp. Ther.*, **129**, 471–475.
Jarman, P. J. (1974). *Behaviour*, **48**, 215–267.
Jaton, A. L., Loew, D. M., & Vigouret, J. M. (1976). *Br. J. Pharmac.*, **56**, 371P.
Jenkins, H. M. (1973). In *Constraints on Learning*. (eds R. A. Hinde & J. Stevenson-Hinde). London: Academic Press, pp. 189–203.
Jirsik, J. (1955). *Saugertierkundiche Mitteilungen*, **3**, 21.
Jones, B. J. & Roberts, D. J. (1968). *J. Pharm. Pharmac.*, **20**, 302–304.
Jones, M. R. (1943). *J. comp. Psychol.*, **35**, 1–10.

Kalat, J. W. & Rozin, P. (1973). *J. comp. physiol. Psychol.*, **83**, 198–207.
Kalmus, H. (1955). *Br. J. Anim. Behav.*, **3**, 25–31.
Kamin, L. J. (1957). *J. comp. psychol.*, **50**, 457.
Kapatos, G. & Gold, R. M. (1972). *Science*, **176**, 685–686.
Karli, P. (1955). *C. r. Soc. Biol.*, **149**, 2227.
Kavanau, J. L. (1962). *Anim. Behav.*, **11**, 263–273.
Kavanau, J. L. (1963). *Behaviour*, **20**, 251–281.
Kavanau, J. L., Ramos, J., & Havenhill, R. (1973). *Behaviour*, **46**, 279–299.
Kelly, P. H. & Miller, R. J. (1975). *Br. J. Pharmac.*, **54**, 115–121.
Kendler, H. H. & Lachman, R. (1958). *J. exp. Psychol.*, **55**, 584–591.
Kennedy, J. S. (1954). *Br. J. Anim. Behav.*, **2**, 12–19.
Khavari, K. A. & Russell, R. W. (1969). *Physiol. Behav.*, **4**, 461–463.
King, A. R. (1970). In *Chemical Influences on Behaviour* (eds R. Porter & J. Birch). Ciba Study Group 35. London: Churchill, pp. 17–24 and 41–52.
King, A. R., Martin, I. L., & Seymour, K. A. (1974). *Br. J. Pharmac.*, **52**, 419–426.
Kissileff, H. (1970). *Physiol. Behav.*, **5**, 163–173.
Knoll, J. & Knoll, B. (1961). *Archs. int. Pharmacodyn. Ther.*, **130**, 141–154.
Koch, A. M. & Warden, C. J. (1936). *J. genet. Psychol.*, **48**, 215–217.
Kotliarevsky, L. I. (1951). *Zh. Vyss. nervn. deiatel.*, **1**, 753–761 (translated in *Pavlov J. Higher Nervous Activity*).
Kral, P. A. & Beggerly, H. D. (1973). *Physiol. Behav.*, **10**, 145–147.
Krebs, J. R., Ryan, J. C., & Charnov, E. L. (1974). *Anim. Behav.*, **22**, 953–964.
Kreezer, G. L. (1949). In *The Rat in Laboratory Investigation.* (eds Farris & Griffith) (2nd ed.). Philadelphia: Lipincott, pp. 203–277.
Krnjević, H. & Videk, M. (1967). *Psychopharmacologia*, **10**, 308–315.
Kršiak, M. (1975). *Br. J. Pharmac.*, **55**, 141–150.
Kršiak, M. & Janků, I. (1971). *Psychopharmacologia*, **21**, 118–130.
Kršiak, M., Steinberg, H., & Stolerman, I. P. (1970). *Psychopharmacologia*, **17**, 258–274.
Kulkarni, A. S., Thompson, T., & Shideman, F. E. (1966). *J. Neurochem.*, **13**, 1143–1148.
Kumar, R. (1969). *Psychopharmacologia*, **16**, 54–72.
Kumar, R. (1970a). *J. comp. physiol. Psychol.*, **70**, 258–263.
Kumar, R. (1970b). *Q. Jl. exp. Psychol.*, **22**, 205–214.
Kumar, R. (1971a). *Psychopharmacologia*, **19**, 163–187.
Kumar, R. (1971b). *Psychopharmacologia*, **19**, 297–312.
Kumar, R., Steinberg, H., & Stolerman, I. P. (1968). *Nature*, **218**, 564–565.
Kumar, R., & Stolerman, I. P. (1977). In *Handbook of Psychopharmacology*, **7**, (ed. Iversen *et al.*). New York: Plenum. pp. 321–367.
Kuo, Z.-Y. (1932). *J. comp. Psychol.*, **14**, 109–122 (cited by Hinde, 1970).

Lal. H. & Brown, R. M. (1969). *Toxic. appl. Pharmac.*, **14**, 41–47.
Lammers. A. J. J. C. & van Rossum, J. M. (1968). *Europ. J. Pharmac.*, **5**, 103–106.
Langham, R. J., Syme, G. J., & Syme, L. A. (1975). *Br. J. Pharmac.*, **55**, 409–413.
Lashley, K. S. (1938). *J. gen. Psychol.*, **18**, 123–193.
Lashley, K. S. (1939). *J. comp. Neurol.*, **70**, 45–67.
Lát, J. (1965). In *Learning, Conditioning & Retention.* Proc. 2nd. Int. Pharmac. Meeting, Prague, **1**, Oxford: Pergamon, pp. 47–63.
Lát. J., Widdowson, E. M., & McCance, R. A. (1960). *Proc. R. Soc.*, B. **153**, 347–356.

Laties, V. G. (1972). *J. Pharmac. exp. Ther.*, **183**, 1–13.
Laties, V. G. & Weiss, B. (1966). *J. Pharmac. exp. Ther.*, **153**, 388–396.
Laties, V. G., Weiss, B., & Weiss, A. B. (1969). *J. expl. Analysis Behav.*, **12**, 43–57.
Lauener, H. (1963). *Psychopharmacologia*, **4**, 311–325.
Le Magnen, J. & Tallon, S. (1966). *J. Physiol.*, (Paris), **58**, 323–349.
Lehrman, D. E. (1956). In *L'instinct dans le comportement des animaux et de l'homme*. Paris: Singer-Polignac Foundation, pp. 284–285.
Levitsky, D. A. & Barnes, R. H. (1972). *Science*, **176**, 68–71.
Lewis, D. J., Bregman, N. J., & Mahan, J. J. (1972). *J. comp. physiol. Psychol.*, **81**, 243-247.
Lewis, M. (1968). *J. comp. physiol. Psychol.*, **65**, 208–212.
Leyhausen, P. (1956). *Z. Tierpsychol.*, Suppl. 2 (Verhaltenstudien an Katzen).
Liebman, J. M. & Butcher, L. L. (1973). *Arch. Tox.*, **277**, 305–318.
Littleton, J. M. (1974). *Acta pharmac. Tox.*, **34**, 92–96.
Locke, N. M. (1936). *J. Psychol.*, **1**, 255–260.
Logan, F. A. & Boice, R. (1969). *Behaviour*, **34**, 161–183.
Lorenz, K. Z. (1937). *Auk*, **54**, 245–273.
Lorenz, K. Z. (1953). *King Solomon's Ring*. London: Methuen.
Lorenz, K. Z. (1968). *On Aggression*. London: Methuen.
Lovett, D. & Booth, D. A. (1970) *Q. Jl. exp. Psychol.*, **22**, 406–419.

McDougal, W. (1923). *An Outline of Psychology*. London: Methuen.
McFarland, D. J. (1969). *Physiol Behav.*, **4**, 987–989.
McFarland, D. J. (1971). *Feedback Mechanisms in Animal Behaviour*. London: Academic Press.
McGill, T. E. (1962). *Behaviour*, **19**, 341–350.
McGaugh, J. L. (1973). *A Rev. Pharmac.*, **13**, 229–242.
Mackintosh, J. H. (1962). *Nature*, **194**, 1304.
Mackintosh, J. H. (1970). *Anim. Behav.*, **18**, 177–183.
Mackintosh, J. H. (1973). *Anim. Behav.*, **21**, 464–470.
Mackintosh, J. H. & Grant, E. C. (1966). *Z. Tierpsychol.*, **23**, 584–587.
Maffii, G. (1959). *J. Pharm. Pharmac.*, **11**, 129–139.
Magos, L. Butler, W. H. (1972). *Fd. Cosmet. Tox.*, **10**, 513–517.
Mainardi, D., Marsan, M., & Pasquali, A. (1965). *Atti. Soc. Sci. Natur. Milano*, **104**, 325–338.
Malick, J. B. (1970). *Physiol Behav.*, **5**, 519–524.
Mallov, S. & Witt, P. N. (1961). *J. Pharmac. exp. Ther.*, **132**, 126–130.
Malthus, T. (1798 revised 1803). *An Essay on Population*.
Margules, D. L. & Stein, L. (1967). In *Neuropsychopharmacology*, (ed. H. Brill *et al.*). **5**, Excerpta Medica Foundation, pp. 108–120.
Margules, D. L., Lewis, M. J., Dragovich, J. A., & Margules, A. S. (1972). *Science*, **178**, 640–643.
Marley, E. & Morse, W. H. (1966). *J. exp. Analysis Behav.*, **9**, 95–103.
Masserman, J. H. & Yum, K. S. (1946). *Psychosom. Med.*, **8**, 36–52.
Meddis, R. (1975). *Anim. Behav.*, **23**, 676–691.
Medved, L. I., Spynu, E. I., & Kagan, Iu. S. (1964). *Residue Rev.*, **6**, 42–74.
Mellgren, R. L., Willison, P. W., & Dickson, A. L. (1973). *Bull. Psychonom. Soc.*, **2**, 37–38.
Mendelson, J. & Chillig, D. (1970). *Physiol. Behav.*, **5**, 535–537.
Michal, K. (1973). *Behaviour*, **44**, 264–285.

Miczek, K. A. (1973). *Pharmac. Biochem. Behav.*, **1**, 401–411.
Miller, N. E. (1964). In *Animal Behaviour and Drug Action.* (ed. Steinberg). Ciba. London: Churchill, pp. 1–8.
Miller, N. E. & Barry, H. III (1960). *Psychopharmacologia*, **1**, 169–199.
Miller, N. E. & Miles, W. R. (1935). *J. comp. Psychol.*, **20**, 397–412.
Milner, P. M. (1977). In *Handbook of Psychopharmacology*, **7** (ed. Iversen *et al.*) New York: Plenum. pp. 181–200.
Montgomery, K. C. (1954). *J. comp. physiol. Psychol.*, **47**, 60–64.
Montgomery, K. C. (1955). *J. comp. physiol. Psychol.*, **48**, 254–260.
Moore, B. R. (1973). In *Constraints on Learning.* (eds R. A. Hinde & J. Stevenson-Hinde). London: Academic Press, pp. 159–186.
Morgan, B. J. T., Simpson, M. J. A., Hanby, J. P., & Hall-Craggs, J. (1976). *Behaviour*, **56**, 1–43.
Morgan, M. J. (1973). *Anim. Behav.*, **21**, 429–442.
Morris, D. (1956). In *L'instinct dans le comportement des animaux et de l'homme.* Paris: Singer-Polignac Foundation, pp. 261–284.
Morrison, C. F. (1967). *Int. J. Neuropharmacol.*, **6**, 229–240.
Morrison, C. F. (1968). *Br. J. Pharmac.*, **32**, 28–33.
Morrison, C. F. & Armitage, A. K. (1967). *Ann. N.Y. Acad. Sci.*, **142**, 268–276.
Morrison, C. F. & Stephenson, J. A. (1970). *Psychopharmacologia*, **18**, 133–143.
Morrison, C. F. & Stephenson, J. A. (1972a). *Psychopharmacologia*, **24**, 456–461.
Morrison, C. F. & Stephenson, J. A. (1972b). *Br. J. Pharmac.*, **46**, 151–156.
Morrison, C. F. & Stephenson, J. A. (1973). *Neuropharmacology*, **12**, 297–310.
Morse, W. H. (1966). In *Operant Behavior: areas of research and application.* (ed. W. K. Honig). New York: Appleton–Century–Croft, pp. 52–108.
Moss, F. A. (1924). *J. exp. Psychol.*, **7**, 165–185.
Mouret, J., Bobillier, P., & Jouvet, M. (1968). *Europ. J. Pharmac.*, **5**, 17–22.
Munn, N. L. & Collins, M. (1936). *J. genet. Psychol.*, **48**, 72–87.
Myer, J. S. & White, R. T. (1965). *Anim. Behav.*, **13**, 430–433.
Myers, A. K. (1959). *J. comp. physiol. Psychol.*, **52**, 381–386.
Myers, R. D. & Carey, R. (1961). *Science*, **134**, 469–470.
Myers, R. D. & Veale, W. L. (1968). *Science*, **160**, 1469–1471.

Nachman, M. & Hartley, P. L. (1975). *J. comp. physiol. Psychol.*, **89**, 1010–1018.
Nigro, M. R. (1967). *Psychol. Rep.*, **21**, 61–69.
Nissen, H. W. (1930). *J. genet. Psychol.*, **37**, 361–376.
Noirot, E. (1964a). *Anim. Behav.*, **12**, 52–58.
Noirot, E. (1964b). *Anim. Behav.*, **12**, 442–445.
Norton, S. (1957). In *Psychotropic Drugs.* (eds Garattini and Ghetti) pp. 73–82. Amsterdam: Elsevier.
Norton, S. & de Beer. E. J. (1956). *Ann. N.Y. Acad. Sci.*, **65**, 249–257.

O'Kelly, L. I. & Steckle, L. C. (1939). *J. Psychol.*, **18**, 125–131.
Oatley, K. & Dickenson, A. (1970). *Anim. Behav.*, **18**, 259–265.
Olds, J. J. & Travis, R. P. (1960). *J. Pharmac. exp. Ther.*, **128**, 397–404.
Olds, J. J., Travis, R. P., & Schwing, R. C. (1960). *J. comp. physiol. Psychol.*, **53**, 23–32.
Olivierio, A., Castellana C., Renzi, P., & Sansone, M. (1973). *Psychopharmacologia*, **29**, 13–20.
Oswald, I. (1968). *Pharmac. Rev.*, **20**, 273–303.

Oswald, I. (1973). *A. Rev. Pharmac.*, **13**, 243–252.
Overton, D. A. (1964). *J. comp. physiol. Psychol.*, **57**, 3–12.

Pavlov, I. P. (1927). *Conditioned Reflexes.* Oxford U.P. (repr. 1960. Dover).
Payne, A. P. & Swanson, H. H. (1970). *Behaviour*, **36**, 259–269.
Peng, S. K., Ho, K. J., & Taylor, C. B. (1972). *Archs Path.*, **94**, 81–89.
Potter, B. (1904). *A tale of two bad mice.* London: F. Warne.
Prescott, R. G. W. (1970). *Anim. Behav.*, **18**, 791–796.
Price, J. S. (1967). *Lancet*, **ii**, 243–246.

Rajalakshmi, R. & Jeeves, M. A. (1965). *Anim. Behav.*, **13**, 203–211.
Randt, C. T., Barnett, B. M., McEwen, B. S., & Quartermain, D. (1971). *Exp. Neurol.*, **30**, 467–474.
Ratner, A. M. & Hoffman, H. S. (1974). *Anim. Behav.*, **22**, 249–255.
Ray, O. S. (1963). *Psychopharmacologia*, **4**, 326–342.
Ray, O. S. (1964). *Psychopharmacologia*, **5**, 136–146.
Raynaud, G., Ducrocq, J., & Raoul, Y. (1966). *J. Physiol.*, (Paris), **58**, 749–761.
Reed, C. F. & Witt, P. N. (1968). *Physiol Behav.*, **3**, 119–134.
Revusky, S. & Garcia, J. (1970). In *Psychology of Learning and Motivation.* (ed. G. H. Bower). **4**, New York: Academic Press, pp. 1–83.
Reynolds, W. F. & Pavlik, W. B. (1960). *J. comp. physiol. Psychol.*, **53**, 615–618.
Richards, M. P. M. (1966). *Anim. Behav.*, **14**, 303–309.
Richards, S. M. (1974). *Anim. Behav.*, **22**, 914–930.
Richter, C. P. (1927). *Q. Rev. Biol.*, **2**, 307–343.
Rohte, O. (1969). *Psychopharmacologia*, **14**, 18–22.
Rosenzweig, M. R., Bennett, E. L., & Diamond, M. C. (1972). *Scient. Am.*, **226**, 22–29.
Rotrosen, J., Angrist, B. M., Gershon, S., Sachar, E. J., & Halpern, F. S. (1976). *Psychopharmacology*, **51**, 1–8.
Rowe, F. P. & Redfern, R. (1969). *Ann. appl. Biol.*, **64**, 425–431.
Rozin, P. (1968). *J. comp. physiol. Psychol.*, **65**, 23–29.
Rozin, P. (1969). *J. comp. physiol. Psychol.*, **69**, 126–132.
Rozin, P. & Kalat, J. W. (1971). *Psychol. Rev.*, **78**, 459–486.
Rushton, R., Steinberg, H., & Tinson, C. (1963). *Br. J. Pharmac.*, **20**, 99–105.
Rushton, R., Steinberg, H., & Tomkiewicz, M. (1968). *Nature*, **220**, 885–889.

Sacra, P., Rice, W. B., & McColl, J. D. (1957). *Can. J. Biochem. Physiol*, **53**, 1151–1152.
Saelens, J. K., Kovacsics, G. B., & Allen, M. P. (1968). *Arch. int. Pharmacodyn. Ther.*, **173**, 411–416.
Sales, G. D. (1972). *Anim. Behav.*, **20**, 88–100.
Salzen, E. A. & Meyer, C. C. (1968). *J. comp. physiol. Psychol.*, **66**, 269–275.
Sayler, A. & Salmon, M. (1971). *Behaviour*, **40**, 62–85.
Schechter, M. D. & Rosecrans, J. A. (1972). *Psychopharmacologia*, **27**, 379–387.
Schiørring, E. (1971). *Behaviour*, **39**, 1–17.
Schmidt, H. & Dry, L. (1963). *J. comp. physiol. Psychol.*, **56**, 179–182.
Schmidt, H., Kleinman, K. M., & Douthitt, T. C. (1967). *Physiol. Behav.*, **2**, 265–271.
Schuster, C. R. & Thompson, T. (1969). *A. Rev. Pharmac.*, **9**, 483–502.
Scott, E. M. & Verney, E. L. (1947). *J. Nutr.*, **34**, 471–480.
Scott, J. P. (1947). *J. comp. physiol. Psychol.*, **40**, 275–282.

Scourse, N. J. S. & Hinde, R. A. (1973). *Behaviour*, **47**, 1–13.
Senault, B., (1977). *Psychopharmacology*, **55**, 135–140.
Sevenster, P. (1973). In *Constraints on Learning*. (eds. R. A. Hinde & J. Stevenson-Hinde). London: Academic Press, pp. 265–283.
Seward, J. P. (1945a). *J. comp. physiol. Psychol.*, **38**, 175–197.
Seward, J. P. (1945b). *J. comp. physiol. Physiol. Psychol.*, **38**, 213–224.
Seward, J. P. (1945c). *J. comp. physiol. Psychol.*, **38**, 225–238.
Seward, J. P. & Raskin, D. C. (1960). *J. comp. physiol. Psychol.*, **53**, 328–335.
Shettleworth, S. (1973). In *Constraints on Learning*. (eds. R. A. Hinde and J. Stevenson-Hinde). London: Academic Press, pp. 243–263.
Shillito, E. E. (1967). *Br. J. Pharmac.*, **30**, 258–264.
Shillito, E. E. (1969). *Br. J. Pharmac.*, **36**, 193–194P.
Shillito, E. E. (1970a). *Br. J. Pharmac.*, **38**, 305–315.
Shillito, E. E. (1970b). *Br. J. Pharmac.*, **40**, 113–123.
Shirley, M. (1929). *Psychol. Bull.*, **26**, 341–365.
Sidman, M. (1953). *J. comp. physiol. Psychol.*, **46**, 253–261.
Sidman, M. (1966). In *Operant Behavior: areas of research and application* (ed. W. K. Honig). New York: Appleton–Century–Croft, pp. 448–498.
Siegel, P. S. & Stuckey, H. L. (1947). *J. comp. physiol. Psychol.*, **40**, 271–274.
Siegel, S. (1956). *Non-parametric Statistics for the Behavioral Sciences*. New York: McGraw-Hill.
Silverman, A. P. (1965). *Br. J. Pharmac.*, **24**, 579–590.
Silverman, A. P. (1966a). *Behaviour*, **27**, 1–38.
Silverman, A. P. (1966b). *Psychopharmacologia*, **10**, 155–171.
Silverman, A. P. (1970). In *Chemical Effects on Behaviour* (ed. Porter and Birch). Ciba Study Group 35. London: Churchill, pp. 25–37.
Silverman, A. P. (1971). *Anim. Behav.*, **19**, 67–74.
Silverman, A. P. (1973). *Archs Pharmac.*, **279**, suppl. p. 35.
Silverman, A. P. (1976). *Br. J. Pharmac.*, **58**, 439–440P.
Silverman, A. P. & Williams, H. (1975). *Br. J. ind. Med.*, **32**, 308–315.
Skinner, B. F. (1966). In *Operant Behavior: areas of research and application*. (ed. W. K. Honig). New York: Appleton–Century–Croft, pp. 12–32.
Slater, P. J. B. & Ollason, J. C. (1972). *Behaviour*, **42**, 248–269.
Small, W. S. (1901). *Am. J. Psychol.*, **12**, 206–239.
Smythies, J. R., Johnson, V. S., & Bradley, R. J. (1967). *Nature*, **216**, 196.
Soane, I. D. & Clarke. B. (1973). *Nature*, **241**, 62–64.
Spalding, D. (1872) repr. 1954. *Br. J. Anim. Behav.*, **2**, 2–11.
Sparber, S. B. & Tilson, H. A. (1971). *J. Pharmac. exp. Ther.*, **179**, 1–9.
Speizer, Z. & Weinstock, M. (1973). *Br. J. Pharmac.*, **48**, 348–349P.
Speizer, Z. & Weinstock, M. (1974). *Br. J. Pharmac.*, **52**, 605–608.
Spragg, S. D. S. (1940). *Comp. Psychol. Monogr.*, **15** (7).
Sprott, R. L. (1972). *J. comp. physiol. Psychol.*, **80**, 327–334.
Spurway, H. & Haldane, J. B. S. (1953). *Behaviour*, **6**, 8–34.
Stein, L. (1964). *Animal Behaviour and Drug Action*. (ed. Steinberg *et al.*) Ciba Foundation. London: Churchill, pp. 91–118.
Stein, L. (1968). In *Psychopharmacology, a review of progress* 1957–1967 (ed. Efron *et al.*). Washington: U.S. Government Printing Office, pp. 105–123.
Steinberg, H., Rushton, R., & Tinson, C. (1961). *Nature*, **192**, 533–535.
Steiniger, F. (1950). *Z. Tierpsychol.*, **7**, 356–379.
Stephens, R. J. (1973). *Br. J. Pharmac.*, **49**, 146P.

Stevens, D. M. (1955). *Br. J. Anim. Behav.*, **3**, 14–16.
Stevens, S. S. (1951). In *Handbook of Experimental Psychology* (ed. Stevens). New York: Wiley.
Stevenson-Hinde, J. (1973). In *Constraints On Learning* (ed. Hinde and Stevenson-Hinde) pp. 285–296. London: Academic Press.
Stewart, W. W. (1972). *Nature*, **238**, 202–209.
Stone, G. C. (1960). *J. comp. physiol. Psychol.*, **53**, 33–37.
Svensson, T. H. & Thieme, L. (1969). *Psychopharmacologia*, **14**, 157–163.
Syme, G. J. (1974). *Anim. Behav.*, **22**, 931–940.
Syme, G. J., Pollard, J. S., Syme, L.A., & Reid, R. M. (1974). *Anim. Behav.*, **22**, 486–500.

Tedeschi, R. F., Tedeschi, D. H., Mucha, A., Cook, L., Mattis, P. A., & Fellows, E. J. (1959). *J. Pharmac. exp. Ther.*, **125**, 28–34.
Terrace, H. S. (1963a). *J. exp. Analysis Behav.*, **6**, 1–27.
Terrace, H. S. (1963b). *J. exp. Analysis Behav.*, **6**, 223–232.
Terrace, H. S. (1963c). *Science*, **140**, 318–319.
Thompson, H. V. (1953). *Br. J. Anim. Behav.*, **1**, 96–111.
Thompson, T. (1961). *J. comp. physiol. Psychol.*, **54**, 398–400.
Thompson, T. & Schuster, C. R. (1964). *Psychopharmacologia*, **5**, 87–94.
Thorpe, W. H. (1963). *Learning and Instinct in Animals*. (2nd edn). London: Methuen.
Tilson, H. A. & Sparber, S. B. (1973). *J. Pharmac. exp. Ther.*, **184**, 376–384.
Tinbergen, N. & Perdeck, A. C. (1950). *Behaviour*, **3**, 1–39.
Tinbergen, N. (1951). *The Study of Instinct*. Oxford: Clarenden Press.
Tinbergen, N. (1952). *Q. Rev. Biol.*, **27**, 1–32.
Tinbergen, N. (1963). *Z. Tierpsychol.*, **20**, 410–433.
Tolman, E. C. (1924). *J. comp. Psychol.*, **4**, 1–18.
Tomkiewicz, M. (1972). *Br. J. Pharmac.*, **44**, 351P.
Torres, A. H. (1961). *J. comp. physiol. Psychol.*, **54**, 347–353.
Trivers, R. L. & Hare, H. (1976). *Science*, **191**, 249–263.
Tryon, R. C. (1931). *J. comp. Psychol.*, **12**, 303–345.
Tsai, C. (1925/6). *J. comp. Psychol.*, **5**, 407–415.
Tušl, M., Stolin, V., Wagner, M., & Ast, D. (1973). In *Adverse Effects of Environmental Chemicals and Drugs* (ed. M. Horváth & E. Frantík), **1**. Amsterdam: Elsevier, pp. 155–160.

Uhrich, J. (1938). *J. comp. Psychol.*, **25**, 373–413.
Ulrich, R. E. & Azrin, N. H. (1962). *J. exp. Analysis Behav.*, **5**, 511–520.
Ulrich, R. E., Azrin, N. H., & Wolff, P. C. (1964). *Anim. Behav.*, **12**, 14–15.
Ulrich, R. E., Stachnik, T. J., Brierton, G. R., & Mabry, J. H. (1966). *Behaviour*, **26**, 124–129.
Ungar, G., Desiderio, D. M., & Parr, W. (1972). *Nature*, **238**, 198–202.
Ungar, G., Galvan, L., & Clark, R. H. (1968). *Nature*, **217**, 1259–1261.
Ungerstedt, U. (1971). *Acta physiol. scand.*, **82** (Suppl. 367). 1–93.
Universities Federation For Animal Welfare. (1976). *UFAW Handbook on the Care of Laboratory Animals* (5th edn.). London: Churchill Livingstone.
Uyeno, E. T. (1960). *J. comp. physiol. Psychol.*, **53**, 138–141.
Uyeno, E. T. & Graham, R. T. (1966). *Behaviour*, **26**, 351–356.

Valzelli, L. (1967). *Adv. Pharmac.*, **5**, 79–108.
Van Oortmersson, G. A. (1971). *Behaviour*, **31**, 1–92.
Van der Poel, A. M. & Remmelts, M. (1971). *Archs int. Pharmacodyn. Ther.*, **189**, 394–396.
Venulet, J. (1967). *Proc. Europ. Soc. Study Drug. Tox.*, **8**, 177–184.
Verhave, T., Owen, J. E., & Robbins, E. B. (1958). *Archs int. Pharmacodyn. Ther.*, **116**, 45–53.
Verhave, T., Owen, J. E., & Robbins, E. B. (1959). *J. Pharmac. exp. Ther.*, **125**, 248–251.
Vogel, J. R., Hughes, R. A., & Carlton, P. L. (1967). *Psychopharmacologia*, **10**, 409–416.
Von Holst, E. & Mittelstaedt, H. (1950). *Naturwissenschaften*, **37**, 464–476.

Wagstaff, D. J. & Streets, J. C. (1971). *Toxic. appl. Pharmac.*, **19**, 10–19.
Walk, R. D. (1965). *Adv. Stud. Behav.*, **1**, 99–154.
Wang, G. H. (1923). *Comp. Psychol. Monogr.*, **11**, 1–27.
Wang, R. I. H., Hasegawa, A. T., Peters, N. J., & Rimm, A. (1969). *Psychopharmacologia*, **15**, 102–108.
Warden, C. J. (1931). *Animal Motivation*. New York: Columbia U.P.
Warden, C. J. & Warner, E. H. (1927). *Archs. Psychol.*, **92**, 1–35.
Warne, M. C. (1947). *J. comp. physiol. Psychol.*, **40**, 371–388.
Wasserman, E. & Jensen, D. (1969). *Science*, **166**, 1307–1309.
Webster, C. D., Willinsky, M. D., Herring, B. S., & Walters, G. C. (1971). *Nature*, **232**, 498–501.
Weidmann, R. & Weidmann, U. (1958). *Anim. Behav.*, **6**, 114.
Weinstock, M. & Speizer, Z. (1973). *Psychopharmacologia*, **30**, 241–250.
Weiss, B. & Laties, V. G. (1960). *J. comp. physiol. Psychol.*, **53**, 603–608.
Weiss, J. M. (1971). *J. comp. physiol. Psychol.*, **77**, 1–30.
Wentworth, K. L. (1936). *J. comp. Psychol.*, **22**, 255–267.
Weyant, R. G. (1966). *Anim. Behav.*, **14**, 480–484.
White, N., Sklar, L., & Amit, Z. (1977). *Psychopharmacology*, **52**, 63–66.
White, R. E. C. (1971). *Behaviour*, **40**, 135–161.
Wiberg, G. S. & Grice, H. L. (1965). *Fd. Cosmet. Tox.*, **3**, 597–603.
Wiepkema, P. (1971). *Behaviour*, **39**, 237–265.
Wilcock, J. & Broadhurst, P. L. (1967). *J. comp. physiol. Psychol.*, **63**, 335–338.
Will, B. (1974). *Anim. Behav.*, **22**, 370–375.
Williams, D. I. (1971). *Anim. Behav.*, **19**, 365–367.
Wilson, C. W. M. & Mapes, R. (1964). *Psychopharmacologia*, **5**, 239–254.
Wilson, E. O. (1975). *Sociobiology: the new synthesis*. Harvard: Belknap Press.
Wilson, E. O. (1976). reviewed in *Anim. Behav.*, **24**, 698–718.
Wootton, R. J. (1972). *Behaviour*, **41**, 232–241.
Wynne-Edwards, V. C. (1964). *Scient. Am.*, **211**, 68–74.

Yen, H. C. Y., Stanger, R., & Millman, N. (1958). *J. Pharmac. exp. Ther.*, **122**, 85A.
Yerkes, R. M. (1907). *The Dancing Mouse*, New York: Macmillan.
Yerkes, R. M. & Watson, J. B. (1911). *Behav. Monogr.*, **1**, 17–28.
Young, P. T. (1945). *J. comp. Psychol.*, **38**, 135–174.

General index

Activity cycles (*see also* Rhythms of behaviour), 15, 37, 80, 85–7, 89–91, 216, 218, 354
  estimates of, 39, 80–4, 88, 249, 321, 333
  motor, 42, 60, 63, 79–92, 170, 208, 218, 234, 245, 273, 321, 332
Adaptation, light/dark, 189
  ecological, evolutionary, 56, 109, 122, 255, 267, 269, 278, 289, 294, 317, 338–48, 361, 364, 370
Addiction, drug dependence, 99–102, 283
Adrenal glands, 47, 101
Age, as a variable in behaviour, 245, 256, 264–5, 267, 272, 298
Aggression (*see also* Fighting), 8, 53, 271–293
  'bizarre' drug-induced, 84, 271, 283
  component of agonistic behaviour, 23, 50, 85, 275, 282, 335, 344
  counter-attack on predator, 31, 287, 344
  interpretation of, 280, 287–9, 292, 318, 322–6, 332, 344, 360
  defensive, shock-induced, 28, 223, 284–5, 288
  territorial, isolation-induced (*see also* Isolation, social), 31, 50, 277, 287–92, 296, 318, 320
  'sham rage', lesion induced (*see also* Brain, Hypersensitivity), 286–8
Agonistic social behaviour, 289, 328, 335
Alarm signals, 26
Alimentary conditioned reflexes, 121, 135
Alley (*see* Maze)
Ambivalence (*see also* Competition), 289, 311
Amnesia, 258, 260
Anaemia, 89
Anaesthesia (*see also* 'Sleep'), 38, 170
Analgesia and pain-killing drugs, 27, 60, 63–4, 101, 224, 285, 292
Anorexia and appetite-reducing drugs, 23, 41, 64–5, 155, 261
Anthropomorphism, 6
Anticonvulsant drugs, 63, 285

Antidepressant drugs, 7, 37, 64, 76–7, 241, 243
Antihistaminic drugs, 23, 78, 185
Anti-predator behaviour (*see also* Anxiety, Avoidance, Escape, 'Fear', Flight, Subjective experience), 175, 197, 264, 344–5, 351, 353, 357, 372
Antivivisection, 25
Anxiety (see also 'Fear'), 58, 71, 201, 206–8, 224–5, 289
Apparatus, for avoidance conditioning, 215, 218, 221, 265
  collection of saliva, 122–3
  electroshock, 195–6
  intravenous drug administration, 102
  measuring activity, 80, 83, 89, 237–8
    barbiturate 'sleep'-time, 66
    circling, 74
    exploration, 241, 265
    light-sensitivity, 187
    motor co-ordination, 67–70
    visual discrimination, 181–2
  observation of social behaviour, 277, 301, 354
  operant conditioning, 141–3, 156, 162, 168
Appetitive/consummatory stages in behaviour, 18, 141, 304
Arousal, 52, 179, 259, 272, 315, 334, 360
'Artificial' behaviour, 18, 20, 120, 122, 146, 165, 178, 249
Ataxis, loss of muscle tone or co-ordination (*see also* Inco-ordination), 9, 38, 60, 67, 100, 170, 221, 244, 256, 264, 322, 336
Attention to stimuli, 190, 232, 279, 325
Automatic recording of behaviour, 17, 249
Autonomic nervous system, signs of drug effect on, 60–1, 135, 292
Autoshaping of operant responses, 146–7

'Beta-blocking' drugs, β-adrenoceptor antagonists, 71–2, 273

General index

Biting, 38, 51, 56, 73, 108, 147, 211, 280, 283–7, 290, 296, 298, 305, 314, 316, 328, 354, 364
Bizarre fighting postures, 84, 283
Blood–brain barrier, 22, 162
Body-build, 236
Brain, anatomy, 104, 287
   chemistry and pharmacology, 55, 89, 99, 149, 210, 236, 239, 256, 274, 284
   electrostimulation of, 52, 103–5, 206–8, 267, 287, 288
   lesions, in amygdala, 287–8
   cerebral cortex, 183, 273
   hypothalamus, 46–7, 72, 287–8
   septum, 286–7
   olfactory bulb, 287, 290
   substantia nigra, 73
   models of, and hypotheses about, 52, 103–4, 173–5, 206–8, 269–70, 281–2, 289, 373
Breathing (*see also* Respiratory depression), 18
Burrows (*see also* Nesting), 110, 231, 241, 266, 317, 353–4, 356–7, 370

Capacitance (electrical) in activity measurement, 82, 89, 245, 334
Catalepsy, 131
Cigarette smoke, 367–71
Classification of elements (qv) into categories, 295, 304, 324, 370
Climbing, 68, 205–6, 219, 299, 315, 354, 358
Cognitive maps, 96, 110, 234
Collateral operant behaviour, 157–8, 168
Colour vision, 140, 183–4, 186, 264
Communal nursing, 57, 355
Comparison between animal species, 168, 266–7, 306, 314–15, 371–2
   animals and man, 2, 7, 12, 29, 31, 76, 153, 168, 170–1, 319, 330, 336, 338, 371, 374
   behavioural methods (*see also* Interpretation), 147, 154, 215, 317
Competition between animals (*see also* Dominance), 278, 282, 339, 358
   kinds of behaviour, motivational conflict (*see also* Ambivalence), 19, 36, 118, 125, 152, 187, 193, 220–9, 246–51, 282, 289–90, 294, 296, 298, 311, 313
Conditioned Avoidance, 29, 48, 105, 161, 187, 204–19, 239, 256–9, 285, 326, 361
   Emotional Response (CER), 200–1, 210
   Stimulus, 22, 41, 106–9, 121, 124, 181, 185, 193, 201, 255, 267, 284, 287, 291, 370

Suppression, 22, 71, 193
Taste Aversion, 41, 43–5, 95, 97, 99, 118, 214, 260, 351, 374–5
Conditioning, classical, Conditioned reflexes, 17, 120–35, 147, 164, 255, 297, 329, 362, 368
Conflict (*see* Competition)
Convulsions (*see also* Electroconvulsive shock), 79, 100, 260
Cost–benefit analysis, 27
Courtship, 19, 106, 108, 147, 263, 287, 354, 363
Critical periods in development, 263–5
Cross-introductions of paired animals, 334
Crouch postures, 252, 299, 310, 313, 357
Curiosity, 43, 147, 160, 234, 313
Cycles of activity (*see* Activity cycles, *see also* Rhythms of behaviour)

Defecation, 47, 175, 196, 237, 287, 298, 353, 360, 367–71
Defensive conditioned reflexes, 121–2, 124, 135, 139, 368–71
Delayed response, 23, 124, 134, 138–9, 152, 214, 216, 242, 246–51, 266–7
Depression, Depressive mood, 31, 64, 75–6, 130, 185, 294, 342, 347
Deprivation of food or water, 23, 40, 88, 93, 96, 112, 128, 145, 147, 152, 182, 188, 220, 226–7
Development of behaviour (*see also* Juvenile behaviour, Learning, 'Instinct'), 21, 51, 76, 106–9, 180, 255, 258–9, 264, 306, 367–71, 374
Discrimination between stimuli, Differentiation, 126–7, 136, 138, 158–9, 170, 179–91, 212, 215
   abilities for, 179–80, 189–90, 275
   criteria for, 182, 267
   reversal learning, 267–8
Disinfectant, detergent, 114, 165, 239
Disinhibition, 159, 201, 207, 215, 222
Displacement activities, 50–2, 57, 168, 280, 299, 373
Distraction, 118, 123, 165, 267, 269
Diuretic drugs, 23
Dominance, Rank-order by access to food, etc., 23, 278–9, 354, 360
   by submission, symbolic act, 274–7, 280, 287, 310, 315–16, 332, 336, 341–2, 344–6, 354–5, 360

General index

Dose and response, 28, 32, 38, 45, 59, 74, 77, 87, 156, 191, 205–6, 226–7, 238, 243, 246, 259, 268, 285, 292, 328, 330
Drinking, 16, 21–3, 83, 100, 150, 152, 248–51, 279, 360–2
'Drive', 5, 35, 41, 57, 93, 172, 222–3, 245, 269, 288, 305, 329
Drugs
   administration of drugs, techniques, 96–7, 99–102, 147, 202, 238
   effect on animal *not* receiving it, 84, 326
   screening (*see* Screening tests for drug activity, Organisation of drug screening)

Eating, 18, 39–47, 108, 150, 223, 246–7, 272, 278–9, 288, 296, 352
Electroencephalogram (EEG), 35, 37, 138, 330
Electroconvulsive shock (ECS) (*see also* Convulsions), 63, 259–60, 285
Electroshock (as reinforcement) (*see also* Negative Reinforcement), 28–9, 46, 49, 124, 130, 135, 161, 173, 192–3, 195–8, 200, 210, 220–6, 239–40, 244, 255, 282, 284–5, 288, 361–2
Electrostimulation (*see* Brain electrostimulation)
Elements in spontaneous behaviour, 17, 49, 240, 275, 277, 282, 284–5, 288, 295–6, 302–4, 315, 368
Emotion, 11, 47, 172, 200, 236, 277
Enriched environment, 54, 267, 274
Error-free discrimination, 186–7
Errors in maze-running, 113
Escape as anti-predator behaviour, 175, 351, 354, 357
   from experimental conditioned stimulus, 193, 196, 204, 210, 215, 218
Ethical questions, 25–31, 33–4, 161, 192, 198, 286
Ethology, 2, 263–4, 288, 372–4
Exploration (*see also* Investigatory reflex), 39, 73, 88–9, 110, 112–13, 116, 177, 194, 201, 218, 230–53, 256, 259, 261, 269, 290, 299, 306, 316, 328, 363, 367
Extinction, ending of non-reinforced response, 126, 139, 149, 165, 201, 208, 214, 218, 282
Euphoria, 78

Falling posture, 68
Fatigue, 231, 252

'Fear' (*see also* Anti-predator behaviour, Anxiety, Avoidance, Emotion, Escape, Flight, Subjective experience), 26, 48, 103, 110, 134, 205, 220–2, 225–6, 234, 239, 279, 290, 360
Fighting (*see also* Aggression), 85, 272, 279–80, 314, 359
Fixed Action Pattern, 19, 106, 370
Flight, running away (e.g. in social behaviour) (*see also* Retreat), 51, 282, 287, 289, 313, 316, 326, 332–3, 336, 354, 357
Free fatty acids, 28, 47
Free Operant Avoidance (*see also* Operant Conditioning), 194, 209, 285
Friendship, 289, 355, 359–60
Frustration, 100, 113–14, 149, 168, 220, 280, 282, 289, 299, 355
Function of behaviour, 84, 88, 165, 172, 200, 294, 306–7, 338–48, 367, 370, 372–3

Generalisation of conditioned reflexes, 127, 263
Genetics, effects of gene differences, 67, 279, 297, 360
   experimental selection, 48, 116, 349, 360, 364
   genetic mechanisms, 343, 364
Gnawing, 40, 157, 271
Grooming, care of body surface, Maintenance, (*see also* Preening in birds), 17, 49–53, 73, 88–9, 96, 108, 157, 168, 177, 201, 245, 280, 284, 290, 299, 367
Group-housing, group size (*see also* Isolation, social), 30, 272–4, 276
Group-toxicity (*see also* Amphetamine), 84, 271, 273

Habit, 47
Habituation, 94, 231, 240, 247, 255, 259, 265–6, 285, 352
Hair-erection, Piloerection, 100, 298, 312, 315
Hallucinogenic drugs, 78, 150, 153, 215, 268
Hampton Court maze, 110
Harness-pulling, 220
Heat output, 79
Height, unconditioned avoidance of by rats, 112, 216, 218
Histology, 138, 366
Hoarding, 40, 111, 287, 357
Holes, response to by rodents, 240–4, 262
Homeostasis, 43, 52, 134, 232, 318

Hormones, 36, 54, 255, 335
Hot-plate test for analgesia, 63–4, 101, 292
Hunting, 79, 97–9, 108, 123, 125, 171–2, 175, 286, 288, 340, 358
Hypersensitivity (*see also* Aggression, Brain, Sensitivity, Irritability), 38, 269, 283, 286, 290, 360
Hypothalamus (*see also* Brain), 46–7, 103
Hypersonic calls by rodents, 55–6, 85, 195
activity-measuring apparatus, 83, 137

Immobility, 37, 52, 79, 122, 157, 200–1, 208, 231, 245, 249, 252, 288, 290, 336, 362, 369
Imprinting, 263–5
Inco-ordination (*see also* Ataxia), 78, 137
Individual differences, 36, 80, 89–91, 131–2, 148, 169, 191, 199, 212–13, 242, 251–2, 273, 280, 289, 291, 296, 329, 330, 332, 353
Induction of conditioned reflexes, 129
Infanticide, 56–7, 286
Infection, 100, 355
Information, communication of, 194, 306, 309, 353
intake of (*see also* Learning, Sensitivity to stimuli), 10, 52, 194, 231–2, 239, 248, 255, 300
Inhibition, 51, 124–6, 130, 133–4, 136, 139, 208, 220, 222, 234, 240, 301, 333, 335, 343, 354
Insomnia, 39
'Instinct' (*see also* Development of behaviour, Learning), 5, 18, 35, 106–9, 280
Intensity of behaviour, 51, 297, 299, 315
of stimuli, 194, 196, 201, 226–7, 239–40, 288, 297
Intention movements, 19–20, 51
Interpretation of behaviour and behavioural experiments, 7, 24, 33, 41, 53, 137–8, 151, 169, 176–8, 190, 216, 251–2, 257–8, 280, 286–7, 292, 317–19, 333–4, 338
Irradiation of conditioned reflexes, 'spreading depression', 128
Irritability (*see also* Hypersensitivity, Sensitivity), 8, 9, 269
Irritant chemicals, 97, 369
Investigation of another animal, 299, 322, 332, 335
Investigatory reflex ('What-is-it?') reflex (*see also* Exploration, Orientation), 121, 125, 127, 194, 230–1, 266

Isolation, social (*see also* Aggression, isolation-induced, Group-housing), 30, 54, 83, 165, 223, 272–4, 289–90, 294, 320, 361–2

Jiggle cage, 82
Jumping, 182
Juvenile behaviour (*see also* Development of behaviour, Learning, 'Instinct'), 37, 51, 56, 94, 106–7, 180, 245, 263, 269, 289, 298, 306, 309, 315, 317, 355, 357
adult effects of juvenile experience or treatment, 54–5, 57, 76, 94, 149, 210, 245, 272, 279, 290, 360

Kidney function, 23, 101, 251
'Kinds of behaviour', 5, 46, 121, 305

Language, semantic questions, 4–5, 8, 20, 49, 61, 179, 192, 200, 269, 282, 286, 305, 315, 360
Latency (*see* Delayed response)
Latent learning, 240, 248, 261
LD_{50}, 28, 60, 271
Learning (*see also* Development of behaviour, Juvenile behaviour, 'Instinct'), 19, 46, 56, 69, 89, 94, 106–9, 113, 116, 197, 206, 210, 212, 216, 240, 244–5, 249, 251, 254–70, 290, 306, 351, 361–2, 368–71, 374
Lever-holding in operant conditioning, 170, 209
Licking, 21
Light intensity, Laboratory illumination, 85, 187–9, 194, 218, 236–7, 268, 275, 301
unconditioned avoidance of light by rodents, 216

Maintenance behaviour (eating, grooming, etc.), 307, 328
Malnutrition, 1, 39, 47, 55, 116, 210, 245, 281, 339
Mazes, Maze-running, 40, 110–19, 181, 260, 269
alley, 114, 118, 199–200, 220–3, 240
Dashiell, 245
elevated, 112, 218, 240
Hampton Court, 110
learning of, 11, 113, 248, 259, 268–9, 274
multiple enclosed, 112, 269
plus, 39, 81, 95
T, 56, 185, 255, 268–9

temporal, 115, 199
Y, 38, 216–18, 238–40, 245
Meals, 42, 223
Memory, 256–8, 259–60, 269–70
Mixtures of drugs, 244, 262
Models, 13, 22, 33, 36, 58, 76, 101, 110, 180, 225, 237, 273, 275, 334, 343, 373
Monotony, 41, 55, 97, 130
Motivation, 42, 172, 307, 322, 373
Motor activity, 42, 60, 63, 65, 79–92, 157, 170, 208, 234, 236, 240, 247, 261, 273, 285, 290, 292, 306, 321–2, 326, 334
Motor control, physiology of, 134
Motor–food conditioned reflexes, 135–9
Muricide, mouse-killing by rats, 56, 282, 286, 288, 358

Natural conditioned reflex, 106, 121, 123, 136, 364
Natural selection, 57, 165, 173, 255, 269, 289, 339, 353, 360, 371–2
Nausea, 26, 41, 45, 64, 78, 124, 152, 332, 369
Negative reinforcement (*see also* Electroshock, Noise, Pain, Swimming), 29, 192–229, 368–70
Neophobia, avoidance of unfamiliar stimuli (*see also* Novelty, Unfamiliarity), 44, 352–3, 359
Nesting, 35, 50, 56, 82, 108, 232, 263, 267, 317, 360–1, 364, 372
Neuroleptic drugs, major tranquillisers, 63, 71, 76, 158, 161, 177, 185, 291
Neurosis, experimental, 100, 133, 181, 193
Noise, as conditioned stimulus, 170, 195, 200–1
  as measure of activity, 84
  as unconditioned stimulus (*see also* Negative reinforcement), 29, 170, 195
Novelty, approach to unfamiliar stimuli (*see also* Aggression, Neophobia, Unfamiliarity), 234, 244–5, 352
Nutrition (*see also* Malnutrition, Eating), 116, 210, 245, 339, 344–6

Objectivity, 11, 120, 249, 292, 295, 367
Observation, 10, 43, 71, 77, 82, 177, 210, 227–9, 235, 282, 287, 295, 367
  comparison of observers, comparison with automatic recording, 82, 88, 157, 221, 227, 236–7, 249, 252, 297, 314–15, 321–2, 367

techniques of, 236–7, 248–9, 295–6, 306, 328, 334
Odour (*see also* Pheromones, Smell, sense of), 54, 114, 189, 235, 252, 290, 317, 335–6, 353, 361, 369
Open Field test, 47, 71, 235–6, 273, 287
Operant conditioning, 40, 89, 91, 93, 103, 141–78, 209, 264, 330, 374
  apparatus, 141–3, 156, 162, 168
  comparison of performance on different schedules, 23, 143, 154–5, 158, 163, 177
  schedules,
    adjusting, 214
    combinations of
      chained, 161
      multiple, 162
      tandem, 160
    conflict, 152, 203, 223–9, 326
    continuous reinforcement (CRF), 40, 147–8, 362
    differential reinforcement of low rate (DRL), 143–4, 152–4, 157, 214
    extinction, 149
    fixed interval (FI), 100, 134, 143, 150–1, 155, 158
    fixed ratio (FR), 134, 143, 149–50, 155, 159, 362
    free operant avoidance, 194, 209, 211–15, 285, 362
    variable interval (VI), 151–2, 158, 286–7, 201–3, 223–4, 226
    variable ratio (VR), 151, 188
Optimal Foraging theory (*see also* Hunting), 171
Organisation of drug screening, 59–60, 63, 75–8
Orientation (*see* Investigatory reflex, Stimuli, arousal and orientation functions)

Pain, (*see also* Negative Reinforcement), 9, 25, 27–8, 174, 192, 196, 221
Palatability (*see also* Preferences), 43
Paradoxical conditioned reflexes, 131, 138
Parathyroid glands, 47
Parental (maternal) behaviour, 37, 51, 56–7, 81, 94, 179, 263, 276, 279, 355, 361
Parkinson's disease, 71, 75
Passive unconditioned avoidance, 194, 215–18, 239–40, 256–8, 270
Pathological behaviour in animals, 100, 133, 138, 168, 273, 283, 338, 347–8

Pecking, 39, 50–1, 107, 142, 274
Perseverance, 118, 268, 273
Pesticides, 27, 139, 210
Pheromones (see also Odour), 114, 290
Photoelectric cells (see also Apparatus), 43, 80, 88–9, 236, 265
Physiological control mechanisms, 23, 41, 43, 52, 134, 174, 206–7, 232–3, 288–9, 373
Placebo, 38
Play, 175, 309
Play-fighting, 38, 284, 286, 306, 315, 355, 360
Plus maze, 39, 81, 95
Poison, 44, 351–2
Pole-climbing conditioned avoidance/escape, 205–6, 209
Polydipsia, 100
Polymorphism, 98–9
Population, dynamics, 339–42
  experiments on, 346–8
Position habit, 45, 95, 182, 267–8
Postures (see Elements) after electroshock, 197, 221
  in social behaviour, 302–3, 360
Predatory behaviour (see also Hunting, Muricide), 286, 358
Predictability of behaviour, 3, 12, 366
Preening in birds (see also Grooming), 50, 106
Preferences, 93–6, 364, 371
  food, (see also Palatability), 40, 45, 95, 352
  light intensity, temperature, 93, 218
  sexual, 54
  other, 56, 94–5
Pregnancy, 55–6
Puberty, 246
Punishment, 29, 104, 173, 188, 193, 202–3, 206, 213

Rank-order (see Dominance)
Rapid-eye-movement (REM) sleep, 36–8, 281
Rate of behavioural response, 23, 39, 143–5, 156, 167, 212, 224, 247, 301, 326, 334
Rating scales, semi-subjective measurement, 60, 296
Rearing on hindlegs, Upright Postures, 89, 236–7, 245, 264, 271, 291, 302–3, 363
Red light, discrimination of, illumination by, 85, 184, 186, 275, 284
Reinforcement, Reward, 22, 104, 142, 145, 168, 173, 206–7, 264, 291, 330
Reflexes, unconditioned, 18, 106, 123
  righting, 60, 66

Reliability of measures, 75, 78, 115, 129, 290–1, 366
Repetition of single responses, 167, 244
Residential maze (see Plus-maze)
Respiratory depression (see also Breathing), 66
Responsiveness (see also Sensitivity to stimuli), 325
Retreat, run away (see also Flight), 240, 282, 302–3, 305, 310
Reversal learning, 267–8, 273, 275, 279
Rhythms of behaviour, activity cycles, 36, 42, 80, 86–7, 89–91, 213, 216, 239, 330, 354, 356, 362
Rotating rod (see also Ataxis, Apparatus), 67–70, 205, 272, 285, 292
Running speed, 86, 118, 136

Saliva, 17, 106, 121–3, 137
Satiation, end of eating, 41, 43, 65, 111, 124, 144, 208
Schedules of reinforcement (see Operant conditioning)
Schizophrenia, 58, 71–2, 185
Scratching (see also Grooming), 108
Screening tests for drug activity (see also Organisation of drug screening), 27, 58–71, 75–8, 285, 291–2
Search image, 98
Sedation, 26, 37, 87, 89, 274, 327
Self-administration of drugs, 102–3, 161, 330
Self-stimulation, electrical, 103–5, 175, 206–8
Sensitivity to stimuli (see also Information intake, Responsiveness), 23, 51, 78, 87, 111, 158, 189–90, 220, 256, 259, 269, 325, 335
  of test methods to low doses, 20, 32, 154, 170, 177–8, 197, 206, 227, 243, 252, 329, 374
Separation and return procedure for observing social behaviour, 330
Sequences of behavioural elements, 20, 35, 52, 54, 172, 227–9, 288, 300, 304, 307–9, 329
Sex differences, 48, 86, 88, 243, 251–2, 275, 317, 335, 341, 354, 363
Sexual behaviour, 20, 36, 53, 85, 88, 93, 108, 125, 255, 272, 278, 284, 287, 299, 300, 312, 327, 335, 354, 356
'Sham rage', 286
Shaping operant responses, 142–3, 146–7, 165

General index

Shuttle-box test of conditioned avoidance, 139, 206–8, 258, 285, 362
Shyness to bait, traps etc. (*see also* Conditioned Taste Aversion), 350, 359
Side-effects of drugs, 58, 71, 77, 205, 291
Signals, morphological and behavioural, 306, 309–10, 314
Sleep, 35–9, 52, 130–1, 188, 231, 266, 281, 327, 357
'Sleep', anaesthesia, 65–6, 205, 272–3, 281
Smell, sense of (*see also* Odour), 54, 95, 189, 202, 288, 356
Social behaviour, 53, 87, 294–319, 354–6, 367
 as a test method, 251, 320–37, 374
Social 'drive', 223, 289, 313
Social organisation, 84, 273, 277–8, 287, 315–16, 332, 341–8, 353
Species differences, 93, 315, 344–6, 358–9, 371
Specific appetites, 43
Spontaneous alternation, 115, 182
Spontaneous behaviour, 20, 87, 89, 91, 123, 165, 178, 249, 283, 294–338
State-dependent learning, 186, 255–6, 259, 262
Statistics, 13, 96, 101, 115, 139, 144–5, 169–70, 182, 277, 291, 308, 321, 326–9, 374
Step-down passive avoidance, 216
Stereotyped behaviour, 38, 73, 75, 237, 244, 271, 283, 287, 329
Stimulant drugs, 60, 177, 271, 330
Stimuli, arousal and orientation functions, 52, 179, 230
 environmental, 15–16, 51–2, 156, 342
 experimental, 53, 98, 156, 158, 179–90
 interaction of with treatment effects, 38, 84, 87, 156, 190, 213, 224–6, 288
 internal, 45, 157, 172, 185–6, 222, 255
 'strength' of, 56, 136, 139, 194–5, 197, 201, 226–7, 288
Stimulus control (*see also* Responsiveness, Sensitivity), 162, 250
Strains (genetic), and strain differences in behaviour, 47–8, 100, 116, 236, 256, 269, 276–7, 314, 330, 358, 363–4
Strangers, response to (*see also* Aggression, Neophobia, Novelty), 84, 290, 314, 316–17, 354, 356
Stress, 28, 100, 145, 212, 214, 271, 315
Subjective experiences, 32, 45, 58, 150, 153, 169, 174, 185, 367
Submission, inhibition of attack, 23, 85, 176, 195, 276, 298, 304, 311, 315, 336, 360

Super-sensitivity of neurotransmitter receptors, 74
'Superstitious' operant behaviour, 157–8, 168
Swimming, 115, 198–9

Tameness, 290
Taste (*see also* Conditioned Taste Aversion), 45, 97, 99, 107, 352
Temperament (*see also* Individual differences), 131–3, 148, 170, 277
Temperature, of body or nest, 271–2, 357, 361
 effects on behaviour, 20, 22, 93, 260
 preferences, 93
Territory, 108, 277–8, 287, 310–11, 316–18, 341, 363
Tetanus, 196
Therapeutic ratio, 62
Thirst (*see also* Drinking), 22, 248
Threat (*see also* Elements), 289, 311
Threshold Limit Value (TLV), 138, 374–5
Thresholds, sensory, 52, 287–9, 202, 267
Tilt-cage for activity measurement, 81, 88
Time Out from operant responding, 158–9, 188
Timing of behaviour, 15, 42, 54, 84–5, 87, 89, 108, 115, 127, 131, 144, 148, 157, 159, 167, 171, 177, 188, 212–13, 216, 231, 237, 239, 242, 248–9, 276–7, 279, 284, 290, 301, 320, 324, 329, 334, 361
 of treatment/drug effect, 77, 87, 89, 147–8, 167, 216–17, 244, 256, 258, 260, 326
Tolerance to drugs, 37, 88, 100–1, 150–1, 251, 268, 332
Toxicity, Industrial hygiene, Occupational medicine, 9, 28, 39–40, 57–8, 66, 69–70, 77, 137, 147, 150, 159, 205, 210, 250, 271, 367–8, 371, 374–5
Tranquillisers (*see also* Benzodiazepines, etc.), 28, 37, 63, 69, 161, 197, 201, 208–9, 212, 225, 289, 330
Traps, 350–2, 361
Tremor, 79, 100, 245
Tunnel-board, 241–2

Ulcers, 212–14
Unfamiliarity (*see also* Aggression, Novelty, Neophobia), 234, 264, 352
Units of behaviour, 17–18, 21, 92, 113, 141–3, 145, 165, 167, 196, 249, 366–7
Urine, 40, 114, 125, 196, 290, 315, 335–6, 353

Variability, 3, 67, 76, 80, 129, 170, 191, 199, 212, 237, 251–2, 273, 289, 290–1, 329, 353, 366
Vibrations, 82
Visual cliff, 68
Visual discrimination, 180–2, 317

Weaning, 245, 315
Wheel, activity apparatus, 30, 80, 86–8
operant manipulandum, 142, 209, 285
Wild, behaviour in the, compared with in the laboratory, 4, 171, 180, 263–5, 315, 349, 352, 354–5, 359–62

Y-maze, 38, 216–18, 238–40, 245
Yoked pairs of animals in conditioned avoidance, 212–14

Chemicals index

Functional classes of drugs are in the general index

Acetone, 139
Acetopromazine, 291
Acetylcholine, 46, 72, 75, 151–2, 175
Alcohol, Ethanol, 23, 66, 70, 78, 99–101, 103, 205–6, 208–9, 220, 272
Ammonia, ammonium chloride, 281, 368
d,l-Amphetamine, 38, 41, 50, 64–6, 72–3, 75, 78, 84, 88–9, 151–3, 160, 201, 206–8, 215, 239, 241, 243, 247, 258–9, 262, 271–2, 281, 283, 324, 326
d-Amphetamine, 23, 74, 89, 103, 151, 155, 158, 186, 217–18, 224, 236, 244, 259
Amyl acetate, 202
Amylobarbitone, 23, 38, 103, 218, 221–2, 237, 262, 279, 281
Aniseed oil, 44
Apomorphine, 26, 45, 73–4, 105, 271, 282–3, 334
Arachis oil, 352
Aspirin, 27
Atropine, 22
Atropine methylbromide, 22

Barbiturate drugs, 23, 32, 38–9, 63, 65–6, 69, 103, 205, 281, 334
Barbitone sodium, 65, 238
Benactyzine, 203, 211, 326
Benzodiazepines, 75, 201
Bromide potassium, 133
Bromlysergide, 268
Butyl acetate, 202
n-Butyl mercaptan, 352
Butyric acid, 202, 352

Caffeine, 60, 118, 127, 131, 160, 281
Calcium, 47
Cannabis, 78, 215, 281, 336
Carbamates, Banol, 210
  Aprocarb, Carbaryl, 269
Carbon dioxide, 18, 79

Carbon disulphide, 170
Carbon monoxide, 147
Chloral hydrate, 131
Chlordiazepoxide, 69, 78, 161, 201, 203, 208, 212, 218, 244, 246, 262
Chlorpromazine, 32, 63, 65–6, 71–2, 78, 103–4, 158, 161, 177, 187, 197, 201, 203, 205–6, 208–9, 215, 218, 225–7, 238, 240, 243, 247, 249, 250, 279, 280, 285, 290, 295, 320–6
p-Chlorophenylalanine, 38, 99, 283
p-Chlororesorcinol, 283
Cholinesterase enzymes, 55, 139, 152, 236, 268–9, 274
Cholinesterase enzyme inhibitors, 27, 210, 269
Cocaine, 89
Codeine, 60
Corticosteroid hormones, 349, 360
Cycloheximide, 256

DDT, 66
Deuterium, heavy hydrogen, 9
Dextromoramide, 291
2,4-Diamino-6-chloro-*s*-triazine, 97, 283
Diazepam, 212, 218
Diphenylhydantoin, Phenytoin, 285
l-Dopa, 72, 74, 105, 283
Dopamine, 71–5, 84, 89, 105, 271, 281, 283, 373

Enkephalins, 27
Ethirimol, 39

Fenfluramine, 247
Ferric ammonium sulphate, Iron, 89
Free Fatty Acids, 28, 197–8

Glucose, 41

Haloperidol, 63, 71, 158, 201, 283

Hexobarbitone, 65
Histamine, 23
Hydrochloric acid, 121
Hydrocortisone, 97
6-Hydroxydopamine, 8, 72, 74
Hydroxyzine, 208

Imipramine, 37, 78, 187, 241, 243
Insulin, 41, 87
Iproniazid, 78

Lactic acid, 281
Lead, 177
Lithium, 43, 45, 118, 260, 375
Lysergic acid diethylamide, LSD, 32, 78, 150, 239, 268, 275, 281

Marijuana, 153, 189, 281
Meprobamate, 104, 161, 203, 208, 224, 264, 285, 295
Mercury, 177
Mescaline, 103, 150, 153, 158, 239, 281
α-Methyl-*p*-Tyrosine, 99
Methyl mercury compounds, 57, 69, 251, 374
Methyl Cellosolve, monomethyl ether of ethylene glycol, 205
Methylphenidate, 177
Mianserin, 76
Monoamine Oxidase Inhibitors, MAOI, 64, 241
Morphine, 27, 60, 64, 101–4, 118, 124, 161, 209, 283, 295

Nalorphine, 161
Naloxone, 102
Neostigmine, 152
Nicotine, 23, 78, 87–8, 103, 151–2, 155, 185, 218, 330, 334, 369
 nicotine derivatives, 185
Nitrazepam, 37
Nitrogen dioxide, 199
Nitroglycerin, Glyceryl Trinitrate, 374
Noradrenaline, NA, norepinephrine, 7, 46, 72, 75, 84, 88, 152, 175, 239, 271, 281–2

Oestrogen, 54, 87
Oxotremorine, 82
Oxygen, 18

Paraquat, 40
Parathion, 139, 210
Pemoline, 103

Pentobarbitone, 39, 155–6, 208, 212, 224, 226, 255–6, 272–3, 295
Pentylenetetrazol, 258
Peppermint oil, 352
Perphenazine, 225
Phenmetrazine, 41, 64–5
Phenobarbitone, 23, 38–9, 63, 87, 201, 224, 247, 285, 290
Phentolamine, 8
Physostigmine, 38, 152
Pimozide, 74
Pipradol, 210
Potassium, 89
Practolol, 71, 273
Progesterone, 54
Promazine, 158, 224
Propranolol, 71–2, 78, 201, 273
Protein, 47, 55, 89, 256

Quinine, 43, 45, 47, 97, 103, 208, 220

Renin, 23
Reserpine, 7, 64, 75–6, 89, 149, 208, 285, 290, 295
Rodenticides (red squill, strychnine, thallium, warfarin, etc.), 351

Saccharine, 45, 103, 118, 260, 375
Salt, sodium chloride, 22, 101
Scopolamine, Hyoscine, 22, 153, 158, 176, 201, 247, 291, 328
Scopolamine methylbromide, 22, 328
Scotophobin, 257
Serotonin, 5-Hydroxytryptamine, 5-HT, 37, 72, 75, 84, 88, 99, 284, 290
Spaghetti, 41, 64
Sodium, 44, 47, 89
Stilboestrol, 97
Strychnine, 259, 260, 351
Sugar, Sucrose, 41, 44, 145

Testosterone, 54, 118
Tetrabenazine, 88
Δ^1-Tetrahydrocannabinol, 153, 215, 271
Δ^9-Tetrahydrocannabinol, 185, 281, 336
Thiamin, 44, 46–7
Thiopropazate, 210
Thioridazine, 72, 200, 240
Thiourea, 271
Tobacco, 367–71
Trichloroethylene, 138, 159, 170, 190, 199, 251, 327, 334

Chemicals index

Tricyclic antidepressants, 64, 185, 241, 243
Tri-ortho-Cresyl phosphate, 70

Vinyl acetate, 330

Vitamins A and D, 47

Warfarin, 45, 351

Zinc sulphate, 288

Species index

Unless otherwise specified in this species index, references are to laboratory rats, Rattus norvegicus albinus. *The index includes references to species causing behavioural change in others.*

Bacteria
   Escherichia coli, 150
   Myobacterium tuberculosis, 66
Protozoa
   Paramecium spp., 266
   Trypanosoma spp., 87
Oligochaeta
   earthworms, *Lumbricus* spp., 266
Mollusca
   cuttlefish, *Sepia officinalis*, 79
Insecta, Hymenoptera, 79
   ants, 343
   digger wasp, *Ammophila pubescens*, 267
   honeybee, *Apis mellifera*, 175, 191, 343
Fish
   electric fish, *Gymnarchus* and *Gymnotus* spp., 194
   goldfish, *Carassius auratus*, 168
   Siamese fighting fish, *Betta splendens*, 275
   3-spined stickleback, *Gasterosteus aculeatus*, 107–8, 146, 166, 359
Amphibia
   newts, *Triturus cristatus*, 19
   T. viridescens, 275
   T. vulgaris, 20
Birds, Aves, 45
   chaffinch, *Fringilla coelebs*, 166, 232, 344
   chickadee, *Parus atricapillus*, 171–2
   doves, Barbary and Ring, *Streptopelia risoria*, 22
   ducks,
     Eider, 264
     mallard, *Anas platyrhynchos*, 264–5, 310
   geese, greylag, *Anser anser*, 263, 265
   grouse, *Lagopus scoticus*, 341
   gulls, 341–2, 372
     black-headed, *L. ridibundus*, 180, 289
     herring, *Larus, argentatus*, 50, 180
     kittiwake, *Rissa tridactyla*, 372
   jackdaw, *Corvus* sp., 275
   pigeon, *Columba livia*, 39, 51, 106, 142, 145–7, 155–6, 158, 167, 186–90, 202
   poultry, domestic hens, 51, 70, 98, 107, 162, 175, 263–4, 274, 278
   ruff, *Philomachus pugnax*, 278
   skylark, *Alauda arvensis*, 52
   zebra finch, *Taeniopygia guttata*, 52
Mammals
   Lagomorphs
     rabbit, *Oryctolagus* sp., 38, 94
   Ungulates
     antelopes, 344–6
     goat, 47
     sheep, *Ovis ovis*, 263
   Rodents
     deermouse, *Peromyscus* spp., 30, 90–1, 146, 285
     Florida packrat, *Sigmodon* sp., 285
     guinea-pig, *Cavia porcellata*, 54, 135, 315, 367–71
     hamster,
        golden, *Mesocricetus auratus*, 30, 56, 88, 93, 108, 147, 166, 273, 287, 295, 306, 309–11, 315, 367–71
        European, *Cricetus cricetus*, 370
     mouse, *Mus musculus*
        (wild), 285, 316, 364
        (laboratory strains), 41–3, 52, 54–6, 60, 64, 66–8, 81, 88–9, 99, 100, 179, 231, 237, 241, 243, 247, 257, 260, 266, 271, 276, 289–91, 306, 311, 314–15, 335–6, 346–7, 363–4, 367–71
     rat,
        Rattus norvegicus (wild), 29, 43, 49, 110, 232, 281, 285–6, 349–63

Species index

black, *R. rattus*, 219, 315, 358
Pacific, *R. exulans*, 358
vole, *Microtus* spp., 358–9
Carnivora
  cat, *Felis domestica*, 35, 61, 79, 96, 100, 107, 110, 139, 175, 203, 221, 266, 284, 286, 295
  dog, *Canis canis*, 17, 31, 35, 55, 106, 121–34, 181, 189
  weasels, 218, 357

Primates
  chimpanzee, *Pan troglodytes*, 31, 35, 102
  monkeys (species unspecified), 23, 29, 31, 146, 197, 232, 267, 278
    Japanese, *M. fusca*, 278
    Rhesus, *Macaca mulatta*, 161, 212–13, 278, 295
    squirrel, *Saimiri sciureus*, 161, 203
  Man, 36, 38, 52, 87, 101, 168, 170–1, 185, 190, 225, 230, 245, 267, 271, 283, 315, 330, 336, 340, 371

Author index

Abramson, H. A., 275
Acetis, L. de, 212
Adams, D. B., 284, 288
Adams, W. J., 101
Ahtee, L., 88
Albert, J. R., 287
Allen, M. P., 88
Allin, J. T., 56
Amit, Z., 118
Anderson, C. O., 94
Anderson, D. C., 83
Andrew, R. J., 118
Andrewartha, H. C., 340
Angrist, B. M., 72
Annau, Z., 57
Anrep, G. V., 128
Archer, J., 49, 118
Armitage, A. K., 143, 155, 330
Ast, D., 199
Azrin, N. H., 29, 158, 195–7, 202, 284

Baenninger, L., 307
Baerends, G. P., 267, 374
Baerends-van Roon, J. M., 374
Bagg, H. J., 363
Baile, C. A., 47
Bailey, C. J., 221
Bainbridge, J. G., 71, 200–1
Balagura, S., 41
Banks, E. M., 56, 291
Bannova, N. V., 138, 191
Barber, D. L., 74
Barnes, R. H., 55
Barnett, B. M., 256
Barnett, S. A., 5, 39, 43, 81, 314, 352–3, 355, 357, 359–60
Barnum, C. P., 85
Barry, H, III, 43, 205, 220–1
Bateson, P. P. G., 171–2
Bättig, K., 199
Bauer, R. H., 258
Beach, F. A., 54, 55

Beer, E. J. de, 295
Beggerly, H. D., 260
Bennet, E. L., 55, 274
Beritashvili, J. S., 135
Besbokaya, 122
Bignami, G., 48, 212, 217
Bindra, D., 177
Blackburn, T. P., 74
Blight, W. C., 54
Bliss, D. K., 256
Blough, D. S., 187–9, 202
Bobillier, P., 284
Boice, R., 49, 281, 285, 353, 361–3
Boissier, J. R., 243
Bol, A. C. A., 51
Bolles, R. C., 22, 49
Booth, D. A., 41
Boreman, J., 281, 360
Boren, J. J., 176
Borgen, L. A., 283
Borgesová, M., 84
Bovet, D., 87, 217
Bovet-Nitti, F., 87
Bradley, D. W. M., 243–4
Bradley, P. B., 38, 267
Bradley, R. J., 153
Brady, J. V., 212–13
Breda, J. B., 259
Bregman, N. J., 260
Brierton, G. R., 285
Broadhurst, P. L., 48, 70, 236, 239
Brodie, R. E., 210
Brown, R. M., 150
Brown, R. V., 100, 272
Bruce, H., 55
Bunnell, B. N., 287
Burcher, L. L., 105
Butler, W. H., 251
Buxton, D. A., 71

Cairns, R. B., 290
Calhoun, J. B., 346–7

Campbell, B. A., 22, 111, 325
Campbell, D., 60, 76
Candland, D. K., 95
Candland, M. H., 95
Cappell, H., 201
Carey, R., 103
Carlier, C., 56
Carlini, E. A., 259, 281–2
Carlton, P. L., 21, 247–8, 268
Casterline, J. L., 210
Caswell, S., 185
Champlin, K., 54
Chance, M. R. A., 10, 68, 84, 114–15, 232, 246, 248, 271, 276–7, 336
Chang, O. L., 89
Chappell, M. N., 147
Charnov, E. L., 171
Chillig, D., 100
Chorny, H., 197
Christenson, J. D., 70
Clark, R., 43, 65
Clark, R. H., 257
Clarke, B., 99
Collins, M., 183–4
Colvin, D. V., 359
Conger, J. J., 138, 220
Conway, F. J., 72
Cook, L., 160, 203–6, 285
Cooper, J., 272
Coppock, J. W., 102
Corbit, J. D., 21
Costa, E., 89
Cox, T., 71
Craig, W., 18
Crow, T. J., 72
Crowcroft, P., 316–17, 346
Cullen, E., 372
Cutler, M., 336

Darwin, C., 339
Davies, J. A., 239
Davis, F. C., 280, 296–7, 314
Davis, J. D., 41
Davis, W. M., 283
Dawkins, M., 95
Dawkins, R., 301
Debiase, P. L., 206
Delius, J. D., 52, 288–9
Denenberg, V. H., 94, 287, 290
Dennis, W., 112
Descartes, R., 120
Dési, I., 268–9

Desiderio, D. M., 257
Dews, P. B., 39, 155–6, 169, 325–6
Dewsbury, D. A., 53
Diamond, M. C., 55, 274
Dickenson, A., 22
Dickson, A. L., 256
Dillow, P. V., 226
Dixon, A. K., 335–6
Domino, E. F., 38
Dorr, M., 246, 262
Doty, B. A., 208–9
Doty, L. A., 208–9
Douglas, M. B., 97
Douthitt, T. C., 23
Dragovich, J. A., 46
Draper, W. A., 49
Dren, T., 38
Driver, P. M., 197, 264
Drori, D., 272
Dry, L., 279
Ducrocq, J., 88
Duncan, I. J. H., 51
Duncan, N. G., 258, 260

Eayrs, J. T., 88
Eddy, N. B., 64
Ericksson, K., 23
Evans, C. R., 36
Evans, H. L., 374
Evans, L. T., 275
Evans, S., 115, 199
Ewer, R. F., 315, 358
Extance, K., 153, 251, 374

Fadeyeva, V. K., 136, 138
Falk, J. L., 100
Farkos, I., 268
Farris, E. J., 360, 363
Faulds, B., 95
Fellows, E. J., 285
Fentress, J. C., 52
Feokritova, I., 125
Ferster, C. B., 160, 168
File, S. E., 244
Fitzsimons, J. T., 23
Fleshler, M., 197
Folman, Y., 272
Formánek, J., 138, 191
Foursikov, D. S., 129
Francis, R. L., 85
Frantík, E., 170, 195
Fremont-Smith, N., 275

Freud, S., 36, 164, 226
Friedman, M. I., 287
Frolov, Iu. P., 135, 138

Gallagher, R. J., 41
Galvan, L., 257
Gandelman, R., 287, 297
Garcia, J., 44–6
Gatti, G. L., 212
Gaulin-Kremer, E., 287, 290
Geller, I., 223–4, 326
Gellerman, L. W., 182
Gerald, M. C., 23
Gerall, A. A., 272
Gerall, H., 272
Gerold, M., 8
Gershon, S., 72
Gillbe, C., 72
Ginsburg, R., 201
Glees, P., 70
Glick, S. D., 23
Glover, J., 89
Gold, P. E., 260
Gold, R. M., 22
Goldberg, A. M., 57
Goldberg, H. D., 147
Goldberg, M. E., 191, 205
Gönczi, L., 268
Govier, W. M., 206
Graham, R. T., 198
Grahame-Smith, D. G., 72
Grandjean, E., 159, 191, 199
Grant, E. C., 49, 276–7, 291, 304, 307, 310, 314–15, 320, 329, 335, 374
Granville-Grossman, K. L., 71–2
Grappetti, A., 89
Green, A. R., 72
Green, K. F., 45
Greenwood, D. T., 71–2, 74, 200–1
Grice, H. L., 272
Griffiths, P. J., 100
Grigoriev, Z. E., 139
Grossman, F. S., 124
Grossman, S. P., 46, 224–5
Grunt, J. A., 54
Gumma, M. R., 93

Haeusler, G., 8
Hailman, J. P., 181
Hake, D. F., 197
Halberg, F., 85
Haldane, J. B. S., 18

Hall, C. S., 47, 235–6, 277, 280, 96–7, 314
Hall, G. H., 330
Hall-Craggs, J., 308, 374
Halliday, M. S., 239
Halliday, T. R., 19–20
Halpern, F. S., 72
Hamaqui, A., 281
Hamilton, W. D., 343
Hanby, J. P., 308, 374
Hare, H., 343, 373
Hartley, P. L., 45, 351
Hasegawa, A. T., 84
Haun, C., 205
Havenhill, R., 218
Headlee, C. P., 102
Hebb, D. O., 274
Hecht, K., 204
Heimstra, N. W., 279
Henton, W. W., 202
Herring, B. S., 153, 215
Herrnstein, R. J., 157, 168, 190
Herxheimer, A., 97
Hess, E. H., 103, 264
Higginson, G. D., 296
Hill, S. Y., 103
Hinde, R. A., 1, 164, 172, 231–2, 244, 266, 270
Ho, K. J., 8
Hoffmann, H. S., 197, 209, 251, 264–5
Hogan, J. A., 107
Holland, H. C., 81
Holloway, F. A., 215–16
Holmes, W., 79
Holst, E. von, 232
Holz, W. C., 29, 158, 195–7, 202
Holz-Tucker, A. M., 54
Honig, W. K., 164, 173–4
Hope, K., 327
Hordern, A., 78
Horváth, M., 138, 170, 191, 195
Hughes, F. W., 208
Hughes, J., 57
Hughes, R. A., 21
Hughes, R. N., 246
Humphries, D. A., 10, 197
Hunt, E., 260
Hunt, H. F., 200
Hunter, W. S., 115
Huntingford, F. A., 286, 374
Hurwitz, H. M. B., 226

Iersel, J. J. A. van, 51

Author index

Irwin, S., 60, 66, 206
Itani, I., 278
Ivanov-Smolensky, 135
Iversen, L. L., 1
Iversen, S. D., 1, 373
Izergina, A. Iu., 136–8

Jacobs, A., 89
Jacobs, B. L., 260
Jageneau, A. H., 285, 291–2, 329
Janků, I., 237, 239
Janssen, P. A. J., 285, 291–2, 329
Jarman, P. J., 344–6, 373
Jarvik, M. E., 23
Jaton, A. L., 75
Jeeves, M. A., 267
Jenkins, H. M., 147
Jensen, D., 114
Jirsik, J., 358
Johnson, H. E., 191
Johnson, V. S., 153
Jones, B. J., 70
Jones, M. R., 87
Jouvet, M., 38, 284
Joyce, D., 243–4, 262
Jung, C., 164

Kadlecová, O., 84
Kagan, Iu. S., 139
Kalat, J. W., 46
Kalmus, H., 189
Kamin, L. J., 213, 216
Kapatos, G., 22
Karki, N., 88
Karli, P., 286
Kavanau, J. L., 31, 90–1, 146, 218
Kelly, P. H., 72
Kendler, H. H., 268
Kennedy, J. S., 18
Khalsa, J. H., 283
Khavari, K. A., 22
King, A. R., 51, 170, 197, 226–9, 268
King, W. T., 283
Kissileff, H., 43
Klein, N., 277, 280, 314
Kleinman, K. M., 23
Kneffel, Z., 268–9
Knoll, B., 82
Knoll, J., 82
Koch, A. M., 116, 118
Koelling, R. A., 46
Kortlandt, A., 50

Kotliarevski, L. I., 135–8, 245
Kovacsics, G. B., 88
Kral, P. A., 260
Krebs, J. R., 171
Krech, D., 55, 274
Kreezer, G. L., 111, 115, 222–3
Kriikovsky, 129
Krnjević, H., 242
Kršiak, M., 84, 236–7, 239, 272, 289–90, 307, 329, 334
Kulak, J. F., 224, 326
Kulkarni, A. S., 149
Kumar, R., 38, 101–2, 216–18, 239, 261, 326
Kuo, Z.-Y., 107

Lachman, R., 268
Ladove, R. E., 41
Lal, H., 150
Lammers, A. J. J. C., 283
Langham, R. J., 44
Lashley, K. S., 182–3
Lát, J., 89, 245
Laties, V. G., 93, 146, 157–8, 374
Lauener, H., 201
Lehrman, D. E., 51, 106, 374
Léimbach, D., 64
Le Magnen, J., 43
Lerwill, C. J., 310
Levine, R., 272
Levitsky, D. A., 55
Lewis, D. J., 260
Lewis, M., 47
Lewis, M. J., 46
Leyhausen, P., 286
Liebman, J. M., 105
Lindsey, C. J., 281
Little, C. C., 363
Littleton, J. M., 100, 271
Locke, N. M., 223
Loew, D. M., 75
Logan, F. A., 285
Lorenz, K. Z., 1, 106, 164, 263, 275, 360, 367
Loveland, D. H., 190
Lovett, D., 41
Luschei, E. S., 21

Mabry, J. H., 285
McCance, R. A., 245
McDougall, W., 121, 175
McEwen, B. S., 256
McFarland, D. J., 22

McGaugh, J. L., 258–60
McGill, T. E., 54
Mackintosh, J. H., 49, 66, 84, 273, 291, 304, 310, 315, 317, 335–6
Madinaveitia, J., 41
Maffii, G., 205
Magos, L., 251
Mahan, J. J., 260
Mahoney, P., 83
Maickel, R. P., 23
Mainardi, D., 54, 95
Malick, J. B., 287
Mallov, S., 197
Malthus, T., 339
Mapes, R., 84
Margules, A. S., 46
Margules, D. L., 46, 208
Marks, D., 185
Marley, E., 162
Marsan, M., 54, 95
Martin, I. L., 268
Marty, H., 350
Märtz, R. M. W., 281
Masserman, J. H., 100, 182
Mattis, P. A., 285
Mead, A. P., 114–15, 246–8
Meddis, R., 36
Medved, L. I., 139
Mellgren, R. L., 256
Mendel, G., 367
Mendelson, J., 100, 177
Meyer, C. C., 264
Michal, K., 287
Miczek, K. A., 201–2
Middlemiss, D. N., 72
Miles, W. R., 118, 220
Miller, N. E., 43, 103, 118, 134, 193, 205, 220–2, 224
Miller, R. J., 72
Millman, N., 291
Misanin, J. R., 22
Mitchell, C. L., 101
Mittelstaedt, H., 232
Montgomery, K. C., 218, 240, 245
Moore, B. R., 147
Morgan, B. J. T., 308, 374
Morgan, M. J., 273
Morris, D., 53
Morrison, C. F., 23, 51, 88, 143, 152, 155, 157, 218, 330
Morse, W. H., 160, 162, 325–6
Moss, F. A., 223

Mouret, J., 38, 284
Mucha, A., 285
Munn, N. L., 183–4
Murcurio, J., 83
Murphy, E. M., 243–4
Myer, J. S., 56
Myers, A. K., 195
Myers, R. D., 99, 103

Nachman, M., 45, 351
Naimzada, M. K., 89
Nash, B. M., 243–4
Navaratnam, V., 239
Navarro, A. P., 176
Nichols, J. R., 102
Niemegeers, C. J. E., 285, 291–2, 329
Nikiforovsky, M. P., 127
Nigro, M. R., 226
Nissen, H. W., 244
Noirot, E., 56–7
Norton, S., 295

Oatley, K., 22
O'Kelly, L. I., 284
Olds, J. J., 103–4
Oliverio, A., 87, 208
Ollason, J. C., 52
Oortmersson, G. A. van, 363–4
Ortiz, A., 100
Oswald, I., 37
Overton, D. A., 255–6
Owen, J. E., 209

Parr, W., 257
Pasquali, A., 54, 95
Pavlik, W. B., 40
Pavlov, I. P., 17, 31, 106, 108, 120–35, 170, 181, 194, 208, 222, 230
Payne, A. P., 306
Penfield, W., 103
Peng, S. K., 9
Perdeck, A. C., 180
Peters, N. J., 84
Petrova, M. K., 133
Poel, A. M. van der, 329
Pollard, J. S., 279
Popper, K., 176
Porsolt, R. D., 243, 262
Potter, B., 351
Powell, B. J., 103
Pozzani, V. C., 191
Prescott, R. G. W., 88

Author index

Price, E., 281, 360
Price, J. S., 342

Quartermain, D., 256

Rajalakshmi, R., 267
Ramos, J., 218
Randt, C. T., 256
Raoul, Y., 88
Raskin, D. C., 200
Ratner, A. M., 264–5
Ray, O. S., 224–6, 326
Raynaud, G., 88
Redfern, P. H., 239
Redfern, R., 316
Reed, C. F., 198
Reese, E., 264
Reid, R. M., 279
Remmelts, M., 329
Renzi, P., 208
Revusky, S., 44
Reynolds, W. F., 40
Rice, W. B., 203
Richards, M. P. M., 56
Richards, S. M., 280
Richter, C. P., 80, 82, 86
Richter, W., 60, 76
Riley, R. A., 367
Rimm, A., 84
Robbins, E. B., 209
Roberts, D. J., 70
Robustelli, F., 217
Rohte, O., 50
Rosecrans, J. A., 185–6
Rosenzweig, M. R., 55, 274
Rossum, J. M. van, 283
Rotrosen, J., 72
Rountree, G. B., 208
Rowe, F. P., 316–17, 346
Rozin, P., 44, 46–7
Rushton, R., 38, 262
Russell, R. W., 22
Ryan, J. C., 171

Sachar, E. J., 72
Sacra, P., 203
Sader, N. F. A., 259
Saelens, J. K., 88
Sales, G. D., 85, 195
Salmon, M., 57, 355
Salzen, E. A., 264
Samson, H. H., 100

Sansone, M., 208
Sayler, A., 57, 355
Schechter, M., 185–6
Schiørring, E., 50
Schmidt, H., 23, 279
Scholtz, S. D., 290
Schuster, C. R., 102–3, 161–2
Schwing, R. C., 104
Scott, E. M., 45
Scott, J. P., 290
Scourse, N. J. S., 231, 266
Seifter, J., 223–4, 326
Senault, B., 283, 334
Sevenster, P., 108, 146, 166
Seward, J. P., 200, 277, 280, 298, 304, 314, 360
Seymour, K. A., 268
Shalloway, D. I., 287
Sheffield, F. D., 111, 325
Shettleworth, S., 108, 166, 146
Shideman, F. E., 149
Shillito, E. E., 38, 240–2, 284
Shirley, M., 80
Sidman, M., 209, 211–12, 214
Siegel, P. S., 22
Siegel, S., 13, 97
Silverman, A. P., 23, 50, 84, 248–52, 280, 304, 320–7, 330–5, 374–5
Simon, G., 268–9
Simon, P., 243
Simpson, M. J. A., 308, 374
Skinner, B. F., 104, 134, 141, 145, 156, 160, 164, 166, 169–74
Sklar, L., 118
Slabok, M., 206
Slater, P. J. B., 52
Small, W. S., 110–11, 118, 235, 240, 244
Smart, J. L., 39, 81
Smyth, H. F., 191, 205
Smythies, J. R., 153
Snyder, S. H., 1
Soane, I. D., 99
Sobotka, T. J., 210
Sodetz, F. J., 287
Sorenson, C. A., 260
South, F. E., 93
Spalding, D., 263–4
Sparber, S. B., 150, 159
Speizer, Z., 273
Spencer, M. M., 352
Spragg, S. D. S., 102
Sprott, R. L., 256

Spurway, H., 18
Spynu, E. I., 139
Stachnik, T. J., 285
Stanger, R., 291
Steckle, F. C., 284
Stein, L., 175, 206–8, 226
Steinberg, H., 38, 102, 118, 236, 238, 244, 262
Steiniger, F., 110, 286, 316, 353–8, 360
Stephens, R. J., 247
Stephenson, J. A., 51, 88, 157, 218
Stevens, D. M., 265
Stevens, S. S., 13
Stevenson-Hinde, J., 164, 167
Stewart, W. W., 257
Stilwell, F. P., 52
Stolerman, I. P., 101–2, 236
Stolin, V., 199
Stone, G. C., 197, 210–11
Streets, J. C., 66
Stuckey, H. L., 22
Summerfield, A., 243–4, 262
Svensson, T. H., 83, 89
Swanson, H. H., 306
Sweatman, H. P. A., 19–20
Syme, L. A., 44, 279
Syme, G. J., 44, 279, 280

Tallon, S., 43
Taylor, C. B., 9
Tedeschi, D. H., 285
Tedeschi, R. H., 285
Terrace, H. S., 120, 186–7
Thieme, L., 83, 89
Thoenen, H., 8
Thomas, D. B., 95
Thompson, H. V., 350–3, 359
Thompson, T., 102–3, 149, 161–2, 282
Thorpe, W. H., 254–5
Tilson, H. A., 150, 159
Tinbergen, N., 1, 17, 35–6, 50–1, 79, 173, 175, 180, 191, 296, 367, 372–4
Tinson, C., 38, 262
Tolman, E. C., 116
Tomkiewicz, M., 23, 244, 262, 279
Torres, A. H., 200
Travis, R. P., 104
Trivers, R. L., 343, 373
Tryon, R. C., 116, 269
Tsai, C., 94
Tufik, S., 281
Turausky, A. J., 41
Turner, P., 71

Tušl, M., 199
Twyman, W. A., 243–4

Uhrich, J., 276
Ulrich, R. E., 284–5
Ungar, G., 257–8
Ungerstedt, U., 72, 74
Universities Federation for Animal Welfare (UFAW), 31
Uyeno, E. T., 198, 279

Valzelli, L., 282, 286
Veale, W. L., 99
Venulet, J., 66
Verduyn, C., 71
Verhave, T., 209
Verney, E. L., 45
Videk, M., 242
Vigouret, J. M., 75
Vogel, J. R., 21–2

Wagner, M., 199
Wagstaff, D. J., 66
Walk, R. D., 68
Wallgren, H., 70
Walters, G. C., 153, 215
Wang, G. H., 86
Wang, R. I. H., 84
Wansley, R., 215–16
Ward, I. L., 272
Warden, C. J., 111–12, 116, 118, 223
Warne, M. C., 276
Warner, E. H., 111–12
Wasserman, E., 114
Watson, R. H. J., 236
Webster, C. D., 89, 153, 201, 215
Weidley, L. E., 204–6
Weidmann, R., 180
Weidmann, U., 180
Weinstock, M., 273
Weiss, A. B., 157
Weiss, B., 93, 146, 157–8, 374
Weiss, J. M., 213
Wentworth, K. L., 116
Weyant, R. G., 268
White, N., 118
White, R. E. C., 301
White, R. T., 56
Wiberg, G. S., 272
Widdowson, E. M., 39, 245
Wiepkema, P., 43, 223
Wilcock, J., 48

Author index

Will, B., 148, 169
Williams, D. I., 238–9
Williams, H., 251, 327, 374
Willinsky, M. D., 153, 215
Willison, P. W., 256
Wilson, C. W. M., 84
Wilson, E. O., 373
Winger, G., 100
Witt, P. N., 27, 197–8
Wolff, P. C., 284
Wood, L. A., 101
Wood-Gush, D. G. M., 51
Wootton, R. J., 359

Wynne-Edwards, V. C., 340–2

Yamamoto, K., 38
Yeh, S. Y., 101
Yen, H. C. Y., 291
Yenkel, E. H., 360, 363
Yerkes, R. M., 182
Young, P. T., 47
Young, W. C., 54
Yum, K. S., 100

Zarrow, M. X., 94, 287, 290
Zitovich, I. S., 121